Windows® Programming
Programmer's Notebook

Mario Giannini

and

Jim Keogh

Upper Saddle River, New Jersey 07458
www.phptr.com

ISBN 0-13-027845-9

90000

9 780130 278456

Library of Congress Cataloging-in-Publication Data

Giannini, Mario.
    The Windows programming programmer's notebook / Mario Giannini and Jim Keogh.
      p. cm.
    ISBN 0-13-027845-9
      1. Microsoft Windows (Computer file)   2. Operating systems (Computers)   I. Keogh,
James Edward, 1948- II. Title.

QA76.76.063 G52 2001
005.4'469—dc21   00-046526

Editorial/production supervision: *Pine Tree Composition, Inc.*
Cover design: *Design Source*
Cover design director: *Jerry Votta*
Manufacturing manager: *Alexis R. Heydt*
Marketing manager: *Debby van Dijk*
Acquisitions editor: *Greg Doench*

©2001 Prentice Hall PTR
Prentice-Hall, Inc.
Upper Saddle River, New Jersey 07458

The publisher offers discounts on this book when ordered
        in bulk quantities. For more information, contact:

Corporate Sales Department
      PTR Prentice Hall
      One Lake Street
      Upper Saddle River, NJ 07458

      Phone: 800-382-3419
      Fax: 201-236-7141
      E-mail: corpsales@prenhall.com

ISBN 0-13-027845-9

Printed in the United States of America

10 9 8 7 6 5 4 3 2 1

Prentice-Hall International (UK) Limited, London
Prentice-Hall of Australia Pty. Limited, Sydney
Prentice-Hall Canada Inc., Toronto
Prentice-Hall Hispanoamericana, S.A., Mexico
Prentice-Hall of India Private Limited, New Delhi
Prentice-Hall of Japan, Inc., Tokyo
Pearson Education Asia Pte. Ltd.
Editora Prentice-Hall do Brasil, Ltda., Rio de Janeiro

Contents

Preface

Windows programming is complex and has many rules that must be obeyed. Learning those rules can be time-consuming, especially for readers who already know how to program in other programming languages. Those readers want to jump into the language and begin writing simple code immediately.

Many programmers who learn Windows programming as their second language have their own philosophy about learning a programming language. "Show me sample code and I'll figure out the rest," is a statement that summarizes their approach. That's what we do in this book.

The picture book concept places the focus of the book on a picture of the code. Around this picture are callouts that describe each keyword and statement. The rules are presented in lists that are positioned near the picture. Furthermore, there is a picture for variations of each topic that is discussed in the chapter.

A reader who wants to jump into Windows programming can study the picture, then copy the code into a compiler and make the executable program without having to sift through pages of text. The rules can be referenced later, when the reader needs to expand the use of the routine.

This approach is not intended to circumvent a thorough presentation of Windows programming. In fact, this book presents Windows programming in its entirety. The picture book approach presents material in a way that makes programmers want to learn a new programming language.

Navigating This Book

We organized this book into traditional chapters. Each chapter covers a topic of Windows programming in a logical progression. So, if you are not familair with the basics of Windows programming, then begin with the first chapter and continue through each chapter in succession. At the end of the last chapter you will have a good foundation in Windows programming and how to build a Windows application.

However, these chapters also can be used for quick reference. Jump to the chapter that discusses the topic that you want to review. The topic within the chapter is presented in its completion with a focus on examples of code.

The most efficient way to use this book is to first study the codes that contain callouts. If you understand the function of each statement in the example, then you can continue and write your own program. Howver, if a statement, keyword, or concept is confusing, then read the callout that describes the item. Still confused? Read the text associated with the example.

There are two ways of building a Windows program: using the Software Development Kit (SDK) or using the Microsoft Foundation Classes (MFC). We show you how to develop a Windows program using both the SDK and the MFC.

We suggest using the MFC because this saves you time from coding standard functionality—no one wants to spend time writing code that already exists. However, you'll need the Microsoft compiler and the MFC library installed on your computer.

You don't need to go out and purchase the Microsoft compiler and the MFC library if you already have a Windows SDK made by another software vendor. In this case, you can copy our SDK examples into your compiler to begin building your own Windows program.

Chapter 1

Preparing Yourself
for Windows Programming

- About Windows
- Windows Messaging
- A Complete SDK Windows Application
- Message Boxes
- Dialog-based Windows Applications
- Creating Programs with Visual C++ and AppWizard
- Creating an SDK program
- Microsoft Foundation Classes
- Running AppWizard
- Enhancing an MFC Framework Application
- Compiling a Windows Program
- Distributing a Windows Program

About Windows

A *Windows program* is composed of visual components called *windows*. Each window can be described as having an *appearance*, can *respond to events* or actions (i.e., mouse clicks or key presses), and has *data* associated with it called *properties* (i.e., the text in an edit box, or the strings in a list box).

For example, the main window of a Windows application has a caption bar and menu and might be able to be resized (see Figure 1–1). The caption bar and menu, along with the color of the window and other such attributes, make up the window's visual appearance. Text in the caption bar and the color of the window are some of the window's properties. Resizing the window occurs as a reaction to an event, such as when the user maximizes the size of the window.

A typical Windows application will use many types of windows. Each type of window is called a *window class* and has a predefined appearance, property set, and action set. Some window classes are not intuitively recognized as windows. Buttons, edit boxes, list boxes, and check boxes are all types of windows. In addition to the predefined windows, you can create your own window classes from scratch or by enhancing a predefined Windows class. You could, for example, create a 3D button window class with a bitmap picture in the center of the button.

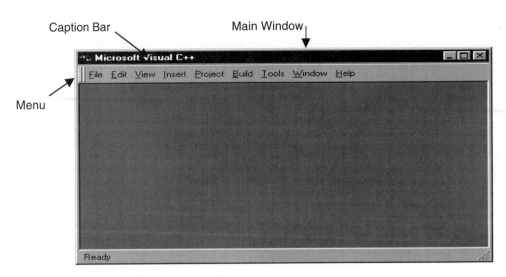

Caption Bar   Main Window

Microsoft Visual C++

File Edit View Insert Project Build Tools Window Help

Menu

Ready

Figure 1–1   A typical Windows application.

Parent and Child Windows

Many Windows applications create a *main window* as the first window of the application. The main window can have a caption bar and a menu, although these are not required. A main window could simply contain one button. Additional windows can be displayed as the user interacts with the application, such as when the user selects a menu item. The main window is referred to as the *parent window* and subsequent windows created from the main window are called *child windows*.

Let's say the menu of the main window contains a File Open menu item. When this item is selected, the window's application displays the open file window that enables the user to select a file. The main window is said to be the parent of the open file window.

Likewise, a child window can also be a parent to its own child window. Typically, the open file window contains other windows such as the OK button. The open file window is then said to be the parent of the OK button, making the OK button a child of the open file window.

Once a parent window creates a child window, the parent and the child become semi-autonomous. Both the parent and child handle their own actions without relying on each other. For example (see Figure 1–2), the user can browse through directories within the open file window without those actions being reported to the main window.

However, there are actions that affect both the parent and the child. When a parent is destroyed, moved, hidden, or disabled, then so is the child window and the child's own child windows. A child window can, if so programmed, send a message to its parent that an action has taken place, such as if the user clicked the mouse button while the cursor is on the child window. The parent may then decide the proper response.

Basic Components of a Windows Program

There are two fundamental components of every Windows program: handles and resources. A *handle* is an identifier of a resource; a *resource* is a component that is used by the application to perform a specific task.

Each resource enhances the functionality of the application by lending its abilities to the application. It is your job as the Windows programmer to select the resources that you require for the application, then acquire a handle to those resources so the resource can be used in your application.

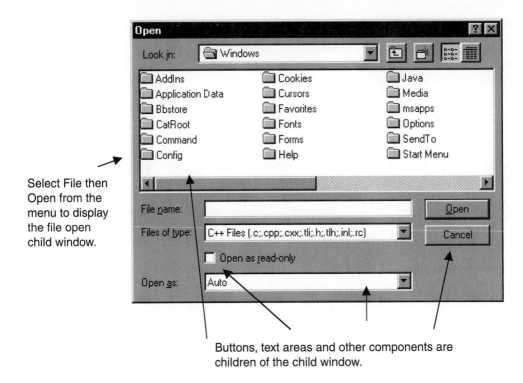

Select File then Open from the menu to display the file open child window.

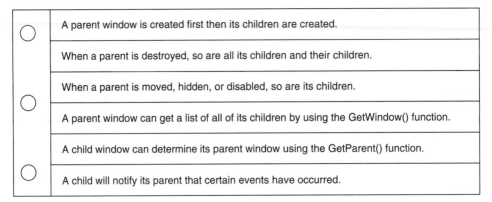

Buttons, text areas and other components are children of the child window.

Figure 1-2 Actions taken by a user in a child window are not necessarily passed back to the parent window.

Remember

○	A parent window is created first then its children are created.
	When a parent is destroyed, so are all its children and their children.
○	When a parent is moved, hidden, or disabled, so are its children.
	A parent window can get a list of all of its children by using the GetWindow() function.
	A child window can determine its parent window using the GetParent() function.
○	A child will notify its parent that certain events have occurred.

Primary Resources

Figures 1–3 and 1–4 show the common resources that are used in a Windows application.

Windows

Each window in your application has a unique *window handle*, which is identified with the HWND data type. The handle obtained by calling the CreateWindow(), GetWindow(), or FindWindow() functions. You can also get a window handle from the window procedure (see Windows Messaging later in this chapter). The window's handle is used to reference the window.

Menus

A *menu* displays options the user can select from a list. There are two kinds of menus: pull-down and pop-up. The HMENU data type is used to identify a handle to a menu and the GetMenu() function is used to get a menu's handle. The handle

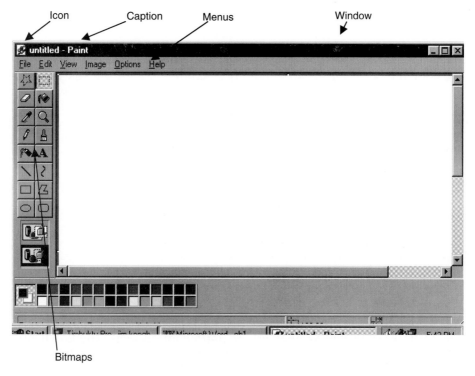

Figure 1–3   Here are various components of a window.

Dialog

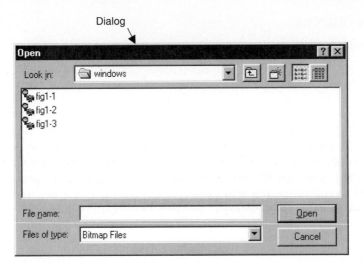

Figure 1–4 Here is a typical dialog window.

can then be used to add, remove, enable, disable, check, and uncheck a selection within a menu.

Dialogs

A *dialog*, sometimes called a *dialog box*, is a simple window that is used for communication between the user and the application. The HWND data type is used to define the handle to a dialog. Dialog windows are typically displayed by calling either the DialogBox() or DialogBoxParam() functions. Since these functions do not return until the dialog is closed, most of the work for a dialog window is performed within its window procedure.

Bitmaps

A *bitmap* is an image or picture and is identified with the HBITMAP handle. The functions such as LoadBitmap(), LoadImage(), CreateBitmap(), SelectObject(), and BitBlt() use the handle to load, create, or display the bitmap.

Icons

An *icon* is a small image that is used to represent a functionality of an application. For example, an icon represents the application itself when the application is minimized. The HICON data type is used as the handle for an icon. The LoadIcon() function is one of the functions that use the icon handle to manipulate an icon from within the application.

Cursors

A *cursor* is an image that indicates the current position on the screen. Cursors appear as an arrow, an hourglass, or other familiar images. The HICON data type identifies a cursor, and the LoadCursor() and SetCursor() functions are two functions used to load and display the cursor.

String Tables

A *string table* is a resource that represents a collection of strings (text data). String tables are often found in international programs, where the end users' languages will vary. Calling the LoadString function, your application can load a desired string from the string table, depending upon the user's locale settings. String tables are often found in DLL files as well, so that you could make a language-specific DLL for your applications use.

Device Context

A *device context,* unlike the other resources above, is not something created at design time with an editor; it is a canvas on which you may draw. The device context is represented with the HDC data type and may refer to the screen, printer, or a memory buffer. You can get a device context for a window by calling BeginPaint(), and when you are done drawing with it, you should release it by calling EndPaint().

Windows Messaging

A Windows application interacts with the Windows environment and the application's windows by sending messages. A *message* is represented by an integer and is sent by a function call. For example, an application can minimize a window by sending the WM_SIZE message using the SendMessage() function call. Window message processing involves three components: the message queue, the message loop, and the window procedure.

All events such as the click of a mouse are detected by the Windows environment, which places the event in the form of a message on the application's message queue. A *message queue* is a storage area for messages. Windows and applications send messages to an application by placing the message on the message queue. An application receives messages by removing messages from the message queue. Every Windows application has a message queue created for it by Windows when the application is started.

Each application must poll the message queue using the GetMessage() or PeekMessage() functions to receive the message. Likewise, an application can place a message on the message queue by using the PostMessage() function.

Windows determines which application is to receive a message. However, your application must forward the message to the proper window within your application. Let's say that the mouse was clicked over your application's main window. Windows places the event on your application's message queue. Your application must retrieve the message and send the message to the main window for processing. If the mouse was clicked over a child window, like a button, then your application must send the message to the child window.

The *message loop* is a series of statements in your application responsible for polling the application's message queue, then sending the message to the appropriate window of your application. A message loop routine (see Code 1–1) must be part of your application unless the Microsoft Foundation Class library is used, which includes a message loop that automatically retrieves messages from the queue and dispatches them to the appropriate window.

Here's how the message loop works:

1. Windows automatically converts an event into a message queue structure called the *MSG structure* and places the MSG structure on the application's message queue. The message queue is accessible by creating an instance of the MSG object (MSG Msg) in the application's message loop. The MSG structure contains data members that describe the type of message (such as as WM_MOUSEMOVE, meaning the mouse was moved) as well as some additional information that may be specific to the message (for example, the coordinate the mouse moved over).
2. The GetMessage() function is passed to the address of the MSG object and gets a message out of the queue and into the MSG object. The MSG structure contains a message and related information such as the type of event, event, destination window, and additional information if necessary, such as the mouse coordinates where a mouse-click occurred, if the mouse was clicked.
3. A sequence of events is sometimes considered a single event such as pressing a keyboard key. The first event is pressing a key down and the second event is releasing the key, called a key up.
4. The TranslateMessage() function translates multiple events into a single event so the event can be processed by the application. The DispatchMessage() function sends the message to the destination window of the application.

Each application window must have a window procedure. A *window procedure* is a function that either reacts to or ignores specific Windows messages. The DispatchMessage function works by identifying which window a message was intended for, and then calling the window procedure for that window. For example, if the mouse was moved over a child window, then the child is notified of that because DispatchMessage() will call the child's window procedure.

Code 1-1

The MSG structure contains data members such as the intended
window, the message itself, when the message was placed in the
queue, message object contains a member structure used to store the
message identifier and additional information that is required by some
messages.and other data specific to the message.

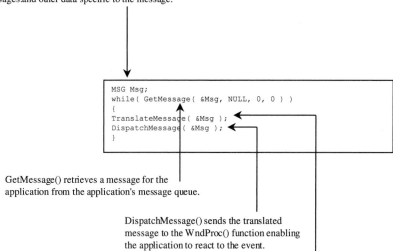

```
MSG Msg;
while( GetMessage( &Msg, NULL, 0, 0 ) )
{
TranslateMessage( &Msg );
DispatchMessage( &Msg );
}
```

GetMessage() retrieves a message for the
application from the application's message queue.

DispatchMessage() sends the translated
message to the WndProc() function enabling
the application to react to the event.

TranslateMessage() combines two or more
events into a single event for the application.

Note: A window procedure is called a *callback function*. This means that you may
write the function, but you don't actually call it directly. Instead, Windows will call
it when needed. This concept is key to understand GUI programming and will be a
new concept to programmers coming from a DOS or procedural-style programming
background. Windows programming is termed *event-driven*, while DOS style is
termed *procedural*.

Window Procedure

A *window procedure* is the function associated with a window class that controls
the appearance and behavior for all windows of that class. You don't normally need
to write a window procedure, as there are predefined ones available for the common
window classes such as edit box, list box, button, etc. You will write window procedures when you create non-dialog, SDK-style main-window applications, or SDK-
style dialogs.

Let's say that you have an edit box in the main window of your application. You
must create the window procedure for the main window. An edit box is a predefined
window class. Therefore, you do not need to create a window procedure for it.

The window procedure is traditionally called WndProc() and must accept a standard parameter list and return type. There are no standards you must follow within the window procedure to process messages. Code 1–2 contains the parameter list and return type you must include in your window procedure.

Code 1–2

```
LRESULT CALLBACK WndProc( HWND hWnd, UINT uMessage, WPARAM wParam, LPARAM lParam )
```

The *LRESULT* is the return type. The *CALLBACK* is a calling method modifier, which states that the function may be called by Windows and uses the Pascal function calling method. The name of the function is *WndProc()*, although any name can be used since your application directly calls this function.

The HWND parameter identifies the handle of the window destined to receive the message; uMessage is an integer that identifies the message type. The wParam and the lParam parameters contain additional information about the message, if any exists. The type of message determines whether the wParam and the lParam contain information.

Code 1–3 contains a sample of a typical window procedure used for the main window of an application. A Windows application can receive hundreds of messages, most of which are ignored by the application. This sample ignores all messages except WM_CLOSE. Later in this chapter we'll enhance this procedure so it will respond to particular messages.

The uMessage parameter is compared to known message types by using the *switch statement. Case statements* (not shown) are used to trap desired message types. The *default statement* is used to trap message types that are ignored by the application.

The DefWindowProc() is called whenever a message is ignored [or not handled by the WndProc()]. The parameters of the window procedure are passed as arguments to the DefWindowProc(). The DefWindowProc() handles most of the default window behavior such as drawing, closing, and moving the window. Basically, you only write code to handle messages of interest to your window. All other messages are passed to DefWindowProc().

The window procedure for your main window does not receive messages destined for child windows of that window. Windows sends messages such as a mouse click on a button directly to the child window (remember a button is a child window). The child window directly responds to the event, then the child window may send a message to the parent window notifying the parent window that an event has occurred.

Code 1-3

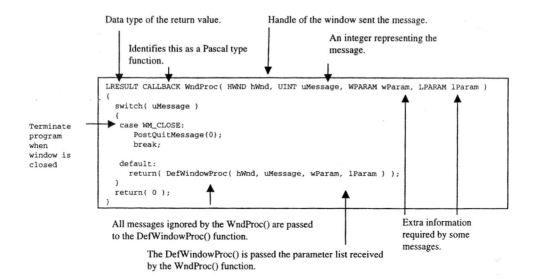

Data type of the return value.

Identifies this as a Pascal type function.

Handle of the window sent the message.

An integer representing the message.

```
LRESULT CALLBACK WndProc( HWND hWnd, UINT uMessage, WPARAM wParam, LPARAM lParam )
{
   switch( uMessage )
   {
   case WM_CLOSE:
        PostQuitMessage(0);
        break;

   default:
        return( DefWindowProc( hWnd, uMessage, wParam, lParam ) );
   }
   return( 0 );
}
```

Terminate program when window is closed

All messages ignored by the WndProc() are passed to the DefWindowProc() function.

The DefWindowProc() is passed the parameter list received by the WndProc() function.

Extra information required by some messages.

Remember

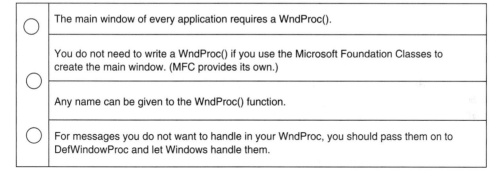

○	The main window of every application requires a WndProc().
○	You do not need to write a WndProc() if you use the Microsoft Foundation Classes to create the main window. (MFC provides its own.)
	Any name can be given to the WndProc() function.
○	For messages you do not want to handle in your WndProc, you should pass them on to DefWindowProc and let Windows handle them.

A Complete SDK Windows Application

A Windows application built using the Software Development Kit requires a minimum number of steps even if a single line of text such as "Hello World" is to be displayed. Fewer steps are required if the Microsoft Foundation Classes are used to build the application, which we'll show you later in this chapter.

Code 1–4 contains the code necessary to build the traditional Hello World Windows application. This same code is repeated—minus the Hello World—in every Windows

---

application that you build. Consider this code as a starting point for building all Windows applications.

1. The entry point in every Windows application is the WinMain() function, which is similar to the main() function in C/C++ programs. Your first step in a Windows application is to define the window class and the resources (i.e., icons and menus) that will be used by the application. We'll explore window classes and resources in depth later in the book.

2. Next, the window application is registered by calling the RegisterClass() function. Buttons, list boxes, and other standard windows are Windows-defined classes. That is, Windows already knows everything about them such as their resources.

3. Your application's window is a new window type to Windows called a *class*. Windows doesn't know anything about your application's window. Therefore, the RegisterClass() function must be called to tell Windows about your application.

4. You assign a name to your class when you define the strClassName variable. The class name of the sample program on the next page is HelloWnd.

5. After the application is registered with Windows, the CreateWindow() function is called to create the application's main window as described earlier in this chapter. The CreateWindow() function uses the strClassName to identify the window.

6. Once the application's main window is created, Windows then starts sending messages to the application's window procedure that is defined as WindProc(). You must create a WndProc() function and a message loop as mentioned previously in this chapter.

7. When the main window is created, the application calls the ShowWindow() and UpdateWindow() functions. The ShowWindow() function displays the window (though it was created, the parent window's visible property is initially false, or invisible). The UpdateWindow() function tells the window that it should update or draw its client area, if needed.

8. The window procedure is designed to handle two specific types of messages: WM_PAINT and WM_CLOSE. *WM_PAINT* is the message sent whenever the window is to be displayed. In response to this message, you must write code to display the text in the window. *WM_CLOSE* is the message sent whenever a window is being closed. Since the demonstration window procedure below is for the main window, we assume that closing the main window means the user wants to close the application. For this reason, the application calls the PostQuitMessage() function, which sends a quit message to Windows acknowledging the close message. PostQuitMessage() places a WM_QUIT message in the message queue, and when the GetMessage() function takes the WM_QUIT message out of the queue, it returns FALSE, which causes the message loop to terminate, therefore causing the main program to

Code 1-4

Define the class name for your application.

Include the windows.h header file.

Declare the WndProc() function

Define your window's class.

Define resources for your application.

Register the customized window class.

Display error if class cannot be registered.

Create the application's main window.

Display error if window cannot be created.

Show the window (make it visible) and update the window (refresh it's the client area of the window)

The window procedure

React to the WM_PAINT message. (our WndProc() determines the window's appearance.)

React to the WM_CLOSE message.

React to any other message

```c
#include <windows.h>
LRESULT CALLBACK WndProc( HWND, UINT, WPARAM, LPARAM );
char strClassName[]= "HelloWnd";
int WINAPI WinMain( HINSTANCE hInst, HINSTANCE hPrevInst, LPSTR
lpszArgs, int nCmdShow )
{
HWND hWnd;
MSG Msg;
WNDCLASS WndClass;
WndClass.hInstance = hInst;
WndClass.lpszClassName = strClassName;
WndClass.lpfnWndProc = WndProc;
WndClass.style = 0;
WndClass.hIcon = LoadIcon( NULL, IDI_APPLICATION );
WndClass.hCursor = LoadCursor( NULL, IDC_ARROW );
WndClass.lpszMenuName = NULL;
WndClass.hbrBackground = (HBRUSH) GetStockObject( WHITE_BRUSH );
          WndClass.cbClsExtra = 0;
WndClass.cbWndExtra = 0;
if( !RegisterClass( &WndClass ) )
{
MessageBox( NULL, "Error registering class", NULL,
MB_ICONEXCLAMATION|MB_OK );
return( 0 );
}
hWnd = CreateWindow( strClassName, "Hello", WS_OVERLAPPEDWINDOW,
CW_USEDEFAULT, CW_USEDEFAULT, CW_USEDEFAULT, CW_USEDEFAULT,
HWND_DESKTOP, NULL, hInst, NULL );
if( !hWnd )
{
  MessageBox(NULL, "Error creating window", NULL,
MB_ICONEXCLAMATION|MB_OK);
return( 0 );
}
ShowWindow( hWnd, nCmdShow );
UpdateWindow( hWnd );
while( GetMessage( &Msg, NULL, 0, 0 ) )
{
TranslateMessage( &Msg );
DispatchMessage( &Msg );
}
return( Msg.wParam );
}
LRESULT CALLBACK WndProc( HWND hWnd, UINT uMessage, WPARAM wParam,
LPARAM lParam )
{
HDC DC;
PAINTSTRUCT PaintStruct;
switch( uMessage )
{
case WM_PAINT:
 DC = BeginPaint( hWnd, &PaintStruct );
 TextOut( DC, 0, 0, "Hello World", 11 );
 EndPaint( hWnd, &PaintStruct );
 break;
case WM_CLOSE:
 if( MessageBox( hWnd, "Are you sure you want to exit?",
  "Confirmation", MB_ICONQUESTION|MB_YESNO|MB_DEFBUTTON1 ) == IDYES )
 DestroyWindow(hWnd);
case WM_DESTROY:
 PostQuitMessage(0);
 break;
default:
  return( DefWindowProc( hWnd, uMessage, wParam, lParam ) );
}
return( 0 );
}
```

The message loop.

Start painting. Gets the device context, which (DC is a device context handle like a canvas to draw on) on the window.

Display text.

End painting (Release the device context handle)

terminate. The WM_CLOSE is sent by Windows when the user tries to close the window (i.e., clicks the "X" window in the upper right corner of the main window).

Message Boxes

A *message box* (see Figure 1–5) is a simple and convenient method to inform users of something or get some basic choices from them. Message boxes have a caption, optional icon, a message, and one or more buttons.

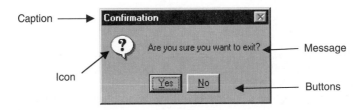

Figure 1–5   Here is a typical message box.

In order to display a message box, you invoke the MessageBox() function. The Message-Box() function has three parameters: The hWnd parameter is the handle of the parent window, which is typically the handle of the application's main window; the lpText parameter is the message string that will be displayed inside the message box; the lpCaption is the caption string that will be displayed as the caption of the message box; and the uType parameter is a bit-mask value. A bit-mask value is a setting of bits that indicates the types and numbers of predefined buttons that are to be displayed in the message box, such as the OK button. The MessageBox() function (see Code 1–5) returns a value that indicates how the user closed the message box and which button was selected.

Code 1–5

```
int MessageBox( HWND hWnd, LPCTSTR lpText, LPCTSTR lpCaption, UINT uType);
```

The value of the hWnd parameter determines if the message box window is modal or modeless.

A *modal window* is one that requires the window to be closed before the user can access another window. A *modeless window* does not need to be closed before a user can access another window.

If the hWnd parameter in the message box is NULL, then the message box is a modeless window, otherwise if the message box is a modal window.

A typical message box is displayed in Figure 1–5 along with the statements that are necessary to generate the message box (see Code 1–6).

Code 1-6

```
if( MessageBox( hWnd, "Are you sure you want to exit?",
        "Confirmation", MB_ICONQUESTION|MB_YESNO|MB_DEFBUTTON1 )
        == IDYES ) PostQuitMessage(0);
```

In the statements in Code 1–6, the hWnd parameter is the handle to the main window of the application. The MessageBox() function is a predefined window and therefore has its own message loop. Furthermore, since the hWnd parameter is not NULL, the message box is modal and the WinMain() message loop stops running until the message box is closed. The WinMain() message loop continues to run if the hWnd parameter is NULL, making the message box a modeless window.

The "Are you sure you want to exit?" parameter (see Code 1–7) is a literal string that contains the message that appears in the center of the message box. The "Confirmation" parameter is the literal string that contains the caption of the message box. MB_ICONQUESTION|MB_YESNO|MB_DEFBUTTON1 is bit-mask value that tells Windows to display the question mark icon, a Yes button, a No button, and make the Yes button (button 1) the default button.

Table 1.1 lists the various bit-mask values that can be used with the MessageBox() function.

Code 1-7

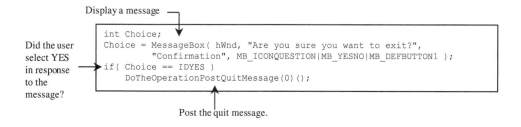

```
Display a message
                        int Choice;
Did the user            Choice = MessageBox( hWnd, "Are you sure you want to exit?",
select YES                      "Confirmation", MB_ICONQUESTION|MB_YESNO|MB_DEFBUTTON1 );
in response          →  if( Choice == IDYES )
to the                      DoTheOperationPostQuitMessage(0)();
message?
                    Post the quit message.
```

Table 1.1   Message Box Bitmask Values

Button Selection

Flag	Buttons Displayed
MB_ABORTRETRYIGNORE	Abort, Retry, and Cancel
MB_OK	OK
MB_OKCANCEL	OK and Cancel
MB_RETRYCANCEL	Retry and Cancel
MB_YESNO	Yes and No
MB_YESNOCANCEL	Yes, No, and Cancel

Icon Selection

Flag	Icon That Appears
MB_ICONEXCLAMATION, MB_ICONWARNING	Exclamation point
MB_ICONINFORMATION, MB_ICONASTERISK	Lowercase I in a circle
MB_ICONQUESTION	Question mark
MB_ICONSTOP, MB_ICONERROR, MB_ICONHAND	Stop sign

Default Button Selection

Flag	Default Button
MB_DEFBUTTON1	The first button. This is the default if nothing else is specified.
MB_DEFBUTTON2	Second button, whatever that may be.
MB_DEFBUTTON3	Third button, whatever that may be.
MB_DEFBUTTON4	Fourth button (see MB_HELP below).

Controlling the Modal Behavior

Flag	Modal Behavior
MB_APPLMODAL	The user can not interact with the parent window (specified by the first parameter to message box) until the user has closed the message box. This is the default if none of the other MODAL options are specified.
MB_SYSTEMMODAL	Similar to MB_APPLMODAL, except that the message box will remain the top-most window (will not be covered up by other windows).
MB_TASKMODAL	The user can not interact with any other window in the program until the user has closed the message box. If there is only one other window (often the case) then this option is just like MB_APPLMODAL.

(continued)

Table 1.1   Continued

<table>
<tr><td colspan="2" align="center">**Additional Options**</td></tr>
<tr><td>*Flag*</td><td>*Option*</td></tr>
<tr><td>MB_DEFAULT_DESKTOP_ONLY</td><td>Insures the user is logged on, in a secured network environment, otherwise the function call will fail.</td></tr>
<tr><td>MB_HELP</td><td>Adds a HELP button (may be the fourth button) to the dialog. Clicking the help button will generate a WM_HELP message for the application.</td></tr>
<tr><td>MB_RIGHT</td><td>Text is right justified.</td></tr>
<tr><td>MB_RTLREADING</td><td>For Hebrew and Arabic installations, displays text right-to-left.</td></tr>
<tr><td>MB_SETFOREGROUND</td><td>Forces the message box into the foreground, even if the application was not active at the time. Unlike being a topmost message box, the user can select another application, which may cover up the message box again.</td></tr>
<tr><td>MB_TOPMOST</td><td>The message box will be topmost, meaning that it will appear and stay above other windows (as long as the other windows are not also topmost).</td></tr>
<tr><td>MB_SERVICE_NOTIFICATION</td><td>Used by Windows NT, this permits a service to display a message box. A service is running even if a user is not logged in.</td></tr>
<tr><td>MB_SERVICE_NOTIFICATION_NT3X</td><td>Similar to MB_SERVICE_NOTIFICATION, but used by Windows NT 3.x.</td></tr>
<tr><td colspan="2" align="center">**Return Values**</td></tr>
<tr><td>*Return Value*</td><td>*Description*</td></tr>
<tr><td>IDABORT</td><td>Abort button was selected.</td></tr>
<tr><td>IDCANCEL</td><td>Cancel button was selected, ESC was pressed, or used closed dialog with the "X" button on the upper right corner.</td></tr>
<tr><td>IDIGNORE</td><td>Ignore button was selected.</td></tr>
<tr><td>IDNO</td><td>No button was selected.</td></tr>
<tr><td>IDOK</td><td>OK button was selected.</td></tr>
<tr><td>IDRETRY</td><td>Retry button was selected.</td></tr>
<tr><td>IDYES</td><td>Yes button was selected.</td></tr>
</table>

Dialog-based Windows Applications

The "Hello World" program on page 19 is considered a *non-dialog-based* Windows application. This means that the program creates a custom window type or class for the main window and is responsible for the behavior and appearance of an application. In this type of program, you must implement the message loop, the window procedure, and call the RegisterClass() function. This type of program is good when your application will not have lots of child windows, like in a paint program.

An alternative to this is a *dialog-based* application. A dialog-based Windows application is an application where the main window coordinates child windows. Child windows are responsible for the behavior and appearance of an application.

A dialog-based application requires at least one dialog, which will serve as the main window. The dialog is created using the dialog editor tool in Visual C++ and is displayed by calling the DialogBox() function in the WinMain() function. A dialog-based application does not register a window class, call the CreateWindow() function, or provide a message loop. Examples throughout the remainder of this book use dialog-based applications.

Dialog-based applications are most like the applications created normally in Visual Basic or Delphi, and are also called "Form-based" applications.

Creating Programs with Visual C++ and AppWizard

Visual C++ has a utility called AppWizard to help you create a starting or skeleton program. When you select the File/New menu items and select a project type, AppWizard will start executing. AppWizard is a series of dialogs that asks you questions about the type of program you want to generate and what basic features you want it to have (such as database access or OLE automation). Once you've completed all the steps, AppWizard will generate the files need to compile the program.

The program that AppWizard generates is a skeleton, or starting point program. For instance, it will give the program a File-Open menu choice that will pop up the file-open dialog box, but it will not load any files. You need to determine where in the program you will be adding the needed code to make the program act specifically the way you want.

Creating an SDK Program

We'll first go through the VC++ steps to create an SDK-style program. The program that it generates will be organized slightly differently from our previous example, and it will look different, but you will find in that program the same basic code that we presented earlier. To create the program, perform the following steps:

1. In Visual C++, select the File/New menu choice.
2. With the Projects tab highlighted, select the Win32 Application project type.
3. Enter the desired name for your project in the Project Name edit box.
4. Click OK.
5. Select "A Typical 'Hello World' Application" from the next dialog and click Finish.
6. Click OK at the next dialog to create the program.

That's it. Press F7 to compile your program and CTRL-F5 to run it, and you should see a Hello World program appear.

You should notice the following differences between this program and the one we presented earlier.

The Use of LoadString

Each Windows program executable file contains resources. Resources might be menus, dialogs, bitmaps, icons, and so on. One type of resource is also called a string table. A string table is just that, a table of strings where each one has a unique ID. The LoadString() function is used to load a string from the string table into memory.

Keeping strings in a string table has several advantages. For one, it saves memory space, loading the string only when needed. Also, if you put your strings into a string table rather than hard coding them (as we did in our first Hello World program), then it makes it easy to change the strings later using a different string table. This makes things like internationalization of your program easier.

Use of TCHAR Instead of char

Also along the lines of internationalization, you will notice the use of TCHAR where you would normally expect char. A TCHAR is a data type that may be either an 8-bit or 16-bit character. The 16-bit characters, or wide characters, are for supporting Unicode. Unicode is the character set that Windows uses for internationalization and is only fully supported on NT (not Win95 or 98). Because the TCHAR is actually part of a conditional compilation in the header files, it will

---

normally be defined as a char, but not always. Note: If you use Unicode, then your program will probably not work on Win9x machines.

The Use of LoadAccelerator

An accelerator is yet another type of resource contained in a Windows executable file. An accelerator table allows you to define key combinations, or hotkeys, that should send a certain message to a program, like a menu item. For example, if you had a menu item with an ID of IDM_BOLD that turned on boldfacing, you could define an accelerator for CTRL-B, which would also send the IDM_BOLD click notification to the program, as if the user selected it from the menu. You can examine the Accelerator table in the resource view of Visual C++.

The Use of lpszMenuName in the WNDCLASS Structure

Unlike our earlier program, this program has a simple menu. The menu has File/Exit and Help/About menu options. The menu itself is also stored in the resource file, and the WndProc() has been modified to pay attention to the user's menu selections [see the case WM_COMMAND in WndProc()].

Microsoft Foundation Classes

The *Microsoft Foundation Classes* (MFC) are a collection of C++ classes from Microsoft that simplify the creation of Windows applications. MFC provides classes to help you work with child windows, files, memory, collections of generic data types, and also to manage the application.

Most MFC-based applications have at least a View class, a Document class, and an Application class. The *Application class* is responsible for the start-up and shutdown of the program, as well as other application-level items such as easy access to registry settings.

The *Document class* is used to hold the data the program works with and has the responsibility of saving and loading the data from and to a disk file. When you want to work against the data of your application—for example, to determine if the data has changed or if any data has been entered—you would work with the Document class.

The *View class* is responsible for displaying the data in the document to the user, as well as interacting with the user in order to create or change the data in the document. This means that while the document class is responsible for holding the data, it is the View class that displays it to the user and gets the users actions that might change it. Think of the View class as a window you look at to see the data.

A typical example of Document/View programming is a spreadsheet. The document class would hold a two-dimensional array of numbers and would provide functions to save, load, or clear out the numbers. The View class would be responsible for handling a File/Open menu choice and getting the filename, but it then asks the Document class to load the data. The View class would also get the numbers from the Document class to display possibly as either a grid of numbers or as a graph of some type. The Document and View classes communicate and work together very closely.

An MFC application provides a framework within which you insert the statements and functions that are necessary to execute your application. You must determine where in framework to place your statements. You will be using a feature called *Class-Wizard* to add the code to respond to user events.

You create an MFC application by running the *AppWizard*, which is a code generator. AppWizard prompts you with one or more dialogs about the type of program you want to create, and then generates a skeleton program with the features you requested. You then go and add whatever additional functionality you want. To run AppWizard, simply select the File/New menu options, then, in the New dialog, select the desired type of project from the Projects tab.

The next two sections address some basics pertaining to an MFC application. These are Running AppWizard, in order to create the base, skeleton, application, and then Enhancing an MFC Framework Application which identifies the basics of how to respond to messages in MFC.

Running AppWizard

As mentioned above, AppWizard can be used to create a skeleton program with some basic features that you select through a series of dialogs. The final result of running AppWizard is a series of files and C++ classes that use MFC classes and fit into the MFC framework, or way of doing things. The project created by AppWizard can be compiled and run immediately after running AppWizard.

The MFC framework (and the skeleton program that AppWizard generates) automatically provides a number of features that are based on choices you made while running AppWizard. Some of the features for a new project include:

- WinMain() is already written and is "hidden" in the framework source code (you will not see it in your source).
- WndProc() is already written and is "hidden" in the framework source code (you will not see it in your source).

- Default Icons for your application and its documents are created (you will see them in the resource editor and be able to change them).

- A default "About" dialog is created (you will see it in the dialog editor and be able to edit it).

- A default menu is provided, with options like File/Open, File/Exit, and Help/About (you will see it in the menu editor and may modify it there).

- The default menu options such as File/Open are handled automatically (you have the ability to replace the default menu handling or add new menu items by adding message handlers, described later).[*]

- The ability to add message handler functions to handle user events and window messages with *ClassWizard* is added. A message handler is a function that gets called when a window message or event occurs. This represents a different way of handling messages like we did with the `switch` statement of the WndProc() earlier. (ClassWizard is availble after the project was created, by selecting the View/ClassWizard menu item).

AppWizard Steps

Select the File/New menu choice. You will see the New dialog above appear. Make sure that the Projects tab (see Figure 1–6) is highlighted, that MFC AppWizard (exe) is highlighted, and that the Location field contains the parent folder of where you want to put your project. Give your project a name, and click the OK button.

Step 1

Figure 1–7 is the first AppWizard dialog to appear. This dialog is presented to allow you to decide on the basic initial appearance of your application. Your choices are:

Single document.   A single document program has a single view and can open only a single document at a time. Notepad is an example of a Single Document Interface, or SDI, program.

Multiple documents.   A multiple document program starts with a single view and can have several documents open at a time. Microsoft Word is an example of a Multiple Document Interface, or MDI, program.

Dialog-based.   A dialog-based application is a simple program with child controls. Though a dialog-based program may have a menu, AppWizard will not create

---

[*]The default handler for the File/Open menu item will pop up the common File/Open dialog to allow the user to open a file, and then open the file for you. It will not, however, read or write data from the file. In the past, when dealing with files, you may have been accustomed to the process of get filename, open file, read/write data, close file. This means that now you only need to worry about the read/write file process and the framework handles the rest.

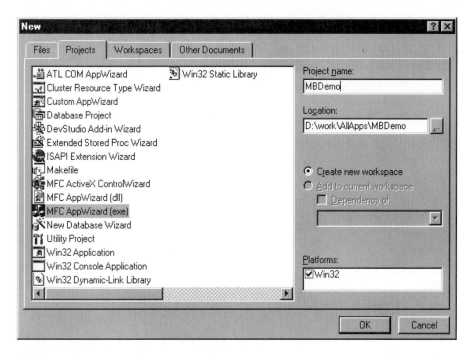

Figure 1–6 Select the type of project you want to create.

a menu for you (in MDI and SDI, it will). The Calculator is an example of a dialog-based application. This is good for small utility programs that don't have data files.

Document/view architecture support. The document/view architecture, if selected, provides an easy ability to save and load data files, as well as provide easy print and print preview features. Dialog-based applications do not provide document/view support; SDI and MDI do provide it by default.

Note: Choices you make in this dialog are extremely difficult to change after the project is generated.

Step 2 (assuming SDI or MDI was selected)

Figure 1–8 dialog allows you to select whether you want database support. If you want to access a database such as Access or SQL Server, you will want to make a selection here, otherwise the None selection is acceptable.

None. Your program will not access any databases.

Header files only. This means that the file afxdb.h will be included in your main project header file. It allows you to access databases but does not create a view or

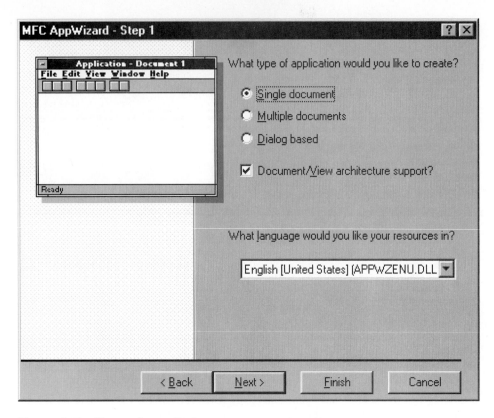

Figure 1–7   Choose the application type you want to create.

display that is specific to a database-style appearance. This is often a good choice when you want to create more robust database applications; this is easy to change after the project is generated.

Database view without file support.   This option means that you will want a simple database view or appearance to your program, with Next Record and Previous Record buttons. It also means that there will be no file menu choices (like File/Open), as it is assumed you will work with a database and not document files.

Database view with file support.   Like the previous option, only the file menu choices will still be available.

Data source.   If you selected a database view option, then you must select one or more tables from a database to work with. By pressing this button, you are led to a dialog where you can select an ODBC or DAO data source and then one or more tables from that data source.

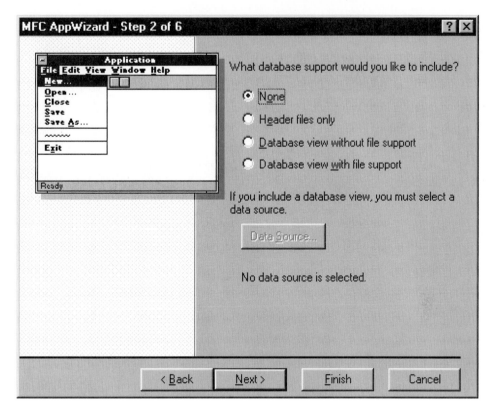

Figure 1–8 Choose the database support you want for your project.

Note: While the Database view options work nicely for very simple search and browse programs, more robust database applications will want to use the Header files only option and have more control over appearance and table control.

Step 3

Figure 1–9 dialog asks if you want to support compound documents. Compound documents are OLE documents. This means that you may let your documents be embedded in other applications like Microsoft Word, or that you might embed other documents (like Microsoft Word documents) in your own documents.

None. OLE documents are not supported.

Container. Documents from other OLE server applications (like Word) may be embedded into your documents.

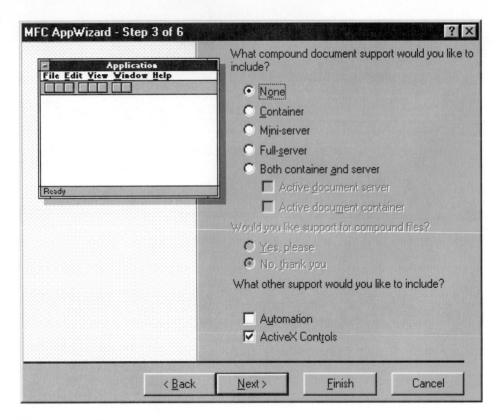

Figure 1–9   Choose the document support you want for your project.

Mini-server.   Other OLE server applications (like Word) may embed your documents within theirs, but your application will not run as a standalone. This is like creating a "plug-in" application whose sole purpose is to provide features to other applications but is not a complete application in itself.

Full-server.   Your documents can be embedded into the documents of other server applications, and your program may also work standalone. The Paint program is an example of this type of program (you can run paint standalone, and you can also embed a Paint picture in a Word document. If you double-click a Paint image in a Word document, then the Paint program will be run to edit it).

Both container and server.   This permits your program to contain other document types, like Word documents, and also let other documents (like Word documents) contain your document type.

Automation.   This provides the ability for your application to be controlled by other applications or your application to control other applications. For example, you could tell Word to print 10 copies of a particular Word document, or Word could tell your program to print 10 copies of one of your documents.

ActiveX controls. This provides the ability for your application to use ActiveX controls. ActiveX controls are a wide range of add-on controls such as a calendar, a multimedia viewer, and a variety of others. This option is default and, for all but the simplest programs, should remain checked.

Note: Selections made in this dialog are hard to undo after the project is generated.

Step 4

Figure 1–10 dialog prompts you for more details about the basic appearance of your application (for SDI and MDI programs only). Your options are:

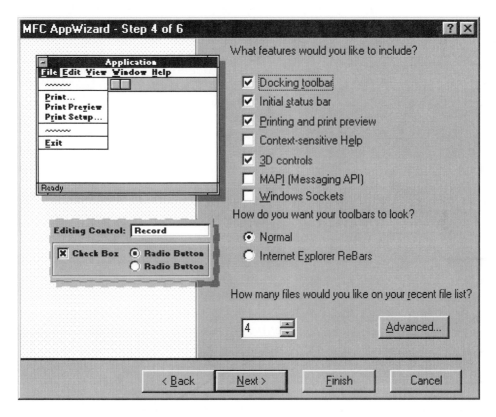

Figure 1–10 Identify the features you want to include in your project.

Docking toolbar.   This option indicates whether a dockable toolbar is provided. Word and Visual C++ are examples of programs with dockable toolbars. This option is recommended and moderately difficult to change after the project is generated.

Initial status bar.   This option indicates whether a status bar should appear at the bottom of the main window. This option is recommended and moderately difficult to change after the project is generated.

Printing and print preview.   This option indicates whether support for print and print preview is to be provided. If you are going to generate reports from this program, you should select this option. It is easy to disable this option after removing the print and print preview menu items. If you are not sure you want reports, consider this: It is easier to select this option now and then just disable the menu items later (if you don't want the feature) than it is to add the code and menu items manually.

Context-sensitive help.   This option indicates whether a default help project and file should be added to the program. If you want to add context-sensitive Help, then this option should be added. Note that this means you will also need to modify the Help file to be specific to your program as well. Adding this feature after the project is generated is moderately difficult but well-documented in the online Help.

3D controls.   If you want your program to have 3D controls (normal appearance), then select this option. This option is moderately difficult to enable after the project is generated; it is highly recommended that you leave it enabled.

MAPI (Messaging API).   This option should be selected if you will want your application to support MAPI for sending email. Also, if you want to support the Send menu item, which is required for a Windows 95 Logo application, you should enable this option. Adding this option after the project is generated is relatively easy.

Windows sockets.   If your program is going to be an internet-type program or use sockets for interprocess communications, this option should be checked. This option is very easy to enable after the project is generated.

How do you want your toolbars to look?   This option controls the appearance of your toolbars. Normal toolbars may be undocked and dragged anywhere within the application window, while Rebars may not be undocked. Rebars also start with a dialog bar that lets you add other controls such as a combo box to them. This option is moderately hard to change after the project is generated.

How many files do would you like on your recent file list?   The application will automatically have the ability to list in the File menu a list of recently used files. This option controls how many recent files should be kept. This option is relatively hard to change after the project is generated.

Advanced. Figures 1–11 and 1–12 illustrate dialogs that allow you to control things about your document, such as the default file extension and the class name that appears in Windows Explorer when the file type is displayed. It also permits you to control other aspects of your main window, such as if it should have a splitter window or the type of frame. These options are moderately difficult to change after the project is generated.

Step 5

Figure 1–13 prompts you for some final appearance questions, as well as source code comments and library usage.

What style of project would you like?   An MFC Standard project is one that has a typical window appearance, while the Windows Explorer style will have two windows, a tree view on the left and a list view on the right, like Windows Explorer. If you want a program that looks like Windows Explorer, then select the appropriate

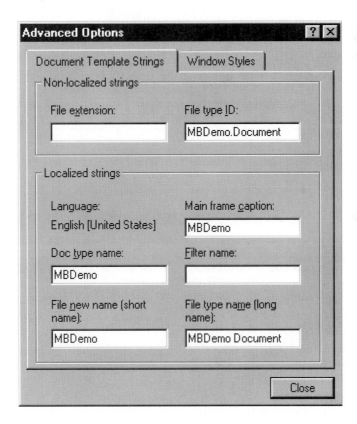

Figure 1–11   Enter the Document String tab for the application.

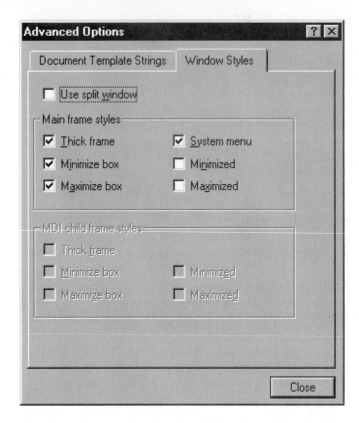

Figure 1–12 Use the Windows Style tab to select the Windows style.

option; otherwise, select MFC standard. This option is hard to undo after the project is generated.

Would you like source file comments? This polite option asks if you want comments added to your source code. If you select "Yes, please," then various To Do comments are inserted in the generated source code to help you make various changes. Use of this option is highly recommended and is pointless to add after the project is generated.

How would you like to use the MFC library? This prompt is not available in all Visual C++ versions—some only provide the "As a shared DLL" option. If you select the shared DLL option, then your EXE file will be small, but you must also provide the MFC42.DLL file when you distribute your executable. If you select statically linked, then your EXE file will be larger, but you won't need to distribute the MFC42.DLL file. Note that other features you use in your application may require you to distribute other DLL files.

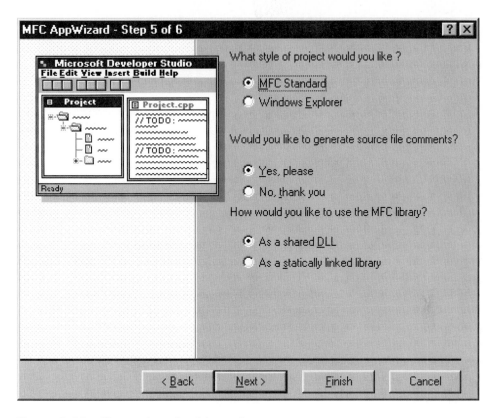

Figure 1–13 Choose the style of the project you want to create.

Step 6

Figure 1–14 is the final dialog with prompts. In this dialog, you will have the ability to select the type of base class you want for your View class. Changing this option after the project is generated is difficult. The View class determines the appearance of your main view window. Your options for a View class are:

CEditView. This view type will create a single edit box on the main view that is automatically sized to fit the main window. In addition, the File and Edit menu choices are linked to the Edit control. In other words, this option will provide you with a fully functional program very similar to Notepad, without your having to write any code.

CFormView. This class creates a view that is similar to a dialog-based application; that is, the main view will be a dialog resource and you can easily drop controls such as edit boxes and buttons on it.

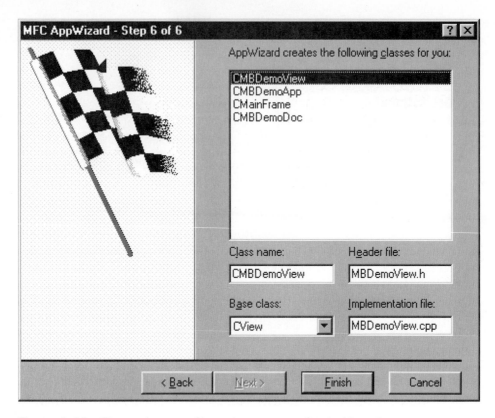

Figure 1–14   Choose the type of base class you want for the View class.

CHtmlView.   This class creates a view that contains an HTML window. It's helpful when you want to create programs similar to a web browser. Unlike CEditView, it does not generate a fully functional browser program.

CListView.   This generates a view whose main window contains a list control. An example of a list control is the right-hand window of Windows Explorer. It has the ability to list items with small icons, large icons, or in a columnar format.

CRichEditView.   This view generates a window whose single child window is a rich edit control. This will be able to display multiple font types and styles and will be able to directly interpret Rich Text Format (RTF) files.

CScrollView.   This class is similar to the CView class, but provides built-in support for scroll bars.

CTreeView.   This generates a view whose main window contains a tree control. An example of a tree control is the left-hand window of Windows Explorer.

CView.   A Cview is a main view that has no special features and creates a view that is similar in appearance to the SDK program we created earlier. It is a simple view appearance.

The two most commonly used views are CFormView and CView. If you want a program that will contain child controls and you can respond to child events like button clicks, select CFormView. If you want a view that you can draw directly on and respond to mouse messages easily, select the CView or CScrollView. Note that once the project is generated, you can add additional features as desired (for example, you can draw on a CFormView, or add controls to a CView). The point of this selection is to simplify the primary purpose of your window.

Creating a Typical MFC Application

1. Select File/New to display the New dialog.
2. Select the Projects tab.
3. Select MFC AppWizard (exe) as the project type.
4. Enter "hello_mfc" or a name of your choice as the project name.
5. Enter the folder name where you want to store the project in the Location field.
6. Click OK and you are prompted to answer a series of questions.
7. Select SDI Document in the Step 1 dialog.
8. Click the Finish button and accept the default values for the remaining questions.
9. Click OK when the project description is displayed to create the framework.
10. Press F7 to compile the framework into a program.
11. Press Ctrl F5 to run the program. The default program has a menu and an About Help box.

Enhancing an MFC Framework Application

We will modify the MFC application framework to display Hello World (see Code 1–8) in the client area of the application's main window. This is similar to the Hello World program using the Windows Software Development Kit.

The AppWizard automatically creates a View class, which is responsible for displaying text in the client area of the application's main window and to process events. The View class is automatically named using the name that you have given to the project. Therefore, the name of the View class in the hello_mfc project is CHello_mfcView.

The definition of the CHello_mfcView class is contained in the hello_mfcview.cpp and hello_mfcview.h files. Open the hello_mfcview.cpp file in the Visual C++ editor and you'll notice that several member functions are defined. These member functions provide various features such as printing [OnPrepareDC(), OnBeginPrinting(), etc.] and screen display [OnDraw()]. We will add code to the function that controls program appearance, OnDraw().

Code 1–8

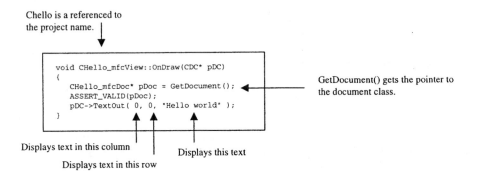

The OnDraw() member function is similar to SDK case statement that responds to the WM_PAINT message. When a WM_PAINT message is sent to the program, the OnDraw() member function is executed. The OnDraw() member function is called each time the windows is displayed. The OnDraw() function is an example of a "message map," where a particular window message is handled by a function, (or we can say the message is mapped to a function).

Find the OnDraw() member function in the hello_mfcview.cpp file and modify the function to reflect statements found in Code 1–8.

The Device Context (DC) is provided as a parameter in the form of a CDC object pointer and not as an HDC device context handle as in the SDK program. As with all MFC class names, CDC starts with "C," meaning "class." Other examples of class names include CString, CListbox, CArray, etc.

The CDC class is a wrapper class that wraps together the DC handle and related Graphical Device Interface (GDI) functions such as TextOut(). In our example on the opposite page, we are calling the TextOut() member function of the CDC class.

Compare the similar two lines between the SDK and MFC program versions shown in Code 1–9. They look very similar, however in the MFC program we only had to write a single line of code.

Code 1-9

```
pDC->TextOut( 0, 0, "Hello world" ); /* In MFC */
TextOut( DC, 0, 0, "Hello World", 11 ); /* In SDK */
```

MFC—"Hello World"—Dialog-Based

Just like the SDK programs had the ability to create dialog-based applications (see Figure 1–15), MFC programs do as well. As a refresher, a dialog-based application is primarily a program that has several child controls that make up the contents of the main window.

MFC provides two ways of making programs like this. The first is in Step 1 in App-Wizard, where we selected SDI application. If we had selected Dialog-based, then we would have had a program whose main window was a dialog.

An alternative would be in Step 6 in AppWizard (see Figure 1–16). In this dialog, you have the option of changing the base class for the View class that AppWizard is about to create. A CView base class means that the main window will most likely not have child controls. However, CFormView means that it will have child controls.

A CFormView-based class, once selected, will automatically add the dialog that will appear as the main window for your application. All you need to do is add controls

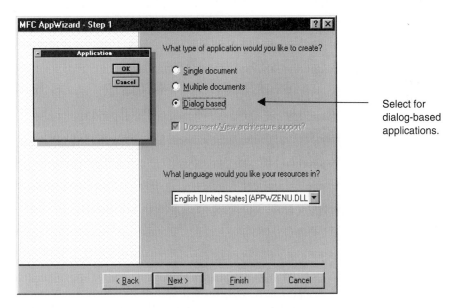

Figure 1–15 Choose the dialog-based radio button to create a dialog-based application.

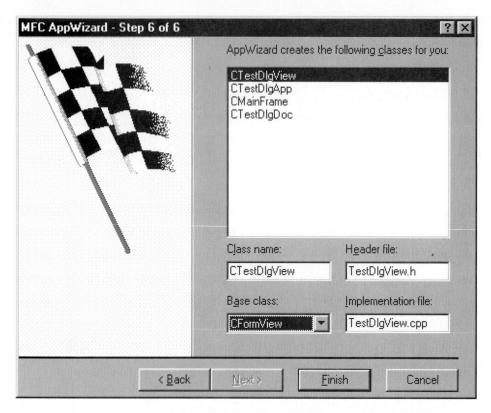

Figure 1–16   The AppWizard creates several classes for you.

for that dialog, and they will appear in the main window when the program runs. Since the child controls are assumed to have the responsibility of window appearance, you will note that CFormView view classes do not have an OnDraw() function automatically, like the default CView does.

To test out the CFormView class, execute steps 1 through 7 from the "Creating a Typical MFC Application" list (make sure to pick a new project name). At step 8, click the "Next" button until you reach "step 6 of 6" of the AppWizard. In this dialog, highlight the view class (its name will end in "View"), and change the Base Class combo box to say CFormView. Then click the Finish button and proceed from step 9 again.

If you select the Dialog-based application in step 1 of AppWizard (method 1 mentioned above), then your program will not have a Document or View class. If you select CForm-View in step 6 of AppWizard, then you will have a Document and View class. Document classes make it easy for your program to work with data files, and View classes make it easy to provide a print and print preview feature. Also, method 1 will not have a menu on the dialog by default, but you can easily add one.

SDI versus MDI

An MDI, or Multi-Document Interface, program is one like MS Word that can open several document files at once. An SDI, or a Single-Document interface, program like Notepad is one that can only open one document at a time (without running several instances of Notepad). From a programming standpoint (especially in MFC), there is very little difference between the two. So, in order to decide whether you want SDI or MDI, simply decide if you want the program to be able to work on several files at once (MDI) or not (SDI). In order to create either an MDI or SDI program in MFC, you simply select the desired option in the first dialog when you run App-Wizard.

Your Program Instance

In 16-bit windows, each program you run would use the same memory address space. But in order to conserve memory, Windows would attempt to reuse some of the resources of the application between the two running programs. Part of the approach in doing this involved assigning each running program a unique "Program instance." This unique program instance was a number that Windows could use to identify a particular program run from another run of the same application. Technically, the instance value was actually the address where the program data was loaded into memory.

In win32, however, each program runs in its own address space. Because of this, a program instance value may no longer be unique in Win32. But for reasons of backward compatibility we see the program instance value being used. Certain functions in the SDK and in MFC may require you to provide an instance value, or an HINSTANCE type, to a function for the program instance handle. The following are all methods by which you can get access to that value.

1. If your program is SDK-based, you can save the hInstance parameter to WinMain() in a global variable and then use that global variable anywhere you want the program instance.
2. If your program is SDK- or MFC-based, you call the GetModuleHandle() parameter with a parameter of NULL and it will return the instance handle for your program.
3. If your program is an MFC program, you can call the AfxGetInstance-Handle() function, and its return value is the instance of your program.
4. If your program is an MFC program, you can get the CWinApp object for your program, and its m_hInstance data member is the instance handle for your program.

Compiling a Windows Program

Press the F7 key to compile a project; press CTRL-F5 to run the application from within the Visual C++ environment.

When Visual C++ compiles a program, it is either a debug or release executable program. By default, programs are compiled as debug executable programs. Debug programs are much larger and slower then release programs, but you can examine them as they run in the Visual C++ environment.

You choose the mode in which to compile the program by selecting Build/Select Active Configuration, then choose the type of program mode. Debug-compiled programs are stored in the Debug subfolder located below the main folder for your project. Release programs are stored in the Release subfolder at the same location.

You should use the debug mode while you develop and test your programs. When you are confident that the program works, you should recompile it in release mode (to make a smaller, faster executable) and then distribute the release mode executable.

Distributing a Windows Program

Distributing a windows program can be as easy as giving someone the executable file on a disk. However, if your program is dynamically linked to a DLL or ActiveX Control file (OCX), then you must also include those files with your executable.

You can determine a list of the files you may legally redistribute by checking the REDIST.TXT file that is in your Program Files\Visual Studio folder. Hundreds of files are listed, most of which are not required to run your program. Certain features and options that you include in your application may require that you distribute other files with your application. Here are some guidelines to follow:

- Include these files if your program uses dynamically linked DLL or OCX files:
  MFC42.DLL   Main MFC class library
  MFCD42.DLL   MFC Database classes, CDatabase, CRecordset, etc.
  MSVCRT.DLL   Microsoft Visual C++ C Runtime library
- If you added an ActiveX Control file to your project, then you must include that file.
- If you are using the DAO record set classes, you should distribute the DAO install disks. This is a set of three disks that can be found in a

folder called DAOSDK\ReDist. The actual CD and location will depend on the version of Visual C++ you own.

- If your project uses ActiveX controls, COM, OLE or OLE Automation, include the following:
    - oleaut32.dll
    - secur32.dll
    - compobj.dll
    - ole2.dll
    - ole32.dll
- If you are using any of the newer common controls, include:
    - COMCTL32.dll

The DLL files above are normally installed in the System32 folder of the user installation. This folder is defined as %SystemRoot%\System32, where %SystemRoot% can be checked by getting the environment setting of SYSTEMROOT [with the getenv() function]. Your executable file can be placed anywhere you like, but is most often placed in a subfolder of the Program Files folder. Later on we will examine the steps needed to create an installation program that comes with the setup utility in Visual C++.

Chapter 2

Menus

- The Menu Resource
- Modifying/Inserting Menu Items
- Enabling/Disabling and Checking/Unchecking Menu Items
- Determining the Status of a Menu Item
- Sample SDK Program with Menu Selections
- Responding to Menu Selections in an MFC Program
- Enabling and Checking Menu Items in an MFC Program
- Pop-up Menus
- Responding to SDK and MFC Messages

A *menu* is method used to make a selection from a series of options. Two steps are required to insert a menu into a Windows application: First, the menu is created using the Visual C++ resource editor or any text editor as long as the file is saved with a .rc file extension. The exact steps for accessing the resource editor, which is integrated with the Visual C++ IDE, are described in later sections. The file is called a *script resource file*. A menu is defined using the resource scripting language, which is illustrated in Code 2–1. The resource file and its menu(s) are then compiled using the resource compiler (a part of the normal compilation process). A script resource file is automatically included in your project if you develop an MFC application or if you create the SDK program with the "A typical Hello World program" option of AppWizard. If your project was not created in this fashion, then you must manually add the .rc file to your Visual C++ project. Second, you must add the code to use the menu (tie it to the main window) as well as add the code that gets performed based on a user selection. To manually add a resource file to your project, perform the following steps (with your project open):

1. From the File menu, select the New menu choice.
2. In the New Dialog, select the Resource Script type in the Files tab and enter a filename (with .rc extension) for the resource.
3. Click OK.

The Menu Resource

An example of a menu definition is displayed in Code 2–1. The menu definition must contain a resource name (IDR_MENU1) and a keyword that specifies the definition as a menu definition (MENU). You should also indicate whether Windows could discard the menu (DISCARDABLE). Discardable means that when Windows is low on memory, the memory for that resource will be discarded temporarily. If the resource is needed again, it is reloaded.

Two menu items are defined in Code 2–1. These are File and Exit. File appears on the menu bar; File is a pop-up menu (POPUP) that contains one item: Exit. The ampersand appears before the letter that is underscored to indicate the shortcut key. A *shortcut key* is used to select the menu item using the keyboard.

You must give the menu (IDR_MENU1) and each menu item that appears on a pop-up menu (ID_MENUEXIT) a unique ID (individual pop-up menus like File and Edit are not assigned IDs). An ID is a numeric value that is associated with a name. The association of the ID's name and number is made using a #define statement contained in the resource.h file as illustrated in Code 2–1. When you create a resource file using the resource editor in Visual C++, the resource.h file is created and maintained automatically for you.

Code 2–1

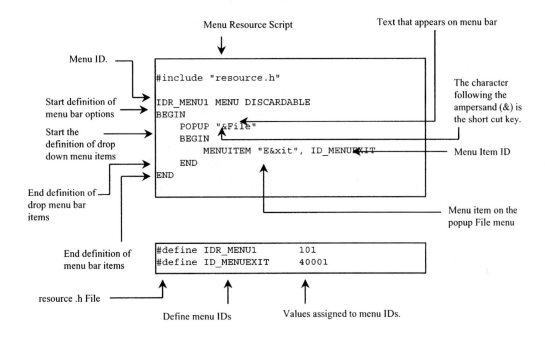

Numeric values used for IDs (101, 40001) are not meaningful, but should be a unique value in the resource.h file. The resource editor automatically assigns ID names and values and enters the IDs in the resource file and resource.h file.

Once the menu is defined, changes must be made to the source code to reflect menu selections. How to do this is described in the *Responding to Menu Selections in an SDK Program* and *Responding to Menu Selections in an MFC Program* sections.

When you compile the application, the resource file is converted into a compiled resource file that contains the .res file extension. The compiled resource file is then linked with the application's executable file.

Modifying/Inserting Menu Items

Once you associate a menu to your project, use the Visual C++ menu editor to change the menu. To access the menu editor, just locate the menu in the Resource View (left of Visual C++ environment) and double-click the menu ID (see Figure 2–1).

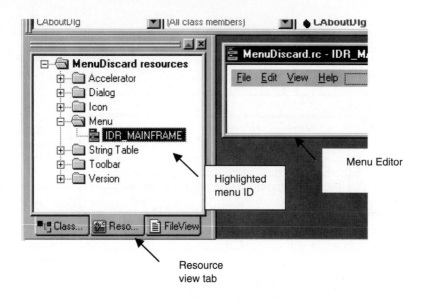

Figure 2–1 Associate a menu with your project using the Resource View.

Table 2.1 Properties of a Menu

Setting	Description
ID	The unique identifier for the menu item (not available for pop-up menus).
Caption	The menu item caption. Use & to indicate the underlined, or hotkey, value. If you add a \t (tab character) to the string, you can present items like shortcut keys (Ctrl+N in the demo above) that appear on the far right of the pop-up menu.
Separator	If checked, then the menu item is simply a dividing line, for appearance. The user will not be able to select it as an option.
Checked	Indicates whether a checkmark should appear next to a menu item.
Popup	Indicates if the menu is a selectable option, or simply a pop-up for another submenu. Common examples of pop-up items in a menu are the top-level items File, Edit, and Help.
Grayed	Indicates if the menu item should be grayed (disabled).
Inactive	Indicates if the menu item should be disabled. If a menu item is grayed, then it is also inactive, but not vice versa. From a visual standpoint, newer programs use the Grayed status to disable a menu item.

(continued)

Table 2.1   Continued

Setting	Description
Help	The menu item is right-justified at runtime. This is most often used with the Help menu item only, when you want it to appear on the far right of the menu bar, by itself.
Break	Indicates if the menu item should appear in its own column or bar section. This option is not commonly used.
Prompt	This is used only in MFC-style programs. Text you put here is displayed in the status bar when the user selects the option, as well as in the tooltips for controls. The string is organized as *statustext\ntooltip text* where *statustext* is the text to display in the status bar, \n is a separator (entered as \n) and *tooltip* is the text to display when the user hovers over the menu item (or toolbar item).

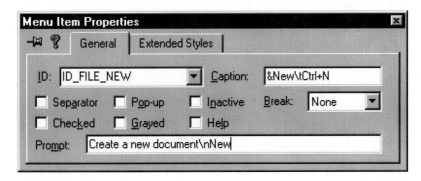

Figure 2–2 Menu Item Properties.

Double-click on a menu item to display the menu item's properties, then modify any property. An example of a property dialog for a menu resource appears in Figure 2–2. Table 2.1 identifies the available menu properties.

You can insert a new menu it by clicking on the menu bar or on a pop-up menu list, then pressing the Insert key. Double-click on the new item, and you can change its properties.

Place an ampersand (&) in the menu item caption to the left of the character you want as the menu hotkey. Windows automatically underlines the hotkey character.

Adding a Menu to an SDK Application

Adding a menu item to an SDK program is the same as adding it to an MFC program. This section will address the changes you need to make to your code for an SDK program to implement the menu.

Associating a menu with an SDK application is a two-step process: First, attach the menu to a window class using the menu's ID; second, write statements within application's WindProc() to respond to menu events.

Attaching the Menu

A menu is attached to a window class rather than to a specific window. Any window object created using that class is created with that menu.

The lpszMenuName property in the WNDCLASS in WinMain() must be modified to reflect the application menu. Assign to the lpszMenuName property either the integer used as the menu ID or the string name you used to identify the menu in the resource file (rc). You can use the MAKEINTRESOURCE macro to convert the menu symbol ID to the menu integer ID (see Code 2–2).

Code 2–2

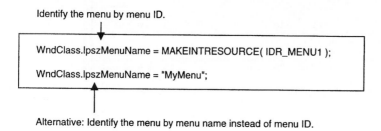

Identify the menu by menu ID.

```
WndClass.lpszMenuName = MAKEINTRESOURCE( IDR_MENU1 );

WndClass.lpszMenuName = "MyMenu";
```

Alternative: Identify the menu by menu name instead of menu ID.

If you opted to assign a string name to your menu instead of a unique integer ID (which was detailed above), then you can use the same string as the lpszMenuName property of the WndClass. However, since using an integer ID improves the ability to catch misspellings (the compiler will not detect if you used strings "IDM_MENU_MAIN" and "IDM_MENUMAIN," but can tell if you used IDM_MAIN_MENU and IDM_MAINMENU), it's recommended that you not use string names.

Responding to Menu Selections in an SDK Program

Several messages are sent when a menu item is selected. These are WM_SYSCOMMAND, WM_INITMENU, WM_MENUSELECT, and WM_INITMENPOPUP. Windows addresses these messages and sends a WM_COMMAND message to your application.

The WM_COMMAND message is sent to WindProc() in the uMessage parameter (see *Windows Messaging* in Chapter 1). For WM_COMMAND, the wParam parameter of the WindProc() is divided into two parts: The *low-word value* contains the ID of the window that sent the message and the *high-word value* indicates whether the selection is made from an accelerator key (the underscore letter in the menu) or by the user's clicking the menu. A value of 1 indicates an accelerator is used and a value of 0 indicates the selection is from clicking the menu. The lParam parameter of the WindProc() contains the handle of the window that generated the message.

Each window (child or parent) has a unique window handle, or HWND. Each window also has an ID that must be unique amongst its siblings (in other words, a parent window cannot have two child windows with the same ID). The GetDlgItem() and GetWindowLong() functions can be used to get the HWND for a child window via its ID, or its ID via its HWND. Most window functions will require an HWND.

When a menu choice is made, the uMessage parameter is evaluated by the switch statement. If the message is WM_COMMAND, the LOWORD() macro is used to evaluate the low-word of the wParam parameter to determine the ID of the selected menu item (see Code 2–3).

Code 2–3

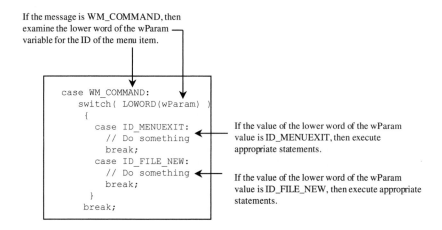

If the message is WM_COMMAND, then examine the lower word of the wParam variable for the ID of the menu item.

```
case WM_COMMAND:
    switch( LOWORD(wParam) )
    {
        case ID_MENUEXIT:
            // Do something
            break;
        case ID_FILE_NEW:
            // Do something
            break;
    }
    break;
```

If the value of the lower word of the wParam value is ID_MENUEXIT, then execute appropriate statements.

If the value of the lower word of the wParam value is ID_FILE_NEW, then execute appropriate statements.

Enabling/Disabling
and Checking/Unchecking Menu Items

Menu items can be enabled, disabled, or grayed, and checked or unchecked depending on the needs of the application. An application should enable menu items only if the menu item is applicable to the current activity. If not, then the menu item should be disabled, which means the text appears normal but is inactive. An inactive menu item should also be grayed, which displays the text of the menu items as a shadow. Current menu selections should be checked and those not currently selected should not be checked.

The EnableMenuItem() function enables, disables, and grays a menu item. Enable-MenuItem() has three parameters. The first parameter is the handle of the menu. The handle is identified by using the GetMenu() function. The GetMenu() function must be passed the hWnd handle as the first argument in the WindProc() function of the window.

The second parameter of the EnableMenuItem() function contains the ID of the menu item that is being enabled or disabled. The third parameter contains a flag that determines if the menu item is enabled, disabled, or grayed. Flags are MF_DIS-ABLED, MF_ENABLED, and MF_GRAYED.

These flags can be combined with a flag that identifies the menu item by using the OR operator (|). The flags are MF_BYCOMMAND and MF_BYPOSITION. MF_BY-COMMAND, which is the default flag, tells the function that the second parameter contains a menu ID. MF_BYPOSITION tells the function that the second parameter contains an integer that represents the position of the menu.

The position of a menu item is indicated by its physical position within the menu. The first item is position 0, the second position 1, and so on. While menu items are most commonly enabled or disabled with the MF_BYCOMMAND option, MF_BY-POSITION can be helpful when you want to enable or disable an array of contiguous menu items (see Code 2–4).

Code 2-4

```
EnableMenuItem(GetMenu(hWnd),ID_ADDBUTTON, MF_ENABLED | MF_BYCOMMAND );
```

This code returns the previous enabled status, or 0xFFFFFFFF upon error. Note how we used MF_GRAYED and not MF_DISABLED. MF_DISABLED will still work, but current user interface guidelines recommend the use of MF_GRAYED. Code 2–5 illustrates this technique.

Code 2-5

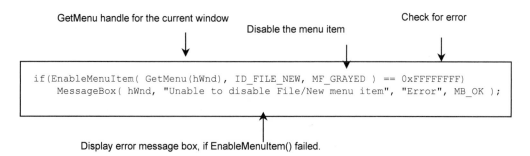

GetMenu handle for the current window

Disable the menu item

Check for error

```
if(EnableMenuItem( GetMenu(hWnd), ID_FILE_NEW, MF_GRAYED ) == 0xFFFFFFFF)
    MessageBox( hWnd, "Unable to disable File/New menu item", "Error", MB_OK );
```

Display error message box, if EnableMenuItem() failed.

The EnableMenuItem() function should only fail if you pass it bad parameters, such as a menu ID that is not in the current menu. This is not a typical occurrence, and errors, like not being able to open a file, should be caught when writing the program.

Checking/Unchecking a Menu Item in an SDK Program

The CheckMenuItem() function (see Code 2–6) is used to check or uncheck a menu item. CheckMenuItem() has three parameters. The first parameter is the handle of the menu, which is identified by using the GetMenu() function. The GetMenu() function must be passed the hWnd handle as the first argument in the WindProc() function.

The second parameter of the CheckMenuItem() function contains the ID of the menu item that is being enabled or disabled. The third parameter contains a flag that determines if the menu item is enabled, disabled, or grayed. Flags are MF_CHECKED and MF_UNCHECKED.

These flags can be combined with a flag that identifies the menu item by using the OR operator (|). The flags are MF_BYCOMMAND and MF_BYPOSITION. MF_BY-COMMAND, which is the default flag, tells the function that the second parameter contains a menu ID. MF_BYPOSITION tells the function that the second parameter contains an integer that represents the position of the menu it.

Returns the previous check status, or 0xFFFFFFFF upon error. Code 2–7 illustrates how this is done. The CheckMenuItem() function should only fail if you pass it bad parameters, such as a menu ID that is not in the current menu. This is not a typical occurrence or errors, like not being able to open a file, and should be caught when writing the program.

Code 2-6

```
CheckMenuItem(GetMenu(hWnd), ID_ADDBUTTON , MF_CHECKED | MF_BYCOMMAND );
```

Code 2-7

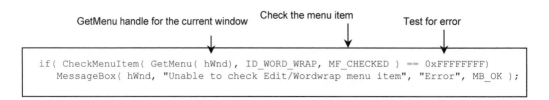

```
if( CheckMenuItem( GetMenu( hWnd), ID_WORD_WRAP, MF_CHECKED ) == 0xFFFFFFFF)
    MessageBox( hWnd, "Unable to check Edit/Wordwrap menu item", "Error", MB_OK );
```

Determining the Status of a Menu Item

Once your application changes the status of a menu item such as checking or enabling, the application should verify that the action is performed. The GetMenuItemInfo() function (see Code 2–8) retrieves detailed information about a menu item and its state. This function and the MENUITEMINFO structure it works with can help you determine if a menu item is currently checked, unchecked, enabled, or disabled; it returns the non-zero for success, zero for failure. Table 2.2 identifies the parameters required by the GetMenuItemInfo() function.

Code 2-8

```
BOOL GetMenuItemInfo(HMENU hMenu, UINT uItem, BOOL fByPosition, LPMENUITEM-
INFO lpmii );
```

Code 2–9 contains code needed in an SDK program to determine the status of a menu item. This code should be placed in the menu handler within the WndProc() function.

The MENUITEMINFO() function contains much more additional information for a menu item, such as bitmaps for menu items and submenus.

Table 2.2   Parameters for the GetMenuItemInfo() Function

Parameter	Meaning
hMenu	Handle to the menu
uItem	ID of the menu item or its position (based on *fByPosition*)
fByPosition	If TRUE, then *uItem* contains the menu item position; if FALSE, then it contains the menu item ID (normally, this is FALSE)
lpmii	Pointer to a MENUITEMINFO structure

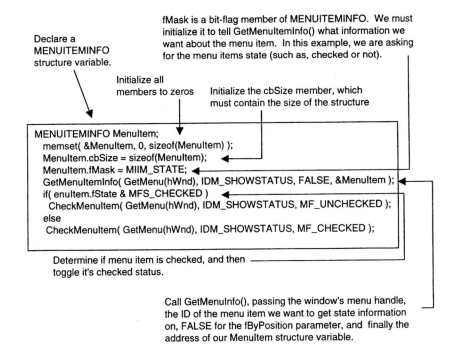

Declare a MENUITEMINFO structure variable.

fMask is a bit-flag member of MENUITEMINFO. We must initialize it to tell GetMenuItemInfo() what information we want about the menu item. In this example, we are asking for the menu items state (such as, checked or not).

Initialize all members to zeros

Initialize the cbSize member, which must contain the size of the structure

```
MENUITEMINFO MenuItem;
  memset( &MenuItem, 0, sizeof(MenuItem) );
  MenuItem.cbSize = sizeof(MenuItem);
  MenuItem.fMask = MIIM_STATE;
  GetMenuItemInfo( GetMenu(hWnd), IDM_SHOWSTATUS, FALSE, &MenuItem );
  if( enuItem.fState & MFS_CHECKED )
    CheckMenuItem( GetMenu(hWnd), IDM_SHOWSTATUS, MF_UNCHECKED );
  else
    CheckMenuItem( GetMenu(hWnd), IDM_SHOWSTATUS, MF_CHECKED );
```

Determine if menu item is checked, and then toggle it's checked status.

Call GetMenuInfo(), passing the window's menu handle, the ID of the menu item we want to get state information on, FALSE for the fByPosition parameter, and finally the address of our MenuItem structure variable.

TIP

More often than not, it's more convenient to create a global variable that reflects the current status of a menu item, which gets modified during menu processing, then to call the GetMenuItem-Info() function.

Sample SDK Program
with Menu Selections

The following example program (see Code 2–10) was created with the AppWizard "A typical Hello World program" option. The source code in bold shows code that was added or changed to implement a menu.

The menu was added with a single entry in the main menu, called Shape, and then four sub-menus, one of which had the Separator property set, and another, which was checked (Rectangle). Its appearance in the menu editor is shown in Figure 2–3.

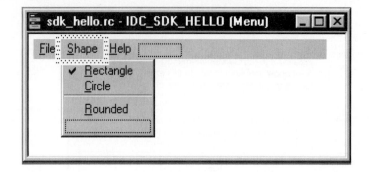

Figure 2–3 Here is the menu for the SDK program.

Code 2–10

```cpp
// sdk_hello.cpp : Defines the entry point for the application.
//

#include "stdafx.h"
#include "resource.h"

#define MAX_LOADSTRING 100

// Data that our program will be needing
int CurrentShape=IDM_RECTANGLE;
int IsRounded = FALSE;

// Global Variables:
HINSTANCE hInst;
TCHAR szTitle[MAX_LOADSTRING];
TCHAR szWindowClass[MAX_LOADSTRING];
ATOM MyRegisterClass(HINSTANCE hInstance);
BOOL InitInstance(HINSTANCE, int);
LRESULT CALLBACK WndProc(HWND, UINT, WPARAM, LPARAM);
LRESULT CALLBACK About(HWND, UINT, WPARAM, LPARAM);

int APIENTRY WinMain(HINSTANCE hInstance, HINSTANCE hPrevInstance,
                     LPSTR     lpCmdLine, int       nCmdShow)
{
        MSG msg;
        HACCEL hAccelTable;
        LoadString(hInstance, IDS_APP_TITLE, szTitle, MAX_LOADSTRING);
        LoadString(hInstance, IDC_SDK_HELLO, szWindowClass, MAX_LOADSTRING);
        MyRegisterClass(hInstance);
        if (!InitInstance (hInstance, nCmdShow))
                return FALSE;
        hAccelTable = LoadAccelerators(hInstance, (LPCTSTR)IDC_SDK_HELLO);
        while (GetMessage(&msg, NULL, 0, 0)) {
                if (!TranslateAccelerator(msg.hwnd, hAccelTable, &msg)) {
                        TranslateMessage(&msg);
```

```
                        DispatchMessage(&msg);
            }
        }
        return msg.wParam;
}

ATOM MyRegisterClass(HINSTANCE hInstance)
{
        WNDCLASSEX wcex;

        wcex.cbSize             = sizeof(WNDCLASSEX);
        wcex.style              = CS_HREDRAW | CS_VREDRAW;
        wcex.lpfnWndProc        = (WNDPROC)WndProc;
        wcex.cbClsExtra         = 0;
        wcex.cbWndExtra         = 0;
        wcex.hInstance          = hInstance;
        wcex.hIcon              = LoadIcon(hInstance, (LPCTSTR)IDI_SDK_HELLO);
        wcex.hCursor            = LoadCursor(NULL, IDC_ARROW);
        wcex.hbrBackground      = (HBRUSH)(COLOR_WINDOW+1);
        wcex.lpszMenuName       = (LPCSTR)IDC_SDK_HELLO;
        wcex.lpszClassName      = szWindowClass;
        wcex.hIconSm            = LoadIcon(wcex.hInstance, (LPCTSTR)IDI_SMALL);

        return RegisterClassEx(&wcex);
}

BOOL InitInstance(HINSTANCE hInstance, int nCmdShow)
{
    HWND hWnd;

    hInst = hInstance; // Store instance handle in our global variable

    hWnd = CreateWindow(szWindowClass, szTitle, WS_OVERLAPPEDWINDOW,
        CW_USEDEFAULT, 0, CW_USEDEFAULT, 0, NULL, NULL, hInstance, NULL);

    if (!hWnd)
        return FALSE;

    ShowWindow(hWnd, nCmdShow);
    UpdateWindow(hWnd);

    return TRUE;
}

LRESULT CALLBACK WndProc(HWND hWnd, UINT message, WPARAM wParam, LPARAM lParam)
{
        int wmId, wmEvent;
        PAINTSTRUCT ps;
        HDC hdc;
        TCHAR szHello[MAX_LOADSTRING];
        LoadString(hInst, IDS_HELLO, szHello, MAX_LOADSTRING);
        switch (message) {
                case WM_COMMAND:    // WM_COMMAND may indicate a menu selection
                        wmId = LOWORD(wParam);
                        wmEvent = HIWORD(wParam);
```

```
// Parse the menu selections:
switch (wmId)
{

        case IDM_ROUNDED:
        // User clicked the 'Rounded' menu item. Toggle its
        // check mark, and toggle the IsRounded variable as
        well
                IsRounded = ! IsRounded;
                CheckMenuItem( GetMenu(hWnd), IDM_ROUNDED,
                        IsRounded?MF_CHECKED:MF_UNCHECKED );
                InvalidateRect( hWnd, 0, TRUE );
                break;
        case IDM_RECTANGLE:
        case IDM_CIRCLE:
        // User selected the Rectangle or Circle menu item.
                {

                        HMENU hMenu = GetMenu( hWnd );
                        // Uncheck both the Circle and Rec-
                        tangle
                        // menu items
                        CheckMenuItem( hMenu, IDM_CIRCLE,
                                MF_UNCHECKED );
                        CheckMenuItem( hMenu, IDM_RECTANGLE,
                                MF_UNCHECKED );
                        // Now, check the menu item speci-
                        fied by
                        // wmId, which will be either the
                        Circle, or
                        // the rectangle.
                        CheckMenuItem( hMenu, wmId,
                                MF_CHECKED );
                        // If the circle menu item was se-
                        lected, then
                        // the 'rounded' menu item should be
                        // disabled.
                        if( wmId == IDM_CIRCLE )
                                EnableMenuItem( hMenu,
                                IDM_ROUNDED,
                                        MF_GRAYED );
                        else
                                EnableMenuItem( hMenu,
                                IDM_ROUNDED,
                                        MF_ENABLED );
                        // Save the current shape based on
                        selection
                        CurrentShape = wmId;
                        // Invalidate the main window, caus-
                        ing a
                        // WM_PAINT
                        InvalidateRect( hWnd, 0, TRUE );
                }
                break;
```

```
                        case IDM_ABOUT:
                            DialogBox(hInst, (LPCTSTR)IDD_ABOUTBOX, hWnd,
                                (DLGPROC)About);
                            break;
                        case IDM_EXIT:
                            DestroyWindow(hWnd);
                            break;
                        default:
                            return DefWindowProc(hWnd, message, wParam, lParam);
                }
                break;
            case WM_PAINT:
                hdc = BeginPaint(hWnd, &ps);
                // TODO: Add any drawing code here...
                RECT rt;
                GetClientRect(hWnd, &rt);
                // Based on the CurrentShape variable, draw a circle or rec-
                tangle
                if( CurrentShape == IDM_RECTANGLE )
                {
                        // If its a rectangle, determine if its rounded
                        if( IsRounded )
                                RoundRect( hdc, rt.left+10, rt.top+10,
                                rt.right-10,
                                        rt.bottom-10, 25, 25 );
                        else
                                Rectangle( hdc, rt.left+10, rt.top+10,
                                rt.right-10,
                                        rt.bottom-10 );
                }
                else
                        Ellipse( hdc, rt.left+10, rt.top+10, rt.right-10,
                                rt.bottom-10 );
                EndPaint(hWnd, &ps);
                break;
            case WM_DESTROY:
                PostQuitMessage(0);
                break;
            default:
                return DefWindowProc(hWnd, message, wParam, lParam);
    }
    return 0;
}


// Mesage handler for about box.
LRESULT CALLBACK About(HWND hDlg, UINT message, WPARAM wParam, LPARAM lParam)
{
        switch (message)
        {
            case WM_INITDIALOG:
                        return TRUE;

            case WM_COMMAND:
                    if (LOWORD(wParam) == IDOK || LOWORD(wParam) == IDCANCEL)
```

```
                                        {
                                                EndDialog(hDlg, LOWORD(wParam));
                                                return TRUE;
                                        }
                                        break;
                        }
                return FALSE;
        }
```

◯	In order to add a menu, you must add, or already have, a resource script in your project.
	Menu items are added without writing code; you use the menu editor.
	Menu items are enabled and disabled with EnableMenuItem().
	Menu items are checked and unchecked with CheckMenuItem().
◯	You must handle the WM_COMMAND to respond to the user's menu selections.
	In the WM_COMMAND message, you can do a LOWORD(wParam) to determine the ID of the menu that was invoked.
◯	To add a menu to your main window, if you created it, make sure to set the lpszMenuName variable of your WNDCLASS (or WNDCLASSEX) struct to the MAKEINTRESOURCE() value of your menu ID.

Responding to Menu Selections in an MFC Program

In order to respond to a user's menu choice, an MFC program does not inspect the window messages directly. Instead, you need to set up a message handler using ClassWizard. A message handler is a function that the MFC framework calls when the user selects that menu item. Message handlers are stored in an array called a *message map*. The demonstration here assumes that you created an MFC SDI application using AppWizard.

To your existing menu, add the following menu items as shown in the *Modifying/ Inserting Menu Items* section in this chapter (see Figure 2–4).

1. Add a Shape top menu item.
2. Add to Shape's drop-down menu the Rectangle, Circle, and Rounded menu items. Give the menu items IDs like IDM_RECTANGLE, IDM_CIR-CLE, and IDM_ROUNDED.

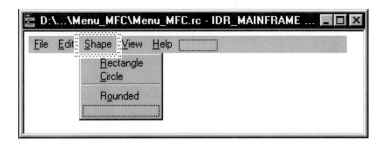

Figure 2–4 These menu items were created earlier in this chapter.

3. Go to ClassWizard by going to the View menu choice and selecting ClassWizard.
4. Go to the MessageMaps tab (see Figure 2–5) in the dialog.

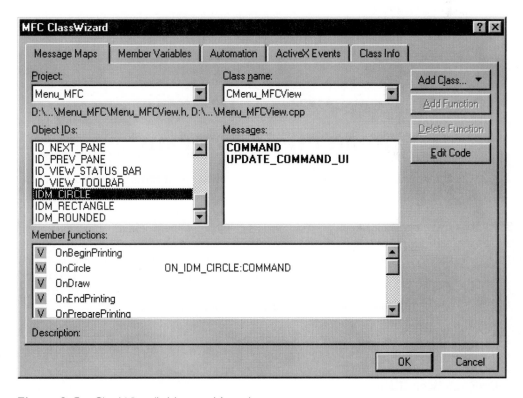

Figure 2–5 ClassWizard's Message Map tab.

5. In the Class Name field, select the name of your View class.
6. In the Object IDs field, select the menu item you want to add a handler for (IDM_CIRCLE, for example).
7. Click the COMMAND item in the Message list.
8. Click the Add Function button.
9. Click OK to the Add Member function dialog (accepting the function name it gives you).
10. Double-click on the new function in the Member functions list.
11. Inside the OnRectangle function, add the following:

```
MessageBox( "You selected Circle" );
```

12. Compile and run your program, testing the Rectangle menu choice.

Remember

◯	In MFC, you respond to menu commands by adding a message map, with ClassWizard.
◯	The Class Name, Object ID, and Message items in the message map tab of ClassWizard should be verified.
◯	The Class Name is normally your view, or mainframe document, for menus.

Enabling and Checking Menu Items in an MFC Program

In an MFC program, you won't be using the SDK functions to enable or check menu items. Instead, you will again be using the ClassWizard message map ability.

Just before a menu item is about to be displayed, the MFC framework calls the function specified as the UPDATE_COMMAND_UI handler. You add functions to handle the UPDATE_COMMAND_UI in the same way you do for handling a user's menu selection, the difference being that the function was not called because the user selected a menu item. However, because the framework is about to display it, it wants the menu item's appearance verified (checked, disabled, etc.).

When you write a function handler for UPDATE_COMMAND_UI, that function will receive a pointer to a CCmdUI object that represents the menu item (or possibly a child control as well). Using this pointer, you can call functions to enable, disable, check, or uncheck the item.

In the same way that our SDK example kept some variables to maintain the status of menu items, our MFC program will as well. For this reason, we add to the View class the following data members as shown in Code 2-11.

Code 2-11

```
int CurrentShape; // Keep track of Rectangle or Circle shape
int IsRounded; // Keep track if rectangle is rounded or not.
```

Now, after adding all the functions for handling the COMMAND and UPDATE_COMMAND_UI using ClassWizard, we will have six functions for each menu item. Make sure your functions look like Code 2-12.

Code 2-12

```
// CMenu_MFCView message handlers

void CMenu_MFCView::OnRectangle()
{
      CurrentShape = IDM_RECTANGLE;
      InvalidateRect( NULL );        // Force re-draw
}

void CMenu_MFCView::OnCircle()
{
      CurrentShape = IDM_CIRCLE;
      InvalidateRect( NULL );        // Force re-draw
}

void CMenu_MFCView::OnRounded()
{
      IsRounded = ! IsRounded;        // Toggle rounded status (our data member)
      InvalidateRect( NULL );         // Force re-draw
}

void CMenu_MFCView::OnUpdateRectangle(CCmdUI* pCmdUI)
{
      if( CurrentShape == IDM_RECTANGLE ) // Check or uncheck menu item
                        pCmdUI->SetCheck( TRUE );
      else
                        pCmdUI->SetCheck( FALSE );
}

void CMenu_MFCView::OnUpdateCircle(CCmdUI* pCmdUI)
{
      if( CurrentShape == IDM_CIRCLE ) // Check or uncheck menu item
            pCmdUI->SetCheck( TRUE );
      else
            pCmdUI->SetCheck( FALSE );
}

void CMenu_MFCView::OnUpdateRounded(CCmdUI* pCmdUI)
{
```

```
        if( IsRounded ) // Check or uncheck menu item
              pCmdUI->SetCheck( TRUE );
        else
              pCmdUI->SetCheck( FALSE );
        if( CurrentShape == IDM_RECTANGLE ) // Enable or disable menu item
              pCmdUI->Enable( TRUE );
        else
              pCmdUI->Enable( FALSE );
}
```

Finally, to complete the example, make sure you modify your OnDraw() function, originally added by AppWizard, to look like Code 2–13.

Code 2-13

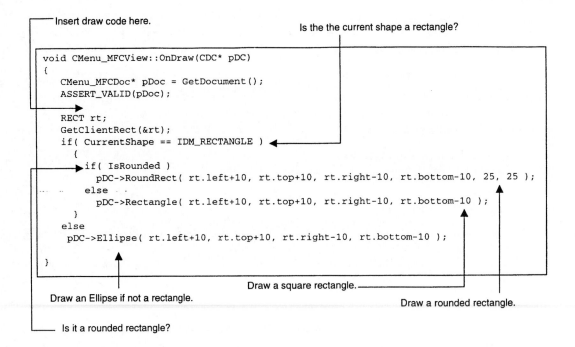

Insert draw code here.

Is the the current shape a rectangle?

```
void CMenu_MFCView::OnDraw(CDC* pDC)
{
    CMenu_MFCDoc* pDoc = GetDocument();
    ASSERT_VALID(pDoc);

    RECT rt;
    GetClientRect(&rt);
    if( CurrentShape == IDM_RECTANGLE )
      {
        if( IsRounded )
            pDC->RoundRect( rt.left+10, rt.top+10, rt.right-10, rt.bottom-10, 25, 25 );
        else
            pDC->Rectangle( rt.left+10, rt.top+10, rt.right-10, rt.bottom-10 );
      }
    else
      pDC->Ellipse( rt.left+10, rt.top+10, rt.right-10, rt.bottom-10 );

}
```

Draw an Ellipse if not a rectangle.

Draw a square rectangle.

Draw a rounded rectangle.

Is it a rounded rectangle?

Remember

○	ClassWizard is used to add a function to handle the appearance of menu items.
○ ○	The Class Name, Object ID, and Message items in the Message Map tab of ClassWizard should be verified.

Pop-up Menus

SDK

A pop-up menu is one that appears when you right-click an item. The keys to generating a pop-up menu are:

1. Create the menu in the resource editor.
2. Add to your code the LoadMenu() and GetSubMenu() items for the new menu.
3. Call TrackPopupMenu() to display the pop-up menu.
4. Call DestroyMenu() when done.

These steps assume you created your SDK program completely using AppWizard options. In VC++, go to the Insert menu option, select Resource, and then Menu from the New dialog. Your menu will be added with no items. Right-click on that menu, and change its name to IDR_POPUPMENU.

In your new menu, there will be only one main menu and a submenu for it. The caption for the top item is not important, but its subitems are important. Add menu items, such as Add, Edit, and Delete, so that the menu looks like Figure 2–6.

The Add, Edit, and Delete menu options should all have IDs like IDM_ADD, IDM_EDIT, and IDM_DELETE.

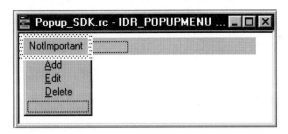

Figure 2–6 Pop-up menu in the menu editor.

In your Window Procedure, you need to add a handler for the WM_CONTEXTMENU item. To your WndProc, in the switch statement, add Code 2–14.

Code 2–14

Get mouse click coordinates, which are window-relative

Load the popup menu

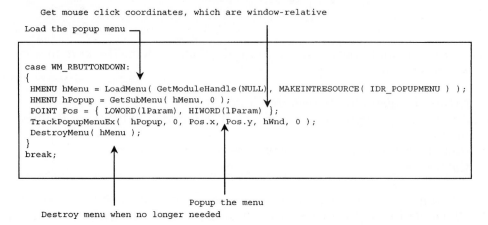

```
case WM_RBUTTONDOWN:
{
 HMENU hMenu = LoadMenu( GetModuleHandle(NULL), MAKEINTRESOURCE( IDR_POPUPMENU ) );
 HMENU hPopup = GetSubMenu( hMenu, 0 );
 POINT Pos = { LOWORD(lParam), HIWORD(lParam) };
 TrackPopupMenuEx( hPopup, 0, Pos.x, Pos.y, hWnd, 0 );
 DestroyMenu( hMenu );
}
break;
```

Popup the menu

Destroy menu when no longer needed

Code 2–14 will display the menu for you. When the user selects an item from the menu, the menu will close and its handle is destroyed. But, the user's selection is also sent back to the main window [the fifth parameter to TrackPopupMenu()]. So, to finish the demonstration, make the "case WM_COMMAND" in your WndProc() look like Code 2–15 (Items in bold are what you need to add):

Code 2–15

Identify the menu item or child control, by its ID

Child control or Menu notification   Parse the menu selections

Add item was selected

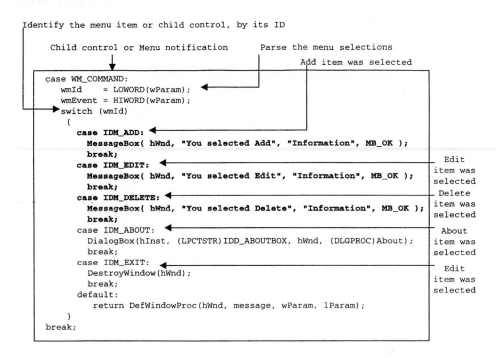

```
case WM_COMMAND:
    wmId    = LOWORD(wParam);
    wmEvent = HIWORD(wParam);
    switch (wmId)
      {
        case IDM_ADD:
          MessageBox( hWnd, "You selected Add", "Information", MB_OK );
          break;
        case IDM_EDIT:
          MessageBox( hWnd, "You selected Edit", "Information", MB_OK );
          break;
        case IDM_DELETE:
          MessageBox( hWnd, "You selected Delete", "Information", MB_OK );
          break;
        case IDM_ABOUT:
          DialogBox(hInst, (LPCTSTR)IDD_ABOUTBOX, hWnd, (DLGPROC)About);
          break;
        case IDM_EXIT:
          DestroyWindow(hWnd);
          break;
        default:
            return DefWindowProc(hWnd, message, wParam, lParam);
      }
    break;
```

Edit item was selected

Delete item was selected

About item was selected

Edit item was selected

Windows CE does not support the TPM_NONOTIFY, TPM_LEFTBUTTON, and TPM_RIGHTBUTTON flags for TrackPopupMenu().

MFC

The following steps are used to generate a pop-up menu using MFC, assuming that you created your MFC program completely using AppWizard options.

1. Create the menu in the resource editor. In VC++, go to the Insert menu option, select Resource, and then Menu from the New dialog. Your menu will be added with no items. Right-click on that menu and change its name to IDR_POPUPMENU.

   In your new menu, there will be only one main menu and a submenu for it. The caption for the top item is not important, but its subitem's is. Add menu items, such as Add, Edit, and Delete, so that the menu looks like Figure 2–7. The Add, Edit, and Delete menu options should all have IDs like IDM_ADD, IDM_EDIT, and IDM_DELETE.

2. Start the ClassWizard and add a message map for the WM_CON-TEXTMENU message for your View class. ClassWizard will look like Figure 2–8. Note the various settings such as Class name, Object ID, and Messages.

3. Click the Add Function button, and a function similar to Code 2–16 will be added for you by Visual C++.

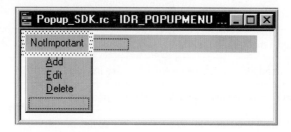

Figure 2–7 Pop-up menu for MFC program.

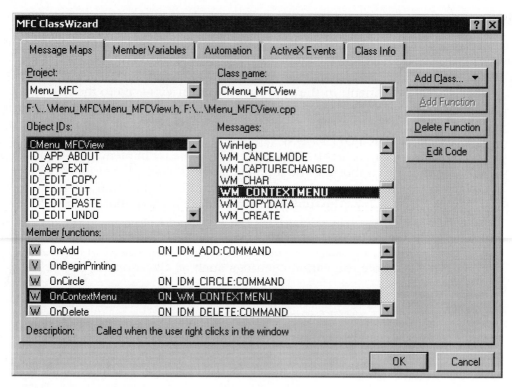

Figure 2–8 ClassWizard Message Map for context menu.

Code 2-16

```
void CMenu_MFCView::OnContextMenu (CWnd* pWnd, CPoint point)
{
        // TODO: Add your message handler code here and/or call default

        CView::OnRButtonDown(pWnd, point);
}
```

    4.   Change the OnContextMenu() function to look like Code 2–17.

Code 2–17

```
void CMenu_MFCView::OnContextMenu (CWnd* pWnd, CPoint point)
{
        // Create a temporary CMenu object, and load the Pop-up menu into
        it.
        CMenu Tmp;
        Tmp.LoadMenu( IDR_POPUPMENU );
        // Get a CMenu pointer to the first item in the pop-up menu
        CMenu* pPopup = Tmp.GetSubMenu(0);
        // Display the pop-up menu.
        pPopup->TrackPopupMenu(0, point.x, point.y, this );
}
```

Code 2–17 will display the menu for you. When the user selects an item from the menu, the menu will close and its handle is destroyed. But, the user's selection is also sent back to the main window (the fourth parameter to TrackPopupMenu). So, to finish the demonstration, you will need to go into ClassWizard again, to the Message Maps tab, and add message handlers for the new pop-up menu choices. In ClassWizard, your work should look like Figure 2–9.

Add the needed functions to handle the new pop-up menu items (three, in this demonstration). The code after adding these three message maps (and your changes) should look like Code 2–18.

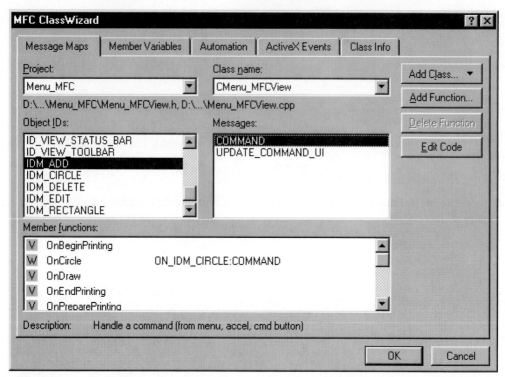

Figure 2–9   ClassWizard Message Map for pop-up menu item.

Code 2–18

```
void CMenu_MFCView::OnAdd() // Message map handler for Add menu selection
{
      MessageBox( "You selected Add" );
}
void CMenu_MFCView::OnDelete()// Message map handler for Delete menu selec-
tion
{
      MessageBox( "You selected Delete" );
}
void CMenu_MFCView::OnEdit()// Message map handler for Edit menu selection
{
      MessageBox( "You selected Edit" );
}
```

> **NOTE**
>
> Windows CE does not support the TPM_NONOTIFY, TPM_LEFTBUTTON, and TPM_RIGHT-BUTTON flags for TrackPopupMenu.

Responding to SDK and MFC Messages

Graphical User Interface (GUI) programs are conceptually different from procedural programs like DOS or console programs in how they interact with the user. A DOS or console program will prompt the user for an option, then wait for the user's selection, and respond to that selection.

A Windows program, however, will set up its main window with buttons and menu items, then ask Windows to display it. Then Windows takes over. When the user makes a menu choice or clicks a button, Windows sends a message to the running program to indicate the event has occurred. A main aspect of writing Windows programs is writing functions to respond to these events.

To handle events in an SDK program, you write a window procedure or a WndProc() that Windows will call when a message is sent to your program. In this function, you are given a Message parameter, which is a normal integer value that identifies the type of message being sent (such as WM_PAINT when you need to redraw your window or WM_LBUTTONDOWN when the user clicks a window). Your Window Procedure normally has a switch statement to help identify the message type and a case statement with the code to handle the message.

To handle events in an MFC program, you create a Message Map using Class-Wizard's Message Map tab. Using ClassWizard in this way, you can specify a function that should be called when a certain event has occurred, such as the user selecting a menu choice. Basically, ClassWizard lets you assign and create a function that is called when an event occurs; it's up to you to write your desired code in the function that ClassWizard adds. This is an aspect of all Rapid Application Development (RAD) tools.

This chapter has presented examples in both SDK and MFC for responding to things like menu selections or button clicks. Other controls, like list boxes and radio buttons, also send messages to the parent window when a list box item selection is changed or when the user clicks the radio button. Now would be a good time to review the examples above and try to make a mental note of the events that are occurring on the user's end and how the programs respond to those events. This concept of responding to messages will be used extensively throughout the book.

Remember

○	In order to add a menu, you must add, or already have, a resource script in your project.
	Menu items are added without writing code; you use the menu editor.
○	A pop-up menu has one main menu item, which is ignored.
	CMenu::TrackPopupMenu() is the function to display a pop-up menu.
	Add menu handlers for the new menu items with ClassWizards Message Map tab.
○	Make sure that each menu item has a unique numeric ID (can be done with the View/Resource Symbols menu item).

Chapter 3

Dialog Boxes

- Adding a Dialog
- Dialog Box Procedure
- Displaying or Popping up a Dialog
- Dialog Box as a Main Window
- Dialog-based Applications
- Using Dialogs for Data Entry
- Adding Code to the Main Dialog
- Creating a Modeless Dialog
- Common Dialogs

A dialog box, also referred to as a dialog, is a window class normally designed to help your program interact with the user. An example of a dialog box is the open dialog box that appears when you select File/Open from the menu bar. The open dialog box appears, and prompts the user for a file name. Dialog boxes make it convenient to create child windows at design time using the dialog editor, rather than having to call CreateWindow() to create a child window, as we did in the in previous chapters.

Dialog boxes are either modal or modeless. A *modal dialog*, like the File/Open example, means that the user cannot return to the main window until he or she has closed the dialog (usually by pressing the OK or Cancel button on the dialog). A *modeless dialog* permits the user to switch freely back and forth between the dialog box and the main application window.

Dialog boxes can have menu and child windows. Many of the attributes of a dialog box are modified in the dialog editor or in the .rc file for your project.

A dialog box requires a Window Procedure that handles messages for the dialog box. This is called the *dialog procedure,* and is a function you create.

The DialogBox() function is called to display the dialog box and the EndDialog() function is called to close the dialog box (for a modal dialog).

Adding a Dialog

In order to add a dialog box to your project, you must create a .rc file by following these steps:

1. From the Insert menu, select the Resource option.
2. Select Dialog from the dialog that appears and click New (see Figure 3–1).
3. Save the Resource Script file, with a filename the same as your project, but with the .rc extension.
4. Go to the Project/Add To Project/Files. . . menu item.
5. Select the new .rc file and click OK.
6. A ResourceView tab appears in the project viewer in the VC++ screen.

Once the dialog box is added to the project, the dialog editor is displayed (Figure 3–2). The window on the left is the dialog box that you are creating; on the right is the tool palette. The tool palette contains controls that are inserted in the dialog box by clicking on a control, then clicking on the dialog box to insert the control on the dialog. A control gives functionality to the dialog box.

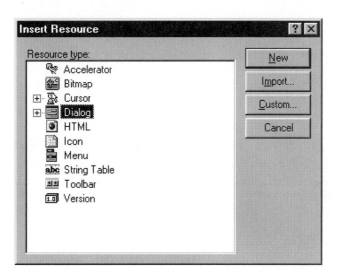

Figure 3–1   Insert Resource Dialog.

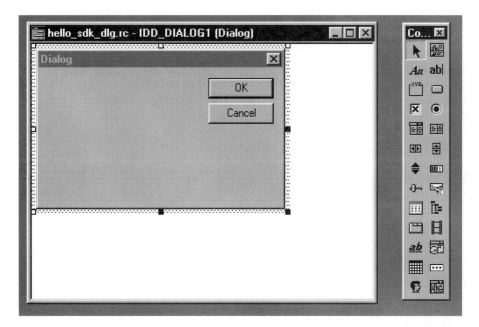

Figure 3–2   The Dialog Editor.

A dialog box has properties such as its caption or menu. Properties can be changed by right-clicking on the client area of the dialog box (the area of the dialog box that does not contain any controls) to display the Dialog Properties editor (Figure 3–3). Caution: If you right-click on a control placed on the dialog box (and not the dialog itself), the Properties editor will display properties for the child control.

Figure 3–3   Dialog Properties.

Dialog Box Procedure

Once a dialog box is added to the project, a dialog box procedure must be written. A dialog box procedure is a function that reacts to events that occur in the dialog box such as a click of the OK button. Typically, each dialog box has its own dialog procedure, but a dialog procedure can be shared by several dialogs. Shared dialog procedures are typically for very simple dialogs that perform very similar tasks; these seldom have more than one or two controls on them.

A dialog box procedure is similar to a Window Procedure in that it reacts to events within the window. Each dialog box procedure requires a prototype that describes the return value, function name, and parameter list to the compiler. Code 3–1 contains a dialog box prototype.

Code 3–1

```
LRESULT CALLBACK DlgProc(HWND hDlg, UINT message, WPARAM wParam, LPARAM
lParam);
```

We called the dialog box procedure DlgProc(), but you use any name that complies with the Windows naming convention for functions.

The return value of the dialog box procedure reflects the outcome of a message it receives, but if the dialog procedure does not handle a particular message, it should return 0 or FALSE (unlike the Window Procedure, which should have passed it on to DefWindowProc()). Code 3–2 is a dialog procedure for a typical dialog-based main window.

Code 3–2

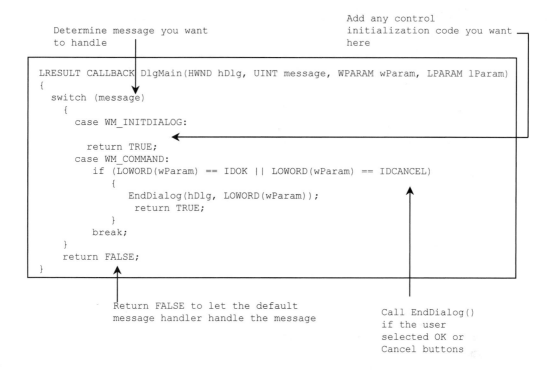

```
                                               Add any control
 Determine message you want                    initialization code you want
 to handle                                      here

LRESULT CALLBACK DlgMain(HWND hDlg, UINT message, WPARAM wParam, LPARAM lParam)
{
   switch (message)
     {
        case WM_INITDIALOG:

          return TRUE;
        case WM_COMMAND:
          if (LOWORD(wParam) == IDOK || LOWORD(wParam) == IDCANCEL)
            {
                EndDialog(hDlg, LOWORD(wParam));
                return TRUE;
            }
          break;
     }
   return FALSE;
}
```

Return FALSE to let the default message handler handle the message

Call EndDialog() if the user selected OK or Cancel buttons

Displaying or Popping up a Dialog

Call either the DialogBox() or DialogBoxParam() function to display a modal dialog box. The DialogBox() function is used when no data is passed to the dialog box. The DialogBoxParam() function is used when data is passed to the dialog box, such as the data the dialog should edit.

Code 3–3 contains the prototypes for both DialogBox() and DialogBoxParam(). The first four parameters of the two functions are identical and described in detail in Table 3.1.

Code 3–3

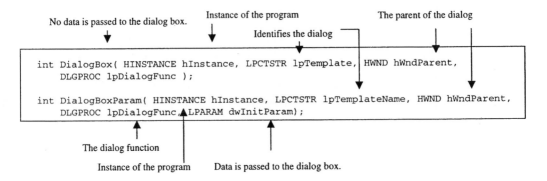

Table 3.1   Parameters for the DialogBox() and DialogBoxParam() Functions

hInstance	Program Instance. See Program Instance in Chapter 1 for more details.
lpTemplate	This identifies the dialog to be displayed. Though it's a string parameter, you can use the MAKEINTRESOURCE macro (demonstrated below) to use the ID for the dialog.
hWndParent	This is the parent window of the dialog and can be 0 if there is no parent. When a modal dialog box is displayed, the parent is disabled until the dialog is closed.
lpDialogFunc	This is the name of the dialog procedure that was described earlier.

Code 3–4 is an example of how to call the dialog we created earlier (IDD_MAIN) and specify its dialog procedure (DlgMain()).

Code 3–4

```
DialogBox( hInstance, MAKEINTRESOURCE(IDD_MAINFORM), 0, (DLGPROC)DlgMain );
```

For the extra parameter in DialogBoxParam(), you can specify any 32-bit value you want. Windows will take this value and pass it to the dialog procedure in its WM_INITDIALOG message as the lParam parameter. The actual use of this value is up to you, but most often it is a pointer to the data that a dialog should work with (for example, it could be a pointer to a Person object, if the dialog was designed to edit Person objects). Code 3–5 is an example of how you might invoke DialogBox-Param.

See the Dialog-based Application—SDK section for a more complete example of how to call both DialogBox() and DialogBoxParam(), as well as how to use the fifth parameter of DialogBoxParam().

Code 3–5

```
DialogBoxParam( hInstance, MAKEINTRESOURCE(IDD_EDIT), hwndDlg,
(DLGPROC)EditDlgProc, (LPARAM)pPerson );
```

Remember

◯	A dialog needs a dialog procedure—a function to handle Windows messages.
	Use DialogBox() or DialogBoxParam() functions to invoke a dialog.
◯	Use the EndDialog() to close a dialog from the dialog procedure.
	Modifying the dialog box properties in the dialog editor can change its appearance and behavior without writing code.
◯	The return value of DialogBox() or DialogBoxParam() indicates how the user closed the dialog, such using the OK or Cancel button.

Dialog Box as a Main Window

The main window of a Windows application can be a dialog box rather than the familiar opening window of a Windows application. Creating a program where the main window is a dialog box is referred to as a *dialog-based application.*

The Calculator program that comes with Windows is a perfect example of a dialog-based application; Notepad is another example. The Notepad main window is the dialog box for it's main window as well with a single edit child control that is resized to fill the main window anytime the main window is resized.

Dialog-based Applications

SDK

A dialog-based application is one where your main window is a dialog, which does not require calling the RegisterClass() and CreateWindow() functions. A dialog-based application also makes it easier to place controls such as buttons and edit boxes on the main window, since you can just drop them into position with the dialog editor.

You create a dialog-based application by first creating a dialog box as is described previously in this chapter. Next, call the dialog box from the WinMain() function.

Using AppWizard, Create the New Application

1. Select the File/New menu choice.
2. Make sure the Projects tab is highlighted in the New dialog.
3. Select Win32 Application from the selection and enter the desired name for your project (for example, dlg_sdk).
4. Click OK.
5. In the Win32 Application—Step 1 of 1 dialog, select A simple Win32 application.
6. Click Finish.

Add the Main Dialog

1. Select the Insert/Resource menu item.
2. Double-click on the Dialog item in the Insert Resource dialog.
3. Before anything else, save the resource file as part of your project:
   a. Find the Script1* window, which was created when you inserted the new dialog.
   b. Select the Script1* window, and select the File/Save menu choice.
   c. A recommended filename is the same as your project, with a .rc extension (for example, dlg_sdk.rc)
   d. Now, close the Script1* window.
4. Select the Project/Add to project/Files... menu item.
5. Double-click on the name that you just saved the resource script as (for example, dlg_sdk.rc).
6. You should now see the ResourceView tab appears on the left, where the ClassView and FileView tab are.

Add Controls on the Dialog

1. Click the ResourceView tab.
2. Expand the tree (see Figure 3–4) until you see the Dialog folder and the IDD_DIALOG1 item.

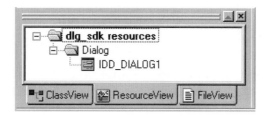

Figure 3–4 The ResourceView tab.

3. Double-click on the IDD_DIALOG1 item, and it will appear in the dialog editor (Figure 3–5).

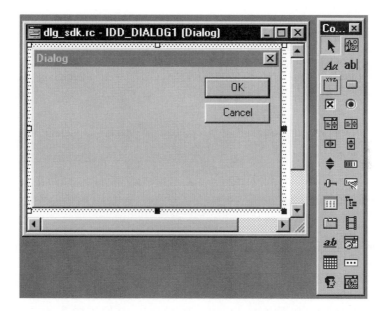

Figure 3–5 The new dialog box in the Dialog editor.

4. Change default properties by double-clicking the body of the dialog to display the property editor.
5. Change the property values as shown in Figure 3–6.

Figure 3–6 The Dialog Properties editor.

6. Click the More Styles tab and select the Center option (Figure 3–7). This will make the dialog automatically center itself when displayed, without your having to write any code.

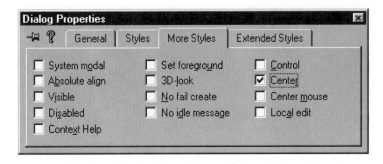

Figure 3–7 The More Styles tab.

7. Delete the OK button from the dialog by selecting the button and hitting the Delete key.
8. Right-click the Cancel button to display the Push Button Properties Editor. This is where you can change the default properties of the Cancel button. Modify the properties as shown in Figure 3–8.

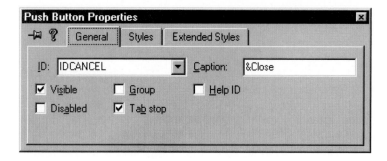

Figure 3–8 The Push Button Properties editor.

9. Define a hotkey for the Cancel button by placing the ampersand (&) in front of the letter of the caption that is used as the hotkey. A hotkey is a letter that when selected in conjunction with the Alt key on the keyboard selects the control.

10. Place another button on the dialog box by clicking the button on the tool palette, then clicking the position on the dialog box where you want the button to appear.

11. Right-click the new button and change its properties so that it looks like the properties in Figure 3–9.

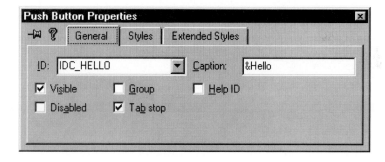

Figure 3–9 The properties window for the Hello button.

Add the C++ Code for the Dialog

1. Open the .cpp file for your project (there will only be one .cpp file).

2. Add the #include for resource.h below the #include for stdafx.h (resource.h was created by the dialog editor).

3. Insert the dialog procedure shown in Code 3–6 above WinMain(). The DialogProc() function responds to messages sent for the dialog box.

Code 3–6

WM_COMMAND indicates a
button was clicked   Was it the Hello button?   Was it the Cancel button?

```
BOOL CALLBACK DialogProc(  HWND hwndDlg,  UINT uMsg, WPARAM wParam, LPARAM lParam )
{
   switch( uMsg )
    {
      case WM_COMMAND:
         if( LOWORD(wParam) == IDC_HELLO )
            {
              MessageBox( hwndDlg, "Why, hello!", "Greetings", MB_OK );
              return( TRUE );
            }
         else if (LOWORD(wParam) == IDCANCEL )
            {
               EndDialog( hwndDlg, IDCANCEL );
               return( TRUE );
            }
    }
   return( FALSE );
}
```

Close the dialog

NOTE

The IDs for the controls like IDC_HELLO were specified when you changed the properties for the control (for example, Figure 3–8). To find the ID of a control while writing a program, just select it in the dialog editor and right-click it to see its properties.

---

4. Add the call to the DialogBox() function to WinMain() as shown in Code 3–7. This call displays the dialog box and makes it modal.
5. Compile and run the program. Experiment with dropping different controls on the dialog in the dialog editor, and trying to interact with them in the DialogProc() function.

Code 3-7

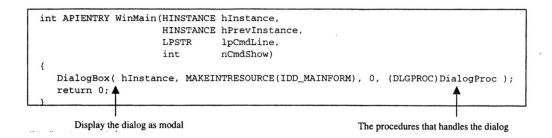

```
int APIENTRY WinMain(HINSTANCE  hInstance,
                     HINSTANCE  hPrevInstance,
                     LPSTR      lpCmdLine,
                     int        nCmdShow)
{
    DialogBox( hInstance, MAKEINTRESOURCE(IDD_MAINFORM), 0, (DLGPROC)DialogProc );
    return 0;
}
```

Display the dialog as modal   The procedures that handles the dialog

Remember

○	The WM_INITDIALOG is the place to initialize dialog variables and child controls. The Using Dialogs for Data Entry section contains more details and examples of initialization.
	In a dialog procedure, your code responds to messages required by the dialog box and ignores other messages.
○	Unlike a window procedure, a dialog procedure does not call DefWndProc(). This is a requirement for windows.
○	You can add a menu to a dialog-based application by creating the menu resource and adding it to the Properties of the dialog (Figure 3–5 shows the property to change for the menu). Once done, you can add message handlers for the menu items.

MFC

Creating a dialog-based application with MFC is simpler than doing so with the SDK. MFC creates features for you such as the dialog resource. With MFC, all you will need to do is to create the project as a dialog-based application, then alter the dialog and add a message map to handle the button click. As described in the Responding to Menu Selections in an MFC Program section (in Chapter 2), a message map is a function you add using ClassWizard that allows you to specify a function to be called when an event occurs (i.e., a menu selection, button click, etc.).

Creating the MFC Dialog Base Application Project

1. Select the File/New menu choice and make sure that Projects is the selected tab.
2. Select MFC Application (exe) and enter the project name (for example, dlg_mfc).
3. Click OK.

4. In the Step 1 dialog of the MFC AppWizard select the Dialog-based radio button and click Next.
5. In the Step 2 dialog, enter a caption for the dialog. The caption will appear at the top of the dialog box.
6. Click Finish then OK to create the project.

Changing the Dialog

1. Select the ResourceView tab (see Figure 3–10; if you don't see the ResourceView, then from the View main menu item, select the Workspace subitem).
2. Expand the tree until you find your main dialog. Your main dialog is usually named IDD_*programname*_DIALOG where *programname* is the name of your project, as shown in Figure 3–10.
3. Double-click on the dialog name, which will open up the dialog editor.

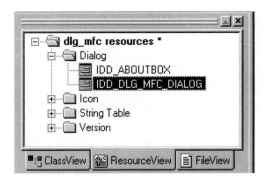

Figure 3–10 Select the dialog box to change.

4. In the dialog editor, remove the OK button.
5. Change the properties of the Cancel button by right-clicking the button, then select Properties from the menu to display the properties editor (Figure 3–8).
6. Add a new button to the dialog, then change its properties so that it looks like the setting in Figure 3–9.

Adding Code to Respond to the New Button's Click Event

1. Select the View/ClassWizard menu bar.
2. Select the Message Maps tab.
3. Make sure the name of the dialog class is displayed in the Class Name field. The name of your dialog class should be formatted as C*Program-Name*Dlg, where *ProgramName* is the name of your project (see Figure 3–10).
4. Select the IDC_HELLO item on the Object IDs list.
5. Select the BN_CLICKED message in the Messages list (Figure 3–11).
6. Click the Add Function button.
7. Accept the default name for the function [OnHello()] by clicking OK. (Note: The function was now added to the source code and will automatically be invoked when the user hits the Hello button at runtime.)
8. Open the dialog .cpp file (named dlg_mfcDlg.cpp, which is the format *ProgramName*Dlg.cpp).

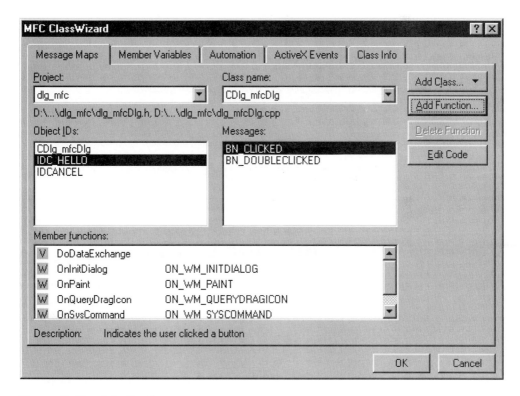

Figure 3–11 Selecting the message map.

9. Look at the end of this file for the function OnHello(). It should look like Code 3–8.

Code 3–8

```
void CDlg_mfcDlg::OnHello()
{
        // TODO: Add your control notification handler code here
}
```

10. Change the function by inserting a call to MessageBox() like Code 3–9.

Code 3–9

```
void CDlg_mfcDlg::OnHello()
{
        MessageBox( "Why, hello!" );
}
```

11. Compile and run your program.

Remember

◯	An MFC dialog-based application is very easy to create using AppWizard.
	You add message handlers to your dialog using the Message Map tab of ClassWizard.
◯	An MFC dialog-based application does not have a dialog procedure like an SDK version.
◯	An MFC dialog-based application does not have a menu by default, but you can easily add one by creating the menu resource and adding it to the Properties of the dialog.

Using Dialogs for Data Entry

Dialog boxes are primarily used to get a set of values from the user. A user is presented with a control showing empty values then asked to enter values. The user can also be presented with values in controls, then asked to modify those values. Data shown in the controls are processed by the application once the user selects the OK button. Changes to the data are abandoned if the user selects the Cancel button.

We will use a very simple example with a Person class that contains a Name, Age, and Eligible flag. These data elements demonstrate how to work with strings, numbers, and flags (checkboxes). Although this example uses data for a single person, you can create an array of persons to have the same program work with more than one person.

SDK Example

Let's create an SDK example of a dialog-based application that displays a person's name, age, and whether the person is enabled in the system. The project will have two dialogs: The main dialog, which will show information for a single person, and an edit dialog that will let us change information for the person. We begin by creating a dialog-based application as discussed previously in this chapter (see Figure 3–4).

We will present this demonstration in several stages. First we will create the dialog-based application, and modify the main dialog to display person information, then we will create the Edit dialog and add controls to it for editing. Then we will create a very simple Person object, and finally add the code needed to make the program work.

Using AppWizard, Create the New Application

1. Select the File/New menu choice.
2. Make sure the Projects tab is highlighted in the New dialog.
3. Select Win32 Application from the selection and enter the desired name for your project (for example, dlgdata_sdk).
4. Click OK.
5. In the Win32 Application—Step 1 of 1 dialog, select A simple Win32 application.
6. Click Finish.

Add the Main Dialog

1. Select the Insert/Resource menu item.
2. Double-click on the Dialog item in the Insert Resource dialog.
3. Before anything else, save the resource file as part of your project:
   a. Find the Script1* window, which was created when you inserted the new dialog.
   b. Select the Script1* window and select the File/Save menu choice.
   c. A recommended filename is the same as your project, with a .rc extension (for example, dlgdata_sdk.rc).
   d. Now, close the Script1* window.
4. Select the Project/Add to project/Files... menu item.
5. Double-click on the name that you just saved the resource script as (for example, dlgdata_sdk.rc).
6. You should now see the ResourceView tab appear on the left, where the ClassView and FileView tab are.

Add Controls to the Main Dialog

1. Click the ResourceView tab.
2. Expand the tree until you see the Dialog folder and the IDD_DIALOG1 item.
3. Double-click on the IDD_DIALOG1 item, and it will appear in the dialog editor.
4. Change default properties by double-clicking the body of the dialog to display the Property editor.
5. Change the property values so that the ID is IDD_MAINFORM and the caption is My Person Editor.
6. Click the More Styles tab of the Properties dialog and select the Center option. This will make the dialog automatically center itself when displayed, without your having to write any code.
7. Delete the OK button from the dialog by selecting the button and hitting the Delete key.
8. Right-click the Cancel button and select Properties to display the Push Button Properties editor. This is where you can change the default properties of the Cancel button. Modify them so that the ID is IDC_CLOSE and the caption is &Close.
9. Add a static control to the form and change its properties so that its ID is IDC_DATA and its caption is Static.
10. Add a button to the form and change its properties so that the ID is IDC_EDIT and its caption is &Edit.
11. See Figure 3–14 for an example of what the dialog will look like.

Add the Edit Dialog

1. Using the Insert/Resource menu item, insert a new dialog.
2. Change the properties of the new dialog so that its ID is IDD_EDIT and its caption is Person Edit.
3. Add controls to the dialog so that it looks like Figure 3–12.
4. Change the properties of the first edit box so that its ID is IDC_NAME.
5. Change the properties of the second edit box so that its ID is IDC_AGE.
6. Change the properties of the checkbox so that its ID is IDC_ELIGIBLE and its caption is &Eligible.
7. Modify the source code to look like Code 3–10.

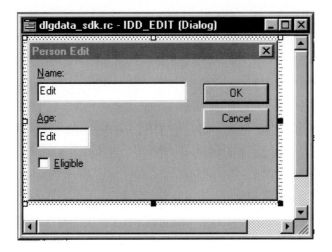

Figure 3-12 The Person Edit dialog box.

Code 3-10

```cpp
// dlgdata_sdk.cpp : Defines the entry point for the application.
//

#include "stdafx.h"
#include "resource.h"
#include <stdlib.h> // For atoi

// The person class, what we will be editing
class Person
{
public:
        void BuildString( char* Dest ) // A helper function, to get person
        as 1 string
        {
                wsprintf( Dest, "%s is %d years old, and %s eligible",
                        Name, Age, Eligible?"is":"is not" );
        }
        char Name[31];
        int Age;
        bool Eligible;
};

// Window procedure for the person edit dialog.
BOOL CALLBACK EditDlgProc( HWND hwndDlg, UINT uMsg, WPARAM wParam, LPARAM
lParam )
{
        static Person* pPerson; // static variable, to keep pointer to data
```

```
we are editing
char Buffer[256];

switch( uMsg )
{
case WM_INITDIALOG:
        // Save address of person we will be editing
        pPerson = (Person*)lParam;
        // Set the text-size limit of the Name edit box
        SendDlgItemMessage( hwndDlg, IDC_NAME, EM_LIMITTEXT,
                sizeof(pPerson->Name)-1, 0 );
        // Place the name of our person to edit in the Name edit box
        SetDlgItemText( hwndDlg, IDC_NAME, pPerson->Name );
        wsprintf( Buffer, "%d", pPerson->Age );
        // Place the age of our person to edit in the Age edit box
        SetDlgItemText( hwndDlg, IDC_AGE, Buffer );
        // Check, or uncheck the Eleigible checkbox, to reflect our
        person to edit
        SendDlgItemMessage( hwndDlg, IDC_ELIGIBLE, BM_SETCHECK, pPer-
        son->Eligible, 0 );
        return( FALSE );
case WM_COMMAND: // User clicked a button
        if( LOWORD(wParam) == IDOK )
        {
                // User hit OK, the following four functions will get
                the values of
                // the user's edits from the edit boxes (dialog con-
                trols) and place // them into the person object (data
                members) we are editing.
                GetDlgItemText( hwndDlg, IDC_NAME, pPerson->Name,
                        sizeof(pPerson->Name) );
                GetDlgItemText( hwndDlg, IDC_AGE, Buffer,
                        sizeof(Buffer) );
                pPerson->Age = atoi( Buffer );
                pPerson->Eligible = SendDlgItemMessage( hwndDlg,
                IDC_ELIGIBLE,
                        BM_GETCHECK, 0, 0 )?true:false;
                // Close the dialog, and specify an IDOK dialog return
                value.
                EndDialog( hwndDlg, IDOK );
                return( TRUE );
        }
        else if (LOWORD(wParam) == IDCANCEL )
        {
                // User hit Cancel, close dialog without saving user
                edits
                // Close the dialog, and specify an IDCANCEL dialog
                return value.
                EndDialog( hwndDlg, IDCANCEL );
```

```
                        return( TRUE );
                }
        }
        return( FALSE );
}


// The main dialog window procedure, displays person information, and in-
vokes the edit
// dialog.
BOOL CALLBACK DialogProc( HWND hwndDlg, UINT uMsg, WPARAM wParam, LPARAM
lParam )
{
        static Person* pPerson;
        char Buffer[256];
        switch( uMsg )
        {
        case WM_INITDIALOG:
                // Initialize dialog by saving pointer to person we will be
                changing,
                // and initializing child controls (the static control)
                pPerson = (Person*)lParam;
                pPerson->BuildString( Buffer );
                SetDlgItemText( hwndDlg, IDC_DATA, Buffer );
                return( FALSE );
        case WM_COMMAND: // Indicates user hit a button, find out which one
                if( LOWORD(wParam) == IDC_EDIT ) // Was it the edit button?
                {
                        // User hit the edit button, invoke the edit dialog.
                        if( DialogBoxParam( 0, MAKEINTRESOURCE(IDD_EDIT),
                        hwndDlg,
                                (DLGPROC)EditDlgProc, (LPARAM)pPerson ) == IDOK )
                        {
                                // If user hit OK, then get user's changes and
                                put into the
                                // static control
                                pPerson->BuildString( Buffer );
                                SetDlgItemText( hwndDlg, IDC_DATA, Buffer );
                        }
                        return( TRUE );
                }
                else if (LOWORD(wParam) == IDC_CLOSE ) // Was it the Close
                button?
                {
                        EndDialog( hwndDlg, IDC_CLOSE );
                        return( TRUE );
                }
        }
        return( FALSE );
```

```
}
int APIENTRY WinMain(HINSTANCE hInstance,
                     HINSTANCE hPrevInstance,
                     LPSTR lpCmdLine,
                     int nCmdShow)
{
        // Create and initialize the person object we will be working with.
        Person P;
        strcpy( P.Name, "Bob" );
        P.Age = 21;
        P.Eligible = true;

        // Invoke the main dialog.
        DialogBoxParam( hInstance, MAKEINTRESOURCE(IDD_MAINFORM), 0,
(DLGPROC)DialogProc, (LPARAM)&P );
        return 0;
}
```

Here is an overview of the functions used in Code 3–10.

GetDlgItemText(hwndDlg, IDC_NAME, pPerson->Name, sizeof(pPerson->Name));

GetDlgItemText() is a function that retrieves text from an edit box and places it into a string. In this example, hwndDlg is the window handle for the dialog, IDC_NAME is the ID of the edit box to get data from, pPerson->Name is a character array, or string, to place the text into, and sizeof(pPerson->Name) is the maximum number of bytes to retrieve.

GetDlgItemText() is also used to get the text from the IDC_AGE control and store it into the Buffer variable, then call the C atoi function to convert it from a string to an integer.

SendDlgItemMessage(hwndDlg, IDC_ELIGIBLE, BM_GETCHECK, 0, 0);

The SendDlgItemMessage() function is used to send a message to a control on a dialog. In this example, hwndDlg specifies the window handle for the dialog and IDC_ELIGIBLE specifies the ID of the desired child control (the checkbox). BM_GETCHECK is the message that we want to send it, and for this message the last two parameters are always zero. When you send the BM_GETCHECK message to a child checkbox control, its return value will tell you whether the checkbox is checked.

The WM_INITDIALOG message

The DlgProc function, in its WM_INITDIALOG case statement, saves the lParam parameter to the pPerson static local variable. This is an example of how to use the last parameter of the DialogBoxParam function. Several things tie in here:

- The WinMain function has a Person local variable named P.
- When WinMain calls DialogBoxParam, it passes the address of the P variable (&P) as its last parameter.
- What the DialogBoxParam now does is take that parameter and pass it to the DlgProc function as its lParam parameter in a WM_INITDIALOG function.
- The DlgProc function, in turn, takes the lParam for a WM_INITDIALOG message, typecasts it back to a Person pointer (Person*), and stores it in its static data member named pPerson.
- Now, the dialog procedure DlgProc has its own pointer to the same Person object (named P) that WinMain has. The two functions can share information.
- The pPerson variable of DlgProc is static, so that in between calls to DlgProc (which correspond to Windows messages), the value stored there will remain valid (until it is changed by the next WM_INITDIALOG message).

Something similar to this is being done in the EditDlgProc() as well, where DlgProc() calls DialogBoxParam() to invoke that edit dialog and initialize its parameter with the same person memory address that it has.

Return Value of DialogBoxParam

In the DlgProc() function, if the user hits the Edit button, Code 3–11 is executed. The DialogBoxParam() function is used to invoke the Edit dialog. The function will not return until the user closes the edit dialog. If the user hits the OK button, then the case statement in EditDlgProc() will call EndDialog() with a value of IDOK. Not only does EndDialog() close the edit dialog, but it also specifies what the return value will be for the DialogBoxParam() function that originally invoked the dialog. So basically, the "if" portion is testing to see if the user hit the OK button.

SetDlgItemText(hwndDlg, IDC_DATA, Buffer);

This function is used inside the main dialog procedure DlgProc(). SetDlgItemText() permits you to place text in an edit box or static control. In this example, hwndDlg is the HWND for the dialog window, and IDC_DATA is the ID for the child control we want to put the string in (this is a static control on the main form). Buffer is the string to be placed into the control.

Code 3-11

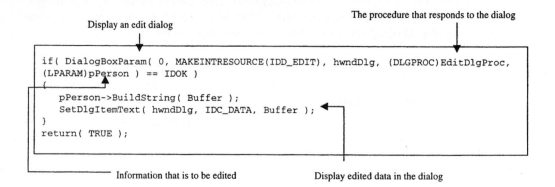

Display an edit dialog

The procedure that responds to the dialog

```
if( DialogBoxParam( 0, MAKEINTRESOURCE(IDD_EDIT), hwndDlg, (DLGPROC)EditDlgProc,
(LPARAM)pPerson ) == IDOK )
{
    pPerson->BuildString( Buffer );
    SetDlgItemText( hwndDlg, IDC_DATA, Buffer );
}
return( TRUE );
```

Information that is to be edited

Display edited data in the dialog

Remember

○	A dialog has a window (or dialog) procedure to handle messages, like any other type of window.
	The WM_COMMAND message indicates the user interacted with some window on a dialog, like clicking a button or selecting a menu item.
	The WM_INITDIALOG message is where you can initialize your dialog, doing things like putting text into edit controls.
○	To keep track of the object a dialog box should change, use DialogBoxParam() to pass the data and use the lParam for WM_INITDIALOG to access the information passed.
	A static variable is best for keeping track of the data you need to edit in the dialog procedure so that it is available throughout various calls (set the static in WM_INITDIALOG).
	Use EndDialog() to close the dialog, specifying the value that the DialogBox() or DialogBoxParam() function should return.
○	AppWizard does not provide a simple SDK dialog-based application template for new projects.

MFC Example

You can create an application similar to the data input dialog box in the previous example by using the Microsoft Foundation Classes. The basic steps are the same, though we will be using some of the Visual C++ environment tools such as Class-Wizard to simplify the handling of messages. Here's how to do this:

Creating the Program

1. Select File/New from the menu choice and then select the Projects tab.
2. Select MFC Application (exe) and enter the project name (for example, dlgdata_mfc).
3. Click OK.
4. In the MFC AppWizard—Step 1 dialog box, select the Dialog-based item.
5. Click Next.
6. In the step 2 dialog box, enter in a caption for the dialog, such as "Dialog Demo in MFC."
7. Click Finish.
8. Click OK to create the project.

Adding a Person Class

1. Create a class called person, the object of which will be edited by using the dialog box.
2. Select Insert from the menu then New Class item to display the New Class dialog box (Figure 3–13).

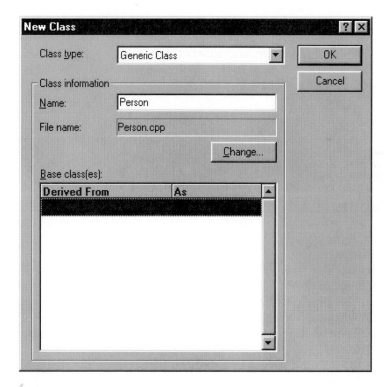

Figure 3–13   The New Class dialog box.

3. Change the Class Type to Generic Class.
4. Type Person in the Name field.
5. Click OK to create the person.h and person.cpp files to the project.
6. Open the person.h file and insert Code 3–12.

Code 3–12

```
class Person
{
public:
// The person class, what we will be editing
        Person();
        ~Person();
        void BuildString( char* Dest )
        {
                wsprintf( Dest, "%s is %d years old, and %s
                eligible",
                        Name, Age, Eligible?"is":"is not" );
        }
        char Name[31];
        int Age;
        bool Eligible;
};
```

7. Save the file.
8. Open the person.cpp and insert Code 3–13.

Code 3–13

```
Person::Person()
{
     Age = 0;
     Name[0]='\0';
     Eligible = false;
}
```

9. Save the file.
10. In the resource view, locate the main dialog box and double-click it to display the dialog box in the dialog editor.
11. Remove the OK button.
12. Change the properties of the Cancel button so that its caption is &Close.
13. Add the Edit button, and change its ID to IDC_EDIT.
14. Add a static control and change its ID to IDC_DATA.
15. Change the dialog properties so that its caption is "My person editor" (Figure 3–14).
16. Create the Edit dialog by selecting Insert from the menu, then by selecting Resource.
17. Double-click on the Dialog item in the New Resource window that appears.

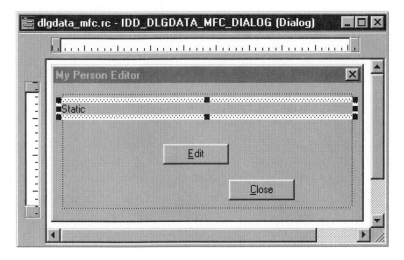

Figure 3–14   The main dialog box in the dialog box editor.

18. Double-click on the new dialog box in the Resource View to edit it in the dialog editor.
19. Modify the new dialog box to appear like Figure 3–15.

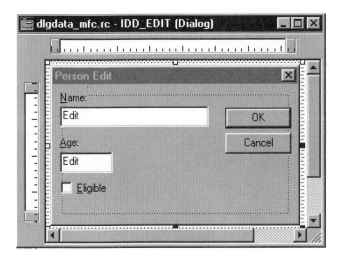

Figure 3–15   The new dialog box in the dialog box editor.

20. Change the dialog properties so that the ID is IDD_EDIT and its caption is Person Edit.
21. Add a static control whose caption is &Name.
22. Add an Edit box whose ID is IDC_NAME.
23. Add a static control whose caption is &Age.
24. Add an edit box whose ID is IDC_AGE.
25. Add a checkbox whose ID is IDC_ELIGIBLE and whose caption is &Eligible.
26. Add a class for the new edit dialog box using ClassWizard. Select View from the menu then select ClassWizard. Class Wizard will recognize that you just created a new dialog and will ask if you want to create a class for it.
27. Select Create a new class.
28. Click the OK button. The New Class dialog box will appear.
29. Make the selections shown in Figure 3–16.

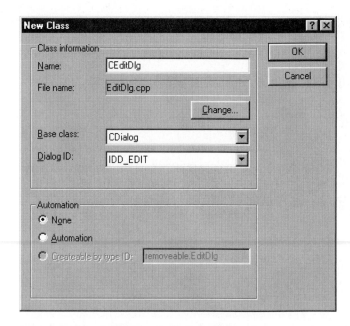

Figure 3–16 The New Class dialog box.

30. Click the OK button to create the new class.
31. Add member variables for edit dialog components using the Class-Wizard to map member variables to child controls (i.e., edit control).
32. Select the Member Variables tab in the ClassWizard as shown in Figure 3–17.

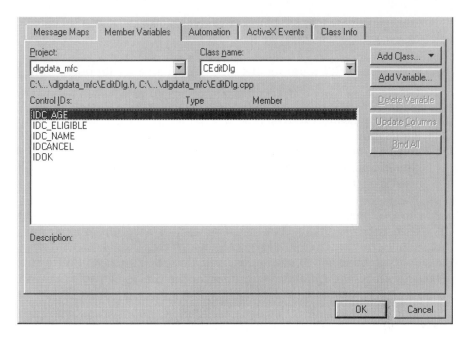

Figure 3–17 The Member Variables tab in the ClassWizard.

33. Highlight the IDC_AGE control.
34. Click the Add Variable button. A new dialog box will appear (Figure 3–18).

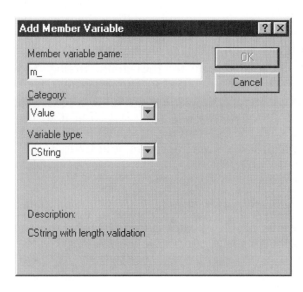

Figure 3–18 Add Member Variable dialog box.

35. Change the Member Variable Name to m_Age.
36. Change the Variable Type to int.
37. Click OK.
38. Repeat steps 32 to 36 for IDC_ELIGIBLE and set its name to m_Eligible and its variable type to BOOL.
39. Repeat steps 32 to 36 for IDC_NAME, making the variable name m_Name and its variable type a CString.
40. Place values into the member variables before invoking the dialog so those values will appear inside the dialog when displayed. Likewise, after the dialog is closed, the values in the member variables will be the results of the user edits (if the user hits the OK button).

Assigning values in step 39 is a straightforward process. For example, in the dialog described above, the CEditDlg class represents the Edit dialog and has a data member of m_Age that was mapped to the Age edit box. If we wanted to have the dialog appear with a value of 10 in the age edit box, we would initialize the m_Age member before calling the DoModal() function of the dialog class as shown in Code 3–14.

Code 3–14

```
CEditDlg Tmp;
Tmp.m_Age = 10; // Initialize member variable
Tmp.DoModal(); // Display dialog. MFC will move data from m_Age to the edit
control.
```

Later, however, we will not just be placing a hard-coded value like 10 into m_Age. Instead, we will make it more practical by getting the Age value from a Person object and placing it into m_Age.

41. Add a Person object to the main dialog box class (CDlgdata_mfcDlg in this demo) by adding the following data member to the main dialog class (in CDlgdata_mfcDlg.h for this demo). You can add the variable the old fashioned way by just typing it in the .h file, or you can right-click on the class name in ClassView and select the Add member variable menu item. In either case, add Code 3–15.

Code 3–15

```
Person m_Person;
```

42. Initialize this object by adding Code 3–16 to the end of the main dialog constructor (in CDlgdata_mfcDlg.cpp for this demo).

Code 3-16

```
strcpy( m_Person.Name, "Bob" );
m_Person.Age=21;
m_Person.Eligible = true;
```

43. Add Code 3–17 to the main dialog so that the information for the person object is displayed in the static text on the main dialog by writing a function called UpdateStatic(). This is a member function of the CDlgdata_mfcDlg class (for this demo) that you can add easily by right-clicking on the class name in ClassView and selecting Add Member function from the pop-up menu. The code is added to the CDlgdata_mfcDlg.cpp file, for this demo.

Code 3-17

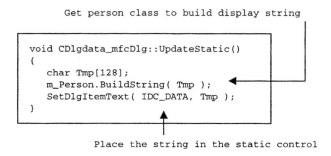

Get person class to build display string

```
void CDlgdata_mfcDlg::UpdateStatic()
{
    char Tmp[128];
    m_Person.BuildString( Tmp );
    SetDlgItemText( IDC_DATA, Tmp );
}
```

Place the string in the static control

44. Add the UpdateStatic() function prototype to the main dialog class header file (CDlgdata_mfcDlg.h for this demo), if you added it manually. If you right-clicked the class in ClassView as described in step 42, then you don't need to do this (VC++ already did it).

45. Add a call to UpdateStatic() to the end of the OnInitDialog() function, before the return statement. It will now look like Code 3–18 in the CDlgdata_mfcDlg.cpp file.

Code 3-18

```
BOOL CDlgdata_mfcDlg::OnInitDialog()
{
    CDialog::OnInitDialog();
    // Add "About..." menu item to system menu.


    ASSERT((IDM_ABOUTBOX & 0xFFF0) == IDM_ABOUTBOX);  ◄──────
    ASSERT(IDM_ABOUTBOX < 0xF000);  ◄──────

    CMenu* pSysMenu = GetSystemMenu(FALSE);
    if (pSysMenu != NULL)
        {
            CString strAboutMenu;
            strAboutMenu.LoadString(IDS_ABOUTBOX);
            if (!strAboutMenu.IsEmpty())
              {
                  pSysMenu->AppendMenu(MF_SEPARATOR);
                  pSysMenu->AppendMenu(MF_STRING, IDM_ABOUTBOX, strAboutMenu);
              }
        }
    SetIcon(m_hIcon, TRUE);  ◄──────
    SetIcon(m_hIcon, FALSE);  ◄──────

    // TODO: Add extra initialization here
    UpdateStatic();  ◄──────
    return TRUE;
}
```

IDM_ABOUTBOX must be in the system command range.

Get Person information into the static control

Set small icon   Set big icon

return TRUE unless you set the focus to a control

Set the icon for this dialog. The framework does this automatically when the application's main window is not a dialog

Adding Code to the Main Dialog

With the dialogs and dialog classes completed, add code to the main dialog to display the edit dialog. First, using ClassWizard, add a handler to the Edit button on the main form. In that handler we will give the Edit dialog all the person information to edit.

1. Using ClassWizard and its Message Map tab, add a message map for the IDC_EDIT object for the BN_CLICKED message. (See Responding to Messages, SDK and MFC in Chapter 1 for more information.)

2. Change the handler to look like Code 3–19 (you must add the code in **bold**). The function was added in step 1, at the bottom of the CDlg-data_mfcDlg.cpp file.

Code 3–19

```
void CDlgdata_mfcDlg::OnEdit()
{
    CEditDlg Tmp;

    Tmp.m_Age = m_Person.Age;
    Tmp.m_Eligible = m_Person.Eligible?TRUE:FALSE;      ◄── Place person data
    Tmp.m_Name = m_Person.Name;                               into the dialog
    if( Tmp.DoModal() == IDOK )                               members
      {
        strcpy( m_Person.Name, Tmp.m_Name );
        m_Person.Eligible = Tmp.m_Eligible?true:false;  ◄──
        m_Person.Age = Tmp.m_Age;                           Retrieve person data
        UpdateStatic();                                     from dialog into person
      }                                                     object
}
```

NOTE

Before the call to DoModal(), which displays the dialog, data members previously added to the dialog class are initialized with data from the person object. If DoModal() returned IDOK (meaning that the user hit the OK button), the user's changes are taken from the same data members and placed back into the person object.

Creating a Modeless Dialog

SDK

A modeless dialog is one that allows the parent window to continue to work while it is displayed (a modal dialog, on the other hand, is one that will disable its parent until you close it). When working with a modal dialog, we used the DialogBox() and DialogBoxParam() functions to display the dialog. For modeless dialogs, we will be using the CreateDialog() and CreateDialogParam() functions.

Unlike DialogBox() and DialogBoxParam(), which will not return until the modal dialog box is closed, CreateDialog() and CreateDialogParam() will return immediately, with the handle of the newly created dialog. When we want the dialog to appear, we simply call ShowWindow() with the HWND that CreateDialog() or CreateDialog-Param() returned.

This demonstration will display a message in the main window. If you click the main window with the mouse, it will display a modeless dialog with an edit box that contains the message to be displayed. If you change the text in the edit box, you will see the text displayed in the main window change with each keystroke. The demonstration (see Figure 3–19) shows how to communicate data between the main window and the modeless dialog, such as a string of text, using CreateDialog-Param() and WM_INITDIALOG.

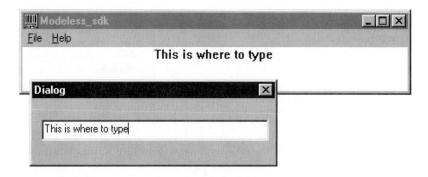

Figure 3–19   Modeless dialog SDK demonstration.

Creating the Program

1. Select the File/New menu choice.
2. Make sure the Projects tab is highlighted.
3. Select Win32Application.
4. Type in the name of the project, Modeless_sdk, in the Project Name field. The dialog should now look like Figure 3–20.
5. Click OK.
6. Select A Typical Hello World application from the Step 1 of 1 dialog.
7. Click Finish.
8. Click OK.

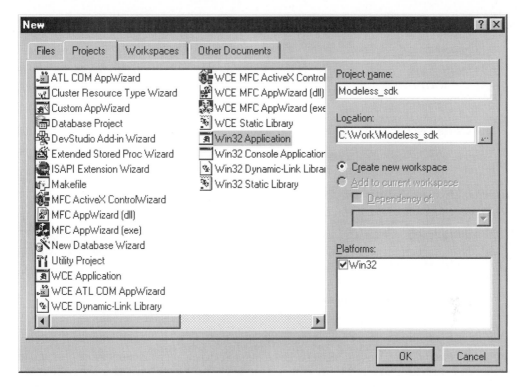

Figure 3–20 AppWizard for new project.

Making the Text Dynamic

Change the Modeless_sdk.cpp file, so that the string it displays is not hard-coded (we will change what is displayed with the modeless dialog).

1. In the .cpp file, locate the declaration for szHello as shown in Code 3–20.

Code 3–20

```
TCHAR szHello[MAX_LOADSTRING];
LoadString(hInst, IDS_HELLO, szHello, MAX_LOADSTRING);
```

2. Delete these two lines and replace them with Code 3–21.

Code 3–21

```
static char Message[128]="Click this window to show modeless
box";
```

3. Locate Code 3–22 in the WndProc() function of modeless_sdk.cpp:

Code 3–22

```
DrawText(hdc, szHello, strlen(szHello), &rt, DT_CENTER);
```

4. Change the line to Code 3–23.

Code 3–23

```
DrawText(hdc, Message, strlen(Message), &rt, DT_CENTER);
```

Adding the Dialog Resource for the Modeless Dialog

1. Go to the Insert menu item, and select Resource....
2. Double-click on the Dialog item (this will create a new blank dialog).
3. Using dialog editor (double-click the dialog name in the ResourceView window to get to it), remove the OK and Cancel buttons from the dialog.
4. Add an Edit box and change its properties so that its ID is IDC_MESSAGE (access its properties by right-clicking on the edit box).

Adding the Dialog Procedure for the Modeless Dialog

The dialog box must do two basic tasks: Initialize its edit box with the current message and retrieve the users changes and notify its parent window (the main window). WM_INITDIALOG is used to initialize the edit box, and WM_COMMAND is used to identify when the user changes the edit box text. When we see that the edit box text has changed, we tell the main window to redraw itself by calling GetParent() to get the parent window and call InvalidateRect() to invalidate the client area of the main window (forcing the redraw). Add Code 3–24 just above your WndProc() function in modeless.cpp.

Having the Main Window Display the Modeless Dialog

We call the CreateDialogParam() to create the dialog and then ShowWindow() to make it visible. First, we check to make sure we haven't already created it, or shown it, by calling the IsWindow() and IsWindowVisible() functions. Add Code 3–25 portion to your WndProc() function in modeless_sdk.cpp just above the default handler in your switch statement.

Code 3-24

Message from child window (the edit box)

Did the user change
the text in the edit box?

Get the last paramer from
CreatedialogParam, a
pointer to the message.

Place the
message in the
edit box.

```
BOOL CALLBACK DlgProc( HWND hwndDlg, UINT uMsg, WPARAM wParam, LPARAM lParam )
{
    static char* pMessage;
    switch( uMsg )
      {
        case WM_INITDIALOG:
            pMessage = (char*) lParam;
            SetDlgItemText( hwndDlg, IDC_MESSAGE, pMessage );
            break;
        case WM_COMMAND:
            if( HIWORD(wParam) == EN_CHANGE )
              {
                GetDlgItemText( hwndDlg, IDC_MESSAGE, pMessage, 128);
                HWND X = GetParent(hwndDlg);
                InvalidateRect( X, NULL, TRUE  );
              }
            break;
        case WM_CLOSE:

            EndDialog( hwndDlg, 0 );
            break;
          }
    return( FALSE );
}
```

Get text from the edit
box, and store into our
message string

Invalidate the main
(parent) window, so
it re-draws using new
message

Let default dialog
procedure deal with
message

Close the dialog by calling EndDialog

Code 3-25

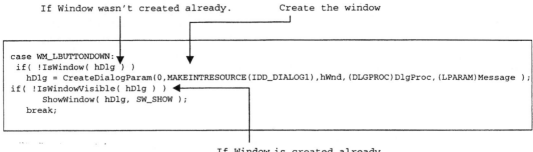

If Window wasn't created already.   Create the window

```
case WM_LBUTTONDOWN:
  if( !IsWindow( hDlg ) )
    hDlg = CreateDialogParam(0,MAKEINTRESOURCE(IDD_DIALOG1),hWnd,(DLGPROC)DlgProc,(LPARAM)Message );
  if( !IsWindowVisible( hDlg ) )
      ShowWindow( hDlg, SW_SHOW );
  break;
```

If Window is created already.

Remember

◯	To create a modeless dialog, use CreateDialog() or CreateDialogParam().
	A modeless dialog must be made visible by calling ShowWindow().
◯	Like modal dialogs, modeless dialogs need their own Dialog Procedure.
	The WM_INITDIALOG is used to initialize your dialog, and the IParam parameter for this window is the value passed in the last parameter to CreateDialogParam().
◯	Variables in your dialog procedure that must retain their values between calls (like pMessage in our example) should be declared as static locals.

MFC

This is the MFC version of the modeless dialog from the previous section. A modeless dialog is one that allows the parent window to continue to work while it is displayed (a modal dialog on the other hand, is one that will disable its parent until you close it). When working with a modal dialog, we used the DoModal() function to display the dialog. For modeless dialogs, we will be using the Create and ShowWindow() to create and display the dialog functions.

Since MFC is based on C++, instead of using the complex parameter passing used by the SDK program, we will instead use data members in a custom dialog class to communicate data between the main window and the modeless dialog.

This demonstration will display a message in the main window. If you click the main window with the mouse, it will display a modeless dialog with an edit box that contains the message to be displayed. If you change the text in the edit box, you will see the text displayed in the main window change with each keystroke. The demonstration (see Figure 3–21) shows how to communicate data between the main window and the modeless dialog, such as a string of text, using a member variable in a dialog class.

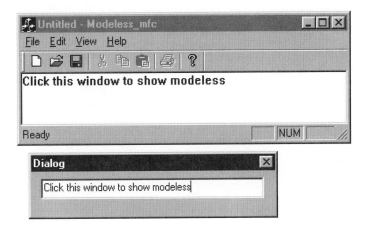

Figure 3–21   Modeless dialog MFC demonstration.

Creating the Program

1. Select the File/New menu choice.
2. Make sure the Projects tab is highlighted.
3. Select Win32Application.
4. Type in the name of the project, Modeless_mfc, in the Project Name field. The dialog should now look like Figure 3–22.
5. Click OK.
6. Select Single Document in MFC AppWizard Step 1.
7. Click Finish.
8. Click OK.

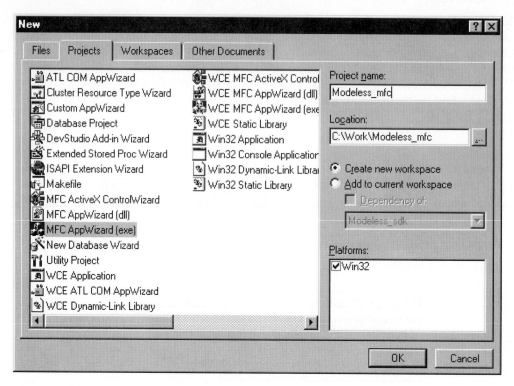

Figure 3–22 AppWizard for New project.

Displaying a Message in the Main Window

In order to display a message in the main window, which can be changed by the modeless dialog at runtime, modify the CModeless_mfcView::OnDraw function of the modeless_mfcView.cpp file, so that it outputs the message to the screen and looks like Code 3–26.

Code 3–26

```
void CModeless_mfcView::OnDraw(CDC* pDC)
{
    CModeless_mfcDoc* pDoc = GetDocument();
    ASSERT_VALID(pDoc);
    // TODO: add draw code for native data here
    pDC->TextOut( 0, 0, m_MessageDlg.m_Message ); // Get text from dialog
}
```

Adding the Modeless Dialog

1. Go to the Insert menu item, and select Resource....
2. Double-click on the Dialog item (this will create a new blank dialog).
3. Using dialog editor (double-click the dialog name in the ResourceView window to get to it), remove the OK and Cancel buttons from the dialog.
4. Add an Edit box and change its properties so that its ID is IDC_MESSAGE (access its properties by right-clicking on the edit box).

Creating a Dialog Class for Your New Dialog

1. While still in the dialog editor from the above, go to the View menu item, and select ClassWizard.
2. The Adding a Class dialog will appear to help you create a class for your new dialog.
3. Make sure that Create a New class is selected in this dialog, and click OK.
4. The New Class dialog will appear. It should look like Figure 3–23.

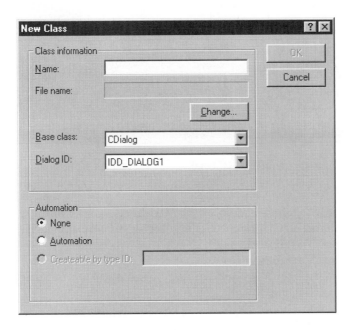

Figure 3–23   New Class dialog.

5. Fill in CMessageDlg for the Name field, and click OK. Note that the Dialog ID is the ID for the dialog we just added, and that the Base Class is CDialog.
6. Click OK again, to get out of ClassWizard.

Adding a Data Member to the New Dialog Class (CMessageDlg) for the Edit Box

1. Go to ClassWizard (from the View menu choice)
2. Select the Member Variable tab. It should look like Figure 3–24.

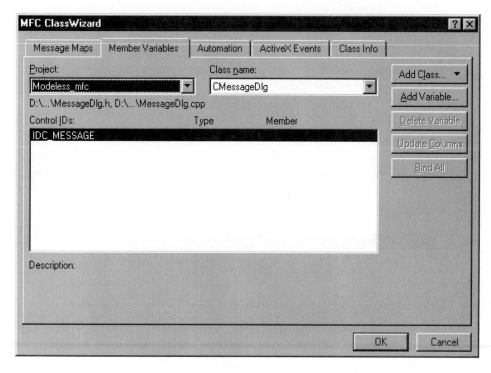

Figure 3–24   ClassWizard, Member Variable tab.

3. Make sure that CMessageDlg is selected in the Class name item.
4. Make sure that IDC_MESSAGE is selected (it should be the only item there, as pictured above).
5. Click the Add Variable button.
6. The Add Member Variable dialog will appear, looking like Figure 3–25.
7. In the Member variable name field, type in m_Message.
8. Hit the OK button.

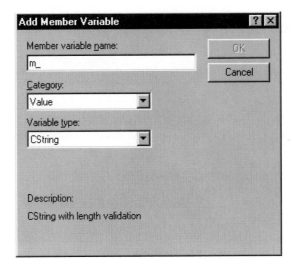

Figure 3–25 Add Member Variable.

NOTE

Dialogs and forms in MFC programs provide the above method to easily associate an on-screen control (like our edit box) with a member variable of a dialog or view class (like our CMessageDlg class). This means that when we want to access the data from the edit box, we can look in the data member variable.

Displaying the Modeless Dialog from the Parent

We will create a member variable in the main window class for the modeless dialog, and modify the main window class (the view) to create and display the dialog as needed.

1. Add a data member of type CMessageDlg to the CModeless_MFCView class, in CModeless_MFCView.h as a "public" data member. Call the data member m_MessageDlg.
2. Go to ClassWizard and select the Message Maps tab.
3. Make sure that the Class name is CModeless_MFCView, the Object ID is CModeless_MFCView, and the Messages is WM_LBUTTONDOWN, as pictured in Figure 3–26.
4. Click the Add Function button.
5. Find the CModeless_mfcView::OnLButtonDown() function, which was added by ClassWizard in step 4. It should look like Code 3–27, in Modeless_MFCView.cpp.

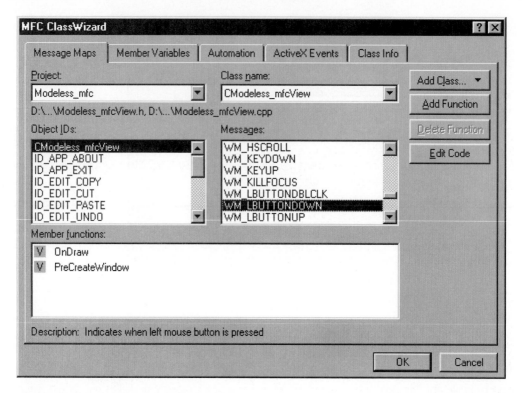

Figure 3–26 ClassWizard, Message Map.

Code 3-27

```
void CModeless_mfcView::OnLButtonDown(UINT nFlags, CPoint point)
{
    // TODO: Add your message handler code here and/or call default

    CView::OnLButtonDown(nFlags, point);
}
```

6.   Modify the code so that it looks like Code 3–28.

Code 3-28

```
void CModeless_mfcView::OnLButtonDown(UINT nFlags, CPoint point)
{
    // TODO: Add your message handler code here and/or call default

    if( !m_MessageDlg.GetSafeHwnd() ) // Have we created the dialog?
        m_MessageDlg.Create( IDD_DIALOG1, this );
```

```
    if( !m_MessageDlg.IsWindowVisible() ) // Is it visible?
        m_MessageDlg.ShowWindow( SW_SHOW );
    CView::OnLButtonDown(nFlags, point);
}
```

Having the Modeless Dialog Box Tell the Parent That the Message Has Changed

We want the modeless dialog to be able to tell the parent (main) window when the user has changed the message in the dialog. In order to do this, we will add a message map to the CMessageDlg class to handle the EN_CHANGE notification from the edit box. In order to do this add the following:

1. Go to ClassWizard.
2. Select the Message Maps tab.
3. Make sure that CMessageDlg is selected in the Class name field.
4. Make sure that IDC_MESSAGE is selected in the Object IDs list.
5. Make sure that EN_CHANGE is selected in the Messages list.
6. The dialog should look like Figure 3–27.

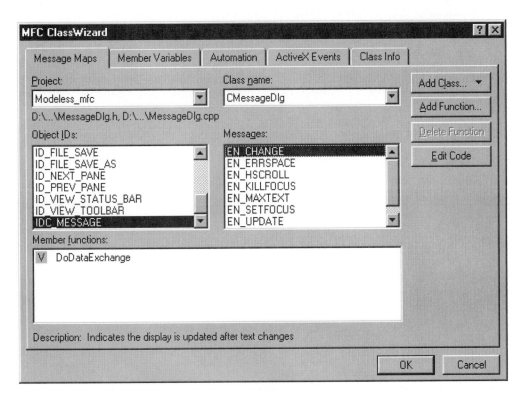

Figure 3–27   ClassWizard Message Map for Edit Box.

7. Click the Add function button.
8. Verify the name of the function about to be added [it should be On-ChangeMessage()] and click OK.
9. Close ClassWizard.
10. Go to the MessageDlg.cpp file, and find the OnChangeMessage() function.
11. Modify the OnChangeMessage() function so that it looks like Code 3–29.

Code 3–29

```
void CMessageDlg::OnChangeMessage()
{
        UpdateData(); // Move data from edit box into member variable
        GetParent()->Invalidate(); // Tell parent to re-draw
}
```

NOTE

The UpdateData() function is used to move data between member variables and on-screen controls. It exchanges the data that you created a Member Variable for using ClassWizard, as we did for m_Message earlier. Where the SDK program might have to call the GetDlgItemText() function ten times if you had ten edit boxes to retrieve their strings, an MFC program just calls UpdateData() once.

If you wanted to remove the modeless dialog, the main window could call the ShowWindow() function for the dialog class with a SW_HIDE parameter, for example:

```
m_MessageDlg.ShowWindow( SW_HIDE );
```

Remember

○	A modeless dialog in MFC is wrapped by a class derived from CDialog.
	To display a modeless dialog, call the Create function.
○	To show or hide a modeless dialog, call the ShowWindow() function.
	You can easily associate a member variable with an on-screen control using the Member Variables tab in ClassWizard.
○	Call UpdateData() when you want to move data from variables to on screen controls, or vice-versa.

Common Dialogs

Common dialogs are a set of predefined, standard dialogs that you can use in your program to permit you to easily do things like a file-open, font selection, or color selection. Because they are predefined, their appearance is consistent with other applications and requires little coding on your part.

While starting with a default appearance is very useful, many applications also need the ability to make slight changes to the default appearance. In order to support this, common dialogs have various flags you can set to control their appearance, as well as providing you with the ability to provide a replacement Dialog Procedure to be used instead of the default one. With your own Dialog Procedure, it's possible to add and modify controls any way you see fit.

All the common dialogs here require you to #include the commdlg.h file. If the ShBrowseForFolder() function is used in the program, then the shlobj.h file must also be included. Common dialog functions and classes use unique data structures. Data members of each structure can be modified to change the behavior of the dialog.

In an MFC application, a series of classes are dedicated to implementing the various common dialogs. These classes are all derived from the CDialog class. In order to display a dialog box that is implemented in a CDialog-derived class, call the DoModal() for an instance of the CDialog (or any of its derived classes). This causes the dialog box to be displayed as a modal dialog box. All MFC Common Dialog classes, except the Find and Replace dialogs, are modal. The Find and Replace dialog boxes are modeless.

File Open

SDK Example

In an SDK program, the GetOpenFileName() function displays the File Open common dialog box (Figure 3–28). You can modify features of the file open dialog box by modifying values in the OPENFILENAME data structure.

Declare an instance of the OPENFILENAME data structure within the DemoGetOpenFileName() function. Set members of the OPENFILENAME data structure as shown in Code 3–30.

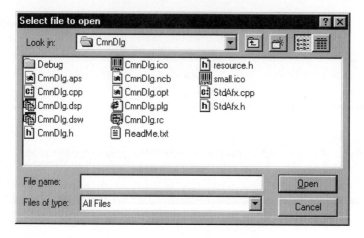

Figure 3–28 The File Open common dialog box.

Code 3–30

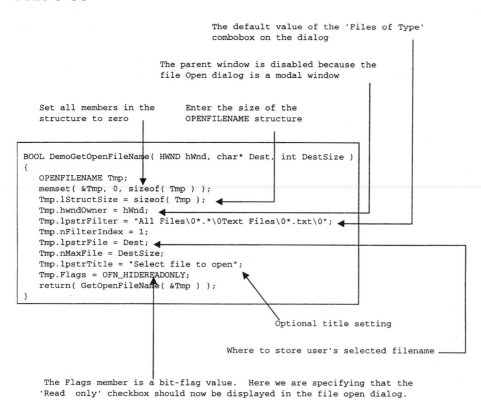

The default value of the 'Files of Type' combobox on the dialog

The parent window is disabled because the file Open dialog is a modal window

Set all members in the structure to zero

Enter the size of the OPENFILENAME structure

```
BOOL DemoGetOpenFileName( HWND hWnd, char* Dest, int DestSize )
{
    OPENFILENAME Tmp;
    memset( &Tmp, 0, sizeof( Tmp ) );
    Tmp.lStructSize = sizeof( Tmp );
    Tmp.hwndOwner = hWnd;
    Tmp.lpstrFilter = "All Files\0*.*\0Text Files\0*.txt\0";
    Tmp.nFilterIndex = 1;
    Tmp.lpstrFile = Dest;
    Tmp.nMaxFile = DestSize;
    Tmp.lpstrTitle = "Select file to open";
    Tmp.Flags = OFN_HIDEREADONLY;
    return( GetOpenFileName( &Tmp ) );
}
```

Optional title setting

Where to store user's selected filename

The Flags member is a bit-flag value. Here we are specifying that the 'Read only' checkbox should now be displayed in the file open dialog.

In this example, the hWnd is the window to the main application window. Dest is a pointer to a string (character array) where the filename selected by the user is stored. DestSize is size of the Dest buffer. The function returns TRUE if the user selected a filename, and FALSE if he or she did not. Before calling this demo function, it is important to ensure that whatever Dest points to is either an empty string or the name of a legitimate file.

The lpstrFiler identifies the type of files that should be displayed in the Files of Type combo box for the file open dialog. Several pairs of strings are enclosed within the single string assigned to the lpstrFiler member. A NULL character (\0) separates each string pair. The Code 3–30 of "All Files\0*.*\0Text Files\0*.txt\0" translates into

All Files	*.*
Text Files	*.txt

The first string (i.e., All Files) is placed into the Files of Type combo box in the File Open dialog box as the default value. If the user selects All Files, then the second string (*.*) is used as a mask for files to be displayed in the file open dialog.

The GetOpenFileName() function is called to display the dialog box. If this function returns TRUE, then the user selected a filename and that filename is stored in the lpstrFile data member.

CAUTION

If any of the members of the OPENFILENAME are not correctly initialized, then when GetOpenFileName() is called, no dialog will appear and the function will return immediately with a FALSE value.

MFC Example

SDI and MDI AppWizard-generated applications already provide a menu item and File Open and File Save dialogs, requiring no additional coding. This section is primarily for dialog-based applications where you might want to invoke these dialogs yourself.

In an MFC program there are several classes provided for displaying common dialogs boxes. The CFileDialog class is used for both File Open and File Save dialogs. Inside this class is an OPENFILENAME structure (the same as used in the SDK example) named as the m_ofn data member. Most of the commonly used features can be set in the constructor for the CFileDialog class as shown in Code 3–31.

Code 3-31

```
CFileDialog( BOOL bIsOpen, LPCTSTR lpszDefExt = NULL, LPCTSTR lpszFileName
= NULL, DWORD dwFlags = OFN_HIDEREADONLY | OFN_OVERWRITEPROMPT, LPCTSTR
lpszFilter = NULL, CWnd* pParentWnd = NULL );
```

Only the first parameter in the CFiledialog constructor is required, which is a flag to indicate whether it should be a File Open type dialog, or a File Save type. The other parameters are default values. The parameters to the constructor are placed into the m_ofn data member of the OPENFILENAME structure with the exception of the lpszFilter parameter.

The lpszFiler parameter is a string similar to the string used in the SDK example previously in this chapter. The lpszFiler string is divided into substrings by using the pipe "|" character, which is similar to how the NULL "\0" character is used in the SDK example. MFC converts lpszFilter into a string compatible with the OPEN-FILENAME structure and then stores it into the structure. An example of a file dialog is shown in Code 3-32.

Once the dialog has been displayed, if the return value from DoModal() is IDOK, then the GetPathName() function is called to get the user's filename choice. The GetPathName() function must be added to the view class of the project, using ClassWizard's Message Map tab.

Code 3-32

```
void CCmnDlg_MFCView::OnGetopenfilename()
{
        static char Filter[]="All Files (*.*)|*.*|Text Files
(*.txt)|*.txt||";

        CFileDialog Tmp( TRUE, NULL, NULL, OFN_HIDEREADONLY |
                OFN_OVERWRITEPROMPT, Filter); // TRUE makes it an 'Open' dia-
                log

        if( Tmp.DoModal()==IDOK ) // Display dialog, and get user's input.
                MessageBox( Tmp.GetPathName() ); // Display user's selection

}
```

File Save

The File Save dialog box (Figure 3-29) allows the user to select a file to be saved and follows the same basic appearance as the File Open dialog.

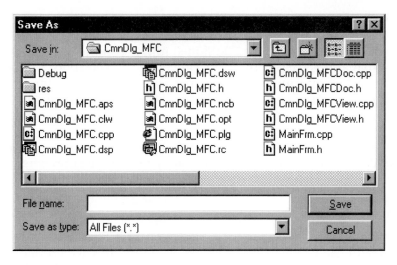

Figure 3–29 The File Save dialog box.

SDK Example

In an SDK program, the GetSaveFileName() function is used to display the File Save common dialog box. Like GetOpenFileName() used to display the File Open dialog box (see previous discussion in this chapter), the GetSaveFileName() function uses an OPENFILENAME data structure, which must be properly initialized before you call GetSaveFileName(). Code 3–33 demonstrates how to write a function to open a common File Save dialog box in your application.

Code 3–33

```
BOOL DemoGetSaveFileName( HWND hWnd, char* Dest, int DestSize )
{
        // Remember to #include <commdlg.h> for Common Dialogs
        OPENFILENAME Tmp;
        memset( &Tmp, 0, sizeof( Tmp ) );
        Tmp.lStructSize = sizeof( Tmp );
        Tmp.hwndOwner = hWnd;
        Tmp.lpstrFilter = "All Files\0*.*\0Text Files\0*.txt\0";
        Tmp.nFilterIndex = 1;
        Tmp.lpstrFile = Dest;
        Tmp.nMaxFile = DestSize;
        Tmp.lpstrTitle = "Select file to save as";
        return( GetSaveFileName( &Tmp ) );
}
```

The DemoGetSaveFileName() function requires three parameters. The first parameter is hWnd, which is the handle to the main application window. The second

---

parameter is Dest, which is a pointer used to store the filename that is selected by the user. The last parameter is DestSize, which is the size of the memory allocated for the filename. The DemoGetSaveFileName() function returns TRUE if the user selected a filename and FALSE if the user cancelled the selection. Before calling the DemoGetSaveFileName() function, make sure that what Dest points to is either an empty string or a name of a legitimate file, otherwise the dialog will not be displayed.

If any of the members of the OPENFILENAME structure are not correctly initialized, the GetSaveFileName() function will immediately return a FALSE when the function is called and no dialog box will be displayed.

MFC Example

The CFileDialog class is used for both File Open and File Save dialog boxes. The first parameter to the CFileDialog constructor determines which dialog box is displayed. If the parameter is TRUE, then the File Open dialog box is displayed. A FALSE value causes the display of the File Save dialog box.

Code 3–34 is an example of how to display a File Save dialog box and retrieve the filename the user has selected. Once you have called the DoModal() function of that class and determined that it has returned IDOK, then you can access the user's file selection by calling the GetPathName() function. Please note that the OnGetSave-File() function itself is just a demonstration and does nothing useful with the file name it retrieves except show it in a MessageBox(). In practical use, you would want to take the CString that is returned by GetPathName() and pass that on to a file-saving function.

Most likely, you will be adding functions to your View or CMainFrame class in an MFC program to respond to user events, like the user clicking the File/Save As menu item, so the function below is in a View class. But, since the Document and View classes work so closely, once the View has successfully gotten a file name to save as, it should ask the Document class to actually save data to that file.

Code 3–34

```
void CCmnDlg_MFCView::OnGetsavefile()
{
        // The filter for files to be displayed in the dialog
        static char Filter[]="All Files (*.*)|*.*|Text Files
        (*.txt)|*.txt||";
        // Construct the CFileDialog object as a 'Save' dialog
        (1st parameter)
        CFileDialog Tmp( FALSE, NULL, NULL, OFN_HIDEREADONLY | OFN_OVER-
        WRITEPROMPT,
                Filter); // FALSE in first param makes it a 'Save' dialog
```

```
if( Tmp.DoModal()==IDOK ) // Invoke the dialog
        MessageBox( Tmp.GetPathName() ); // Display user's selec-
        tion
}
```

Page Setup

The Page Setup dialog box (Figure 3–30) is a common dialog box that enables the user of your application to specify page setup information. This dialog does not actually do anything but provide a method for you to show settings for page setup and permit the user to make changes. It is assumed that you are writing some sort of function to create a report and that the function needs to know page setup values.

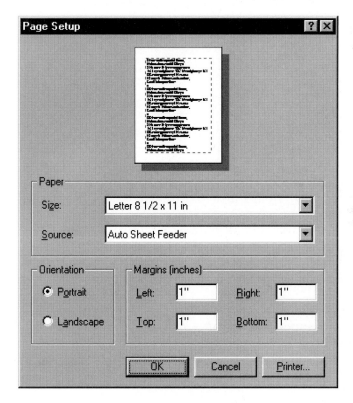

Figure 3–30 The Page Setup dialog box.

SDK Example

The PageSetupDlg() function is used to display the Page Setup dialog box in your application and requires the initialization of the PAGESETUPDLG structure. The PageSetup PAGESETUPDLG structure is a global structure in our example that reflects the current values for the page setup. The values from the PageSetup structure are used to specify what is displayed in the dialog when it is first displayed, as well as where to store the changes the user makes to the settings. Values stored in members of the PageSetup structure are also available to other functions in the application such as a report printing function. This is illustrated in Code 3–35.

Code 3–35

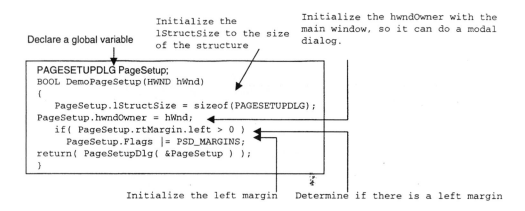

```
PAGESETUPDLG PageSetup;
BOOL DemoPageSetup(HWND hWnd)
{
    PageSetup.lStructSize = sizeof(PAGESETUPDLG);
PageSetup.hwndOwner = hWnd;
    if( PageSetup.rtMargin.left > 0 )
        PageSetup.Flags |= PSD_MARGINS;
return( PageSetupDlg( &PageSetup ) );
}
```

Declare a global variable

Initialize the lStructSize to the size of the structure

Initialize the hwndOwner with the main window, so it can do a modal dialog.

Initialize the left margin   Determine if there is a left margin

Code 3–35 assumes that the hWnd parameter is the HWND for the main window similar to the WndProc(). Remember that the HWND is a handle to a window and is how you interact with the window. The PageSetupDlg() function will use this hWnd to disable and enable the parent window while it is running. The structure size (lStructSize) and parent window (hwndOwner) data members are initialized and if the PageSetup structure member rtMargin already has a value other than zero then this value is used as the default setting when the Page Setup dialog box is displayed.

The PageSetupDlg() function returns TRUE if the user clicked OK and FALSE if Cancel is clicked. If the Printer button is clicked, the dialog will invoke the printer selection dialog, but will not return from the PageSetupDlg() function (until OK or Cancel clicked). Here are the most commonly used members of the PAGESETUPDLG structure:

PageSetup.rtMargin.left	=	Left margin, in 1/1000″ (by default)
PageSetup.rtMargin.top	=	Top margin, in 1/1000″ (by default)
PageSetup.rtMargin.bottom	=	Bottom margin, in 1/1000″ (by default)

PageSetup.rtMargin.right	=	Right margin, in 1/1000″ (by default)
Pagesetup.ptPaperSize.cx	=	Width of selected paper, in 1/1000″ (by default)
Pagesetup.ptPaperSize.cy	=	Height of selected paper, in 1/1000″ (by default)

Other fields in the printer selection dialog, such as page orientation and paper source, handle printer specifications directly and are not normally needed by your application. For example, if the user were to select landscape orientation in the printer selection dialog, it would be reflected in the ptPaperSize data member.

NOTE

SDI and MDI AppWizard-generated applications automatically provide a menu item that contains the Page Setup dialog box, therefore you are not required to write additional code. However, you will be required to write code to include the Page Setup dialog box if you create a dialog-based application.

MFC Example

The CPageSetupDialog class is the MFC class used to display the Page Setup dialog box in an application created using the MFC. Instead of creating a global variable as we did in the SDK example, we will create a data member for the View class to enable storage of the page specification. The following is an example of how to add the Page Setup dialog box to your application using the MFC. The CPageSetupDialog class is defined in the afxdlgs.h file, which you may or may not need to include, based on your project type.

First, we add Code 3–36 to our View class (though it can also be in the CMain-Frame class or a global variable):

Code 3–36

```
CPageSetupDialog m_PageSetup; // Add this to your view class header file as
a data member
```

Next, we add a message map handler that will invoke the Page Setup dialog, using our m_PageSetup data member. Code 3–37 is the handler for a menu item named "Page Setup," which was added via ClassWizard. Note how all it does is call the Do-Modal() function.

Code 3–37

```
// Add this function to your view class, call it when you need to display
dialog
```

```
void CCmnDlg_MFCView::OnPagesetup()
{
        m_PageSetup.DoModal();
}
```

The OnInitialUpdate() is called each time an MFC program loads a document. It is normally already defined for the View class in your project, as shown in Code 3–38.

Code 3–38

```
void CCmnDlg_MFCView::OnInitialUpdate()
{
        CView::OnInitialUpdate();

        if( m_PageSetup.m_psd.rtMargin.bottom==0 )
        {
                m_PageSetup.m_psd.rtMargin.bottom = 1000;
                m_PageSetup.m_psd.rtMargin.top = 1000;
                m_PageSetup.m_psd.rtMargin.left = 1000;
                m_PageSetup.m_psd.rtMargin.right = 1000;
        }

}
```

You can access the following members of the m_PageSetup data member of the view class to get to the user's selections:

m_PageSetup.m_psd.rtMargin.left	=	Left margin, in 1/1000" (by default)
m_PageSetup.m_psd.rtMargin.top	=	Top margin, in 1/1000" (by default)
m_PageSetup.m_psd.rtMargin.bottom	=	Bottom margin, in 1/1000" (by default)
m_PageSetup.m_psd.rtMargin.right	=	Right margin, in 1/1000" (by default)
m_Pagesetup.m_psd.ptPaperSize.cx	=	Width of selected paper, in 1/1000" (by default)
m_Pagesetup.m_psd.ptPaperSize.cy	=	Height of selected paper, in 1/1000" (by default)

NOTE

Other values from the dialog such as page orientation and paper source deal with the printer directly and are not typically required by your application. For example, page orientation is automatically reflected in the ptPaperSize data member.

Color Selection

The Color Selection dialog box (Figure 3–31) allows the user to select a color from a standard dialog box or display the entire color grid, with the option of standard or custom colors. The color selection dialog doesn't actually change the color of anything, it simply presents the user with the ability to choose a color, and it is up to your code to decide how to use that color selection. Exactly what the color is for—i.e., a Font, Button, window background, etc.—is not important to the Color Selection dialog, it merely gets the color selection from the user.

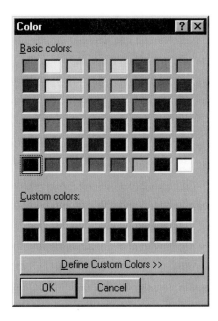

Figure 3–31   The Color Selection dialog box.

SDK Example

In order to display a color selection dialog box, you must use the CHOOSECOLOR structure and the ChooseColor() function in your program. As with all common dialogs, you can insert your own enhancement, called a hook, by creating your own "hook" function to take control for added functionality that you want to incorporate or you can choose not to (most often, you won't). You can also modify various values in the CHOOSECOLOR structure to get different behavior and appearance from the color selection dialog.

Code 3–39 is a function that accepts the HWND of the main window and a pointer to a color (a COLORREF data type) called DestColor. DestColor will be the pointer to the currently selected color, and if the user selects a different color, then Dest-Color will be changed to that selection.

Code 3–39

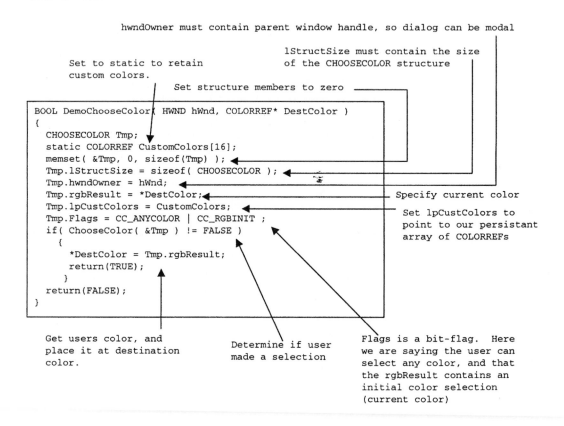

hwndOwner must contain parent window handle, so dialog can be modal

lStructSize must contain the size of the CHOOSECOLOR structure

Set to static to retain custom colors.

Set structure members to zero

```
BOOL DemoChooseColor( HWND hWnd, COLORREF* DestColor )
{
    CHOOSECOLOR Tmp;
    static COLORREF CustomColors[16];
    memset( &Tmp, 0, sizeof(Tmp) );
    Tmp.lStructSize = sizeof( CHOOSECOLOR );
    Tmp.hwndOwner = hWnd;
    Tmp.rgbResult = *DestColor;
    Tmp.lpCustColors = CustomColors;
    Tmp.Flags = CC_ANYCOLOR | CC_RGBINIT ;
    if( ChooseColor( &Tmp ) != FALSE )
    {
        *DestColor = Tmp.rgbResult;
        return(TRUE);
    }
    return(FALSE);
}
```

Specify current color

Set lpCustColors to point to our persistant array of COLORREFs

Get users color, and place it at destination color.

Determine if user made a selection

Flags is a bit-flag. Here we are saying the user can select any color, and that the rgbResult contains an initial color selection (current color)

MFC Example

The CColorDialog class must be used for an MFC program that needs to display the Color Selection dialog box. The CColorDialog class constructor takes three parameters as shown in Code 3–40.

Code 3–40

```
CColorDialog( COLORREF clrInit=0, DWORD dwFlags=0, CWnd* pParentWnd=NULL );
```

The clrInit parameter specifies what color should be the currently selected color when the dialog is displayed.

The dwFlags parameter is a bitmask combination of optional flags. Our example will only use the CC_ANYCOLOR and CC_RGBINIT flags, which mean that the user may select any color (users are not limited to a small palette of colors) and that we have specified an RGB color for initializtion (the clrInit value).

The pParentWnd parameter is the pointer to the parent window of the dialog. Since this function is in a View class, then this is assumed to be a pointer to the view window and serves well for this parameter, which must be the parent window handle. The parent window is disabled while the color selection is displayed and enabled when the dialog is closed.

Code 3–41 is similar to the SDK version in that you pass the address of a COLORREF variable to it, and it will invoke the color selection dialog with that color displayed. If the user changes the color selection and hits the OK button, then the new color choice will be stored at the COLORREF variable whose address you originally provided.

Code 3–41

```
BOOL CCmnDlg_MFCView::SelectColor(COLORREF *CurColor)
{
        // CC_ANYCOLOR means dialog will display all available colors
        // CC_RGBINIT means that the first parameter should be show as the
        current color.
        CColorialog Tmp( *CurColor, CC_ANYCOLOR | CC_RGBINIT, this );

        if( Tmp.DoModal() == IDOK )
        {
                CString Msg;
                Msg.Format( "You selected color %d", Tmp.GetColor() );
                *CurColor = Tmp.GetColor();        // Get user's choice
                return( TRUE );
        }
        return( FALSE );
}
```

Text Find and Replace Dialogs

The text Find (see Figure 3–32) and Replace (see Figure 3–33) dialog boxes are different from other common dialog boxes, in that they are not modal dialog boxes but are instead modeless dialog boxes. This means they do not need to be closed in order to set focus to (work with) the main window while the user performs a search. The Find and Replace dialog boxes do not perform a search or replace. They merely capture data used in the search or replace. Your application performs the search or replace.

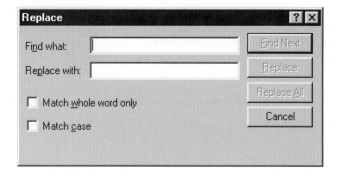

Figure 3–32   The Replace dialog box.

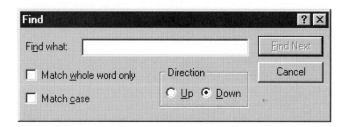

Figure 3–33   The Find dialog box.

The Find and Replace dialog boxes send messages to the parent window to do a search or replace operation. This means they are much more interactive with the main window than other common dialog boxes, which merely disable the parent window until they are closed.

SDK Example

In order to implement the Find or Replace dialog box, you must register a window message for the Find dialog box, which is passed to the main window. In addition, you must display the dialog box and process messages the dialog box sends to the parent window. Here is what you need to do to use the Find or Replace dialog box in your application:

1.   Add the following global variables to your SDK program as shown in Code 3–42.

Code 3-42

```
UINT FindMsg; // The Find window message, passed by dialog to
parent
HWND FindWnd; // HWND for the Find or Replace dialog
char FindWhat[81], ReplaceWith[81]; // Find and Replace
strings
FINDREPLACE FindData; // Data for holding find and replace in-
formation
```

2. In WinMain, register the FINDMSGSTRING message with your window by calling RegisterWindowMessage() and save the return value in the FindMsg global variable as shown in Code 3-43.

Code 3-43

```
FindMsg = RegisterWindowMessage( FINDMSGSTRING );
```

3. Modify the message loop in WinMain() so that messages from the Find dialog box are processed. Modifications to the message loop are illustrated in bold in Code 3-44.

Code 3-44

```
while (GetMessage(&msg, NULL, 0, 0))
{
        if( FindWnd && IsDialogMessage( FindWnd, &msg ) )
                //Global variable continue;
        if (!TranslateAccelerator(msg.hwnd, hAccelTable,
        &msg))
        {
                TranslateMessage(&msg);
                DispatchMessage(&msg);
        }
}
```

4. Modify the WndProc() to handle the FindMsg message. You cannot use the FndMsg variable in the case statement since the case statements require a constant value and the FndMsg is a variable. Instead, add Code 3-45 to your WndProc(), placing it above your switch statement.

Code 3-45

```
if( message == FindMsg ) // Respond to Find/Replace dialog messages
{
        char Str[256];
        // Get access to the FINDREPLACE struct, in the lParam for the mes-
        sage
        FINDREPLACE* pFindReplace = (FINDREPLACE*)lParam;
        if( pFindReplace->Flags & FR_DIALOGTERM ) // Was dialog closed?
        {
```

```
                FindWnd = 0;
                return(0);
        }
        if( pFindReplace->Flags & FR_FINDNEXT ) // Was a FindNext request?
        {
                wsprintf( Str, "Asked to find '%s'", pFindReplace->lp-
                strFindWhat );
                if( pFindReplace->Flags & FR_DOWN )
                        strcat( Str, " (down)" );
                else
                        strcat( Str, " (up)" );
        }
        else if( pFindReplace->Flags & FR_REPLACE ) // Was a Replace re-
        quested?
                wsprintf( Str, "Asked to replace '%s' with '%s'",
                        pFindReplace->lpstrFindWhat,
                        pFindReplace->lpstrReplaceWith );
        else if( pFindReplace->Flags & FR_REPLACEALL ) // Was it a Replace
        All?
        {
                wsprintf( Str, "Asked to replace all '%s' with '%s'",
                        pFindReplace->lpstrFindWhat,
                        pFindReplace->lpstrReplaceWith );
                if( pFindReplace->Flags & FR_DOWN )
                        strcat( Str, " (down)" );
                else
                        strcat( Str, " (up)" );
        }
        else // Must have been a normal find
                wsprintf( Str, "Asked to find '%s'", pFindReplace->lp-
                strFindWhat );
        MessageBox( hWnd, Str, "Information", MB_OK );
}
else
switch (message) // Your normal switch for message processing follows...
{
```

5. Display either dialog boxes by creating one or both of the following functions. Notice that both use the FindData global variable are shown in Code 3–46.

Code 3–46

```
HWND DemoFindText(HWND hWnd )
{
        // Note: This function pops up a dialog, but it is not modal. The
        dialog
        // will send messages to the parent window, as the user makes vari-
        ous selections.
        // See the 'if( message == FindMsg )' in the WndProc for an exam-
```

```
        ple.
        memset( &FindData, 0, sizeof( FINDREPLACE ) ); // Init members to
        zero
        FindData.lStructSize = sizeof( FINDREPLACE ); // Setup the needed
        lStructSize
        FindData.hwndOwner = hWnd; // Indicate parent window to get mes-
        sages
        FindData.Flags = FR_DOWN; // Default the search direction to Down
        FindData.lpstrFindWhat = FindWhat; // Buffer of what to search for
        FindData.wFindWhatLen = sizeof(FindWhat); // How large is the
        buffer
        return( FindText( &FindData ) );
}

HWND DemoReplaceText( HWND hWnd )
{
        // Note: This function pops up a dialog, but it is not modal. The
        dialog
        // will send messages to the parent window, as the user makes vari-
        ous selections.
        // See the 'if( message == FindMsg )' in the WndProc for an exam-
        ple.
        memset( &FindData, 0, sizeof( FINDREPLACE ) );
        FindData.lStructSize = sizeof( FINDREPLACE );
        FindData.hwndOwner = hWnd;
        FindData.Flags = FR_DOWN;
        FindData.lpstrFindWhat = FindWhat;
        FindData.wFindWhatLen = sizeof(FindWhat);
        FindData.lpstrReplaceWith = ReplaceWith;
        FindData.wReplaceWithLen = sizeof( ReplaceWith );
        return( ReplaceText( &FindData ) );
}
```

MFC Example

In order to implement a Find or Replace dialog box in MFC, you will need to use the CFindReplaceDialog class and its members to display and interact with the dialog box.

1. Declare a single protected data member to the View class as shown in Code 3–47. The data member must be a pointer because when the dialog box is closed, the CFindReplaceDialog object automatically does a delete (as in release dynamic memory) on itself. If you don't dynamically allocate the data structure, (as shown in step 9) then you will get a General Protection Fault. In the constructor for your View class, remember to initialize the m_pFindData data member to zero.

Code 3-47

```
CFindReplaceDialog *m_pFindData;
```

2. Since there is no standard window message for a Find, we need to register our own, which we do with the RegisterWindowMessage() function. We are doing this here in the View class, not the MainFrame class. This is OK for SDI programs, but it should be done in the MainFrame class if you are going to create an MDI program. In the top of your view .cpp file, add Code 3-48.

Code 3-48

```
static UINT WM_FINDREPLACE = ::RegisterWindowMessage(FINDMSG-
STRING);
```

3. Manually add the WM_FINDREPLACE message handler to the message map. You can't use ClassWizard to do it automatically because this message is not a standard Windows message and will not appear in your list of possible messages.
4. Insert the line shown in bold in Code 3-49 to the bottom of the message map in your view classes .cpp source file.

Code 3-49

```
//}}AFX_MSG_MAP
ON_REGISTERED_MESSAGE( WM_FINDREPLACE, OnFindReplace )
        // Standard printing commands
        ON_COMMAND(ID_FILE_PRINT, CView::OnFilePrint)
        ON_COMMAND(ID_FILE_PRINT_DIRECT, CView::OnFilePrint)
        ON_COMMAND(ID_FILE_PRINT_PREVIEW, CView::OnFilePrint-
        Preview)
END_MESSAGE_MAP()
```

5. Insert the prototype as shown in Code 3-50 for the OnFindReplace() function into the class definition in your .h file for the view class of the project. This makes the OnFindReplace() function work like other message maps that are normally added with ClassWizard (that is, that they will handle a Windows message and invoke a special function in response to that message).

Code 3-50

```
//}}AFX_MSG
afx_msg LONG OnFindReplace(WPARAM wParam, LPARAM
lParam);
DECLARE_MESSAGE_MAP()
};
```

6. Add the OnFindReplace() function shown in Code 3–51, which is the message handler for the messages sent by the Find and Replace dialog boxes.

Code 3–51

```
LONG CCmnDlg_MFCView::OnFindReplace(WPARAM wParam, LPARAM lParam)
{
        CString Str;
        FINDREPLACE* pFindReplace = (FINDREPLACE*)lParam;

        if( pFindReplace->Flags & FR_FINDNEXT ) // Asked to find next
        {
                Str.Format("Asked to find '%s'", pFindReplace->lpstrFindWhat
                );
                if( pFindReplace->Flags & FR_DOWN )
                        Str += " (down)";
                else
                        Str += " (up)";
        }
        else if( pFindReplace->Flags & FR_REPLACE ) // Asked to replace
                Str.Format( "Asked to replace '%s' with '%s'",
                        pFindReplace->lpstrFindWhat,
                        pFindReplace->lpstrReplaceWith );
        else if( pFindReplace->Flags & FR_REPLACEALL ) // Asked to replace
        all
        {
                Str.Format( "Asked to replace all '%s' with '%s'",
                        pFindReplace->lpstrFindWhat,
                        pFindReplace->lpstrReplaceWith );
                if( pFindReplace->Flags & FR_DOWN )
                        Str += " (down)";
                else
                        Str += " (up)";
        }
        else // Asked to do a simple find
                Str.Format( "Asked to find '%s'", pFindReplace->lpstrFind-
                What );
        MessageBox( Str );
          return(0);
}
```

7. The sample code above does not actually perform a search and replace. Instead, for demonstration purposes it will display a message box that shows what the function has been requested to do. Depending on the type of your program, you will need to modify the function above to perform the actual search and/or replace.

8. Add menu items and message handlers for the menu items, using ClassWizard, to display the Find and Replace dialog boxes. The Menu handling section of this boOK contains examples of how to accomplish this. A typical menu item handler for search and replace will look like Code 3–52.

Code 3–52

```
// This function would have been added via a Message Map in ClassWizard for the
// Find Text menu item.
void CCmnDlg_MFCView::OnFindtext()
{
        if( m_pFindData ) // Already open? If so, close it
              m_pFindData->EndDialog( IDOK ); // Does a 'delete' automati-
              cally
        m_pFindData = new CFindReplaceDialog();
        m_pFindData->Create( TRUE, "", NULL, FR_DOWN, this );

}
// This function would have been added via a Message Map in ClassWizard for the
// Find Text menu item.
void CCmnDlg_MFCView::OnReplacetext()
{
        if( m_pFindData ) // Already open? If so, close it
              m_pFindData->EndDialog( IDOK ); // Does a 'delete' automati-
              cally
        m_pFindData = new CFindReplaceDialog();
        m_pFindData->Create( FALSE, "", NULL, FR_DOWN, this );

}
```

Font Selection

The Font Selection common dialog box (Figure 3–34) permits the user to make a font selection. When using the Font Selection dialog box, your application needs to track the select font and its color. In an MFC application, the font selection is stored in the CFont variable and the font color is stored in the COLORREF variable. In an SDK application, the HFONT and COLORREF variable types are used to store the font and color selected by the user.

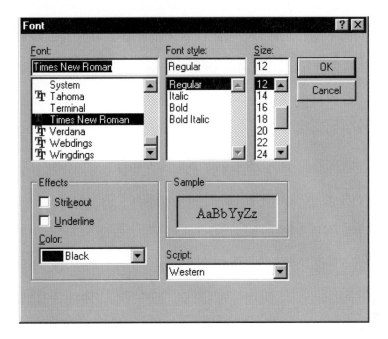

Figure 3–34   The Font Selection dialog box.

NOTE

The color of a font is not a part of the Windows font definition. This means that when you work with font selection dialogs, you will be retrieving two separate pieces of data from the dialog: font description and color. You will note that examples for the font selection will actually return two values to match this.

SDK Example

In order to display the Font Selection dialog box in an SDK program, you will need to create an instance of the structure CHOOSEFONT then call the ChooseFont() function.

1. Create a function that creates an instance of and initializes the CHOOSEFONT structure and calls the ChooseFont() to display the Font Selection dialog box as illustrated in Code 3–53. We called this the Demo-ChooseFont() function. Notice that this function requires three parameters. These are the handle of the parent window that requested the

---

Font Selection dialog box, a pointer to the handle of the active font, and a pointer to the active color of the font.

2. Initialize (see Code 3–53) the lpLogFont and rgbColors members of the CHOOSEFONT structure with the font and color parameters that are passed to the DemoChooseFont() function. This sets the initial values of the Font Selected dialog box when the dialog box first appears on the screen.

Code 3–53

```
BOOL DemoChooseFont( HWND hWnd, HFONT* DestFont, COLORREF* CurColor )
{
CHOOSEFONT Tmp;
        LOGFONT LogFont;
        HFONT CurFont = *DestFont;
        // Set all members to zero
        memset( &Tmp, 0, sizeof(Tmp) );
        // This must be the size of the CHOOSEFONT structure
        Tmp.lStructSize = sizeof( CHOOSEFONT );
        // Specify the parent window - it will be disabled when the dialog
        is displayed
        Tmp.hwndOwner = hWnd;
        if( *DestFont == 0 ) // If DestFont has not been initialized yet…
        {
                // Then, get the current font from the parent window
                HDC hDC = GetDC( hWnd );
                SetMapMode( hDC, MM_TWIPS );
                CurFont = (HFONT)GetCurrentObject( hDC, OBJ_FONT );
                ReleaseDC( hWnd, hDC );
        }
        else
                CurFont = *DestFont; // Otherwise, use the font we had
        // GetObject is used to get information about the font via its han-
        dle, into a
        // LOGFONT structure. This is used by ChooseFont, and Create-
        FontIndirect
        GetObject( CurFont, sizeof(LOGFONT), (void*) &LogFont );
        // Set flags to tell the dialog to display both printer and screen
        fonts, and
        // to initialize the dialogs font with the lpLogFont member
        Tmp.Flags = CF_BOTH | CF_INITTOLOGFONTSTRUCT;
        // Specify information to be displayed when the
        // dialog pops up (font type and color)
        Tmp.lpLogFont = &LogFont;
        Tmp.rgbColors = *CurColor;
        if( ChooseFont( &Tmp ) != FALSE )// Invoke dialog, and check if user
        hot 'OK'
        {
                if( *DestFont ) // If there was already a font there,
```

```
            DeleteObject( *DestFont ); // then delete it first
            // Create a font from users selection
            *DestFont = CreateFontIndirect( &LogFont );
            *CurColor = p.rgbColors;    // And set its color
            return(TRUE);
    }
    return(FALSE);
}
```

3. Create two static variables (see Code 3–54) in the application's Wnd-
    Proc() to track the current font and color as illustrated below. A COLOR-
    REF stores a 24-bit color value, and an HFONT is a handle to a font
    object (much like HWND is a handle to a Window object).

Code 3-54

```
    static COLORREF TextColor;
    static HFONT TextFont;
```

4. Use the TextColor and TextFont variables in the application's WM_
    PAINT message contained in the application's WndProc() as illustrated
    in Code 3–55. Changes to the font and color options in the Font Se-
    lected dialog box are stored in the TextColor and TextFont variables,
    which are referenced whenever the WM_PAINT message is received to
    repaint the screen.

Code 3-55

```
    case WM_PAINT:
            hdc = BeginPaint(hWnd, &ps);
            RECT rt;
            GetClientRect(hWnd, &rt);
            SetTextColor( hdc, TextColor ); // Select the 'current'
            color
            if( TextFont )
                    SelectObject( hdc, TextFont ); // Select the
                    'current' font
            DrawText(hdc, szHello, strlen(szHello), &rt, DT_CEN-
            TER);
            EndPaint(hWnd, &ps);
            break;
```

5. The DemoFontSelection() function is called from a menu. In this example,
    we created a menu item with the ID of IDM_CHOOSEFONT. Place Code
    3–56 beneath the IDM_CHOOSEFONT in the WM_COMMAND message of
    the application's WndProc(). When the user selects the menu item, the
    IDM_CHOOSEFONT message is sent to the WndProc() and is processed
    by the WM_COMMAND handler. The DemoChooseFont() function is
    called and displays the Font Selection dialog box. If the user clicks OK to

close the Font Selection dialog, then DemoChooseFont() returns TRUE and the InvalidateRect() function is called, which sends the WM_PAINT messages to repaint the screen using the new font and color. If the user clicks Cancel to close the Font Selection dialog, then DemoChooseFont() returns FALSE and the font is not changed.

Code 3-56

```
case IDM_CHOOSEFONT:
      if( DemoChooseFont( hWnd, &TextFont, &TextColor ) )
         InvalidateRect( hWnd, NULL, TRUE );
   break;
```

MFC Example

In an MFC application, the CFontDialog class is used to display the Font Selection dialog box and is illustrated in the following CView application. A CView type view is a simplistic window that is easy to draw on, as described in Chapter 1.

1. Declare the CFont and COLORREF variables as shown in Code 3-57 and place them in the View class definition found in its .h header file (the actual name of the header file will depend on your project name). You can make the entries in a protected section of the class, but for purposes of our demonstration the exact category is not important (in other words, it will work correctly as public or private).

Code 3-57

```
CFont m_Font;
COLORREF m_FontColor;
```

2. Modify the OnDraw() member function that was automatically added to your project by AppWizazrd. OnDraw() uses the selected font and color to display when displaying text as shown in Code 3-58.

Code 3-58

```
void CCmnDlg_MFCView::OnDraw(CDC* pDC)
{
      CCmnDlg_MFCDoc* pDoc = GetDocument();
      ASSERT_VALID(pDoc);
      // TODO: add draw code for native data here

      if( !m_Font.GetSafeHandle() ) // Font not created yet
      {
          m_Font.CreatePointFont( 120, "Times New Roman" ); // Set de-
          fault font
          m_FontColor = 0; // Set black font color
      }
```

```
pDC->SelectObject( &m_Font ); // Select the font
pDC->SetTextColor( m_FontColor ); // Select the text color

pDC->TextOut( 0, 0, "Hello World" ); // Output text in selected font
and color
}
```

3. Add a function to your View class to handle the display of the Font Selection dialog. You can name the function whatever you want, but we
   have called it SelectFont(), as shown in Code 3–59.

Code 3-59

```
BOOL CCmnDlg_MFCView::SelectFont(CFont *CurFont, COLORREF* CurColor)
{
        LOGFONT LogFont;
        // Initialize LogFont with information from the font we were given.
        CurFont->GetLogFont( &LogFont );
        // Construct the CFontDialog, and initialize it
        // with information from the LogFont structure
        CFontDialog Tmp( &LogFont );

        // Place the current color selection into the CFontDialog object.
        Tmp.m_cf.rgbColors = *CurColor;

        if( Tmp.DoModal() == IDOK )        // Invoke the dialog, and check if
        user hit 'OK'
        {
            CurFont->DeleteObject(); // Delete old font
            CurFont->CreateFontIndirect( &LogFont );
            // Create new font from user selection
            *CurColor = Tmp.m_cf.rgbColors; // Retrieve users color selection
            return( TRUE );
        }
        return( FALSE ); // Return FALSE if user hit Cancel
}
```

4. Add a menu item to your menu and identify the menu item as
   IDM_CHOOSEFONT. This will be the menu item that invokes the Font
   Selection dialog.
5. Add a message map handler for it with ClassWizard and call the message map handler OnChoosefont(). Make sure that in ClassWizard that
   you select the View class in the Class Name field, that Object IDs is set
   to IDM_CHOOSEFONT (from step 4), and that the Messages has COM-
   MAND selected when you add the handler.
6. Modify the OnChoosefont() function so that the function is identical to
   the following code. When the menu item is selected, the application
   calls the OnChooseFont() function, which calls the our SelectFont()
   function (from step 3). The SelectFont() (see Code 3–60) function calls

the ChooseFont() function, which displays the Font Selection dialog box. The ChooseFont() function returns a TRUE if the Font Selection dialog box is closed using the OK button and a FALSE if the Cancel button is used to close the dialog box. If a TRUE is returned, then the OnChooseFont() function is called, which causes the OnDraw() function to be called to repaint the window using the new font and color.

Code 3–60

```
void CCmnDlg_MFCView::OnChoosefont()
{
        if( SelectFont( &m_Font, &m_FontColor ) ) // Invoke
        with address of 2 data members
                InvalidateRect(NULL); // Force text to be re-
                drawn, if font changed
}
```

Printer Selection

The Printer Selection dialog box (Figure 3–35) is user to get the settings for a print job and to start a printing. Calling the PrintDlg() function displays the Printer Selection dialog box and gets the Device Context of the printer. The Device Context is a Windows handle that represents a sort of canvas. When you have a Device Context for a printer, or the screen, if you do a TextOut using that device context then the text will appear on either the printer or the screen.

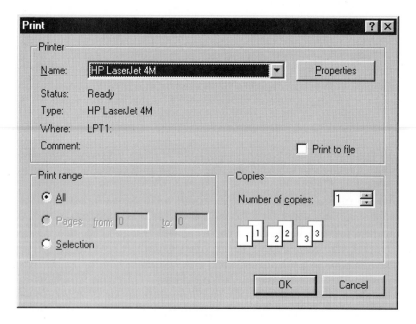

Figure 3–35 The Printer Selection dialog box.

The Printer Selection dialog box uses the PRINTDLG structure. Members of the PRINTDLG structure store printing options such as "from" page (nFromPage) and "to" page (nToPage). You can assign default values to members, which are displayed when the Printer Selection dialog box is displayed. Likewise, you can find the user's selection in the member of the PRINTDLG structure when the dialog box is closed using the OK button.

SDK Example

In an SDK application, you must create a function that will display the Printer Selection dialog box, retrieve the user's selections, and retrieve the Device Context of the printer so your application can print to the printer. A separate process performs printing. Here's what you need to do to create this function.

1. Create an instance of the PRINTDLG structure as global as illustrated in Code 3–61.

Code 3–61

```
PRINTDLG Print;        // For the print dialog
```

2. Insert a menu item that will display the Printer Selection dialog box. Identify the menu item as IDM_PRINTDLG. Make sure that you set up the menu item in the main menu.

3. Create a handler for the menu item in the application's WndProc() function as shown in Code 3–62.

Code 3–62

```
switch (message)
  {
    case WM_COMMAND:
      wmId = LOWORD(wParam);
      wmEvent = HIWORD(wParam);
      // Parse the menu selections:
      switch (wmId)
        {
          case IDM_PRINTDLG:
            if( DemoPrintDlg( hWnd, &hPrinterDC ) )
              {
                MessageBox( hWnd, "Could now print using the
global Print struct, for printing destination", "Information",
MB_OK );
                // We could, but we won't for this demo....
                DeleteDC( hPrinterDC );
                hPrinterDC = 0;
              }
            break;
```

4. Define the variable hPrinterDC within the WndProc() function as shown in Code 3–63. The value of the hPrinterDC variable is the same value as the hDC data member of the global Print structure declared in step 1. This was done for simplicity more than anything, else since the hDC member of the Print variable will contain the same value as the hPrintDC variable (see step 5 also). The hPrinterDC was declared in the WndProc() as shown in Code 3–63.

Code 3–63

```
static HDC hPrinterDC;
```

5. Call the Printer Selection dialog box by using the PrintDlg() function as shown in Code 3–64.

Code 3–64

```
BOOL DemoPrintDlg( HWND hWnd, HDC* phPrinterDC )
{
        BOOL Ret;
        // Uses the global 'Print' variable
        Print.lStructSize = sizeof(PRINTDLG); // Setup its size
        Print.hwndOwner = hWnd; // Identify parent window in-
        voking the dialog
        Print.Flags = PD_RETURNDC; // Tell PrintDlg we want the
        hDC member initialized
        Ret = PrintDlg( &Print ); // Show dialog
        if( Ret ) // Did user hit OK?
                *phPrinterDC = Print.hDC; // If so, save our
                printer Device Context.
        return( Ret );
}
```

6. The hPrinterDC variable is used to reference the printer when printing.

MFC Example

For non-dialog-based applications, the AppWizard automatically generates a menu item and Printer Selection dialog box, so no additional coding is necessary. However, you'll need to write code for a dialog box application to display the Printer Selection dialog box. Here's what you need to do.

An MFC program uses the CPrintDialog class to display the Printer common dialog box and to get a Device Context class (CDC) for the current printer without actually displaying the common dialog. The CPrintDialog constructor has several parameters, only one of which is required. The required parameter is TRUE to have the Printer Setup dialog displayed and FALSE to have the Printer Selection dialog displayed.

1. Add a data member to the view class (which was created by AppWizard when you created your project) as illustrated in Code 3–66.

Code 3–66

```
CPrintDialog m_Print;
```

2. Modify the view class constructor so that it contains an initializer list as shown in bold in Code 3–67. The initializer list contains the parameter required by the CPrintDialog constructor. With this initializer list, we are specifying the parameters needed by the CPrintDialog constructor. The CPrintDialog constructor looks like Code 3–68. The bPrintSetupOnly option determines whether the dialog will be a Print Setup dialog box or a Printer dialog box. The flags define the basic display items and behavior for the dialog.

Code 3-67

```
CCmnDlg_MFCView::CCmnDlg_MFCView() : m_Print(FALSE)
{
        // Rest of the view constructor
```

Code 3-68

```
CPrintDialog( BOOL bPrintSetupOnly, DWORD dwFlags = PD_ALL-
PAGES |
PD_USEDEVMODECOPIES | PD_NOPAGENUMS | PD_HIDEPRINTTOFILE |
PD_NOSELECTION, CWnd* pParentWnd = NULL );
```

3. Add a menu item to your menu using the menu editor. The menu item will be used to invoke the Print dialog. The caption for the menu item should be Print Dialog, and its ID should be IDM_PRINTDLG.
4. Use ClassWizard and the Message Maps tab to add a message handler for the menu item added in step 3. The handler you add will need to be modified to call the DoModal() member function of the CPrintDialog class from a handler function that was added to a menu item such as in Code 3-69. The DoModal() function displays the Print Selection dialog box. The function returns an IDOK if the user closes the Print dialog box using the OK button. You also need to create an instance of the CDC class, which is used to print reports.

Code 3-69

```
// Function added via ClassWizard Message Map for menuitem:
void CCmnDlg_MFCView::OnPrintdlg()
{
        if( m_Print.DoModal() == IDOK ) // If user clicked OK
        {
                CDC PrinterDC;
                PrinterDC.Attach( m_Print.GetPrinterDC() );
                // Use PrinterDC to do printing.
                // When done, clean up
                // We don't need to call Detach or DeleteDC for Print-
                erDC, because
                // its destructor does it for us.
        }
}
```

Browse for Folder

The Browse for Folder dialog box (Figure 3–36) allows the user to select a folder. The ShBrowseForFolder() function used to display this folder is part of the Shell Objects library and requires the use of the shlobj.h file. Make sure to #include this file.

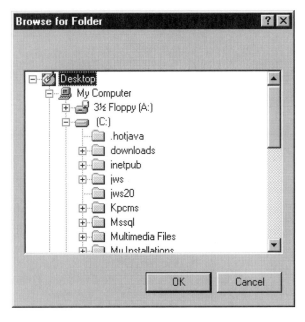

Figure 3–36   The Browse for Folder dialog box.

The Browse for Folder dialog box is displayed the same way regardless if the application is built using the SDK or the MFC. Create a function that will require a window handle (for the parent window), a title string, as well as a char array where it should store the user folder name. The function can be added by right-clicking the view class name in the ClassView window, specifying BOOL as the Function Type, and the function name as parameters in the Function Declaration field. The function is as shown in Code 3–71. Several of the items in Code 3–71 are a bit complex for detailed description here. The primary issues are the fact that the IMalloc interface is used to free memory returned by SHBrowseForFolder() and that you must call SHGetPathFromIDList() to extract the selected path from the pointer that SHBrowseForFolder() returns. IMalloc is a COM interface implemented by the operating system and works with the pointer that SHBrowseForFolder() returns. The function pictured in Code 3–71 is defined as part of the View class of your project (CCmnDlg_MFCView in this example), but you can also use the same code to implement the browse for folder dialog from an SDK program.

Code 3–71

```
BOOL CCmnDlg_MFCView::DemoBrowseForFolder( HWND hWnd, const char* Title,
char* Dest )
{
        // Dest is assumed to be _MAX_PATH characters in length
        // Remember to #include <shlobj.h>
        BROWSEINFO bi;
        ITEMIDLIST * pItemIDList;
        IMalloc * pMalloc;

        if( CoGetMalloc( 1, &pMalloc ) <> S_OK )
                return( FALSE );

        // Folder Only will contain the folder name, without full path
        char FolderOnly[_MAX_PATH];
        // Initialize all members to zero
        memset( &bi, 0, sizeof(bi) );
        bi.hwndOwner=hWnd; // Window handle from the view class
        bi.lpszTitle = Title; // Caption to appear above the tree control
        bi.pszDisplayName=FolderOnly; // Where to store folder name
        if( (pItemIDList=SHBrowseForFolder( &bi )) != NULL )
        {
                //ShBrowseForFolder doesn't get you the actual folder name, but
                // an ITEMIDLIST struct pointer. The SHGetPathFromIDList
                function
                // converts this structure pointer into a valid pathname.
                SHGetPathFromIDList( pItemIDList, Dest );
                pMalloc->Free( pItemIDList );
                return( TRUE );
        }
        return( FALSE );
}
```

Chapter 4

Windowing

- Creating a Window at Runtime
- Creating a Window at Design Time
- Getting a Child Window from a Parent—MFC and SDK
- Positioning and Sizing a Window
- Hiding and Showing a Window
- Enabling and Disabling a Window
- Controlling Windows Fonts
- Focus

As mentioned earlier, a Windows program is made up of a parent window and usually several child windows. Each window has a Window Procedure that is responsible for its appearance and behavior. For example, a button that flashes when you click it has a different Window Procedure from a static text window, which does nothing when you click it.

In this section, we will be performing tasks that are shared by almost all the window classes, such as creating, moving, hiding, and resizing. Since these basic tasks are common across different types or classes of windows (such as buttons, edit boxes, list boxes, etc.), the same functions and approaches can be used with the various window types.

Also mentioned earlier, every window has a window handle associated with it by the operating system. In an SDK program, a programmer uses the HWND data type to track and work with a window, while in an MFC program you would use a CWnd or CWnd-derived object instance. You will find the functions described in this section in both the SDK and as member functions of the CWnd class.

Creating a Window at Runtime

SDK

If you are writing a program similar to our first hello world program, one that is not dialog-based, you will be creating the your windows at runtime. We are going to call the CreateWindowEx() function to create windows. Even if you have created a dialog-based application, you can dynamically add and remove windows at runtime using the code demonstrated in this section.

NOTE

Creating windows at design time using the resource editor, as discussed in Chapter 3, "Dialog Boxes," normally eliminates the need to create windows at runtime. You can also create windows at design time and set their properties so that they are invisible initially. This gives you the ability to see the control on the form at design time, then selectively hide and show the control, rather than create and destroy it at runtime.

The CreateWindowEx() function has an older counterpart called CreateWindow(), which was used in 16-bit windows programs. You can still use CreateWindow(), but CreateWindowEx() permits you to create windows with an extended style attribute (more features, particularly a 3D-like appearance). Though we will be using

CreateWindowEx(), CreateWindow() will also work with most demonstrations presented here. Code 4–1 contains the CreateWindowEx() function.

Code 4–1

```
HWND CreateWindowEx( DWORD dwExStyle, LPCTSTR lpClassName,
    LPCTSTR lpWindowName, DWORD dwStyle, int x, int y, int nWidth,
    int nHeight, HWND hWndParent, HMENU hMenu, HINSTANCE hInstance,
    LPVOID lpParam);
```

CreateWindowEx() will return an HWND to the newly created window if successful or a zero if the window cannot be created.

The dwExStyle parameter references the extended styles or properties for the new window. Some of the most common styles include the following.

- WS_EX_ACCEPTFILES

  Indicates that the window will accept files that are dropped on it from the Explorer file manager. However, you must write the code to accept the files. Windows will modify the cursor when a file is dragged to the program.

- WS_EX_APPWINDOW

  The newly created window will appear on the taskbar even if the window is not the application's main window.

- WS_EX_CONTEXTHELP

  Indicates that the window (if a top-level window) should have the question mark help button on its upper-right corner. If you click the question mark button, the cursor will change to a question mark symbol. If you then click on another control, that control will be sent the WM_HELP message, which is used for context-sensitive help. This option cannot be used with the minimize or maximize button.

- WS_EX_MDICHILD

  Creates an MDI (Multiple Document Interface) child window. The window will have an appearance similar to a main window (caption, resizable, etc.), but will be a child window and can not be moved outside the parent window. (MS Word is an example of an MDI program.)

- WS_EX_CLIENTEDGE

  Creates the window with a sunken border.

- WS_EX_WINDOWEDGE

  Creates a window with a raised border.

  The lpClassName parameter indicates the window type or class. If you created your own main window class or even your own child window class, you would replace lpClassName with the string of your class name. You can also use a stock window styles using its name in place of lpClassName such as "EDIT," "BUTTON," LISTBOX," "COMBOBOX," and "STATIC." Using the newer common controls such as the treeview and list view requires some extra initialization; these will be discussed in their respective sections.

The lpWindowName parameter indicates the window text associated with the new window. It is not needed for all window classes. For example, on a static button, checkbox, and radio button, this text will appear as the text displayed in the window such as OK for a button. Other windows, such as a list box, ignore this parameter.

The dwStyle parameter indicates the styles or properties for the new window. Some of the most common styles are outlined here for generic windows. Some windows however have styles unique to them. For example, the Edit box window has a custom style of ES_PASSWORD where the user's text will be displayed as asterisks when he or she types.

- WS_CHILD

  Indicates that the child will be the child window of another. The parent must be created before the child window is created. Normally this is used when creating child windows, not parent windows.

- WS_DISABLED

  Creates a window that is initially disabled or grayed. The window can be enabled later. This is used when creating child windows only.

- WS_GROUP

  Indicates that the window is the first control of a group. An item such as a radio button where one button being selected deselects all the others occurs within a group. A parent window may have many groups and this option is only used with child controls.

- WS_DLGFRAME

  Indicates the window should have a dialog-like frame that consists of a border and title by default but it will not be resizable. This is used for parent windows but not child windows.

- WS_HSCROLL and WS_VSCROLL

  Creates a window with a horizontal and/or vertical scrollbar. The scroll bars may later be made visible or invisible. Though the scroll bars are present, you must write the code to make them functional. These styles are used for parent windows and list boxes.

- WS_MAXIMIZE and WS_MINIMIZE

  Creates a window that is initially maximized or minimized. The window may be resized later. This is used only for parent windows and with the WS_OVERLAPPED style.

- WS_MAXIMIZEBOX and WS_MINIMIZEBOX

  Causes the window to be displayed with a maximize and/or minimize button on its upper right corner. This is used only for parent windows.

- WS_OVERLAPPED

  An overlapped window is used only with parent windows and normally for programs that are not dialog-based, such as the Hello World program shown in Chapter 1, "A Complete SDK Application."

- WS_OVERLAPPEDWINDOW

  A combination of the WS_OVERLAPPED, WS_CAPTION, WS_SYSMENU, WS_THICKFRAME, WS_MINIMIZEBOX, and WS_MAXIMIZEBOX styles.

- WS_POPUP

  Used to create dialog-like window where a caption is optional. Dialog-based programs use this style to create their main window.

- WS_POPUPWINDOW

  Actually a combination of WS_BORDER, WS_POPUP, and WS_SYS-MENU.

- WS_SYSMENU

  Causes a system button to appear in the upper left corner of the window. This is used only with parent windows and windows that have a caption bar.

- WS_TABSTOP

  Indicates that the new window can be selected when the user presses the tab key to move from window to window. This is used only with child windows.

- WS_THICKFRAME

  Indicates that the window appears with a thick frame to permit the user to resize the window by grabbing the window edges with the mouse cursor. This is used for parent windows only.

- WS_VISIBLE

  Creates a window that is initially visible by can be hidden later. This is used with child windows.

The x and y parameters simply indicate the x and y coordinate of the upper left hand of the window. The coordinates are relative to the parent window if it's a child window.

The nWidth and nHeight parameters contain the width and height of the desired window.

The hMenu parameter serves two purposes. For parent windows, it holds the menu handle of the parent window and can also be specified in the class for the window. For child windows, this parameter should be the unique ID for the child. A unique ID is a unique integer you assign to each child control to identify it later. For child windows you will want to typecast the integer for this parameter, such as (HMENU) 1000.

The hInstance parameter identifies the instance of the program. This parameter can be zero or it can be the hInstance parameter received by the WinMain() function. You can also use the return value of the GetModuleHandle() function to set this parameter.

The lpParam parameter is an extra parameter. It's not used by Windows directly but is used to pass data to the Window Procedure for the child window. The lpParam can be used to initialize a child window created using your own window classes. The lpParam is not often used and usually set to zero.

A program can call CreateWindowEx() function to create child and/or parent windows. We will assume that you have a program generated using AppWizard for a Win32 Application (dialog 1 of AppWizard) with the "A Typical Hello World! Application" option set and will be inserting the code below (Code 4–2) immediately after the original call to CreateWindow(), which created the main parent window (in the InitInstance() function) and stored its result into a variable called hWnd.

Code 4–2

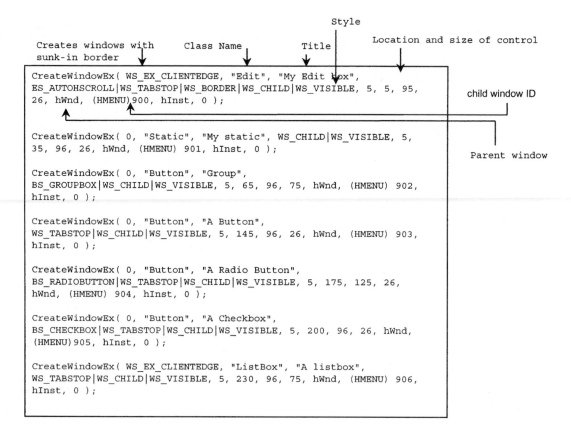

```
CreateWindowEx( WS_EX_CLIENTEDGE, "Edit", "My Edit Box",
ES_AUTOHSCROLL|WS_TABSTOP|WS_BORDER|WS_CHILD|WS_VISIBLE, 5, 5, 95,
26, hWnd, (HMENU)900, hInst, 0 );

CreateWindowEx( 0, "Static", "My static", WS_CHILD|WS_VISIBLE, 5,
35, 96, 26, hWnd, (HMENU) 901, hInst, 0 );

CreateWindowEx( 0, "Button", "Group",
BS_GROUPBOX|WS_CHILD|WS_VISIBLE, 5, 65, 96, 75, hWnd, (HMENU) 902,
hInst, 0 );

CreateWindowEx( 0, "Button", "A Button",
WS_TABSTOP|WS_CHILD|WS_VISIBLE, 5, 145, 96, 26, hWnd, (HMENU) 903,
hInst, 0 );

CreateWindowEx( 0, "Button", "A Radio Button",
BS_RADIOBUTTON|WS_TABSTOP|WS_CHILD|WS_VISIBLE, 5, 175, 125, 26,
hWnd, (HMENU) 904, hInst, 0 );

CreateWindowEx( 0, "Button", "A Checkbox",
BS_CHECKBOX|WS_TABSTOP|WS_CHILD|WS_VISIBLE, 5, 200, 96, 26, hWnd,
(HMENU)905, hInst, 0 );

CreateWindowEx( WS_EX_CLIENTEDGE, "ListBox", "A listbox",
WS_TABSTOP|WS_CHILD|WS_VISIBLE, 5, 230, 96, 75, hWnd, (HMENU) 906,
hInst, 0 );
```

Code 4–2 creates child windows on the main window. Notice how the "BUTTON" class is actually a button, radio button, and checkbox, based on the styles passed to it. The return value from the CreateWindowEx() does not need to be saved in this demonstration because the window handle for a specific child can be retrieved using its unique ID. Also, when the parent window is closed, these windows will automatically be closed as well.

You need to make another small change to the program to enhance the program's appearance. By default, the main window has a white background. In keeping with the standard user interface, the main window should be the same color as that of a button (i.e., grey, by default). In order to do this, locate the following line in Code 4–3 in the MyRegisterClass() function and change it to the line shown in Code 4–4.

Code 4–3

```
wcex.hbrBackground   = (HBRUSH)(COLOR_WINDOW+1);
```

Code 4–4

```
wcex.hbrBackground   = GetSysColorBrush( COLOR_3DFACE );
```

NOTE

Though it's possible to create windows at runtime like in the example above, using dialogs or forms at design time is easier and faster. Whether a window is created at design time or runtime, the methods for manipulating the child control and responding to its events are identical. This can include hiding and showing windows, giving the illusion that the windows are created and destroyed during user operations.

MFC

As with SDK programs, an MFC program permits you to create controls dynamically at runtime. Instead of creating windows with the CreateWindowEx() function, however, use the set of classes provided by MFC as shown in Table 4.1.

In order to create the window at runtime, first instantiate the class for the type of window. For example, you need a CEdit object if you want to dynamically create an edit box. The best place to create this object is as a data member in either the View class or Dialog class, because it must be in existence during the entire life of the parent window. This is illustrated in Code 4–5. Notice that data members are declared inside the Dialog class, which is the main window of the program.

Table 4.1   Microsoft Foundation Classes

Control	MFC Class	Description
animation	CAnimateCtrl	Displays and plays an AVI file.
button	CButton	Buttons, also used for checkboxes, radio buttons, and group boxes.
combo box	CComboBox	Combination of an edit box and a list box. Also has a style where user cannot type in edit box.
edit box	CEdit	Edit boxes for typing text.
header	CHeaderCtrl	Button that appears above a column of text and controls width of text displayed. Primarily used with List controls.
hotkey	CHotKeyCtrl	Invisible window that enables user to create a "hot key" to perform an action quickly.
image list	CImageList	Collection of images used to manage large sets of icons or bitmaps (image list isn't really a control; it supports lists used by other controls).
list	CListCtrl	Window that displays a list of text with icons. The appearance has several variations, such as snaking columns and columnar.
list box	CListBox	A list of strings displayed as lines of text.
progress	CProgressCtrl	A bar that indicates the current completion state of a process.
rich edit	CRichEditCtrl	An edit box for typing text that also supports mixed fonts and the Rich Text Format.
scroll bar	CScrollBar	Scroll bar used as a control inside a dialog box (not on a window). Scrollbars can be added to a window as a style option.
slider	CSliderCtrl	Appears like a slider control from audio equipment.
spin button	CSpinButtonCtrl	Pair of arrow buttons user can click to increment or decrement a value.
static	CStatic	Text for labeling other controls. To create a variable for a static control, you must change its ID from the default of IDC_STATIC. Static controls can contain bitmaps as well as text.
status bar	CStatusBarCtrl	Window for displaying status information, similar to MFC class CStatusBar. AppWizard will normally add one of these to your new projects.
tab	CTabCtrl	Appears as tabs from a physical notebook, used in "tab dialog boxes" or property sheets.
toolbar	CToolBarCtrl	Window with command-generating buttons, similar to MFC class CToolBar. AppWizard will normally add one of these to your new projects.

Control	MFC Class	Description
tool tip	CToolTipCtrl	Small pop-up window that describes purpose of a toolbar button or other tool.
tree	CTreeCtrl	Window that displays a hierarchical list of items.

Code 4-5

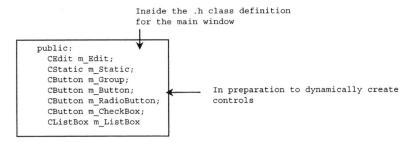

```
public:
    CEdit m_Edit;
    CStatic m_Static;
    CButton m_Group;
    CButton m_Button;
    CButton m_RadioButton;
    CButton m_CheckBox;
    CListBox m_ListBox
```

Inside the .h class definition for the main window

In preparation to dynamically create controls

Once data member objects are declared, the program calls the Create() or Create-Ex() member function for each object, which creates the window and associates the window with that object. The Create() function calls CreateWindow(), and the CreateEx() function calls CreateWindowEx(). Each class has a slightly different form of the Create() function that is unique to the class; however, the CreateEx() function is always the same. Parameters passed to these functions mimic the parameters passed to the CreateWindow() and CreateWindowEx() functions. The Create function for the CEdit class specifically, looks like the following (Code 4-6):

Code 4-6

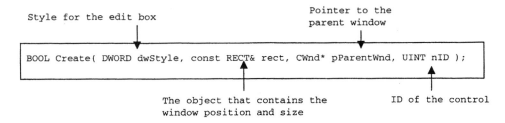

Style for the edit box

Pointer to the parent window

```
BOOL Create( DWORD dwStyle, const RECT& rect, CWnd* pParentWnd, UINT nID );
```

The object that contains the window position and size

ID of the control

When you create the child control dynamically, it may have a font that is different than the dialog or form. You can make the font the same as the parent by calling the GetFont() function of the parent window object, then passing the return value to the SetFont() function of the child window object. Examples of creating the controls dynamically include are shown in Code 4-7.

Note that the same basic process is used:

1. Initialize a CRect object with the desired size relative to parent window.
2. Call the Create() or CreateEx() function to create the window.
3. Set the font of the child window with the same font as its parent.

Code 4–7 can be placed anywhere as either in response to a button click or in the WM_INITDIALG message handler using the OnInitDialg() handler function.

Code 4–7

```
CRect Rect;
Rect.SetRect(5, 5, 95, 26);
m_Edit.CreateEx( WS_EX_CLIENTEDGE, "EDIT", "",
        ES_AUTOHSCROLL|WS_TABSTOP|WS_BORDER|WS_CHILD|WS_VISIBLE,
        Rect, this,900 );
m_Edit.SetFont( GetFont() );//Note: GetFont() is this -> GetFont

Rect.SetRect(5, 35, 105, 61);
m_Static.Create( "My Static", WS_CHILD|WS_VISIBLE, Rect, this, 901 );
m_Static.SetFont( GetFont() );

Rect.SetRect(5, 65, 105, 140 );
m_Group.Create( "Group", BS_GROUPBOX|WS_CHILD|WS_VISIBLE, Rect,
this, 902 );
m_Group.SetFont( GetFont() );

Rect.SetRect( 5, 145, 105, 169 );
m_Button.Create( "A Button", WS_TABSTOP|WS_CHILD|WS_VISIBLE, Rect,
this, 903 );
m_Button.SetFont( GetFont() );

Rect.SetRect( 5, 175, 130, 200 );
m_RadioButton.Create( "A Radio Button",
        BS_RADIOBUTTON|WS_TABSTOP|WS_CHILD|WS_VISIBLE, Rect, this,
        904 );
m_RadioButton.SetFont( GetFont() );

Rect.SetRect( 5, 200, 105, 226 );
m_CheckBox.Create( "A CheckBox", BS_CHECKBOX|WS_TABSTOP|WS_CHILD|
        WS_VISIBLE, Rect, this, 905 );
m_CheckBox.SetFont( GetFont() );

Rect.SetRect( 5, 230,105, 305 );
m_ListBox.CreateEx( WS_EX_CLIENTEDGE, "LISTBOX", "",
        WS_TABSTOP|WS_CHILD|WS_VISIBLE, Rect, this, 906 );
m_ListBox.SetFont( GetFont() );
```

Creating a Window at Design Time

Creating child windows at design time is much easier than at runtime. It requires you to write no code. Instead, we assume that the program is either dialog-based or that you will be placing the controls on a dialog box. A dialog can be the main window of a dialog-based application. The resource editor permits you to simply drop controls on a form, enables you to assign a control a unique ID, and let's you change various properties for the control.

TIP

Often features that a programmer wants to change for a child window can be set by changing its properties in the dialog editor and requires no code.

Getting a Child Window from a Parent—MFC and SDK

In the next few sections, you will learn how to move windows and also how to hide and show them. In order to do this, the program needs the window handle (HWND in SDK, or CWnd in MFC) for the target window. The GetDlgItem() function is called to retrieve the window handle for a child window and has a prototype shown in Code 4–8.

Code 4–8

```
HWND GetDlgItem( HWND hParent, int nChildID );
```

For MFC, it's:

```
CWnd* CWnd::GetDlgItem(int nChildID );
```

Here, hParent is the window handle of the parent window, and nChildID is the unique ID for the desired child.

The GetDlgItem() function works on any type of window, not just dialog parent windows. In Code 4–7, an edit box is created with a unique ID of 900. This ID can be used to obtain the edit box window handle, later in the program.

Code 4–9 is an SDK example that retrieves text from that edit box and should be placed in the Window Procedure of the main window. Note that the function GetDlgItemText() combines GetDlgItem() and GetWindowText() into one function.

Code 4–9

```
char EditText[128];
HWND hEdit = GetDlgItem( hWnd, 900 ); // Retrieve window handle for child
ID 900
GetWindowText( hEdit, EditText, sizeof(EditText) );
```

The CWnd class of MFC also has a GetDlgItem() member function. However, this function requires one parameter, which is the ID of the control and the function returns a CWnd pointer. Code 4–10 is an example of using this function, which can be placed in a message-map handler of an MFC program.

Code 4–10

```
CString EditText;
CEdit* pEdit = (CEdit*)GetDlgItem( IDC_EDIT1 );
pEdit->GetWindowText( EditText );
```

Positioning and Sizing a Window

When positioning or moving a window, there are two types of positions: The Z-Order and the X-Y coordinate. The Z-Order of a window determines whether that window is displayed in front of or behind another window. Programs that provide a Bring to Front or Send to Back operation like MS Word for its graphic elements do so by changing the Z-Order of their child windows.

The X-Y coordinate determines the x and y coordinates of the upper-left corner of a window relative to either its parent or the screen if the window has no parent.

Changing the Position or Size of a Window

In order to change the position or size of a window, you can use the MoveWindow() or SetWindowPos() functions. The MoveWindow() function requires you to change both the position and size of a window at the same time while SetWindowPos() allows you to change either or both. SetWindowPos() also permits you to change the Z-Order of a window.

The MoveWindow() prototype in the SDK looks like Code 4–11. MoveWindow() returns TRUE if it was successful, otherwise it returns FALSE. The SetWindowPos() prototype in the SDK looks like Code 4–12. SetWindowPos returns TRUE if it was successful, otherwise it returns FALSE.

Code 4-11

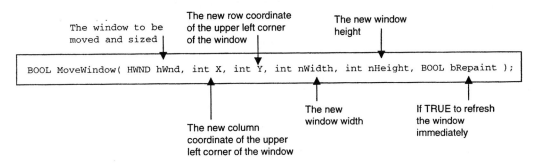

The window to be moved and sized

The new row coordinate of the upper left corner of the window

The new window height

```
BOOL MoveWindow( HWND hWnd, int X, int Y, int nWidth, int nHeight, BOOL bRepaint );
```

The new column coordinate of the upper left corner of the window

The new window width

If TRUE to refresh the window immediately

Code 4-12

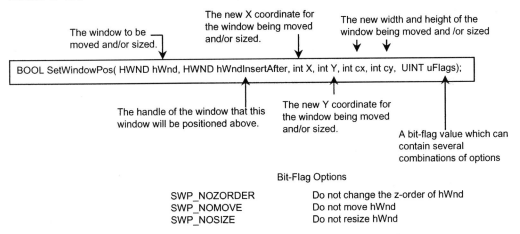

The window to be moved and/or sized.

The new X coordinate for the window being moved and/or sized.

The new width and height of the window being moved and /or sized

```
BOOL SetWindowPos( HWND hWnd, HWND hWndInsertAfter, int X, int Y, int cx, int cy, UINT uFlags);
```

The handle of the window that this window will be positioned above.

The new Y coordinate for the window being moved and/or sized.

A bit-flag value which can contain several combinations of options

Bit-Flag Options

SWP_NOZORDER   Do not change the z-order of hWnd
SWP_NOMOVE   Do not move hWnd
SWP_NOSIZE   Do not resize hWnd

Moving, Resizing, and Making a Window Topmost

SDK

Be sure that you have created a dialog-based application that contains three controls that will be resized and moved. The controls are:

1. A button with an ID of IDC_CLOSE.
2. A static control with an ID of IDC_STATUS.
3. A checkbox with the ID IDC_ONTOP.

Make sure the style property for the dialog itself is set to Resizing frame: The dialog is illustrated in Figure 4–1.

Add a handler (i.e., the case statement in Code 4–13) for the WM_SIZE message in the dialog procedure. WM_SIZE is sent whenever the user resizes the dialog. This

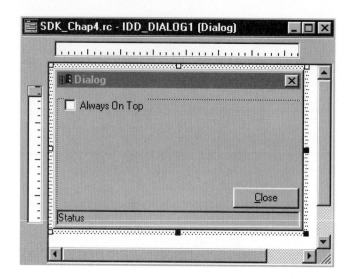

Figure 4–1   Creating a dialog window.

handler moves and resizes the static control so that it always appears at the bottom of the dialog and occupies the width of the dialog. The handler also moves but doesn't resize the button so that it always appears at the bottom right of the dialog.

The WM_COMMAND handler (Code 4–13) is enacted when the user clicks the Always On Top checkbox as well as the Close button. The checkbox shows how to create a topmost window, which stays on top of other windows even if the program is not the active application.

Code 4–13 uses the SendMessage() function to send a BM_GETCHECK message to the checkbox to see if it's checked or not. The IsDlgButtonChecked() function can also be used for this same purpose. The SendMessage() function is used here to show that the SendMessage() function often has easier-to-use counterpart functions that perform the same task. IsDlgButtonChecked() function is used later in this chapter.

Code 4–13

```
LRESULT CALLBACK DialogProc( HWND hwndDlg, UINT uMsg, WPARAM wParam, LPARAM
lParam )
{
    int wID;
    int wNotification;
    RECT ChildRect;
    int Width;
    int Height;
    HWND hChild;
```

```
switch( uMsg )
{
    case WM_CLOSE:
        EndDialog( hwndDlg, 0 ); // Close the dialog
        break;

    case WM_COMMAND: // A message from a control or menu item

        // Parse out WM_COMMAND parameters to be more readable
        wID = LOWORD(wParam);
        wNotification = HIWORD(wParam);
        hChild = (HWND) lParam;

        // Was the 'Always On Top' checkbox clicked?
        if( wID == IDC_ONTOP && wNotification==BN_CLICKED )
        {   // If so, get current check state
            int CheckedState = SendMessage( hChild, BM_GETCHECK, 0, 0 );
            // call SetWindowPos to make top most or not
            if( CheckedState == BST_CHECKED )
                    SetWindowPos( hwndDlg, HWND_TOPMOST, 0, 0, 0, 0,
                            SWP_NOMOVE|SWP_NOSIZE );
            else
                    SetWindowPos( hwndDlg, HWND_NOTOPMOST, 0, 0, 0, 0,
                            SWP_NOMOVE|SWP_NOSIZE );
        }
        else
        // Was the Close button clicked?
        if( wID == IDC_CLOSE && wNotification == BN_CLICKED )
            EndDialog( hwndDlg, 0 ); // Close the dialog
        break;

    case WM_SIZE:
            // Determine new window size
            Width = LOWORD(lParam);
            Height = HIWORD(lParam);
            // Get handle to the 'status' STATIC control
            hChild = GetDlgItem( hwndDlg, IDC_STATUS );
            // And Move and size it, based on new height and width
            MoveWindow( hChild, 0, Height-18, Width, 18, TRUE );
            // Now, get the handle to the Close button
            hChild = GetDlgItem( hwndDlg, IDC_CLOSE );
            // Get the buttons dimensions, so we can right-justify the
            // control
            GetClientRect( hChild, &ChildRect );
            // And, position it
            SetWindowPos( hChild, NULL, Width - ChildRect.right,
                    Height - 20 - ChildRect.bottom, 0, 0,
                    SWP_NOZORDER|SWP_NOSIZE);
            // Note: The hWndInsertAfter, cx, and cy parameters are NULL
            // and 0,
```

```
        // and the uFlags parameter is a combination of SWP_NOZORDER
        // and SWP_NOSIZE.

        break;

    }
    return( FALSE );
}
```

MFC

This MFC example shows how to move and resize controls and how to make a window topmost on the screen (Figure 4–2). A topmost window is a window that stays above other windows even when it does not have the input focus. The example is a dialog-based application created using AppWizard. It assumes that you have done the following:

In the main dialog:

1. Add a checkbox control and changed its properties so that its caption is Always on Top and its ID is IDC_ONTOP.
2. Add a button control and change its properties so that its caption is &Close and its ID is IDC_CLOSE.
3. Add a static control and change its properties so that its caption is Status, its ID is IDC_STATUS, and it has a sunken border.

Since this is an MFC program, we will add message handlers using the ClassWizard Message Map tab for handling the WM_SIZE message. The message handler is

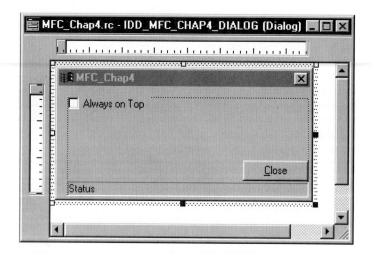

Figure 4–2 Dialog for moving and sizing demonstration in Dialog Editor.

added to the dialog class called CMFC_Chap4Dlg. The dialog resource you add the controls to, in our sample, is called IDD_MFC_CHAP4_DIALOG.

Add three message handlers—one for the WM_SIZE message, one for the user checking or unchecking the Always On Top checkbox, and another for the user clicking the Close button. We will also make a slight change to the dialog initialization code in the OnInitDialog() function in the MFC_Chap4Dlg.cpp file.

Adding the WM_SIZE Handler

1. Go to the View menu item and select ClassWizard to display the Class-Wizard.
2. Make sure the Message Maps tab is the current tab in ClassWizard.
3. Make sure the name of your dialog class is displayed in the Class Name field (CMFC_Chap4Dlg in our sample).
4. In the Object IDs list, select the first item, which should also be the name of the dialog class (from step 3).
5. In the Messages list, scroll down until you find the WM_SIZE entry and highlight it.
6. Click the Add Function button and click OK to accept the name it suggests, which is OnSize().
7. Go to the OnSize() function in your .cpp file. This will be at the end of the MFC_Chap4Dlg.cpp file in our example and will look like Code 4–14.
8. Change the function to look like Code 4–15.

Code 4-14

```
void CMFC_Chap4Dlg::OnSize(UINT nType, int cx, int cy)
{
        CDialog::OnSize(nType, cx, cy);
}
```

Code 4-15

Get CWnd pointer for the Status static control

If available, then move and size the window accordingly

Don't call the default OnSize() handler.

Get CWnd pointer for the Close button control

```
void CMFC_Chap4Dlg::OnSize(UINT nType, int cx, int cy)
{
//  CDialog::OnSize(nType, cx, cy);
    CWnd* pChild;
    pChild = GetDlgItem( IDC_STATUS );
    if( pChild->GetSafeHwnd() )
        pChild->MoveWindow( 0, cy - 18, cx, 18, TRUE );
    pChild = GetDlgItem( IDC_CLOSE );
    if( pChild->GetSafeHwnd() )
    {
      CRect ChildRect;
      pChild->GetClientRect( &ChildRect );
      pChild->SetWindowPos( 0, cx - ChildRect.right,
        cy - 20 - ChildRect.bottom, 0, 0,
        SWP_NOZORDER|SWP_NOSIZE );
    }
}
```

If available, then move (don't size) the window accordingly

NOTE

- The original OnSize() call to the CDialog base class is commented out. This is done because the default OnSize() calls the default window procedure for the dialog. Since we will be calling this function from our own OnInitDialog() routine, we do not want the normal default handling to occur.
- The OnSize() function is invoked when a WM_SIZE message is received for a window. The handler of that function should resize and reposition child windows as needed.
- GetDlgItem() is used to get the CWnd pointer for a window object by its ID.
- GetSafeHWnd() is used to verify we have a successful child window CWnd pointer. The On-Size() function is called several times by the MFC framework, and it may be called before the child controls are available for manipulation. This function helps tell us whether those controls are available.
- The CWnd::MoveWindow() and CWnd::SetWindowPos() functions are called to move and size or just move the desired controls.

The prototype for the GetSafeHwnd() function is illustrated in Code 4–16.

Code 4–16

```
CWnd* CWnd::GetSafeHwnd();
```

The GetSafeHwnd() function verifies if the pChild is a CWnd pointer to a valid window. CWnd is merely a C++ wrapper class for the HWND data type and the CWnd class has a member called m_hWnd, which is the HWND the class wraps. The GetSafeHwnd() function not only tells you if the m_hWnd parameter is non-NULL, it also tells you if the pointer (pChild in our example) is not NULL as well.

Adding the Close Button Handler

1. Select the Message Maps tab in the Class Wizard.
2. Make sure that the Class name is the Dialog class (CMFC_Chap4Dlg in our sample).
3. In the Object IDs list, highlight the IDC_CLOSE item (selecting the control you want to respond to).
4. In the Messages list, select the BN_CLICKED item.
5. Click the Add Function button and add click OK to accept the suggested function name of OnClose().
6. Go to the OnClose() function (this is at the end of the MFC_Chap4Dlg. cpp file in our sample) and change the function so that it looks like Code 4–17.

Code 4–17

```
void CMFC_Chap4Dlg::OnClose()
{
    EndDialog( IDC_CLOSE );
}
```

Close the dialog, and indicate how it was closed

NOTE

The EndDialog() function is used to close the main dialog, which terminates this program.

Adding the Always on Top Handler to Your Code

Using ClassWizard similar to the examples above, add a handler for the BN_CLICKED message of the IDC_ONTOP object ID to the Dialog class (CMFC_Chap4Dlg in our sample). The function added is called whenever the user checks or unchecks the checkbox. Change the code in the function so that it resembles Code 4–18.

Code 4–18 uses the GetDlgItem() function to get a pointer to the checkbox control's CWnd object. This pointer is typecast to a CButton pointer. Since a button control is really also a checkbox or radio control, you will find functions in the CButton class for working with these window types, such as the GetCheck() function. We called GetCheck() to determine if the checkbox was checked or not.

Code 4-18

Get pointer to CWnd
for the Check Box
control

Determine if it's checked or not, then
set top-most status of this window.

```
void CMFC_Chap4Dlg::OnOntop()
{
  CButton* pButton = (CButton*)GetDlgItem( IDC_ONTOP );
  if( pButton->GetCheck() )
    SetWindowPos( &wndTopMost, 0, 0, 0, 0, SWP_NOMOVE|SWP_NOSIZE );
  else
    SetWindowPos( &wndNoTopMost, 0, 0, 0, 0, SWP_NOMOVE|SWP_NOSIZE );
}
```

If the checkbox is not checked, then SetWindowPos() is called with a first parameter of &wndNoTopMost, otherwise it is called with a first parameter of &wndTopMost. Notice how the other parameters are zeros, and the last parameter states we don't want to move or resize the window. This demonstrates how to make a window top-most or not.

Since the OnOnTop() function is a member of the Dialog class and the Dialog class is the class for the main window, then when the SetWindowPos() is called, it is using the C++ *this* implied parameter. This means the window we are setting to be topmost or not is the "this" object. If we wanted to do it with another window, we would have to preceded the SetWindowPos() with the wrapper object for that window as we did in the WM_SIZE handler earlier.

Hiding and Showing a Window

Once a window has been created, it can be either shown or hidden. When a window is hidden, it isn't visible to the user, but you can still do things such as move it, resize it, and get text and a selection from it. If you hide a window, then all its child windows are also hidden. When you show a window, then its child windows are shown (unless the child window itself is set to hidden).

Hiding a window is often used as an easy shortcut for controlling user interface. For example, you can create a dialog that has many controls on it and then create that dialog as a child window of another dialog. You can simple show the child dialog to display all the controls at once, or hide the child dialog to remove all the controls all at once. This is how tab controls work, where each page on a tab control is really a separate dialog that is made visible or invisible as the tab selection changes.

The ShowWindow() function is used to show or hide a window. This function is also used to minimize, maximize, or restore a window, but we will primarily be concerned here with its ability to show and hide a window. The prototype for the ShowWindow() function is illustrated in Code 4–19.

Code 4–19

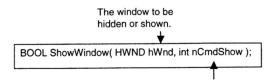

The window to be
hidden or shown.

```
BOOL ShowWindow( HWND hWnd, int nCmdShow );
```

Specifies how we want the window shown

Options for nCmdShow

SW_HIDE	Hides the window
SW_MAXIMIZE	Maximizes the window
SW_MINIMIZE	Minimizes the window
SW_RESTORE	Restores the window to it's original size
SW_SHOW	Activates and shows the window at its current size
SW_SHOWDEFAULT	Show the window according to application defaults
SW_SHOWMAXIMIZED	Activates and maximizes the window
SW_SHOWMINIMIZED	Activates and minimizes the window
SW_SHOWNA	Shows window at its current size (no activate)
SW_SHOWNOACTIVATE	Displays window in its current size
SW_SHOWNORMAL	Activates and displays the window in its original size

SDK

The following code sample assumes that you have a dialog-based application with two controls on a dialog: A checkbox with the ID of IDC_HIDEBUTTON and a button with the ID of IDC_CLOSE. This code fragment (see Code 4–20) will show you how to respond to the user clicking the checkbox, and then hiding or showing the button based on the state of the checkbox. Portions of the code have been eliminated to save space.

Notice how Code 4–20 uses ShowWindow() to hide and show the desired window. The first parameter to ShowWindow() is the handle or HWND to the window you want to show or hide. Since we don't have the HWND for the Close button on the dialog, we use the GetDlgItem() function to determine its HWND using its unique ID (ID_CLOSE).

Code 4-20

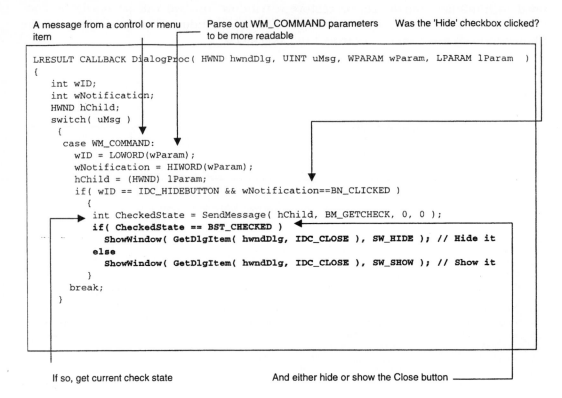

A message from a control or menu item   Parse out WM_COMMAND parameters to be more readable   Was the 'Hide' checkbox clicked?

```
LRESULT CALLBACK DialogProc( HWND hwndDlg, UINT uMsg, WPARAM wParam, LPARAM lParam  )
{
    int wID;
    int wNotification;
    HWND hChild;
    switch( uMsg )
      {
      case WM_COMMAND:
        wID = LOWORD(wParam);
        wNotification = HIWORD(wParam);
        hChild = (HWND) lParam;
        if( wID == IDC_HIDEBUTTON && wNotification==BN_CLICKED )
          {
          int CheckedState = SendMessage( hChild, BM_GETCHECK, 0, 0 );
          if( CheckedState == BST_CHECKED )
            ShowWindow( GetDlgItem( hwndDlg, IDC_CLOSE ), SW_HIDE ); // Hide it
          else
            ShowWindow( GetDlgItem( hwndDlg, IDC_CLOSE ), SW_SHOW ); // Show it
          }
        break;
      }
```

If so, get current check state   And either hide or show the Close button

MFC

The following code sample (Code 4–21) assumes you have a dialog-based application with two controls on the main dialog: a checkbox with the ID of IDC_HIDE-BUTTON and a button with the ID of IDC_CLOSE. If your using the MFC_Chap4Dlg sample project from the previous MFC example, you can simply add the checkbox to the main dialog, since it already has a Close button.

Using ClassWizards Message Maps tab, add a function for the BN_CLICKED message of the IDC_HIDEBUTTON Object ID. This function will need to determine the current check status of the checkbox and then either hide or show the Close button. You should make that function look like Code 4–21.

In Code 4–21, the GetDlgItem() member function is used to get pointers to the CButton and CWnd for the checkbox and the Close button. We typecast the checkbox to a CButton because we must call a member function specific to the CButton class. Even though both controls are Button objects, we don't have to typecast the Close buttons pointer to a CButton because we are calling the ShowWindow() function, which is a member of the CWnd class (a base class of the CButton).

Code 4–21

Get pointer to CWnd for the
Check Box control

```
void CMFC_Chap4Dlg::OnHidebutton()
{
  CButton* pButton = (CButton*)GetDlgItem( IDC_HIDEBUTTON );
  CWnd* pClose = GetDlgItem( IDC_CLOSE );
  if( pButton->GetCheck() )
    pClose->ShowWindow( SW_SHOW );
  else
    pClose->ShowWindow( SW_HIDE );
}
```

Determine if it's checked or not, then hide or show the Close button

Enabling and Disabling a Window

When a window is disabled, it will not accept any input from either the mouse or keyboard. It cannot be the active or focused control. Many windows also have a slightly different appearance when disabled, such as having a grayed appearance. While input is disabled, output remains enabled, which means the program can still change the appearance or content of a window.

The central function for enabling or disabling a window is the EnableWindow() function. This function exists in both the SDK as well as a member function of the CWnd class. As with the MoveWindow(), SetWindowPos(), and ShowWindow() functions described earlier, the EnableWindow() function can be used with any window type as long as it has the ability to react to mouse or keyboard input.

If you disable a parent window, then all its children are automatically disabled. If you enable a parent window, then any of its child windows are re-enabled as long as they were enabled when the parent was first disabled.

SDK

In order to call the EnableWindow() function to enable or disable a window, we first need its HWND. If you haven't stored the HWND somewhere already, such as in a global variable, you can use the GetDlgItem function as long as you know the ID of the control itself.

The HWND for a window is not guaranteed to remain the same throughout program run. There are certain operations that may cause the window to be destroyed and re-created. The ID of a window, however, never changes. For this reason, it can be considered a safe practice to get the HWND of a window at any time by using the

GetDlgItem() function. If the child window does not exist, then GetDlgItem() returns NULL or zero.

In this example, we will not create a complete program. Instead, we will assume that you have a program such as the SDK_Chap4 sample program, which is a dialog-based application. The program should have a checkbox with an ID of IDC_ENABLECLOSE and a button with the ID of IDC_CLOSE.

The SDK_Chap4 sample program has a WM_COMMAND section, which parses information from a WM_COMMAND message (notification from a child window or menu item) into several easy-to-use variables by the code fragment in Code 4–22.

Code 4–22

```
// Our Dialog Procedure
LRESULT CALLBACK DialogProc( HWND hwndDlg, UINT uMsg, WPARAM wParam, LPARAM
lParam )
{
    int wID;
    int wNotification;
    HWND hChild;
    // Portions removed to reduce size of demonstration
    switch( uMsg )
    {
        // Portions removed to reduce size of demonstration
        case WM_INITDIALOG:
            // Place check in the Checkbox, since Close button starts as
            // enable
            CheckDlgButton( hwndDlg, IDC_ENABLECLOSE, BST_CHECKED );
            return( TRUE );
        case WM_COMMAND: // A message from a control or menu item
            // Parse out WM_COMMAND parameters to be more readable
            wID = LOWORD(wParam);
            wNotification = HIWORD(wParam);
            hChild = (HWND) lParam;

            // Portions removed to reduce size of demonstration
            if( wID == IDC_ENABLECLOSE && wNotification==BN_CLICKED )
            // Enable clicked?
            { // If so, get current check state
                int CheckedState = IsDlgButtonChecked( hwndDlg, IDC_ENABLE-
                CLOSE );
                // And either Enable or Disable the Close button
                hChild = GetDlgItem( hwndDlg, IDC_CLOSE );
                if( CheckedState == BST_CHECKED )
                        EnableWindow( hChild, TRUE );
                else
                        EnableWindow( hChild, FALSE );
            }
            break;
```

```
    // Portions removed to reduce size of demonstration
    }
    return( FALSE );
}
```

Notice how once broken into wID and wNotification just under the case WM_COM-MAND, the if test checks to see if the ID of the child window was IDC_ENABLE-CLOSE, then checks wNotification to see if the notification from that child was a BN_CLICKED event.

Once it has been determined that the event was a click on the desired checkbox, the code uses the IsDlgButtonChecked() function to determine if the control is checked or not. It then calls the EnableWindow() with the HWND of the Close button and passes a TRUE to enable the Close button or FALSE to disable the Close button.

In Code 4–22, notice the CheckDlgButton() function in the WM_INITDIALOG handler. As you may recall from the section on dialogs, the WM_INITDIALOG message is used after a dialog and its child windows are created, but before it is displayed. This is the opportunity for you to initialize the child windows as you see fit. For this example, this means placing a check in the checkbox. Since the Close button starts out enabled, we want to make sure there is a check in the checkbox to accurately reflect its state.

MFC

As with the SDK example, we assume that you have a dialog-based application like the MFC_Chap4 sample program and that there are at least two controls on it: a checkbox with the ID of IDC_ENABLECLOSE and a button with the ID of IDC_CLOSE. Most of the code for the MFC_Chap4 program can be found in the previous MFC example.

For purposes of this example we will show how to enable and disable a window by checking or unchecking a checkbox. There are two key items that must be changed in the MFC program:

1. When the dialog is initialized, the default value for the checkbox must be set.
2. When the user changes the check status, we must enable or disable the Close button.

Initializing the Check Status

Since the checkbox reflects the enabled status of the Close button and the Close button is enabled by default, we must make sure the checkbox is checked. Since this is not a property that can be set for the check control, we need to do it with code during dialog initialization.

We normally add a handler to handle the dialog initialization, which is the WM_INIT-DIALOG message. However this is a dialog-based application and the AppWizard already created an OnInitDialog() function for us that handles the message. If we created a dialog class on our own, then we would have to add the handler via ClassWizard.

Instead of running ClassWizard this time, locate the OnInitDialog() function for the main dialog (not the About dialog) in the class source code (MFC_Chep4Dlg.cpp in our sample). At the end of this function and before the return statement, add Code 4–23.

Code 4–23

```
CheckDlgButton( IDC_ENABLECLOSE, TRUE );
```

CheckDlgButton() is a CWnd class member function. Since we call this in the Dialog class, the "this" pointer is a CWnd for the main dialog window. In other words, we don't see the HWND parameter as we did in the SDK usage of CheckDlgButton() because it's the implied "this" parameter of a C++ member function.

Code 4–23 will check the IDC_ENABLECLOSE control of the dialog. If the second parameter is false, the checkbox appears unchecked, which is the default.

Responding to User's Changing the Check

We need to respond to the user checking or unchecking the control, which should in turn enable or disable the Close button. In order to do that, we first need to use the ClassWizards Message Map tab to add a new message map.

The ClassName for the handler should be the name of the main dialog class (MFC_Chap4Dlg in our sample), the Object IDs should have the IDC_ENABLE-CLOSE item highlighted, and the Messages list should have the BN_CLICKED item selected. Once these are set, click the Add Function button to add the function and click OK to accept its suggested function name of OnEnableclose(). Now, go to that function in the .cpp file and make it look like the following (Code 4–24).

In Code 4–24, the GetDlgItem() function is used to get CWnd pointers to the IDC_ENABLECLOSE checkbox and the IDC_CLOSE button. Once retrieved, the GetCheck() function is used for the CButton class to determine if the control is checked or not. Finally, based on the checked state, the EnableWindow() function for the Close button is called to enable or disable the button.

Note how the EnableWindow() function is called for the pClose pointer. If the pClose-> portion were left off these two lines of code, it would still compile cleanly, but when the program was run, it would use the "this" pointer, which would really refer to the entire dialog and not just the Close button. This means that when you unchecked the control, it would disable the program, and you couldn't enable it again because the checkbox would be disabled!

Code 4-24

Get Pointers to window objects

```
void CMFC_Chap4Dlg::OnEnableclose()
{
  CButton* pButton = (CButton*)GetDlgItem( IDC_ENABLECLOSE );
  CWnd* pClose = GetDlgItem( IDC_CLOSE );
  if( pButton->GetCheck() )
    pClose->EnableWindow( TRUE );
  else
    pClose->EnableWindow( FALSE );
}
```

Determine if it's checked or not, then enable or disable the Close button

Controlling Windows Fonts

When you work with fonts in Windows, you will once again be using a handle. In the SDK, there is an HFONT data type, which is a handle to a font, and in the MFC framework there is a CFont class (which is a wrapper class for the HFONT data type). We will cover fonts in a cursory fashion here, as our main goal is to show how to apply fonts to window controls. When we discuss printing and reports, we will dive deeper into the aspects of font creation.

Whether you have an HFONT for an SDK program or a CFont for an MFC program, the basic principles are the same when it comes to windows controls. Each window control (such as a button, static, or edit control) can be set to use a particular font. The HFONT or CFont we use must remain in existence for as long as the control using it is in existence and several controls can share a single font.

When you work with the dialog editor, you can control the font of the dialog by altering its properties. The font you select is inherited by all the controls in the dialog. This means that in order to have two controls with different fonts from each other or the dialog itself, you must write code to do so.

Our first example in here will demonstrate a simple function that can be called to create a font. It will call the CreateFont() function, which actually creates the font. The reason we won't call CreateFont() directly is simply because of its complexity. It has fourteen parameters, many of which can use default values so that we can easily avoid them. If you feel the need to use any of the parameters that our Simple-CreateFont() function hides from you, simply call the CreateFont() function directly.

As we discuss the setting of fonts for an individual window, we will also examine when to create the font, when to select it into the child window, and when to destroy it.

Simple Font Creation—SDK and MFC

The function presented below (Code 4–25) is a simple function for creating fonts called SimpleCreateFont(). The function uses the SDKs CreateFont() function, which can be used from either an SDK or an MFC program.

Code 4–25

```
HFONT SimpleCreateFont ( int Height, BOOL Bold, BOOL Italic,
      BOOL Underline, BOOL StrikeOut, DWORD Family,
      char* FaceName )
{

      HFONT Ret;
      int Weight;

      Weight = Bold ? FW_BOLD : FW_NORMAL;
      // Call CreateFont
      Ret = CreateFont ( Height, 0, 0, 0, Weight, Italic,
            Underline, StrikeOut, DEFAULT_CHARSET,
            OUT_DEFAULT_PRECIS, CLIP_DEFAULT_PRECIS,
            DEFAULT_QUALITY, DEFAULT_PITCH | Family,
            FaceName );

      return ( Ret );
}
```

Setting a Control Font—SDK

In order to set a font for a specific control, we will need to first create the desired font, then use it for as many windows as we want. When the program is done or the windows are about to be closed, the fonts are deleted. Our example demonstrates each of these steps. This demonstration program is dialog-based similar to the SDK_Chap4 sample discussed throughout this chapter. We assume that you have at least one control you want with a unique font (our sample will change the font of a checkbox with the ID of IDC_ENABLECLOSE).

Creating the Font and Initializing the Window

Since the font must be referenced by an HFONT variable and this variable must exist both before the window is shown and just prior to closing the program, we will declare it as a static local variable in our dialog procedure.

Since this is a dialog-based application, the best place to perform this type of font creation and initializing the window with the new font using the WM_INITDIALOG message. Remember that WM_INITDIALOG is sent to a dialog after the controls are created, but before they are made visible, so you can initialize them (see Code 4–26).

Code 4–26

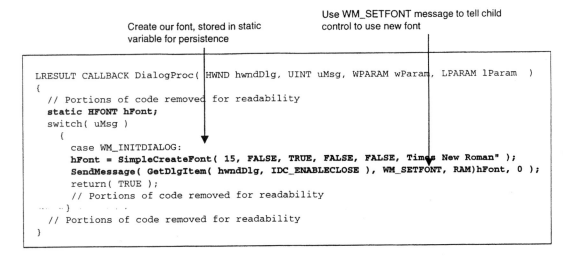

Create our font, stored in static variable for persistence

Use WM_SETFONT message to tell child control to use new font

```
LRESULT CALLBACK DialogProc( HWND hwndDlg, UINT uMsg, WPARAM wParam, LPARAM lParam )
{
    // Portions of code removed for readability
    static HFONT hFont;
    switch( uMsg )
    {
        case WM_INITDIALOG:
        hFont = SimpleCreateFont( 15, FALSE, TRUE, FALSE, FALSE, Times New Roman" );
        SendMessage( GetDlgItem( hwndDlg, IDC_ENABLECLOSE ), WM_SETFONT, RAM)hFont, 0 );
        return( TRUE );
        // Portions of code removed for readability
    }
    // Portions of code removed for readability
}
```

In Code 4–26 the bold code demonstrates the main points. The hFont variable is made static so that it can retain its value between calls. The WM_INITDIALOG case calls the SimpleCreateFont() function to create the font and places the return value into hFont. SendMessage() is then used to tell the IDC_ENABLECLOSE control that it should set its font to be hFont (the third parameter to SendMessage() in our example).

The hFont must be a static or global variable, so that we can use it later on when we need to destroy the font. We will do this in the WM_CLOSE message.

Deleting the Font When No Longer Needed

Once the child window has had its font set, it will continue to display that font until changed or the window is destroyed. Since we created the font in the example code, we need to release the font handle when the font is no longer needed. We will do this in the WM_CLOSE message.

The following code (Code 4–27) fragment is from the same DialogProc() function as the code above, but again with portions removed for ease of readability.

Notice how the DeleteObject() function is used to delete the font we previously created in response to the WM_CLOSE message, which means the parent window is being closed.

Code 4–27

```
LRESULT CALLBACK DialogProc( HWND hwndDlg, UINT uMsg, WPARAM wParam, LPARAM
lParam )
{
// Portions of code removed for readability
        static HFONT hFont;

        switch( uMsg )
        {
                case WM_CLOSE:
                        EndDialog( hwndDlg, 0 ); // Close the dialog
                        DeleteObject( hFont );
                        break;
// Portions of code removed for readability
        }
// Portions of code removed for readability

}
```

Setting a Control Font—MFC

In order to set a font for a specific control in MFC, we will need to use a CFont object, along with the SimpleCreateFont() function described above (Code 4–25). We will need to create the desired font so that it stays in existence as long as the dialog itself, and we will want to tell the desired child control to use that new font and not the default font.

Creating the Persistent Font and Setting the Control to Use It

Rather than create a static local or a global variable for the MFC program as we did in the SDK program, we will create a data member in the main dialog class because the data member will exist for as long as the dialog object instance exists.

To create the data member, add the following (Code 4–28) to the class definition for your main dialog (in the MFC_Chap4Dlg.h file for our sample). It doesn't matter whether you make the member a public, private, or protected data member.

Code 4-28

```
CFont m_Font;
```

Next, we need to add code to the OnInitDialog() function of our class. Remember this is the function MFC calls after all the controls are created in response to the WM_INITDIALOG window message, but before the dialog is displayed. The code we need to add should initialize the m_Font data member using SimpleCreateFont() and pass the new font to the controls. Add the following lines (Code 4-29) of code to the OnInitDialog() member function, just before the return of that function:

Code 4-29

```
// Set font for our 'Enable' checkbox
m_Font.Attach( SimpleCreateFont( 15, FALSE, TRUE, FALSE, FALSE, 0,
        "Times New Roman" ) );
GetDlgItem( IDC_ENABLECLOSE )->SetFont( &m_Font );
```

In Code 4-29 we are using the Attach() function of the CFont class. The Attach() function is used to specify the data value that an MFC class is to wrap. In this example, the Attach() function of the CFont class must specify the HFONT that is to be wrapped by the class (its m_Font data member).

After the Attach() function is called, the SetFont() function is used to tell the control to start using the new font. The GetDlgItem() is called to get a CWnd pointer to the desired control, which is then used to call the SetFont() function. The m_Font data member is the SetFont() function's only parameter.

Once SetFont() function is called, the control continues to use that font until it is either destroyed or the control is told to use another font.

Deleting the Font When No Longer Needed

When a CFont object goes out of scope, its destructor is called and it automatically performs a DeleteObject() on the font it wraps, which releases the resource. Since the m_Font is a CFont object, and we attached it to the HFONT we created by calling SimpleCreateFont(). When the m_Font object goes out of scope, the font is automatically released. The m_Font data member goes out of scope when the main dialog object goes out of scope or when the program terminates. In other words, no additional clean up to do here, thanks the destructor of the CFont class.

Focus

Focus is defined as the window that will receive mouse or keyboard focus. It can be considered the currently active window. If a window is disabled, it cannot receive focus.

As you tab from child control to child control, or if you use the mouse to select a new child control, focus is changed from window to window. You can also set the focus to a specific window programmatically by calling the SetFocus() function. While you can control the tab order of a dialog by using SetFocus(), it is much easier to specify the tab order in the dialog resource editor by selecting the Layout and then the Tab Order menu items and click the controls in the desired order.

When focus moves from one window to the next, the parent window gets several notification messages indicating that focus is happening. The type of messages sent when a control loses or gains focus depends on the type of control. For the built-in control types, there are specific windows messages for each control, and for the common controls there is a shared notification message.

> ## NOTE
>
> A child window itself is sent a WM_KILLFOCUS and WM_SETFOCUS as it loses and gains focus. In this manner, if you subclass a window, then you can have the window refuse to lose focus unless it meets some special value. While this is possible, this type of "Force user to make selection before proceeding" processing can be undesirable, because the control wouldn't let the user hit a Cancel button.

Focus Notification and Predefined Windows

The built-in controls, which send a WM_COMMAND to their parent, are listed in Table 4.2. When these controls lose focus, they send a WM_COMMAND message to the parent, along with the notification code specified in the high word of the WPARAM parameter. Examples later on will use the above window types to demonstrate how to handle window focus.

Table 4.2   Parameters for Controls

Control	Set Focus Message	Lose Focus Message
BUTTON	BN_SETFOCUS	BN_KILLFOCUS
COMBOBOX	CBN_SETFOCUS	CBN_KILLFOCUS
EDIT	EN_SETFOCUS	EN_KILLFOCUS
LISTBOX	LBN_SETFOCUS	LBN_KILLFOCUS
RICHEDIT_CLASS	EN_SETFOCUS	EN_KILLFOCUS

Focus Notification and Common Control Windows

Common controls are newer Windows-style control types such as the date time picker, tree, and listview controls. Rather than sending specialized messages like the above, they send the information to the parent window via a WM_NOTIFY message (not a WM_COMMAND).

When any of the common controls lose focus, they send a WM_NOTIFY message to the parent, and the lParam parameter is a pointer to an NMHDR structure (notification message). The NMHDR structure has the following data members:

HWND hwndFrom;
UINT idFrom;
UINT code;

The hwndFrom is the window handle of the child window sending the WM_NOTIFY. The idFrom is the ID of the same control. The code data member contains the notification message from the child control and may depend on the type of the control. For our discussion however, we are using the NM_KILLFOCUS in our code. An example of an SDK case statement in a window or dialog procedure to work with this information would appear as shown in Code 4–30.

Code 4–30

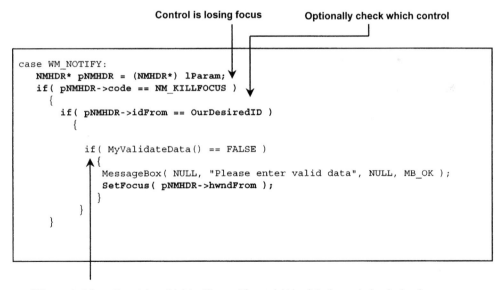

```
case WM_NOTIFY:
    NMHDR* pNMHDR = (NMHDR*) lParam;
    if( pNMHDR->code == NM_KILLFOCUS )
      {
        if( pNMHDR->idFrom == OurDesiredID )
          {

            if( MyValidateData() == FALSE )
              {
                MessageBox( NULL, "Please enter valid data", NULL, MB_OK );
                SetFocus( pNMHDR->hwndFrom );
              }
          }
      }
```

Control is losing focus   **Optionally check which control**

If the control doesn't contain valid data, Then set focus right back to the control we're leaving.

The code above is partially pseudo code. There is no MyValidateData() function, but we use it to demonstrate how a program might validate data from a control that is losing focus, then, if it appears that the data is not valid, it would set focus back to the control.

Example Focus Changing

SDK

This example will assume that we have an edit box in a dialog-based application, similar to the SDK_Chap4 sample program. Code 4–31 shows how to handle the focus leaving the edit box, then validating whether the edit box has any data and if not, giving a warning message and then setting focus back to the edit box.

Code 4–31

```
LRESULT CALLBACK DialogProc( HWND hwndDlg, UINT uMsg, WPARAM wParam, LPARAM
lParam )
{
// Portions of code removed for readability
    int wID;
    int wNotification;
    HWND hChild;

    switch( uMsg )
    {
// Portions of code removed for readability
        case WM_COMMAND: // A message from a control or menu item

            // Parse out WM_COMMAND parameters to be more readable
            wID = LOWORD(wParam);
            wNotification = HIWORD(wParam);
            hChild = (HWND) lParam;

            if( wID == IDC_REQUIRED && wNotification == EN_KILLFOCUS ) {
                // If the edit box lost focus, let's see if it's empty
                if( GetWindowTextLength( hChild ) == 0 ) {
                    // If it is, then display error and set focus back to the
                    // control
                    MessageBox( NULL, "Please enter some text",
                    "Field cannot be blank",
                        MB_OK );
                    SetFocus( hChild );
                }
            }
        // Portions of code removed for readability
        }
    }
}
```

The primary code is in bold font. The code checks the ID to make sure it's the ID of our desired edit box, and if it's a EN_KILLFOCUS notification, meaning the user is leaving that field. Inside the if test, the GetWindowTextLength() function is called getting length of the text in the edit box (hChild was initialized from lParam). If the length of the text was zero, then the MessageBox() is displayed, and the SetFocus() function is used to set focus back to the edit box.

MFC

In order to handle and respond to focus changing in an MFC program, we will use the Class Wizard MessageMap abilities to add a handler. If the control in question is a common control, then Class Wizard will offer the WM_NOTIFY handlers, and if it's a built-in control, it will offer the WM_COMMAND handler automatically. Basically, this means there is a fairly intuitive interface for handling the various classes.

Rather than going through the normal Class Wizard Message Map tab, we'll use an alternative method for creating a message map, though the end result will be the same. This sample will assume that you have an edit control in a dialog-based application, like our MFC_Chap4 sample program. While in the dialog editor, right-click on the edit box and select the Events... menu item. This will display the event message handler dialog shown in Figure 4–3.

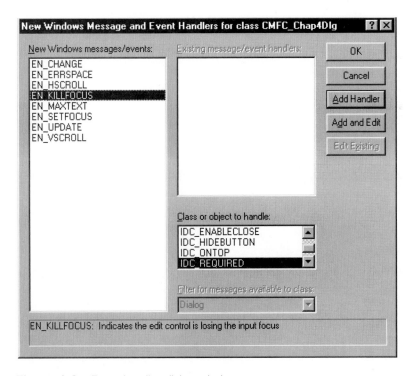

Figure 4–3   Event handler dialog window.

In this window, highlight the notification message you want (EN_KILLFOCUS) and the control that you want to handle that message for (IDC_REQUIRED), and click Add and Edit button. You will want to click OK at the next dialog to accept the suggested function name of OnKillFocusrequired(). Once you have done this, you will be placed automatically inside the newly added function, where you can make your changes. The function should look like Code 4–32.

Code 4–32

```
void CMFC_Chap4Dlg::OnKillfocusRequired()
{
        // TODO: Add your control notification handler code here

}
```

Modify this code so that it tests the length of the text in the edit box and then sets focus back to it if it does not contain any text. It should look like Code 4–33. Notice how in this example the pEdit variable once again uses the GetDlgItem() function to get a CWnd pointer to the desired edit control object. Also note how the SetFocus() function is called, with the pEdit-> in front, specifying the window that should have focus (this is normal C++ calling convention, but looked different in our C SDK example where SetFocus() took a parameter).

Code 4–33

```
void CMFC_Chap4Dlg::OnKillfocusRequired()
{
        // Get pointer to the Edit box control class
        CEdit* pEdit = (CEdit*)GetDlgItem( IDC_REQUIRED );
        // Determine if the edit box is empty
        if( pEdit->GetWindowTextLength() == 0 )
        {
                // If so, display error message
                MessageBox( "Edit box can not be blank" );
                // And set focus back to the edit control
                pEdit->SetFocus();
        }
}
```

Remember

○	There are a number of functions that affect all windows in the same fashion, such as EnableWindow(), ShowWindow(), SetWindowPos(), and MoveWindow().
	You can change the properties of a control in the dialog resource editor to make it initially invisible or disabled.
	Built-in controls send a WM_COMMAND message when they are about to lose focus along with a special notification code based on the window type. Common controls send a WM_NOTIFY message along with a NMHDR structure pointer.
○	A window is sent a WM_KILLFOCUS when it loses focus and a WM_SETFOCUS before it receives focus. A parent window, however, is sent a WM_COMMAND or a WM_NOTIFY message when its child windows change focus.
	Use GetDlgItem() to get the window handle or CWnd pointer to a child window to modify or work with that child window.
	You can easily set the font a child window should use at runtime (with either WM_SETFONT message in the SDK or the SetFont() function in MFC), but you must create a font and make sure that the font persists for the life of the child window. You cannot change fonts for individual controls from within the dialog editor.
○	While it is possible to force the user to return back to a control if it contains invalid data by using the Kill Focus notifications, it can lead to a poor user interface. You might find it more helpful to create a ValidateData() function that can be called at any time to validate fields and set focus to a control with bad data.

Chapter 5

Basic Controls

- Creating a Form-based Sample Program
- Styles
- Window Text
- Fonts
- Changing Control Colors
- Dynamically Created Controls
- Buttons
- Checkboxes
- Radio Buttons
- Combo Boxes
- List Boxes
- Edit Boxes
- Static Controls

In this chapter, we will take a closer look at window controls such as edit boxes, buttons, and radio buttons. We will see some of the features that are unique to these types and some of the common programming requirements for working with them.

Creating a Form-based Sample Program

Controls are used in form-based programming where a dialog box or form serves as the primary screen to the user. Rather than create controls at runtime, we will drop them onto the dialog box at design time, then size and position them as needed. Follow any of the paths listed here to create a form-based program that enables you to easily work with controls on the form.

Dialog-based SDK Program

1. From the main menu, select the File menu choice, then New.
2. Make sure the Projects tab is selected in the New dialog. Select the Win32 Application option in the New dialog, and type your new project name into the Project Name edit box (our demo is SDK_Controls), then click OK.
3. Select A Simple Win32 Application. (Note: This will create a project that allows you to use MFC classes, but no initial code. If you wanted to develop a "straight C" SDK program, then you should select An Empty Project, and you can add the .c source files as you like.)
4. When you click Finish, and then OK, AppWizard will create a set of files for you, most important being the .cpp file that contains an empty Win-Main function. There will only be one .cpp file, with the same name as your project (SDK_Controls.cpp for our demo).
5. You will need to add a dialog:
    a. From the File menu item, select New.
    b. In the New dialog, make sure the Files tab is selected, then select the Resource Script item.
    c. Enter the name of the resource file you want VC++ to create in the File Name box, such as SDK_Controls.rc (it should have a .rc extension, and it's a good idea to name it the same as your project) and click OK.
    d. From the Insert menu item, select the Resource sub-item.
    e. Double-click on the Dialog item. VC++ will create a default dialog and place you in the dialog editor, where you can add, remove, and change properties for various controls.
6. Go back to the .cpp file (SDK_Controls.cpp in our demo, and add the following line, just under the #include "stdafx.h" line:

```
#include "resource.h"
```

7. Next, add a Dialog procedure to handle the dialog messages, in the same .cpp file. The function should look like Code 5–1 for now:

Code 5-1

Close the dialog

A message from a control or menu item

```
LRESULT CALLBACK DialogProc( HWND hwndDlg, UINT uMsg, WPARAM wParam, LPARAM
lParam  )
{
  int wID;
  int wNotification;
  HWND hChild;
  switch( uMsg )
   {
    case WM_INITDIALOG:
      return( TRUE );
    case WM_CLOSE:
      EndDialog( hwndDlg, 0 );
      break;
    case WM_COMMAND:
      wID = LOWORD(wParam);
      wNotification = HIWORD(wParam);
      hChild = (HWND) lParam;
      if( (wID == IDOK || wID==IDCANCEL) && wNotification == BN_CLICKED )
        EndDialog( hwndDlg, wID );
      break;
   }
  return( FALSE );
}
```

Parse out WM_COMMAND parameters   Close the dialog

8. Add the following line of code in WinMain, just above the return state-
    ment:

    ```
    DialogBox( hInstance, MAKEINTRESOURCE(IDD_DIALOG1), 0,
    (DLGPROC)DialogProc );
    ```

9. Compile and run your program.

We are now ready to start adding controls to the dialog box–based application and
respond to Windows events. The rest of this chapter assumes for SDK examples
that you have followed the above steps and have a working dialog box–based application and a dialog procedure such as the one above.

MFC-based Form Program

For MFC programs, you can create either a dialog-based program, or an MDI or SDI
program-type program. This option is presented to you in the very first dialog when
you run AppWizard. Dialog-based programs will be just that—their main window
will be based on a dialog, and you will be able to add controls to the dialog using
the dialog editor.

Basic Controls

For SDI or MDI programs, however, AppWizard will utilize the Document/View architecture for the program. This means that the program will have a main window (supported by the CMainFrame class), a main View window that is responsible for appearance and user interaction, and a Document class that is responsible for saving and loading data. The view window can be created based on several view styles, such as HTML view, Tree View, Edit View, or Form View. The Form View will also create dialog that will appear as the window that you can edit using the dialog editor.

So, what's the difference between a dialog-based program and an MDI/SDI program that uses a CFormView class for its class? The CFormView method will also have a menu, Print and Print Preview functionality, and a Document object for saving and loading data files. You can select the CFormView view type from the last dialog of AppWizard be changing the BaseClass item for the view class. SDI and MDI mean Single Document Interface and Multiple Document Interface and determine whether your program can have a single or multiple documents open at once (like NotePad, which is an SDI program, vs. Word, which is an MDI program).

When you select the CFormView View class, AppWizard creates a dialog for you that serves as the main window for your application (technically, the view is the child of the main window, or main frame, but it will occupy the entire main frame client area). The steps are as follows:

1. From the File menu choice, select New.
2. Make sure that Projects is highlighted in the New dialog, then select the MFC AppWizard (EXE) item, and enter a project name (MFC_ Controls in our sample).
3. Click OK.
4. Select the Single Document option in the Step 1 dialog and click Next.
5. Just click Next at the Step 2 of 6 dialog that appears.
6. Just click Next at the Step 3 of 6 dialog that appears.
7. Just click Next at the Step 4 of 6 dialog that appears.
8. Just click Next at the Step 5 of 6 dialog that appears.
9. In the Step 6 of 6 dialog, highlight the View class (its name will end in 'View' and its base class will be Cview).
10. Change the Base Class select from CView to CFormView.
11. Click Finish, and then OK.

Following the above steps creates a sample program that can be used for the MFC samples in this chapter. Unlike the SDK version, this MFC program has a menu, Help About box, icons, and various other resources to make it a more robust program.

Special Note on Controls and MFC Programs

We have previously stated that in order to interact with controls, you need to know the handle for the desired window. In SDK that handle was an HWND data type and in MFC it is the CWnd class type. Your program needs to get the handle of the desired window in order to work with it (i.e., move it, enable, hide it, get text from it, etc.).

In MFC programs, the CWnd::GetDlgItem() member function is used to find a CWnd pointer to a child window. Another approach is to use member variables for the View or Dialog class that MFC automatically associates with the on-screen control.

The ClassWizard can also be used to create a member variable for an on-screen control and automatically associate it with that on-screen control. The following demonstration shows how to create an CEdit member variable in a View class and associate it with an on-screen edit box.

This program is a CFormView-type program as described in the beginning of this chapter; the sample is called MFC_Controls.

1. Place an edit box on the main form of your application. Make sure its properties are set so that its ID is IDC_EDIT1 (which is the default for the first edit box).
2. Run ClassWizard from the View menu choice then select the Member Variables tab. Make sure the Class Name item represents the main View or Dialog class for your project (CMFC_ControlsView in our sample), and the ID for the edit control in the IDC_EDIT1 control is highlighted, as shown in Figure 5–1.
3. Click the Add Variable button to display the Add Member Variable dialog (see Figure 5–2). Notice that we have entered a Member Variable Name of m_Edit and also changed the default Category to Control. The Variable Type is CEdit.

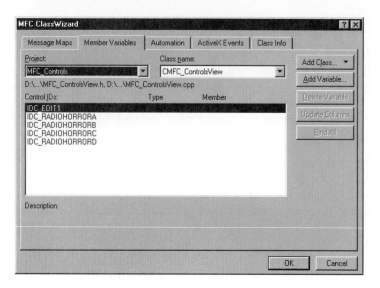

Figure 5–1 Highlight the ID for the edit control.

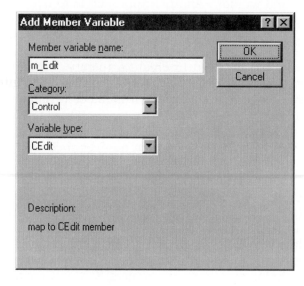

Figure 5–2 Change the default category to control.

4. Click OK and ClassWizard will create the CEdit type object as a data member in your .h file for your View/Dialog class and will add code to the DoDataExchange() function to associate the two. From the .h file, ClassWizard added the item in bold (see Code 5-2).

In the views .cpp file the ClassWizard also added the code shown in bold in Code 5-3 to the DoDataExchange() function.

Code 5-2

```
public:
        //{{AFX_DATA(CMFC_ControlsView)
        enum { IDD = IDD_MFC_CONTROLS_FORM };
        CEdit   m_Edit;
        //}}AFX_DATA
```

Code 5-3

```
void CMFC_ControlsView::DoDataExchange(CDataExchange* pDX)
{
        CFormView::DoDataExchange(pDX);
        //{{AFX_DATA_MAP(CMFC_ControlsView)
        DDX_Control(pDX, IDC_EDIT1, m_Edit);
        //}}AFX_DATA_MAP
}
```

Since the Control category in the ClassWizard was selected, the ClassWizard created a data member of CEdit type (see Code 5-2). CEdit is derived from CWnd, which is the same type of information that GetDlgItem() returned. There are now two methods available for working with a window: calling GetDlgItem() function and accessing a member variable using the ClassWizard. Both methods in Code 5-4 will work.

Code 5-4

```
        // How to work with child window using GetDlgItem:
        CEdit* pEdit = (CEdit*)GetDlgItem(IDC_EDIT);
        pEdit->SetWindowText( "My Edit box" );

        // How to work with child window using member variable:
        m_Edit.SetWindowText( "My Edit box" );
```

If you expect to often hide, move, get, and set control values, then use the member variable method. If you will be performing the same operations infrequently, then call the GetDlgItem() function. Neither method provides a noticeable difference in speed or memory space.

Throughout much of this chapter we will be using GetDlgItem(), but you may want to experiment with creating a member variable as described above then try using that member variable directly rather than using the return value of GetDlgItem().

Windows Subclassing with MFC

You'll find that the ability to subclass a Windows control is a fairly straightforward process when MFC is used. A subclassed window is normally a child window that acts and looks like a normal Windows control. You might want to alter or enhance a particular behavior of the subclassed window by using C++ classes and the MFC framework.

The Image with Text Button—MFC example later in this chapter gives specific details on how to create a subclassed window, but here we will discuss the basic technique.

As already discussed, one aspect or feature of MFC is a message map that is responsible for handling window messages as well as certain MFC framework activities such as PreCreateWindow(). Normally, if you want to handle a message map, you add a message map using ClassWizard in the class you want to handle the message. Adding a handler for a button click event to either your View or Dialog class (depending on whether your program is View or dialog box–based) is a common message map. In this example, a parent window handles the WM_COMMAND message from one of its child windows. Whatever you do in that handler (function) is not important for this discussion. What is important is that you can create a function in the parent View or Dialog window class and MFC will invoke that function when the button is clicked. You use the ClassWizard's Message Map tab to add handler functions to respond to various events.

In Windows subclassing, we create a class derived from one of the standard MFC control classes such as a CButton or a CEdit. Inside that control class we add functions again using the Message Map tab, to be invoked to handle certain Windows messages and MFC framework events.

For an example, the Image with Text Button – MFC example creates a class derived from CButton. In that new class (called CPNImageButton) we add a message map to handle the drawing of the button control. In that handler, we will display the button, the button image, and its caption. We will not provide handling for things like the button click event where the mouse-down and mouse-up events trigger a BN_CLICKED event to the parent window. Notice that we are selectively taking over certain behaviors of the BUTTON window control.

Using the CPNImageButton class is very simple as it is for other types of subclassed window classes. First, place a control on the form, then create a member variable for that control using ClassWizard and the new derived C++ class. No statements must be added to use the new control once the derived C++ class (CPNImageButton) is added to the program, and the member variable created.

Styles

All windows have a style that is unique to that type of window. The style often controls the window's appearance, but can also define how it behaves under certain user actions. An example of a window style is the ES_PASSWORD, or Password style for an edit box.

If an edit box does not have this style, then text is displayed normally. But if it does have this style, then as the user types, he or she will not see the text but instead will see an asterisk for each letter in the text.

Styles for a window are controlled at several times. At design time, the control style can be set by changing the properties of the control from within the dialog editor (right click on the control and select Properties from the pop-up menu). When changed this way, you will only be presented with styles that reflect the type of control you are working with. Figures 5–3 and 5–4 are examples of the property editor for an edit box and the property editor for a button control. It is strongly recommended that controls' styles are set at design time, which reduces the amount of coding you need to do.

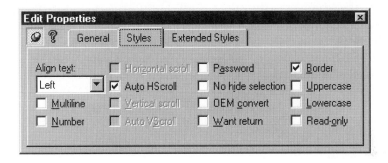

Figure 5–3   The edit box property editor.

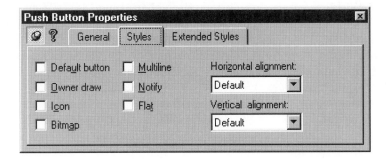

Figure 5–4   The button control property editor.

You can also change the style for a window at runtime. For example, the user may select an option that requires that the password style be turned on or off for an edit box.

Changing styles for a control at runtime is a relatively a straightforward process and is described below for the SDK and the MFC methods of developing a Windows application. However, not all styles can be set at runtime. Some styles need to be specified at design time or when a program calls CreateWindow(), and cannot be set or cleared after the window is created.

An example is the ES_PASSWORD style for the edit box. You can't simply change that style at runtime. Instead, when you set the password character that the edit box uses to asterisk, it changes style automatically. If you set the password character to zero (\0), then it will go back to normal mode. Code 5–6 shows how this is done with the EM_SETPASSWORDCHAR message. In addition, some styles may not take effect until the window is modified or resized with a call to the SetWindowPos() function.

SDK

An SDK program can call the GetWindowLong() and SetWindowLong() functions to get and set window styles. GetWindowLong() and SetWindowLong(), when used with window styles, work with bitmask values. This means that if you want to turn on or off a particular style, you need to use the bitwise operators in C/C++ such as AND (&), OR (|), and XOR(^). First the program gets the current window style by calling GetWindowLong(), then turns on or off the desired style before calling SetWindowLong() to update the window style.

Code 5–5 illustrates this technique and assumes an edit box has been placed on the window and is assigned the ID IDC_EDIT1. This example turns on, then off, the uppercase style for the edit box.

Not all styles can be set simply by changing the style as shown in Code 5–5. For example, to turn on and off the ES_PASSWORD style, you can't user SetWindowLong() and GetWindowLong(). Instead, a special message is sent to the control to facilitate the style change. In the case of the ES_PASSWORD style, sending an EM_SETPASSWORDCHAR message to the child control turns the style on or off (see Code 5–6). This code may be placed in the WM_INITDIALOG message handler or a handler that responses to a menu selection or button click.

Code 5-5

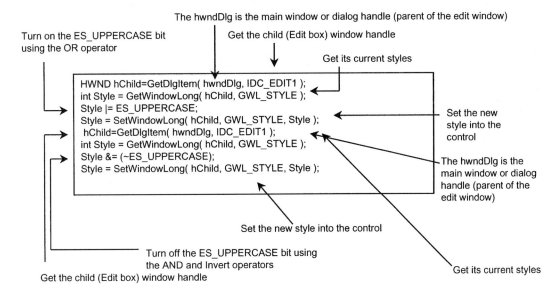

The hwndDlg is the main window or dialog handle (parent of the edit window)

Turn on the ES_UPPERCASE bit using the OR operator

Get the child (Edit box) window handle

Get its current styles

```
HWND hChild=GetDlgItem( hwndDlg, IDC_EDIT1 );
int Style = GetWindowLong( hChild, GWL_STYLE );
Style |= ES_UPPERCASE;
Style = SetWindowLong( hChild, GWL_STYLE, Style );
hChild=GetDlgItem( hwndDlg, IDC_EDIT1 );
int Style = GetWindowLong( hChild, GWL_STYLE );
Style &= (~ES_UPPERCASE);
Style = SetWindowLong( hChild, GWL_STYLE, Style );
```

Set the new style into the control

The hwndDlg is the main window or dialog handle (parent of the edit window)

Set the new style into the control

Turn off the ES_UPPERCASE bit using the AND and Invert operators

Get its current styles

Get the child (Edit box) window handle

Code 5-6

```
// The hwndDlg is the main window or dialog handle (parent of the edit window)
// To turn on the password style:
SendDlgItemMessage( hwndDlg, IDC_EDIT1, EM_SETPASSWORDCHAR, (WPARAM)'*', 0 );
// Top turn off the password style:
SendDlgItemMessage( hwndDlg, IDC_EDIT1, EM_SETPASSWORDCHAR, 0, 0 );
```

MFC

MFC programs use the GetStyle() and ModifyStyle() functions in the CWnd class to alter styles for a control. Our example in this section assumes you created a CForm-View or a dialog-based application and placed an edit box on the form with the ID of IDC_EDIT1.

The GetStyle() function (see Code 5–7) returns the styles value for the control. You can determine if a particular style is on or not with the bitwise AND (&) operator. The ModifyStyle() function (see Code 5–8) is used to set or clear one or more styles.

Code 5-7

```
CWnd* pWnd = GetDlgItem( IDC_EDIT1 );
if( pWnd->GetStyle() & ES_PASSWORD ) // Is password on?
        // Do some processing
```

Code 5-8

```
BOOL CWnd::ModifyStyle( DWORD dwRemove, DWORD dwAdd, UINT nFlags = 0 );
```

The dwRemove parameter contains one or more styles of the control that are to be turned off (combined with the OR (|) operator). The dwAdd parameter references one or more styles to turn on (combined with the OR operator). The nFlags parameter determines how the SetWindowPos() function should be called to refresh the window.

An example (see Code 5-9) that might turn off the ES_UPPERCASE style for an edit box, and turn on its ES_LOWERCASE style.

Code 5-9

```
CWnd* pWnd = GetDlgItem( IDC_EDIT1 );
pWnd->ModifyStyle( ES_UPPERCASE, ES_LOWERCASE );
```

Window Text

Many windows have a single text or caption property that can change at runtime and are described in the following list:

- The Main Window: Whether dialog-based or view-based, the main window has a text property that appears on the title bar. Changing the window text will change the caption on the title bar.

- Edit Windows: The edit window's text property contains text entered by the user. By setting the text, the program places text into the edit box. Retrieving the edit window's text property returns text that appears in the edit window.

- Buttons: The text property for a button control is the text displayed on the button. There isn't a need to retrieve the text of a button control because the user doesn't change the text. However, it is common to change the text at runtime. For example, the program could display a Run button, then once the button is selected, change the text to Cancel. The same process also pertains to check boxes and radio button controls.

- STATIC Windows: Static windows are windows that contain nothing but text. While you may not often get text from a static control since the user can't change the text, the program can update the text. For example, you may be writing a database and want to show a unique ID for a record, but not let the user change it.

Changing or Retrieving Window Text

SDK

Four basic functions available for getting and setting the text of an Edit box, as illustrated in Code 5–10. The first two functions work with a window handle (HWND) to an edit box, which is *hEdit* in both of these examples. SetWindowText() sets the text that lpText points to (LPCSTR means "Long Pointer to a Constant String") into the desired edit box. GetWindowText() extracts text from the edit box and stores up to *nMax* characters at lpText (LPTSTR means "Long Pointer to a Text String").

Code 5–10

```
BOOL SetWindowText( HWND hEdit, LPCSTR lpText );
BOOL GetWindowText( HWND hEdit, LPTSTR lpText, int nMax );
BOOL SetDlgItemText( HWND hParent, int nID, LPCSTR lpText );
BOOL GetDlgItemText( HWND hParent, int nID, LPTSTR lpText, int nMax );
```

The second two functions work best when you have a handle to a parent window of an edit box such as a dialog window handle. Since this is most often the case, you will probably find yourself using these functions more often than the first two functions. SetDlgItemText() and GetDlgItemText() work the same as SetWindowText() and GetWindowText(), except instead of an edit box window handle as the first parameter, they use the window handle of the parent (or dialog most likely) window and the ID of the child edit box.

These functions can be called any time you want to get or set the text of an edit box, as long as the edit box exists. Examples from our sample SDK_Controls are shown in Code 5–11. In Code 5–11, the Tmp variable is declared and contains the string from the edit box before calling the GetDlgItemText() function. The array is fixed in size (32 characters), but the edit box may contain more than this. It is possible to limit the amount of text an edit box holds.

MFC

An MFC program uses class functions shown in Code 5–12. In the functions below, rString is a CString object used to receive the text from a window, as in (GetWindowText and GetDlgItemText).

lpStr is an LPTSTR (Long Pointer to a Text STRing) used to get text from the window. Functions like GetWindowText() and GetDlgItemText(), which use the lpStr parameter, also have an nMaxCount parameter that indicates how much text to retrieve. lpcStr is an LPCTSTR (Long Pointer to a Constant Text STRing) parameter, used to put text into a window. Functions like SetWindowText() and SetDlgItemText()use the lpcStr parameter. For functions that set the window text and use an

---

Code 5-11

Parse out WM_COMMAND parameters
to be more readable

If 'Hello' button is clicked,
then display their text

A message from a control or menu item

```
LRESULT CALLBACK DialogProc( HWND hwndDlg, UINT uMsg, WPARAM wParam, LPARAM lParam )
{
    int wID;
    int wNotification;
    HWND hChild;
    switch( uMsg )
       {
        // Portions of code removed for readability
        case WM_COMMAND:
            wID = LOWORD(wParam);
            wNotification = HIWORD(wParam);
            hChild = (HWND) lParam;
            if( (wID == IDC_BUTTONNAME) && wNotification == BN_CLICKED )
               {
                char Tmp[32];
                GetDlgItemText( hwndDlg, IDC_EDITNAME, Tmp, sizeof(Tmp) );
                MessageBox( hwndDlg, Tmp, "You entered", MB_OK );
               }
            if( (wID == IDC_BUTTONNAMECLEAR) && wNotification == BN_CLICKED )
                SetDlgItemText( hwndDlg, IDC_EDITNAME, "" );
```

Clear the edit box if the user clicked the clear button.

Code 5-12

```
int CWnd::GetWindowText( LPTSTR lpStr, int nMaxCount ) const;
void CWnd::GetWindowText( CString& rString ) const;

int CWnd::GetDlgItemText( int nID, LPTSTR lpStr, int nMaxCount ) const;
int CWnd::GetDlgItemText( int nID, CString& rString ) const;

void CWnd::SetWindowText( LPCTSTR lpcStr );
void CWnd::SetDlgItemText( int nID, LPCTSTR lpcStr );
```

LPCTSTR type, you can still use a CString object as a parameter because the CString class has a type-conversion function (an aspect of C++) that will let you use it anywhere you need an LPCSTR.

The nID parameter found in the GetDlgItemText() and SetDlgItemText() functions is used with a parent window object (such as a form or dialog) that have child controls. It specifies the ID of the child control to get or set the text for.

Code 5–13 illustrates the use of these functions. Although this example uses an edit box window type, any window type listed at the beginning of this section can be used. Code 5–13 assumes that ChildID is an integer value (variable or constant) of the desired control. For example, if you had an edit box with the ID of IDC_USER-NAME, then you could substitute IDC_USERNAME for ChildID.

Remember that in an MFC program that has a view, the View class is not the main window—instead, the CMainFrame is the main window. The View class is actually a child window of the CMainFrame class. This means the window text for the Main-frame (not view) is the caption for your program.

Code 5–13

```
CWnd* pWnd = GetDlgItem( ChildID );
CString CStr;
char Text[128];

// Examples to get text
pWnd->GetWindowText( CStr );
pWnd->GetWindowText( Text, sizeof(Text) );
GetDlgItemText( ChildID, CStr );
GetDlgItemText( ChildID, Text, sizeof(Text) );

// Example to set the text
pWnd->SetWindowText( "" ); // Make text empty
SetDlgItemText( ChildID, "" ); // make text empty
```

Fonts

Each window control has the ability to keep track of its own font setting. Normally, with dialog-based applications, you would set the font property of the dialog and child controls on the dialog box, enabling each control to inherit and use the same font. If you create the controls at runtime, then you will need to set the font for the child controls to be the same as their parent window.

Since this font-management method is user for all types of windows, you can use the functions described here to change the font of any type of child control such as a STATIC control, Edit box, or List box.

Changing Font

SDK

The two functions shown in Code 5–14 will simplify how we manage fonts for child controls. The PNSetFont() function creates the type of font as specified in its parameters, then uses the WM_SETFONT window message to tell the child window to

---

begin using that font. The font created by PNSetFont() is released from memory by PNClearFont() function. PNSetFont() is called in the WM_INITDIALOG handler and PNClearFont() is called in the WM_DESTROY handler as shown in Code 5–15.

Code 5–14

```
// PNSetFont - Sets a font for a child window
// Parameters:
//      hParent - Window handle to parent of control
//      nID - ID for the child window
//      lpszFontName - String with name of font to use
//      nHeight - Height of font in device units
//      bBold - If TRUE then use bold font, otherwise use normal font
//      bItalic - TRUE for italic font, FALSE for normal
//      bUnderline - TRUE for underlined font, FALSE for normal
// Returns: TRUE if succesful, or FALSE upon failure
BOOL PNSetFont( HWND hParent, int nID, const char* lpszFontName, int
nHeight, BOOL bBold, BOOL bItalic, BOOL bUnderline )
{
    HFONT ParentFont, CurFont;
    HWND hChild = GetDlgItem( hParent, nID );

    if( !hChild )
        return(FALSE);

    ParentFont = (HFONT)SendMessage( hParent, WM_GETFONT, 0, 0 );
    CurFont = (HFONT)SendMessage( hChild, WM_GETFONT, 0, 0 );
    // If the font is not the parent or dsystem font, we can delete it.
    if( CurFont != ParentFont && CurFont != (HFONT)GetStockObject(SYSTEM_FONT) )
        DeleteObject( CurFont );

    HFONT NewFont = CreateFont( nHeight, 0, 0, 0, bBold?FW_BOLD:FW_NORMAL,
            bItalic, bUnderline, FALSE, DEFAULT_CHARSET, OUT_DEFAULT_PRECIS,
            CLIP_DEFAULT_PRECIS, DEFAULT_QUALITY, FF_DONTCARE|DEFAULT_PITCH,
            lpszFontName );
    if( NewFont )
    {
        SendMessage( hChild, WM_SETFONT, (WPARAM) NewFont, TRUE );
        return( TRUE );
    }
    return(FALSE);
}

// PNClearFont - Removes font created by PNSetFont
// Parameters:
//      hParent - Window handle to parent of control
//      nID - ID for the child window
void PNClearFont( HWND hParent, int nID )
{
```

```
    HFONT ParentFont, CurFont;
    HWND hChild = GetDlgItem( hParent, nID );

    if( !hChild )
        return;

    ParentFont = (HFONT)SendMessage( hParent, WM_GETFONT, 0, 0 );
    CurFont = (HFONT)SendMessage( hChild, WM_GETFONT, 0, 0 );

    // If the font is not the parent or dsystem font, we can delete it.
    if( CurFont != ParentFont && CurFont != (HFONT)GetStockObject(SYS-
    TEM_FONT) )
{
        SendMessage( hChild, WM_SETFONT, (WPARAM)ParentFont, 1 );
        DeleteObject( CurFont );
}
}
```

Code 5-15

```
LRESULT CALLBACK DialogProc( HWND hwndDlg, UINT uMsg, WPARAM wParam, LPARAM lParam  )
{
   switch( uMsg )
   {
     case WM_INITDIALOG:
        PNSetFont( hwndDlg, IDC_STATICSOMETEXT, "Times New Roman", 18,
                   TRUE, TRUE, FALSE );
        return( TRUE );
     case WM_DESTROY:
        PNClearFont( hwndDlg, IDC_STATICSOMETEXT );
         break;
        // Portions of code removed for readability
```

Set control to use a Times New Roman 18 pixel (not point) font

MFC

The two functions shown in Codes 5–16 and 5–17 simplify the dynamic setting and clearing of fonts for individual controls. With these two functions (which you can either create as member functions of your View or Dialog class, or make standalone functions outside your class), you can now easily set or clear fonts on a control-by-control basis.

In order to set the font of a control, you might want to do it in the OnInitialUpdate() function of a CFormView project (the MFC_ControlsView.cpp file in our example), or in the OnInitDialog() function if it's a dialog-based application. An example of calling it is shown in Code 5–18.

Code 5–16

```
BOOL CPNSetFont( CWnd* pParent, int nID, const char * lpszFontName, int
nHeight, BOOL bBold, BOOL bItalic, BOOL bUnderline )
{
    CFont* pCurFont, *pParentFont;
    CWnd* pChild = pParent->GetDlgItem( nID );

    // Make sure we have valid child control
    if( !pChild )
        return( FALSE );

    // Get current font from child and parent windows
    pCurFont = pChild->GetFont();
    pParentFont = pParent->GetFont();

    // If the font is not the same as the parent font or the system font, then
    // we probably created it. Remove it.
    if( pCurFont != pParentFont &&
        pCurFont->GetSafeHandle() != GetStockObject(SYSTEM_FONT) )
    {
        delete pCurFont;
        pChild->SetFont( pParentFont );
    }

    // Create the new font dynamically.
    CFont* pFont = new CFont;
    if( !pFont )
        return( FALSE );
    if( pFont->CreateFont( nHeight, 0, 0, 0, bBold?FW_BOLD:FW_NORMAL,
            bItalic, bUnderline, FALSE, DEFAULT_CHARSET, OUT_DEFAULT_PRECIS,
            CLIP_DEFAULT_PRECIS, DEFAULT_QUALITY, FF_DONTCARE|DEFAULT_PITCH,
            lpszFontName ) == FALSE )
                return( FALSE );

    // Tell the child control to use that font from now on
    pChild->SetFont( pFont );
    return(TRUE);
}
```

Code 5–17

```
void CPNClearFont( CWnd* pParent, int nID )
{
    CFont* pCurFont, *pParentFont;
    CWnd* pChild = pParent->GetDlgItem( nID );
    // Make sure we have a valid child font
```

```
    if( !pChild )
        return;

    // Get child and parent fonts
    pCurFont = pChild->GetFont();
    pParentFont = pParent->GetFont();

    // If the current font is not the parents font, and not the system font,
    // then delete it
    if( pCurFont != pParentFont &&
        pCurFont->GetSafeHandle() != GetStockObject(SYSTEM_FONT) )
    {
        delete pCurFont;
        // And make sure we leave the control with a valid font to use
        pChild->SetFont( pParentFont );
    }
}
```

Code 5–18

```
void CMFC_ControlsView::OnInitialUpdate()
{
        CFormView::OnInitialUpdate();
        GetParentFrame()->RecalcLayout();
        ResizeParentToFit();
        // Portions of code removed for readability
        // Set unique font for a control
        CPNSetFont( this, IDC_STATICSOMETEXT, "Times New Roman", 18, TRUE,
        TRUE, FALSE );

        // Portions of code removed for readability
}
```

In Code 5–18, the font for the IDC_STATICSOMETEXT control is set to Times New Roman 18-pixel high bold italic font. In the case of a CFormView-based project such as in Code 5–18, the OnInitialUpdate() was already created by AppWizard and we would only have to add the highlighted line.

In order to clear the font when the main window is closed, you need to add the PN-ClearFont() for the desired control on one of the window close handlers as shown in Code 5–19.

Code 5–19

```
        CPNClearFont( this, IDC_STATICSOMETEXT );
```

The PNClearFont() function can be called at other times in a program, depending on the type of program. In a CFormView-type program, a message map is then added, using ClassWizard for the View class to handle the WM_DESTROY message (this

---

would add a function call OnDestroy(). In a dialog-based application, a message map is added using ClassWizard for the DestroyWindow() of the main dialog window (the new function would be called DestroyWindow()). You would add the call to CPNClearFont() to each of these functions.

Changing Control Colors

SDK

If you want to be able to change the color of a control on the fly (at the user's request for example) or in a dialog, then you need to respond to the WM_CTLCOLOR-family messages in your window procedure. These messages are sent just prior to drawing the controls in the window, and passes in the *wParam* parameter the HDC that will be used to draw the item. In response to the message, you should return the brush (as an HBRUSH) to be used for drawing. This is illustrated in Code 5–20.

Code 5–20

```
static HBRUSH hBrush;
switch( Message )
{
        // Portions of code removed for readability
        case WM_CTLCOLORDLG:
        case WM_CTLCOLORSTATIC:
        case WM_CTLCOLORBTN:
        case WM_CTLCOLOREDIT:
        case WM_CTLCOLORLISTBOX:
        case WM_CTLCOLORSCROLLBAR:
        if( !hBrush )
              hBrush=CreateSolidBrush( RGB(192,0,0) ); /Red
        SetBkColor( (HDC)wParam, RGB(192,0,0) );
        SelectObject( (HDC)wParam, hBrush );
        return( (LONG)hBrush);
        // Portions of code removed for readability
}
```

MFC

To change colors of a control at runtime for an MFC program, you need to add a handler to the parent window for the WM_CTLCOLOR message. Once you have done this, it will add a function similar to Code 5–21.

Code 5–21

```
HBRUSH CWhateverDlg::OnCtlColor(CDC* pDC, CWnd* pWnd, UINT nCtlColor)
{
        HBRUSH hbr = CDialog::OnCtlColor(pDC, pWnd, nCtlColor);
```

```
        // TODO: Return a different brush if the default is not desired
        return hbr;
}
```

The framework will now call this function just before a child control or the parent window is displayed, giving you the ability to change its color. The pDC parameter is the device context object that will be used to draw the window; the pWnd parameter is a pointer to the CWnd object for the window being displayed; and the nCtl-Color indicates the type of window. nCtlColor will be one of the following and is used in Code 5–22.

CTLCOLOR_BTN	Button control
CTLCOLOR_DLG	Dialog box
CTLCOLOR_EDIT	Edit control
CTLCOLOR_LISTBOX	List-box control
CTLCOLOR_MSGBOX	Message box
CTLCOLOR_SCROLLBAR	Scroll-bar control
CTLCOLOR_STATIC	Static control

Code 5–22

```
HBRUSH CWhateverDlg::OnCtlColor(CDC* pDC, CWnd* pWnd, UINT nCtlColor)
{
        HBRUSH hbr = CDialog::OnCtlColor(pDC, pWnd, nCtlColor);

        static CBrush MyBrush;
        if( !MyBrush.GetSafeHandle() )
              MyBrush.CreateSolidBrush( RGB( 192, 0, 0 ) );

        if( pWnd != this )
        {
              pDC->SetBkMode( TRANSPARENT );
              return( (HBRUSH)MyBrush );
        }
        // TODO: Return a different brush if the default is not desired
        return hbr;
}
```

Dynamically Created Controls

Though you can create controls such as buttons or edit boxes at runtime by calling various SDK or MFC functions, it is better to create them using the dialog editor. The dialog editor enables you to visually place and size controls, which cannot be done when creating the controls at runtime.

If you want controls that appear and disappear, it is better to create the controls on the dialog with the dialog editor then hide and show them by calling the ShowWindow() function at runtime. This approach is strongly recommended.

An additional issue on dynamically created controls is that with MFC and ClassWizard there are extra steps to add event processing for them. Consider the example of a button on a dialog. With ClassWizard, it is easy to go to the Message Map tab and select the ID of the button, then add a handler function for when the button is clicked. But if the button were created at runtime then ClassWizard would have no idea it existed at design time. You won't see the button in the list of objects to add message map handlers. Instead you must manually create a message map for the dynamically created button control.

Follow these steps when manually making an entry in the message map for your view in an MFC program.

Step 1: Modify the Message Map Portion of Your Header File

Add to the View or Dialog class definition a prototype for the new handler. Find a section of code commented with //{{AFX_MSG in the header file for the parent window of the new control. This is where to make entries for new message map handlers. An example of this code fragment is shown in Code 5–23.

Add a function prototype for the handler. Don't touch the code between //{{AFX_MSG and //}} because this is the area where ClassWizard inserts its definitions. Add your own prototypes for our handlers after the //}}AFX_MSG and before the DECLARE_MAP() ending as shown in Code 5–24 in bold.

The afx_msg is standard for message map handlers. The return type and parameter list will depend on the type event you want to handle. We called our example OnClickDynamic because we will want to add a handler for when the user clicks a dynamic button, but you are free to call the function whatever you like.

Code 5–23

```
// Generated message map functions
protected:
    //{{AFX_MSG(CMFC_ControlsView)
    afx_msg int OnCreate(LPCREATESTRUCT lpCreateStruct);
    //}}AFX_MSG
    DECLARE_MESSAGE_MAP()
```

Code 5-24

```
// Generated message map functions
protected:
        //{{AFX_MSG(CMFC_ControlsView)
        afx_msg int OnCreate(LPCREATESTRUCT lpCreateStruct);
        //}}AFX_MSG
        afx_msg void OnClickDynamic();
        DECLARE_MESSAGE_MAP()
```

Step 2: Add the Handler Function to Your .cpp File Message Map

In the .cpp file for the View or Dialog class (the parent window of the dynamically created control), search for the message map, which starts with BEGIN_MES-SAGE_MAP and ends with END_MESSAGE_MAP(). Code 5–25 is typical of what you might find.

Add your handler to this message map. The message map is an array of IDs and pointers. The items with all uppercase letters are macros. Add your new handler after the //}}AFX_MSG_MAP and before the END_MESSAGE_MAP as shown in Code 5–26.

Code 5–26 assumes that 4000 refers to the unique ID of the control you are going to create (this is something you must specify when you create the control at run-time—the unique ID).

The ON_BN_CLICKED(4000, OnClickDynamic) macro breaks down to: "When the child control ID # 4000 sends us a BN_CLICKED notification, we call the OnClick-Dynamic() function." Many of the macros supported in this message map will work in the same manner.

Code 5-25

```
BEGIN_MESSAGE_MAP(CMFC_ControlsView, CFormView)
        //{{AFX_MSG_MAP(CMFC_ControlsView)
        ON_WM_CREATE()
        //}}AFX_MSG_MAP
        // Standard printing commands
        ON_COMMAND(ID_FILE_PRINT, CFormView::OnFilePrint)
        ON_COMMAND(ID_FILE_PRINT_DIRECT, CFormView::OnFilePrint)
        ON_COMMAND(ID_FILE_PRINT_PREVIEW, CFormView::OnFilePrintPreview)
END_MESSAGE_MAP()
```

Code 5-26

```
BEGIN_MESSAGE_MAP(CMFC_ControlsView, CFormView)
        //{{AFX_MSG_MAP(CMFC_ControlsView)
```

```
ON_WM_CREATE()
//}}AFX_MSG_MAP
// Standard printing commands
ON_BN_CLICKED(4000, OnClickDynamic)
ON_COMMAND(ID_FILE_PRINT, CFormView::OnFilePrint)
ON_COMMAND(ID_FILE_PRINT_DIRECT, CFormView::OnFilePrint)
ON_COMMAND(ID_FILE_PRINT_PREVIEW, CFormView::OnFilePrintPreview)
END_MESSAGE_MAP()
```

Step 3: Add the Function Itself

The final step is to add the handler function that is called when the user clicks the button. We called it OnclickDynamic() throughout our examples, but it can be called whatever you like (as long as it matches what you used in steps 1 and 2). The code for this function must be manually added to the view .cpp file, and it would look Code 5–27.

Code 5–27

```
void CWhateverView::OnClickDynamic()
{
        // Perform whatever processing you want.

}
```

TIP

Sometimes it can be difficult to determine what type of macro (such as ON_BN_CLICKED) to add to the message map manually for a specific type of event notification from a certain type of dynamically created child window. Here's a trick to use. Take the type of dynamic control you want to create and place on a form. Add a message map handler for it using the ClassWizard. Then, go to the three source code locations described in this section and see how the ClassWizard modified these locations. Copy and paste the code generated by the ClassWizard into the source code locations for your program. Be sure to change the ID and the function name to correlate with IDs and functions used in your program. Delete the message handler created by the ClassWizard and the control you added.

Buttons

Button controls like those pictured in Figure 5–5 are in just about every Windows program. Button controls are created by the button window class that includes checkboxes and radio buttons. Even though checkboxes and radio buttons are of

---

Figure 5–5 A sample of button controls.

the same class as buttons, we will cover them as different types of controls later in this chapter. This section explores the standard push-style button.

Notice in Figure 5–5 that the OK button is highlighted with a dark rectangle and the others are not. This identifies that button as the *default button*. When the user typing in a dialog hits the Enter key, the dialog box responds as if the user had clicked the default button. A dialog box may have no default button if after placing the button on the dialog box you change the button property.

Buttons have a caption with an underlined character that indicates the hotkey for the button. For example, if the user presses ALT-O in Figure 5–5, that would be the same as clicking the OK button. Hot keys are identified by placing an ampersand (&) in front of the character used as the hotkey. The caption for the OK button is really "&OK". You can set the caption or get the caption of a button by calling the SetWindowText() and GetWindowText() functions either in the SDK library or the MFC CWnd class.

When the user clicks on a button, the button sends a WM_COMMAND message to its parent. It will send a notification code of either BN_CLICKED or BN_DBLCLK along with the WM_COMMAND. The BN_DBLCLK notification is only sent if the button has one the BS_USERBUTTON, BS_RADIOBUTTON, BS_OWNERDRAW or BS_NOTIFY styles.

Responding to a Button Click—SDK

An SDK function receives a WM_COMMAND message at its window or dialog procedure when a button is clicked. WM_COMMAND is used for many controls and menu items to notify the parent window that an event has occurred. Information for a click is illustrated in Code 5–28. Notice how the wID, wNotification, and hChild values are set by the code right under the case WM_COMMAND section.

When a WM_COMMAND is sent to a window/dialog procedure, the wParam contains the ID in the low word of the control or menu item that sent the message. The high word of wParam contains the notification code, such as BN_CLICKED, and the lParam really contains the child window handle. All of this information is sent to

---

Code 5-28

A message from a control or menu item

```
LRESULT CALLBACK DialogProc( HWND hwndDlg, UINT uMsg, WPARAM wParam, LPARAM lParam  )
{
    int wID;
    int wNotification;
    HWND hChild;
    switch( uMsg )
      {
        case WM_COMMAND:
          wID = LOWORD(wParam);
          wNotification = HIWORD(wParam);
          hChild = (HWND) lParam;
          if( (wID == ButtonID ) && wNotification == BN_CLICKED )
            {
            }
```

Parse out WM_COMMAND parameters to be more readable

Enter code you want executed when the button is clicked

your window/dialog procedure to identify what control the user worked with, and what they did with it.

Creating a Button at Runtime

Dynamically creating a button at runtime is not a complex process. It involves calling the *CreateWindow()* function. However, it is more efficient if you create buttons using the dialog editor then rather than at runtime. Once the button is created, you can hide and display it as needed. Refer to the ShowWindow() function in the previous chapter to see how to hide and display buttons using ShowWindow().

When you create a button at runtime, you need to make sure that the button has a unique ID from all other controls on the same form. You need to control its position and size, font, its selection of styles, and also make sure there is a handler to process button events.

We'll create a button dynamically when the dialog box is created. The button will be destroyed when the user clicks the button. You will have to rerun the program to see the button again. With MFC programs, you can only use ClassWizard to add an event handler (message map) for a button that is *not* dynamically created.

Dynamic Button Creation, Response, and Destruction

SDK

First, we will create the button then write a reusable function called CreateButton()
(see Code 5–29), which simplifies the creation of the button and manages the font
used for the button caption.

Code 5–29

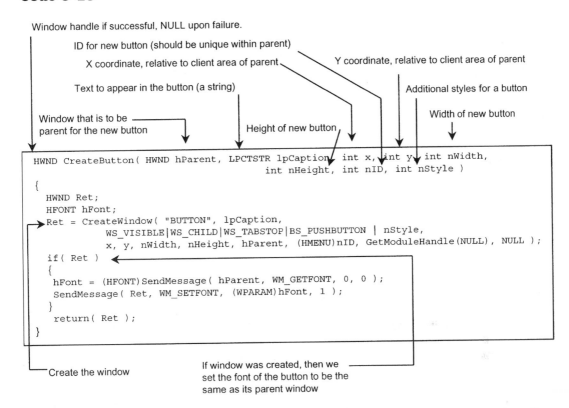

Window handle if successful, NULL upon failure.

ID for new button (should be unique within parent)

X coordinate, relative to client area of parent

Y coordinate, relative to client area of parent

Text to appear in the button (a string)

Additional styles for a button

Window that is to be parent for the new button

Width of new button

Height of new button

```
HWND CreateButton( HWND hParent, LPCTSTR lpCaption, int x, int y, int nWidth,
                   int nHeight, int nID, int nStyle )
{
  HWND Ret;
  HFONT hFont;
  Ret = CreateWindow( "BUTTON", lpCaption,
          WS_VISIBLE|WS_CHILD|WS_TABSTOP|BS_PUSHBUTTON | nStyle,
          x, y, nWidth, nHeight, hParent, (HMENU)nID, GetModuleHandle(NULL), NULL );
  if( Ret )
  {
   hFont = (HFONT)SendMessage( hParent, WM_GETFONT, 0, 0 );
   SendMessage( Ret, WM_SETFONT, (WPARAM)hFont, 1 );
  }
   return( Ret );
}
```

Create the window

If window was created, then we
set the font of the button to be the
same as its parent window

The CreateButton() function is called from the WM_INITDIALOG message handler
and creates the button at run time, just before the dialog becomes visible. This
function could be called anytime while the program is running as long as there is a
parent window on which to create the button. Code 5–30 shows how to call Code
5–29 in the WM_INITDIALOG handler.

Code 5–30

```
case WM_INITDIALOG:
        // Call Helper function to create button at runtime
        hChild = CreateButton( hwndDlg, "&Remove Me", 4, 4, 100, 24,
        4000, 0 );
        return( TRUE );
```

The next example (Code 5–31) adds a message handler to respond to the user's clicking the new button, which will respond by deleting the new button control. In order to add the handler, we check for the ID of the child button, which is 4000. Button events (like a click) are sent to the parent window or dialog procedure as a WM_COMMAND message (see the Responding to a Button Click section).

The ID and window handle of the child control is divided into wID and hChild and the notification code it sent is placed into wNotification.

Code 5–31

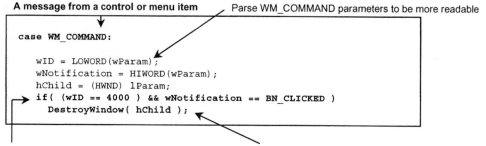

```
case WM_COMMAND:

    wID = LOWORD(wParam);
    wNotification = HIWORD(wParam);
    hChild = (HWND) lParam;
    if( (wID == 4000 ) && wNotification == BN_CLICKED )
        DestroyWindow( hChild );
```

A message from a control or menu item

Parse WM_COMMAND parameters to be more readable

If is was our dynamically-created button, then we destroy itDestroy the window

MFC

We'll use the MFC_Controls demo program to illustrate how to create a button at runtime that will be destroyed when the user clicks the button. The CButton class is used to create and destroy the window. MFC normally makes it very easy to respond to button clicks by using the message map facility of ClassWizard. But since we are dynamically creating the button, we will need to add the message map manyally, without the help of ClassWizard.

Before a button is created, we need to declare a CButton object. The CButton object should be a data member of the View class. The CButton object is initialized in the application's main dialog class if we were creating a dialog-based application. The reason we create the CButton member variable in the View class is because the object must exist for the duration of the program. If the CButton object were a local variable of a function, then the CButton object is destroyed when function ends, and the object goes out of scope.

To create the data member, go to ClassView on the left pane of VC++, then right-click the name of your View class (CMFC_Controls in our example). Select Add Member Variable then enter information into the Add Member Variable dialog as shown in Figure 5–6. Selecting public, private, or protected will work equally well for this example.

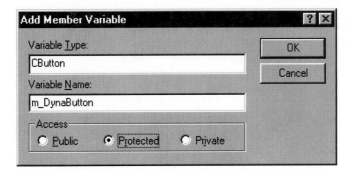

Figure 5–6 Create a data member for the class using Add Member Variable.

Next, a handler must be added for the OnCreate() function or for the WM_CREATE message. In the View class (CMFC_ControlsView in Figure 5–6), add the creation of the button in the OnCreate(),then add the font change code in the OnInitialUpdate() function, which is also in the View class. This forces the button to use the default Windows font rather than the font normally used by the dialog.

Create the button in the OnCreate() function, then change button's font to reflect the parent window by calling OnInitialUpdate(). We do this because the font the dialog uses isn't available when the window is created by calling OnCreate(). On-InitialUpdate is called whenever a document is loaded or created; this could create the button several times. Code must be added to both handlers to prevent duplicate buttons from appearing. However, if this were a dialog-based application, then we could just add all the code to the WM_INITDIALOG message without a problem.

Using ClassWizard, go to the Message Map tab. Make sure that the View class is selected in the Class Name item, that the View class name (CMFC_ControlsView in this example) is selected in the Object IDs field, and that WM_CREATE is selected in the Messages list. Click the Add Function button, then click OK to accept the function name of OnCreate(). Modify the OnCreate() function so it looks like Code 5–32.

Code 5–32

```
int CMFC_ControlsView::OnCreate(LPCREATESTRUCT lpCreateStruct)
{
    if (CFormView::OnCreate(lpCreateStruct) == -1)
       return -1;

    // TODO: Add your specialized creation code here

    // Initialize the m_DynaButton object, creating the window.
```

```
// See OnInitialUpdate also
CRect PosAndSize( 4, 4, 100, 24 );
m_DynaButton.Create( "&Remove me", WS_VISIBLE|WS_CHILD|WS_TABSTOP|
    BS_PUSH BUTTON, PosAndSize, this, 4000 );

    return 0;
}
```

Notice how an CRect object is created and how it holds the x, y, width, and height values, which are passed to the Create() function in the CButton class. The parameters to the CButton::Create() function are: button caption (string), button styles (integer), rectangle with position and size, the parent window CWnd pointer, the unique ID for the new button.

When AppWizard created the View class, it already added an OnInitialUpdate() function. The code inside the default OnInitialUpdate() sizes the main form to fit the size of the view. Locate the OnInitialUpdate() function in your source code (the MFC_ControlsView.cpp file in our example) and change it to reflect the statements in Code 5–33.

Code 5–33

```
void CMFC_ControlsView::OnInitialUpdate()
{
        CFormView::OnInitialUpdate();
        GetParentFrame()->RecalcLayout();
        ResizeParentToFit();

        // Since this is a CFormView, the font changes after the window is
        // created in OnCreate. So we need to set the font for our child window
        // to be like the parent here, and not in OnCreate.
        m_DynaButton.SetFont( GetFont() );

}
```

The GetFont() function gets the font for the view window and returns a CFont pointer, which is a parameter to the SetFont() function for the m_DynaButton object. The m_DynaButton object is our dynamically created button.

The final step is to add the handler for responding to the user clicking the dynamic button. ClassWizard cannot be used to add the handler because the button was created dynamically. Instead, the handler must be added manually.

First, add to the View class definition a prototype for a handler (see the bold statements in Code 5–34) similar to the way ClassWizard inserts the prototype.

Code 5-34

```
// Generated message map functions
protected:
        //{{AFX_MSG(CMFC_ControlsView)
        afx_msg int OnCreate(LPCREATESTRUCT lpCreateStruct);
        //}}AFX_MSG
        afx_msg void OnClickDynamic();
        DECLARE_MESSAGE_MAP()
```

Notice that between //{{ and //}} is where ClassWizard inserts its own code. You should not change anything inside that section. Place the prototype after the //}} comment and before the DECLARE_MESSAGE_MAP macro.

Next, add the OnClickDynamic() function (called the function whatever you like) to the .cpp file. The OnClickDynamic() function needs to be added in the Message Map array and as an actual function body. For the message map array, look for the BEGIN_MESSAGE_MAP in your .cpp file (called MFC_ControlsView.cpp for our sample) and change it so it looks like Code 5-35.

Code 5-35

```
BEGIN_MESSAGE_MAP(CMFC_ControlsView, CFormView)
        //{{AFX_MSG_MAP(CMFC_ControlsView)
        ON_WM_CREATE()
        //}}AFX_MSG_MAP
        // Standard printing commands
        ON_BN_CLICKED(4000, OnClickDynamic)
        ON_COMMAND(ID_FILE_PRINT, CFormView::OnFilePrint)
        ON_COMMAND(ID_FILE_PRINT_DIRECT, CFormView::OnFilePrint)
        ON_COMMAND(ID_FILE_PRINT_PREVIEW, CFormView::OnFilePrintPreview)
END_MESSAGE_MAP()
```

Placed the code below the //{{ and //}} section and but above the END_MESSAGE_MAP macro. ON_BN_CLICKED is a macro that takes the ID of a control, which is 4000 in our example, and the name of the function to call (OnClickDynamic() for this example). Notice there is no semicolon at the end of the line because this is a macro and not a statement. Add the handler function that gets called when the user clicks the button. We call it OnclickDynamic(), but it can be called whatever you like. The code for this function must be manually added to the view .cpp file and should look like Code 5-36. The steps used to create the button apply for all dynamic created controls.

Code 5–36

```
void CMFC_ControlsView::OnClickDynamic()
{
        // Destroy the dynamically-created window
        m_DynaButton.DestroyWindow();

}
```

TIP

If you are not sure what ClassWizard does for you in response to certain child window messages, then simply add a temporary window of the type you want to handle dynamically to your dialog. Add the handler using ClassWizard and examine the .h and .cpp files to see what ClassWizard did. Replace the IDs and names of the statically created control with that of your dynamically created control. Make sure to move your changed code out of the ClassWizard-controlled areas (they have comments with //{ and //}. Remove the statically created control from the dialog.

Buttons with Bitmaps

Pushbuttons may have bitmap or icon images associated with them. However, buttons with images do not provide a text caption along with the image. Buttons that use bitmap or icon images have four images—Up, Down, Selected, and Disabled—for the matching control states.

Images used with a button are created in the bitmap or icon editor of Visual C++. You can create images by using the Insert menu item, selecting Resource, and then double-clicking either the Bitmap or Icon item in the dialog box. Icons are sometimes easier to create than bitmaps because they automatically support transparency in a button. However, icons are limited in colors.

About Icons

Various examples in this section assume that you can create a 16×16 image icon. Notice that when you first create an icon, the program starts with a 32×32 icon. Make sure that you create a 16×16 image by clicking the Create image button and selecting the 16×16 item (see Figure 5–7), and then also changing the editor to use the 16×16 image.

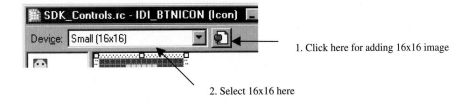

1. Click here for adding 16x16 image

2. Select 16x16 here

Figure 5–7   Create and modify 16 × 16 icon.

Simple Image without Text Button

SDK

Our first example is for a simple button that displays an image, with no text, and only one image for all possible states. It assumes that you have placed a button on a dialog whose properties are:

> ID = IDC_IMGBUTTON
> Icon in the Styles tab is checked
> The Caption property is not important, it will not be displayed in this demo.

We also assume that you have created a 16x16 Icon that will be displayed in the button, with an ID of IDI_BTNICON. Create two functions (see Codes 5–37 and 5–38) to simplify the management of the image button.

PNSetButtonImage() takes three parameters: the handle to the parent window of the button control, the ID of the button control, and the ID of the bitmap or icon resource to use as an image. The function begins by calling the GetlgItem() function to get a handle to the button control itself.

If the GetlgItem() function finds the control, it proceeds to call GetWindowLong() for that button specifying GWL_STYLE as its second parameter. GWL_STYLE means Get Window Long Style and it allows us to get the styles that you selected for the button in the dialog editor at designtime. The GetlgItem() function calls GetWindowLong() twice to see if the desired control has either the Icon or Bitmap properties set (one of the two must be set for this to work).

Based on either the Icon or Bitmap property, the LoadImage() function is used to load the bitmap or icon image. The LoadImage() function can be used to load an icon or bitmap from a separate file. In this demonstration, the function loads the image from the resources of your application. Notice that the LoadImage() function specifies the dimensions of the image as 16x16 in the fourth and fifth parameters.

Once the image is loaded, the SendMessage() function (see Code 5–38) is used to send a BM_SETIMAGE message to the button. Along with the message, the wParam parameter informs the control if it's a bitmap or an icon image and the lParam image is the handle for the image. Except for removing the image from memory when no longer needed, this is all that's needed to place an image on a button.

The PNClearButtonImage() function is used to remove an image from a button then release the image resource from memory. This function is normally called just before the child button is destroyed, such as when the parent window receives the WM_DESTROY message.

Code 5–37

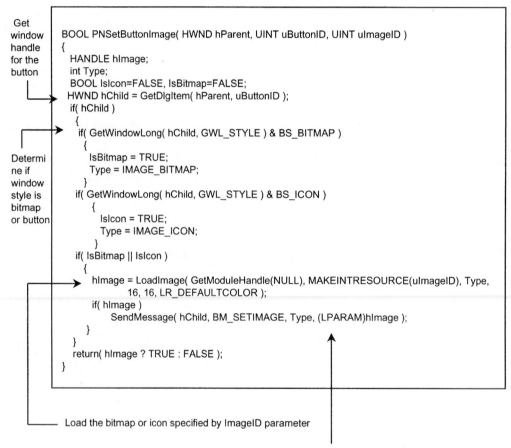

Get window handle for the button

Determine if window style is bitmap or button

```
BOOL PNSetButtonImage( HWND hParent, UINT uButtonID, UINT uImageID )
{
    HANDLE hImage;
    int Type;
    BOOL IsIcon=FALSE, IsBitmap=FALSE;
    HWND hChild = GetDlgItem( hParent, uButtonID );
    if( hChild )
        {
        if( GetWindowLong( hChild, GWL_STYLE ) & BS_BITMAP )
            {
            IsBitmap = TRUE;
            Type = IMAGE_BITMAP;
            }
        if( GetWindowLong( hChild, GWL_STYLE ) & BS_ICON )
            {
            IsIcon = TRUE;
            Type = IMAGE_ICON;
            }
        if( IsBitmap || IsIcon )
            {
            hImage = LoadImage( GetModuleHandle(NULL), MAKEINTRESOURCE(uImageID), Type,
                16, 16, LR_DEFAULTCOLOR );
            if( hImage )
                SendMessage( hChild, BM_SETIMAGE, Type, (LPARAM)hImage );
            }
        }
    return( hImage ? TRUE : FALSE );
}
```

Load the bitmap or icon specified by ImageID parameter

Tell the button to display it (set the button image)

Code 5-38

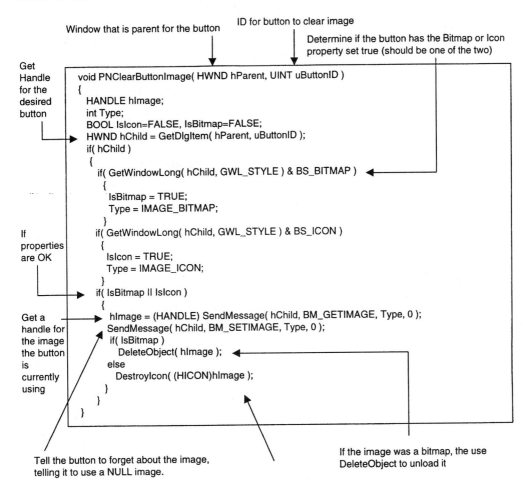

Window that is parent for the button

ID for button to clear image

Determine if the button has the Bitmap or Icon property set true (should be one of the two)

Get Handle for the desired button

```
void PNClearButtonImage( HWND hParent, UINT uButtonID )
{
    HANDLE hImage;
    int Type;
    BOOL IsIcon=FALSE, IsBitmap=FALSE;
    HWND hChild = GetDlgItem( hParent, uButtonID );
    if( hChild )
    {
        if( GetWindowLong( hChild, GWL_STYLE ) & BS_BITMAP )
        {
            IsBitmap = TRUE;
            Type = IMAGE_BITMAP;
        }
        if( GetWindowLong( hChild, GWL_STYLE ) & BS_ICON )
        {
            IsIcon = TRUE;
            Type = IMAGE_ICON;
        }
        if( IsBitmap || IsIcon )
        {
            hImage = (HANDLE) SendMessage( hChild, BM_GETIMAGE, Type, 0 );
            SendMessage( hChild, BM_SETIMAGE, Type, 0 );
            if( IsBitmap )
                DeleteObject( hImage );
            else
                DestroyIcon( (HICON)hImage );
        }
    }
}
```

If properties are OK

Get a handle for the image the button is currently using

Tell the button to forget about the image, telling it to use a NULL image.

If the image was a bitmap, the use DeleteObject to unload it

If the image was an Icon, the use DestroyIcon to unload it

With the two functions (see Codes 5–37 and 5–38) added to your program and the button and icon added as described above the code, we can now modify the program to have an image button.

Here are the three events handled in Code 5–39:

- In the WM_INITDIALOG, PNSetButtonImage() is called to set the image.
- In the WM_DESTROY, PNClearButtonImage() is called to release the image from memory.
- In the WM_COMMAND, we respond to the button click.

Code 5-39

A message from a control or menu item

Release the image we loaded for button   Close the dialog

```
LRESULT CALLBACK DialogProc( HWND hwndDlg, UINT uMsg, WPARAM wParam, LPARAM lParam )
{
  int wID;
  int wNotification;
  HWND hChild;
  switch( uMsg )
    {
      case WM_INITDIALOG:
          PNSetButtonImage( hwndDlg, IDC_IMGBUTTON, IDI_BTNICON);
          return( TRUE );
      case WM_DESTROY:
          PNClearButtonImage( hwndDlg, IDC_IMGBUTTON );
          break;
      case WM_CLOSE:
          EndDialog( hwndDlg, 0 );
          break;
      case WM_COMMAND:
          wID = LOWORD(wParam);
          wNotification = HIWORD(wParam);
          hChild = (HWND) lParam;
          if( (wID == IDC_IMGBUTTON ) && wNotification == BN_CLICKED )
            MessageBox( hwndDlg, "You clicked the simple image button",
            "Information", MB_OK );
          break;
    }
  return( FALSE );
}
```

Parse out WM_COMMAND parameters to be more readable

Our Image button, show a nice message

CAUTION

Portions of Code 5–39 have been removed to emphasize features discussed in this section. Code 5–39 should not be considered a Complete Dialog Procedure.

MFC

This MFC program demonstrates how to create a simply image button without text and uses one image for all possible states. We assume that you have placed a button on a dialog whose properties are:

ID = IDC_IMGBUTTON
Icon in the Styles tab is checked
The Caption property is not important, it will not be displayed in this demo.

We will also assumed that you have created a 16×16 Icon that will be displayed in the button, with an ID of IDI_BTNICON. (See the SDK example for more details on the icon.)

Notice that the code used in this example is much smaller than the SDK version of the program. This is because we used the MFC framework and the Document/View architecture. In this example, you will add data member to the View/Dialog class along with adding a few lines of code to several functions. We will be using the CButton MFC class, which wraps the BUTTON window class.

First, create a member variable of CButton type for our button control. The button control should have been placed on the form before beginning this step. The button control has the ID of IDC_IMGBUTTON. Use the ClassWizard's Member Variable tab to create the button and associate the button with the IDC_IMGBUTTON button control.

Select ClassWizard then select the Member Variables tab. When you highlight the View class name in the Class name control, the screen will look like Figure 5–8. Make sure that the IDC_IMGBUTTON item is selected, and hit the Add Variable button. You will presented with the dialog shown in Figure 5–9.

In Figure 5–9, we have already entered m_ImgButton for the Member variable name field. Click OK to add this member variable. Refer to the section on ClassWizard Member Variables for details on how the ClassWizard modified the code. But for now, you will find that it added the declaration shown in Code 5–40 to the view class:

Code 5–40

```
CButton m_ImgButton;
```

It has also made a programmatic association between this member variable and the on-screen control. Now with that association established, we can invoke Cbuttonand CWnd functions like SetIcon() or EnableWindow() on the m_ImgButton object, and they will affect the on-screen control.

In the OnInitialUpdate function of your view class, add the code needed to load the icon and set the button to use it. OnInitialUpdate() is called when a document is first associated with a view such as when a Document/View program first starts up or when the user picks the File/New or /Open choices. Since OnInitialUpdate() can be called several times based on users' actions, add code so that the icon is only loaded once. OnInitialUpdate() was added by AppWizard and should already be in

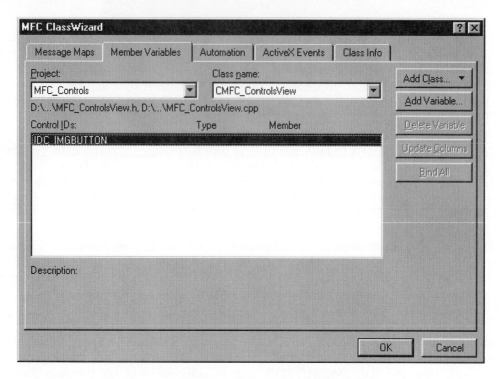

Figure 5–8 The MFC ClassWizard displays a list of on-screen controls.

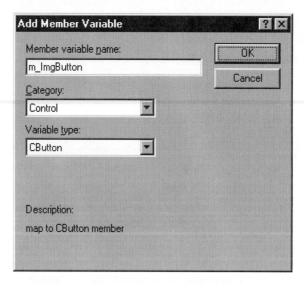

Figure 5–9 Select IDC_IMGBUTTON and click Add
Variable to display the Add Member Variable dialog.

your view .cpp file (MFC_ControlsView.cpp for our sample). Add Code 5–41 to the end of your OnInitialUpdate() function. For a dialog-based application, place Code 5–41 in the OnInitDialog() function.

Code 5–41

```
if( ! m_ImgButton.GetIcon() )
{
        // Load Icon for simple button demo and set it in the button
        // (See OnDestroy also)
        HICON hIcon;
        hIcon = (HICON)LoadImage( GetModuleHandle(NULL),
              MAKEINTRESOURCE(IDI_BTNICON),
              IMAGE_ICON, 16, 16, LR_DEFAULTCOLOR );
        m_ImgButton.SetIcon( hIcon );
}
```

Code 5–41 uses the LoadImage() function to load the IDI_BTNICON icon from the resource information. LoadImage() can also be used to load a bitmap from resource information or an icon or bitmap from an external file as well (the resource information we refer to here is embedded in the EXE file of your program). Once the icon is loaded with LoadImage(), call the CButton::SetIcon() function to set the icon to display for the desired button.

That's all you need to set the image. The image will now appear on the form when the program runs. Now, we need to respond to the button click, and finally we have to destroy the icon we loaded when our program terminates.

Use the Message map tab of ClassWizard to respond to the user clicking the button. Make sure that the View class is in the Class Name field and that the IDC_IMGBUTTON control is highlighted in the Object IDs list. Once the IDC_IMG-BUTTON is selected, you should see BN_CLICKED appear in the Message IDs list. Select that, and click Add Function. Click OK to accept the suggested function name of OnImgbutton().

Go to the newly added function in your view .cpp file and modify the OnImgbutton() function to look like Code 5–42.

Code 5–42

```
void CMFC_ControlsView::OnImgbutton()
{
        MessageBox( "You clicked the simple image button", "Information",
        MB_OK );

}
```

Finally, we need to release our icon. We only want to do it when our program is terminating. While there are several ways of doing this, we are going to add a handler for the WM_DESTROY message, which is sent when a window is being destroyed (but it and its child windows have not yet been destroyed).

Once again, go to the Message map tab of ClassWizard. Make sure that the View class is in the Class Name field and that the View class name (CMFC_ControlsView for our demo) is highlighted in the Object IDs list. Once the View class is selected, scroll to the WM_DESTROY item in the Message IDs list and select it. Click the Add Function button, and click OK to accept the suggested function name of OnDestroy(). Modify the OnDestroy() function to look like Code 5–43.

In Code 5–43, the CButton::GetIcon() function is called to get the icon handle (an HICON) for the button. If the icon was successfully gotten, the DestroyIcon() function is called to release the icon handle from memory.

Code 5–43

```
BOOL CMFC_ControlsView::DestroyWindow()
{
        // Remove our loaded Icon from memory
        HICON hIcon = m_ImgButton.GetIcon();
        if( hIcon )
                DestroyIcon( hIcon );

        return CFormView::DestroyWindow();
}
```

Image with Text Button

SDK

Creating a button with an image and with text at the same time is not a trivial matter in the SDK. In the property editor, buttons are either images or text but not both. The default design of windows simply doesn't provide it. What we will do to provide this feature will demonstrate several interesting aspects of SDK programming, and we will be able to wrap up the code into easier reusable functions that you can use in your own code.

First, we will need to have several images for a button. These include a normal "up" appearance for the image and a "disabled" appearance. Our example code will also permit you to optionally specify two other images for the "down" and "focus" state images for your buttons. The first problem to overcome is how to associate up to four images with a single button. If you want to skip the rather complex details of how it all works, go to the Using the PNImageButton() Functions section.

Storing Additional Information with a Window

Each window in a program has an extra 32-bit value associated with it, called either "item data" or "user data." The interesting thing about this value is that Windows doesn't use it at all. It is completely up to the program how to use this value and what to use it for. In fact, for many simple controls like buttons and edit boxes, the value is never used (we will see interesting values for combo boxes and list boxes later). To reiterate: Each window has an extra 32-bit value that we can get and set, and it's completely up to us to decide what we want to do with it.

In order to get or set that extra data, we use the GetWindowLong() and SetWindowLong() functions as shown in Code 5–44.

Code 5–44

```
// To retrieve the value:
Some32bitValue = GetWindowLong( hWnd, GWL_USERDATA );
// To set the value:
SetWindowLong( hWnd, GWL_USERDATA, (LPARAM) Some32BitValue );
```

For as long as the hWnd window exists, it will carry around that value we store in Some32bitValue. We need to store four images. In fact, we will be storing several extra pieces of data. Since we have several pieces of data, we will store them in a structure, or a "struct," as a convenient container (see Code 5–45).

In the struct in Code 5–45, we conveniently have our four bitmaps, along with some information that will help us draw our images when needed. What we are going to do is dynamically create the structure above and then store the pointer for the structure in the button windows extra 32-bit value "user data." This enables us to retrieve the same struct anytime we want.

Our first function is the PNImageButtonSetData() function. This function loads the desired images for the button and creates a PNImageButtonInfo structure (see Code 5–45), storing it into the button windows "user data" value as shown in Code 5–46.

Code 5–45

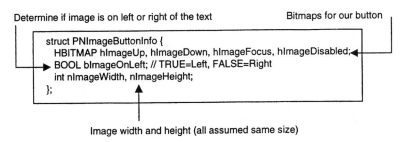

Determine if image is on left or right of the text   Bitmaps for our button

```
struct PNImageButtonInfo {
    HBITMAP hImageUp, hImageDown, hImageFocus, hImageDisabled;
    BOOL bImageOnLeft; // TRUE=Left, FALSE=Right
    int nImageWidth, nImageHeight;
};
```

Image width and height (all assumed same size)

Code 5-46

```
// PNImageButtonSetData - Sets images for an Image with Text button
// Parameters:
// hParent - Window handle to parent of button
// ImageOnLeft - If TRUE then image appears to left of text, otherwise it
// appears to right
// ID - ID for the child window
// IDUp - ID for bitmap to used for button up image (must not be zero)
// IDDown - ID for bitmap to used for button down image (if zero, then Up image
//         is used)
// IDFocus - ID for bitmap to used for button focus image (if zero, then Up image
//         is used)
//   IDDisabled - ID for bitmap to used for button disabled image (if zero, then
//               Up image is used)
// Returns: TRUE if succesful, or FALSE upon failure
BOOL PNImageButtonSetData( HWND hParent, BOOL ImageOnLeft, int ID, int IDUp,
    int IDDown, int IDFocus, int IDDisabled )
{
    PNImageButtonInfo * pInfo=0;
    HWND hChild = GetDlgItem( hParent, ID );

    // If we can't find the child window, we can't continue
    if( !hChild )
       return( FALSE );

    // If the window already has it's 32-bit 'user data' in use, we can't do it.
    if( GetWindowLong( hChild, GWL_USERDATA ) )
       return( FALSE );

    // Standard 'new' now throws an exception, handle it here in case compiler
    // adapts this standard
    try {
        pInfo = new PNImageButtonInfo;
    } catch( ... ) { return( FALSE ); }

    // And handle here in case it doesn't
    if( !pInfo )
       return( FALSE );

    pInfo->hImageUp = pInfo->hImageDown = pInfo->hImageFocus = 0;
    pInfo->bImageOnLeft = ImageOnLeft;
    // Load bitmap information for the 'button up' image
    pInfo->hImageUp = LoadBitmap( GetModuleHandle(NULL), MAKEINTRESOURCE( IDUp ) );

    // Determine the height and width of the images (they are all assumed
    // to be the same)
    BITMAP BM;
    GetObject( pInfo->hImageUp, sizeof(BM), &BM );
    pInfo->nImageWidth = BM.bmWidth;
```

```
        pInfo->nImageHeight = BM.bmHeight;

    // Now, load the rest of the images, if they are available
    if( IDDown )
        pInfo->hImageDown = LoadBitmap( GetModuleHandle(NULL),
            MAKEINTRESOURCE( IDDown ) );
    if( IDFocus )
        pInfo->hImageFocus = LoadBitmap( GetModuleHandle(NULL),
            MAKEINTRESOURCE( IDFocus ) );
    // If they specified a disabled image, use that, otherwise
    // we create an embossed version of the 'up' image.
    if( IDDisabled )
        pInfo->hImageDisabled = LoadBitmap( GetModuleHandle(NULL),
            MAKEINTRESOURCE( IDDisabled ) );
    else
        pInfo->hImageDisabled = PNImageButtonEmboss(
        (HBITMAP)pInfo->hImageUp );

    // Store the pointer to the structure with the window, as the 'user data'
    SetWindowLong( hChild, GWL_USERDATA, (LPARAM) pInfo );
    return( TRUE );
}
```

Here are the steps used in the function in Code 5–46:

- Call GetDlgItem() to determine the window handle (HWND) for the button.

- Call GetWindowLong() to see if the window is already using its user data (if it is, then the function can't work, and returns FALSE).

- Use new to dynamically allocate a PNImageButtonInfo structure.

- Use LoadBitmap() to load a bitmap from the resources (Remember: The resources are all stored in your EXE file when it was compiled) for the Up image.

- Call GetObject() to get information about the bitmap, such as height and width.

- Repeat similar calls to LoadBitmap() for the down, focused, and disabled images.

- If a disabled image was not specified, then the PNImageButtonEmboss() function is called to create an embossed version of the up button.

- SetWindowLong() is used to store the PNImageButtonInfo pointer in the button windows "user data" value for later use.

Creating the Embossed or Disabled Image.   Though you can specify four different images for the button, you need only specify the Up button image. For the

Down and Focus states, the same image usually works nicely. However, a disabled image looks different. You have two options: Create and use your own disabled version of the bitmap or programmatically create an embossed version of the Up button, in which case, you only to create the Up state image.

If you pass a zero in the IDDisabled parameter for PNImageButtonSetData() function, then the PNImageButtonEmboss() function is called to create an embossed version of the Up button at runtime. While the PNImageButtonEmboss() function is a rather "brute-force" method, it should work quite well in most circumstances, considering bitmaps on buttons are not usually very large. While there are other methods to turn an image into a disabled appearance, we want ours to have three color values, so we take a slightly unusual approach as shown in Code 5–47.

Code 5–47

```
// PNImageButtonEmboss - Basic embossing ability
// Parameters:
//       bmSource - Source bitmap to be embossed
// Returns: Embossed version of Source bitmap
// Comments: Uses brute force so we can maintain 3 colors on a disabled bitmap:
// the highlight, dark, and transparent colors
HBITMAP PNImageButtonEmboss( HBITMAP hbmSource )
{
    HDC memDC, memDCEmbossed;
    HBITMAP hbmEmbossed, hbmOldBM, hbmOldBMEmbossed;
    BITMAP bmInfo;
    COLORREF crTransparent, crLo = GetSysColor(COLOR_3DHILIGHT);
    COLORREF crHi=GetSysColor(COLOR_3DSHADOW);
    COLORREF crCur, crNewTransparent = GetSysColor( COLOR_3DFACE );
    int Row, Col, ColorAvg=0, Total=0;

    // Determine information for the bitmap passed
    GetObject( hbmSource, sizeof(bmInfo), &bmInfo );

    // Create memory DCs, and the return bitmap, for drawing and creation
    memDC = CreateCompatibleDC(NULL);
    memDCEmbossed = CreateCompatibleDC(NULL);
    hbmOldBM = (HBITMAP)SelectObject(memDC, hbmSource );
    hbmEmbossed = CreateCompatibleBitmap( memDC, bmInfo.bmWidth,
    bmInfo.bmHeight );

    // Select the new bitmap into the memory DC. Now, when we draw on the
    memory DC, it
    // will manipulate the bitmap that is selected into it.
    hbmOldBMEmbossed = (HBITMAP)SelectObject( memDCEmbossed, hbmEmbossed );

    // Perform some basic color analisys, to determine what colors to use
    crTransparent = GetPixel( memDC, 0, bmInfo.bmHeight-1 );
```

```
for( Row=0; Row < bmInfo.bmHeight; Row++ )
    for( Col=0; Col < bmInfo.bmWidth; Col++ )
    {
        crCur = GetPixel( memDC, Row, Col );
        if( crCur != crTransparent )
        {
          ColorAvg+=(GetGValue(crCur)+GetBValue(crCur)+
          GetRValue(crCur));
          Total++;
        }
    }
ColorAvg /= Total;

// Draw the original bitmap into the memory DC, which will set the
color depth and
// dimensions of the new bitmap.
BitBlt( memDCEmbossed, 0, 0, bmInfo.bmWidth, bmInfo.bmHeight, memDC, 0,
0, SRCCOPY);

// Now, go through each pixel, and make it one of 3 colors:
//     Dark, light, and transparent
for( Row=0; Row < bmInfo.bmHeight; Row++ )
    for( Col=0; Col < bmInfo.bmWidth; Col++ )
    {
        crCur = GetPixel( memDC, Col, Row );
        if( crCur != crTransparent )
        {
          if( (GetGValue(crCur)+GetBValue(crCur)+GetRValue(crCur)) >
          ColorAvg )
                  SetPixel( memDCEmbossed, Col, Row, crHi);
              else
                  SetPixel( memDCEmbossed, Col, Row, crLo);
        }
        else
            SetPixel( memDCEmbossed, Col, Row, crNewTransparent );
    }

// Return the memory DCs to their previous state, and delete them from
memory
SelectObject( memDC, hbmOldBM );
SelectObject( memDCEmbossed, hbmOldBMEmbossed );
DeleteDC( memDC );
DeleteDC( memDCEmbossed );

// Return the new bitmap
return( hbmEmbossed );
}
```

Here's what is happening in Code 5–47:

- Calls GetObject() to get information about the bitmap passed, such as height and width.
- Creates memory Device Contexts and Bitmaps, so that we can "draw" on the bitmap to be returned. You will see calls to CreateCompatibleDC() and CreateCompatibleBitmap() here.
- Uses SelectObject() to select the bmEmbossed bitmap into the memDCEmbossed memory DC. Now, any drawing on the memDCEmbossed Device Context will change the bmEmbossed bitmap.
- Uses GetPixel() to determine the color of the lower left pixel, which is used in our code as the transparent color.
- Enters a *for* loop to get the average color brightness for each pixel from the original bitmap.
- Uses BitBlt to transfer the image from the memDC (and the original bitmap) into the memDCEmbossed (and the new bitmap we are creating)
- Enters another *for* loop, this time setting pixels in the memDCEmbossed Device Context (and therefore, the bmEmbossed bitmap) to one of our three colors, based on its basic color weight.
- Calls SelectObject() to deselect the bitmaps from the memory DCs.
- Calls DeleteDC() to release the memory Device Contexts we created from memory.
- Returns the new HBITMAP handle for our new bitmap.

Cleaning up the Images for a Button.   Once a form is about to be destroyed, we should unload any of the bitmaps that we loaded for the button. In order to do this, we have provided the PNImageButtonClearData() function, which releases all the memory and bitmaps that the PNImageButtonSetData() data function created as shown in Code 5–48.

Here's what is happening in Code 5–48:

- Calls GetDlgItem() to get the window handle for the button.
- Calls GetwindowLong() to retrieve the PNImageButtonInfo pointer from the button window's "user data" value (placed there by PNImageButtonSetData()).
- Checks each bitmap handle, and if non-zero calls DeleteObject() to release the bitmap from memory.
- Uses delete to release the structure itself from memory.
- Uses SetWindowLong() to set the "user data" value for the window back to zero.

Code 5-48

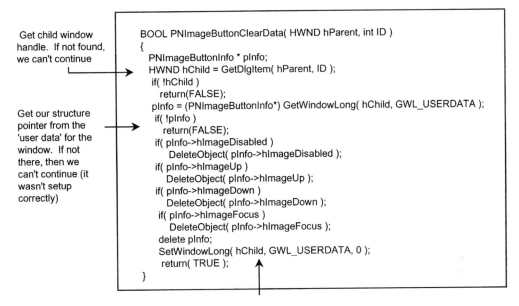

Get child window handle. If not found, we can't continue

Get our structure pointer from the 'user data' for the window. If not there, then we can't continue (it wasn't setup correctly)

```
BOOL PNImageButtonClearData( HWND hParent, int ID )
{
    PNImageButtonInfo * pInfo;
    HWND hChild = GetDlgItem( hParent, ID );
    if( !hChild )
        return(FALSE);
    pInfo = (PNImageButtonInfo*) GetWindowLong( hChild, GWL_USERDATA );
    if( !pInfo )
        return(FALSE);
    if( pInfo->hImageDisabled )
        DeleteObject( pInfo->hImageDisabled );
    if( pInfo->hImageUp )
        DeleteObject( pInfo->hImageUp );
    if( pInfo->hImageDown )
        DeleteObject( pInfo->hImageDown );
    if( pInfo->hImageFocus )
        DeleteObject( pInfo->hImageFocus );
    delete pInfo;
    SetWindowLong( hChild, GWL_USERDATA, 0 );
    return( TRUE );
}
```

Set user data back to zero.

Drawing the Button and Text.   Since there is no standard Windows button with the text and image together, we have to redraw the entire window ourselves. This gets rather complicated in view of the fact that there are so many states to the button and various characteristics of each state. The function we have created (see Code 5–49) to provide this drawing ability is called PNImageButtonDrawItem().

Code 5-49

```
// PNImageButtonDrawItem - Handles owner-draw requirements for PN Image
   with Text buttons
// Parameters:
//     hParent - Window handle to parent of button
//     ID - ID for the child window
//     lpDrawItem - Pointer to a DRAWITEMSTRUCT structure
// Returns: TRUE if succesful, or FALSE upon failure
BOOL PNImageButtonDrawItem( HWND hParent, int ID, LPDRAWITEMSTRUCT
lpDrawItem )
{
    HDC DC = lpDrawItem->hDC;
    RECT Rect = lpDrawItem->rcItem;
    SIZE DrawArea;
    int XOffset, YOffset, YTextOffset=0, YImageOffset=0;
    UINT nOffset = 0;
    UINT nFrameStyle=0;
```

```c
    int nStateFlag;
    HANDLE hImage;

    char Text[128];
    PNImageButtonInfo * pInfo;

    // Get child window handle. If not found, we can't continue
    HWND hChild = GetDlgItem( hParent, ID );
    if( !hChild )
        return(FALSE);

    // Get our structure pointer from the 'user data' for the window. If
       not there,
    // then we can't continue (it wasn't setup correctly)
    pInfo = (PNImageButtonInfo*) GetWindowLong( hChild, GWL_USERDATA );
    if( !pInfo )
        return(FALSE);

    // Based on the size of the button text, and the images, determine drawing
    // positions of each.
    GetWindowText( hChild, Text, sizeof(Text) );
    GetTextExtentPoint32(DC, Text, strlen(Text), &DrawArea );
    DrawArea.cx += (pInfo->nImageWidth+4);
    if( DrawArea.cy > pInfo->nImageHeight )
        YTextOffset = ( pInfo->nImageHeight - DrawArea.cy ) /2;
    else
    {
        YImageOffset = (DrawArea.cy - pInfo->nImageHeight) /2;
        DrawArea.cy = pInfo->nImageHeight;
    }
    XOffset = (Rect.right - DrawArea.cx)/2;
    YOffset = (Rect.bottom - DrawArea.cy)/2;

    // Determine if button is in the selected state
    if ( lpDrawItem->itemState & ODS_SELECTED)
    {
        nFrameStyle = DFCS_PUSHED;
        hImage = pInfo->hImageDown ? pInfo->hImageDown : pInfo->hImageUp;
        nOffset += 1;
    }

    // Determine if button is disabled
    if( lpDrawItem->itemState & ODS_DISABLED )
    {
        nStateFlag = DSS_DISABLED;
        hImage = pInfo->hImageDisabled?pInfo->hImageDisabled : pInfo->hImageUp;
    }
    else
    {
```

```
        nStateFlag = DSS_NORMAL;
        hImage = pInfo->hImageUp;
    }


    // Determine if button has the focus state
    if ( lpDrawItem->itemState & ODS_FOCUS )
        if( (hImage = pInfo->hImageFocus) == 0 )
            hImage = pInfo->hImageUp;

    // If button is selected, the use DrawFrameControl to display its frame
    if( ! (lpDrawItem->itemState & ODS_SELECTED) )
    {
        // If the button is focused, then we need to draw the black rectangle,
        // and shrink the button a tiny bit (visual appearance of all buttons)
        if( lpDrawItem->itemState & ODS_FOCUS )
        {
            Rectangle(DC, Rect.left, Rect.top, Rect.right, Rect.bottom );
            Rect.left++;
            Rect.top++;
            Rect.bottom--;
            Rect.right--;
        }
        DrawFrameControl(DC, &Rect, DFC_BUTTON, DFCS_BUTTONPUSH | nFrameStyle);
    }
    else
    {
        // If it's not selected, then drawing is more complex
        // Create out pens and brushes for drawing, and draw a rectangle.
        HBRUSH NewBrush = CreateSolidBrush( GetSysColor( COLOR_3DFACE ) );
        HBRUSH hOldBrush = (HBRUSH)SelectObject( DC, NewBrush );
        Rectangle(DC, Rect.left, Rect.top, Rect.right, Rect.bottom );
        HPEN NewPen = CreatePen( PS_SOLID, 1, GetSysColor(COLOR_3DSHADOW) );
        HPEN hpOldPen = (HPEN)SelectObject( DC, NewPen );

        // Then, shrink the rectangle a tiny bit, and draw the inner rectangle
        Rect.left++;
        Rect.top++;
        Rect.bottom--;
        Rect.right--;
        Rectangle(DC, Rect.left, Rect.top, Rect.right, Rect.bottom );
        SelectObject( DC, hpOldPen );
        SelectObject( DC, hOldBrush );
        DeleteObject( NewPen );
    }

    if( pInfo->bImageOnLeft )
    {
        // Draw the bitmap image, transparently, and then the text
        PNDrawTransparent( DC, XOffset+nOffset, YOffset+nOffset+
```

```
    YImageOffset, (HBITMAP)hImage, TRUE, 0 );
    DrawState( DC, 0, 0, (LPARAM)Text, 0, XOffset+pInfo-
    >nImageWidth+4+nOffset, YOffset+nOffset+YTextOffset, DrawArea.cx,
    DrawArea.cy, DST_PREFIXTEXT|nStateFlag );
    }
    else
    {
        // Draw the text, and then the bitmap image transparently
        DrawState( DC, 0, 0, (LPARAM)Text, 0, XOffset+nOffset, YOffset+
        nOffset+YTextOffset, DrawArea.cx, DrawArea.cy, DST_PREFIXTEXT
        |nStateFlag );
        PNDrawTransparent( DC, XOffset+nOffset+DrawArea.cx-pInfo->nImage-
        Width, YOffset+nOffset+YImageOffset, (HBITMAP)hImage, TRUE, 0 );
    }
    // Draw the focus rectangle for the button
    if( ( lpDrawItem->itemState & ODS_FOCUS ) )
    {
        RECT Rect2;
        Rect2 = Rect;
        Rect2.left += 3;
        Rect2.right -= 3;
        Rect2.top += 3;
        Rect2.bottom -= 3;
        DrawFocusRect( DC, &Rect2 );
    }
    return(TRUE);
}
```

Here's what's happening in Code 5–49:

- Uses GetDlgItem() to get a window handle to the desired child button window.

- Uses GetWindowLong() to retrieve the PNImageButtonInfo pointer that was created for the specific button by the PNImageButtonSetData() function.

- Uses GetWindowText() to retrieve the text that was specified for the button caption.

- Uses GetTextExtentPoint32 to determine the display area needed to display the text, so we can judge its positioning relative the image and button sides.

- Calculates a drawing area inside the button for the text and the image together, to be centered.

- Tests the lpDrawItems itemState member to determine the state of how the button should be drawn.

- Calls the Rectangle function to draw some basic frames for the button.

- Possibly calls the DrawFrameControl() function to display a normal button frame.

- Calls PNDrawTransparent() to draw the selected bitmap transparently.

- Calls DrawState() to display the text for the button in either a normal or disabled state.

- Calls the DrawFocus() function to display the focus rectangle for the button (if focused).

The Transparent Bitmap. The PNImageButtonDrawItem() function calls the PNDrawTransparent() function to display its bitmap as a transparent image. PNDrawTransparent() lets you specify that the lower-left corner of the bitmap contains the transparent color, which will not be shown during display. This function will also work with larger images as well. Note: There is a simplified function called TransparentBlt in win98 and WinNT/2000, but it does not exist in Win95. The PNDrawTransparent() function is as shown in Code 5-50.

Code 5-50

```
// PNDrawTransparent - Draws a bitmap with transparency
// Parameters:
//     DC - HDC to draw bitmap on
//     x - X coordinate on DC to draw bitmap at
//     y - Y coordinate on DC to draw bitmap at
//     hbmImage - Handle to bitmap to display
//     LowerLeft - If True, then transparency color is taken from lower
//     left of bitmap
//     crColor - If LowerLeft is false, then this must specify transparent
//     color for bitmap
void PNDrawTransparent(HDC DC, int x, int y, HBITMAP hbmImage,
    BOOL LowerLeft, COLORREF crColor)
{
    HDC hdcImage;
    HDC hdcTrans;
    HBITMAP hbmTrans;
    BITMAP bmBitmap;
    GetObject( hbmImage, sizeof(bmBitmap), &bmBitmap );
    // Change Background and text color, saving values for end
    COLORREF crOldBack = SetBkColor(DC, RGB(255,255,255));
    COLORREF crOldText = SetTextColor(DC, RGB(0,0,0) );

    // Create Memory DCs to do our work in
    hdcImage = CreateCompatibleDC(DC);
    hdcTrans = CreateCompatibleDC(DC);

    // Select passed Image bitmap into Image memory DC
    SelectObject(hdcImage, hbmImage);
```

```
// Create transparent bitmap, and select into transparent DC
hbmTrans = CreateBitmap( bmBitmap.bmWidth, bmBitmap.bmHeight, 1, 1, NULL);
SelectObject(hdcTrans, hbmTrans);

// If LowerLeft is true, then determine transparent color from bitmap
// passed
if( LowerLeft )
    crColor = GetPixel( hdcImage, 0, bmBitmap.bmHeight-1 );

// Select background color (transparent color) for our image memory DC
SetBkColor(hdcImage, crColor);

BitBlt(hdcTrans, 0, 0, bmBitmap.bmWidth, bmBitmap.bmHeight, hdcImage,
    0, 0, SRCCOPY);

// Perform BitBlt operations (this is where the Masking occurs)
BitBlt(DC, x, y, bmBitmap.bmWidth, bmBitmap.bmHeight, hdcImage, 0, 0,
    SRCINVERT);
BitBlt(DC, x, y, bmBitmap.bmWidth, bmBitmap.bmHeight, hdcTrans, 0, 0,
    SRCAND);
BitBlt(DC, x, y, bmBitmap.bmWidth, bmBitmap.bmHeight, hdcImage, 0, 0,
    SRCINVERT);

// Release our memory DCs and Bitmap we created
DeleteDC( hdcImage );
DeleteDC( hdcTrans );
DeleteObject( hbmTrans );

// Retore original background and text colors for the passed DC
SetBkColor(DC, crOldBack);
SetTextColor(DC, crOldText);
}
```

Here's what is happening in Code 5–50:

- Calls SetBkColor() and SetTextColor() to alter the destination DC in preparation for drawing.
- Calls CreateCompatibleDC() to create memory Device Contexts for us to draw in before going to the screen.
- Calls CreateBitmap() to create a bitmap that we can use for creating the transparent mask bitmap.
- Calls GetPixel() to determine the color of the pixel on the lower left corner, to be used for transparency (based on the LowerLeft parameter).
- Calls the BitBlt() function, moving the bitmap image from the original bitmap, and the transparent bitmap, and the screen, in a series of masked drawings.
- Deletes the memory device contexts made previously.

- Calls the SetBkColor() and SetTextColor() functions to restore the screen DC to its previous state.

Using the PNImageButton() Functions. The previous sections outlined a set of functions that can be used to implement buttons that contain both text and images. In this section, we will describe how you can use that code to add these image and text buttons to your own programs.

Here are the steps to follow to use the PNImageButton() functions in your application.

1. **Create your bitmap(s).** Create at least one bitmap in the bitmap editor in VC++. You may create as many as four for the following states of the button: Up, Down, Focused, and Disabled. Of the four, only Up is required.
2. **Place a normal button on the form.** In the dialog editor, place a button on your form. Change the properties of the button so that the Owner Draw property is checked. Make note of the ID for the button (our example will use IDC_BUTTONIMG2)
3. **Set the Button User Data to remember its own images.** In the WM_INITDIALOG message handler for your dialog box (or after you create the button if its not a dialog-based program), call PNImageButton-SetData function, such as:

   ```
   PNImageButtonSetData( hwndDlg, TRUE, IDC_BUTTONIMG2,
       IDB_CHECKUP, 0, 0, 0 );
   ```

   In this example, hwndDlg is the parent window (dialog) window handle. TRUE means image will appear to left of the text. FALSE places the image on the right. IDC_BUTTONIMG2 is the ID of the button we want to have text with images. IDB_CHECKUP is the image we want for the Up state of the button. The three zeros after are the Down, Focus, and Disabled bitmap IDs, and we are specifying none here.
4. **Add a handler to the WM_DRAWITEM message.** In your dialog or window procedure, add a handler for the WM_DRAWITEM message, similar to Code 5-51.

Code 5-51

```
case WM_DRAWITEM:
      if( wParam == IDC_BUTTONIMG2 ) // Our owner draw button
      {
            PNImageButtonDrawItem( hwndDlg, wParam, (LPDRAWITEMSTRUCT)lParam);
            return( 0 );
      }
      break;
```

Notice how wParam is checked to make sure the message is for our desired button. Then, PNImageButtonDrawItem() is called to actually display the button. The parameters to the PNImageButtonDrawItem() won't change as it passes the handle to the parent window (the dialog) of the button, and then to the wParam and the lParam parameters that came with the WM_DRAWITEM function.

NOTE

If you have no other Owner Draw style controls on your form, then you can simply call PN-ImageButtonDraw() without the *if* test shown above, and it will handle any number of PNImage-Button style buttons.

MFC

While MFC wraps a great number of things for you, it currently does not support the ability to have a button contain both image and text on its surface. In order to implement this type of control, we will create a new MFC class derived from the CButton and have that derived class handle the display of the button (but the rest of the normal BUTTON behavior is still handled by the normal windows class). This technique is called windows subclassing.

The following section will give details on how to create the new class. If you want to skip the details and see how to use the class, just skip to the Using the CPNImage-Button Class section. Note that you must have the class added to your project in order to use it.

In the ClassWizard:

1. Click the Add Class button.
2. Select New.
3. In the New Class dialog (see Figure 5–10), enter CPNImageButton for the class name.
4. In the Base Class field, select CButton.
5. Click OK.

Once the new class called CPNImageButton is created, add functions (Code 5–52) to the class.

Code 5–52

```
BOOL SetData( BOOL ImageOnLeft, UINT IDUp, UINT IDDown=0, UINT IDFocus=0,
   UINT IDDisabled=0);
void DrawTransparent(CDC* pDC, int x, int y, CBitmap* hbmImage,
   BOOL LowerLeft, COLORREF crColor);
```

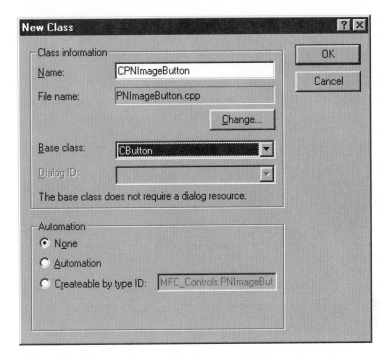

Figure 5–10 Create a new class for the CPNImageButton.

```
void Emboss( CBitmap& Dest, CBitmap& bmSource );
void DrawItem(LPDRAWITEMSTRUCT lpDrawItemStruct);
```

You can manually add these functions to the .h and .cpp files (called CPNImage-Button.h and CPNImageButton.cpp) or you can right-click on the CPNImageButton class in the ClassView window and then select the Add Member Function menu item in the pop-up menu that is displayed. Each function is detailed below.

We will also need to add several data members to the CPNImageButton class. Again, the member variables can be added either by manually editing the CPNImageButton.h file or you can right-click on the CPNImageButton class in ClassView and then click the Add Member Variable menu item in the pop-up menu. The data members are shown in Code 5–53.

Code 5–53

```
// Bitmaps for image display
CBitmap m_Up, m_Down, m_Focus, m_Disabled;
// Bitmap height and width information
int m_ImageWidth, m_ImageHeight;
// Flag for image on left or right
BOOL m_ImageOnLeft;
```

The SetData() Function. The SetData() function for CPNImageButton sets up information about the images that the button should use. The prototype is shown in Code 5–54 and the actual function is defined in Code 5–55.

The SetData() function will first see if there are already any bitmaps loaded for the button, using the GetSafeHandle() function of the m_Up, m_Down, m_Focus, and m_Disabled CBitmap data members. If these bitmaps are already loaded, then the DeleteObject() function is called to release them from memory.

After cleaning up whatever bitmaps may already be in use, it loads the new Up state image. The Up state image must be specified as it will serve as the image that the other states use if nothing is specified for them. It also determines the height and width of the images (all must be the same height and width for a single button).

Finally, it loads the other bitmaps if their IDs were specified in the parameter list, by calling the LoadBitmap() member function of the CBitmap class. The Disabled state image is slightly different. If there is no disabled bitmap specified for the control, then the Emboss function is called to create an embossed version of the Up bitmap.

The final result of this function is the initialization of the m_Up, m_Down, m_Focus, and m_Disabled bitmap data members to contain the images that should be displayed on these various states.

Code 5–54

```
BOOL SetData( BOOL ImageOnLeft, UINT IDUp, UINT IDDown=0, UINT IDFocus=0,
    UINT IDDisabled=0);
```

Code 5–55

```
// CPNImageButton::SetData - Sets image information for the CPNImageButton
// class
//      ImageOnLeft - If TRUE then image appears to left of text, otherwise
//      image appears to the right
//      IDUp - Must specified the ID for the bitmap to display when in the
//         normal, 'Up' state.
//      IDDown - Specifies the image to use for the down state of the button.
//         May be zero.
//      IDFocus - Specifies the image to use for the focus state of the
//      button.
//         May be zero.
//      IDDisabled - Specifies the image to use for the disabled state of
//      the button.
//         May be zero.
// Returns: TRUE if succesful, FALSE if not
```

```
// Comments: If IDDown or IDFocus are zero, then the Up image is used for
// those states. If the IDDisabled value is zero, then an embossed version
// of the up image is created and used.
BOOL CPNImageButton::SetData(BOOL ImageOnLeft, UINT IDUp, UINT IDDown, UINT
IDFocus, UINT IDDisabled)
{
        // If button already has data loaded, then delete the bitmaps
        if( m_Up.GetSafeHandle() )
            m_Up.DeleteObject();
        if( m_Down.GetSafeHandle() )
            m_Down.DeleteObject();
        if( m_Focus.GetSafeHandle() )
            m_Focus.DeleteObject();
        if( m_Disabled.GetSafeHandle() )
            m_Disabled.DeleteObject();

        // Load the 'Up' state bitmap (required). Use it to specify height
        // and width of all images
        m_Up.LoadBitmap( IDUp );
        BITMAP BM;
        m_Up.GetObject( sizeof(BM), &BM );
        m_ImageHeight = BM.bmHeight;
        m_ImageWidth = BM.bmWidth;

        // Store the ImageOnLeft value
        m_ImageOnLeft = ImageOnLeft;

        // Load other bitmaps as needed
        if( IDDown )
            m_Down.LoadBitmap( IDDown );
        if( IDFocus )
            m_Focus.LoadBitmap( IDFocus );

        // If a disabled image was specified, then load it, otherwise create an
        // embossed version of the 'Up' image.
        if( IDDisabled )
            m_Disabled.LoadBitmap( IDDisabled );
        else
            Emboss( m_Disabled, m_Up );

        return(TRUE);
}
```

The DrawTransparent() Function.   The DrawTransparent() function inside the
CPNImageButton class is responsible for drawing the bitmaps for the various states
in a transparent mode. It has the ability to treat the pixel on the lower left corner of
the bitmap as the transparent color or you can specify the desired color yourself.
The prototype of the function is shown in Code 5–56 and the actual function is
shown in Code 5–57.

Code 5-56

```
void DrawTransparent(CDC* pDC, int x, int y, CBitmap* hbmImage,
       BOOL LowerLeft=TRUE, COLORREF crColor=0);
```

Code 5-57

```
// DrawTransparent - Draws a bitmap with transparency
// Parameters:
//     DC - HDC to draw bitmap on
//     x - X coordinate on DC to draw bitmap at
//     y - Y coordinate on DC to draw bitmap at
//     hbmImage - Handle to bitmap to display
//     LowerLeft - If True, then transparency color is taken from lower
//     left of bitmap
//     crColor - If LowerLeft is false, then this must specify transparent
//     color for bitmap
void CPNImageButton::DrawTransparent(CDC* pDC, int x, int y, CBitmap*
hbmImage, BOOL LowerLeft, COLORREF crColor)
{
       CDC hdcImage;
       CDC hdcTrans;
       CBitmap hbmTrans;
       BITMAP bmBitmap;

       hbmImage->GetObject( sizeof(bmBitmap), &bmBitmap );
       // Change Background and text color, saving values for end
       COLORREF crOldBack = pDC->SetBkColor(RGB(255,255,255));
       COLORREF crOldText = pDC->SetTextColor(RGB(0,0,0) );

       // Create Memory DCs to do our work in
       hdcImage.CreateCompatibleDC(pDC);
       hdcTrans.CreateCompatibleDC(pDC);

       // Select passed Image bitmap into Image memory DC
       hdcImage.SelectObject(hbmImage);

       // Create transparent bitmap, and select into transparent DC
       hbmTrans.CreateBitmap( bmBitmap.bmWidth, bmBitmap.bmHeight, 1, 1, NULL);
       hdcTrans.SelectObject( hbmTrans);

       // If LowerLeft is true, then determine transparent color from
       bitmap passed
       if( LowerLeft )
           crColor = hdcImage.GetPixel( 0, bmBitmap.bmHeight-1 );

       // Select background color (transparent color) for our image memory DC
       hdcImage.SetBkColor(crColor);
       hdcTrans.BitBlt( 0, 0, bmBitmap.bmWidth, bmBitmap.bmHeight,
       &hdcImage, 0, 0, SRCCOPY);
```

```
// Perform BitBlt operations (this is where the Masking occurs)
pDC->BitBlt( x, y, bmBitmap.bmWidth, bmBitmap.bmHeight, &hdcImage,
0, 0, SRCINVERT);
pDC->BitBlt( x, y, bmBitmap.bmWidth, bmBitmap.bmHeight, &hdcTrans,
0, 0, SRCAND);
pDC->BitBlt( x, y, bmBitmap.bmWidth, bmBitmap.bmHeight, &hdcImage,
0, 0, SRCINVERT);

// Retore original background and text colors for the passed DC
pDC->SetBkColor(crOldBack);
pDC->SetTextColor(crOldText);

}
```

Here's what is happening in Code 5–57.

- It uses the CGdiObject::GetObject() member function of the hbmImage parameter (the bitmap to display) to determine the height and width of the passed CBitmap.

- It uses the CDC::SetBkColor() and CDC::SetTextColor() member functions of the pDC parameter to set the background and text colors for the output Device Context.

- It calls the CDC::CreateCompatibleDC() member functions for hdcImage and hdcTrans to create memory device contexts for them (A "device context" should be pictured as a canvas where you can draw with functions like TextOur or Rectangle). A memory Device Context will perform your drawing and output into a memory buffer, not actually to the screen.

- The CDC::SelectObject() member function is called for the hdcImage variable, to associate the passed bitmap (hbmImage) with the hdcImage device context.

- The CBitmap::CreateBitmap() function for hdmTrans is called to create a bitmap of a specified height and width.

- The SelectObject() member function for the hdcTrans variable is called, to associate the new bitmap with the hdcTrans memory device context.

- The CDC::GetPixel() function is called for the hdcImage variable, if the LowerLeft parameter were not FALSE. This retrieves the color of the pixel at the lower left corner of the passed bitmap.

- A series of masked CDC::BitBlt() operations are performed, which copies the passed bitmap to the output device context (the pDC parameter) in a transparent manner.

- The original background color and text color for the passed pDC parameters are restored.

The Emboss() Function. Th Emboss() function creates an embossed (grayed, or disabled in appearance) version of the bitmap passed to it. The function prototype is shown in Code 5–58 and the actual function is shown in Code 5–59.

This function implements an unusual form of embossing because we need to be left with three colors: highlight, shadow, and transparent. Normal embossing techniques only leave two colors, highlight and shadow. This function uses a very simplistic method to perform this conversion, which, while not optimal in performance, should be more than adequate for small bitmaps such as those used on buttons.

Code 5-58

```
void Emboss( CBitmap& Dest, CBitmap& bmSource );
```

Code 5-59

```
// Emboss - Basic embossing ability
// Parameters:
//      bmDest - Destination bitmap
//      bmSource - Source bitmap to be embossed
// Comments: Uses brute force so we can maintain 3 colors on a disabled bitmap:
//    the highlight, dark, and transparent colors
void CPNImageButton::Emboss( CBitmap& Dest, CBitmap& bmSource )
{
    CDC memDC, memDCEmbossed;
    CBitmap hbmOldBM, hbmOldBMEmbossed;
    BITMAP bmInfo;
    COLORREF crTransparent,
        crLo = ::GetSysColor(COLOR_3DHILIGHT),
        crHi=::GetSysColor(COLOR_3DSHADOW);
    COLORREF crCur, crNewTransparent = ::GetSysColor( COLOR_3DFACE );
    int Row, Col, ColorAvg=0, Total=0;

    // Determine information for the bitmap passed
    bmSource.GetObject( sizeof(bmInfo), &bmInfo );

    // Create memory DCs, and the return bitmap, for drawing and creation
    memDC.CreateCompatibleDC(NULL);
    memDCEmbossed.CreateCompatibleDC(NULL);
    memDC.SelectObject(&bmSource );
    Dest.CreateCompatibleBitmap( &memDC, bmInfo.bmWidth, bmInfo.bmHeight );

    // Select the new bitmap into the memory DC. Now, when we draw on the
    memory DC, it
    // will manipulate the bitmap that is selected into it.
    memDCEmbossed.SelectObject( Dest );

    // Perform some basic color analisys, to determine what colors to use
    crTransparent = memDC.GetPixel( 0, bmInfo.bmHeight-1 );
    for( Row=0; Row < bmInfo.bmHeight; Row++ )
```

```
        for( Col=0; Col < bmInfo.bmWidth; Col++ )
        {
                crCur = memDC.GetPixel( Row, Col );
                if( crCur != crTransparent )
                {
                        ColorAvg+=(GetGValue(crCur)+GetBValue(crCur)+GetRValue
                        (crCur));
                        Total++;
                }
        }
ColorAvg /= Total;

// Draw the original bitmap into the memory DC, which will set the
color depth and
// dimensions of the new bitmap.
memDCEmbossed.BitBlt( 0, 0, bmInfo.bmWidth, bmInfo.bmHeight, &memDC, 0,
0, SRCCOPY);

// Now, go through each pixel, and make it one of 3 colors: Dark,
// light, and transparent
for( Row=0; Row < bmInfo.bmHeight; Row++ )
    for( Col=0; Col < bmInfo.bmWidth; Col++ )
    {
            crCur = memDC.GetPixel( Col, Row );
            if( crCur != crTransparent )
            {
                if( (GetGValue(crCur)+GetBValue(crCur)+GetRValue(crCur)) >
                ColorAvg )
                    memDCEmbossed.SetPixel( Col, Row, crHi);
                else
                    memDCEmbossed.SetPixel( Col, Row, crLo);
            }
            else
                memDCEmbossed.SetPixel( Col, Row, crNewTransparent );
    }
// Destructors clean up for us.
}
```

Here's what is happening in Code 5–59.

- It calls GetSysColor() to determine the users personal color settings for highlight, shadow, and normal colors.
- It calls CGdiObject::GetObject() to get information about the CBitmap passed, such as height and width.
- It creates memory Device Contexts and Bitmaps, so that we can "draw" on the bitmap to be returned. You will see calls to CreateCompatibleDC() and CreateCompatibleBitmap() here.

- It uses the CDC::SelectObject() function to select the bmEmbossed bitmap into the memDCEmbossed memory DC. Now, any drawing on the memDCEmbossed Device Context will change the bmEmbossed bitmap.

- It uses CDC::GetPixel() to determine the color of the lower left pixel, which is used in our code as the transparent color. The pixel comes from the bitmap image associated with the memory Device Context.

- It enters a for loop to get the average color brightness for each pixel from the original bitmap.

- It uses CDC::BitBlt() to transfer the image from the memDC (and the original bitmap) into the memDCEmbossed (and the new bitmap we are creating).

- It enters another for loop, this time setting pixels in the memDCEmbossed Device Context (and therefore, the bmEmbossed bitmap) to one of our three colors, based on its basic color weight.

The DrawItem() Function.   The DrawItem() function is the routine that will be called by the framework to draw the actual button. Controls that have the Owner Drawn style set will have the DrawItem() function called when subclasses as we have done with the CPNImageButton class. The prototype for the function is shown in Code 5–60 and the actual function is shown in Code 5–61.

Much of the work of the DrawItem() function is to determine the size and display area of the control to be displayed, as well as determine the current state of the button (i.e., up, down, disabled). It then calls functions near the end of the function to actually display the control.

Code 5–60

```
void DrawItem(LPDRAWITEMSTRUCT lpDrawItemStruct);
```

Code 5–61

```
void CPNImageButton::DrawItem(LPDRAWITEMSTRUCT lpDrawItemStruct)
{
    CRect Rect = lpDrawItemStruct->rcItem;
    SIZE DrawArea;
    int XOffset, YOffset, YTextOffset=0, YImageOffset=0;
    UINT nOffset = 0;
    UINT nFrameStyle=0;
    int nStateFlag;
    CBitmap* pImage;

    CString Text;

    CDC DestDC;
    DestDC.Attach( lpDrawItemStruct->hDC );
```

```
// Based on the size of the button text, and the images, determine drawing
// positions of each.
GetWindowText( Text );
DrawArea = DestDC.GetTextExtent(Text);
DrawArea.cx += (m_ImageWidth+4);
if( DrawArea.cy > m_ImageHeight )
   YTextOffset = ( m_ImageHeight - DrawArea.cy ) /2;
else
{
   YImageOffset = (DrawArea.cy - m_ImageHeight) /2;
   DrawArea.cy = m_ImageHeight;
}
if( Text.Find( "&" ) >= 0 )
{
   CSize Tmp;
   Tmp = DestDC.GetTextExtent( "&" );
   DrawArea.cx -= Tmp.cx;
}
XOffset = (Rect.right - DrawArea.cx)/2;
YOffset = (Rect.bottom - DrawArea.cy)/2;

// Determine if button is in the selected state
if ( lpDrawItemStruct->itemState & ODS_SELECTED)
{
   nFrameStyle = DFCS_PUSHED;
   pImage = m_Down.GetSafeHandle() ? &m_Down : &m_Up;
   nOffset += 1;
}

// Determine if button is disabled
if( lpDrawItemStruct->itemState & ODS_DISABLED )
{
   nStateFlag = DSS_DISABLED;
   pImage = m_Disabled.GetSafeHandle() ? &m_Disabled : &m_Up;
}
else
{
   nStateFlag = DSS_NORMAL;
   pImage = &m_Up;
}

// Determine if button has the focus state
if ( lpDrawItemStruct->itemState & ODS_FOCUS )
   pImage = m_Focus.GetSafeHandle() ? &m_Focus : &m_Up;
// If button is selected, the use DrawFrameControl to display its frame
if( ! (lpDrawItemStruct->itemState & ODS_SELECTED) )
{
   // If the button is focused, then we need to draw the black rectangle,
   // and shrink the button a tiny bit (visual appearance of all buttons)
   if( lpDrawItemStruct->itemState & ODS_FOCUS )
```

```
        {
            DestDC.Rectangle(Rect.left, Rect.top, Rect.right, Rect.bottom );
            Rect.DeflateRect(1,1);
        }
        DestDC.DrawFrameControl( &Rect, DFC_BUTTON, DFCS_BUTTONPUSH |
        nFrameStyle);
    }
    else
    {
        // If it's not selected, then drawing is more complex
        // Create out pens and brushes for drawing, and draw a rectangle.
        CBrush NewBrush;
        NewBrush.CreateSolidBrush( ::GetSysColor( COLOR_3DFACE ) );
        CBrush* pOldBrush = (CBrush*)DestDC.SelectObject( &NewBrush );
        DestDC.Rectangle(Rect.left, Rect.top, Rect.right, Rect.bottom );
        CPen NewPen;
        NewPen.CreatePen( PS_SOLID, 1, GetSysColor(COLOR_3DSHADOW) );
        CPen* pOldPen = (CPen*)DestDC.SelectObject( &NewPen );
        // Then, shrink the rectangle a tiny bit, and draw the inner rectangle
        Rect.left++;
        Rect.top++;
        Rect.bottom--;
        Rect.right--;
        DestDC.Rectangle( Rect.left, Rect.top, Rect.right, Rect.bottom );
        DestDC.SelectObject( pOldPen );
        DestDC.SelectObject( pOldBrush );

    }
    if( m_ImageOnLeft )
    {
        // Draw the bitmap image, transparently, and then the text
        DrawTransparent( &DestDC, XOffset+nOffset, YOffset+nOffset+
        YImageOffset, pImage );
        DestDC.DrawState( CPoint(XOffset+m_ImageWidth+4+nOffset,
            YOffset+nOffset+YTextOffset),
            DrawArea, Text, DST_PREFIXTEXT|nStateFlag, TRUE, 0, (HBRUSH)0
);
    }
    else
    {
        // Draw the text, and then the bitmap image transparently
        DestDC.DrawState( CPoint(XOffset+nOffset, YOffset+nOffset+
        YTextOffset), DrawArea,
            Text, DST_PREFIXTEXT|nStateFlag, TRUE, 0, (HBRUSH)0 );
        DrawTransparent( &DestDC, XOffset+nOffset+DrawArea.cx+m_ImageWidth,
            YOffset+nOffset+YImageOffset, pImage );
    }
    // Draw the focus rectangle for the button
    if( ( lpDrawItemStruct->itemState & ODS_FOCUS ) )
    {
```

```
        RECT Rect2;
        Rect2 = Rect;
        Rect2.left += 3;
        Rect2.right -= 3;
        Rect2.top += 3;
        Rect2.bottom -= 3;
        DestDC.DrawFocusRect( &Rect2 );
    }
    DestDC.Detach();

//  CButton::OnDrawItem(nIDCtl, lpDrawItemStruct);
}
```

Here's what is happening in Code 5–61.

- CDC:GetTextExtent() is called to determine the height and width of the text that needs to be displayed (the buttons caption).
- The itemState member of the lpDrawItemStruct parameter is checked to determine the state of the control (up, down, disabled, etc.).
- The CGdiObject::GetSafeHandle() function is called to determine if the specified bitmap is actually loaded or not (for example, if the m_Down bitmap is loaded, the pImage is sent to point to it, othewise it is set to point to the m_Up bitmap).
- The CDC:Rectangle() function is used to draw the frame of the button if it is down.
- The CDC::DrawFrameControl() function is used to display the frame for the button. This will draw the button frame and surface, but no text or image.
- The CPNImageButton::DrawTransparent() function is called to draw the bitmap image (specified by pImage) in a transparent fashion.
- The CDC::DrawState() is used to display the text or caption of the button in either a normal ir disabled state.

Using the CPNImageButton Class.   Using the CPNImageButton Class is much easier than creating it. Once you have a class like this defined (as in, a custom class derived from a standard MFC window class with some additional features), you can simply use ClassWizard to map a member variable to it of Control category. This will require practically no lines of code!

Here's how to create the member variable:

1. Drop a normal button on your dialog.
2. Change the properties of that button so that it is Owner Draw.
3. Go to ClassWizard, and the Member Variable tab (see Figure 5–11).

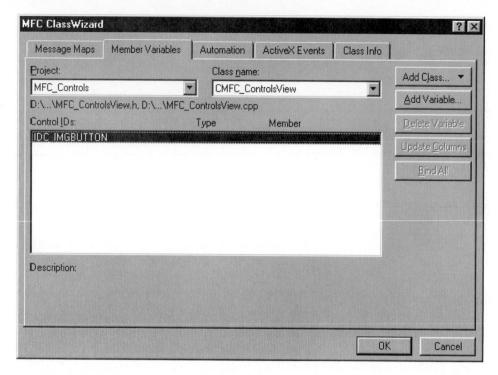

Figure 5–11 The MFC ClassWizard displays a list of on-screen controls.

4. Make sure your main dialog or View class is highlighted in the Class-Name field.
5. Select the button contol in the Control IDs list that you had added in step 1.
6. Click the Add Variable button.
7. The Add Member Variable dialog should be displayed.
8. Fill in the name of the member variable, such as m_ImageWithText.
9. Make sure the Category field says Control.
10. In the Variable Type, make sure you select CPNImageButton (see Figure 5–12).
11. Click the OK button.
12. Add #include "CPNImageButton.h" to the view or dialog class after creating the member variable.

Now with the member variable of Control category associated with the on-screen button, the only thing left to do is to set the bitmap to be used with the button. You

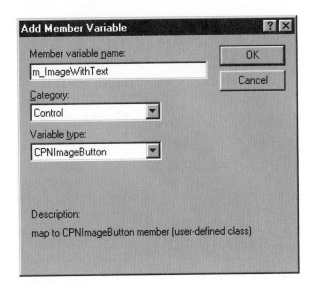

Figure 5–12 Add the m_ImageWithText variable to the class.

should call the SetData() function for the new member variable to set the image to be used. A good place to do this in the OnCreate() function of the View class, or the OnInitDialog() function of a dialog-based application. This is shown in Code 5–62. The code above assumes that you have created a bitmap with the bitmap editor of Visual C++, and change its properties so that its ID is IDB_CHECKUP.

Code 5–62

```
int CMFC_ControlsView::OnCreate(LPCREATESTRUCT lpCreateStruct)
{
        if (CFormView::OnCreate(lpCreateStruct) == -1)
                return -1;

        // TODO: Add your specialized creation code here
        // Image with Text button
        m_ImageWithText.SetData( TRUE, IDB_CHECKUP );
        return 0;
}
```

Checkboxes

Checkboxes (see Figure 5–13) provide the ability for the user to make a yes/no type selection easily. Checkboxes also support a "tri-state" property where the user may select between three different states: checked, not checked, and grayed.

An example of tri-state logic might be a street fair database with a "Within City" criteria. By checking the option, the user indicates that he or she wants to see information for events within his or her city. If the user unchecked the option, then the user wants to see events for outside his or her city. If the user grayed the option, then he or she wants to see all events inside and outside the city.

The example checkboxes in Figure 5–13 will all change the style properties of the checkbox on the right. The sample code demonstrates how to respond to user changes, as well as to determine how to retrieve the checked state of a checkbox and set an image for a checkbox.

Like buttons, checkboxes can also have icon or bitmap images associated with them, which is displayed instead of text. We will be using the same logic for enabling the images for a checkbox as we did for the button control.

You can also place an "&" in front of any character of the caption of a checkbox to make that character act as the hotkey for the checkbox. For example, if the caption for a checkbox was "&Hot," then it would appear on screen as H̲ot and if the user press Alt-H then that checkbox would be selected.

Creating a Checkbox at Runtime

SDK

It is easier to create, position, and size checkboxes using the dialog editor than it is to dynamically create and destroy windows. However, the following functions are a simplified manner of dynamically creating a child combo box control as shown in Code 5–63.

Code 5–63 uses the CreateWindow() function to create a BUTTON control, with at least the BS_AUTOCHECKBOX style, thereby creating a checkbox control. If the window was successfully created, then the font for the parent window is retrieved and the new control is set to use that font via the WM_GETFONT() and WM_SET-FONT messages. Finally, the default state is set for the check status (from the nState parameter).

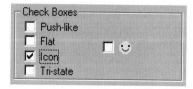

Figure 5–13   Common checkboxes.

Code 5-63

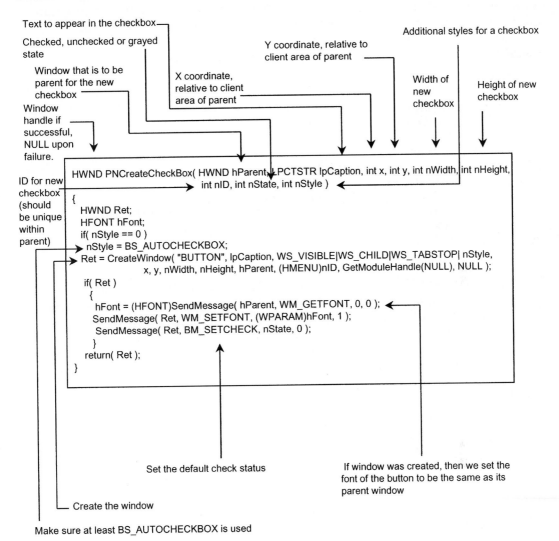

Text to appear in the checkbox

Checked, unchecked or grayed state

Window that is to be parent for the new checkbox

Window handle if successful, NULL upon failure.

X coordinate, relative to client area of parent

Y coordinate, relative to client area of parent

Additional styles for a checkbox

Width of new checkbox

Height of new checkbox

ID for new checkbox (should be unique within parent)

```
HWND PNCreateCheckBox( HWND hParent, LPCTSTR lpCaption, int x, int y, int nWidth, int nHeight,
                       int nID, int nState, int nStyle )
{
    HWND Ret;
    HFONT hFont;
    if( nStyle == 0 )
        nStyle = BS_AUTOCHECKBOX;
    Ret = CreateWindow( "BUTTON", lpCaption, WS_VISIBLE|WS_CHILD|WS_TABSTOP| nStyle,
                        x, y, nWidth, nHeight, hParent, (HMENU)nID, GetModuleHandle(NULL), NULL );
    if( Ret )
    {
        hFont = (HFONT)SendMessage( hParent, WM_GETFONT, 0, 0 );
        SendMessage( Ret, WM_SETFONT, (WPARAM)hFont, 1 );
        SendMessage( Ret, BM_SETCHECK, nState, 0 );
    }
    return( Ret );
}
```

Set the default check status

If window was created, then we set the font of the button to be the same as its parent window

Create the window

Make sure at least BS_AUTOCHECKBOX is used

MFC

In order to create a checkbox at runtime, declare a CButton data member for our View or Dialog class (CMFC_ControlsView.h in our sample project) and then call the Create() member function for it. Begin by adding Code 5-64 to the .h file.

Code 5-64

```
CButton m_DynaCheck;
```

Call the CButton::Create() member function to create the child window on screen. We will do this in the CFormView::OnCreate() function of our sample program, in CMFC_ControlsView.cpp. This function would be made to look Code 5–65.

Code 5–65

```
int CMFC_ControlsView::OnCreate(LPCREATESTRUCT lpCreateStruct)
{
        if (CFormView::OnCreate(lpCreateStruct) == -1)
                return -1;

        CRect PosAndSize;

        // Dynamically create Checkbox
        PosAndSize.SetRect( 411, 275, 485, 299 );
        m_DynaCheck.Create( "Dynamic", WS_VISIBLE|WS_CHILD|BS_AUTOCHECKBOX,
            PosAndSize, this, 4006 );
        return( 0 );
}
```

The Create() function in Code 5–65 eventually calls the CreateWindow() function. The last step is to set the font of the child window to match that of its parent. In order to do this, add code to the CFormView::OnInitialUpdate() function for our View class (CMFC_ControlsView.cpp in our sample). In a dialog-based application you would do so in the OnInitDialog() function. The code to set the child control to use the same font as its parent dialog is shown in Code 5–66.

Code 5–66

```
void CMFC_ControlsView::OnInitialUpdate()
{
        CFormView::OnInitialUpdate();
        GetParentFrame()->RecalcLayout();
        ResizeParentToFit();

        // Set our dynamically create checkbox font
        m_DynaCheck.SetFont( GetFont() );
}
```

The code above calls the GetFont() function to retrieve the CFont object used by the View class. Keep in mind that the C++ *this* pointer is available because the Code 5–66 is a View class member function. So the this pointer refers to the parent window class. Calling GetFont() will retrieve the parents font, and calling m_DynCheck.SetFont will tell that child window to use that font.

Responding to Checkbox Events

SDK

The child checkbox sends a WM_COMMAND message to its parent window with a BN_CLICKED notification code. Given the nature of the checkbox, you don't have to respond to user clicks on it unless you want to provide immediate feedback for the control.

For example, if there is a set of checkboxes a user might select before proceeding to the next step of a program, you may simply wait for them to click a Next button before handling the check statuses. You then get the check states for each of the checkboxes. Alternatively, you might want to provide immediate feedback to the user, as they check and uncheck the checkboxes (where you would handle the WM_CMMAND message).

Code 5-67 is an example of handling the checkbox events also demonstrates how you would retrieve the current setting for the checkbox

Code 5-67

```
LRESULT CALLBACK DialogProc( HWND hwndDlg, UINT uMsg, WPARAM wParam, LPARAM
lParam )
{
    int wID;
    int wNotification;
    HWND hChild;

    switch( uMsg )
    {
        // Portions of code removed for readability
        case WM_COMMAND: // A message from a control or menu item
                // Parse out WM_COMMAND parameters to be more readable
                wID = LOWORD(wParam);
                wNotification = HIWORD(wParam);
                hChild = (HWND) lParam;

                // Check Boxes
                if( (wID == IDC_CHECKPUSHLIKE ) && (wNotification ==
                BN_CLICKED) )
                {
                    if( IsDlgButtonChecked( hwndDlg, IDC_CHECKPUSHLIKE ) )
                            // Do something when it's checked
                    else
                            // Do something when its unchecked
                }
        // Portions of code removed for readability
```

Code 5–67 is in the WM_COMMAND message handler for your dialog procedure. The if test will test to see if the control that generated the message is the IDC_CHECKPUSHLIKE control (our sample checkbox) and that its notification code was that it was clicked. If that's true, then inside the if body we call the IsDlgButtonChecked() function, which tells you if the checkbox is checked.

Notice that within the code there is nothing needed to toggle the checkbox state on and off. This is done automatically by the control itself when it has the BS_AUTO-CHECKBOX style.

MFC

Responding to a checkbox doesn't need to be an immediate-response action. Checkboxes will retain their value as long as they are displayed and will automatically toggle their states (from check to unchecked to checked, etc.) as the user clicks on them. Often a program will not respond immediately to checkboxes and instead wait for some other action, such as clicking a button, after which the program determines the status of all checkboxes at that time.

In order to respond to user events for a checkbox, go to the ClassWizard dialog by selecting the View/ClassWizard main menu items. Then, in ClassWizard, select the Message Map tab. Once in the Message Map tab, make sure that the Class Name field contains the view or dialog class that you want to handle the message map (CMFC_ControlsView in our sample). Also be sure that the Object IDs item has the ID for the checkbox you want to respond to and that the BN_CLICKED is selected in the Message IDs list box as shown in Figure 5–14.

Once the items are selected, click the Add Function button and click OK to select the suggested function name. Now, when the user clicks the checkbox, it will invoke this newly added function. The function in Figure 5–14 is called OnCheck-flat(). Once you've added the message map handler, it will look like Code 5–68. You can now do whatever you want in response to the checkbox click, within the OnCheckflat() function.

Code 5–68

```
void CMFC_ControlsView::OnCheckflat()
{
        // TODO: Add your control notification handler code here

}
```

Dynamically Created Controls

Your application requires a handler for each dynamically created control. You will need to create the handler manually. ClassWizard's Message Map tab cannot be used with controls created dynamically at runtime control because ClassWizard

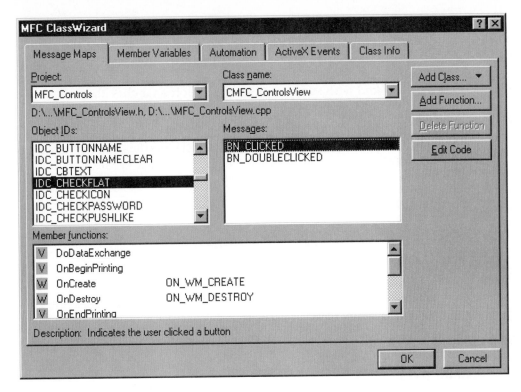

Figure 5–14 ClassWizard Message Maps tab for a checkbox.

does not know these controls exist at designtime. Here's how to manually add a message map.

1. Add handler function prototype in the message map section of the class definition. The main View or Dialog class has a section in its .h file that contains a comment of //{{AFX_MSG. This is where ClassWizard stores its handler function prototypes. Add your own handler just after the closing comment of //}}AFX_MSG, as shown in Code 5–69. The code in boldface is the line we added. Notice that it has an "afx_msg void" prefix and accepts no parameters. Code 5–69 is in the CMFC_ControlsView.h file for our sample project.

Code 5-69

```
protected:
        //{{AFX_MSG(CMFC_ControlsView)
        afx_msg int OnCreate(LPCREATESTRUCT lpCreateStruct);
        afx_msg void OnDestroy();
        //}}AFX_MSG
        afx_msg void OnClickDynamicCheck();
        DECLARE_MESSAGE_MAP()
};
```

2. Add the Message Map entry in the .cpp file. Locate the BEGIN_MES-SAGE_MAP macro in the main view or dialog class .cpp file (our sample is called CMFC_ControlsView.cpp) as illustrated in Code 5–70. This is where ClassWizard inserts its message map entries to associate a function to be invoked with various messages (such as a checkbox click). We will add an entry after the //}}AFX_MSG_MAP line, to invoke our new handler as shown in Code 5–71.

Code 5–71 states that when a BN_CLICKED notification comes from child ID 4006 (as we used in our dynamic checkbox creation example), that the OnClickDynamicCheck() function should be invoked.

Code 5–70

```
BEGIN_MESSAGE_MAP(CMFC_ControlsView, CFormView)
    //{{AFX_MSG_MAP(CMFC_ControlsView)
    //}}AFX_MSG_MAP
    // Standard printing commands
    ON_COMMAND(ID_FILE_PRINT, CFormView::OnFilePrint)
    ON_COMMAND(ID_FILE_PRINT_DIRECT, CFormView::OnFilePrint)
    ON_COMMAND(ID_FILE_PRINT_PREVIEW, CFormView::
    OnFilePrintPreview)
END_MESSAGE_MAP()
```

Code 5–71

```
BEGIN_MESSAGE_MAP(CMFC_ControlsView, CFormView)
    //{{AFX_MSG_MAP(CMFC_ControlsView)
    //}}AFX_MSG_MAP
    // Standard printing commands
    ON_BN_CLICKED(4006, OnClickDynamicCheck)
    ON_COMMAND(ID_FILE_PRINT, CFormView::OnFilePrint)
    ON_COMMAND(ID_FILE_PRINT_DIRECT, CFormView::
    OnFilePrint)
    ON_COMMAND(ID_FILE_PRINT_PREVIEW, CFormView::
    OnFilePrintPreview)
END_MESSAGE_MAP()
```

3. Add the actual handler function. Add the handler function that we created the prototype for in the .h file and the manual entry for in the message map. The function is illustrated in Code 5–72. With the above steps, the manually added OnClickDynamicCheck() will be invoked when the user clicks the dynamically created checkbox (again, the ID of 4006 for the checkbox is from the Dynamic checkbox create example).

Code 5–72

```
void CMFC_ControlsView::OnClickDynamicCheck()
{
    MessageBox( "You clicked the dynamic checkbox" );
}
```

Changing or Determining Checkbox Status

SDK

In order to determine if a checkbox is checked, you can either send the BM_GETCHECK directly to the child window handle of the checkbox or you can call the IsDlgButtonChecked(). Code 5–73 uses the BM_GETCHECK message. This method is useful when you already have the child window handle, such as when you might check it in response to a WM_COMMAND message as in Code 5–74. Using IsDlgButtonChecked() function, its easier to get a checkbox status for a controls that may not have sent the notification—for example, getting the state from several checkboxes when the user clicks a button as shown in Code 5–75. In either of these methods, the return value will be one of the values shown in Table 5.1.

Code 5–73

```
int State = SendMessage( hChild, BM_GETCHECK, 0, 0 );
```

Code 5–74

```
LRESULT CALLBACK DialogProc( HWND hwndDlg, UINT uMsg, WPARAM wParam, LPARAM
lParam )
{
    int wID;
    int wNotification;
    HWND hChild;

    switch( uMsg )
    {
        case WM_COMMAND: // A message from a control or menu item
            // Parse out WM_COMMAND parameters to be more readable
            wID = LOWORD(wParam);
            wNotification = HIWORD(wParam);
            hChild = (HWND) lParam;

            // Did the message come from the IDC_CHECKPUSHLIKE checkbox?
            if( (wID == IDC_CHECKPUSHLIKE ) && (wNotification == BN_CLICKED) )
            {
                // If so, determine if checked or not
                if( SendMessage( hChild, BM_HETCHECK, 0, 0 ) = BST_CHECKED )
                    // The checkbox is checked
                else
                    // It's not checked
```

Code 5–75

```
LRESULT CALLBACK DialogProc( HWND hwndDlg, UINT uMsg, WPARAM wParam, LPARAM
lParam )
{
```

```
int wID;
int wNotification;
HWND hChild;

switch( uMsg )
{
    case WM_COMMAND: // A message from a control or menu item
        // Parse out WM_COMMAND parameters to be more readable
        wID = LOWORD(wParam);
        wNotification = HIWORD(wParam);
        hChild = (HWND) lParam;

    if( (wID == IDC_BUTTONNAMECLEAR) && wNotification == BN_CLICKED )
    {

        if( IsDlgButtonChecked( hwndDlg, IDC_CHECKPUSHLIKE ) ==
        BST_CHECKED )
            // The IDC_CHECKPUSHLIKE is checked
        else
            // The IDC_CHECKPUSHLIKE is not checked

        if( IsDlgButtonChecked( hwndDlg, IDC_CHECKFLAT ) ) ==
        BST_CHECKED )
            // The IDC_CHECKFLAT is checked
        else
            // The IDC_CHECKFLAT is not checked
        // Do whatever other button processing is needed
    }
    // Portions of removed for readability
```

Table 5.1   Return Values Used to Determine the Status of a Checkbox

Value	Meaning
BST_CHECKED	Checkbox is checked
BST_INDETERMINATE	Checkbox is grayed (only for checkboxes with the BS_3STATE or BS_AUTO3STATE style)
BST_UNCHECKED	Checkbox is not checked

To set the checkbox state, you can send a BM_SETCHECK message (see Code 5–76) to the child control or you can call CheckDlgButton() function (see Code 5–77). As with the previous example, the BM_SETCHECK message is handy when you already have the child control window handle, and the CheckDlgButton is handy when you want to set a number of checkbox items at once (calling Check-DlgButton repeatedly).

Code 5-76

```
SendMessage( hChild, BM_SETCHECK, BST_CHECKED, 0 );
```

Code 5-77

```
CheckDlgButton( hParent, IDC_CHECKPUSHLIKE, BST_CHECKED );
CheckDlgButton( hParent, IDC_CHECKFLAT, BST_UNCHECKED );
```

The third parameter to SendMessage() with BM_SETCHECK, or the third parameter to CheckDlgButton(), is BST_CHECKED, BST_INDETERMINATE, or BST_UNCHECKED.

Be sure to set your checkbox status when your dialog starts up in the WM_INITDIALOG handler as shown in Code 5-78.

Code 5-78

```
LRESULT CALLBACK DialogProc( HWND hwndDlg, UINT uMsg, WPARAM wParam, LPARAM
lParam )
{
    int wID;
    int wNotification;
    HWND hChild;

    switch( uMsg )
    {
    // Portions of code removed for readability
        case WM_INITDIALOG:
            // Note: Default for checkboxes is already unchecked
            CheckDlgButton( hwndDlg, IDC_CHECKPUSHLIKE, BST_UNCHECKED );
            CheckDlgButton( hwndDlg, IDC_CHECKFLAT, BST_UNCHECKED );
            CheckDlgButton( hwndDlg, IDC_CHECKICON, BST_UNCHECKED );
            CheckDlgButton( hwndDlg, IDC_CHECKTRISTATE, BST_UNCHECKED );
            return( TRUE );
    // Portions of code removed for readability
```

MFC

Call the CWnd::IsDlgButtonChecked() function (see Code 5-79) to determine the status of a checkbox. Call the CWnd::CheckDlgButton() function to change the setting of a checkbox. Both functions are in the CWnd class and will be inherited by the View or Dialog class.

Code 5-79

```
void CMFC_ControlsView::OnCheckflat()
{
        // Get pointer to the IDC_SAMPLE checkbox
        CButton* pSample = (CButton*)GetDlgItem( IDC_CHECKSAMPLE );
        if( pCheckBox )
```

```
{
        // Determine if the IDC_CHECKFLAT checkbox is checked or not
        if( IsDlgButtonChecked( IDC_CHECKFLAT ) )
                pSample->ModifyStyle( 0, BS_FLAT );
        else
                pSample->ModifyStyle( BS_FLAT, 0 );
        pSample->InvalidateRect( 0 );
}

}
```

In the example Code 5–79, the OnCheckflat() function might be a function that was a message map handler for the IDC_CHECKFLAT checkbox, which is called when the user clicks that checkbox. In response to the click, CWnd::GetDlgItem() is called to retrieve a CButton pointer for the IDC_CHECKSAMPLE checkbox. IsDlgButtonChecked() is called next with the ID of the checkbox that we are checking the status of (IDC_CHECKFLAT in this example).

As an alternative, you can also call the CButton::GetCheck ()function for the CButton object itself as shown in Code 5–80. Both the IsDlgButtonChecked() and Getcheck() functions return a value shown in Table 5.2.

Code 5–80

```
CButton* pCheck = (CButton*)GetDlgItem( IDC_CHECKFLAT );
if( pCheck->GetCheck() == BST_CHECKED )
        // it's checked
else
        // it's not checked
```

Table 5.2   Values for Getting or Setting Checkbox Statuses

Value	Meaning
BST_CHECKED	Checkbox is checked
BST_INDETERMINATE	Checkbox is grayed (only for checkboxes with the BS_3STATE or BS_AUTO3STATE style)
BST_UNCHECKED	Checkbox is not checked

The CWnd::CheckDlgButton() is used to set or clear the status of a checkbox as illustrated in Code 5–81. You can call this function from any member function of your view or dialog class that contains the checkbox.

You can also call the CButton::SetCheck() member function for the CButton class to set or clear the check status as shown in Code 5–82.

Code 5-81

```
CheckDlgButton( IDC_CHECKFLAT, BST_CHECKED );
```

Code 5-82

```
CButton* pCheck = (CButton*) GetDlgItem( IDC_CHECKFLAT );
pCheck->SetCheck( BST_CHECKED );
```

Radio Buttons

Radio buttons allow easy selection of one out of several possible items. They can be automatically mutually exclusive. In Figure 5–15, we have six groups of radio buttons divided into various appearance styles. Note that they can be laid out horizontally or vertically. The sixth column contains simple radio buttons that were created dynamically but have the same style as the first column. Radio buttons are really a BUTTON class control, but with the BS_AUTORADIOBUTTON style. Only one item from each column may be selected by the user in the any of the columns in Figure 5–15.

The Default column is how radio buttons normally look when dropped on the form. The Push-like column has the Push-like property for each radio button set on. The Icon column has the Icon property set for each control, and the Icon and Push-like column has both Icon and Push-like property set for each control. The Flat column shows radio buttons with the Flat property set. These properties can be set for the individual control when the radio buttons are on a dialog by changing the properties of the control in the dialog editor. Other properties such as Client Edge can also change appearance; we suggest you experiment with different styles to see their effects.

The two Icon columns that have an image require additional programming. Controls with images must have their image set at runtime, the image cannot be selected at design time with the dialog editor. But, we will be reusing the PNSetButtonImage function from the Buttons section to set the image for the button easily (i.e., one line of code) for SDK programs; MFC programs have some basic support to set the button image easily.

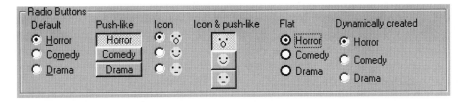

Figure 5–15 Common radio buttons.

The presence of the underlined characters in the text (such as "H" in Horror in the first column) acts as a hotkey—pressing Alt-H will automatically select that item. In order to do this, simply make the caption of the radio button "&Horror." If you precede a letter or window text with an ampersand (&), then the letter that follows serves as its hotkey.

When the user clicks a button, it sends a WM_COMMAND message to the parent window and in the wParam and lParam parameters indicates the ID of the control, the handle to the child window, and the notification code that a click occurred. In the sections below we will give examples in SDK and MFC format of how to respond to these messages. But, keep in mind that unlike a normal button, you don't necessarily need to respond to each click. Since radio buttons are normally mutually exclusive, you can simply determine later on (for example, in response to another button click) the radio button the user selected.

For example, imagine there may be three radio buttons and a normal pushbutton. When the user clicks the pushbutton, the program can inspect the radio buttons and determine how to proceed. It wouldn't need to add the handler to respond to radio selection events. If, however, you wanted some other on-screen controls to be enabled or disabled (for example) as different choices were made, then you might want to respond to the radio button events.

Grouping Radio Buttons and Tabbing

In order to group radio buttons so that only one button in a set can be on at a time, the first button of the set must have the WS_GROUP or Group style set. Then, subsequent buttons in creation or tab order without the WS_GROUP style are considered a part of that group. The next radio button with the WS_GROUP style set begins a whole new group. In the example at the beginning of this topic, the first item in each of the six columns has the Group property set, and the ones below it do not. You can change the style of the buttons easily by checking the Group option in the properties for the radio buttons. Also, if you want the user to be able to tab into the radio group, then make sure you apply the WS_TABSTOP property to the first radio button (along with the Group property).

Creating a Radio Button at Runtime

SDK

In order to create a radio button dynamically at runtime, we will call the CreateWindow() function specifying "BUTTON" as the window class and the desired type of radio button. We have a simplified function, as illustrated in Code 5–83. Now, with this function, we can easily create radio buttons. An example of creating the button with the helper function Code 5–83 is shown in Code 5–84.

Notice how the first call specifies the WS_GROUP option, bsut the second call does not. These two buttons will now be mutually exclusive in selection. You could also specify the BS_PUSHLIKE and/or BS_ICON styles for the last parameter to PN-CreateRadioButton to apply those styles. Note: BS_PUSHLIKE is not currently documented in VC++ online help.

Also note that there were bugs in VC++ prior to version 6 where once you selected the Push-like style in the dialog editor, you couldn't undo it. While fixed in version 6, in previous versions you need to call up the .rc file for your project with a text editor like Notepad and manually remove the BS_PUSHLIKE flag from the control.

Code 5–83

```
// PNCreateRadioButton - Simplified radio button creation function.
// Parameters:
//      hParent - Window that is to be parent for the new button
//      lpCaption - Text to appear in the button (a string)
//      x - X coordinate, relative to client area of parent
//      y - Y coordinate, relative to client area of parent
//      nWidth - Width of new button
//      nHeight - Height of new button
//      nID - ID for new button (should be unique within parent)
//      nStyle - Additional styles for a button
// Returns: Window handle if succesful, NULL upon failure.
HWND PNCreateRadioButton( HWND hParent, LPCTSTR lpCaption, int x, int
      y, int nWidth, int nHeight, int nID, int nStyle )
{
      HWND Ret;
      HFONT hFont;

      // Create the window
      Ret = CreateWindow( "BUTTON", lpCaption,
            WS_VISIBLE|WS_CHILD|WS_TABSTOP|BS_AUTORADIOBUTTON | nStyle,
            x, y, nWidth, nHeight, hParent, (HMENU)nID,
            GetModuleHandle(NULL), NULL );
      if( Ret )
      {
            // If window was created, then we set the font of
            // the button to be the same as its parent window
            hFont = (HFONT)SendMessage( hParent, WM_GETFONT, 0, 0 );
            SendMessage( Ret, WM_SETFONT, (WPARAM)hFont, 1 );
      }
      return( Ret );
}
```

Code 5–84

```
LRESULT CALLBACK DialogProc( HWND hwndDlg, UINT uMsg, WPARAM wParam, LPARAM
lParam )
{

      switch( uMsg )
```

```
{
    case WM_INITDIALOG:
        PNCreateRadioButton( hwndDlg, "DynaCreated1", 4, 80,
        100, 24, 4001, WS_GROUP );
        PNCreateRadioButton( hwndDlg, "DynaCreated2", 4, 100,
        100, 24, 4002, 0 );
        return( TRUE );
```

MFC

In order to create a window dynamically in MFC, we are going to add CButton member variables to the View class (it would be the main dialog class if this were a dialog-based application). We will call the Create member variable for these member variables in the OnCreate() handler and we set up their font in the OnInitialUpdate() function. All this takes place in the View class, which is CMFC_ControlsView.cpp for our sample. You can also do it in a dialog-based application's OnInitDialog function.

In order to add the data members, add Code 5–85 inside the class definition for your View class (in CMFC_ControlsView.h for our sample):

Code 5–85

```
CButton m_DynaRadio1, m_DynaRadio2;
```

Next, go to the OnCreate() function for the View class or OnInitDialog() function if your main window was a dialog object. If the OnCreate() function is not already in your View class, add it using the ClassWizard (this is described alone in the Dynamic Button Creation, Response, and Destruction, MFC section). Add Code 5–86 to the OnCreate() function.

Code 5–86

```
int CMFC_ControlsView::OnCreate(LPCREATESTRUCT lpCreateStruct)
{
    if (CFormView::OnCreate(lpCreateStruct) == -1)
        return -1;

    // Initialize the m_DynaRadio1 and m_DynaRadio2 object2, creating
    // the window.
    // See OnInitialUpdate also
    CRect PosAndSize;
    PosAndSize.SetRect(4, 80, 4+100, 80+24);
    m_DynaRadio1.Create( "DynaCreate1",
        WS_VISIBLE|WS_CHILD|WS_GROUP|WS_TABSTOP|BS_AUTORADIOBUTTON,
        PosAndSize, this, 4001 );
    PosAndSize.SetRect(4, 100, 4+100, 100+24);
    m_DynaRadio2.Create( "DynaCreate2", WS_VISIBLE|WS_CHILD|BS_AUTORA-
    DIOBUTTON, PosAndSize, this, 4001 );
    return 0;
}
```

In the OnInitialUpdate(), add the code to set the font of the new child windows to the same as their parent. Remember that this is a Document/View program, and we created our dynamic radio buttons on the view form. So, if we call GetFont() directly in one of the view member functions, it will get the font for the view, or our primary display window. This code is illustrated in Code 5–87.

Code 5–87

```
void CMFC_ControlsView::OnInitialUpdate()
{
        CFormView::OnInitialUpdate();
        GetParentFrame()->RecalcLayout();
        ResizeParentToFit();

        // Since this is a CFormView, the font for the main window changes
        // after it is created in the OnCreate function. So we need to set
        // the font for our child window to be like the parent here, and
        // not in OnCreate

        m_DynaRadio1.SetFont( GetFont() );
        m_DynaRadio2.SetFont( GetFont() );
}
```

Responding to Radio Button Clicks

SDK

For an SDK program to respond to a radio button selection, it adds code in the WM_COMMAND handler (and adds a WM_COMMAND handler if one is not already present) as shown in Code 5–88.

Code 5–88

```
LRESULT CALLBACK DialogProc( HWND hwndDlg, UINT uMsg, WPARAM wParam, LPARAM
lParam )
{
    int wID;
    int wNotification;
    HWND hChild;

    switch( uMsg )
    {
      case WM_COMMAND: // A message from a control or menu item
          // Parse out WM_COMMAND parameters to be more readable
          wID = LOWORD(wParam);
          wNotification = HIWORD(wParam);
          hChild = (HWND) lParam;
          // Was the IDC_RADIOCOMEDYA radio button clicked?
          if( (wID == IDC_RADIOCOMEDYA) && wNotification == BN_CLICKED )
```

```
MessageBox( hwndDlg, "You selected 'Comedy'", "Information",
MB_OK );
```

Code 5–88 demonstrates how the WM_COMMAND message is handled and the wParam and lParam parameters are processed to get the ID, notification code, and window handle of the child control sending the WM_COMMAND.

The "if" test shows how to determine if the child ID is the radio button we are interested in (IDC_RADIOCOMEDYA in this example) and was the BN_CLICKED notification code. Code 5–88 uses a Message Box to inform the user. We could, however, enable or disable other controls on the same form. This code above would be placed in the Window or Dialog Procedure for the parent window that contains the radio buttons.

MFC

In order to respond to user clicks on a radio button (which will select that button), add a message map using ClassWizard for that button. Repeat these steps for each radio button. Remember that the application does not need to respond to buttons once they are selected. Instead, you can simply inspect the values of the buttons when you wanted to determine which one was selected. Figure 5–16 shows how this is done using the ClassWizard.

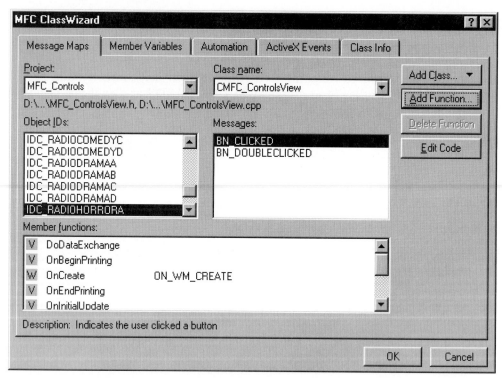

Figure 5–16 ClassWizard Message Maps for a radio button.

To respond to a single button:

1. Select the View menu choice, and then ClassWizard to get into the ClassWizard.
2. Go to the Message Maps tab of the ClassWizard screen.
3. Make sure the view or dialog for your project is selected in the Class-Name item in ClassWizard (CMFC_ControlsView in our sample).
4. Highlight the ID of the desired radio button in the Object IDs list.
5. Highlight the BN_CLICKED item in the Messages list.
6. Click the Add Function button.
7. Click the OK button on the next dialog that suggests a new function name.

Once you complete these steps, the handler for the BN_CLICKED event of the desired control is added to your View class .cpp file (MFC_ControlsView.cpp in our sample). The function is empty and will look like Code 5–89. You can perform the tasks you want here.

Code 5–89

```
void CMFC_ControlsView::OnRadiohorrora()
{
        // TODO: Add your control notification handler code here

}
```

Determining if Radio Button Is Checked

SDK

In order to determine if a radio button is checked, we can simply use either the Is-DlgItemChecked() function or we can send the child control a BM_GETCHECK message as illustrated in Code 5–90.

Both the SendMessage() and the IsDlgButtonChecked() can return one of the following values:

BST_CHECKED	The radio button is checked
BST_INDETERMINATE	Button is grayed (only in 3-State buttons
BST_UNCHECKED	Button is not checked

Code 5–90

```
// Assumes that hChild is the HWND for the radio button
if( SendMessage( hChild, BM_GETCHECK, 0, 0 ) & BST_CHECKED )
        // Button is checked

// Assumes that hWnd is the parent window HWND for the radio button,
```

```
// and IDC_RADIO1 is the ID of the radio button.
if( IsDlgButtonChecked( hWnd, IDC_RADIO1 ) == BST_CHECKED)
        // Button is checked
```

You can use Code 5–90 anywhere in your program, as long as hChild or hWnd are valid. For example, hWnd might be the window handle to the parent window (from the Window or Dialog Procedure's first parameter) or hChild might have been initialized using GetDlgItem, as illustrated in Code 5–91. hwndDlg is the main (parent) window handle and IDC_RADIOHORRORA is the ID for the radio button.

Code 5–91

```
HWND hRadio = GetDlgItem( hwndDlg, IDC_RADIOHORRORA );
```

MFC

In order to determine if a radio button is checked, we can simply use either the CWnd::IsDlgButtonChecked() message, or we can use the CButton class along with the GetDlgItem() function to retrieve a pointer for the desired radio button control. Examples of both methods are illustrated in Code 5–92.

Code 5–92

```
// Method one: Using a CButton pointer and GetDlgItem
CButton* pButton= (CButton*)GetDlgItem( IDC_RADIOHORRORB );

if( pButton->GetCheck() == 1 )
     MessageBox( "HorrorB is checked" );

// Method two: Using IsDlgButtonChecked function
if( IsDlgButtonChecked( IDC_RADIOCOMEDYB ) == 1 )
     MessageBox( "ComedB is checked" );
```

NOTE

MFC is just a set of wrapper classes, for the SDK data types, and functions. We can also use the SendMessage method from the SDK example to accomplish the same task.

Setting a Radio Button Programmatically

SDK

When you place a radio button on a form in your dialog editor, you can't set its checked status as a property. Instead, to define the initial checked item in a group, you need to do so programmatically. The WM_INITDIALOG message is a good place

---

to do this, and we will use the CheckRadioButton() function as shown in Code 5–93.

Code 5–93

```
LRESULT CALLBACK DialogProc( HWND hwndDlg, UINT uMsg, WPARAM wParam, LPARAM
lParam )
{

    switch( uMsg )
    {
        case WM_INITDIALOG:
            CheckRadioButton( hwndDlg, IDC_RADIOHORRORA, IDC_RADIODRAMAA,
                IDC_RADIOHORRORA );
```

Code 5–93 shows how a WM_INITDIALOG might call the CheckRadioButton() function. CheckRadioButton has four parameters: first is the parent window handle, next is the ID of the first radio button of a group, followed by the ID of the last radio button in the group. The fourth parameter is the ID of the button in that group to make selected. CheckRadioButton() in Code 5–93 will check the IDC_RADIO-HORRORA control for the group of buttons between and including IDC_RADIO-HORRORA and IDC_RADIODRAMAA and removes the check from any other button in that range.

MFC

When you place a radio button on a form in your dialog editor, you can't set its checked status as a property. Instead, you will need to define the initial checked item in a group using code.

In an MFC program you would do this in the OnInitDialog() function of your main dialog if your project were a dialog-based application, or in the OnInitialUpdate() function of your View class if it were a document-view based program (this depends on how you created the project with AppWizard). Regardless if it is a view or a dialog-based application, however, you call the CWnd::CheckRadioButton() function as shown in Code 5–94.

Code 5–94

```
void CMFC_ControlsView::OnInitialUpdate()
{
        CFormView::OnInitialUpdate();
        GetParentFrame()->RecalcLayout();
        ResizeParentToFit();

        // Portions of code removed for readability
        CheckRadioButton( IDC_RADIOHORRORA, IDC_RADIODRAMAA, IDC_
        RADIOHORRORA );
}
```

Code 5–94 shows how the OnInitialUpdate() handler function can call the Check-RadioButton() function. CheckRadioButton() has three parameters. Two of the parameters are the IDs of the first and last radio buttons in a group. The third parameter is the ID of the button in that group to make selected. CheckRadioButton() in the example above will check the IDC_RADIOHORRORA control for the group of buttons between (and including) IDC_RADIOHORRORA, and IDC_RADIO-DRAMAA and will remove the check from any other button in that range.

Using Images with Radio Buttons

SDK

Our example radio buttons at the start of this section showed some with images. In order to assign an image to a button, we will assume that we have an Icon created in the resource editor that is a 16×16 image (not the default 32×32). The steps for assigning an image to a radio button are identical to that of assigning an image to a pushbutton. This means that we can use the PNSetButtonImage() function to load and assign the icon to a radio button. Here are the steps for adding an image to a button using the SDK. Code 5–95 is a typical dialog procedure used to display and destroy a button. In Code 5–95, we assume you have icons with IDs of IDI_ICON-HORROR, IDI_COMEDY, and IDI_ICONDRAMA.

1. Create your icon in the icon resource editor.
2. In the WM_INITDIALOG handler for your dialog, or at any point after the radio button window has been created, call the PNSetButtonImage() function.
3. In the WM_DESTROY handler for your dialog (or, at any time you want to remove or change the icon for the button), call the PNClearButtonIm-age() function.

Code 5–95

```
LRESULT CALLBACK DialogProc( HWND hwndDlg, UINT uMsg, WPARAM wParam, LPARAM
lParam )
{

    switch( uMsg )
    {
    case WM_INITDIALOG:
        // Set images for our buttons
        PNSetButtonImage( hwndDlg, IDC_RADIOHORRORC, IDI_ICONHORROR );
        PNSetButtonImage( hwndDlg, IDC_RADIOCOMEDYC, IDI_ICONCOMEDY );
        PNSetButtonImage( hwndDlg, IDC_RADIODRAMAC, IDI_ICONDRAMA );
        return( TRUE );
    case WM_DESTROY:
        PNClearButtonImage( hwndDlg, IDC_RADIOHORRORC );
        PNClearButtonImage( hwndDlg, IDC_RADIOCOMEDYC );
        PNClearButtonImage( hwndDlg, IDC_RADIODRAMAC );
```

```
        // Portions of code removed for readability
    }
    return( FALSE );
}
```

MFC

Our example radio buttons at the start of this section showed some with images. In order to assign an image to a button, we assume that we have an Icon created in the resource editor that is a 16×16 image. The steps for assigning an image to a radio button are identical to that of assigning an image to a pushbutton. This means that we can use the PNSetButtonImage (defined in the *Simple Image Without Text Button, SDK* section) function to load and assign the icon to a radio button. Here is how to add an image to a button using MFC.

1. Create your icon in the icon resource editor.
2. In the OnInitialUpdate function (if your program is Document/View based) or the OnInitDialog() function (if your program is dialog-based), call the PNSetButtonImage() function to select the image.
3. In the OnDestroy() handler for your dialog (or, at any time you want to remove or change the icon for the button), call the PNClearButtonImage() function. You will need to add the OnDestroy() handler via Class-Wizards Message Map tab (the Message ID should be WM_DESTROY).

Since the PNSetButtonImage() and PNClearButtonImage() functions are really SDK functions and won't understand the CWnd class, we will use the CWnd::m_hWnd data member, which is the HWND that the CWnd contains or "wraps," as shown in Code 5–96.

If we wanted a more "MFC-like" approach, then we can also use the CButton classes SetIcon function to set the image of a button to be a particular image, such as Code 5–97.

Since MFC currently has no wrapper class for icons, we still use the HICON data type. As with PNSetButtonImage, call the LoadImage() function to load the icon into memory. Call the SetIcon() function of the CButton class to associate that icon with the button (the CButton* refers to a CButton for the IDC_RADIOHORRORC button in our example and was initialized first with GetDlgItem()).

Code 5–96

```
void CMFC_ControlsView::OnInitialUpdate()
{
        CFormView::OnInitialUpdate();
        GetParentFrame()->RecalcLayout();
        ResizeParentToFit();
        // Set image for radio button. note use of m_hWnd (this->m_hWnd)
```

```
        PNSetButtonImage( m_hWnd, IDC_RADIOHORRORC, IDI_ICONHORROR );
}

void CMFC_ControlsView::OnDestroy()
{
        CFormView::OnDestroy();

        PNClearButtonImage( m_hWnd, IDC_RADIOHORRORC );
}
```

Code 5–97

```
CButton* pButton = (CButton*)GetDlgItem( IDC_RADIOHORRORC );
HICON hIcon= (HICON)LoadImage( GetModuleHandle(NULL),
MAKEINTRESOURCE(IDI_ICONHORROR), IMAGE_ICON, 16, 16, LR_DEFAULTCOLOR );
pButton->SetIcon( hIcon );
```

Combo Boxes

A combo box provides a convenient way to have the user select one or more possible string values. As with all controls, several properties will affect the appearance and behavior of the combo box. In Figure 5–17, there are four combo boxes. There is no visual difference between the controls in Figure 5–17, but their behavior is described in this section.

The combo box is an interested control because it actually is composed of three different controls wrapped into one Combo Box window class. For example, there is the main ComboBox control, as seen on the right in Figure 5–17 with the down arrow. There is a list box control, which is made visible when the user wants to select something (it can also always be displayed; this is the Simple property for the combo box). There is an EDIT control, where the user can type in the desired string. There are three properties of a combo box.

Figure 5–17   Common combo boxes.

Type	*Simple*—List box is always displayed under the selection item.
	Dropdown—User can type into selection area freely or display dropdown list.
	Drop List—User cannot type in selection freely and must make selection from dropdown list.
Sort	If checked, then items are automatically sorted.
Data	List of strings to be placed in the combo box.

Figure 5–18 is an example of the Data property in the property editor. In an MFC program, these strings are automatically placed into the combo box, but in an SDK program we will need to write the code to get information from the Data property and place it into the combo box. When entering in items into the Data properties selection for a combo box, press CTRL-ENTER to end a line, not ENTER.

A combo box is an example of a control that does not require immediate response when the user works with it. For example, consider a dialog filled with combo boxes and a button. The button requires immediate event handling, because when the user clicks the button, something should happen. However, as the user makes a choice in a combo box, you may not need to provide immediate feedback (as you would for a button). It may simple be enough so that when the user hits the button, you query each of the combo boxes for what its current selection is.

The combo box will send WM_COMMAND messages to its parent as the user makes various choices in the combo box. Various notification codes will go with that WM_COMMAND message, including the commonly used CBN_SELCHANGE (which tells you the user made a selection in the combo box). We will address how to do the "immediate response" handling in case you want to perform an action as the user makes selections, and we will also show how to determine which row in the combo box is selected.

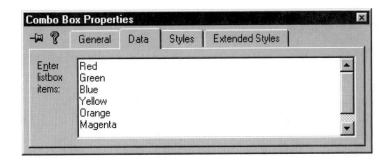

Figure 5–18 Enter data to be displayed in the combo box.

Item Data

Combo boxes have a very useful feature. They permit you to store a 32-bit value with each line of text in the combo box. The thing to note is that there is no predefined purpose for this 32-bit value, and you are free to use it as you please. When we start working with database tables, we will do things like populate a combo box with a list of person names, and then for each name string we will store the unique ID for the person record in the item data for that string. This way, when the user selects an item, we can quickly access its unique ID in the database.

The item data stays with the line you associate it with, even if (because of sorting) the line moves up or down in the combo box.

Populating Combo Box from the Data Property

SDK

MFC programs have the ability to automatically place the strings in the Data property for a combo box into the combo box window itself. But SDK programs do not. We will provide a function that will simplify the ability to do so.

The PNDlgInit() function presented below can be fairly complex to comprehend. If you want to see how to use it, skip to the Using PNDlgInit section.

PNDlgInit() works on the principle that the resources for a program are included in the executable file itself. In the case of the combo box Data property, the strings are stored separately from the combo box itself. There are two types of resource files: .rc files, which are text-based definitions for dialogs and menus, and .aps files, which are binary type resource files. You can load the .rc file into notepad and read along logically through the file. But the .aps file will appear as a mixture of strange characters and symbols. (You can find some of the initialization information for a dialog in .rc file, but the strings themselves are in the APS file).

But both types of resource files are compiled and placed into your executable file. Basically, the APS file is actually an array of data organized as a control ID, a message to send to that control, and additional information for the control.

The PNDlgInit() function will load the APS data at runtime from the executable file itself (the APS is not needed to run the program but is needed to create the executable, so don't delete the APS file, just don't distribute it with your executable file). It will load the resource for a specific dialog and then iterate through that resource, getting the initialization values for combo boxes as shown in Code 5–98.

Code 5-98

```
// PNDlgInit - Initializes dialog box members, like strings in comboboxes
// Parameters:
//      hParent - Window handle for dialog to initialize
//       ID - Dialog resource ID
// Returns: TRUE if succesful, FALSE upon failure
// Comments: Loads strings from dialog editor into combobox controls.
BOOL PNDlgInit( HWND hParent, int ID )
{
    // Find the initializer resource for dialog controls, with same
    // Resource name as this dialog
    HRSRC hDlgInit = ::FindResource(GetModuleHandle(NULL),
    MAKEINTRESOURCE(ID), MAKEINTRESOURCE(240) );
    if( !hDlgInit )
        return( FALSE );

    // Load the initializer resource, and get its handle
    HGLOBAL hResource = NULL;
    hResource = LoadResource(GetModuleHandle(NULL), hDlgInit);
    if( !hResource )
        return( FALSE );

    // Lock the resource, which gives us a pointer to the data
    LPVOID lpResource = NULL;
    lpResource = LockResource(hResource);
    if( !lpResource )
    {
        FreeResource(hResource);
        return(FALSE);
    }

    // Now, we can 'walk through' the loaded resource which is an array
    // of initializer items. The format of each item in the array is:
    // Window ID, Window Message, Length of Data, Data for message
    // We enter a loop to iterate this array, extracting the needed
    // data and sending the Window Message to the desired child control

    // Data to help our iteration
    UNALIGNED WORD* lpnRes = (WORD*)lpResource;
    WORD nIDC;
    WORD nMsg;
    DWORD dwLen;
    BOOL bSuccess = TRUE;

    // Iterate the elements in the initializer array (from resource)
    while( bSuccess && *lpnRes != 0 )
    {
        nIDC = *lpnRes++;
```

```
        nMsg = *lpnRes++;
        dwLen = *((UNALIGNED DWORD*&)lpnRes)++;

        // The hard-coded numbers deal with the fact that the resource editor
        // stores strings in the resource file with Win16 messages. So here
        // we convert them to Win32 messages
        if( nMsg == 0x1234 )
              nMsg = CBEM_INSERTITEM;
        else if( nMsg == 0x0401 )
              nMsg = LB_ADDSTRING;
        else if( nMsg == 0x0403 )
              nMsg = CB_ADDSTRING;

        if( nMsg == CBEM_INSERTITEM ) // Insert into Extended Combobox?
        {
              COMBOBOXEXITEM item;
              item.mask = CBEIF_TEXT;
              item.iItem = -1;
#if defined(_UNICODE)
                {
                USES_CONVERSION;
                WideCharToMultiByte(acp, 0, lpw, -1, lpa, nChars, NULL, NULL);
                item.pszText = A2T(LPSTR(lpnRes));
                }
#else
              item.pszText = (LPSTR)lpnRes;
#endif
              if( SendDlgItemMessage( hParent, nIDC, nMsg, 0, (LPARAM)
              &item) == -1 ) bSuccess = FALSE;
        }
        // Add string to List box or Combo box?
        else if( nMsg == LB_ADDSTRING || nMsg == CB_ADDSTRING )
        {
              if( SendDlgItemMessageA(hParent, nIDC, nMsg, 0, (LPARAM)
              lpnRes) == -1 ) bSuccess = FALSE;
        }
        // skip past data, in preparation for next string
        lpnRes = (WORD*)((LPBYTE)lpnRes + (UINT)dwLen);
    }

    // Unlock and release our resrouces
    UnlockResource(hResource);
    FreeResource(hResource);
    return( TRUE );
}
```

Here's is how the PNDlgInit() function works.

- It calls FindResource() to determine if there is additional APS resource information for the desired dialog. (The MAKEINTRESOURCE(240) identifies the type of resource we want to load (such as Bitmap or Cursor), and in this case the "240" means "APS data").

- If the resource is found, then LoadResource() is called, which loads the resource into memory and gives us a memory handle to the resource.

- The LockResource() function is used to lock a resource handle, which guarantees that the resource data is loaded into memory, and returns a pointer to where it was loaded into memory (lpResource in our example above).

- One the lpResource pointer is initialized, it starts "walking" through the array of elements loaded from the APS data. Each element is defined as a control ID, a control message for that ID, the length of any additional information for the message, and finally the additional data for that message.

- Just within the "while" loop, you can see where the ID, Message, and length of data are extracted.

- The message ID is examined and converted into the Win32 counterpart, because APS still stores its information as Win16 messages and some message IDs changed between Win16 and Win32.

- Once the message is converted, it is determined if it is an addstring message for a combo box, extended combo box, or a list box.

- The additional data should be a string, and that string is added using the SendMessage() fnuction to the destination ID.

- The process continues until the entire array is iterated.

For additional background, you can image the APS file looks something like the following. PNDlgInit loads the APS information into memory and then iterates through the array.

```
IDC_COMBOBOX1, CBM_ADDSTRING, 5, "Hello"
IDC_COMBOBOX1, CBM_ADDSTRING, 5, "there"
IDC_COMBOBOX1, CBM_ADDSTRING, 5, "buddy"
IDC_COMBOBOX2, CBM_ADDSTRING, 3, "Red"
IDC_COMBOBOX2, CBM_ADDSTRING, 5, "Green"
IDC_COMBOBOX2, CBM_ADDSTRING, 4, "Blue"
```

Using PNDlgInit

In order to use the PNDlgInit() function, all you need to do is have the WM_INITDIALOG handler of your program call PNDlgInit() and pass to it the window handle of the dialog itself, along with the ID for the dialog as shown in Code 5–99.

Code 5–99

```
LRESULT CALLBACK DialogProc( HWND hwndDlg, UINT uMsg, WPARAM wParam, LPARAM
lParam )
{
        // Portions removed for readability
        switch( uMsg )
        {
                case WM_INITDIALOG:
                        PNDlgInit( hwndDlg, IDD_DIALOG1 );
                        return( TRUE );
        // Portions removed for readability
```

Notice how in the call to PNDlgInit() in Code 5–99, the first parameter is hwndDlg, which is also the parameter to DialogProc(). The second parameter is the ID for the dialog itself, which you can determine by right-clicking the dialog in the dialog editor and checking its properties.

PNDlgInit() should be called in the WM_INITDIALOG for any dialog procedure you invoke. Thus, if you have four dialogs, each will have its own dialog procedure and each dialog procedure should call PNDlgInit() in its WM_INITDIALOG handler. If the dialog doesn't have a combo box, or that combo box doesn't have Data property strings, then there is no need to call PNDlgInit().

Creating a Combo Box at Runtime

SDK

It is much easier to create, position, and size your controls in the dialog editor and then make them hidden or visible at runtime than it is to dynamically create and destroy the control. However, we will present the technique for dynamically creating a combo box. In order to hide and show it, use the ShowWindow () function, which will both hide or show a window.

The function listed in Code 5–100 simplifies your requirements for creating a combo box. It is closely modeled after other dynamic control creation functions with the notable exceptions:

- There is no Caption parameter.
- The nRows parameter dictates the height of the drop-down list in lines.
- There is no Height parameter because all combo boxes are the same height.

Code 5–100

```
// PNCreateComboBox - Simplified combo box creation function.
// Parameters:
```

```
//      hParent - Window that is to be parent for the new combo box
//      x - X coordinate, relative to client area of parent
//      y - Y coordinate, relative to client area of parent
//      nWidth - Width of new combo box
//      nRows - Number of rows to appear in dropdown list
//      nID - ID for new combo box (should be unique within parent)
//      nStyle - Additional styles for a combo box
// Returns: Window handle if successful, NULL upon failure.
HWND PNCreateComboBox( HWND hParent, int x, int y, int nWidth, int nRows,
    int nID, int nStyle )
{
        HWND Ret;
        HFONT hFont;
        int LineHeight;
        // Create the window
        Ret = CreateWindow( "COMBOBOX", NULL,
                WS_VISIBLE|WS_CHILD|WS_TABSTOP|WS_VSCROLL|CBS_AUTOHSCROLL |
                nStyle, x, y, nWidth, 1, hParent, (HMENU)nID,
                GetModuleHandle(NULL), NULL );
        if( Ret )
        {
                // If window was created, then we set the font of the button
                // to be the same as its parent window
                hFont = (HFONT)SendMessage( hParent, WM_GETFONT, 0, 0 );
                SendMessage( Ret, WM_SETFONT, (WPARAM)hFont, 1 );

                nRows++;

                // Determine height of the font
                LOGFONT LogFont;
                GetObject( hFont, sizeof(LogFont), &LogFont );

                // Determine Height of the current window
                RECT Rect;
                GetWindowRect( Ret, &Rect );
                Rect.bottom -= Rect.top;
                Rect.right -= Rect.left;
                // Determine line height based on font
                if( LogFont.lfHeight < 0 )
                        LineHeight = (-LogFont.lfHeight)+2;
                else
                        LineHeight = LogFont.lfHeight+4;

                // Increase window size to hold as many lines as requested
                Rect.bottom += (nRows * LineHeight);
                // Resize window, making it taller adds to list box height
                SetWindowPos( Ret, NULL, 0, 0, Rect.right, Rect.bottom,
                    SWP_NOMOVE|SWP_NOZORDER );
```

```
        }
        return( Ret );
}
```

Code 5–100 calls CreateWindow() to create the combo box. Note how the Height parameter to the CreateWindow() function is 1. This is because all combo boxes are the same height. When you change or specify the height of a combo box, you are really changing the height when the drop-down list is displayed (thereby changing the height of the drop-down list). Even a combo box created with a height of 1 pixel would be displayed normal size, but its drop-down list would be a single thin black line.

Once the window has been created, we set the font of the child control to be the same as the parent control (the dialog), using WM_GETFONT and WM_SETFONT. We then use GetObject() to get information about the font, such as its height. Once we have the height of the font, we multiply that times nRows, add it to the current window height (gotten by the GetWindowRect() function), then resize the windows height to match the callers request.

In order to use the PNCreateComboBox() function, you can place it in the WM_INIT-DIALOG handler of your dialog procedure as shown in Code 5–101. Note: If you create the control when the dialog initializes, and then destroy the control before the dialog terminates, then you have basically re-invented all the work that the dialog editor already does for you.

Code 5–101

```
LRESULT CALLBACK DialogProc( HWND hwndDlg, UINT uMsg, WPARAM wParam, LPARAM
lParam )
{
    HWND hChild;
    // Portions of code removed for readability
    switch( uMsg )
    {
        case WM_INITDIALOG:
            // Dynamically create a ComboBox
            hChild = PNCreateComboBox( hwndDlg, 300, 300, 100, 3, 4004,
                CBS_DROPDOWNLIST );
            SendMessage( hChild, CB_ADDSTRING, 0, (LPARAM)"Line1" );
            SendMessage( hChild, CB_ADDSTRING, 0, (LPARAM)"Line2" );
            SendMessage( hChild, CB_ADDSTRING, 0, (LPARAM)"Line3" );
            SendMessage( hChild, CB_ADDSTRING, 0, (LPARAM)"Line4" );
    // Portions of code removed for readability
```

MFC

In order to create a combo box at runtime, we will declare a member variable of CCombobox type in the View or Dialog class that serves as the parent window where we want to create our control. In our example, the CMFC_ControlsView.h file is modified. Add Code 5–102 as a data member to the View class.

Code 5-102

```
CComboBox m_DynaCombo;
```

If your program is view-based, add the creation code to the OnCreate() member function of the view. If your program is dialog-based, then add the code to the OnInitDialog() function. The creation code invokes the CcomboBox::Create() member function to actually create the window on screen as shown in Code 5-103.

Code 5-103

```
int CMFC_ControlsView::OnCreate(LPCREATESTRUCT lpCreateStruct)
{
    if (CFormView::OnCreate(lpCreateStruct) == -1)
        return -1;

    CRect PosAndSize;
    // Dynamically create a combo box
    PosAndSize.SetRect(126, 230, 196, 300);
    m_DynaCombo.Create(WS_VISIBLE|WS_CHILD|WS_TABSTOP|CBS_DROPDOWNLIST,
        PosAndSize, this, 4004 );

    return 0;
}
```

The code above will create the combo box window, which is wrapped by the m_DynaCombo data member of the View class. Next, set the font for the new window to match that of its parent. We will accomplish this in the OnInitialUpdate() function for view-type programs. Both the Create () above and the SetFont() Code 5-104 are done in the OnInitDialog() function for dialog-based applications.

Since the GetFont() function is called from a View class member function, remember that it's like saying "this->GetFont()." This retrieves the font for view or parent window and then sets it into the new child control.

Code 5-104

```
void CMFC_ControlsView::OnInitialUpdate()
{
    CFormView::OnInitialUpdate();
    GetParentFrame()->RecalcLayout();
    ResizeParentToFit();

    static bool DoneOnce = false;

    //Set our dynamically created combo box font
    m_DynaCombo.SetFont( GetFont() );
}
```

Responding to Combo Box Selections and Changes

SDK

When the user types in text in the edit box of a combo control or makes a selection from the drop-down list, the child combo box sends a WM_COMMAND message to the parent window or dialog. In order to know when these events occurred, add a handler to the window/dialog procedure for the parent window.

The WM_COMMAND message will specify the notification code in the high word of the wParam parameter to the dialog procedure and the ID in the low word as shown in Code 5–105. In this example, the WM_COMMAND handler has code added to identify the control as our combo box (IDC_COMBOEDIT in our sample), and then checks for the CBN_EDITCHANGE or CBN_SELCHANGE notification codes from that child combo box.

Code 5–105

```
LRESULT CALLBACK DialogProc( HWND hwndDlg, UINT uMsg, WPARAM wParam, LPARAM
lParam )
{
    int wID;
    int wNotification;
    HWND hChild;

    switch( uMsg )
    {
        case WM_COMMAND: // A message from a control or menu item
            // Parse out WM_COMMAND parameters to be more readable
            wID = LOWORD(wParam);
            wNotification = HIWORD(wParam);
            hChild = (HWND) lParam;

            if( wID == IDC_COMBOEDIT && wNotification == CBN_EDITCHANGE )
            {      // User typed in text, retrieve what they typed
                char Text[64];
                GetWindowText( hChild, Text, sizeof(Text) );
              // Text now contains the users text
            }
            else if( wID == IDC_COMBOEDIT && wNotification == CBN_SELCHANGE)
            {  // User selectd an item in dropdown list, retrieve their
               // selection
                int Selection = SendMessage( hChild, CB_GETCURSEL, 0, 0 );
                if( Selection != CB_ERR )
                {
                    // Selection is now the index of the line selected by the
                    // user
                }
            }
    }
```

MFC

Responding to combo box events such as changes in the user selection are done by adding a message map with ClassWizard. Here are the steps to add a function to your project that will get invoked when the user makes a selection in a combo box.

1. Make sure that the Message Map tab is selected (see Figure 5–19).
2. Make sure that the View class (CMFC_ControlsView.cpp in our sample) is selected in the Class Name field, or the dialog class name if your project is dialog-based.
3. In the Object IDs list, highlight the desired combo box control (IDC_COMBEDIT in example).
4. In the Messages list, select the CBN_SELCHANGED message (if this is the one you want handled).
5. Click the Add Function button to actually add the function.

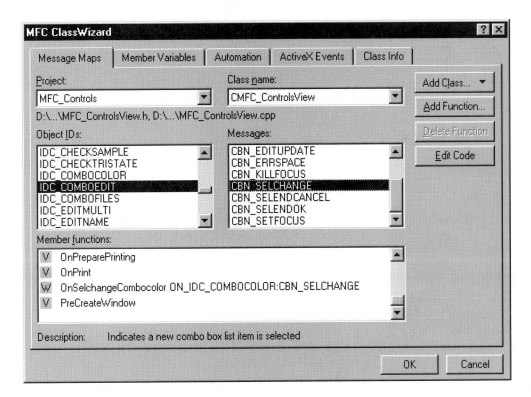

Figure 5–19 ClassWizard Message Maps for a combobox.

Inside this function (see Code 5–106), add the code that you want to be executed when the user changes the selection in a combo box. See Retrieving Text and/or Current Selection, MFC for examples on determining what the user selected.

Code 5-106

```
void CMFC_ControlsView::OnSelchangeComboedit()
{
// TODO: Add your control notification handler code here

}
```

NOTE

ClassWizard Message maps can not be added for controls created dynamically. Refer to Code 5–69 and 5–70 for details on dynamically created controls.

Retrieving Text and/or Current Selection

SDK

In order to retrieve the values a user has typed or selected in a combo box, you can either determine what item in the drop-down list is selected, or you can get the selected text from the control. Code 5–107 shows how to do both. To get the text from the combo box, use the GetWindowText() function:

Code 5-107

```
char Text[64];
GetWindowText( hChild, Text, sizeof(Text) );
```

Code 5–107 assumes that hChild is the window handle for the combo box to get the text from. It will place the text from the combo box into the Text variable.

In order to get the current selection from a combo box, send the CB_GETCURSEL message to the child window using SendMessage(). The return value will be the currently selected item, or CB_ERR if no item has been selected, as shown in Code 5–108.

Code 5-108

```
char Text[64];
int Selection = SendMessage( hChild, CB_GETCURSEL, 0, 0 );
if( Selection != CB_ERR )
{
    int ItemData;
    SendMessage( hChild, CB_GETLBTEXT, Selection, (LPARAM)Text );
    // Text now contains the text of the users selection
    ItemData = SendMessage( hChild, CB_GETITEMDATA, Selection, 0 );
    // ItemData now contains the extra 'user data' for the selected item }
```

In Code 5–104, we are actually retrieving two pieces of data for the selected item. The SendMessage() of CB_GETCURSEL to the combo box window will return to us the selected item. If no item is selected, it will return CB_ERR.

Once we have the index of the selected item from the combo box, we can use that to either get the text selected, or we can also use it to retrieve the "user data" for that item. This means that you can also use these methods to iterate through the items or strings in a combo box.

Remember that each row in a combo box has an extra 32-bit value called "user data" or "item data." That 32-bit value has no predefined usage and is yours to do with as you please. When you add a string to the list box, you then have the ability to store a 32-bit value (which would include pointers) with that item. We will see examples of how to do this when we add strings to the combo box. Code 5–108 above also assumes that hChild is the window handle to the combo box.

MFC

In order to determine the text or current selection for a combo box, we will use the CWnd::GetWindowText() or CComboBox::GetCurSel() and CComboBox::GetLBText() functions as shown in Code 5–109.

Code 5–109 is invoked when the user makes a change in the edit box of a combo box. GetDlgItem() is called to get a CWnd pointer to the combo box and then call GetWindowText() to retrieve its current text.

Code 5–109

```
void CMFC_ControlsView::OnEditchangeComboedit()
{
        CString Text;

        // Get CWnd pointer for combo box, and retrieve its text
        CWnd* pWnd = GetDlgItem( IDC_COMBOEDIT );
        pWnd->GetWindowText( Text );

        // Get CWnd pointer for static control, and place text into it.
        pWnd = GetDlgItem(IDC_CBTEXT); // pWnd now points to another control
        pWnd->SetWindowText( Text );

}
```

Code 5–110 calls GetDlgItem() to get a CComboBox pointer to the combo box control. Notice that this time we type-casted the return value to a CComboBox pointer and stored it into that type of pointer (pCombo).

Code 5-110

```
void CMFC_ControlsView::OnSelchangeComboedit()
{
        // Get CWnd pointer for combo box
        CComboBox* pCombo = (CComboBox*) GetDlgItem( IDC_COMBOEDIT );

        // Get its current selection, if any
        int i = pCombo->GetCurSel();
        if( i != CB_ERR )
        {
                CString Text;
                // Get the text of the selected item
                pCombo->GetLBText( i, Text );
                // And place the text into static control
                GetDlgItem(IDC_CBTEXT)->SetWindowText(Text);
        }
}
```

Once we have the CComboBox pointer, we can call the GetCurSel() function to determine which item is selected by the user. If GetCurSel() returns CB_ERR, then nothing is selected. If it's not CB_ERR, then it is the row (zero-relative) the user selected. We then use GetLBText() to retrieve that line of text from the drop-down list: The row number is passed as its first parameter, and a destination CString is passed as its second parameter. The resulting string from the list box is left in the Text CString.

Setting the Current Selection Programmatically

SDK

In order to set the current selection in a combo box, you can send the CB_SETCURSEL item to the window control as shown in Code 5-111 and Code 5-112. Both examples assume that Index is an integer that contains the row number that you want to select in the combo box. If Index were CB_ERR, then it would clear whatever the current selection was and leave it with no row selected.

Code 5-111

```
SendMessage( hChild, CB_SETCURSEL, Index, 0 );
```

Code 5-112

```
SendDlgItemMessage( hwndDlg, IDC_COMBFILES, CB_SETCURSEL, Index, 0 );
```

MFC

In order to set the current selection in a combo box, you can either send the control a CB_SETCURSEL message (see Code 5-113) or you can call the CCombo-Box::SetCurSel() function (see Code 5-114). The first method is good when you want to set several combo boxes sequentially where SetCurSel() is usually easier when you want to work with a specific control. You can set the combo box to have no selection by setting its index to CB_ERR as shown in Code 5–115.

Code 5–113

```
SendDlgItemMessage( IDC_COMBOFILES, CB_SETCURSEL, Index, 0 );
```

Code 5–114

```
CComboBox* pCombo = (CComboBox*) GetDlgItem( IDC_COMBOEDIT );
pCombo->SetCurSel( Index );
```

Code 5–115

```
pCombo->SetCurSel( CB_ERR ); // Clear selection
```

Adding Strings and User Data to a Combo Box

SDK

The strings that you want to add to a combo box may not be known at design time. You then need to populate the combo box at runtime. You can add strings at runtime by sending a CB_ADDSTRING message to the child control as shown in Code 5–116. Code 5–116 shows how to add a string to a combo box. The return value is where in the combo box list the string was actually added.

Code 5–116

```
int AddedAt = SendMessage( hChild, CB_ADDSTRING, 0, (LPARAM)"Smith, John");
```

Once we know where the string was added based on the value of AddedAt variable, we can use the item data for the new line (see ItemData section at the start of the Combo Box section for more information). Imagine that the "John Smith" person added previously had a unique database ID of 8. We want to store this unique ID in the combo box without showing it to the user, so that it is easy to identify the item selected when the user made a selection in the combo box. Code 5–117 contains two variables used in this example. These are the ID and Name. In order to add the data shown in Code 5–117 to the combo box, we use the code illustrated in Code 5–118.

Code 5–117

```
int PersonID=8;
char PersonName[]="Smith, John";
```

Code 5–118

```
int AddedAt = SendMessage( hChild, CB_ADDSTRING, 0, (LPARAM) PersonName );
if( AddedAt != CB_ERR && AddedAt != CB_ERRSPACE )
      SendMessage( hChild, CB_SETITEMDATA, AddedAt, PersonID );
```

Storing the string and the item data is just part of the operation. At some point the user will make a selection and the program needs to determine the item the user selected. The CB_GETCURSEL message is used to determine the item selected and then the CB_GETITEMDATA is used to retrieve the item data from the user choice as shown in Code 5–119. The PersonID integer has the unique ID for the person selected by the user.

You can also insert strings at a specific column by sending a child control the CB_INSERTSTRING message instead of a CB_ADDSTRING message. In this case, the wParam parameter indicates where to insert the string as shown in Code 5–120. This would insert the string in NewStr into the combo box list at row zero (the third parameter), whether the combo box is sorted or not.

Code 5–119

```
int PersonID=0;
int Selection = SendMessage( hChild, CB_GETCURSEL, 0, 0 );
if( Selection != CB_ERR )
        PersonID = SendMessage( hChild, CB_GETITEMDATA, Selection, 0 );
```

Code 5–120

```
SendMessage( hChild, CB_INSERTSTRING, 0, NewStr );
```

MFC

We can add strings to a combo box using either the CB_ADDSTRING message (see Code 5–121) or the CComboBox::AddString() function (see Code 5–122). The CWnd::SendDlgItemMessage() function is called because we assume that the code is in a View or Dialog class member function. CWnd::SendDlgItemMessage(), which is a member function of the CWnd class, should not be confused with ::SendDlgItemMessage(), which is the Windows API we would use for SDK-style programs. The CWnd version only needs four parameters; the SDK version requires five parameters.

Code 5–121

```
int Index = SendDlgItemMessage( IDC_COMBOEDIT, CB_ADDSTRING, 0,
(LPARAM)"Line1");
```

Code 5–122

```
// Assumes that m_DynaCombo is a CComboBox object
int Index = m_DynaCombo.AddString( "Line1" );
```

In Codes 5–121 and 5–122, the string "Line1" is added to a combo box. The return value of both is stored in Index. If the combo box were sorted, then the string could be inserted anywhere within the combo box list. The return value represents the line or index where the string was placed.

The index for the newly inserted item can be used to set the Item Data for that new item, in the combo box. You may recall that the "item data" or "user data" is an extra 32-bit value that is ours to use as we please. As the strings are moved up or down in the combo box because of additions or deletions, the item data remains associated with the string as shown in Code 5–123.

In Code 5–123, assume the person name and ID were retrieved from a database and the ID was the unique ID for the person in the database. When the user selects a person from the combo box, we have access to the selected person's unique ID immediately in the form of item data.

Code 5–123

```
int PersonID=35;
CString PersonName = "Smith, Joe";

// Adding a string with Item Data (i.e., Initialization):
CComboBox* pBox = GetDlgItem( IDC_COMBOPERSONS);
int Index = pBox->AddString( PersonName );
pBox->SetItemData( Index, PersonID );

// Retrieving the Item Data for the users selection:
CComboBox* pBox = GetDlgItem( IDC_COMBOPERSONS);
int Index = pBox->GetCurSel();
if( Index != CB_ERR )
{

        PersonID = pBox->GetItemData( Index );

}
```

Populating a Combo Box with a List of Filenames

SDK

The combo box class supports the ability to easily fill it with a list of file names from which the user makes a selection. While this is not a replacement for the common File Open dialog, the combo box is an easy-to-implement feature. In order to accomplish the file list, you can send a CB_DIR message to the child combo box control (see Code 5–124) or you can call the DlgDirListComboBox() function (see Code 5–125).

Code 5–124

```
SendDlgItemMessage( hwndDlg, IDC_COMBOFILES, CB_RESETCONTENT, 0, 0 );
SendDlgItemMessage( hwndDlg, IDC_COMBOFILES, CB_DIR, DDL_READWRITE,
        (LPARAM)"C:\\*.*" );
```

Code 5-125

```
char Path[MAX_PATH] = "C:\\*.*"
DlgDirListComboBox( hwndDlg, Path, IDC_COMBOFILES, 0, DDL_READWRITE );}
```

In Code 5–124, we used the SendDlgItemMessage() function, but we could have used the SendMessage() function. The SendDlgItemMessage() function is the parent window handle for the combo box and the ID of the combo box where in the SendMessage() function, only the child window handle is passed. The following describes the last three parameters, which are the same for both functions.

- CB_DIR is the Windows message that is used to populate the list with filenames.
- DDL_READWRITE contains one of several file-attributes that can be combined as a bitmask. This is the default file attribute that selects all normal read/write files. Here are the other possible file attributes: DDL_ARCHIVE, DDL_DIRECTORY, DDL_DRIVES, DDL_EXCLUSIVE, DDL_HIDDEN, DDL_READONLY, and DDL_SYSTEM.
- C:*.*" contains the file path with or without wild card characters.

DlgDirListComboBox() (see Code 5–125) is more flexible than the SendDlgItemMessage() function. The fourth parameter of DlgDirListComboBox(), which is zero in our example, allows you to specify a STATIC control. When called, DlgDirListComboBox() places the starting path (C:\ in our example) into that static control.

DlgDirListComboBox() sends a CB_RESETCONTENT and then a CB_DIR message to the combo box. DlgDirListComboBox() also requires that the second parameter is an array because this function uses the array for both the starting path and return the path of the filename in the array.

The filename is a path that can include wild cards. For example, "C:\\work*.cpp" would populate the combo box with a list of files with a .cpp extension from the c:\work folder. Notice that our example uses the "\\" for a single slash. Because the C++ "\\" conversion is done at compiletime, the end user would not need to type in two slashes.

NOTE

For typical file selection, use of the FileOpen common dialog is recommended.

MFC

In order to populate a combo box with a list of files, we can send the CB_DIR message to the control or use the CWnd::DlgDirListComboBox() or CComboBox::Dir() functions.

Windows Programming Programmer's Notebook

Using the DlgDirListComboBox() function also allows you to specify a STATIC control that is set with the path name of the folder. You also can specify zero to indicate no STATIC control. The DlgDirListComboBox() function expands the passed path into a complete path as shown in Code 5–126. DlgDirListComboBox() also empties the destination combo box before populating it with filenames.

Code 5–126

```
int DlgDirListComboBox( LPTSTR lpPathSpec, int nIDComboBox,
    int nIDStaticPath, UINT nFileType );
```

Here are descriptions of the parameters used in the DlgDirListComboBox() function:

- lpPathSpec: The path to search for. This string is also used for output from the function and therefore should never be a static string.
- nIDComboBox: The ID of the Combo box to populate with filenames.
- nIDStaticPath: The ID of a STATIC control to receive the path, or zero for no STATIC control.
- nFileType: Types of files.

The file attributes are specified in Code 5–127 wherever you see DDL_READWRITE (in the 3 various methods). You select from the following values, and can combine them with the OR (|) operator: DDL_ARCHIVE, DDL_DIRECTORY, DDL_DRIVES, DDL_EXCLUSIVE, DDL_HIDDEN, DDL_READONLY, DDL_READWRITE, and DDL_SYSTEM.

Code 5–127

```
// Three different methods to get file list into a combo box:
char Path[MAX_PATH]="C:\\*.*";

// Method 1: DlgDirListComboBox
DlgDirListComboBox( Path, IDC_COMBOFILES, 0, DDL_READWRITE );

// Method 2: Messages to reset content and get file list
SendDlgItemMessage( IDC_COMBOFILES, CB_RESETCONTENT, 0, 0 );
SendDlgItemMessage( IDC_COMBOFILES, CB_DIR, DDL_READWRITE, (LPARAM) Path );

// Method 3: CCombo class and ResetContent and Dir functions
CComboBox* pCombo = (CComboBox*)GetDlgItem(IDC_COMBOFILES);
pCombo->ResetContent();
pCombo->Dir( DDL_READWRITE, Path );
```

Notice in the DlgDirListComboBox() function, the Path parameter also serves as return data for the function. Make sure you pass an array that can hold more data than you originally passed. You would *never* pass a static string to this function such as shown in Code 5–128.

Code 5-128

```
DlgDirListComboBox( "C:\\*.*", IDC_COMBOFILES, 0, DDL_READWRITE ); // Big
mistake!
```

NOTE

For typical file selection, use of the FileOpen common dialog is recommended.

Clearing a Combo Box

SDK

Send the CB_RESETCONTENT message to remove all items contained in a combo box as shown in Code 5–129.

All text currently in the drop-down list of the combo box will be removed, along with any item data the items would have had. If you don't have the child window for the control and you only have the window handle for the parent dialog of the combo box, you can use SendDlgItemMessage() to clear the combo box as shown in Code 5–130.

Code 5-129

```
SendMessage( hChild, CB_RESETCONTENT, 0, 0 );
```

Code 5-130

```
SendDlgItemMessage( hwndDlg, IDC_COMBOFILES, CB_RESETCONTENT, 0, 0 );
```

MFC

Send the CB_RESETCONTENT message to clear a combo box or we can call the CComboBox::ResetContent() function. Both methods are shown in Code 5–131.

Code 5–131 assumes that the ID for our desired combo box to clear out is IDC_COMBOFILES. The SendDlgItemMessage() would be the CWnd::SendDlg-ItemMessage() function, and we assume that the example code was called from a member of the View or Dialog class that is the parent of the combo box (in other words, think of it as *this*->SendDlgItemMessage(...)).

Code 5-131

```
CComboBox* pBox = (CComboBox*)GetDlgItem( IDC_COMBOFILE );

// Method 1:
pBox->SendMessage( CB_RESETCONTENT );
```

```
SendDlgItemMessage( IDC_COMBOFILES, CB_RESETCONTENT );

// Method 2:
pBox->ResetContent();
```

Determining the Count of Items in a Combo Box

SDK

To determine the number of items in a combobox, you can send the CB_GET-COUNT message to the control using either SendMessage () or SendDlgItemMessage() functions. The SendMessage() is used if you know the child window's handle (see Code 5–132). If you only have the parent window's handle, then use the SendDlgItemMessage() function shown in Code 5–133. This function is also used to count items in a combo box. In Code 5–133 the IDC_COMBOFILES is the ID of the combo box whose items we want to count.

Code 5–132

```
int Count = SendMessage( hChild, CB_GETCOUNT, 0, 0 );
```

Code 5–133

```
int Count = SendDlgItemMessage( hwndDlg, IDC_COMBOFILES, CB_GETCOUNT, 0, 0 );
```

MFC

To determine the count of items in a combo box we can either send the control a CB_GETCOUNT message or call the CComboBox::GetCount() function as shown in Code 5–134.

Code 5–134 assumes that the ID for our desired combo box to clear out is IDC_COMBOFILES. The SendDlgItemMessage() is the CWnd::SendDlgItemMessage() function. We assume Code 5–134 is called from a member of the View or Dialog class that is the parent of the combo box (in other words, think of it as *this*->SendDlgItemMessage(...)).

Code 5–134

```
CComboBox* pBox = (CComboBox*)GetDlgItem( IDC_COMBOFILE );
int Count;

// Method 1:
Count = pBox->SendMessage( CB_GETCOUNT );
Count = SendDlgItemMessage( IDC_COMBOFILES, CB_GETCOUNT );

// Method 2:
Count = pBox->GetCount();
```

Finding a String in a Combo Box

SDK

In order to search the drop-down list of a combo box for a string (i.e., to avoid duplicates before adding), you can send the control a CB_FIND or CB_FINDEXACT message to the control as shown in Code 5–135.

CB_FINDSTRINGEXACT finds an exact match and CB_FINDSTRING finds the first string that starts with the characters in the passed search string.

Code 5–135

```
if( SendMessage( hChild, CB_FINDSTRINGEXACT, 0, NewStr ) == CB_ERR )
    SendMessage( hChild, CB_ADDSTRING, 0, (LPARAM)NewStr );
```

MFC

In order to search the drop-down list of a combo box for a string, send a CB_FIND or CB_FINDEXACT message to the control or call the CComboBox::FindString () or CComboBox::FindStringExact() functions as shown in Code 5–136.

Code 5–136

```
CComboBox* pBox = (CComboBox*)GetDlgItem( IDC_COMBOFILE );
int Found;
// Method 1: Uses CB_FINDSTRINGEXACT message
Found = pCombo->SendMessage( CB_FINDSTRINGEXACT, -1, (LPARAM)(LPCSTR)Text );
Found = SendDlgItemMessage( IDC_COMBOEDIT, CB_FINDSTRINGEXACT, -1,
        (LPARAM)(LPCSTR)Text );
// Method 2: Calls CComboBox::FindStringExact function
Found = pCombo->FindStringExact( -1, Text );
```

List Boxes

List boxes (see Figure 5–20) provide the user with a list of items that they may select one or more items from. List boxes should not be confused with the ListView control, which is a covered in the next chapter. The ListView control provides much more functionality than the list box.

As with the Combo Box control, the List Box control allows you to store a set of strings but also permits you to store "item data" or "user data" with that string in the control. This item data is a 32-bit value that is yours to do with as you please. See the Item Data section of the Combo Box section for some more details.

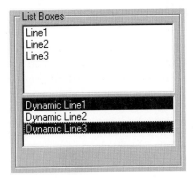

Figure 5–20 Common list boxes.

The bottom list box in Figure 5–20 has multiple selections. In order to do this, the Multiple selection or LBS_EXTENDEDSEL style should be selected, or you can set it in the dialog editor by changing the properties of the list box (right-click on the control in the dialog editor).

The list box control sends a WM_COMMAND message to its parent to notify it of certain events, such as when the user makes a selection, or when the user leaves the list (focus changes to another control).

Important properties for the list box can be set in the properties of the dialog in the dialog editor by right-clicking on the control and selecting Properties. Some items that you can change are:

Selection
- Single—Users can select only one item
- Multiple—Users can select multiple items
- Extended—Users can select multiple items, and extend selection using the SHIFT or CONTROL keys.
- None—Users can select any items

Sort: If checked, items added to the listbox with LB_ADDSTRING are sorted (but not with LB_INSERTSTRING).

Creating a List Box at Runtime

SDK

Creating a control with dialog editor, and then hiding and showing the window as desired, is a much easier method to control user interface than dynamically creating and destroying controls. However, Code 5–137 is a simplified list box window creation function that calls the CreateWindowEx() function and then sets the font of the window to match its parent window. PNCreateListBox will help you create listbox controls at runtime.

Code 5–138 is an example how to call the function in Code 5–137, which might be placed in the WM_INITDIALOG handler for your dialog procedure.

Code 5-137

```
// PNCreateListBox - Creates a list box at runtime
// Parameters:
//      hParent - Parent window handle (usually the dialog to create on)
//      x - X coordinate for location
//      y - Y coordinate for location
//      nWidth - Width of control
//      nHeight - Height of control
//      nID - Unique ID for the list box (must be unique on the parent window)
//      nStyle - Additional list styles (start with 'LS_')
// Returns: HWND of new window of NULL upon failure
HWND PNCreateListBox( HWND hParent, LPCTSTR lpCaption, int x, int y, int
nWidth, int nHeight, int nID, int nStyle )
{
    HWND Ret;
    HFONT hFont;

    // Create the window
    Ret = CreateWindowEx( WS_EX_CLIENTEDGE, "LISTBOX", lpCaption,
        WS_VISIBLE|WS_CHILD|WS_TABSTOP| nStyle, x, y, nWidth, nHeight,
        hParent, (HMENU)nID, GetModuleHandle(NULL), NULL );
    if( Ret )
    {
        // If window was created, then we set the font of the button to be
        // the same as its parent window
        hFont = (HFONT)SendMessage( hParent, WM_GETFONT, 0, 0 );
        SendMessage( Ret, WM_SETFONT, (WPARAM)hFont, 1 );
    }
    return( Ret );
}
```

Code 5-138

```
hChild = PNCreateListBox( hwndDlg, NULL, 19, 315, 175, 80, 4006,
    LBS_EXTENDEDSEL );
```

MFC

Follow the steps below to create a list box at runtime. Add a data member to our parent View or Dialog class where we want to place the list box. In our example, we will be doing so in the CMFC_ControlsView.cpp file.

Once the member variable is declared, call its Create() function to create the window itself in the View class's OnCreate() function (it would be in OnInitDialog() if it were a dialog-based application). Next call the its SetFont() function in the OnInitialUpdate() function of the View class (we would do so in the OnInitDialog() function if it were a dialog-based application).

1. Add to your View class (in CMFC_CONTROLSView.h in our example) Code 5–139.

Code 5–139

```
CListBox m_DynaList;
```

2. In the OnCreate() function for the vew class (CMFC_ControlsView.cpp for out example), call the Create() member function of the CListBox class as shown in Code 5–140. Notice that this example calls CreateEx() instead of Create() as other MFC examples. This is to implement the 3D appearance of the listbox, with the WS_EX_CLIENTEDGE style. The CWnd::CreateEx() function calls the SDKs CreateWindowEx() function.

Code 5–140

```
// Dynamically create listbox
CRect PosAndSize(19, 315, 161, 395);
m_DynaList.CreateEx( WS_EX_CLIENTEDGE, "LISTBOX", NULL,
        WS_VISIBLE|WS_CHILD|WS_TABSTOP|WS_VSCROLL|LBS_SORT|LBS_EXTENDEDSEL,
        PosAndSize, this, 4005 );
```

3. Change the font of the new control to match its parent window font. In the View class of the OnInitialUpdate() handler, call the SetFont() function for the new object. Use the return value from the parent windows GetFont() function as shown in Code 5–141. Remember that the GetFont() function call is in a member function and be thought of as this-> GetFont().

Code 5–141

```
void CMFC_ControlsView::OnInitialUpdate()
{

        CFormView::OnInitialUpdate();
        GetParentFrame()->RecalcLayout();
        ResizeParentToFit();

        // Set listbox font to match the parent (the parent is 'this')
        m_DynaList.SetFont( GetFont() );
}
```

Adding Strings

SDK

Adding strings to a list box involves sending the LB_ADDSTRING message to the child control. You can use SendMesssage() or SendDlgItemMessage() as illustrated in Codes 5–142 and 5–143.

Code 5–142

```
SendMessage( hChild, LB_ADDSTRING, 0, (LPARAM)"Dynamic Line1" );
```

Code 5–143

```
SendDlgItemMessage( hwndDlg, IDC_LIST1, LB_ADDSTRING, 0, (LPARAM)"Line1" );
```

You can call SendMessage() when you have the handle to the child window, or call SendDlgItemMessage() when working with one or more child windows or when you don't have the window handle. For SendDlgItemMessage(), the first two parameters are the parent (dialog) window handle and the ID of the list box control.

You can also use the LB_INSERTSTRING message to insert instead of append or place at the end of strings in a list box. In this case, the wParam (third) parameter of SendMessage() indicates where in the list control to insert the string, as shown in Code 5–144.

Code 5–144 inserts NewStr as the first string in the list box, at row zero, which is the third parameter.

Code 5–144

```
SendMessage( hChild, LB_INSERTSTRING, 0, NewStr );
```

MFC

Adding strings to a list box involves either sending an LB_ADDSTRING or LBINSERTSTRING message to the child control or calling the CListBox::AddString() or CListBox::InsertString() functions as illustrated in Code 5–145.

Code 5–145

```
CString Str = "Line2";
CListBox* pList = (CListBox*) GetDlgItem( IDC_LIST1 );

// Method 1: Send a message
pList->SendMessage( LB_ADDSTRING, 0, (LPARAM)"Line1");
// Method 2: Call AddString
pList->AddString( Str );
// Slight variation, Method 2 using a mapped member variable.
```

```
// If your class had mapped a member variable to the list named
// m_List, then you could also:
m_List.AddString( "Line3" );
```

The LB_ADDSTRING message expects the third parameter (lParam) to be a pointer to a string. The AddString() functions needs a const char* to the string as its only parameter. We are passing a CString object to one of the AddStrings() in the examples in Code 5–145. This is possible because the CString class has a conversion operator that returns a const char*, so we can use the CString class anywhere we need a const char*.

For the InsertString function and the LB_INSERTSTRING message, there is an extra parameter that indicates where to insert the new string. The string is then inserted at that point even if the list box has the sorted style as shown in Code 5–146.

Code 5–146

```
int InsertAt = 1;
pList->SendMessage( LB_INSERTSTRING, InsertAt++, "New Line 2" );
pList->InsertString( InsertAt, "New Line 3" );
```

Responding to User Selections

SDK

The list box control sends a WM_COMMAND message to its parent and the notification code of LBN_SELCHANGE when the user makes a selection within the list box. Add code in the WM_COMMAND handler to process this selection (see Code 5–147). Notice that the list box retains its selection. So unlike controls that need immediate feedback, such as a button or menu item, you can determine what items were selected by the user some time after the selection rather than respond immediately to each selection.

Code 5–147

```
LRESULT CALLBACK DialogProc( HWND hwndDlg, UINT uMsg, WPARAM wParam, LPARAM
lParam )
{
    int wID;
    int wNotification;
    HWND hChild;

    switch( uMsg )
    {
        case WM_COMMAND: // A message from a control or menu item
            // Parse out WM_COMMAND parameters to be more readable
            wID = LOWORD(wParam);
```

```
wNotification = HIWORD(wParam);
hChild = (HWND) lParam;

// Was item selected by user in the IDC_LIST1 listbox?
if( wID == IDC_LIST1 && wNotification == LBN_SELCHANGE )
{
    // Determine the item selected by the user
    int Selection = SendMessage( hChild, LB_GETCURSEL, 0, 0 );
    if( Selection != LB_ERR )
    {
        char Text[128];
        int ItemData;
        SendMessage( hChild, LB_GETTEXT, Selection, (LPARAM)Text );
        ItemData = SendMessage( hChild, LB_GETITEMDATA,
        Selection, 0 );
        MessageBox( hwndDlg, Text, "You selected", MB_OK );
    }
}
// Portions of code removed for readability
```

MFC

In order to respond to a user choice in a list box control, add a message map with ClassWizard for the LBN_SELCHANGED message from the child window by following these steps. The ClassWizard creates Code 5–148 after completing these steps. Place inside Code 5–148 any code that you want to execute when the user makes a selection.

1. From the View menu choice, select ClassWizard.
2. Make sure the Message Map tab (see Figure 5–21) is highlighted in your ClassWizard dialog.
3. Make sure the Class Name contains the name of your View or Dialog class (CMFC_ControlsView in our example).
4. Highlight the desired list box ID in the Object IDs list.
5. Highlight the LBN_SELCHANGED item in the Messages list.
6. Click Add Function.
7. Click OK at the next dialog that suggestions a function name.

Here are other types of messages that the list control will also send to its parent:

LBN_DBCLK	Double-click
LBN_ERRSPACE	Out of space to store strings
LBN_KILLFOCUS	Control is losing keyboard focus
LBN_SELCANCEL	Selection was cancelled (if Notify property is on)
LBN_SETFOCUS	Control has received keyboard focus

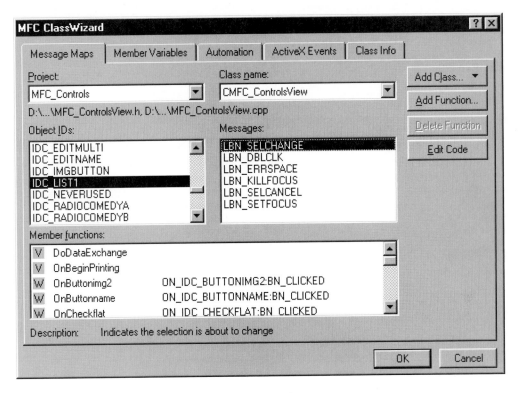

Figure 5–21 Class Wizards Message Map for a list box.

Code 5-148

```
void CMFC_ControlsView::OnSelchangeList1()
{
}
```

Emptying the List

SDK

Any time you want to empty out the list of strings in a list box send the window an LB_RESETCONTENT message calling either SendMessage() (see Code 5–149) or SendDlgItemMessage() (see Code 5–150).

Use the SendMessage() function if you have the window handle for the child list control (hChild). Use the SendDlgItemMessage() if you want to reset several list box controls in a loop. The hwndDlg is the parent dialog window handle for the list control, and the second parameter is the ID for the list control.

Code 5-149

```
SendMessage( hChild, LB_RESETCONTENT, 0, 0 );
```

Code 5-150

```
SendDlgItemMessage( hwndDlg, IDC_LIST1, LB_RESETCONTENT, 0, 0 );
```

MFC

To empty out a list in MFC, send the LB_RESETCONTENT to the list box window or call the CListBox::ResetContent() function as shown in Code 5-151.

Code 5-151

```
CListBox* pList = (CListBox*) GetDlgItem( IDC_LIST1 );

// Method 1: SendMessage with LB_RESETCONTENT
pList->SendMessage( LB_RESETCONTENT );
SendDlgItemMessage( IDC_LIST1, LB_RESETCONTENT );

// Method 2: Call ResetContent
pList->ResetContent();
```

Adding a File Listing to a List Box

SDK

In order to populate a list control with a list of filenames, you can either send it an LB_DIR message or you can call the DlgDirList() function. DlgDirList() is flexible and allows you to specify a STATIC control that will retrieve the path string of the file listing (a single folder). Both methods are shown in Code 5-152.

See the Combo Box section on populating a file list for more details on file paths and the user of the DlgDirList(). For typical file selection, however, use of the FileOpen common dialog is recommended.

Code 5-152

```
LRESULT CALLBACK DialogProc( HWND hwndDlg, UINT uMsg, WPARAM wParam, LPARAM
lParam )
{
    int wID;
    int wNotification;
    HWND hChild;

    char Path[MAX_PATH] = "C:\\*.*";

    switch( uMsg )
    {
        case WM_INITDIALOG:
            DlgDirList( hwndDlg, Path, IDC_LIST1, 0, DDL_READWRITE );
```

```
    // Portions of code removed for readability

LRESULT CALLBACK DialogProc( HWND hwndDlg, UINT uMsg, WPARAM wParam, LPARAM
lParam )
{
    int wID;
    int wNotification;
    HWND hChild;

    char Path[MAX_PATH] = "C:\\*.*";

    switch( uMsg )
    {
        case WM_INITDIALOG:
            SendDlgItemMessage( hwndDlg, IDC_LIST1, LB_RESETCONTENT, 0, 0 );
            SendDlgItemMessage( hwndDlg, IDC_LIST1, LB_DIR, 0, (LPARAM)Path );
    // Portions of code removed for readability
```

MFC

To populate a list of files into a list box, send a LB_DIR message to the control or
we can call the CWnd::DlgDirList() or the CListBox::Dir() functions as illustrated in
Code 5–153.

Code 5-153

```
char Path[MAX_PATH]="C:\\*.*";
CListBox* pList = (CListBox*)GetDlgItem(IDC_LIST1 );

// Method 1: LB_DIR message
pList->SendMessage( LB_RESETCONTENT );
pList->SendMessage( LB_DIR, DDL_READWRITE, (LPARAM)Path );

// Method 1 Variation: SendDlgItemMessage
SendDlgItemMessage( IDC_LIST1, LB_RESETCONTENT );
SendDlgItemMessage( IDC_LIST1, LB_DIR, DDL_READWRITE, (LPARAM)Path );

//Method 2: DlgDirList
DlgDirList( Path, IDC_LIST1, 0, DDL_READWRITE );

// Method 3: ResetContent and Dir funcitons
pList->ResetContent();
pList->Dir( DDL_READWRITE, Path );
```

In Code 5–153, IDC_LIST1 is assumed to be the unique ID for the list box control.
The Path variable is a character array with a path in it. Of the functions listed here,
only the DlgDirList() function requires the passed path to be an array because it
will reuse the string for output of the actual path. The other functions will only use
the Path parameter for input, and you could therefore pass them a constant string
as shown in Code 5–154.

The DDL_READWRITE parameter determines the file types to find and can be one or more of the following: DDL_ARCHIVE, DDL_DIRECTORY, DDL_DRIVES, DDL_EXCLUSIVE, DDL_HIDDEN, DDL_READONLY, DDL_READWRITE, and/or DDL_SYSTEM.

For typical file selection, however, use of the FileOpen common dialog is recommended.

Code 5–154

```
pList->Dir( DDL_READWRITE, "C:\\*.*" );
```

Determining the Count of Items in List Box

SDK

To determine the count of items in a list box (not the count of selected items), send a LB_GETCOUNT message (see Code 5–155) or call the SendDlgItemMessage() (see Code 5–156). In both examples, hChild is the window handle for the desired list box or hwndDlg is the parent dialog window handle and IDC_LIST1 would be the ID of the desired list box child window.

Code 5–155

```
int Count = SendMessage( hChild, LB_GETCOUNT, 0, 0 );
```

Code 5–156

```
int Count = SendDlgItemMessage( hwndDlg, IDC_LIST1, LB_GETCOUNT, 0, 0 );
```

MFC

In order to determine the count of items in a list box (not the count of selected items), you can either send an LB_GETCOUNT message to the list box control or you can call the CListBox::GetCount() function as shown in Code 5–157. This example assumes that IDC_LIST1 is the unique ID for a list box.

Code 5–157

```
CListBox* pList = (CListBox*)GetDlgItem(IDC_LIST1 );
int Count;

// Method 1: LB_GETCOUNT message
Count = pList->SendMessage( LB_GETCOUNT );

// Method 1 Variation: SendDlgItemMessage
Count = SendDlgItemMessage( IDC_LIST1, LB_GETCOUNT );

//Method 2: CListBox::GetCount
Count = pList->GetCount();
```

Getting the User's Selection from a List Box

SDK

If a window has a single select, send a LB_GETCURSEL message to determine the currently selected item as illustrated in Code 5–158.

The LB_GETCURSEL message returns the selected row, or LB_ERR id no row is selected by the user. For list boxes that support multiple selections, see the *Working with Multiple Selections* section.

Code 5–158

```
int Selection = SendMessage( hChild, LB_GETCURSEL, 0, 0 );
if( Selection != LB_ERR )
{
        // Selection is the row in the listbox that is selected
        }
```

MFC

For list box controls with single-selection ability, send an LB_GETCURSEL message to the window or call the CListBox::GetCurSel() function as shown in Code 5–159. This example assumes that IDC_LIST1 is a unique ID for a list box control. All of the methods above will return the current user selection, and if nothing is selected, they will return LB_ERR (demonstrated in the if test).

Code 5–159

```
CListBox* pList = (CListBox*)GetDlgItem(IDC_LIST1 );
int Selection;

// Method 1: LB_GETCURSEL message
Selection = pList->SendMessage( LB_GETCURSEL );

// Method 1 Variation: SendDlgItemMessage
Selection = SendDlgItemMessage( IDC_LIST1, LB_GETCURSEL );

//Method 2: CListBox::GetCurSel
Selection = pList->GetCurSel();

if( Selection != LB_ERR )
        // Selection is valid
```

Setting the Currently Selected Item in the List Box

SDK

If you want to set the selection for a list box using code, send the LB_SETCURSEL message to the window as illustrated in Code 5–160.

In this example, the hChild is the child window handle, the third parameter is the row we want to select (zero would be the first row, and one as in our example would be the second row), and the fourth parameter is always zero.

Code 5–160

```
SendMessage( hChild, LB_SETCURSEL, 1, 0 );
```

MFC

In order to make a selection in a list box using code, send the LB_SETCURSEL message to the child, or you can call the CListBox::SetCurSel function() as shown in Code 5–161. This example assumes that IDC_LIST1 is the unique ID for a list control.

Code 5–161

```
CListBox* pList = (CListBox*)GetDlgItem(IDC_LIST1 );
int Selection=0; // Make first row selected

// Method 1: LB_SETCURSEL message
pList->SendMessage( LB_GETCURSEL, Selection );

// Method 1 Variation: SendDlgItemMessage
SendDlgItemMessage( IDC_LIST1, LB_SETCURSEL, Selection );

//Method 2: CListBox::SetCurSel
pList->SetCurSel( Selection );
```

Setting User Selection to a Certain String

SDK

You can select an item in a list box by string value as well as by row. To do this, send the LB_SELECTSTRING message to the window as illustrated in Code 5–162.

Code 5–162

```
if( SendMessage( hChild, LB_SELECTSTRING, -1, (LPARAM)"Apples" ) == LB_ERR )
    MessageBox( hwndDlg, "Text not found", "Information", MB_OK );
```

In this example, the hChild parameter is the window handle to the child list box. The third parameter indicates the item *before* the row to start searching on. This means that if we pass –1, it will start searching at row zero (this is done to easily permit continued searching after the first item found). The fourth parameter is the search string.

If the string is found, then that row is set as the selected row and the SendMessage() routine return value is the new selected row. If the string isn't found, no selection changes and the return value of SendMessage() is LB_ERR.

MFC

To select a row in a list box based on string value and not row, send a LB_SELECTSTRING message or call the CListBox::SelectString() function shown in Code 5–163.

In this example, the Selection parameter is the string you wanted to select in the list box. The –1 parameter indicates the row before where the function should start searching for the string (so, if we use –1, that means start at zero, or the first row). This example assumes that IDC_LIST1 is the unique ID for a list control.

Code 5–163

```
char Selection[]="Apple";
CListBox* pList = (CListBox*)GetDlgItem(IDC_LIST1 );

// Method 1: LB_SELECTSTRING message
pList->SendMessage( LB_SELECTSTRING, -1, (LPARAM)Selection );

// Method 1 Variation: SendDlgItemMessage
SendDlgItemMessage( IDC_LIST1, LB_SELECTSTRING, -1, (LPARAM)Selection );

//Method 2: CListBox::SelectString
pList->SelectString( -1, Selection );
```

Working with Multiple Selections

SDK

Retrieving Multiple Selected Items.   In order to determine the selections in a multiple selection list box, iterate through all the rows and send a LB_GETSEL message to the control (see Code 5–164) or you can send a LB_GETSELITEMS message and get an array of integers for the selected rows (see Code 5–165).

Code 5–164 assumes that hChild is the window handle for the list box you want to work with. The first thing it does is determine the number of rows in the list, then enters a for loop to cycle through each row and determine if that row is selected with the LB_GETSEL message.

Code 5–165 retrieves the count of selected items (not the complete count of items) from the list control using the LB_GETSELCOUNT message. It then dynamically allocates an array of integers, using "new" to hold the list of rows selected. It then sends a LB_GETSELITEMS message to the list box control, also passing the count of selected items to retrieve and the address of where to store the information. The LB_GETSELITEMS will store an array of integers, where each integer is a row that is selected in the list box.

Code 5–164

```
int Count = SendMessage( hChild, LB_GETCOUNT, 0, 0 );
for( int Index=0; Index < Count; Index++ )
{
        if( SendMessage( hChild, LB_GETSEL, Index, 0 ) > 0 ) // Is selected
        {
                // Process selected item as desired
        }
}
```

Code 5–165

```
int Count = SendMessage( hChild, LB_GETSELCOUNT, 0, 0 );
int *pSelected = new int[Count];
SendMessage( hChild, LB_GETSELITEMS, Count, (LPARAM)pSelected);
for( int Index=0; Index < Count; Index++ )
{
        // pSelected[Index] would be a selected row
}
delete [] pSelected;
```

Selecting or Clearing Multiple Selected Items. If you want to set or clear a range of selection items, you can use the LB_SELITEMRANGE message. Code 5–166 selects all the rows in a multiple-selection list box. In this example hChild is the window handle for the list control. It determines how many items in the list are using LB_GETCOUNT, then sends the LB_SELITEMRANGE message to the child list box using SendMessage().

The wParam (third) parameter for LB_SELITEMRANGE is TRUE if you want to make the range selected or FALSE if you want to remove the selection from the range.

The final parameter for the LB_SELITEMRANGE message is actually two values combined as one: The lower 16 bits of the parameter must contain the starting row for the range and the upper 16 bits must contain the ending row for the range. The MAKELPARAM macro is used to combine the two values as needed.

Code 5–166

```
int Count = SendMessage( hChild, LB_GETCOUNT, 0, 0 );
SendMessage( hChild, LB_SELITEMRANGE, TRUE, MAKELPARAM(0, Count) );
```

MFC

Retrieving Multiple Selected Items.   In order to determine what selections are made in a multiple selection list box, iterate through all the rows and send a LB_GETSEL message to the window (see Code 5–167) or send a LB_GETSELITEMS message and get an array of integers for the selected rows (Code 5–168).

The CListBox class also provides member functions CListBox::GetSelCount() to determine how many items are selected, CListBox::GetSel() to determine the selected state of a row, and CListBox::GetSelItems() to get all the selected items at once.

Code 5–167

```
CListBox* pListBox = (cListBox*) GetDlgItem (IDC_LIST1);
int Count = pListBox -> SendMessage( LB_GETCOUNT );
for( int Index=0; Index < Count; Index++ )
{
      if( pListBox -> SendMessage( LB_GETSEL, Index ) > 0 ) // Is selected
      {
            // Process selected item as desired
      }
}
```

Code 5–168

```
CListBox* pListBox = (CListBox*)GetDlgItem(IDC_LIST1 );
int Count = pList->GetSelCount();
for( int Index=0; Index < Count; Index++ )
{
      if( pList->GetSel( Index ) > 0 )
            // If true, then this row was selected, process as desired

}
```

Code 5–168 assumes that IDC_LIST1 is the unique ID for the list box. The first thing it does is determine the number of rows in the list, then it enters a for loop to cycle through each row and determine if that row is selected with the LB_GETSEL message or the CListBox::GetSel () function in the variation as in Code 5–169.

Code 5–169

```
CListBox* pListBox = (cListBox*) GetDlgItem (IDC_LIST1);
int Count = pListBox -> SendMessage( LB_GETSELCOUNT );
int *pSelected = new int[Count];
pListBox -> SendMessage( LB_GETSELITEMS, Count, (LPARAM)pSelected);
for( int Index=0; Index < Count; Index++ )
{
      // pSelected[Index] would be a selected row
}
delete [] pSelected;
```

Code 5–170 retrieves the count of selected items (not the complete count of rows) from the list control using the LB_GETSELCOUNT message (or the CListBox::GetSelCount function() in the variation). It then dynamically allocates an array of integers using new to hold the list of rows selected and sends a LB_GETSELITEMS message to the list box control (or calls the CListBoix::GetSelItems() function in the variation), also passing the count of selected items to retrieve and the address of where to store the information.

Code 5–170

```
CListBox* pListBox = (CListBox*)GetDlgItem(IDC_LIST1 );
int Count = pListBox->GetSelCount();
int *pSelected = new int[Count];
pListBox->GetSelItems( Count, pSelected );
for( int Index=0; Index < Count; Index++ )
{
        // pSelected[Index] would be a selected row
}
delete [] pSelected;
```

Both the LB_GETSELITEMS message and the CListBox::GetSelItems() function will store an array of integers, where each integer is a row that the user selected in the list box.

Selecting or Clearing Multiple Selected Items.   If you want to set or clear a range of selection items, then use the LB_SELITEMRANGE message (see Code 5–171) or call the CListBox::SelItemRange() function (see Code 5–172). The following code example would select all the rows in a multiple-selection list box:

Code 5–171

```
int Start=0;
CListBox* pListBox = (CListBox*)GetDlgItem(IDC_LIST1 );
int Count = pListBox->GetCount();
pList->SendMessage(LB_SELITEMRANGE, TRUE, MAKELPARAM(Start, Count) );
```

Code 5–172

```
CListBox* pListBox = (CListBox*)GetDlgItem(IDC_LIST1 );
int Count = pListBox->GetCount();
pList->SelItemRange( TRUE, Start, Count );
```

Codes 5–171 and 5–172 assumes that IDC_LIST1 is the unique ID for the list control. It first determines how many items are in the list using LB_GETCOUNT or CListBox::GetCount(). Then it sends the LB_SELITEMRANGE message to the child list box in Code 5–171 or calls the CListBox::SelItemRange function in Code 5–172.

The final parameter for the LB_SELITEMRANGE message is actually two values combined as one: The lower 16 bits of the parameter must contain the starting row for the range, and the upper 16 bits must contain the ending row for the range. The MAKELPARAM macro is used to combine the 2 16-bit values into a single 32-bit value.

In Code 5–172, the TRUE that you see in the second parameter to SendMessage() and the first parameter in SelItemRange() determines if you are selecting (TRUE) or de-selecting (FALSE) the range. Where you see Start in the code, that indicates the starting row for the range. Count in the code indicates the ending row of the range.

Storing Extra Information for Each Line of a List Box

SDK

As with combo boxes, list boxes have a very handy feature where each row of the list box can contain an extra 32-bit value that is yours to use as you please. Read the Item Data section in the Combo Box section for more details, and we will see this information used practically when we discuss database programs.

To store or retrieve the extra item data for a list box use the LB_SETITEMDATA LB_GETITEMDATA message. As with combo boxes, set the item data after you have inserted an item into the list. If the list is sorted with the LBS_SORT style and you use LB_ADDSTRING to add the string to the list box, the SendMessage() function returns the actual insertion point where the string was added. That value should be used with the LB_SETITEMDATA message as illustrated in Code 5–173.

Code 5–173

```
int PersonID=5;
char PersonName[] = "Smith, John";

int Row = SendMessage( hChild, LB_ADDSTRING, 0, (LPARAM)PersonName);
SendMessage( hChild, LB_SETITEMDATA, Row, (LPARAM) PersonID );
```

Code 5–173 adds "Smith, John" to the list box as a string using the LB_ADDSTRING message then saves the return value from that addition, which is now the row where the string was added. Code 5–173 also sets the PersonID variable as the "Item Data" for that row using LB_SETITEMDATA. Imagine that the list box is populated with the names of many people and each name has a unique person ID as the item data for that row. To determine the person ID for the user's current selection, use LB_GETITEMDATA as shown Code 5–174.

We have used a Person ID example here, but the value you store as the item data for a row can be whatever you want, including pointers to objects or structures. As long as you implement it consistently (i.e., you use LB_SETITEMDATA to store a Person ID and LB_GETITEMDATA to retrieve a person ID), you can store any type of data you please in the item data.

Code 5–174

```
int PersonID;
int Selection = SendMessage( hChild, LB_GETCURSEL, 0, 0 );
if( Selection != LB_ERR )
{
        PersonID = SendMessage( hChild, LB_GETITEMDATA, Selection, 0 );
                // PersonID is now the ID for the currently selected person.
}
```

MFC

As with combo boxes, list boxes have a handy feature where each row of the list box can contain an extra 32-bit value that is yours to use as you please. Read the Item Data section in the Combo Box section for more details.

To store or retrieve the extra item data for a list box, use the LB_SETITEMDATA or LB_GETITEMDATA messages or the CListBox::SetItemData() and CListBox::GetItemData() functions. As with combo boxes, set the item data after you have inserted it into the list. If the list is sorted (with the LBS_SORT style) and you used LB_ADDSTRING to add the string to the list box, the insertion point where the string was added is returned. The return value is used with the LB_SETITEMDATA message as shown in Code 5–175.

Code 5–175

```
CListBox* pList = (CListBox*)GetDlgItem( IDC_LIST1 );
int Row;
int PersonID=5;
char PersonName[] = "Smith, John";

// Method 1: Using LB_SETITEMDATA
Row = SendMessage( hChild, LB_ADDSTRING, 0, (LPARAM)PersonName);
SendMessage( hChild, LB_SETITEMDATA, Row, (LPARAM) PersonID );

// Method 2: Using CListBox::SetItemData
Row = pList->AddString( PersonName );
pList->SetItemData( Row, PersonID );
```

Code 5–175 adds "Smith, John" to the list box as a string using the LB_ADDSTRING message in method 1 and CListBox::AddString() in method 2. Then it saves the return value from that addition, which is now the row where the string was added. Code 5–175 sets the PersonID variable as the "item data" for that row, using the LB_SETITEMDATA message in method one and the CListBox::SetItemData() function in method 2.

Imagine that the list box is populated with the names of many people and each name also has a unique person ID as the item data for that row. To determine the person ID for the user's current selection use LB_GETITEMDATA, as illustrated in Code 5–176. Code 5–177 retrieves the item using CListBox::GetItemData().

Code 5-176

```
CListBox* pList = (CListBox*) GetDlgItem (IDC_LIST1);
int PersonID;
int Selection = pList -> SendMessage( LB_GETCURSEL );
if( Selection != LB_ERR )
{
        PersonID = pList -> SendMessage( LB_GETITEMDATA, Selection );
                // PersonID is now the ID for the currently selected person.
}
```

Code 5-177

```
CListBox* pList = (CListBox*)GetDlgItem(IDC_LIST1);
int PersonID;
int Selection = pList->GetCurSel();
if( Selection != LB_ERR )
{
        PersonID = pList->GetItemData( Selection );
                // PersonID is now the ID for the currently selected person.
}
```

In Code 5–177, we use CListBox::GetCurSel() to determine the selected row, and then we use CListBox::GetItemData() to retrieve the Item Data from that row. The parameter passed to GetItemData() is the row you want the item data from.

We have used a Person ID example here, but the value you store as the item data for a row can be whatever you want, including pointers to objects or structures. As long as you implement it consistently (i.e., you use LB_SETITEMDATA to store a Person ID and LB_GETITEMDATA to retrieve a person ID), you can store any type of data you please in the item data.

Edit Boxes

Edit boxes are perhaps the most common and simplistic element in forms-based programming, after the button. Figure 5–22 has several window controls (the Edit group box, the Name STATIC control, the Password and Read-only checkboxes, the Hello and Clear buttons, the edit box with Bob in it, and the Multi-line edit box).

Figure 5–22   Common edit boxes.

The edit box with Bob in it is our main center of attention, but the other controls demonstrate how we might interact with the edit box. On the right there is also an edit control with the Multi-line and Want Return properties displayed.

In the examples that follow, we will demonstrate how to respond to user events such as the user's typing into the edit box. You might want to enable and disable a button if the user text is blank or not. We'll also place text into the edit box, retrieve text from the edit box, change the properties of the edit box, and work with the clipboard or copy and paste operations.

Before we begin, notice the STATIC control in front of the Edit box that contains <u>N</u>ame text. This is a separate control from the EDIT control. The STATIC control has a caption of "&Name," which, when displayed on screen, underlines the letter immediately after the ampersand. This special caption identifies the hotkey for that control.

Normally, pressing Alt-N brings us to the control that has a caption with an underlined N. But, STATIC controls are not able to get focus. The hotkey specified by the underlined character of a STATIC text control sets focus to the next control in the tab order. This ability is specified at design time in the dialog editor and no coding is needed. In this example, pressing alt-N will set focus to the edit box.

Edit controls have a default size limit of 32K, but you can limit the amount of text to be a smaller or larger number. An issue not addressed here is creating an edit control that can contain more than 32K. In order to do this, your program must maintain its own dynamic memory for the control and use the EM_SETHANDLE message.

Creating an Edit Box at Runtime

SDK

Dynamically creating and destroying windows at runtime is much more complex than creating them in the dialog editor, and then using ShowWindow to hide or show them.

In order to get the correct 3D appearance of the typical edit box when creating controls dynamically, we need to call the CreateWindowEx() function, not CreateWinow(). Code 5–178 creates the window with normal window styles and permits you to specify various EDIT box styles, such as ES_PASSWORD, and sets the font correctly for the edit box. An example of calling this function is illustrated in Code 5–179.

Code 5-178

```
// PNCreateEditBox - Creates an edit box at runtime
// Parameters:
//      hParent - Parent window handle (usually the dialog to create on)
//      lpCaption - String to store in edit box after created, may be NULL
//      x - X coordinate for location
//      y - Y coordinate for location
//      nWidth - Width of control
//      nHeight - Height of control
//      nID - Unique ID' for the new edit box (must be unique on the parent
//      window)
//      nStyle - Additional edit styles (start with 'ES_')
// Returns: HWND of new window of NULL upon failure
HWND PNCreateEditBox( HWND hParent, LPCTSTR lpCaption, int x, int y, int
    nWidth, int nHeight, int nID, int nStyle )
{
    HWND Ret;
    HFONT hFont;

    // Create the window
    Ret = CreateWindowEx( WS_EX_CLIENTEDGE, "EDIT", lpCaption,
        WS_VISIBLE|WS_CHILD|WS_TABSTOP| nStyle, x, y, nWidth, nHeight,
        hParent, (HMENU)nID, GetModuleHandle(NULL), NULL );
    if( Ret )
    {
        // If window was created, then we set the font of the button to be
        // the same as its parent window
        hFont = (HFONT)SendMessage( hParent, WM_GETFONT, 0, 0 );
        SendMessage( Ret, WM_SETFONT, (WPARAM)hFont, 1 );
    }
    return( Ret );
}
```

Code 5-179

```
PNCreateEditBox( hwndDlg, "Dynamic", 290, 80, 75, 24, 4006, 0 );
```

where hwndDlg is the dialog window handle for the dialog you want to place the edit box on.

MFC

In order to create an edit box at runtime, add a data member to our parent View or Dialog class where we want to place the list box. In our example, we will be doing so in the CMFC_ControlsView.cpp file.

Once the member variable is declared there, call its Create() function to create the window itself in the View class's OnCreate() function (it would be in OnInitDialog() if it were a dialog-based application). Then call the its SetFont() function in the OnInitialUpdate() function of the View class (we would do so in the OnInitDialog() function if it were a dialog-based application). Here are the steps you need to follow:

1. Add to your View class (in CMFC_CONTROLSView.h in our example) Code 5–180.

Code 5–180

```
CEdit m_DynaEdit;
```

2. In the OnCreate() function for the View class (CMFC_ControlsView.cpp for out example), call the Create() member function of the CListBox class as illustrated in Code 5–181. Notice that this example calls CreateEx(), instead of Create() as other MFC examples. This is to implement the 3D appearance without a lot of overhead. The CWnd:: CreateEx() function will call the SDK's CreateWindowEx() function.

Code 5–181

```
// Dynamically create edit box
CRect PosAndSize;
PosAndSize.SetRect( 290, 80, 365, 104 );
m_DynaEdit.CreateEx( WS_EX_CLIENTEDGE, "EDIT", NULL,
        WS_VISIBLE|WS_CHILD|WS_TABSTOP, PosAndSize, this, 4007 );
```

3. Change the font of the new control to match its parent window's font. In the View class in the OnInitialUpdate() handler, call the SetFont() function for the new object with the return value from the parent window's GetFont() function. This is illustrated in Code 5–182. Remember that the GetFont() function call is in a member function and can be thought of as *this*->GetFont().

Code 5–182

```
void CMFC_ControlsView::OnInitialUpdate()
{

        CFormView::OnInitialUpdate();
        GetParentFrame()->RecalcLayout();
        ResizeParentToFit();

        // Set listbox font to match the parent (the parent is
        'this')
        m_DynaEdit.SetFont( GetFont() );
}
```

Getting Text into and from an Edit Box

SDK

For single-line edit boxes see the *Window Text* section at the beginning of this chapter, and the SetWindowText function.

Multi-Line Edit Boxes.   When you add text to a multi-line edit control, you separate lines with a carriage return ("\r") and line feed character ("\n") as shown in Code 5–183. Text retrieved from a multi-line edit control contains only the carriage return character still in the string as a line separator. Also, you can get the number of lines of text in an edit control—not just the number of lines visible—by sending the edit control a EM_GETLINECOUNT message as shown in Code 5–184.

Code 5–183

```
SetDlgItemText( hwndDlg, IDC_EDITMULTI, "Multi-line\r\nEdit control" );
```

Code 5–184

```
int LineCount = SendDlgItemMessage( hwndDlg, IDC_EDITMULTI,
EM_GETLINECOUNT, 0, 0 );
```

Code 5–184 returns the lines using the IDC_EDITMULTI ID, a child of the hwndDlg window. To retrieve a line from a multi-line edit box, use the EM_LINEINDEX message to first retrieve the index of the character at the start of a line. Then use the EM_LINELENGTH message to determine the length of that line. There will be no null ("\0") terminator character. Finally, send an EM_GETLINE message to retrieve the text and properly null-terminate the text.

Because of the added complexity—getting a line of text from a multi-line edit control has no maximum width and when gotten has no null terminator—we will provide a helper function shown in Code 5–185.

Code 5–185

```
//PNMLEditGetLine - Gets a specific line from a multi-line
//   edit box.
// Parameters:
//     hchild - Window handle for multi-line edit control
//     Line - Which line to retrieve
//     Dest - Where to store the gotten line
//     MaxLen -  Maximum number of characters to retrieve
//Returns: TRUE if successful, FALSE upon failure
BOOL PNMLEditGetLine( HWND hChild, int Line, char* Dest, int MaxLen )
{
  char *Tmp;
  int LineSize, LineIndex;
```

```
    // Determine the starting character position of the line
    LineIndex = SendMessage( hChild, EM_LINEINDEX, Line, 0 );
    if( LineIndex == -1 ) // Line parameter was bad
        return( FALSE );
    // Determine the length of line that character is on.
    LineSize = SendMessage( hChild, EM_LINELENGTH, LineIndex, 0 );
    // Dynamically allocate space for the string
    // Note: C programmers use malloc() here
    if( (Tmp=new char[max(LineSize+1,sizeof(WORD))]) == NULL )
        return( FALSE );
    // Store the # of characters to in our input buffer
    *(WORD*)Tmp=LineSize;
    // Retrieve the string from the control
    SendMessage( hChild, EM_GETLINE, Line, (LPARAM) Tmp );
    // Copy it into the Dest parameter
    strncpy( Dest, Tmp, min( MaxLen, LineSize ) );
    // Properly null-terminate the Dest parameter
    Dest[ min( MaxLen, LineSize ) ] = '\0';
    delete[] Tmp; // Note: C programmers use free here.
    return( TRUE );
}
```

To retrieve a line from a multi-line edit control, call the PNMLEditGetLine() function. The first parameter should be the EDIT control window handle, the second parameter is the desired line to get, the third parameter is the destination where to store the string, and the final parameter is the maximum number of characters to get. This is illustrated in Code 5–186.

Code 5–186

```
char Tmp[32];
PNMLEditGetLine( GetDlgItem(hwndDlg, IDC_EDITMULTI), 1, Tmp, sizeof(Tmp) );
MessageBox( hwndDlg, Tmp, "Line 1", MB_OK );
```

Notice how GetDlgItem() is used to get the window handle for the desired multi-line edit control (IDC_EDITMULTI) and as the first parameter to PNMELEditGetLine(). A multi-line edit control also has no method for setting a specific line of text. So again we will create a help function called PNMLEditSetLine() (see Code 5–187) to help you set a line of text in a multi-line edit. Simply call this function to change a specific line in a multi-line edit control as shown in Code 5–188.

Code 5–187

```
// PNMLEditSetLine - Sets a specific line in a multi-line edit box.
// Parameters:
//      hChild - Window handle for multi-line edit control
//      Line - Which line to set
//      Src - String to place into edit box
// Returns: TRUE if successful, FALSE upon failure
BOOL PNMLEditSetLine( HWND hChild, int Line, char* Src )
```

```
{
        int LineStart, LineSize;

        // Determine the starting character position of the line
        LineStart = SendMessage( hChild, EM_LINEINDEX, Line, 0 );
        if( LineStart == -1 ) // Line parameter was bad
                return( FALSE );
        // Determine the length of the line to be replaced
        LineSize = SendMessage( hChild, EM_LINELENGTH, LineStart, 0 );
        // Select the text on that line (like a Cut&Paste operation)
        SendMessage( hChild, EM_SETSEL, LineStart, LineStart+LineSize );
        // Then replace selected text with our new string
        SendMessage( hChild, EM_REPLACESEL, FALSE, (LPARAM) Src );
        return( TRUE );
}
```

Code 5–188

```
PNMLEditSetLine( GetDlgItem(hwndDlg, IDC_EDITMULTI), 1, "A Test" );
```

MFC

For Single-line edit boxes, see the *Window Text* section at the beginning of this chapter.

Multi-Line Edit Boxes.   When you add text to a multi-line edit control, you would separate lines with a carriage return ("\r") and line feed character ("\n"). An example in a View or Dialog class is illustrated in Code 5–189. When text is retrieved from a multi-line edit control, you will only find the carriage return character still in the string as a line separator. Also, you can get the number of lines of text in an edit control—not just the number of lines visible—by calling CEdit::GetLineCount() as shown in Code 5–190.

Code 5–189

```
SetDlgItemText(IDC_EDITMULTI, "Multi-line\r\nEdit control" );
```

Code 5–190

```
CEdit* pEdit = (CEdit*)GetDlgItemText( IDC_EDITMULTI );
int LineCount = pEit->GetLineCount();
```

Code 5–190 returns the lines held by the edit box with the IDC_EDITMULTI ID and assumes that the code was in a View or Dialog member function, which would be the parent window and object to the edit box.

To retrieve a line from a multi-line edit box, you can use the CEdit::GetLine() and CEdit::GetLineLength() functions. Then use the CEdit::LineLength() function to

---

determine the length of that line, because when you retrieve it there will be no null ("\0") terminator there. Next use the CEdit::GetLine() function to retrieve the text for the line and remember to null-terminate it. This is illustrated in Code 5–191.

In Code 5–191, the IDC_EDITMULTI would be the ID of the child control we wanted to work with. The LineNum would be the line number you wanted to retrieve from the multi-line edit box.

Code 5–191

```
CString Text;
pEdit = (CEdit*)GetDlgItem( IDC_EDITMULTI );
int Len = pEdit->LineLength( LineNum );
pEdit->GetLine( LineNum, Text.GetBuffer(Len+1), Len );
Text.ReleaseBuffer(Len+1);
Text.SetAt(Len, '\0');
```

Limiting Text Length

SDK

You can limit the amount of text an EDIT control will contain by sending it an EM_LIMITTEXT message. In this case, the wParam parameter for SendMessage() contains the size limitation of the edit box. Operations like this are normally carried out in the WM_INITDIALOG handler. Code 5–192 illustrates this technique, setting a 32-character limit.

If you set the limit to be smaller then the amount of text already in the control, the text will not be truncated. For this reason, you should set this value before the user has a chance to type data, like in the WM_INITDIALOG handler.

Code 5–192

```
LRESULT CALLBACK DialogProc( HWND hwndDlg, UINT uMsg, WPARAM wParam, LPARAM
lParam )
{
    // Portions of code removed for readability
    switch( uMsg )
    {
        case WM_INITDIALOG:
            // Portions of code removed for readability
            SendDlgItemMessage( hwndDlg, IDC_EDITNAME, EM_LIMITTEXT, 32, 0 );
            return( TRUE );
    // Portions of code removed for readability
```

MFC

To limit the amount of text a user can type into an edit box, send an EM_SETLIMITTEXT message (see Code 5–193) or call the CEdit::SetLimitText() function (see Code 5–194).

In both examples, the IDC_EDITNAME refers to the unique ID of the desired edit control. Max refers to the maximum size, not including the null terminator (i.e., a max of 3 would mean the user could type in 'ABC').

Code 5–193

```
CEdit* pEdit = (CEdit*)GetDlgItem( IDC_EDITNAME );
pEdit->SetLimitText( Max );
```

Code 5–194

```
SendDlgItemMessage( IDC_EDITNAME, EM_SETLIMITTEXT, Max );
```

Determining When User Changes Text

SDK

More often than not, you may not need to respond to notifications from an edit control. However, one common user interface technique is to disable a button until the user types some data in an edit box. For example, in a "Find" operation, a Find button may be disabled until the user types in some text. As the user types in text, the button becomes enabled as shown in Figure 5–23.

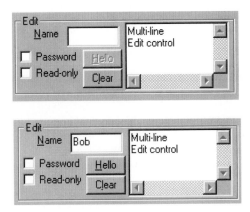

Figure 5–23   As the user enters text, the button becomes enabled.

Notice how the Hello button is disabled when Name is blank, but not when it contains text. To accomplish this, we need to add a WM_COMMAND handler for our main event switch, and test for the EN_CHANGE notification code as shown in Code 5–195.

In Code 5–195, notice how in the WM_INITDIALOG handler we first disable the button. This could also have been done in the dialog editor by changing the button's property to Disabled. Then, in the WM_COMMAND, we make sure the notification message came from the IDC_EDITNAME (our edit control). Next we make sure it was the EN_CHANGE code, which edit boxes send to their parent every time their text changes. Finally, we use GetWindowTextLength() to determine if the string is empty, then enable or disable the IDC_BUTTONNAME control.

Code 5–195

```
LRESULT CALLBACK DialogProc( HWND hwndDlg, UINT uMsg, WPARAM wParam, LPARAM
lParam )
{
    int wID;
    int wNotification;
    HWND hChild;

    switch( uMsg )
    {
        case WM_INITDIALOG:
            // Start button for Edit demonstration in disabled mode
            EnableWindow( GetDlgItem(hwndDlg, IDC_BUTTONNAME), FALSE );
            // Portions of code removed for readability
            return( TRUE );
        case WM_COMMAND: // A message from a control or menu item
            // Parse out WM_COMMAND parameters to be more readable
            wID = LOWORD(wParam);
            wNotification = HIWORD(wParam);
            hChild = (HWND) lParam;

            // Our edit control text changed. Determine to enable button or
            not
            if( (wID == IDC_EDITNAME ) && wNotification == EN_CHANGE )
            {
                if( GetWindowTextLength( hChild ) > 0 )
                        EnableWindow( GetDlgItem(hwndDlg, IDC_BUTTONNAME), TRUE );
                else
                        EnableWindow( GetDlgItem(hwndDlg, IDC_BUTTONNAME),
                        FALSE );
            }
        // Portions of code removed for readability
```

MFC

In order to respond to changes in an edit box, such as when the user types a letter or performs a Paste operation, you will want to respond to the EN_CHANGE notification when the edit control sends to the parent in a WM_COMMAND message. Here are the steps you need to follow when using the ClassWizard. Begin from the View menu selection. The ClassWizard will generate code shown in Code 5–196.

1. Make sure that the Message Maps tab (see Figure 5–24) is highlighted.
2. In the Class name field, make sure your parent window class is selected (CMFC_ControlsView.cpp in our example).
3. In the Object IDs list, make sure you select the ID for the edit box you want to intercept.
4. In the Messages list, select the type of notification you want to handle (our example is EN_CHANGE).
5. Click the Add Function button.
6. Click OK to accept the name for the new function suggested by the compiler.

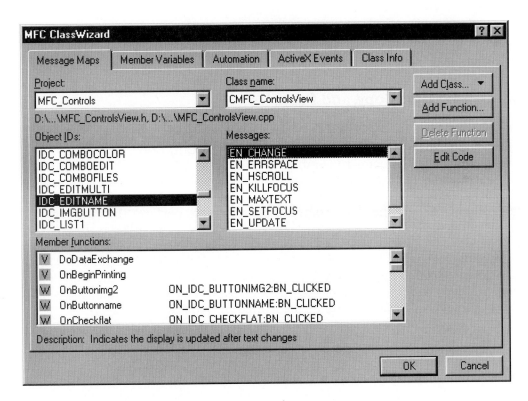

Figure 5–24   ClassWizard Message Map for edit boxes.

Code 5-196

```
void CMFC_ControlsView::OnChangeEditname()
{
        // TODO: Add your message handler here
}
```

To further demonstrate the processing, add code to the handler so that as the user types another button window is enabled or disabled. If the user removes all the text, then the button is disabled, if the user types in text, the button is enabled. This is illustrated in Code 5-197.

Code 5-197

```
void CMFC_ControlsView::OnChangeEditname()
{
        // Based on user typing into an edit box, this show how to disable
        // or enable another control (a button) if the text is blank or not.
        CEdit* pEdit = (CEdit*)GetDlgItem( IDC_EDITNAME );
        CWnd* pButton = GetDlgItem( IDC_BUTTONNAME );
        if( pEdit->GetWindowTextLength() > 0 ) // Is there anything in the
        // edit box?
                pButton->EnableWindow( TRUE );
        else
                pButton->EnableWindow( FALSE );
}
```

Implementing Cut, Copy, and Paste

SDK

Edit controls will automatically be able to support the Cut, Copy, and Paste functionality using standard keyboard combinations such as CTRL-C to copy or CTRL-V to paste. However, standard Windows user interface guidelines are that you include an Edit menu choice with these features. The issue arises of how a menu handler can tell another control (the EDIT control in this case) to perform the cut, copy, or paste.

The simple answer is that you simply send a WM_CUT, WM_COPY, WM_PASTE, or WM_CLEAR message to the current (focused) window. We can use the GetFocus() function to determine the currently focused control, and then SendMessage() to send these messages to that control as illustrated in Code 5-198.

Code 5-198

```
LRESULT CALLBACK DialogProc( HWND hwndDlg, UINT uMsg, WPARAM wParam, LPARAM
lParam )
{
        int wID;
        int wNotification;
```

```
HWND hChild;

switch( uMsg )
{
// Portions of code removed for readability
        case WM_COMMAND: // A message from a control or menu item
                // Parse out WM_COMMAND parameters to be more readable
                wID = LOWORD(wParam);
                wNotification = HIWORD(wParam);
                hChild = (HWND) lParam;

                // Did user select one of the Edit menu items?
                if( (wID == IDM_EDITCUT ) )
                        SendMessage( GetFocus(), WM_CUT, 0, 0 );
                if( (wID == IDM_EDITCOPY ) )
                        SendMessage( GetFocus(), WM_COPY, 0, 0 );
                if( (wID == IDM_EDITPASTE ) )
                        SendMessage( GetFocus(), WM_PASTE, 0, 0 );
                if( (wID == IDM_EDITUNDO ) )
                         SendMessage( GetFocus(), WM_UNDO, 0, 0 );
// Portions of code removed for readability
```

In Code 5–198, we are assume that you have menu items that you added with the menu resource editor with the IDs of IDM_EDITCUT, IDM_EDITPASTE, IDM_EDIT-COPY, and IDM_EDITUNDO. The code above sends the desired WM_CUT, WM_COPY, WM_PASTE, or WM_UNDO Message to the currently focused control.

It is possible to support several formats in the clipboard (this is where things are stored when copied or cut). We are not taking any special steps here to ensure that the operation being performed will work. For example, if someone does a Copy of an image from another program, and then attempts to Paste it into our edit box, nothing will happen. It might be a nice feature to identify whether a Paste operation will really work, based on the contents of the clipboard. There will be examples of this in the Clipboard section of this book.

MFC

Edit controls will automatically be able to support the Cut, Copy, and Paste functionality using standard keyboard combinations, such as CTRL-C to copy or CTRL-V to paste it. However, standard Windows user interface guidelines are that you include an Edit menu choice with these features. The issue arises of how a menu handler can tell another control (the EDIT control in this case) to perform the cut, copy, or paste.

To further complicate matters, menu handlers in MFC fall into two categories: COMMAND messages that mean the menu item was selected by the user and

UPDATE_COMMAND_UI handlers that are called to determine the status of a menu item, such as enabled or not.

The reason this becomes important in a clipboard operation such as copy or paste is that we don't want the Copy menu item enabled when a button is the active control, only when an edit box is the active control. Because of this, we will need to add to menu handlers for each clipboard operation: one for the COMMAND and one for the UPDATE_COMMAND_UI.

The actual interaction with the clipboard will be quite easy, because there are Cut, Copy, and Paste functions inside the CEdit class to perform these operations with one line of code. Because the tasks are similar for the various clipboard operations, we will only demonstrate the Copy capability in this section.

Knowing When an Edit Control Has Focus

First, identify when an edit control is the currently active control. We will need to do this in the UPDATE_COMMAND_UI handler so we can determine if we should enable or disable the clipboard menu item. We will use the CWnd::GetFocus() function to determine which window has the focus, and then we will call the GetClassName() function (an SDK function, not MFC, but still usable) to determine if it's an EDIT control.

Using ClassWizard, add a message map for the UPDATE_COMMAND_UI for the Copy menu item. The function it adds should be called OnUpdateEditCopy(). Modifying this is illustrated in Code 5–199.

Code 5–199

```
void CMFC_ControlsView::OnUpdateEditCopy(CCmdUI* pCmdUI)
{
        // Get the currently focused window
        CEdit* pEdit = (CEdit*)GetFocus();

        if( !pEdit )
                pCmdUI->Enable( FALSE ); //Nothing focused, disable menu item
        else
        {
                // Get its class name
                char Text[32];
                ::GetClassName( pEdit->m_hWnd, Text, sizeof(Text));

                // Was it an Edit box?
                if( stricmp( Text, "EDIT" ) == 0 )
                {
                        // At this point, we know it's an edit box.
                        // Now we see if the user has selected some text in the
                        // edit box.
                        int nStart, nEnd;
                        pEdit->GetSel( nStart, nEnd );
```

```
        // If they have, then the Edit/Copy menu item should be
        // enabled
        if( nStart != nEnd )
                pCmdUI->Enable( TRUE );
        else
                pCmdUI->Enable( FALSE ); // If not, it should be
                // disabled
    }
    }

}
```

Here's what is happening in Code 5–199.

- It calls CWnd::GetFocus() to determine the currently focused window.
- If there is no currently focused window, then it calls pCmdUI->Enabled (FALSE) to disable the menu item.
- If there is a window focused, then it calls the ::GetClassName() SDK function to retrieve the window class name(such as EDIT or BUTTON) and store it into the Text array.
- It then compares the window class name with "EDIT," using stricmp.
- If the control was an EDIT box, then it calls the CEdit::GetSel() function to determine the start and end of the selection in the edit box, to determine if the user selected text in the edit box.
- If the start and end are different, then the edit box has selected text and pCmdUI->Enable(TRUE) is called, which enables the menu item.
- If the start and end are the same, then nothing is selected (and therefore, nothing can be copied), then pCmdUI->Enable(FALSE) is called to disable the menu item.

The CCmdUI class has menu functions to control the appearance of a control or menu item. When you call the Enable function for the passed pCmdUI pointer, then you can enable or disable the menu item that invoked. You can also check it or uncheck it. Since this function is called before every time a menu is dropped down, the state set here will be current when the menu actually appears.

Performing the Copy/Responding to the Menu Selection

We will need to add a message map for the COMMAND message of the Edit/Copy menu item. Using ClassWizard, add the handler and make sure that the message map is added to the View class (or the Dialog class for dialog-based applications). The function that you add should be called OnEditCopy by default (because it is a handler for ID_EDITCOPY). Change the code to make it similar to Code 5–200.

Code 5–200 performs the same CWnd::GetFocus() to get the CWnd pointer for the control. Then with that pointer, it calls the CEdit::Copy() function, which copies the currently selected text into the clipboard.

Code 5-200

```
void CMFC_ControlsView::OnEditCopy()
{
        // Get focused window
        CEdit* pEdit = (CEdit*)GetFocus();

        // If found the focused window, then do the copy
        // Note: Because of the OnUpdateEditCopy function, this menu item
        // would only have been enabled if an edit box were focused. Other
        // wise we would check to see if pEdit really pointed to an edit box.
        if( pEdit )
                pEdit->Copy();
}
```

Password and Read-Only Edit Boxes

SDK

While the best time to make edit boxes password or read only style is at design time in the dialog editor (they are both properties of the edit box), it can also be useful to change them at runtime. Even though these items refer to a style on the edit box, you don't change the style the way you do with some other styles and controls (using GetwindowLong() and SetwindowLong()). Instead, we will send messages to the EDIT control as shown in Code 5–201.

Code 5-201

```
LRESULT CALLBACK DialogProc( HWND hwndDlg, UINT uMsg, WPARAM wParam, LPARAM
lParam )
{
    int wID;
    int wNotification;
    HWND hChild;

    switch( uMsg )
    {
    // Portions of code removed for readability
        case WM_COMMAND: // A message from a control or menu item
                // Parse out WM_COMMAND parameters to be more readable
                wID = LOWORD(wParam);
                wNotification = HIWORD(wParam);
                hChild = (HWND) lParam;

                if( (wID == IDC_CHECKPASSWORD ) && wNotification ==
                BN_CLICKED )
                {
                    if( IsDlgButtonChecked( hwndDlg, IDC_CHECKPASSWORD ) )
                            SendDlgItemMessage( hwndDlg, IDC_EDITNAME,
                            EM_SETPASSWORDCHAR, '*', 0 );
```

```
                else
                        SendDlgItemMessage( hwndDlg, IDC_EDITNAME,
                                EM_SETPASSWORDCHAR, 0, 0 );
                InvalidateRect( GetDlgItem(hwndDlg, IDC_EDITNAME), 0, 0);
        }
        if( (wID == IDC_CHECKREADONLY ) && wNotification ==
            BN_CLICKED )
        {
                if( IsDlgButtonChecked( hwndDlg, IDC_CHECKREADONLY ) )
                        SendDlgItemMessage( hwndDlg, IDC_EDITNAME,
                                EM_SETREADONLY, 1, 0 );
                else
                        SendDlgItemMessage( hwndDlg, IDC_EDITNAME,
                                EM_SETREADONLY, 0, 0 );
                InvalidateRect( GetDlgItem(hwndDlg, IDC_EDITNAME), 0, 0
                );
        }
// Portions of code removed for readability
```

Code 5–201 demonstrates the use of the SendDlgItemMessage() function to send either a EM_SETPASSWORDCHAR or EM_SETREADONLY message to an edit box control. In the case of EM_SETPASSWORDCHAR, the fourth parameter is the character to use for password (hidden text) entry. If this parameter is zero, then the edit box is returned to a normal non-password mode (user can see what they type), otherwise the edit box will display the character passed in the fourth parameter as the user types. For EM_SETREADONLY, the fourth parameter is either 1 to turn on read-only mode, or zero to turn it off.

Code 5–201 shows how to turn on and off the features and counts on the two checkbox controls (IDC_CHECKPASSWORD and IDC_CHECKREADONLY) to be in our dialog. This is why the code sits inside an if test that checks those IDs. The code above is from the SDK_Controls sample.

MFC

In order to change an edit box to password mode or out of password mode, call the CEdit::SetPasswordChar() function. To set it into read-only or read-write mode, call the CEdit::SetReadOnly() function as shown in Code 5–202.

Code 5–202

```
void CMFC_ControlsView::OnCheckpassword()
{
        // When user clicks the Password checkbox, toggle edit control
        // between normal and password mode
        CEdit* pEdit = (CEdit*)GetDlgItem( IDC_EDITNAME );
        if( IsDlgButtonChecked( IDC_CHECKPASSWORD ) )
                pEdit->SetPasswordChar( '*' ); // Make password mode
        else
```

```
        pEdit->SetPasswordChar( 0 ); // Make normal mode
    pEdit->InvalidateRect( 0 );
}

void CMFC_ControlsView::OnCheckreadonly()
{
    // When user clicks Readonly checkbox toggle edit control between
    normal
    // and read-only mode.
    CEdit* pEdit = (CEdit*)GetDlgItem( IDC_EDITNAME );
    if( IsDlgButtonChecked( IDC_CHECKREADONLY ) )
        pEdit->SetReadOnly( TRUE ); // Make read only mode
    else
        pEdit->SetReadOnly( FALSE ); // Make normal mode
}
```

Static Controls

Static controls (see Figure 5–25) are simple text or image type controls that do not normally change, or that the user does not normally interact with or change. Static controls cannot get the focus (receive keyboard input), but they can be clicked on with the mouse of the control has its NOTIFY property set to TRUE.

Figure 5–25 has four STATIC controls: the group box that surrounds the other controls, the "Some Text" control, the smily face icon, and the "Some Other Text" sunken static control.

The smily face icon requires no coding, and the selected image (bitmap or icon) can be chosen all with the properties for the control. The same holds true for the sunken text. For the "Some Text" control, which has a different font, we have changed the font within the program. There is no Font property for static controls.

Remember that one aspect of a STATIC control is that when you drop them on a dialog, they are all given the same ID: IDC_STATIC. If you want to interact with the control at runtime, then you must change the ID to be a unique ID on the dialog.

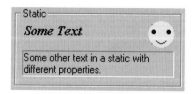

Figure 5–25   Common static controls.

Getting and Setting the Text for the Static Control

SDK and MFC

See the *Window Text* section at the beginning of this chapter to see how to change or retrieve the text in a static control, and the SetWindowText/GetWindowText functions.

Responding to User Clicks on Static Controls

SDK

In order for a STATIC control to send click notifications to its parent, you must make sure that its ID has been changed from IDC_STATIC to some unique ID, and you must also make sure that its Notify property was checked in its Properties dialog.

When the STATIC is clicked, it sends a WM_COMMAND message to its parent window, with an STN_CLICKED notification. An example handler for this in your dialog procedure is shown in Code 5–203.

Code 5–203

```
LRESULT CALLBACK DialogProc( HWND hwndDlg, UINT uMsg, WPARAM wParam, LPARAM
lParam )
{
    int wID;
    int wNotification;
    HWND hChild;

    char Path[MAX_PATH] = "C:\\*.*";

    switch( uMsg )
    {
        case WM_COMMAND: // A message from a control or menu item
            // Parse out WM_COMMAND parameters to be more readable
            wID = LOWORD(wParam);
            wNotification = HIWORD(wParam);
            hChild = (HWND) lParam;
            // Our Static control:
            if( wID == IDC_STATICSOMETEXT && wNotification == STN_CLICKED )
            {
                MessageBox( hwndDlg, "You clicked the static control",
                        "Information", MB_OK );
            }
    // Portions of code removed for readability
```

MFC

In order to respond to a static control, you need to change its ID from IDC_STATIC to some unique ID, like IDC_STATICIMAGE. You also need to make sure that the Notify property for the static control is checked (otherwise it won't notify its parent of clicks).

Once this is done, you can add a message map for it in ClassWizard and handle the BN_CLICKED message that it will generate. Simply add the handler with Class-Wizard. Code 5–205 is an example. This particular example uses the ShellExecute SDK function to launch the default web browser and send it to a specific web site:

Code 5–205

```
void CMFC_ControlsView::OnStaticicon()
{
ShellExecute( m_hWnd, NULL, "http://www.openroad.org", NULL, NULL,
    SW_SHOWNORMAL );
}
```

NOTE

To have your program run or launch another program or document, use the ShellExecute function. This permits you to launch web pages as well.

The first parameter to ShellExecute() is the window handle of the parent window (which can be NULL). The second parameter is a "Verb," which is a string with the operation you want to perform, such as "OPEN," or "PRINT." If the second parameter is NULL, then it defaults to "OPEN." The third parameter is the file to execute (more on this below). The fourth parameter specifies parameters to pass to the program, as if from the command line. The fifth parameter specifies what folder should be made the current folder before starting the program. The final parameter is how the window should be displayed; this is the same parameter you would pass to ShowWindow(), such as SW_NORMAL or SM_MAXIMIZE.

An interesting trait to ShellExecute() is that the filename (the third parameter) does not have to be an executable file name. If its not the name of an executable file, then Windows will launch the program that has been associated with that file type. So, for example, if the file parameter were "C:\\work\resume.doc," and you had Microsoft Word installed, which handles .DOC files, then Word would be launched to open the resume.doc file. This sort of association works for the web interfaces as well. For example, if the third parameter were "mailto://mario@openroad.org," then it would launch your default email program and create a new message to that person.

Remember

○	When working with controls, a great number of things can be controlled simply by changing the properties in the dialog editor.
	You can use SendMessage() or SendDlgItemMessage() to send messages to child controls. Use SendDlgItemMessage() when you want to work with more than one control.
○	List boxes and combo boxes both allow you to specify an extra 32-bit value for each row they contain. You can use this extra value anyway you please.
	Creating windows dynamically at runtime is possible, but it is usually easier to create them with the dialog editor and then hide and show them as needed.
○	Many controls like buttons, checkboxes, and static controls can implement icon and bitmap images with little or no coding by using the Picture tool in the dialog editor (which is really a static control).

Chapter 6

Common Controls

- About Common Controls
- Spin (Up/Down) Controls
- Progress Bars
- Sliders (Trackbar) Controls
- Image Lists
- Tree View Controls
- Tab Control
- Animation Controls
- Date Time Picker and Month Controls

About Common Controls

Common Controls differ from standard controls as discussed in the previous chapter in that they are defined within a DLL file. Controls discussed in Chapter 5 are fundamental controls that have been a core part of Windows since its conception. Common Controls are a standard set of add-on controls that are a part of the Windows Operating System itself, included in every 32-bit version of Windows including Win95, WinNT 4.0, and Windows 2000. The current release is version 5.81 and is in CommCtl32.DLL.

It is important when using the Common Controls to keep track of both the version of the DLL installed on a machine and the version that is required by the application. Your program must determine the version of the DLL installed on a machine then only make use of the functionality available in that version.

Demonstration programs in this chapter are dialog- or form-based. Take a moment to review the first few sections of Chapter 3 on how to create dialog- or form-based programs using either SDK or MFC.

Because Common Controls are stored in a set of DLL files, you need to call an initialization routine to enable use the DLL file in your program. Code 6–1 shows the functions InitCommonControls() or InitCommonControlsEx() that are used to initialize the DLL file.

Code 6–1

```
void InitCommonControls( void );
BOOL InitCommonControlsEx( LPINITCOMMONCONTROLSEX lpInitCtrls );
```

Either the InitCommonControls() and InitCommonControlsEx() functions can be called to initialize your common controls, but one of the two must be called for SDK programs. The InitCommonControls function initializes all controls, while InitCommonControlsEx lets you specify which controls you want to initialize. InitCommonControlsEx is a newer function used in Win98, NT, and Win95 with Internet Explorer 3.0 or later installed. MFC programs generated by the AppWizard already call this function in their CWinApp::InitInstance() function that was generated for your program.

Creating Controls Dynamically

In this chapter, we will discuss creating controls dynamically at runtime. However, it is easier to create the controls on a form using the dialog editor and then hide and show them as needed, rather than dynamically create and destroy them.

WM_NOTIFY vs. WM_COMMAND

The built-in Windows controls such as edit boxes, buttons, and list boxes send a WM_COMMAND message to their parent windows to inform the parent of certain events. Code 6–2 contains code useful in a WM_COMMAND handler for SDK programming to parse out the information about the WM_COMMAND message.

Code 6–2

```
int wID;
int wNotification;
HWND hChild;

// Portions of code removed for readability
case WM_COMMAND: // A message from a control or menu item
        // Parse out WM_COMMAND parameters to be more readable
        wID = LOWORD(wParam);
        wNotification = HIWORD(wParam);
        hChild = (HWND) lParam;
```

With the Common Controls such as Spin Buttons, ListViews, and DateTime Picker, the child window sends a WM_NOTIFY message and not a WM_COMMAND to its parent.

In MFC programs, the ClassWizards Message Map ability handles parsing information on the WM_NOTIFY message. SDK programs need to parse the information similarly to the WM_COMMAND message.

When a WM_NOTIFY message is sent to a window or dialog procedure, the wParam parameter contains the ID of the control sending the message. The lParam parameter contains a pointer to an NMHDR structure. The NMHDR is predefined for you and is illustrated in Code 6–3.

Code 6–3

```
typedef struct tagNMHDR {
        HWND hwndFrom; // Window generating the notification
        UINT idFrom; // ID of control generating the notification
        UINT code; // Notification code being generated.
} NMHDR;
```

NOTE

For other types or versions of controls, the lParam parameter points to a structure other than an NMHDR. But the other type of structure will contain an NMHDR as its first data member, so you can always rely on an NMHDR at least being present. An example of this is the ListView control, which often passes a NMLVDISPINFO structure. The first member of this structure is an NMHDR.

Code 6–4 contains code to parse information from a WM_NOTIFY message. In Code 6–4, the wParam parameter is used to get the ID of the control sending the notification. The lParam parameter is then typecast to an NMHDR pointer, and the *code* and *hwndFrom* data members of that structure are retrieved and stored in the wNotification and hChild local variables. We will use this code throughout the demonstrations in this chapter.

Code 6–4

```
int wID;
int wNotification;
HWND hChild;

// Portions of code removed for readability
case WM_NOITIFY: // A message from a control or menu item
        // Parse out data from a WM_NOTIFY message
        wID = (int) wParam;
        wNotification = ((NMHDR*)lParam)->code;
        hChild = ((NMHDR*)lParam)->hwndFrom;
```

Spin (Up/Down) Controls

Spin controls, also known as the Up/Down controls, normally represent two controls doing one job. They allow the user to select a numeric value with a simplified increment or decrement ability. Spin controls normally work with either an edit or static control to display the current value to the user, as shown in Figure 6–1, where there are two edit controls and one static control. Figure 6–1 also has a dynamically created spin control with a dynamically created static control as its buddy.

The control a spin control works with is called its buddy control. The buddy control is a static or edit control that can automatically display the integer value of a spin control. Buddy controls can easily be associated with a spin control by setting the properties of the spin control. For simple spin control requirements (just integers), implementing them can be as simple as dropping two controls (the spin and its buddy), setting the properties, and writing one line of code to set the range values for the control. In other cases, like in the noninteger (Figure 6–1), more code needs to be added.

Figure 6–1   Spin Controls.

The properties important for managing a buddy control are listed below. These controls are accessible by right-clicking on the control in the dialog editor and selecting Properties from the pop-up menu. The buddy properties are:

Alignment: Indicates if the spin control should automatically be aligned to the left or right of its buddy. If unattached, then the control will appear where you place it. Otherwise, the spin control is moved to the right or left of the buddy control automatically.

AutoBuddy: If selected, then the previous control in the ZOrder (or Tab Order) is defined as the buddy of the spin control. You can determine or alter the ZOrder in the dialog editor by selecting the Layout menu choice, and then selecting the Tab Order sub-menu item. This option determines what control the Alignment and Set Buddy Integer properties work with.

Set Buddy Integer: If checked, when the position of the spin control is changed, it will automatically update the text caption of its buddy control, as long as it's a static or edit control.

When the user clicks a spin control, the event generates a series of messages to its parent window. First, there is a UDN_DELTAPOS message indicating the type of change to take place. The spin control then sends either a WM_HSCROLL or WM_VSCROLL message, which changes the position of the spin control. Normally, you will only need to handle the UDN_DELTAPOS notification code.

In Figure 6–1, only the UDN_DELTAPOS notification code for the non-integer demonstration is handled. Figure 6–1 shows how to deal with noninteger values such as a margin setting, which might be a floating point value displayed in inch measurements. Notice the double quotation (") in the edit box. This is used to indicate that the value indicates inches, purely for the end user's information.

The UDN_DELTAPOS message notification code sends information about the change in position, in a NMUPDOWN or NM_UPDOWN structure pointer in the lParam parameter. This structure is defined in Code 6–5.

Code 6–5

```
typedef struct _NM_UPDOWN {
        NMHDR hdr;
        int iPos;
        int iDelta;
} NMUPDOWN;
```

The hdr member is the NMHDR passed with every common control notification message. The iPos is the current position value for the spin control, and iDelta is the change about to take place. iDelta is a negative value if the user hit the down button, or a positive value if he or she hits the up button.

Retrieving Spin Control Values

When you want to retrieve the value of a spin control, it is usually best to get it from the buddy control. This way, if the buddy control is an edit box, you can get any value that the user may have typed directly into the control. See *Retrieving Text from an Edit Box* in the previous chapter for more details. The MFC library provides a CSpinButtonCtrl class to help you work with a spin control.

Creating a Spin Control at Runtime

SDK

To create the Spin (a.k.a. up-down control) control at runtime, call the CreateWindowEx() function. The SDK also provides a simplified function called CreateUpDownControl() that is specifically designed for the Up-Down control (see Code 6–6 and Table 6.1).

Code 6–7 is an example of calling the CreateUpDownControl() function from the WM_INITDIALOG handler for a dialog. In Code 6–7, the CreateWindowEx() function is called to first create the buddy control, which is a static control with a client edge, for the spin control. Next, the CreateUpDownControl() function is called to create the actual spin control. Finally, the font for the new static control is set using the WM_SETFONT and WM_GETFONT messages to be the same font as its parent dialog.

Code 6–6

```
HWND CreateUpDownControl( DWORD dwStyle, int x, int y, int cx, int cy,
       HWND hParent, int nID, HINSTANCE hInst HWND hBuddy,
       int nUpper, int nLower, int nPos );
```

Table 6.1   Function Paramters for the Spin Control

Parameter	Description
dwStyle	Combination of styles for window controls (WS_ prefix) and UpDown controls (UDS_ prefix).
x	X coordinate for window display, within parent window.
y	Y coordinate for window display, within parent window.
cx	Width of new window.
cy	height of new window.
hParent	Parent window handle.
nID	Unique ID to given to new window. Must be unique within the parent window.
hInst	Program instance handle.
hBuddy	Window handle to buddy window, or 0 if no buddy is desired.

Parameter	Description
nUpper	Upper range limit that spin will go to.
nLower	Lower range limit that spin will go to.
nPos	Initial position of the spin control.

Code 6–7

```
                Called when you are going to use the common controls

LRESULT CALLBACK DialogProc( HWND hwndDlg, UINT uMsg, WPARAM wParam, LPARAM lParam  )
{
  int wID;
  int wNotification;
  HWND hChild;
  switch( uMsg )
   {
    case WM_INITDIALOG:
      InitCommonControls();
      hChild = CreateWindowEx( WS_EX_CLIENTEDGE, "STATIC", "0", WS_VISIBLE|WS_CHILD,
             164, 46, 25, 22, hwndDlg, (HMENU)4000, 0, 0 );
      CreateUpDownControl( WS_CHILD|WS_VISIBLE|UDS_AUTOBUDDY|UDS_SETBUDDYINT,
             189,46,14,22, hwndDlg, 4001, 0, hChild, 100, 0, 0 );
      SendMessage( hChild, WM_SETFONT, (SendMessage(hwndDlg,WM_GETFONT,0,0)), 0);
      return( TRUE );
    // Portions of code removed for readability
```

Dynamically create a static control and an UpDown control

Make sure static control has same font as other controls

MFC

In order to create a dynamic buddy and spin control using MFC, we are going to add data members to the Dialog or View class for each control and then add some code to the OnInitDialog() dialog function to create and initialize the controls.

The example program in Code 6–8 is a dialog-based application named MFC_Cmn-Control. This means that our Dialog class (the main window) is called CMFC_Com-nControlDlg. If this were a Document/View-based program, then we would place the creation code in the OnCreate() function for our View class and the initialization code within the OnInitialUpdate() function.

Step 1: Create the data members. To your dialog class (CMFC_CmnControlDlg in our example) definition, add the following data member (see Code 6–8).

Code 6–8

```
class CMFC_CmnControlDlg : public CDialog
{
// Construction
public:

        // For dynamic Spin control creation:
        CSpinButtonCtrl m_Spin;
        CStatic m_Static;
// Portions of code removed for readability
```

Step 2: Create and initialize the controls. Because this is a dialog-based application, we will perform the creation in the OnInitDialog() function, which AppWizard created for us when we specified a dialog-based application. If this were a Document/View-style program, we would put the creation code in the OnCreate() function for the View class and the initialization code in the OnInitialUpdate() function. Add the code shown in Code 6–9.

Code 6–9

```
  ┌─ Create the control

  ┌───────────────────────────────────────────────────────────────┐
  │  BOOL CMFC_CmnControlDlg::OnInitDialog()                       │
  │  {                                                             │
  │    CDialog::OnInitDialog();                                    │
  │    // Potions of code removed for readability                  │
  │    m_Static.CreateEx( WS_EX_CLIENTEDGE, "STATIC", "0", WS_VISIBLE|WS_CHILD, │
  │                     CRect(164, 46, 189, 68), this, 4000, 0 ); │
  │──► m_Spin.Create( WS_CHILD|WS_VISIBLE|UDS_AUTOBUDDY|UDS_SETBUDDYINT, │
  │                     CRect(189,46,193,68), this, 4001);        │
  │──► m_Spin.SetRange32( 0, 100 );                               │
  │    m_Static.SetFont( GetFont() );                             │
  │    return TRUE;  // return TRUE  unless you set the focus to a control │
  │  }                                                            │
  └───────────────────────────────────────────────────────────────┘

  └─ Initialization the control
```

Code 6–9 calls the m_Static.CreateEx() function to create the static control and then calls the m_Spin.Create() function to create the spin control. Since the static control is created just before the spin control, the static control precedes the spin control in ZOrder, meaning that we can use the UDS_AUTOBUDDY window style.

Once the two controls are created, initialize them by calling m_Spin.SetRange32() to set the lower and upper range limits for the spin control, and then call the m_Static.SetFont() function to set the static control font to match its parent window font (the dialog).

Responding to Spin Control Notifications

SDK

Spin controls automatically update their buddy controls. This means that you normally don't have to worry about responding to notifications from spin controls that their position has changed. You respond to a notification from a spin control when special formatting is required for the buddy control, such as the inch measurement used in Figure 6–1. Likewise, you do the same if you want to provide dynamic feedback to the user as the spin control value changes, such as a graphical preview of what the inch measurement might be. Code 6–10 demonstrates how to perform the noninteger formatting for the inch measurement example shown in Figure 6–1.

It is worth noting that since we are implementing the function of the auto-buddy feature, our spin control does not have the auto-buddy properties set. This is a stand-alone spin control without a buddy. We will respond to the WM_NOTIFY message from the spin control and have it modify the edit box next to it, making it look like a buddy control.

Our goal is to have the spin and edit control display an inch measurement. This doesn't fit into a normal spin control and buddy because the measurement is a floating point value, not a whole integer, and there must be an inch measurement indicator (") inside the edit box.

The spin control can only hold integers for its values and not floats as we need. However, we want the spin control to be adjusted between 0.00 and 10.00 in this example. To do this, we set the range of the control to be between 0 and 1000 then divide the actual value for the spin control by 100 to convert the value of 1000 into 10.00. That is why you will see values divided, or multiplied by 100 in Code 6–10.

Code 6-10

```
Base new value on Value from Edit box ─────────┐
                                               │
Set default for the Inch    Parse out data from a    │
spin control demo           WM_NOTIFY message        │
                                                     │
  ┌─────────────────────────────────────────────────────────────┐
  │ LRESULT CALLBACK DialogProc( HWND hwndDlg, UINT uMsg, WPARAM wParam, LPARAM lParam)
  │ {
  │ int wID;
  │ int wNotification;
  │ HWND hChild;
  │ switch( uMsg )
  │   {
  │   case WM_INITDIALOG:
  │     // Portions of code removed for readability
  │     SetDlgItemText( hwndDlg, IDC_EDITINCH, "1.00\"" );
  │     return( TRUE );
  │   case WM_NOTIFY:
  │     wID = (int) wParam;
  │     wNotification = ((NMHDR*)lParam)->code;
  │     hChild = ((NMHDR*)lParam)->hwndFrom;
  │     if( wID == IDC_SPININCH && wNotification == UDN_DELTAPOS )
  │       {
  │       char Text[16];
  │       NMUPDOWN* UpDown = (NMUPDOWN*)lParam;
  │       GetDlgItemText( hwndDlg, IDC_EDITINCH, Text, sizeof(Text) );
  │       int NewPos = int(atof( Text ) * 100) + UpDown->iDelta;
  │       int Upper, Lower;
  │       SendMessage( hChild, UDM_GETRANGE32, (WPARAM)&Lower, (LPARAM)&Upper );
  │       if( NewPos<Lower )
  │         NewPos=Lower;
  │       else if (NewPos > Upper )
  │         NewPos = Upper;
  │       sprintf( Text, "%-2.2f\"", NewPos/100.0 );
  │       SetDlgItemText ( hwndDlg, IDC_EDITINCH, Text );
  │       return( FALSE );
  │       }
  │     break;
  │   // Portions of code removed for readability
  └─────────────────────────────────────────────────────────────┘

Insure minimum and
maximum values are        Put value into the Edit box
enforced
```

In Code 6–10, the WM_INITDIALOG handler sets the default inch measurement and displays the measurement in the edit box (IDC_EDITINCH). In the WM_NOTIFY handler, we parse the parameters into the wID and wNotification variables to help identify the information sent by the control.

Next, within the *if* test, we determine if the IDC_SPININCH control sent the UDN_DELTAPOS notification. That is, did the user click either the up or down button on the spin control? Once this is determined, we assume that the lParam parameter is a pointer to a NM_UPDOWN structure, which indicates the type of change in position. Code 6–11 contains the NM_UPDOWN structure.

Code 6–11

```
typedef struct _NM_UPDOWN {
        NMHDR hdr;
        int iPos;
        int iDelta;
} NMUPDOWN;
```

We create and initialize the UpDown local variable to help us access the iDelta data member by including Code 6–12.

Code 6–12

```
NMUPDOWN* UpDown = (NMUPDOWN*)lParam;
```

Once the change information is known, we retrieve the current value from the edit box and store the value into the Text local variable as shown in Code 6–13.

Code 6–13

```
GetDlgItemText( hwndDlg, IDC_EDITINCH, Text, sizeof(Text) );
```

Next we determine what the new inch measurement should be based on the text in the edit box and the spin control's iDelta value as shown in Code 6–14.

Code 6–14

```
int NewPos = int(atof( Text ) * 100) + UpDown->iDelta;
```

Once we have the new value for the spin control, we insure that it fits within the range we previously set (0 to 1000) using Code 6–15.

Code 6–15

```
int Upper, Lower;
SendMessage( hChild, UDM_GETRANGE32, (WPARAM)&Lower, (LPARAM)&Upper );
if( NewPos<Lower )
    NewPos=Lower;
else if (NewPos > Upper )
        NewPos = Upper;
```

After we have insured that the new value is within our range, we convert the position back to a floating point string and place it back into the edit box as shown in Code 6–16.

Code 6–16

```
sprintf( Text, "%-2.2f\"", NewPos/100.0 );
SetDlgItemText ( hwndDlg, IDC_EDITINCH, Text );
```

MFC

The spin control automatically updates its buddy control and requires little interaction from you except to get the current spin position value. Our example (see Figure 6–2) illustrates a case where we will be doing special formatting for an inch measurement that the default buddy handling does not implement correctly. Read the *Responding to Spin Control Notifications, SDK* section for additional information on our logic and approach to this situation. Begin by adding the function shown in Code 6–17.

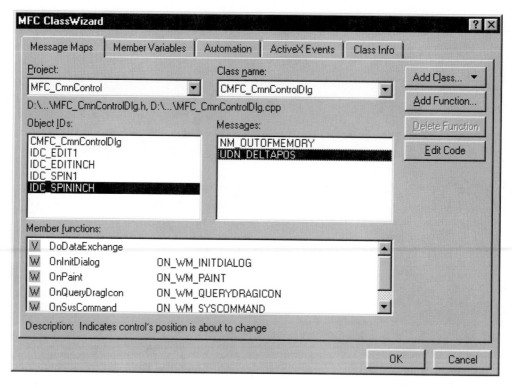

Figure 6–2   ClassWizard Message Maps for a spin control.

Code 6-17

```
void CMFC_CmnControlDlg::OnDeltaposSpininch(NMHDR* pNMHDR, LRESULT* pResult)
{
        NM_UPDOWN* pNMUpDown = (NM_UPDOWN*)pNMHDR;
        // TODO: Add your control notification handler code here

        *pResult = 0;
}
```

Notice how the function added by ClassWizard (Figure 6-2) creates an NM_UP-DOWN structure pointer for you. This is the same as the NM_UPDOWN structure defined in the SDK program. Next, add the code shown in Code 6-18.

Code 6-18

Insure minimum and maximum values are enforced

Base new value on Value from Edit box

```
void CMFC_CmnControlDlg::OnDeltaposSpininch(NMHDR* pNMHDR, LRESULT* pResult)
{
  NM_UPDOWN* pNMUpDown = (NM_UPDOWN*)pNMHDR;
  CString Text;
  GetDlgItemText( IDC_EDITINCH, Text );
  int NewPos = int(atof( Text ) * 100) + pNMUpDown->iDelta;
  int Upper, Lower;
  SendDlgItemMessage( IDC_SPININCH, UDM_GETRANGE32, (WPARAM)&Lower, (LPARAM)&Upper );
  if( NewPos<Lower )
    NewPos=Lower;
  else if (NewPos > Upper )
    NewPos = Upper;
  Text.Format( "%-2.2f\"", NewPos/100.0 );
  SetDlgItemText( IDC_EDITINCH, Text );
  *pResult = 0;
}
```

Put value into the Edit box

Code 6-18 first gets the current inch measurement from the edit box using Code 6-19. It then retrieves the change by inspecting the iDelta member of the passed NM_UPDOWN structure pointer and determines what the new edit box value should be by using Code 6-20. Next, it determines if the new value is within the range set for the spin control using Code 6-21. And finally, places the new measurement back into the edit box using Code 6-22.

Code 6–19

```
GetDlgItemText( IDC_EDITINCH, Text );
```

Code 6–20

```
int NewPos = int(atof( Text ) * 100) + pNMUpDown->iDelta;
```

Code 6–21

```
// Insure minimum and maximum values are enforced
int Upper, Lower;
SendDlgItemMessage( IDC_SPININCH, UDM_GETRANGE32, (WPARAM)&Lower,
(LPARAM)&Upper );
if( NewPos<Lower )
    NewPos=Lower;
else if (NewPos > Upper )
    NewPos = Upper;
```

Code 6–22

```
// Put value into the Edit box
Text.Format( "%-2.2f\"", NewPos/100.0 );
SetDlgItemText( IDC_EDITINCH, Text );
```

Progress Bars

Progress bars (Figure 6–3) are used to indicate the current progress of a lengthy process. It gives visual feedback to the user about how much of the process has been completed.

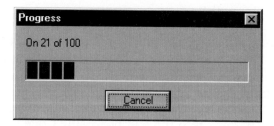

Figure 6–3   Progress bars.

A progress bar is a single control. But progress bars are usually implemented in a progress dialog, which typically has a static control, a progress control, and a button control (for Cancel). An example of such a dialog appears on the right in Figure 6–3. We will demonstrate how to implement both uses of the progress bar.

Like a Spin control, the Progress Bar control maintains minimum and maximum values, and a position somewhere between these two values. Typically, most people think of the minimum as 0, and the maximum as 100, making percentages easy to display. However, the maximum could be any 32-bit value. For example, if you have to export 30,000 records, you would not have to determine what percentage you were at in the conversion, you could simply set the maximum to be 30,000, and then set the position to be the number of records output so far.

The position you set in a progress bar is relative to the minimum and maximum values. For example, if the minimum value were set to 30,000 and the maximum set to 40,000, then setting the position to 35,000 would make the progress bar appear halfway in the child control.

Message Pumps

The Progress Bar control is usually displayed to the user when the program is performing some lengthy process, like exporting a large number of records. This implies that your program is in some sort of loop, repeating a process over and over, such as exporting a single record.

If your program is busy in a loop, then the message loop for your application is not being executed. Since the message loop is where all messages are handled, no messages get processed until the message loop executes. Thus, if you displayed a Cancel button during this lengthy loop processing and never executed the message loop to process messages, then the user hitting the Cancel button would not be processed until the end of the loop. This would completely defeat the purpose of the Cancel button's being there.

In order to work around this issue, our Progress Dialog example implements a message pump. A message pump is another form of message loop that is executed by your loop. We will discuss message pumps in more detail in Chapter 11. For now, we will simply point out where the message pump is being executed in our example.

Setting the Progress Range

SDK

The application sends a PBM_SETRANGE32 message to set the range of a progress bar control as shown in Code 6–23. The SendDlgItemMessage() function is called to send the PBM_SETRANGE32 message. See Table 6.2 for a description of the para-

---

Common Controls

meters of this function. You can also call the SendMessage() function if you already have the child window handle. The SendMessage function is described in the *Window's Messaging* section of Chapter 1. The progress range is often set in response to the WM_INITDIALOG function, but it can be set at any time.

Code 6–23

```
SendDlgItemMessage( hwndDlg, IDC_PROGRESS1, PBM_SETRANGE32, 0, 100);
```

MFC

In order to set the range of a progress bar control, you can send a PBM_SET-RANGE32 message (see Code 6–24), or you can use the CProgressBarCtrl::Set-Range32() function (see Code 6–25). You would normally do this within the OnInitDialog() function for a dialog-based program, or in the OnInitialUpdate() function for a CView-based application.

Code 6–24

```
SendDlgItemMessage( IDC_PROGRESS1, PBM_SETRANGE32, 0, 100 );
```

Code 6–25

```
CProgressBarCtrl* pProgress = GetDlgItem( IDC_PROGRESS1 );
pProgress->SetRange32( 0, 100 );
```

Setting the Progress Position

SDK

To set the position for a Progress bar, send a PBM_SETPOS message to the child control. When you send this message, the wParam parameter indicates the new position for the control.

Table 6.2 Parameters for the SendDlgItemMessage() Function

Parameter	Description
hWndDlg	Window handle to parent (dialog) window.
IDC_PROGRESS1	Unique ID for the Progress Bar control in the dialog.
PBM_SETRANGE32	The Message to send to the child control (to set its range).
0	The minumum range value for the control (may be from 0 to 4 billion).
100	The maximum range value for the control (may be from 0 to 4 billion).

Code 6–26 demonstrates how a dialog procedure is performing a looping process to update a progress bar control indicating the status of the loop. SendDlgItemMessage() is used in the code to set the position of the progress bar.

Code 6–26

The 'Go' button for progress bar demo,

Parse out WM_COMMAND parameters to be more readable

A message from a control or menu item

```
LRESULT CALLBACK DialogProc( HWND hwndDlg, UINT uMsg, WPARAM wParam, LPARAM lParam )
{
  int wID;
  int wNotification;
  HWND hChild;
  switch( uMsg )
  {
    // Portions of code removed for readability
    case WM_COMMAND:
      wID = LOWORD(wParam);
      wNotification = HIWORD(wParam);
      hChild = (HWND) lParam;
      if( wID == IDC_PROGRESSGO && wNotification==BN_CLICKED )
      {
        SetCursor( LoadCursor(0, MAKEINTRESOURCE(IDC_WAIT)) );
        for( int i=0; i < 100; i++ )
        {
          Sleep( 10 );
          SendDlgItemMessage( hwndDlg, IDC_PROGRESS1, PBM_SETPOS, i, 0 );
        }
      }
```

Turn cursor to an hour glass

Update progress bar with new position

Simulate a delay

Enter our loop (simulated processing)

MFC

To set the position for a Progress bar, you can send a PBM_SETPOS message to the child control, or you can call the CProgressCtrl::SetPos() function. When you send this message, the wParam parameter indicates the new position for the control.

Code 6–27 demonstrates how a dialog procedure performs a looping process and updates a progress bar control to indicate its status within the loop. SendDlg-ItemMessage() is used in the code to set the position of the progress bar.

Common Controls

Code 6–27

```
void CMFC_CmnControlDlg::OnProgressgo()
{
        // TODO: Add your control notification handler code here
        CWaitCursor Tmp

        // Enter our loop (simulated processing)
        for( int i=0; i < 100; i++ )
        {
                // Simulate a delay:
                Sleep( 10 );
                // Update progress bar with new position:
                SendDlgItemMessage( IDC_PROGRESS1, PBM_SETPOS, i, 0 );
        }

}
```

Code 6–27 could be a message map handler function for when the user clicks a button. Code 6–28 is an alternative to calling the SendDlgItemMessage() function. Replace the bold line in Code 6–27 with Code 6–28. Using the CProgressCtrl class function is helpful when you have a member variable mapped for the progress control (using the Member Variable tab of ClassWizard).

Code 6–28

```
CProgressCtrl* pProgress = GetDlgItem( IDC_PROGRESS1);
pProgress->SetPos( i );
```

Progress Dialog

There is no common dialog for a progress dialog (Figure 6–4), so we will need to create one manually, but it will not be a complicated task. We will need to implement a message pump, as described in the *Message Pumps* section above to perform the standard behavior of a progress dialog. We want the dialog to appear to be a modal dialog so the user can't access the parent window until the dialog is closed. However, like a modeless dialog, we don't want the main flow of execution that invokes the dialog to be disabled or halted while the dialog is displayed.

In order for us to create a dialog that is a hybrid of both modal and modeless, we will disable the parent window to stop the user from interacting with it, but we will actually be implementing the dialog in a modeless fashion with code.

We will present both the SDK and MFC methods for creating a progress dialog. While there is already a progress dialog in MFC provided in the Component Gallery that you could easily add to your projects, we would provide a simpler MFC version here.

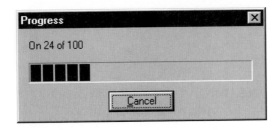

Figure 6–4 The progress dialog.

Both the SDK and MFC versions of the Progress Dialog require you to create a dialog resource like the one pictured in Figure 6–4. Our examples assume that you have created the dialog in the resource editor and that the ID for the dialog is IDD_PROGRESSDLG. You must also add a static text control with an ID of IDC_LABEL, a progress control with an ID of IDC_DLGPROGRESS, and a Cancel button with the ID of IDCANCEL. If you want to use the code in other projects, you will have to copy the dialog to the new project as well.

SDK

The first function to write for a progress dialog is the Window Procedure for the dialog itself. This function will only handle the Cancel button click, which is the same message as the user hitting the X (Close) button on the upper-right corner of the dialog. The function is shown in Code 6–29.

Code 6-29

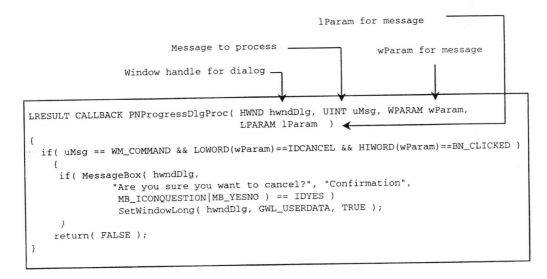

```
                                              lParam for message
                  Message to process ─────────┐        wParam for message
          Window handle for dialog ─┐         │             │
                                    ▼         ▼             ▼
LRESULT CALLBACK PNProgressDlgProc( HWND hwndDlg, UINT uMsg, WPARAM wParam,
                          LPARAM lParam )  ◄─
{
  if( uMsg == WM_COMMAND && LOWORD(wParam)==IDCANCEL && HIWORD(wParam)==BN_CLICKED )
    {
      if( MessageBox( hwndDlg,
              "Are you sure you want to cancel?", "Confirmation",
              MB_ICONQUESTION|MB_YESNO ) == IDYES )
              SetWindowLong( hwndDlg, GWL_USERDATA, TRUE );
    }
    return( FALSE );
}
```

As is the case with all Window Procedure functions, you will not be calling this function directly. Instead, when we create the progress dialog, we will specify the function as the callback function for the dialog. In Code 6–29, the only thing that is done when the user clicks the Cancel or Close button for the dialog is to ask if they want to cancel processing. If they respond Yes, the message box function returns IDYES, then the GWL_USERDATA for the dialog is set to TRUE. If the response is No, then nothing happens and the progress continues.

The next step is to create the function that creates the pop-up progress dialog. In order to create a modeless dialog, call the CreateDialog() function, which creates the window, then call the ShowWindow() function to make it visible. But before the function returns to the caller, the function will also call the EnableWindow() function to disable the parent window. This behavior is like a modal dialog box, but, like a modeless dialog, this will not hang up the processing of the calling function. Instead, this function will return right away. This is illustrated in the PNProgress-DlgPopup() function shown in Code 6–30.

Code 6–30

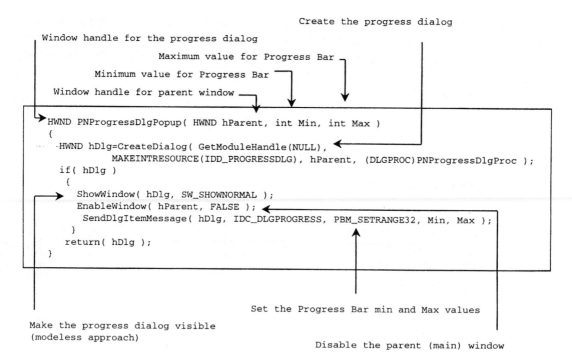

```
HWND PNProgressDlgPopup( HWND hParent, int Min, int Max )
{
    HWND hDlg=CreateDialog( GetModuleHandle(NULL),
            MAKEINTRESOURCE(IDD_PROGRESSDLG), hParent, (DLGPROC)PNProgressDlgProc );
    if( hDlg )
    {
        ShowWindow( hDlg, SW_SHOWNORMAL );
        EnableWindow( hParent, FALSE );
        SendDlgItemMessage( hDlg, IDC_DLGPROGRESS, PBM_SETRANGE32, Min, Max );
    }
    return( hDlg );
}
```

Create the progress dialog

Window handle for the progress dialog

Maximum value for Progress Bar

Minimum value for Progress Bar

Window handle for parent window

Set the Progress Bar min and Max values

Make the progress dialog visible
(modeless approach)

Disable the parent (main) window

Next add functions to help make it easier to use the progress dialog. These functions give you the ability to set the progress bar position if the user hasn't hit the Cancel button, determine if the user hit the cancel button, and close the dialog.

The function to set the progress bar dialog is shown in Code 6–31. In this function, you have the option of setting the dialog bar position as well as the text for the static control. The function will return TRUE or FALSE. If the user chooses the Cancel option of the dialog, it will return FALSE, indicating you should stop whatever processing you are doing. If it returns TRUE, then it means the user has not hit the Cancel button. This function also implements the message pump that is used to permit the processing of window messages such as the user hitting the Cancel key.

Code 6–31

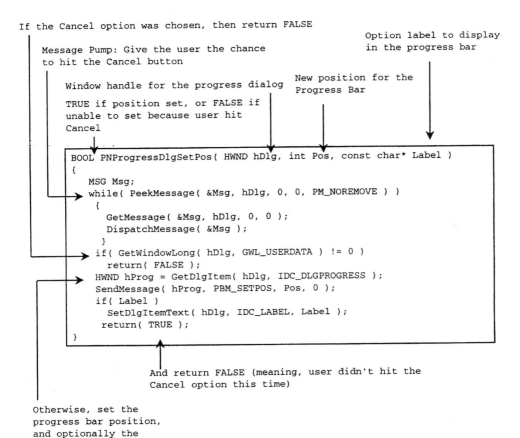

If the Cancel option was chosen, then return FALSE

Option label to display in the progress bar

Message Pump: Give the user the chance to hit the Cancel button

Window handle for the progress dialog

New position for the Progress Bar

TRUE if position set, or FALSE if unable to set because user hit Cancel

```
BOOL PNProgressDlgSetPos( HWND hDlg, int Pos, const char* Label )
{
    MSG Msg;
    while( PeekMessage( &Msg, hDlg, 0, 0, PM_NOREMOVE ) )
    {
        GetMessage( &Msg, hDlg, 0, 0 );
        DispatchMessage( &Msg );
    }
    if( GetWindowLong( hDlg, GWL_USERDATA ) != 0 )
        return( FALSE );
    HWND hProg = GetDlgItem( hDlg, IDC_DLGPROGRESS );
    SendMessage( hProg, PBM_SETPOS, Pos, 0 );
    if( Label )
        SetDlgItemText( hDlg, IDC_LABEL, Label );
    return( TRUE );
}
```

And return FALSE (meaning, user didn't hit the Cancel option this time)

Otherwise, set the progress bar position, and optionally the STATIC control text.

Notice that to use the function shown in Code 6–32, you call it once for each iteration of the processing loop. The PNProgressDlgCanceled() function (see Code 6–32) is a helper function that tells you if the user selected the Cancel option for the dialog. Notice that in this implementation you can only call this function while the progress dialog is visible and not after the PNProgressDlgClose() function has been called.

Code 6–32

```
// PNProgressDlgCanceled - Determines if user hit Cancel for
//        Progress Dialog
// Parameters:
//        hDlg - Window handle for the progress dialog
// Returns: TRUE if user hit Cancel button, or FALSE if not
BOOL PNProgressDlgCanceled( HWND hDlg )
{
        return( GetWindowLong( hDlg, GWL_USERDATA ) ? TRUE : FALSE );
}
```

Notice that the PNProgressDlgCanceled() function uses the dialog windows extra 32-bit value to store whether it was canceled or not. Each window has an extra 32-bit value that is yours to use as you see fit.

The final helper function is PNProgressDlgClose(), which will close the progress dialog and re-enable the parent window is shown in Code 6-33. Now, the code shown in Code 6–33 is used in Code 6–34.

Code 6–33

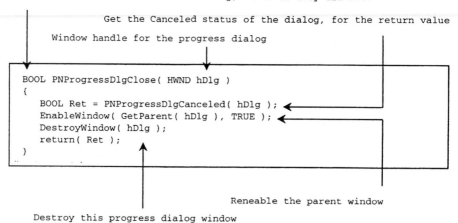

TRUE if user had Canceled the dialog, FALSE if they did not.

Get the Canceled status of the dialog, for the return value

Window handle for the progress dialog

```
BOOL PNProgressDlgClose( HWND hDlg )
{
    BOOL Ret = PNProgressDlgCanceled( hDlg );
    EnableWindow( GetParent( hDlg ), TRUE );
    DestroyWindow( hDlg );
    return( Ret );
}
```

Reneable the parent window

Destroy this progress dialog window

Code 6-34

The user hit Cancel option

Simulate a delay:

Update progress bar with new position

```
char Text[16];
HWND hDlg=PNProgressDlgPopup(hwndDlg, 0, 100);
for( int i=0; i < 100; i++ )
{
  Sleep( 100 );:
  sprintf( Text, "On %d of %d", i+1, 100 );
  if( PNProgressDlgSetPos( hDlg, i, Text ) == FALSE )
    break;
  // Do actual processing here.
}
if( PNProgressDlgCanceled(hDlg) )
  MessageBox( hwndDlg, "You canceled that operation", "Information",
            MB_ICONINFORMATION|MB_OK   );
PNProgressDlgClose( hDlg );
```

MFC

The Component Gallery already has a progress dialog component. We are creating one here to demonstrate how to create your own progress dialog. As mentioned in the start of this section, you must create a dialog in the dialog editor for the progress dialog, with a static text, a Progress Bar, and a Cancel button.

Once you have created the dialog, create a class for it. We will be adding functionality to that class to update the progress bar and determine if the user has hit the Cancel option. With the dialog still in the dialog editor, go to ClassWizard from the View menu. Before ClassWizard appears, it will recognize the fact that there is a new dialog and ask you if you want to create a class for it (see Figure 6-5). Making sure that Create a new class is selected, click the OK (Figure 6-5) button, which will bring you to the New Class dialog (see Figure 6-6).

In the New Class dialog, enter a name for your class such as CPNProgressDlg. Make sure that the Base Class option is CDialog and that the Dialog ID option shows the ID of the progress dialog you just added. Click OK and a new class is created. We will now modify that class as needed.

Our first change is to modify the constructor of the new dialog class so the pParent parameter that ClassWizard created does not have a default parameter of NULL. We do this to safeguard anyone from accidentally creating the object without a parent window. Make the change shown in Code 6-35 in the header file for your new dialog class. We use the CPNProgressDlg.h in our example.

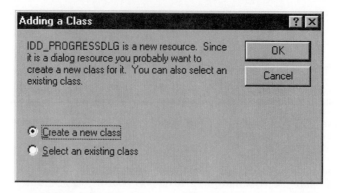

Figure 6–5 Click OK to add a new class.

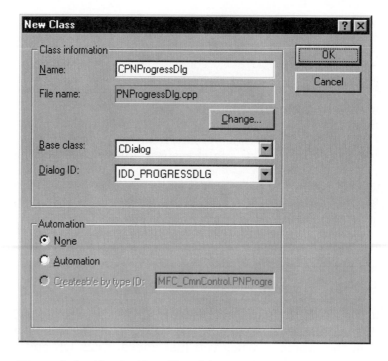

Figure 6–6 Use the New Class dialog to add the class.

Next, add two member variables to the CPNProgressDlg class. One is a normal bool data member as shown in Code 6–36.

Code 6–35

```
// We modified constructor below, to require parent window
CPNProgressDlg(CWnd* pParent /*= NULL*/ ); // standard constructor
```

Code 6–36

```
bool m_bCancel;
```

The other will be a Control Category member variable, so we can easily interact with the progress bar. To do this, go to the Member Variables tab in ClassWizard. Make sure that the CPNProgressDlg class appears in the Class Name field and that the IDC_DLGPROGRESS control (the progress bar) is highlighted in the Control IDs list. Then click the Add Variable button. The next dialog that appears is the Add Member Variable dialog.

In the Add Member Variable dialog, enter m_Prog for the Member variable name field. Make sure that the Category field says Control and that the Variable Type field is CProgressCtrl. Click *OK*. Go to the CPNProgressDlg class file (PNProgress-Dlg.cpp) and modify its constructor function to look like Code 6–37.

Code 6–37

Create our Dialog window (it's not visible yet though)

```
CPNProgressDlg::CPNProgressDlg(CWnd* pParent /*=NULL*/)
    :CDialog(CPNProgressDlg::IDD, pParent)
{
    //{{AFX_DATA_INIT(CPNProgressDlg)
    // NOTE: the ClassWizard will add member initialization here
    //}}AFX_DATA_INIT
    Create( IDD, pParent );
    pParent->EnableWindow( FALSE );
    m_bCancel = false;
    m_prog.SetPos(0);
}
```

Disable the parent window   Start Progress control off at zero (using member variable) m_Prog.SetPos(0); and set the m_bCancel data member to false

The Create function will create the dialog window, but it is not visible yet. The EnableWindow() function for the passed parent window is called to disable the parent window, the SetPos() function is called for the progress bar to set it to zero, and the m_bCancel flag is set to zero.

Next, add the function prototype shown in Code 6–38 to your CPNProgressDlg.h header file, to add a new function to the CPNProgressDlg class as a public function.

The SetPos() function permits you to set a new position and label for the dialog and also informs you if the user selected the Cancel option. The code for the function should be added to the PNProgressDlg.cpp file, as shown in Code 6–39.

Code 6–38

```
bool SetPos( int Pos, LPCSTR Label=0 );
```

Code 6–39

If Window is hidden, then show it

```
bool CPNProgressDlg::SetPos(int Pos, LPCSTR Label)
{
  MSG Msg;
  if( ! IsWindowVisible() )
    ShowWindow( SW_NORMAL );
  while( ::PeekMessage( &Msg, 0, 0, 0, PM_NOREMOVE ) )
    AfxGetApp()->PumpMessage();
  if( !m_bCancel )
      {
        m_Prog.SetPos( Pos );
        if( Label )
          SetDlgItemText( IDC_LABEL, Label );
      }
  return( !m_bCancel );
}
```

If not cancelled yet, then set the position

Message Pump, to permit messages to be processed, like the Cancel button click

The function in Code 6–39 will determine if the window is visible by calling IsWindowVisible() and will make it appear if it is not visible. Then, the function performs a message pump to let the program process messages such as the user hitting the Cancel button. If the user hasn't selected the Cancel option (determined by the m_bCancel flag), it uses the SetPos() function for m_Prog to set the progress bar position, then sets the label for the static control IDC_LABEL (if Label was not zero). It returns TRUE if it worked, or FALSE if the user selected the Cancel option.

We add two helper functions (see Code 6–40) to make the CPNProgressDlg class easier to work with. One determines if the user has selected the Cancel option, and the other permits you to set the minimum and maximum range values for the progress bar. You need to add these functions to your header and class files, as we did for SetPos().

Code 6–40

```
bool CPNProgressDlg::WasCancelled()
{
        return( m_bCancel );
}

void CPNProgressDlg::Reset( int Min, int Max )
{
        m_bCancel = false;
        m_Prog.SetRange( Min, Max );
        m_Prog.SetPos( Min );
        ShowWindow( SW_NORMAL );
}
```

Finally, we need to add a message map handler for the user's hitting the Cancel button. This is created using the ClassWizard from the View menu choice. Make sure that ClassWizard has the Message Map tab selected. Then make sure that CPNProgressDlg is selected in the Class Name field, that the IDCANCEL item is selected in the Object IDs list, and that BN_CLICKED is selected in the Messages list. Hit the Add Function button and accept the default function name of OnCancel when prompted for the function name. Change this function so that it looks like Code 6–41.

Code 6–41

```
void CPNProgressDlg::OnCancel()
{
        if( MessageBox( "Are you sure you want to cancel?",
                "Confirmation", MB_ICONQUESTION|MB_YESNO ) == IDYES )
                m_bCancel = true;

        // Don't call OnCancel, which would close the
        // window (ClassWizard added it):
        // CDialog::OnCancel();
}
```

Note that we commented out the CDialog::OnCancel() function that ClassWizard added for us. If we didn't comment it out, then the dialog would close when the user hit the Cancel button.

Common Controls

With the dialog class defined, we can now test it as shown in Code 6–42. Make sure that whatever source code module you will be using to test has included the CPN-ProgressDlg.h file.

Code 6–42

```
Enter our loop (simulated processing)          Simulate a delay:

    void CMFC_CmnControlDlg::OnDlgprogdemo()
    {
      CPNProgressDlg Prog( this );
      Prog.Reset( 0, 100 );
      CString Tmp;
      for( int i=0; i < 100; i++ )
      {
        Sleep( 10 );
        Tmp.Format( "%d of %d", i+1, 100 );
        if( Prog.SetPos( i, Tmp ) == false )
          break;
        // Perform actual processing here
      }
      if( Prog.WasCancelled() )
        MessageBox( "Processing canceled" );
    }

          Break out of loop if user canceled

        Update progress bar with new position and label
```

Sliders (Trackbar) Controls

A Slider or Trackbar control (see Figure 6–7) is a control that appears like a slider and is often user to allow the user to select a value from a certain range. Like Spin controls, a Slider control has buddy controls, which control the placement of the slider on the parent window. There is no buddy feature, however, that will automatically set the value of the buddy control.

Figure 6–7   Slider controls.

Sliders have a minimum value, a maximum value, and a position that you can change programmatically. If you don't change them, the defaults are zero for minimum and current position and 100 for maximum position. The slider also has values defined as line size and page size. These properties determine how much the slider changes when the user changes its position using the arrow or page up/down keys. The defaults are a line size of 1 and a page size of 20.

Sliders also have tick marks; they are shown on the slider control on the left in Figure 6–7. Tick marks can be set manually or set to appear at an automatic distribution. When you change the range of a slider, you should also change its page size and tick mark frequency to match. Page sizes are usually about one-fifth of the range and ticks frequency about one-tenth of the range.

As the user changes the value for a slider either with the mouse or with the keyboard, the control sends a WM_HSCROLL message to the parent window if it's a horizontal slider, or WM_VSCROLL messages if it's a vertical slider. Since many controls do this or there can be several slider controls on the same parent window, it also sends the ID of the child control for identification purposes.

There are a variety of properties that will affect the appearance of the slider, so make sure you look at the properties in the dialog editor for them by right-clicking on the slider control and selecting the Properties menu choice. One example of such a property is the selection ability where the user can see a certain selection range, as demonstrated by the control on the right, pictured in Figure 6–7. The user does not set the selection property, as in an edit box. Instead, when you set a selection range programatically, the control will only return selections within that range.

Also note that in Figure 6–7, where the slider is in the middle, below it is a static text that displays the number 50 (indicating 50% for our demo). While the slider control does not have the ability to set the value for the buddy control, this feature is not hard to implement.

Controls also have tick marks, which appear as marks along the edge of the slider, indicating increment and decrement positions for the user selection.

When the slider control sends a WM_HSCROLL or WM_VSCROLL message to indicate that the position has changed, it also sends additional information as to what caused the value to change. The low-order word of the wParam parameter of the WM_HSCROLL or WM_VSCROLL message contains the method for what caused the change (scroll). For the TB_THUMBPOSITION and TB_THUMBTRACK methods, the high-order word of the wParam parameter specifies the position of the slider. Table 6.3 represents possible values for the methods.

As with many controls, the value for the slider position is maintained by the control. This means that depending upon your need you may or may not want to provide immediate feedback as the user makes selections.

Table 6.3   Possible Values for the Slider Control

Notification Message	Meaning
TB_BOTTOM	VK_END (End key pressed)
TB_ENDTRACK	WM_KEYUP (the user released a key)
TB_LINEDOWN	VK_RIGHT or VK_DOWN
TB_LINEUP	VK_LEFT or VK_UP
TB_PAGEDOWN	VK_NEXT (the user clicked below or to right of slider knob)
TB_PAGEUP	VK_PRIOR (the user clicked the above or to left of slider knob)
TB_THUMBPOSITION	WM_LBUTTONUP following a TB_THUMBTRACK notification message
TB_THUMBTRACK	Slider movement (the user dragged the slider knob)
TB_TOP	VK_HOME

Responding to User's Changes/Determining Slider Position

SDK

Since the slider sends a WM_HSCROLL message to its parent, we will need to add a WM_HSCROLL to our Window Procedure case statement, for incoming messages. A vertical slider send a WM_VSCROLL messages, but in our demo we use a horizontal scrollbar. Code 6–43 illustrates how to respond immediately to the user selection.

The code shown in Code 6–44 uses the GetDlgCtrlID() function to retrieve the ID of the child window that sent the WM_HSCROLL message passed in the lParam parameter. Once we have determined the ID for the desired control (the IDC_SLIDERH control), we begin processing. Inside the if body, we use SendDlgItemMessage() to send the slider control a TBM_GETPOS message, which will return the current position of the slider. We use sprintf() to format that into a string and SetDlgItemText() to place the text into a static control. Finally, we set the position of another slider control (IDC_SLIDERV) to match that of the horizontal slider.

If you wanted to simply get the position of the slider at any time, you can send the TBM_GETPOS message to the control as shown in Code 6–44. The code shown in Code 6–44 would be used where hwndDlg was the window handle of the parent window of the slider control and IDC_SLIDERH is the unique ID for the slider control.

Code 6-43

Verify the message came from the desired control

```
LRESULT CALLBACK DialogProc( HWND hwndDlg, UINT uMsg, WPARAM wParam, LPARAM lParam)
{
  switch( uMsg )
   {
    case WM_HSCROLL:
     if( GetDlgCtrlID( (HWND)lParam ) == IDC_SLIDERH )
       {
         int i= SendDlgItemMessage( hwndDlg, IDC_SLIDERH, TBM_GETPOS, 0, 0 );
         char Text[4];
         sprintf( Text, "%d", i );
         SetDlgItemText( hwndDlg, IDC_SLIDERVAL, Text );
         SendDlgItemMessage( hwndDlg, IDC_SLIDERV, TBM_SETPOS, TRUE, i );
       }
      break;
   // Potions of code removed for readability
```

Update the vertical slider, to be at the same position

Send message to the control to determine it's new position

Format position as a string, and place it in the STATIC text control

Code 6-44

```
int Pos = SendDlgItemMessage( hwndDlg, IDC_SLIDERH, TBM_GETPOS,
     0, 0 );
```

MFC

Since the slider sends a WM_HSCROLL message to its parent, we will need to add a WM_HSCROLL message map using ClassWizard. Remember that a vertical slider will send WM_VSCROLL messages, but in our demo, we will use a horizontal scrollbar.

Go to ClassWizard (from the View menu option) and make sure that the Message Map tab is selected. In the Message Map tab, make sure that the class selected in the Class name option is the name of your main View or Dialog class. In the Object IDs list, make sure that you select the same View or Dialog class name that you selected for Class name. In the Messages list, scroll down to select the WM_HSCROLL message and click the Add Function button. Click OK to accept the default function name the next dialog suggests. This will add a function similar to Code 6-45. Modify the code to look like Code 6-46.

Code 6–45

```
void CMFC_CmnControlDlg::OnHScroll(UINT nSBCode, UINT nPos,
     CScrollBar* pScrollBar)
{
     CDialog::OnHScroll(nSBCode, nPos, pScrollBar);
}
```

The WM_HSCROLL handler message map in Code 6–46 is passed these parameters: nSBCode, which describes the method of change, like a click, as listed in Table 6–3; nPos, which is the new slider position, but may be zero for certain notification codes; and pScrollBar, which is a pointer to a scroll bar window. The nSBCode indicates the type of operation that caused the message to be sent, such as the user dragging the slider or clicking it with the mouse or keyboard. nSBCode also affects how nPos is interpreted. For example, a TB_THUMBPOSITION notification has nPos set to the new position, but TB_ENDTRACK will have nPos set to zero. This means is that to get the current position of the control, call the CSliderCtrl::GetPos() function as demonstrated in Code 6–46.

Code 6–46

Typecast the CScrollBar pointer to a CSliderCtrl pointer

Make sure it's the control we want

```
void CMFC_CmnControlDlg::OnHScroll(UINT nSBCode, UINT nPos, CScrollBar* pScrollBar)
{
   if( pScrollBar->GetDlgCtrlID() == IDC_SLIDERH )
   {
     CSliderCtrl* pSlider = (CSliderCtrl*)pScrollBar;
     nPos = pSlider->GetPos();
     CString Tmp;
     Tmp.Format( "%d", nPos );
     SetDlgItemText( IDC_SLIDERVAL, Tmp );
     SendDlgItemMessage( IDC_SLIDERV, TBM_SETPOS, TRUE, nPos );
   }
   CDialog::OnHScroll(nSBCode, nPos, pScrollBar);
}
```

For demo purposes, update another slider with the same position. This would be useful when you update a slider from an edit box.

Place the position into a static control, for additional user feedback:

Setting and Getting Slider Ranges

SDK

You can set a slider range by either sending the control a TBM_SETRANGE message for both maximum and minimum values, or you can set them individually with by sending TBM_SETRANGEMAX and TBM_SETRANGEMIN messages, respectively.

To retrieve the range values, you can send the control either a TBM_GETRANGE-MAX or TBM_GETRANGEMIN message to get the maximum or minimum values as shown in Code 6–47.

The TRUE in the wParam (fourth) parameter indicates whether the control should be redrawn. See the *Setting and Getting Slider Pages Sizes, SDK* section below for a function that sets the page size as well as the minimum and maximum ranges.

Code 6-47

```
SendDlgItemMessage( hwndDlg, IDC_SLIDERH, TBM_SETRANGE, TRUE,
    MAKELONG( 0, 100 ) );
```

MFC

You can set a slider range by either sending the control a TBM_SETRANGE message for both maximum and minimum values, or you can set them individually with by sending TBM_SETRANGEMAX and TBM_SETRANGEMIN messages, respectively (see Code 6–48). You can also use the CSliderCtrl::SetRange(), CSliderCtrl::SetRangeMin(), or CSliderCtrl::SetRangeMax() functions (in the CSliderCtrl MFC class).

In order to get the range values, you can send the control either a TBM_GET-RANGEMAX or TBM_GETRANGEMIN message to get the maximum or minimum values, or you can call the CSliderCtrl::GetRange(), CSliderCtrl::GetRangeMin() or CSliderCtrl::GetRangeMax() functions. Code 6–49 illustrates how to get the range using the CSliderCtrl class. This code would appear in the Dialog or View class that is the parent window class for the slider control.

Code 6–48

```
// Initialize the slider control with it's range values (defaults
// to 0 to 100 anyway)
SendDlgItemMessage( hwndDlg, IDC_SLIDERH, TBM_SETRANGE, TRUE,
    MAKELONG( 0, 100 ) );
// Alternative method, using the CSliderCtrl:
CSliderCtrl* pSlider = GetDlgItem( IDC_SLIDERH );
pSlider->SetRange( 0, 100, TRUE );
```

Code 6–49

```
int Min, Max;
pSlider->GetRange( Min, Max ); // Get values we just set
```

Setting and Getting Slider Pages Sizes

SDK

A slider's page size indicates the size of each jump when the user presses the page up/down keys or clicks on the sides of the slider knob. The default is 20, but when the slider contains large values, this is not adequate. The average rule is to create a page size one-fifth the size of the entire range.

To set the page size, send the slider control a TBM_SETPAGESIZE message and set the lParam parameter to be the desired page size. For example, the help function shown in Code 6–50 sets the minimum and maximum range values and then set the page size to the one-fifth average value. In order to get the current page size, simply send the child control a TBM_GETPAGESIZ as shown in Code 6–51.

Code 6–50

```
void PNSetSliderRange( HWND hWnd, int Min, int Max, BOOL Redraw )
{
        // Set minimum and maximum range values
        SendMessage( hWnd, TBM_SETRANGE, Redraw, MAKELONG(Min,Max) );

        int Step = (Max-Min) / 5;
        // Set the typical page size:
        SendMessage( hWnd, TBM_SETPAGESIZE, 0, Step );

        // If it has tick mark style, adjust tick mrk gaps as well
        if( GetWindowLong( hWnd, GWL_STYLE ) & TBS_AUTOTICKS )
                SendMessage( hWnd, TBM_SETTICFREQ, (Max-Min)/10, 0 );
}
```

Code 6-51

```
int Page = SendDlgItemMessage( hwndDlg, IDC_SLIDERH, TBM_GETPAGESIZE,
        0, 0 );
```

MFC

You can send the slider control a WM_SETPAGESIZE message to set the page size. As a guideline, the page size is one-fifth the size of the range between the minimum and maximum ranges of the control. You can also use the CSlider::SetPageSize() function to set the controls size. Two examples are shown in Code 6–52.

To get the slider page size, simply send it a TBM_GETPAGESIZE message, or call the CSliderCtrl::GetPageSize() function. The code should appear in the Dialog or View class that is the parent window class for the slider control.

Code 6–52

```
int Min, Max;

Min = SendDlgItemMessage( IDC_SLIDERH, TBM_GETRANGEMIN, 0, 0 );
Max = SendDlgItemMessage( IDC_SLIDERH, TBM_GETRANGEMAX, 0, 0 );

int Step = (Max-Min) / 5;

// Method using a message:
SendDlgItemMessage( IDC_SLIDERH, TBM_SETPAGESIZE, 0, Step );
// Method using CSliderCtrl class:
m_SliderH.SetPageSize( Step ); // Assumes that m_SliderH is a CSliderCtrl
// member variable

int Page;
Page = SendDlgItemMessage( IDC_SLIDERH, TBM_GETPAGESIZE, 0, 0 );
// or
Page = m_SliderH.GetPageSize();
```

Image Lists

Image Lists are not visual controls like the others we have discussed so far. This means that they are not dropped onto a form like the other controls, nor do they have a visual appearance on a form. Instead, Image lists represent a collection of images, either bitmaps or icons, that are used by other controls such as the tree or list control. The image list control and functions provide the ability to add, remove, copy, or merge images in an image list.

The images in an image list must all be of the same height and size and can be thought of as laid out in a short wide format. That is, image 1 is to the right of image 0, and image 2 is to the right of image 1. It is possible to create and load a bitmap that is properly formatted to appear as several images in an image list. You can also load individual bitmaps or icons and add or remove them to an image list at runtime.

Image lists are defined as either "masked" or "non-masked." A non-masked image list contains only the images you want to display, and they are displayed in just that fashion. A masked image list actually contains two images per displayed image. The first image is the normal image, and the second image is a monochrome mask image. The monochrome image mask is used to draw the image in a transparent fashion.

Image lists also provide the ability to specify an overlay image within the image list for another image, also within the image list. For example, if you had four "real" images, you might actually have eight, four for the real images, and four for the overlay images. Overlay images are images that are drawn transparently over the real image after the real image is drawn. This overlay transparent drawing is done when the image list drawing functions are invoked.

Image lists also have the ability to draw an individual image onto a device context, but are most commonly used as the source of images for either a tree or list control or as the source image for drag-and-drop operations when a drag image is needed.

In addition to image lists that your program can create, you can also gain access to the image list that Windows maintains for drive and file icons. The SGGetFileInfo() function (in both SDK and MFC programs) is how you can determine the image list handle that Windows uses. This is the same image list that Explorer uses when it shows icons for drives and files.

This section will describe how to easily create an image list that can be used with list and tree controls. This topic will also be addressed briefly in each the list and tree control sections.

To Create a Bitmap with Multiple Images

1. From the Insert menu choice, select Resource.
2. Double-click on the Bitmap item in the Insert Resource Dialog (this adds bitmap).
3. With the new bitmap, change its properties so that the ID is IDB_FACEIMGLIST.
4. Change (see Figure 6–8) the image width to 64 and the height to 16 (we will have four 16 × 16 bitmaps).
5. Close the bitmap properties window.
6. Draw the four images on the single bitmap, equally spaced (see Figure 6–9).

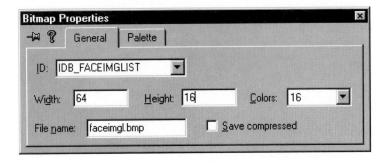

Figure 6–8 Modify the bitmap properties by changing values in the Bitmap Properties dialog box.

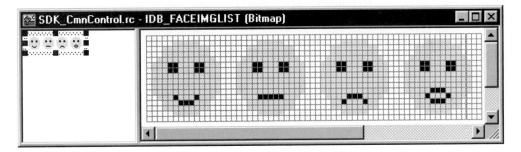

Figure 6–9 Create four images, equally spaced. (See the "Creating and Adding Images" section for details on how to use this bitmap in an image list.)

Retrieving Windows' Image List — SDK and MFC

Windows maintains its own image list of icons for drives, folders, and files. The image list contains the individual images that are associated with each type (drives, folders, and files). Unlike image lists that you create, Windows creates this and you should not destroy the image list when you're done with it. In other words, the image list that Windows uses is a shared resource between programs and should not be destroyed.

The SHGetFileInfo() SDK function will permit you to determine the image not only for a specific file, but the image list used by the system as well. These are the two-helper functions shown in Code 6–53. One returns to the caller the HIMAGELIST handle for the Windows system image list, and the other retrieves the image for a specific drive, folder, or file.

The PNGetSysImageList retrieves the shared image list that Windows uses to store the icons for a drive, folder, or file. The PNGetPathIcons() function returns either

---

the large or small icons for a specific file. PNGetPathIcons() returns two image indices into the system image list for the normal and selected icons for the desired file. Code 6–53 shows how to use these functions.

Code 6–53

```
HIMAGELIST hImageList;
BOOL LargeSize;

hImageList = PNGetSysImageList( LargeSize );
ListView_SetImageList( hWnd, hImageList,
   LargeSize ? LVSIL_NORMAL : LVSIL_SMALL );

// Setup ListView appearance
ListView_DeleteAllItems( hWnd );
PNListViewDeleteColumns( hWnd );
PNListViewInsertColumn( hWnd, 0, "Drives", 100 );

//Determine valid drive letters
char Drives[128], *pRoot;
char Volume[64], FileSystem[64];
char Descr[128];
DWORD Flags, MaxLength;
int iIcon, iIconSel;
int Row=0;

GetLogicalDriveStrings( sizeof(Drives), Drives );

// Iterate through drive letters, determine icons, and
// add to list view control
for( pRoot=Drives; *pRoot; pRoot++ )
{

    PNGetPathIcons( pRoot, iIcon, iIconSel, LargeSize, FALSE );
    PNListViewInsertItem( hWnd, Row++, pRoot, iIcon );

    whle( *pRoot )
        pRoot++;
}
return( Row );
```

Creating and Adding Images

SDK

There are a variety of image list helper macros and functions that all start with ImageList_ to help you manage image lists. We will examine only the most commonly used ones here. Of special note, the ImageList_Create(), ImageList_LoadImage(), ImageList_Add(), and ImageList_Destroy().

HIMAGELIST ImageList_Create(int Width, int Height, UINT Flags, int Initial, int Grow). This function creates an empty image list, where Width and Height are the width and height of each image in the list. The Flags parameter indicates the color details of the images, as well as whether the image list has a mask. The Flags parameter can be one or more of the values shown in Table 6–4.

The Initial parameter indicates the number of initial images the image list will contain. If anything other than 0, then the initial images are created as blank images. The Grow parameter indicates how the image list is grown when an image is added. For efficiency purposes, when an image list is added, the bitmap that contains the images is expanded by the Grow factor if there was no more space to add images. This is illustrated in Code 6–54.

Code 6–54

```
HIMAGELIST hImageList;
hImageList = ImageList_Create( 16, 16, ILC_COLOR, 0, 1 );
```

Table 6.4 The Flags Parameters

Value	Meaning
ILC_COLOR	If you don't specify and of the other ILC_COLOR?? values, this indicates that the color should default to either ILC_COLOR4 or ILC_COLORDIB for older video drivers.
ILC_COLOR4	Use a 4-bit color device-independent bitmap section as the bitmap for the image list.
ILC_COLOR8	Use an 8-bit color device-independent bitmap section. The colors used for the color table are the same colors as the halftone palette.
ILC_COLOR16	Use a 16-bit color device-independent bitmap section.
ILC_COLOR24	Use a 24-bit color device-independent bitmap section.
ILC_COLOR32	Use a 32-bit color device-independent bitmap section.
ILC_COLORDDB	Use a device-dependent bitmap.
ILC_MASK	Use a mask. The image list will contain two bitmaps, one for the real image and another for a monochrome bitmap used as a mask. If not specified, the image list contains only one bitmap (has no mask)

HIMAGELIST ImageList_LoadImage (HINSTANCE hInstance, LPCTSTR lp-Name, int iSize, int iGrow, COLORREF crMask, UINT uType, UINT uFlags).
Creates an image list from a bitmap, cursor, or icon resource. The image may be stored in either the resources for your project or an external file (such as a .BMP or .ICO file). An image list created in this manner does not need to have ImageList_Create() called. The hInstance is the instance handle of your program, or zero to use a file or Windows resource. lpName is either a file name or resource ID (with MAKEINTRESOURCE) that indicates the bitmap, cursor, or icon to be loaded.

iSize indicates the size, both height and width, of each item in the image loaded. cr-Mask is a color indicating the mask color for when the images are drawn. uType indicates the type of image and must be either IMAGE_BITMAP, IMAGE_CURSOR, or IMAGE_ICON. The uFlags parameter is one or more of the values in Table 6.5. Code 6–55 illustrates how to load a bitmap resource from a program.

This program creates and loads the image list from the IDB_FACEIMGLIST bitmap, which is a set of 16×16 images. White (RGB(255,255,255)) is defined as the transparent color.

Code 6–55

```
HIMAGELIST hImageList;
hImageList = ImageList_LoadImage( GetModuleHandle(NULL),
     MAKEINTRESOURCE( IDB_FACEIMGLIST ), 16, 1, RGB(255,255,255),
     IMAGE_BITMAP, LR_DEFAULTCOLOR );
```

int ImageList_Add(HIMAGELIST hImageList, HBITMAP hBitmap, HBITMAP hBitmapMask). This function adds a bitmap to the image list. hImageList is the handle to the image list to be added to. The hBitmap and hBitmapMask are bitmap handles for the image and an image mask. If the image list is nonmasked, then the hBitmapMask is ignored. The previous images stored in the image list are not removed before adding the new image (an image is added, not replaced). This is illustrated in Code 6–56.

Code 6–56

```
HBITMAP hBitmap;
LoadBitmap( GetModuleHandle(NULL), MAKEINTRESOURCE(IDB_IMAGE2) );
HIMAGELIST hImageList;
hImageList = ImageList_Create( 16, 16, ILC_COLOR, 0, 1 );
ImageList_Add( hImageList, hBitmap, 0 );
```

Table 6.5   The uFlags Parameter

Value	Meaning
LR_CREATEDIBSECTION	If uType is IMAGE_BITMAP, then the function will return a DIB section bitmap rather than a compatible bitmap.
LR_CREATEDIBSECTION	Causes the function to load a bitmap without mapping it to the colors of the display device.
LR_DEFAULTCOLOR	Uses the color format of the display.
LR_LOADDEFAULTSIZE	If the iSize parameter is 0, uses the width or height specified by the system metric values for cursors and icons. If not specified and iSize is 0, the function uses the size as defined by the resource. If the resource contains multiple images, the function sets the size to that of the first image.
LR_LOADFROMFILE	Indicates that lpName contains a filename to be loaded (i.e., a .BMP or .ICO file).
LR_LOADMAP3DCOLORS	Indicates that the image, once loaded, should have its colors mapped to the system colors as defined by the users configuration.
LR_LOADTRANSPARENT	Indicates that the first color value (pixel) in the loaded resource should be used as the transparent color.
LR_MONOCHROME	Loads the image in black and white.
LR_SHARED	If the image is loaded multiple times, this flag indicates that the same image handle should be returned each time. Be sure to destroy this handle only once, when no longer needed by any of the pieces of code needs it.

BOOL ImageList_Destroy(HIMAGELIST hImageList).   Removes an image list and its bitmap(s) from memory. hImageList is the handle to the image list to be released.

MFC

MFC provides a CImageList class to assist in managing image list objects. All of the functions in the SDK Image_List family will have counterparts in the CImageList object. In an MFC program, where there is either a Cview- or Cdialog-based class used to display the main interface window, we create a CImageList as a data member of that class. In our MFC example (MFC_CmnControls), there is a CMFC_CmnControlDlg class. To this class, we would add the declaration shown in Code 6–57.

Code 6–57

```
CImageList m_SmileyImages;
```

CImageList::Create(). This function is a combination of the ListView_Create() and ListView_LoadImage() functions from the SDK family. It provides you with the ability to create an empty image list, or to create and load a CImageList from a file or resource. Code 6–58 contains a list of the overloaded Create() functions.

Code 6–58

```
BOOL Create( int cx, int cy, UINT nFlags, int nInitial, int nGrow );
BOOL Create( UINT nBitmapID, int cx, int nGrow, COLORREF crMask );
BOOL Create( LPCTSTR lpszBitmapID, int cx, int nGrow, COLORREF crMask );
BOOL Create( CImageList& imagelist1, int nImage1, CImageList& imagelist2,
       int nImage2,
int dx, int dy );
BOOL Create( CImageList* pImageList );
```

In Code 6–58, cx and cy define the width and height of the image to be loaded or initialized. nFlags are the same flag definitions as described in the ImageList_Create() function of the SDK section above. The nInitial parameter is the number of initial images to create (they will be created as blank images). nGrow indicates the number of images to add when a new image is added to the image list and there is no more space for it. crMask indicates the transparency color for displaying the image list images. lpszBitmapID is the image resource ID (with MAKEINTRESOURCE), or the name of a file to be loaded.

The last two versions of the Create function permit you to create an image list based on other image list objects.

Code 6–59 loads the IDB_FACEIMGLIST bitmap into the CImageList, making images 16×16 pixels in size, with a transparency color of white (RGB(255,255,255)).

Code 6–59

```
m_SmileyImages.Create( IDB_FACEIMGLIST, 16, 1, RGB(255,255,255) );
```

CImageList::Add(). This function permits the addition of new images to an existing CImageList object. The function is overloaded as illustrated in Code 6–60.

Code 6–60

```
int Add( CBitmap* pbmImage, CBitmap* pbmMask );
int Add( CBitmap* pbmImage, COLORREF crMask );
int Add( HICON hIcon );
```

CImageList::DeleteImageList().   This function permits you to destroy the images currently held by a CImageList object. Normally, the destructor will do this for you.

Using the System ImageList

SDK

The System ImageList is an image list that Windows maintains. Inside this image list, you will find all the images that are associated with the items that you would see in Explorer, such as drives, folders, and files. An example of the images kept in this system image list can be seen in the List View demonstration at the beginning of the List View section (drive images only).

The key function used in obtaining these images is the SHGetFileInfo() function, which will return the image list handle to you, as well as the icons or images associated with a file. The icons are returned as the index position within the system image list where they can be found (this will be used in the ListView section that follows). Rather than present the complete details on how this is implemented, we will provide two help functions (see Code 6–61) that will make it easier for you to retrieve and work with the System ImageList.

Code 6–61

```
// PNGetSysImageList - Retrieves the Image list handle used by
//      the Window system
// Returns: The HIMAGELIST handle
// Note: The returned image list handle is shared between windows
//      applications. Do not destroy it!
HIMAGELIST PNGetSysImageList( BOOL LargeImages )
{
        char Drives[128];
        SHFILEINFO shFileInfo;
        // Get list of drives on the system
        GetLogicalDriveStrings( sizeof(Drives), Drives );

        HIMAGELIST hImageList;

        // Call SHGetFileInfo to retrieve the system image list
        hImageList = (HIMAGELIST)SHGetFileInfo( Drives, 0, &shFileInfo,
            sizeof( shFileInfo ), SHGFI_SYSICONINDEX |
            (LargeImages?SHGFI_LARGEICON:SHGFI_SMALLICON) );

        // Return the image list handle
        return( hImageList );
}
```

```
// PNGetPathIcons - Retrieves index into the system image
//      list for a file, folder, or drive
// Parameters:
//      Path - Path of drive, folder, or file to retrieve image for
//      iIcon - Index of icon within the system index (returned)
//      iIconSel - Index of selected icon within the system
//              index (returned)
//      Large - TRUE or FALSE to retrieve the large or small system icon
//      MustSlash - TRUE if the path must end in a slash, false if not
// Returns: TRUE if succesful, false if not
// Note: Files must not end in a slash, and drive letters and
//      folders should end in a slash.
BOOL PNGetPathIcons( const char* Path, int& iIcon, int& iIconSel,
        BOOL Large, BOOL MustSlash )
{
        SHFILEINFO shFileInfo;
        char strPath[MAX_PATH];
        int ImageSize = Large ? SHGFI_LARGEICON : SHGFI_SMALLICON;

        // Make sure path has an ending slash or doesn't
        strcpy( strPath, Path );
        if( MustSlash )
        {
                if( strPath[strlen(strPath)]!='\\' &&
                    strPath[strlen(strPath)]!='/' )
                {
                if( strchr( strPath, '/' ) )
                    strcat( strPath, "/" );
                    else
                        strcat(strPath, "\\" );
                }
        }
        else
        {
                if( strPath[strlen(strPath)]=='\\' ||
                    strPath[strlen(strPath)]=='/')
                    strPath[strlen(strPath)-1] = '\0';
}

        // Get icons for the path
        if( SHGetFileInfo( strPath, 0, &shFileInfo, sizeof( shFileInfo ),
            SHGFI_ICON | ImageSize ) == 0 )
            return( FALSE );
        iIcon = shFileInfo.iIcon;
        if( SHGetFileInfo( strPath, 0, &shFileInfo, sizeof( shFileInfo ),
            SHGFI_ICON | SHGFI_OPENICON | ImageSize ) == 0 )
```

```
            return( FALSE );
        iIconSel = shFileInfo.iIcon;
        return( TRUE );
}
```

The PNGetSysImageList() function takes a single parameter that indicates the size of the images you are interested in, large or small. It will return the system image list that Windows uses for that image size. Note that this is a shared image list, and you should not destroy it when done with it.

The PNGetPathIcons() functions parameters are a path name to a drive, folder, or filename, two integers to receive the normal and selected icon image index (into the system image list), a parameter indicating if you want large or small icons, and finally a parameter that indicates whether the passed Path parameter should have a slash at the end or not.

These two functions will make it very easy to populate a list view control with drive letters and icons, which will be done in the following List View control section.

MFC

The System ImageList is an image list that Windows maintains. Inside this image list, you will find all the images that are associated with the items that you would see in Explorer, such as drives, folders, and files. An example of the images kept in this system image list can be seen in the List View demonstration at the beginning of the List View section (drive images only).

Given the object-oriented nature of MFC, we are going to take a different approach to demonstrate how to use the system Image List in an MFC program. Rather than create individual functions to load the system Image List, we will use subclassed controls. A subclassed control is a class created from a normal MFC window class that changes the behavior of the class somewhat. In the List View class, we will create a class that is derived from the CListCtrl List View class, but its default behavior will be to populate the list control with the drive names and images from the system Image List. See the MFC List View section for more details.

List View Controls

List View controls (see Figure 6–10) have a variety of appearances and are intended to present the user with a list of items, optionally with images for each item. Perhaps the best example of the appearance of a list view control is the right pane of Windows explorer (see Figure 6–10). The list view has the following basic appearance properties or styles, which can be set in the dialog editor by changing the properties of the list view (see Table 6.6)

Full Row Selection and Grid Lines

These properties are not accessible in the dialog editor, so they cannot be set with the other properties at design time. Instead, you must set the properties programmatically at runtime. The full row selection (where the entire row is highlighted when selected) and the Grid Lines properties are set by calling the ListViewSetExtendedListViewStyle() function for the List View control.

Another important property to the list view control is the Shared Image List property. Normally, if an image list is associated with a list view control, when the list view control is destroyed, the image list it is associated with is also destroyed. In the case of a shared image list, this can cause problems. Set this property to TRUE to have the image list not destroyed when the list view is destroyed.

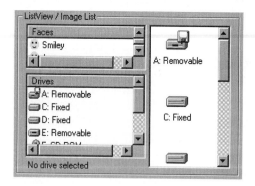

Figure 6–10   The List View control.

Table 6.6   Properties of the List View

View type	Description
Icon	Large icons with single item text displayed.
Small Icon	Small icons with single item text displayed.
List	View small icons and single item text.
Report	Small icons with columns of text and column headers. Columns must be added programmatically to the control when this style is selected. This format can look like a grid.

The images displayed in a list view control are implemented using an image list (described in the previous section). Once an image list has been initialized, it may be associated with a list view control. Once associated, you can set the image to display for a list view item by programmatically changing the image index for the item.

Like other controls, the list view is available on the normal tool palette when you are using the dialog editor. Drop the list view control on your dialog form and right-click it to change its properties.

Extra Item Data

As with the normal list box control, the List View control also has the ability to store an extra 32-bit value for each item or row in the list. Windows will not use or alter this value, and it is there solely for your use. For example, if you populated the List View with the names of people from a database table, you might want to put the unique ID for each person in this extra 32-bit value so that you can easily retrieve the person's record later. Of course, this is just one example—you can store whatever you want into the item data. If you want to store a struct or class object with each item, then you simply store a pointer to that object in the item data.

Adding Columns to a List View

SDK

A list view control that is in the Report style (set by the property editor in the dialog resource for the list view control) appears with column headers that can be grabbed and resized. Before inserting items into a list view control that has the Report Style, you must add columns to the list control.

The typical way to do this in an SDK program is to call the ListView_InsertColumn() function and pass it an LVCOLUMN data structure you have set up. Since this can be a bit complicated, we will present a simple helper function (see Code 6–62) to permit you to easily insert new columns into a list view control.

Code 6–62 gets the width of the client area of the window by calling GetClientRect(). It uses this width, along with the Percent parameter, to determine how wide the new column should be. Next, it populates an LVCOLUMN data structure named lvColumn and initializes the mask, fmt, pszText, iSubItem, and cx members of the structure according to parameters you passed. It then calls the ListView_InsertColumn() to actually insert the new column.

Code 6–63 illustrates how to call this function. This adds two columns: "Name" occupying 75% of the List View window, and "Age" occupying 25%. "Name" and "Age" would appear inside the column headers of the list view control.

Code 6–62

```
                    Column number to be added          Text for column header
                                                        Percentage of window
Handle to list view to add column to                    header the column
                                                        should occupy

int PNListViewInsertColumn( HWND hWnd, int Column, char* Header, int Percent )
{
  RECT Client;
  GetClientRect( hWnd, &Client );
  int Width = (int) (Client.right * (percent/100.0));
  LVCOLUMN lvColumn;
  lvColumn.mask = LVCF_FMT | LVCF_TEXT | LVCF_SUBITEM|LVCF_WIDTH;
  lvColumn.fmt=LVCFMT_LEFT;
  lvColumn.pszText = Header;
  lvColumn.iSubItem = Column;
  lvColumn.cx = Width;
  return( ListView_InsertColumn( hWnd, Column, &lvColumn ) );
}
```

Code 6–63

```
PNListViewInsertColumn( hChild, 0, "Name", 75 );
PNListViewInsertColumn( hChild, 1, "Age", 25 );
```

MFC

A list view control that is in the Report style (set by the property editor in the dialog resource for the list view control) appears with column headers that can be grabbed and resized. Before inserting items into a List View control that has the Report Style, you must add columns to the list control.

The CListCtrl class is the MFC class that serves as a wrapper class for the List View control. In this class, we find the InsertColumn() function (see Table 6.7), over-loaded as illustrated in Code 6–64. Notice that in the second form, all but the first two parameters have default values.

Code 6–64

```
int InsertColumn( int nCol, const LVCOLUMN* pColumn );
int InsertColumn( int nCol, LPCTSTR lpszColumnHeading, int nFormat =
LVCFMT_LEFT, int nWidth = -1, int nSubItem = -1 );
```

A CListCtrl object needs to be associated with the on-screen window before calling this function. This can be done in one of two ways: We can use ClassWizards Member Variable tab to declare a CListCtrl Control category member variable, or we can use GetDlgItem() to retrieve a CListCtrl pointer.

Table 6.7   Parameters for the InsertColumn() Function

Parameter	Meaning
nCol	Column number or position to insert at.
pColumn	Pointer to an LVCOLUMN struct with information on column to insert.
lpszColumnHeading	Pointer to constant string with header text for the new column.
nFormat	Flags for the colum alignment: LVCFMT_LEFT, LVCFMT_CENTER, or LVCFMT_RIGHT.
nWidth	Width of the column in device units, −1 (default) means don't set width.
nSubItem	Index of a subitem associated with the column. −1 (default) means don't make an association.

Using ClassWizard requires no lines of code and makes available a data member that can be used with the InsertColumn(). Notice that in the second version of the function, all but the first two parameters have default values. Code 6–65 shows how to call the GetDlgItem() function.

Code 6–65

```
CListCtrl* pList = (CListCtrl*)GetDlgItem( IDC_FACELIST );
pList->InsertColumn( 0, "Faces" );
```

Code 6–65 might be executed in the OnInitDialog() function of the main dialog window for dialog-based applications, or called in the OnInitialUpdate() function of the View class. However, this function cannot be called in the OnCreate() function because the parent window (view) has been created, but the child window hasn't as yet.

The trick to place the code in the OnInitialUpdate() function of the View class so the function is called each time the user loads a data file or performs a File/New menu selection. Make sure the code only gets executed once as shown in Code 6–66.

Code 6–66

```
static bool WasDone = false;
if( !WasDone )
{
        WasDone = true;
        CListCtrl* pList = (CListCtrl*)GetDlgItem( IDC_FACELIST );
        pList->InsertColumn( 0, "Faces" );
        // Any other initialized code for common controls
}
```

Setting Column Widths

SDK

To set the column width of a specific column in a list view control, use the ListView_SetColumn Width() function as shown in Code 6–67.

Code 6–67

```
BOOL ListView_SetColumnWidth( HWND hwnd, int iCol, int cx );
```

In Code 6–67, hWnd refers to the window handle of the List View control, iCol refers to the column to be sized, and the cx parameter indicates the desired width in device units (commonly, pixels). Code 6–68 illustrates how to set the column width to be equal to the size of the entire window.

Code 6-68

```
//Get window handle to the list view control
HWND hList = GetDlgItem( hwndDlg, IDC_FACELIST );
// Determine rectangle (and therefore, size) of the list view
// control:
RECT Rect;
GetClientRect( hList, &Rect );
// Set the list view width for column 0 to the same as client
//width (Rect.right)
ListView_SetColumnWidth( hList, 0, Rect.right );
```

MFC

We use the CListCtrl classes SetColumnWidth() function to set the width of a specific column. We need a CListCtrl object, which we can either get via a pointer with GetDlgItem(), or we could have created a member variable for the control using ClassWizards Member Variable tab to create a Control category variable. Code 6–69 illustrates the use of the GetDlgItem() function.

Code 6-69

```
CListCtrl* pList = (CListCtrl*)GetDlgItem( IDC_FACELIST );
pList->InsertColumn( 0, "Faces" );
CRect Rect;
pList->GetClientRect( &Rect );
pList->SetColumnWidth( 0, Rect.Width() );
```

Code 6–70 uses GetDlgItem() to get a CListCtrl pointer to the desired list view window. It then uses the CListCtrl::InsertColumn() function to add a column (so there is something to size), and calls the CWnd::GetClientRect() function to retrieve the dimensions of the list view window. With those dimensions, CListrCtrl::SetColumnWidth() is called to set column 0 to the same width as the client area of the List View control (using the CRect::Width() function).

Code 6-70

```
CListCtrl* pList = (CListCtrl*)GetDlgItem( IDC_FACELIST );
pList->InsertColumn( 0, "Faces" );
CRect Rect;
pList->GetClientRect( &Rect );
pList->SetColumnWidth( 0, Rect.Width() );
```

As with the Insert a column section, the code presented above would be in the OnInitDialog() function if the parent window were a dialog or dialog-based program, or in the OnInitialUpdate() function if it were a view-based program.

Adding Items to a ListView

SDK

In order to add items to a list view, we need to call the ListView_InsertItem() function. This function requires an LVITEM structure to be properly initialized for the insertion. The helper function in Code 6-71 illustrates how this is accomplished.

Code 6-71

```
Index (row) where item was inserted

                                      Text to be inserted (appears in first column)

    Row to be inserted at (-1 means at end of list)

                                                      Image index into image
    Handle to list view to                            list control for list
    add item to                                       view

    int PNListViewInsertItem( HWND hWnd, int Row, char* Text, int Image )
    {
        LVITEM lvItem;
        if( Row == -1 )
          Row = ListView_GetItemCount( hWnd );
        lvItem.mask = LVIF_TEXT;
        if( Image >=0 )
            lvItem.mask |= LVIF_IMAGE;
        lvItem.iItem = Row;
        lvItem.iSubItem = 0;
        lvItem.pszText = Text;
        lvItem.iImage = Image;
        return( ListView_InsertItem( hWnd, &lvItem ) );
    }
```

The PNListViewInsertItem() function is called by passing the window handle to the list view control you want to add an item to, then the desired row for insertion. If Row is -1, it gets the count of items in the row by calling ListView_GetItemCount() and then uses that value as the insertion point (places item at the end of the list). The Text parameter will be the text for the item inserted in the List View control, and the Image parameter is an optional parameter that indicates the image index in an image list, if it's > = 0.

By specifying a valid Image parameter to the function for a list view control that has an image list associated with it, when the item is inserted, that particular image will also appear in the List View control.

MFC

In order to add items to a list view window in an MFC project, we will utilize the CListView::InsertItem() function. We need a CListCtrl object, which we can get by adding a data member for the list view control using the Member VariableI tab of the ClassWizard, or we can also just call GetDlgItem() as shown in Code 6-72. CListCtrl::InsertItem() (see Table 6-8) has the following overloaded versions available.

The simplest versions of the functions are the second and third versions as used in Code 6-73. Code 6-73 can be used anywhere you want to place items into a CListCtrl object (List View control, on screen).

Code 6-72

```
int InsertItem( const LVITEM* pItem );
int InsertItem( int nItem, LPCTSTR lpszItem );
int InsertItem( int nItem, LPCTSTR lpszItem, int nImage );
int InsertItem( UINT nMask, int nItem, LPCTSTR lpszItem, UINT nState, UINT
          nStateMask, int nImage, LPARAM lParam );
```

Code 6-73

```
CListCtrl* pList = (CListCtrl*)GetDlgItem( IDC_FACELIST );
pList->InsertColumn( 0, "Faces" );
pList->InsertItem( 0, "Smiley" );
pList->InsertItem( 1, "Average" );
pList->InsertItem( 2, "Frowny" );
pList->InsertItem( 3, "Surprise" );
```

Table 6.8   Parameters for the InsertItem() Function

Parameter	Meaning
pItem	Pointer to an LVITEM to be used to insert the new item.
nItem	Where in the list to perform the insertion of the new item.
lpszItem	The text to insert for the new item.
nImage	The image index for the new item, if there is a CImageList object associated with the List View control.
nState	The item, image, and overlay state for the new item. See the online documentation for the List View Item States for more details.
nStateMask	Indicates which bits of the state member of the LVITEM object are to be utilized. See the online documentation for the List View Item States for more details.
lParam	Extra 32-bit value that is yours to use as you see fit. Not used by Windows.

Performing In-Place Item Editing

SDK

To have the ability to let the user edit the items of a list view control (like Explorer does when you rename files), you need to set the LVS_EDITLABELS property on for the control by selecting the Edit Labels property in the dialog editor for the control. The list view control will handle all of the details except the actual setting of the text to the user's new entry.

When the user is done with the editing of the label (by pressing ENTER or selecting another item or control in the program), the parent window of the List View control is sent a LVN_ENDLABELEDIT notification code via a WM_NOTIFY message. In that message, the lParam parameter will contain an NMLVDISPINFO structure with information about the user's changes.

You don't need to be concerned about the structure, except that if the item.pszText data members parameter is not NULL. If it isn't, then you can pass the address of the item data member from that structure to the ListView_SetItem() function to set the new text (see Code 6–74).

Code 6–74

Parse out data from a WM_NOTIFY message

```
LRESULT CALLBACK DialogProc( HWND hwndDlg, UINT uMsg, WPARAM wParam, LPARAM lParam)
{
  int wID;
  int wNotification;
  HWND hChild;
  switch( uMsg )
    {
    case WM_NOTIFY:
      wID = (int) wParam;
      wNotification = ((NMHDR*)lParam)->code;
      hChild = ((NMHDR*)lParam)->hwndFrom;
      if( wID == IDC_FACELIST && wNotification == LVN_ENDLABELEDIT )
        {
          NMLVDISPINFO* pTreeItem = (NMLVDISPINFO*)lParam;
          if( pTreeItem->item.pszText )
            ListView_SetItem( hChild, &pTreeItem->item );
        }
      // Portions of code removed for readability
```

Handle user editing a list view items text.

Using a Custom Image List with a List View

SDK

To have images appear within the items of a list view control, we need to create the image list (as described in the previous Image List section) and associate it with the list view control.

This can be as simple as using the ListView_SetImageList() function to make the association. Then, when we insert items into the list view control, we specify where in the list to place them, what the text for the new item is, and what the image list index is for the item as shown in Code 6–75.

Code 6–75

```
// Get handle to the image list
HWND hList = GetDlgItem(hwndDlg, IDC_FACELIST);

// Create and load a static image list
HIMAGELIST hImageList = ImageList_LoadImage( GetModuleHandle(NULL),
        MAKEINTRESOURCE( IDB_FACEIMGLIST ), 16, 1, RGB(255,255,255),
        IMAGE_BITMAP, LR_DEFAULTCOLOR );

// Set an image list to use the newly-loaded image list
ListView_SetImageList( hList, hImageList, LVSIL_SMALL );

PNListViewInsertColumn(, 0, "Faces", 100 );
PNListViewInsertItem( hList, 0, "Smiley", 0 );
PNListViewInsertItem( hList, 1, "Average", 1 );
PNListViewInsertItem( hList, 2, "Frowny", 2 );
PNListViewInsertItem( hList, 3, "Surprise", 3 );
```

Code 6–75 assumes that IDC_FACELIST is the ID for the list control on the parent window and hwndDlg is the window handle for the parent window. IDC_FACEIMGLIST is assumed to be the ID of a bitmap made up of smaller same-sized images, laid out side to side (as discussed in the previous Image List section).

The ListView_SetImageList() macro makes that list control use the image list, and when we insert items into the list, we use the helper function PNListViewInsertItem(), which was discussed in the previous section.

The PNListViewInsertItem() is a helper function that creates and initializes an LVITEM structure named lvItem. It populates that structure as needed to add a new item into a list view control, with a text and image index into its selected image list. It calls ListView_InsertItem() to actually perform the insertion.

MFC

To have images appear within the items of a list view control, we need to create the image list (as described in the previous Image List section) and associate it with the list view control. We will be using the CImageList and CListCtrl MFC classes to assist in the coding.

The first step is to make the CImageList object. Since the list view control is a child window of a CDialog or CView-derived main window class, we will add the CImageList object as a data member to that class. Add the following to the CDialog or CFormView derived class object that represents your main view window (CMFC_CmnControlDlg in Code 6–76, in the CMFC_CmnControlDlg.h file).

Code 6–76

```
// ImageList for first listview dmeonstration
CImageList m_SmileyImages;
```

Next, we need to initialize this data member by loading the bitmap of images from the resource. The following code can be added to the OnCreate handler if your project is CView based, or in the OnInitDialog function of your main dialog class if your project was dialog-based. Our example (see Code 6–77) (CMFC_CmnControlDlg) is dialog-based, so we will add it to the end of CMFC_CmnControlDlg::OnInitDialog(), before the return statement:

Code 6–77

```
        // Image List loading
        m_SmileyImages.Create( IDB_FACEIMGLIST, 16, 1, RGB(255,255,255) );
        // ListView initialization
        CListCtrl* pList = (CListCtrl*)GetDlgItem( IDC_FACELIST );
        pList->SetImageList( &m_SmileyImages, LVSIL_SMALL );
        pList->InsertColumn( 0, "Faces" );
        pList->InsertItem( 0, "Smiley", 0 );
        pList->InsertItem( 1, "Average", 1 );
        pList->InsertItem( 2, "Frowny", 2 );
        pList->InsertItem( 3, "Surprise", 3 );
        CRect Rect;
        pList->GetClientRect( &Rect );
        pList->SetColumnWidth( 0, Rect.Width() );

        return TRUE; // return TRUE unless you set the focus to a control
}
```

Code 6–77 first calls the CImageList::Create() function to initialize the m_SmileyImages data member from our bitmap. Then it gets the List View control window handle, in the form of a CListCtrl pointer by calling GetDlgItem() (note the typecast). Then, for the pList pointer, it calls the CListCtrl::SetImageList() function to tell the child list view control to start using our newly loaded CImageList object (m_Smiley-Images).

A series of CListCtrl::InsertItem() functions follows next, passing the desired insertion point, the text to insert, and the image index to use in the image list when displayed. Notice that there are several overloaded versions of InsertItemText() in the CListCtrl class, and the image index is an option parameter. In other words, if you just wanted to set up the list and insert items without images, you just wouldn't call the CListCtrl::SetImageList() function, and you wouldn't pass a third parameter to CListCtrl::InsertItemText().

Using the System Image List

SDK

If you want a list view control to contain drive names, folder, or files on your local machine, you can use the same system image list that Windows uses for Explorer (the right-side window pane in Explorer is a List View control). In order to implement this behavior, we will reuse the functions PNGetPathIcons() and PNGetSysImageList() discussed in the *Image List* section.

We will provide another helper function, named PNListViewInitDrives(). This function will take any list view control and initialize it with a list of drive letters and types, as well as the images for the drives. In order to call this help function, all you need to do is pass to it the window handle of the List View class to be initialized as illustrated in Code 6–78.

Code 6–78 might is called in the WM_INITDIALOG message in your dialog procedure. The helper function is shown in Code 6–79. This code uses the PNGetPathIcons() and PNListViewInsertItem() helper functions as described and also uses the GetLogicalDrives() SDK function to get a list of valid drive letters and types for the system.

Code 6–78

```
PNListViewInitDrives( GetDlgItem(hwndDlg,IDC_DRVLIST) );
```

Code 6–79

```
int PNListViewInitDrives( HWND hWnd )
{
    HIMAGELIST hImageList;
    BOOL LargeSize;

    // Determine if small or large icons are needed based on
    // window style
    if( GetWindowLong( hWnd, GWL_STYLE )
    & (LVS_SMALLICON|LVS_REPORT) )
```

```
        LargeSize = FALSE;
else
        LargeSize = TRUE;

// Use Windows own image list for drive and file icons
hImageList = PNGetSysImageList( LargeSize );
ListView_SetImageList( hWnd, hImageList,
        LargeSize ? LVSIL_NORMAL : LVSIL_SMALL );

// Setup ListView appearance
ListView_DeleteAllItems( hWnd );
PNListViewDeleteColumns( hWnd );
PNListViewInsertColumn( hWnd, 0, "Drives", 100 );

// Determine valid drive letters
char Drives[128], *pRoot;
char Volume[64], FileSystem[64];
char Descr[128];
DWORD Flags, MaxLength;
int iIcon, iIconSel;
int Row=0;

// Use GetLogicalDrives to get list of drive letters
GetLogicalDriveStrings( sizeof(Drives), Drives );

// Iterate through drive letters, determine icons, and
// add to list view control
for( pRoot=Drives; *pRoot; pRoot++ )
{
    switch( GetDriveType( pRoot ) )
    {
            case DRIVE_UNKNOWN:
                sprintf( Descr, "%c: Unknown", *pRoot );
                break;
            case DRIVE_NO_ROOT_DIR:
                sprintf( Descr, "%c: Can't determine", *pRoot );
                break;
            case DRIVE_REMOVABLE:
                sprintf( Descr, "%c: Removable", *pRoot );
                break;
            case DRIVE_FIXED:
                sprintf( Descr, "%c: Fixed", *pRoot );
                break;
            case DRIVE_REMOTE:
                GetVolumeInformation( pRoot, Volume, sizeof(Volume),
                    NULL, &MaxLength, &Flags, FileSystem,
                    sizeof(FileSystem) );
                sprintf( Descr, "%c: Network drive %s (%s)", *pRoot,
                    Volume, FileSystem );
```

```
            break;
        case DRIVE_CDROM:
            sprintf( Descr, "%c: CD-ROM", *pRoot );
            break;

        case DRIVE_RAMDISK:
            sprintf( Descr, "%c: RAM Disk", *pRoot );
            break;
    }

    // Determine system image for drive (using helper functions)
    PNGetPathIcons( pRoot, iIcon, iIconSel, LargeSize, FALSE );
    PNListViewInsertItem( hWnd, Row++, Descr, iIcon );
    while( *pRoot ) // Move to next drive in string
            pRoot++;
    }
    return( Row );
}
```

MFC

If you want an list view control to contain drive names, folder, or files on your local machine, you can use the same system image list that Windows uses for Explorer (the right-side window pane in Explorer is a list view control). Instead of presenting a stand-alone function to assist in this, at the end of this section we will write a class derived from CListCtrl that provides this functionality. Once this is done, we will be able to use this class to place a list view control on a form and populate it with drive information, *using zero lines of code*. The *CPNDriveList Class* section in the Appendix gives full source code.

Responding to Selections

SDK

The list view control sends several specialized notifications for when an item selection has changed in the list view, as well as the common control standard double-click notification. To respond to these notification messages you must add a WM_NOTIFY message handler to your window procedure. This is illustrated in Code 6–80.

Code 6–80 determines that the IDC_DRVLIST control sent the double-click notification message NM_DBCLK. Inside the *if* test, it sends a LVM_GETNEXTITEM message to the child list view control, to determine the selected item if any. If no item is selected, the message will return –1; otherwise, it will return the index of the item.

The ListView_GetItemText() function is called to get the text from the selected row and column zero of the list view control, into the Text variable. This function is covered in more detail in the *Getting and Setting Individual "Cells"* section.

Code 6-80

Parse out data from a WM_NOTIFY message

Determine if notification came from specific control, and if it was a double-click notification

```
LRESULT CALLBACK DialogProc( HWND hwndDlg, UINT uMsg, WPARAM wParam, LPARAM lParam )
{
    int wID;
    int wNotification;
    HWND hChild;
    switch( uMsg )
    {
      case WM_NOTIFY:
        wID = (int) wParam;
        wNotification = ((NMHDR*)lParam)->code;
        hChild = ((NMHDR*)lParam)->hwndFrom;
        if( wID == IDC_DRVLIST && wNotification == NM_DBLCLK )
          {
            int Index = ListView_GetNextItem( hChild, -1, LVNI_SELECTED );
            if( Index != -1 )
              {
                char Text[128];
                ListView_GetItemText( hChild, Index, 0, Text, sizeof(Text) );
                MessageBox( hwndDlg, Text, "You selected", MB_OK );
              }
          }
        break;
        // Portions of code removed for readability
```

As with many windows control, there may not be a need to respond immediately to user events, such as when they change the selected item(s). If you want to determine what item is selected, you may do so at any time by calling the ListView_GetNextItem() function on the control, as demonstrated in the code above. See *Setting and Getting Individual "Cells"* for more details on how to retrieve the selected text.

Code 6-81 contains another example, which would handle the events each time the user changed the selection in a list view.

It is similar to the previous example, except that instead of the double-click event, it handles whenever the user changes the selection with the mouse or keyboard. In this example, the ListView_GetItemText() function is again called, and this time its text value is placed into the STATIC control IDC_DRVSELECTED.

Code 6-81

Parse out data from a WM_NOTIFY
message

```
LRESULT CALLBACK DialogProc( HWND hwndDlg, UINT uMsg, WPARAM wParam, LPARAM lParam )
{
    int wID;
    int wNotification;
    HWND hChild;
    switch( uMsg )
      {
        case WM_NOTIFY:
        wID = (int) wParam;
        wNotification = ((NMHDR*)lParam)->code;
        hChild = ((NMHDR*)lParam)->hwndFrom;
        if( wID == IDC_DRVLIST && wNotification == LVN_ITEMCHANGED )
          {
            NMLISTVIEW* pNMList = (NMLISTVIEW*)lParam;
            if( pNMList->iItem == -1 )
              SetDlgItemText( hwndDlg, IDC_DRVSELECTED, "No drive selected" );
            else
              {
                char Text[128];
                ListView_GetItemText( hChild, pNMList->iItem, 0, Text, sizeof(Text) );
                SetDlgItemText( hwndDlg, IDC_DRVSELECTED, Text );
              }
          }
        // Portions of code removed for readability
```

MFC

In order to respond to user selections, we will be looking at two different types of selections: Double-clicking on an item with the mouse and selecting a new item with the mouse or keyboard. To handle the double-click event, go to ClassWizard (from the View menu) and make sure the Message Map tab is highlighted. Then, make sure that the parent Dialog or View class of the List control is selected in the Messages field, that the IDC_DRVLIST ID is selected in the Object IDs list, and that the NM_DBCLICK ID is selected in the Messages list. Click Add Function and then

---

NOTE

Like many other controls, you don't have to provide immediate feedback when the user makes a selection, except in the case of a double-click (if you to decide to implement the double-click). Instead, you can just get the user's selection when he or she is finished with making selections.

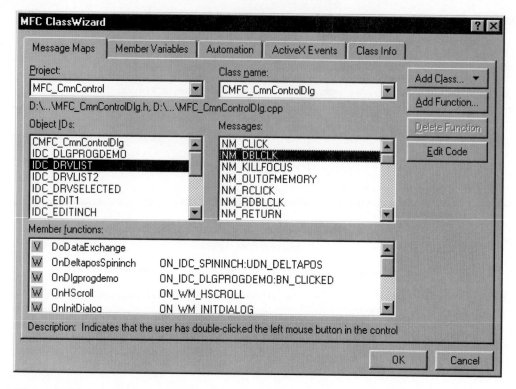

Figure 6–11 ClassWizard Message Maps for list view controls.

click OK to accept the suggested function name (see Figure 6–11) (OnDblclk-Drvlist()).

The OnDblclkDrvlist() function will look like the Code 6–82. Change the Code 6–82 so that it looks like Code 6–83.

Code 6–82

```
void CMFC_CmnControlDlg::OnDblclkDrvlist(NMHDR* pNMHDR,
     LRESULT* pResult)
{
     // TODO: Add your control notification handler code here

     *pResult = 0;
}
```

Code 6-83

```
void CMFC_CmnControlDlg::OnDblclkDrvlist(NMHDR* pNMHDR,
     LRESULT* pResult)
{
     // TODO: Add your control notification handler code here

     CString Text;
     int i= m_DrvList.GetNextItem( -1, LVNI_SELECTED );
     if( i >=0 )
     {
          Text = m_DrvList.GetItemText( i, 0 );
          MessageBox( Text, "You selected" );
     }

     *pResult = 0;
}
```

Code 6–83 (in bold) calls the CListCtrl::GetNextItem() function to determine the currently selected item in the List View control. If it's –1, then nothing is selected, otherwise we enter the body of the if test. Inside the if test, the CListCtrl::GetItemText() function is used to retrieve the first column (subitem) of the list view control, at the specified row ("i"). The text is then displayed in a message box.

In order to handle the changing of the user selections by keyboard or mouse, but not a double-click, we add a handler for the LVN_ITEMCHANGED function, which is sent after the item has changed on screen. As you did in the previous example, add a message map to the main Dialog or View class for the desired list control, and this time make sure that the Messages list has the LVN_ITEMCHANGED selection highlighted.

Add the message map (function) by clicking the Add Function button, and selecting OK at the function name prompt. Modify the new function it creates as shown in Code 6–84.

Code 6-84

```
void CMFC_CmnControlDlg::OnItemchangedDrvlist(NMHDR* pNMHDR,
     LRESULT* pResult)
{
     NM_LISTVIEW* pNMListView = (NM_LISTVIEW*)pNMHDR;

     CString Text;
     int i= m_DrvList.GetNextItem( -1, LVNI_SELECTED );
     if( i >=0 )
     {
          Text = m_DrvList.GetItemText( i, 0 );
          SetDlgItemText( IDC_DRVSELECTED, Text );
```

```
    }

        *pResult = 0;
}
```

The code in bold (see Code 6–84) retrieves the current selected item from the list view, and then call the CListCtrl::GetItemText() function to retrieve the text in the user's selection. It then places that text into the STATIC control with the ID of IDC_DRVSELECTED.

Getting and Setting Individual "Cells" in a List View

SDK

When a list view control is in Report style (as set in the dialog editor, the properties of the list view), it can appear to have columns. In list view controls that have Report style, each column is referred to as a subitem, and these subitems are numbered starting at zero as the first column on the left. When a row already exists in the list control, it is possible to get or set the text of the row and subitem using the ListView_GetItemText() and ListView_SetItemText() functions. Code 6–85 contains the prototype of the ListView_GetText() function.

NOTE

Like many other controls, you don't have to provide immediate feedback when the user makes a selection, except in the case of a double-click (if you to decide to implement the double-click). Instead, you can just get the user's selection when he or she is finished making selections.

Code 6–85

```
void ListView_GetItemText( HWND hWnd, int iItem, int iSubItem, LPTSTR
        pszText, int nMax );
```

In Code 6–85 the hWnd parameter identifies the window handle to the list view. iItem is the item or row to retrieve data from. iSubItem is the column or subitem of text to retrieve (zero if the control is not in Report style). pszText is a pointer to where to store the string, and nMax is the maximum number of character to retrieve. This is illustrated in Code 6–86.

Code 6–86

```
char Text[128];
HWND hList;
// Find the List View control
```

```
hList = GetDlgItem( hwndDlg, IDC_DRIVELIST );
// Find it's selected item
int Index = ListView_GetNextItem( hList, -1, LVNI_SELECTED );
// If an item was selected get text from tirst column (main item)
if( Index >=0 )
        ListView_GetItemText( hList, Index, 0, Text, sizeof(Text) );
```

To set the text of a particular cell in a list view control (remember: Only report-style list view controls have cells, the other styles have a single text item, which would be considered column zero), we will call the ListView_SetItemText() function as shown in Code 6–87.

Code 6–87

```
VOID WINAPI ListView_SetItemText( HWND hWnd, int iIndex, int iSubItem, LPC-
STR pszText );
```

In Code 6–87 hWnd is the window handle to the list view control where the text is to be changed. iItem is the row or item we wanted to change. iSubItem is the column of text we wanted to change (zero for the first row), and lpszText is the string we wanted to put into the cell. Code 6–88 illustrates how to change the text of an item (after the item was inserted).

Code 6–88

```
ListView_SetItemText( GetDlgItem( hwndDlg, IDC_FACELIST), 0, 0,
        "First");
```

Code 6–88 sets the string "First" into the first item (row or cell) of a list view control. This assumes that hendDlg was the window handle to the parent window of the List View control and that the List View controls ID was IDC_FACELIST.

MFC

We will be using the CListCtrl::SetItemText() and CListCtrl::GetItemText() functions to set and get the text items of a list view control with an MFC program. In the various appearances of the list view control (defined by its Style property), text in it can appear as a single row or a grid or set of columns. When in Report format, its appearance looks columnar, and each column is referred to as a subitem. When not in Report format, the single item of text is still referred to as subitem zero. CListCtrl::GetItemText() is overloaded as shown in Code 6–89.

Code 6–89

```
int GetItemText( int iItem, int iSubItem, LPTSTR lpszText, int iLen ) const;
CString GetItemText( int iItem, int iSubItem ) const;
```

In Code 6–89 item is the row or item to retrieve, and iSubItem is the column to retrieve from. In the first version, lpszText is a pointer to a character array to store the retrieved string and iLen is the size of that array (indicates maximum number of characters to retrieve). In the second version, GetItemText() will simply return the string as a CString value. Code 6–90 contains an example of how to use these functions.

Code 6–90

```
CString Text;
int Index= m_DrvList.GetNextItem( -1, LVNI_SELECTED );
if( Index >=0 )
{
        Text = m_DrvList.GetItemText( Index, 0 );
        MessageBox( Text );
}
```

Code 6–90 assumes that m_DrvList is a member variable of Control category that was mapped to the on-screen List View control with the Member Variable tab of ClassWizard. To set the text of a particular item or subitem the CListCtrl::SetItemText() function is called, whose prototype is shown in Code 6–91.

Code 6–91

```
BOOL SetItemText( int iItem, int iSubItem, LPTSTR lpszText );
```

In Code 6–91 the iItem and iSubItem also represent the row and cell to store the text at. lpszText represents the string to put there. Since the CString class provides a conversion operator (aspect of C++, not MFC) to use it where a const char * is needed, we can use either a CString or a normal C-style string for the last parameter. This is illustrated in Codes 6–92 and 6–93.

Code 6-92

```
m_DrvList.SetItemText( 0, 0, "First" );
```

Code 6-93

```
CString Text = "First";
m_DrvList.SetItemText(0, 0, Text );
```

Determining the User's Selection

SDK

To determine what item is currently selected, we can use the ListView_GetNextItem() function. This function actually searches the list view control for items that match a certain flag status, such as "Selected." We can cause the search to start anywhere within the List View, go either up or down during the search, and specify several types of flags to search for. The function prototype is shown in Code 6-94.

Code 6-94

```
int ListView_GetNextItem( HWND hWnd, int iStart, UINT iFlags );
```

In Code 6-94, hWnd is the List View control to search. iStart is the index of the item *before* where the search begins. If you want to start at the first (zero) item, then make this parameter –1. iFlags is a combination of at least one item each from Tables 6.9 and 6.10.

If the item is not found, the function returns –1, otherwise it returns the row or index into the list view control where it was found. A typical example of this function is illustrated in Code 6-95, which determines the selected item in the list.

Code 6-95 assumes that hwndDlg is the window handle to the parent window of the List View control window, and that the List View controls ID was IDC_DRVLIST.

Code 6-95

```
int Index = ListView_GetNextItem( GetDlgItem(hwndDlg, IDC_DRVLIST),
        -1, LVNI_SELECTED);
if( Index == -1 )
{
        // Nothing selected
}
else
{
        // Index now contains index of selected item
}
```

Table 6.9 Where to Start the Search

Flag Option	Meaning
LVNI_ABOVE	Searches for an item that is above the specified item (iStart).
LVNI_BELOW	Searches for an item that is below the specified item (iStart).
LVNI_TOLEFT	Searches for an item to the left of the specified item (iStart).
LVNI_TORIGHT	Searches for an item to the right of the specified item (iStart).

MFC

To determine what item is currently selected, we can use the CListCtrl::GetNext-Item() function (see Code 6–96). This function actually searches the list view control for items that match a certain flag status, such as Selected. We can cause the search to start anywhere within the list view, go either up or down during the search, and specify several types of flags to search.

Code 6–96

```
int GetNextItem( int iStart, int iFlags ) const;
```

In Code 6–96 the iStart parameters and the iFlags are the same as described in the previous SDK section. See the tables there for possible values and usage. Code 6–97 illustrates how this function is used. Code 6–97 assumes that m_DrvList is a CListCtrl member variable for the List View control, added with the Member Variable tab of ClassWizard.

Code 6–97

```
CString Text;
int i= m_DrvList.GetNextItem( -1, LVNI_SELECTED );
if( i >=0 ) // A Selected item was found
{
      Text = m_DrvList.GetItemText( i, 0 );
      // Do more procesing
}
```

Table 6.10 What to Search For

Flag Option	Meaning
LVNI_CUT	Next item with the LVIS_CUT state flag set.
LVNI_DROPHILITED	Next item with the LVIS_DROPHILITED state flag set.
LVNI_FOCUSED	Next item with the LVIS_FOCUSED state flag set.
LVNI_SELECTED	Next item with the LVIS_SELECTED state flag set (selected item)

Setting Full Row and Grid Styles

SDK and MFC

The row select and grid lines properties are extended properties of the list view control that are not accessible in the dialog editor when you change the properties of a list view control. Instead, you must set or clear them at runtime, programmatically.

MFC provides no direct functions for implementing these new styles, so the topic discussed here applies to both SDK and MFC programs. Code 6–98 sets both these options.

Code 6–98

```
// SDK version:
hChild = GetDlgItem( hwndDlg, IDC_FACELIST );
ListView_SetExtendedListViewStyle(, hChild,
      LVS_EX_FULLROWSELECT | LVS_EX_GRIDLINES );

// MFC version:
CListCtrl* pList = (CListCtrl*)GetDlgItem( IDC_FACELIST );
ListView_SetExtendedListViewStyle( pList->m_hWnd,
      LVS_EX_FULLROWSELECT|LVS_EX_GRIDLINES );
```

The ListView_SetExtendedListViewStyle() function is used to set extended window styles for a list view control. The first parameter is the list view child window to set the style for and the second parameter is a group of styles to apply.

A number of extended list view styles are useful, including checkboxes for items. To see a detailed list of these items and the versions of the Common Control Version in which they appeared, refer to the online documentation for "Extended List View Styles."

Storing Extra Item Data

SDK

In order to store or retrieve an extra 32-bit value with each item or row in list view control, we need to invoke the ListView_SetItem() function. This function requires an LVITEM structure to be properly initialized, so we will create helper functions to simplify getting and setting the 32-bit data value as shown in Code 6–99.

Notice that the 32-bit value is not used by Windows. It is intended to be used for whatever purpose you can imagine. See *Storing Additional Information with a Window* in Chapter 5 for more details.

Code 6-99

```
        TRUE if successful, FALSE if not

                    Row or Item to set the idem data for

            Handle of the List View to            32 bit value to store
            set item data for

    BOOL PNListViewSetItemData( HWND hWnd, int Index, int Data )
    {
        LVITEM lvi;
        lvi.mask = LVIF_PARAM;
        lvi.iItem = Index;
        lvi.lParam = Data;
        return ListView_SetItem( hWnd, &lvi );
    }


    int PNListViewGetItemData( HWND hWnd, int Index )
    {
        LVITEM lvi;
        lvi.mask = LVIF_PARAM;
        lvi.iItem = Index;
        ListView_GetItem( hWnd, &lvi );
        return( (int)lvi.lParam );
    }


            Handle of the List View to get item data for

The item data value          Row or Item to get the item data for
```

MFC

The CListCtrl class provides function GetItemData() and SetItemData() to simplify our task of setting and getting 32-bit extra data items for each item or row in a list. The functions are prototyped in Code 6–100.

Code 6-100

```
DWORD GetItemData( int iItem ) const;
BOOL SetItemData( int iItem, DWORD dwData );
```

In these functions, iItem refers to an item in the list view control. dwData is a 32-bit data value we want to set into the item. The GetItemData() function will retrieve the value for us. An example using these functions is shown in Codes 6–101 and 6–102.

Code 6–102 assumes that we have a data CListCtrl data member named m_DrvList that is associated with the on-screen List View control. This member would have been added via ClassWizards Member Variable tab.

Code 6–101

```
m_DrvList.SetItemData( 0, 'A' );
m_DrvList.SetItemData(1, 'C' );
m_DrvList.SetItemData(2, 'D');
```

Code 6–102

```
int Selected = m_DrvList.GetNextItem( -1, LVNI_SELECTED );
char Drive = m_DrvList.GetItemData( Selected );
// Drive now contains the drive letter selected by the user
```

Determining the Count of Items

SDK and MFC

To determine the count of items for a List View control in SDK, call the ListView_GetItemCount() function as shown in Code 6–103. To determine the count of items for a List View control in MFC, use the CListCtrl::GetItemCount() function illustrated in Code 6–104.

Code 6–103

```
int Count;
Count = ListView_GetItemCount( GetDlgItem( hwndDlg, IDC_DRVLIST ) );
```

Code 6–104

```
int Count = m_DrvList.GetItemCount();
```

TreeView Controls

TreeView controls (Figure 6–12) permit you to display information in a hierarchical structure. Perhaps the best-known example of a tree control is the left window of Explorer that lists drives and paths on a computer system. While the TreeView does not have automatic support for displaying drive letters and paths, we will demonstrate the code needed to do so.

The TreeView control is organized as a set of nodes or items. Items may appear at the root (top) of the control or may be children of other items. Items in the TreeView may have an image, checkbox, text, and/or state image associated with them. The user has the ability to collapse or expand an item, hiding or showing the children items of that item. Depending on the style, the user may double-click a node to

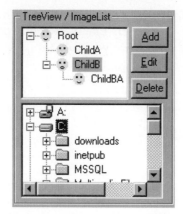

Figure 6-12 TreeView Controls

collapse or expand it, or may click a button to the left of the item (if the TVS_HAS-
BUTTONS style is on for the control). Table 6.11 provides a list of TreeView styles.

Both examples of the TreeView control in Figure 6-12 use image lists. The example
on top uses a custom image list, and the one below uses the system image list. The
custom image list was created by drawing a bitmap with all the images in it. The
system image list is the image list used by Windows itself to display images for drives, folders, and files, in programs like Explorer.

While the TreeView is represented with an HWND data type as with all other controls, it also makes consistent use of another data type, an HTREEITEM. An
HTREEITEM is a value that represents a node within the TreeView control. When a
new item is added to a TreeView, an HTREEITEM is normally the result. Functions
that allow you to search the TreeView, or return a child node in a Tree View will
also return an HTREEITEM. When you add a node, you will also need to specify the
node position to insert it at, and you will need to pass an HTREEITEM to the add
function to do this.

TreeViews also support in-place editing. This means that if the user selects an item
and then clicks again on it, an edit box will appear for the user to edit the item text.
You must handle the TVN_ENDLABELEDIT notification message to implement this
feature.

Adding Items to a TreeView

SDK

The TreeView_InsertItem() function is used to add a node to a TreeView control.
Since the function requires a TVINSERTSTRUCT structure and the initialization of
that structure, we will provide a helper function for adding items to the control as
shown in Code 6-105.

Table 6.11   Styles for the TreeView

Style	Meaning
TVS_HASELINES	Indicates that lines should be drawn to connect various nodes.
TVS_LINESATROOT	Indicates that lines for the root level should also be displayed.
TVS_HASBUTTONS	Indicates the control has a small "–" or "+" button to the left of the item text, that the user can click to collapse or expand an item. This style must be combined with the two styles above to work.
TVS_EDITLABELS	Indicates that the user can edit the text label for an item. Most of the work for editing the label is performed by the control, except for the actual changing of the text.
TVS_SHOWSELALWAYS	Indicates that even when the control does not have the focus, the user's current selection should be indicated.
TVS_CHECKBOXES	Indicates that the control has checkboxes to the left of the item. Note that this style cannot be added or removed after the window is created. To alter this style, you would need to destroy and then re-create the window with or without the style. This style requires either IE5 or Win98 or Win2000 to be installed.

Code 6–105

```
HTREEITEM PNTreeViewInsertItem( HWND hWnd, LPTSTR Text,
    HTREEITEM hParent=TVI_ROOT, HTREEITEM hInsertAt = TVI_SORT,
    int iImageIndex=-1, int iSelectedImageIndex=-1 );

// PNTreeViewInsertItem - Inserts new item into a tree control
// Parameters:
//      hWnd - Window handle for Tree View to insert into
//      Text - Text for new insertion
//      hParent - HTREEITEM for insertion point, or zero for root
//      hInsertAt - Determines insertion position: TVI_LAST,
//                   TVI_FIRST, or TVI_SORT
//      iImageIndex - Index into image list for item, if image
//                    list is available. -1 means no image.
//      iSelectedImageIndex - Index into image list for item
//                    when selected, if image list is
//                    available. -1 means no image.
// Returns: TRUE if succesful, false if not
HTREEITEM PNTreeViewInsertItem( HWND hWnd, LPTSTR Text,
    HTREEITEM hParent, HTREEITEM hInsertAt, int iImageIndex,
    int iSelectedImageIndex )
{
    TVINSERTSTRUCT tvInsertStruct;

    // Initialize tvInsertStruct
```

```
   tvInsertStruct.hParent = hParent;
   tvInsertStruct.hInsertAfter = hInsertAt;
   tvInsertStruct.item.mask = TVIF_TEXT;
   if( iImageIndex!=-1 )
   {
      // If image was specified, then use it
      tvInsertStruct.item.iImage = iImageIndex;
      tvInsertStruct.item.mask |= TVIF_IMAGE;
   }
   if( iSelectedImageIndex !=-1 )
   {
      // If selected image was specified, then use it
      tvInsertStruct.item.mask |= TVIF_SELECTEDIMAGE;
      tvInsertStruct.item.iSelectedImage = iSelectedImageIndex;
   }

   tvInsertStruct.item.pszText = Text;
   // Perform the actual insert
   HTREEITEM Ret = TreeView_InsertItem( hWnd, &tvInsertStruct );
   // Refresh window, looks nicer
   InvalidateRect(hWnd, NULL,FALSE);
   return(Ret);
}
```

The hWnd parameter identifies the TreeView control where the item should be added. The Text parameter indicates the text for the new node. hParent indicates where the new node should be inserted. If hParent is the HTREEITEM of another node, then the new node is created as a child of that node; if it is 0, then the new node is created as a child of the root.

The hInsertAt is a means of specifying where the insertion should take place within the children of the hParent node. If hInsertAt is TVI_LAST, then it is added as the last node; if it is TVI_FIRST, it is added as the first node; and if TVI_SORT is used, then the new node is added to the tree in sorted order.

The iImageIndex and iSelectedImageIndex items are the indices to what images are to be used for the normal and selected image. iImageIndex will be the displayed image normally, and iSelectedImageIndex will be the displayed image when the item is the currently selected node. If the TreeView does not have an image list associated with it, these values are ignored. If you specify –1 for these values, they are not set by PNTreeViewInsertItem().

PNTreeViewInsertItem() returns the HTREEITEM for the newly inserted node. This can be helpful when you are placing child nodes into a newly added parent node. This is illustrated in Code 6–106.

Code 6–106

```
HTREEITEM hItemCountry, hItemState;
HCWND hChild = GetDlgItem(hwndDlg, IDC_STATETREE);
// Insert top node for country
hItemCountry = PNTreeViewInsertItem( hChild, "USA" );
// Insert 1 state
hItemState = PNTreeViewInsertItem( hChild, "NY", hItemCountry );
// Insert a city for that state
PNTreeViewInsertItem( hChild, "New York", hItemState );
// Insert another state
hItemState = PNTreeViewInsertItem( hChild, "CA", hItemCountry );
// Insert a city for that state
PNTreeViewInsertItem( hChild, "Los Angeles", hItemState );
```

MFC

Inserting items into the TreeView control in MFC is done with the help of the CTreeCtrl::InsertItem() function (see Table 6.12). The function has several overloaded versions, as listed in Code 6–107.

Code 6–107

```
HTREEITEM InsertItem( LPTVINSERTSTRUCT lpInsertStruct );
HTREEITEM InsertItem(UINT nMask, LPCTSTR lpszItem, int nImage, int
nSelectedImage,
        UINT nState, UINT nStateMask, LPARAM lParam, HTREEITEM hParent,
        HTREEITEM hInsertAfter );
HTREEITEM InsertItem( LPCTSTR lpszItem, HTREEITEM hParent = TVI_ROOT,
HTREEITEM hInsertAfter = TVI_LAST );
HTREEITEM InsertItem( LPCTSTR lpszItem, int nImage, int nSelectedImage,
HTREEITEM hParent = TVI_ROOT, HTREEITEM hInsertAfter = TVI_LAST);
```

The return value for these functions is the HTREEITEM to the newly added item, so that you can easily create the hierarchy of tree by adding child nodes to newly added nodes. This is illustrated in Code 6–108.

Code 6–108

```
HTREEITEM hItemCountry, hItemState;
CTreeCtrl* pTree = (CTreeCtrl*)GetDlgItem( IDC_STATETREE );
// Insert top node for country
hItemCounty = pTree->InsertItem( "USA" );
// Insert 1 state
hItemState = pTree->InsertItem ( "NY", hItemCountry );
// Insert a city for that state
pTree->InsertItem ( "New York", hItemState );
// Insert another state
hItemState = pTree->InsertItem ( "CA", hItemCountry );
// Insert a city for that state
pTree->InsertItem ( hChild, "Los Angeles", hItemState );
```

Table 6.12   Parameters for the InsertItem() Function

Parameter	Meaning
lpInsertStruct	A pointer to an initialized TVINSERTSTRUCT structure, with item to be inserted.
nMask	A bit mask value that indicates the items that are valid values:
	TVIF_IMAGE - The nImage parameter is valid.
	TVIF_PARAM - The lParam parameter is valid.
	TVIF_SELECTEDIMAGE - The nSelectedImage parameter is valid.
	TVIF_STATE - The nstate and nstateMask parameters are valid.
	TVIF_TEXT - The lpszText parameter is valid.
lpszItem	Is the text for the new item.
nImage	Is the normal image for the new item, if an image list is associated with the control.
nSelectedImage	Is the selected image for the new item, if an image list is associated with the control.
nState	Indicates the state to be used for the new item (i.e., if checkboxes are enabled).
nStateMask	Indicates the mask to be used for determining the checkbox or status state.
lParam	An extra 32-bit value that will be associated with the item.
hParent	The HTREEITEM for the parent node to add this new item as a child to.
hInsertAfter	One of the following: TVI_FIRST, TVI_LAST, or TVI_SORT that controls where in the list of child nodes this new item should be added.

Code 6–108 assumes that you have a TreeView control with the ID of IDC_STATE-TREE that you will be adding items too. We also could have mapped a member variable to the TreeView control and used that member variable, instead of using the GetDlgItem() function to retrieve a pointer to it. The code above would most likely be in the Dialog or View class that represents the parent window of the Tree-View control.

Removing Items from a TreeView

SDK

To remove a single item from a TreeView, use the TreeView_DeleteItem() function shown in Code 6–109.

Code 6–109

```
BOOL TreeView_DeleteItem( HWND hWnd, HTREEITEM hItem );
```

In Code 6-109, hWnd represents the child window to remove the item from, and hItem represents the item to be removed. If the item has any child items, they are also removed. To delete all the items from a TreeView, call the TreeView_DeleteAllItems() function (see Code 6–110). Here, hWnd again represents the window handle to the child TreeView control. All nodes in the tree will be removed.

Code 6–110

```
BOOL TreeView_DeleteAllItems( HWND hWnd );
```

MFC

To remove a single item from a TreeView control, use the the CTreeCtrl::DeleteItem() function as shown in Code 6–111. Here, hItem is the item to delete from the TreeView control. Any children of the item are also deleted. You can remove all items in a TreeView by calling the CTreeCtrl::DeleteAllItems() function illustrated in Code 6–111. Code 6–112 demonstrates how to call both functions.

Code 6–111

```
BOOL CTreeCtrl::DeleteItem( HTREEITEM hItem );
BOOL CTreeCtrl::DeleteAllItems( );
```

Code 6–112

```
CTreeCtrl* pTree = (CTreeCtrl*) DetDlgItem( IDC_GENTREE );
// To remove single item (the selected item):
HTREEITEM hItem = pTree->GetSelectedItem();
pTree->DeleteItem( hItem );

// To remove them all:
pTree->DeleteAllItems();
```

Determining the Currently Selected Item

SDK

In order to determine the currently selected item for a TreeView control, call the TreeView_GetSelection() function (see Code 6–113). This function will return the currently selected item in the TreeView control specified by the window handle hWnd. It returns the HTREEITEM for the node, or NULL if no node is selected.

Code 6–113

```
HTREEITEM TreeView_GetSelection( HWND hWnd );
```

MFC

To determine the currently selected item in a TreeView control, call the CTreeCtrl::GetSelectedItem() function (see Code 6–114). This function returns the

---

HTREEITEM value for the selected item, or 0 if there is no currently selected item in the TreeView control. This is illustrated in Code 6–115.

Code 6–114

```
HTREEITEM CTreeCtrl::GetSelectedItem();
```

Code 6–115

```
CTreeCtrl* pTree = (CTreeCtrl*) DetDlgItem( IDC_GENTREE );
// To remove single item (the selected item):
HTREEITEM hItem = pTree->GetSelectedItem();
pTree->SetItemText( hItem, "New text" );
```

Associating a Custom Image List with a TreeView

SDK

As with the List View control, associating an image list with a TreeView control for displaying images is fairly straightforward. When an item is inserted into a Tree-View control, it will show one of two images if it has an image list: a normal image and a selected image.

The selected image is displayed if the user has selected that node. When the item was inserted, the normal and selected parameters were the index to the respective images in the image list associated with the control. The TreeView_SetImageList() function is used to associate an image list with a TreeView.

The Code 6–116 demonstrates how to load an image list and associated it with a TreeView control. Code 6–116 assumes that IDB_FACEIMGLIST is the ID for a bitmap that can be loaded as an image list (composed of several same-sized images across the bitmap).

The ID for the tree want to set the image list for is IDC_GENTREE. The TVSIL_NOR-MAL parameter indicates we are setting the normal image list, not the state image list (which would be TVSIL_STATE). The prototype for TreeView_SetImageList is shown in Code 6–117. Here, hWnd is the window handle to the TreeView control, hImgList is the handle to the image list, and iType is either TVSIL_NORMAL for normal images or TVSIL_STATE for state image lists.

Code 6–116

```
HWND hChild;
HIMAGELIST hImageList = ImageList_LoadImage( GetModuleHandle(NULL),
      MAKEINTRESOURCE( IDB_FACEIMGLIST ), 16, 1, RGB(255,255,255),
      IMAGE_BITMAP, LR_DEFAULTCOLOR );
hChild = GetDlgItem( hwndDlg, IDC_GENTREE );
TreeView_SetImageList( hChild, hImageList, TVSIL_NORMAL );
```

Code 6–117

```
HIMAGELIST TreeView_SetImageList( HWND hWnd, HIMAGELIST hImgList, int iType );
```

MFC

In order to associate a custom image list with a TreeView control, we will need to create a CImageList object to retain the images and then associate it with the TreeView control. Since the CImageList object must be persistent, we will make it a data member of the Dialog or View class that serves as the parent for the TreeView control. This might be the Dialog class in a dialog-based application, or a CView class in a Document/View application.

To add a CImageList object, add the Code 6–118 to the parent window class's header file (CMFC_CmnControlDlg.h in our demo program).

Code 6–118

```
CImageList m_SmileyImages;
```

Next, we need to initialize the CImageList with a bitmap that was created using the Visual C++ bitmap editor. A good place to do this is in the OnInitDialog() function for dialog-based applications, or in the OnInitialUpdate() function for view-based applications. The code would look something like Code 6–119.

Code 6–119

```
m_SmileyImages.Create( IDB_FACEIMGLIST, 16, 1,
     RGB(255,255,255) );
```

Code 6–119 assumes that IDB_FACEIMGLIST is the ID for a bitmap that contains several small images laid out horizontally. See the *Image Lists* section of this chapter for more details. Finally, we need to associate the image list with the TreeView control, by calling the CTreeCtrl::SetImageList() function as shown in Code 6–120.

Here, a CTreeCtrl pointer is created for the IDC_GENTREE TreeView control, and then the CTreeCtrl::SetImageList() function is called on the next line. The parameters passed to SetImageList are the address of a CImageList and either TVSIL_NORMAL or TVSIL_STATE if setting either the normal or state image list.

Code 6–120

```
        CTreeCtrl* pTree = (CTreeCtrl*)GetDlgItem( IDC_GENTREE );
        pTree->SetImageList( &m_SmileyImages, TVSIL_NORMAL );
```

Associating the System Image List with a TreeView (Drive and Folder Browsing)

SDK

The system image list is the image list that Windows itself uses for drives, folders, and files in programs like Explorer. If you wanted to create a control similar to the left window of Explorer that lists the drives and folders, you need to associate the system Image List with your TreeView control. You also need to be able to populate a tree item (node) with a list of folders.

In order to do this, we will be adding several helper functions: PNTreeViewExpand-Path(), PNTreeViewGetDrivePath(), and PNTreeViewInitDrives(), as shown in Code 6–121.

Code 6–121

```c
// PNTreeViewInitDrives - Populates a TreeView control with a list of
//        Drive letters and icons
// Parameters:
//        hWnd - Window handle for Tree control to initialize
// Returns: Number of rows (drives) added to list
// Note: Call this function to setup a drive list, but also call the
//        PNTreeViewExpandPath function when a folder in the Tree
//        View control is expanded (TVN_EXPANDING)
int PNTreeViewInitDrives( HWND hWnd )
{
   HIMAGELIST hImageList;
   HTREEITEM hTreeItem;
   BOOL LargeSize=FALSE;

   // Use Windows own image list for drive and file icons
   hImageList = PNGetSysImageList( FALSE );
   TreeView_SetImageList( hWnd, hImageList, TVSIL_NORMAL );

   // Setup TreeView appearance
   TreeView_DeleteAllItems( hWnd );

   // Determine valid drive letters
   char Drives[128], *pRoot;
   char Descr[128];
   int iIcon, iIconSel;
   int Row=0;

   GetLogicalDriveStrings( sizeof(Drives), Drives );

   // Iterate through drive letters, determine icons, and add
   // to TreeView control
   for( pRoot=Drives; *pRoot; pRoot++ )
```

```
    {
          sprintf( Descr, "%c:", *pRoot );

          // Determine system image for drive
          PNGetPathIcons( pRoot, iIcon, iIconSel, LargeSize, FALSE );
          hTreeItem = PNTreeViewInsertItem( hWnd, Descr, TVI_ROOT,
               TVI_SORT, iIcon, iIconSel );
          // Add an empty child item, to place a "+" next to drive
          PNTreeViewInsertItem( hWnd, "", hTreeItem );
          while( *pRoot )
               pRoot++;
    }
    return( Row );
}
```

The PNTreeViewInitDrives() function takes only the handle to the child window you want to initialize. It will store into the TreeView control a list of drive letters and will also place the same icons used by Explorer next to the drives.

In Code 6–121, the PNGetSysImageList() helper function is called to get the system image list, and then TreeView_SetImageList() is called to associate that image list with that TreeView control. Next, TreeView_DeleteAllItems() is called to make sure that the TreeView control is empty.

The GetLogicalDriveStrings() function is called to get a list of drive letters into a string, and a loop is entered to iterate through all the drive letters in the string. Inside that loop, the PNGetPathIcons() helper function is called to retrieve the normal and selected icons for the drive.

Finally, PNTreeViewInsertItem() is called to add the drive and its images to the root of the TreeView control, and then an empty subnode is added to the drive node. This is done so that the drive letter has at least one sub child, so that it can be expanded.

The PNTreeViewInitDrives() function would be called in the WM_INITDIALOG function to initialize the TreeView control you wanted to contain the drive and folder information. This is illustrated in Code 6–122.

Code 6–122

```
LRESULT CALLBACK DialogProc( HWND hwndDlg, UINT uMsg, WPARAM wParam, LPARAM
lParam )
{
    int wID;
    int wNotification;
    HWND hChild;

    switch( uMsg )
```

```
{
    case WM_INITDIALOG:
        // InitCommonControls should be called when you are
        // going to use the common controls
        InitCommonControls();
        hChild = GetDlgItem( hwndDlg, IDC_DRVTREE );
        PNTreeViewInitDrives( hChild );
        break;
    // Portions of code removed for readability
```

Part of the strategy for implementing this drive and folder browsing is to avoid the lengthy process of scanning the entire directory structure of the drive(s). So we will only scan one folder level at a time. Whenever the user expands a node, then and only then will we go out and get a list of folders in that node and then add them as children. This means that we need to respond to the TreeView control's TVN_ITEM-EXPANDING notification message. In order to assist in the expansion handling, we provide the helper function shown in Code 6–123.

Code 6–123

```
// PNTreeViewExpandPath - Used with Drive Path TreeViews,
//       to populate a tree node with a list of folders within a path.
// Parameters:
//       hWnd - Window handle for Tree control with drive
//               path information
//       lParam - lParam parameter for LVN_ITEMEXPANDING message
//               (an NMTREEVIEW pointer)
// Returns: TRUE if folders add, FALSE if not
// Note: This function is used to expand folders for a tree
//       control that has had drive letters added to it by
//       calling the PNTreeViewInitDrives function
BOOL PNTreeViewExpandPath( HWND hWnd, LPARAM lParam )
{
    char Path[MAX_PATH]="";
    int Icon, IconSel;
    HTREEITEM hTreeItem;
    NMTREEVIEW* pNMTreeView = (NMTREEVIEW*) lParam;
    BOOL Ret=FALSE;

    if( pNMTreeView->action == TVE_EXPAND )
    {
        // Remove current listing
        while( (hTreeItem=TreeView_GetChild( hWnd,
            pNMTreeView->itemNew.hItem ) ) != 0 )
            TreeView_DeleteItem( hWnd, hTreeItem );

        // Get Path string for the node
        PNTreeViewGetDrivePath( hWnd, Path, pNMTreeView->itemNew.hItem );
```

```
        // List Folders in the Path
        strcat( Path, "*.*" );
        WIN32_FIND_DATA FindFileData;
        HANDLE hFind;
        hFind = FindFirstFile( Path, &FindFileData);
        if (hFind != INVALID_HANDLE_VALUE)
        {
            do {
                if( FindFileData.dwFileAttributes &
                FILE_ATTRIBUTE_DIRECTORY &&
                FindFileData.cFileName[0]!='.' &&
                !(FindFileData.dwFileAttributes & FILE_ATTRIBUTE_HIDDEN)
                )
                {
                    PNGetPathIcons( Path, Icon, IconSel, FALSE, TRUE );
                    hTreeItem = PNTreeViewInsertItem( hWnd,
                        FindFileData.cFileName, pNMTreeView->itemNew.hItem,
                        TVI_SORT, Icon, IconSel );
                    PNTreeViewInsertItem( hWnd, "", hTreeItem );
                    Ret = TRUE;
                }
            }while( FindNextFile( hFind, &FindFileData ) );
        }
    FindClose(hFind);
    }

    return( Ret );
}
```

The function above should be used in response to the TreeView control's sending the TVN_ITEMEXPANDING notification to the parent window. It uses the FindFirstFile() and FindNextFile() functions to retrieve a list of file names in a loop and determine which ones are child folders. It also uses the PNGetPathIcons() functions described in the Image List section of this chapter to determine the icons for the folders. The handling of the TVN_ITEMEXPANDING notification would be handled in the dialog procedure for the parent dialog of the TreeView. Code 6–124 is an example.

Code 6–124

```
LRESULT CALLBACK DialogProc( HWND hwndDlg, UINT uMsg, WPARAM wParam,
    LPARAM lParam )
{
    int wID;
    int wNotification;
    HWND hChild;

    switch( uMsg )
    {
        case WM_NOTIFY:
            // Parse out data from a WM_NOTIFY message
```

```
        wID = (int) wParam;
        wNotification = ((NMHDR*)lParam)->code;
        hChild = ((NMHDR*)lParam)->hwndFrom;

        if( wID==IDC_DRVTREE && wNotification == TVN_ITEMEXPANDING )
            PNTreeViewExpandPath( hChild, lParam );
    // Portions removed for readability
```

The PNTreeViewExpandPath() function also makes use of another helper function, PNTreeViewGetDrivePath(), which is a function that, when given a particular node in the TreeView control, will build a full path string for the folder that node represents.

Since each node in our demonstration TreeView only holds a folder name, when we want the complete pathname for the folder we need to concatenate the text from all its parent nodes. For example, the path C:\Data\July would represent a node with the text "July," which was a child node of "Data." which was in turn a child node of "C." The PNTreeViewDrivePath helper function in Code 6–125 will build the path for us, from any node. Code 6–126 illustrates how to implement full drive and folder browsing in a TreeView control, using our helper functions.

Code 6–125

```
// PNTreeViewGetDrivePath - Retrieves full path from a node in
//      a DrivePath TreeView
// Parameters:
//      hWnd - Window handle for Tree control to retrieve path from
//      Path - Where to store the path retrieved
//      hItem - Node item to retrieve path for
// Returns: Number of rows (drives) added to list
// Note: This is a recurdsive function, that builds up a string
//      from all the parent nodes.
void PNTreeViewGetDrivePath( HWND hWnd, char* Path, HTREEITEM hItem )
{
    static int Recurse=0;

    if(Recurse == 0 ) // Make sure first recursive call clears Dest
            *Path='\0';
    Recurse++;
    if( hItem )
    {
            // This is a recusive function:
            PNTreeViewGetDrivePath( hWnd, Path,
                TreeView_GetParent( hWnd, hItem ) );
            PNTreeViewGetItemText( hWnd, Path+strlen(Path),
                MAX_PATH-strlen(Path), hItem );
            if( *Path )
                strcat(Path, "\\" );
    }
    Recurse--;
}
```

Code 6-126

```
LRESULT CALLBACK DialogProc( HWND hwndDlg, UINT uMsg, WPARAM wParam,
    LPARAM lParam )
{
    int wID;
    int wNotification;
    HWND hChild;

    switch( uMsg )
    {
        case WM_INITDIALOG:
            // InitCommonControls should be called when you are
            // going to use the common controls
            InitCommonControls();
            hChild = GetDlgItem( hwndDlg, IDC_DRVTREE );
            PNTreeViewInitDrives( hChild );
            break;
        case WM_NOTIFY:
            // Parse out data from a WM_NOTIFY message
            wID = (int) wParam;
            wNotification = ((NMHDR*)lParam)->code;
            hChild = ((NMHDR*)lParam)->hwndFrom;

            if( wID==IDC_DRVTREE && wNotification == TVN_ITEMEXPANDING )
                PNTreeViewExpandPath( hChild, lParam );
        // Portions removed for readability
```

MFC

The System ImageList is the image list that Windows itself uses for drives, folders, and files in programs like Explorer. If you wanted to create a control similar to the left window of Explorer that lists the drives and folders, you need to associate the System ImageList with a TreeView control. You then need to populate a tree item (node) with a list of folders.

Because of the object-oriented nature of MFC, rather than implement various support functions as we did in the SDK example, we will create a class named CPNDirTree. This class is listed and commented in the Appendix.

Finding Items in a TreeView

SDK

There is no search function to search the items of a TreeView control for a specific item text, so we will provide one. Since the TreeView represents a tree, we will find that recursion will help us perform our search. The function is illustrated in Code 6-127. Notice its use of other PNTreeView() functions.

Code 6-127

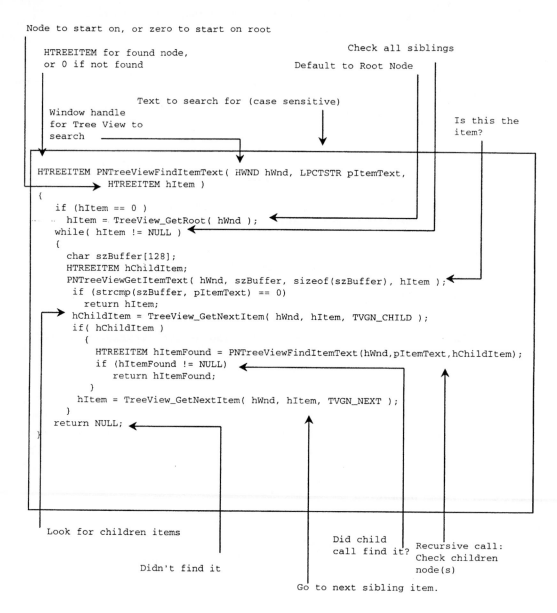

Node to start on, or zero to start on root

HTREEITEM for found node,
or 0 if not found

Check all siblings

Default to Root Node

Text to search for (case sensitive)

Window handle
for Tree View to
search

Is this the
item?

```
HTREEITEM PNTreeViewFindItemText( HWND hWnd, LPCTSTR pItemText,
              HTREEITEM hItem )
{
  if (hItem == 0 )
    hItem = TreeView_GetRoot( hWnd );
  while( hItem != NULL )
  {
    char szBuffer[128];
    HTREEITEM hChildItem;
    PNTreeViewGetItemText( hWnd, szBuffer, sizeof(szBuffer), hItem );
    if (strcmp(szBuffer, pItemText) == 0)
      return hItem;
    hChildItem = TreeView_GetNextItem( hWnd, hItem, TVGN_CHILD );
    if( hChildItem )
    {
      HTREEITEM hItemFound = PNTreeViewFindItemText(hWnd,pItemText,hChildItem);
      if (hItemFound != NULL)
        return hItemFound;
    }
    hItem = TreeView_GetNextItem( hWnd, hItem, TVGN_NEXT );
  }
  return NULL;
}
```

Look for children items

Did child
call find it?

Recursive call:
Check children
node(s)

Didn't find it

Go to next sibling item.

The PNTreeViewFindItemText() function will search through nodes and subnodes looking for the desired text. The hWnd parameter indicates the child window to search. The pItemText parameter is the string to search for, and the hItem parameter is the item to begin the search. If you pass 0 for hItem, then the search begins at the root. If the function finds the text, it will return the HTREEITEM for the node in which it was found and will return NULL if not found.

Notice that the text is limited to 128 characters for searching, which should be more than sufficient.

MFC

There is no search function to search the items of a CTreeCtrl object for a specific item text, so we will provide one. Since the TreeView represents a tree, we will find that recursion will help us perform our search. The helper function is illustrated in Code 6–128 and is called in Code 6–129.

Code 6–128

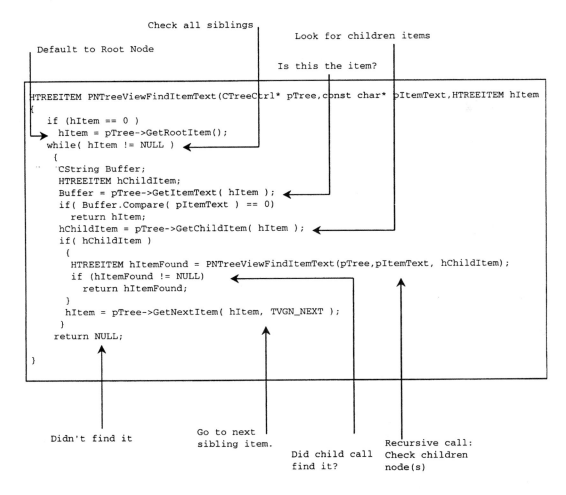

Code 6–129

```
CTreeCtrl* pTree = (CTreeTrl*)GetDlgItem( IDC_DRVTREE );
HITEM hItem = PNTreeViewFindItemText( pTree, "Joe", 0 );
if( !hItem )
      MessageBox("Node not found");
else
      // Found item
```

Getting and Setting Extra Item Data

SDK

As with the List and List View controls, the TreeView control gives you the ability to store an extra 32-bit value with each item it maintains. In the case of the TreeView control that means that each node can have this extra value.

The purpose of this value is completely up to you to determine. You may store a unique ID from a database table there or a pointer to another dynamically created data object. To simplify the getting and setting of these values, we present the following two helper functions in Code 6–130. Examples of using these functions are illustrated in Code 6–131.

Code 6–130

```
// PNTreeSetItemData - Stores an extra 32-bit value with a
//      TreeView item
// Parameters:
//      hWnd - Window handle for TreeView to store data to
//      dwData - Value to be stored
//      hNode - Node within tree to store to (0 means to
//              currently selected node)
// Returns: TRUE if succesful, false if not
BOOL PNTreeViewSetItemData( HWND hWnd, DWORD dwData, HTREEITEM hNode )
{
    if( hNode == 0 )
        hNode = TreeView_GetSelection( hWnd );
    if( hNode == 0 )
        return( FALSE );

    TVITEM tvItem;
    tvItem.hItem = hNode;
    tvItem.mask = TVIF_PARAM;
    tvItem.lParam = dwData;

    return( TreeView_SetItem( hWnd, &tvItem ) );

}

// PNTreeGetItemData - Retrieves extra 32-bit value for a node
```

```
// Parameters:
//      hWnd - Window handle for TreeView to get data from
//      hNode - Node within tree to retrieve (0 means from
//              currently selected node)
// Returns: Value retrieved from node
DWORD PNTreeViewGetItemData( HWND hWnd, HTREEITEM hNode )
{
    if( hNode == 0 )
        hNode = TreeView_GetSelection( hWnd );
    if( hNode == 0 )
        return( FALSE );

    TVITEM tvItem;
    tvItem.hItem = hNode;
    tvItem.mask = TVIF_PARAM;
    TreeView_GetItem( hWnd, &tvItem );
    return( tvItem.lParam );
}
```

Code 6-131

```
// Storing a pointer to a string:
HWND hChild = GetDlgItem( hwndDlg, IDC_NAMETREE );
HTREEITEM hItem = TreeView_GetSelection( hChild );
char* p = new char[ strlen(FullName+1);
strcpy( p, FullName );
PNTreeViewSetItemData( hChild, (DWORD)p, hItem );

// Retrieving pointer back, later on:
HWND hChild = GetDlgItem( hwndDlg, IDC_NAMETREE );
HTREEITEM hItem = TreeView_GetSelection( hChild );
char* p = (char*)PNTreeViewGetItemData(DWORD)p, hItem );
MessageBox( hwndDlg, p, "Selected Person", MB_OK );
```

MFC

In an MFC program, to get or set the extra 32-bit value item for an item or node in a TreeView control, we can use the CTreeCtrl::SetItemData() and CTreeCtrl::GetItemData() functions (see Code 6–132). The exact usage of the 32-bit value is up to you.

Code 6-132

```
BOOL CTreeCtrl::SetItemData( HTREEITEM hItem, DWORD dwData );
DWORD CTreeCtrl::GetItemData( HTREEITEM hItem ) const;
```

In the two functions shown in Code 6–132, hItem is the item in the control to set or get. dwData is the value when setting. GetItemData() returns the value from the selected item. Examples of their use are shown in Code 6–133.

Code 6–133 assumes that m_PersonTree is a member variable of "Control" category for the TreeView control that was added via ClassWizards Member Variable tab. We also could have used GetDlgItem() to retreive a pointer to a CTreeCtrl object for the desired TreeView control.

Code 6–133

```
// To set the data:
CPerson * pPerson = new CPerson( "Joe", "Shmoe" );
HTREEITEM hItem = m_PersonTree.InsertItem( "Joe" );
m_PersonTree.SetItemData( hItem, (DWORD)pPerson );

// To get the data:
HTREEITEM hItem = m_PersonTree.GetSelectedItem();
CPerson * pPerson = (CPerson*)m_PersonTree.GetItemData( hItem );
// pPerson is now valid pointer to CPerson object
```

Selecting, Expanding, and Collapsing a Node—SDK

When the user selects an item in a tree control, you can respond to the TVN_SELCHANGED notification code, sent in a WM_NOTIFY message to the parent window of the TreeView control. You would only need to do this if you wanted to supply immediate feedback to the user as the selection changes in the TreeView. If you weren't interested in immediate feedback, you could simply determine what item was selected by calling the TreeView_GetSelection() function. An example of how to handle this notification in showed in Code 6–134.

Code 6–134

Parse out data from a WM_NOTIFY message

```
LRESULT CALLBACK DialogProc(HWND hwndDlg,UINT uMsg,WPARAM wParam,LPARAM lParam  )
{
    int wID;
    int wNotification;
    HWND hChild;
    switch( uMsg )
      {
        case WM_NOTIFY:
          wID = (int) wParam;
          wNotification = ((NMHDR*)lParam)->code;
          hChild = ((NMHDR*)lParam)->hwndFrom;
          if (wID == IDC_DRVTREE && wNotification == TVN_SELCHANGED )
            {
              char Text[MAX_PATH];
              NMTREEVIEW* pNMTreeView = (NMTREEVIEW*)lParam;
              PNTreeViewGetDrivePath( hChild, Text, pNMTreeView->itemNew.hItem );
              SetDlgItemText( hwndDlg, IDC_DRVSELECTEDTREE, Text );
            }
        // Portions of code removed for readability
```

Code 6–134 uses the TVN_SELCHANGED notification on WM_NOTIFY message to indicate that the user has changed the selected node in the TreeView control. When this notification is received, the lParam parameter to the dialog procedure is in reality a pointer to an NMTREEVIEWITEM data structure. Inside this data structure is an itemOld and itemNew data member, each of type TVITEM, which represent the previous and new selected items. Within the itemNew member is an HTREEITEM data member named hItem, which identifies the new node that was selected.

In Code 6–134, we are using the PNTreeViewGetDrivePath() helper function we created to extract the full path from a drive/folder TreeView control we set up. However, you can call PNGetItemText() to simply get the text for that node.

The expanding and collapsing of a node are all indicated by the TVN_ITEMEXPANDING notification for WM_NOTIFY. If you want to respond to the user's expanding or collapsing a folder, you can add a handler for this specific notification code.

When this notification is received, the lParam of the parent dialog's window procedure is really a pointer to an NMTREEVIEW data structure. Inside that data structure is an action data member that indicates what the person is doing (see Table 6.13).

When the user selects an item in a tree control, you can respond to the TVN_SELCHANGED notification code, sent in a WM_NOTIFY message to the parent window of the TreeView control. You would only need to do this if you wanted to supply immediate feedback to the user as the selection changes in the TreeView. If you weren't interested in immediate feedback, you could simply determine what item was selected by calling the CtreeCtrl::GetSelectedItem() function.

To add a handler to be invoked when the user changes the tree selection, go into Class Wizard from the View menu choice, and make sure the Message Map tab is

Table 6.13   Data Members of the Tree

Action	Meaning
TVE_COLLAPSE	Collapses the list.
TVE_COLLAPSERESET	Collapses and removing the child items. The TVIS_EXPANDEDONCE state flag is reset.
TVE_EXPAND	Expands the list.
TVE_EXPANDPARTIAL	Partially expands the list. In this state, the child items are visible and the parent items plus symbol is displayed. Used in combination with the TVE_EXPAND flag.
TVE_TOGGLE	Collapses the list if it is expanded or expands it if it is collapsed.

highlighted. Then, make sure that the Class Name field is set to the parent window of the TreeView control, that the Object IDs item has the desired TreeView control ID highlighted, and that the Messages list has the TVN_SELCHANGED item selected (Figure 6–13).

Click the Add Function button, and then click OK to respond to the suggested name for the new function. The function will be added looking like Code 6–135.

Modify Code 6–135 to do whatever you want to do in response to the user selection as shown in Code 6–136.

Code 6–135

```
void CMFC_CmnControlDlg::OnSelchangedDrvtree(NMHDR* pNMHDR,
    LRESULT* pResult)
{
    NM_TREEVIEW* pNMTreeView = (NM_TREEVIEW*)pNMHDR;
    // TODO: Add your control notification handler code here

    *pResult = 0;
}
```

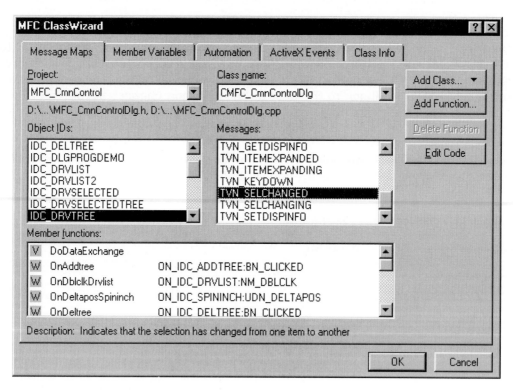

Figure 6–13 ClassWizard's Message Maps for tree controls.

Code 6-136

```
void CMFC_CmnControlDlg::OnSelchangedDrvtree(NMHDR* pNMHDR,
    LRESULT* pResult)
{
    NM_TREEVIEW* pNMTreeView = (NM_TREEVIEW*)pNMHDR;
    // TODO: Add your control notification handler code here

    HTREEITEM hItem = m_DirTree.GetSelectedItem();
    if( hItem )
        SetDlgItemText( IDC_DRVSELECTEDTREE,
            m_DirTree.GetFullPath( hItem ) );

    *pResult = 0;
}
```

Code 6–136 uses the m_DirTree object, which is a CPNDirTree class object. (Figure 6–14 shows how the variable was added with Class Wizard). This class is listed in the Appendix and has a member function called GetFullPath(), which returns the full path from the root of the tree to the selected node. The return value of that function (a CString) is passed to SetDlgItemText(), which is used to change the text of the static control with the ID of IDC_DRVSELECTEDTREE.

If you just want to determine the text of the currently selected node, you could use GetItemText(). This is illustrated in Code 6–137.

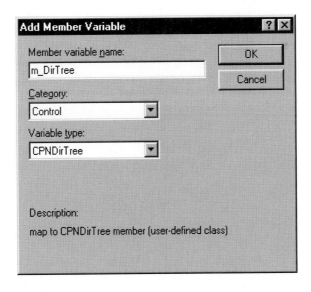

Figure 6–14 Adding m_DirTree with ClassWizard.

Code 6-137

```
HTREEITEM hItem = m_DirTree.GetSelectedItem();
MessageBox( m_DirTree.GetItemText( hItem ) );
```

The expanding and collapsing of a node are all indicated by the TVN_ITEMEX-PANDING notification for WM_NOTIFY. If you want to respond to the user's expanding or collapsing a folder, you can add a handler for this specific notification code. When this notification is received, the lParam of the parent dialog's window procedure is really a pointer to an NMTREEVIEW data structure. Inside that data structure is an action data member that indicates what the person is doing. See the SDK example for more details on the values of the action data member.

The CPNDirTree makes use of the TVN_ITEMEXPANDING notification to populate the child nodes of a drive or folder when, and only when, the user expands a node. This eliminates the need to perform a lengthy search of the drive to build the entire directory structure at once.

A detailed description of the CPNDirTree class is beyond the scope of this chapter. You can find the full source code for it in the Appendix.

Handling User-editing of Items

SDK

As in Explorer, the TreeView can permit the user to edit the text in an item with very little interaction on your part. You simply need to make sure that the TVS_ED-ITLABELS property is set for the control (which can be set at design time with the properties of the control in the dialog editor) and then add a handler for the TVN_ENDLABELEDIT notification code.

To handle the TVN_ENDLABELEDIT notification code (which is sent in the WM_NO-TIFY message to the parent dialog's dialog procedure), add the handler shown in Code 6-138.

Code 6-138

```
LRESULT CALLBACK DialogProc( HWND hwndDlg, UINT uMsg, WPARAM wParam,
      LPARAM lParam )
{
    int wID;
    int wNotification;
    HWND hChild;

    switch( uMsg )
    {
        case WM_NOTIFY:
            // Parse out data from a WM_NOTIFY message
```

```
    wID = (int) wParam;
    wNotification = ((NMHDR*)lParam)->code;
    hChild = ((NMHDR*)lParam)->hwndFrom;

    if( wID==IDC_GENTREE && wNotification == TVN_ENDLABELEDIT )
    {
        NMTVDISPINFO* pTreeItem = (NMTVDISPINFO*)lParam;
        if( pTreeItem->item.pszText )
            TreeView_SetItem( hChild, &pTreeItem->item );
    }

    // Portions of code removed for readability
```

For the TVN_ENDLABELEDIT notification code of WM_NOTIFY, the lParam is in reality a pointer to an NMTVDISPINFO structure. This structure contains a TVITEM data structure named item, which contains the new text the user has typed (or the text will be NULL if the user canceled their edits). In the code above, we first perform an if test to see if it's the right control ID and notification message. Then, inside is another if test to see if we have received valid text from the user. Finally, we use the TreeView_SetItem() function to set the new item into the tree (with the new text).

MFC

To permit the user to change the text within an item, you only have to set the Edit Labels property for the TreeView control and respond to the TVN_ENDLABELEDIT message to actually update the text in the item. The TreeView control will take care of getting the user's edits and handling the clicks to go into edit mode.

To add the TVN_ENDLABELEDIT message, go into ClassWizard from the View menu choice and make sure the Message Map tab is highlighted. Then make sure that the parent class of the window that is the parent of your TreeView control is selected in the Class Name field (CMFC_CmnControlDlg in our example). Also make sure that the desired control is selected in the Object IDs list and that the TVN_ENDLABELEDIT item is selected in the Messages list. Then click the Add Function button, and then click OK to accept the suggested function name.

Modify the added function to look like Code 6–139.

Code 6–139

```
void CMFC_CmnControlDlg::OnEndlabeleditGentree(NMHDR* pNMHDR,
        LRESULT* pResult)
{
    TV_DISPINFO* pTVDispInfo = (TV_DISPINFO*)pNMHDR;

    CTreeCtrl* pTree = (CTreeCtrl*)GetDlgItem( IDC_GENTREE );
    if ( pTVDispInfo->item.pszText)
```

```
    pTree->SetItem( &pTVDispInfo->item );

    *pResult = 0;
}
```

Code 6–139 assumes that IDC_GENTREE is the ID for a TreeView control and that TreeView control is the one that this message handler was added to. The TVN_END-LABELEDIT notification handler passes a TV_DISPINFO pointer that ClassWizard has already broken into a pointer for you. Inside this structure is a TVITEM member named item. This item structure has the user's changes from his or her edit. By passing that on to SetItem for that CTreeCtrl pointer (pTree), we update the text in that item.

Tab Control

A Tab control (Figure 6–15) is a control that displays tabs along the top (in later versions, also the bottom) of a rectangular window. Programmatically, you can add tabs to the control. Tab controls are used when screen space is limited or you need to organize a lot of controls into swapable pages for the user to view.

The tab control has no built-in ability to swap pages. Instead, it sends a notification message to its parent window when the user has changed the tabs (it does handle the changing of the tabs). A common practice is to create a dialog with other controls, or just another control, and make those controls child windows of the tab control. Then, as the user changes the tab, you simply make certain child windows visible or invisible.

Tab controls also support image lists as the List View and TreeView controls do, as well as a 32-bit extra value item per page.

Figure 6–15   Tab control.

Adding Tabs to a Tab Control

SDK

Adding tabs requires the use of the TCITEM structure and initializing its data members, so we will write a helper function for the insertion of tabs into a Tab control as illustrated in Code 6–140.

Code 6–140 initializes a TCITEM structure from the parameters passed to it and calls the TabCtrl_InsertItem() to actually perform the insertion. An example of using this function is shown in Code 6–141.

Code 6–140

```
// PNTabControlInsertItem - Inserts new tab in a tab control
// Parameters:
//      hWnd - Tab control window to add to
//      Item - Position to insert new tab
//      pItemText - Text for the new tab control
// Returns: TRUE if succesful, FALSE otherwise
BOOL PNTabControlInsertItem( HWND hWnd, int Item, LPCTSTR pItemText )
{
        TCITEM tcItem;

        tcItem.mask = TCIF_TEXT;
        tcItem.pszText = (LPTSTR)pItemText;
        return( TabCtrl_InsertItem( hWnd, Item, &tcItem ) );
}
```

Code 6–141

```
// Tab Control
HWND hChild = GetDlgItem( hwndDlg, IDC_TABDEMO );
PNTabControlInsertItem( hChild, 0, "Animation" );
PNTabControlInsertItem( hChild, 1, "RichEdit" );
PNTabControlInsertItem( hChild, 2, "DateTime" );
PNTabControlInsertItem( hChild, 3, "IP Address" );
```

MFC

In order to add tabs to a tab control, use the CTabCtrl::InsertItem() function of the CTabCtrl class. The InsertItem() function in the class is overloaded as shown in Code 6–142.

Code 6–142

```
BOOL InsertItem( int nItem, LPCTSTR lpszItem );
BOOL InsertItem( int nItem, LPCTSTR lpszItem, int nImage );
BOOL InsertItem( UINT nMask, int nItem, LPCTSTR lpszItem, int nImage,
LPARAM lParam );
BOOL InsertItem( int nItem, TCITEM* pTabCtrlItem );
```

In Code 6–142, nItem is the position to insert the new tab at. lpszItem is the text to use for the label. nImage is the index of the image to use for the tab if the tab has an image list associated with it. lParam indicates the 32-bit value "item data" to be used for the tab. pTabCtrlItem is a pointer to a TCITEM structure with information needed to insert the item. Mask indicates which items of nItem, lpszItem, nImage, and lParam are valid. A typical example of using InsertItem might look like Code 6–143.

Code 6–143

```
// Tab Control initialization
CTabCtrl* pTab = (CTabCtrl*)GetDlgItem( IDC_TABDEMO );
pTab->InsertItem( 0, "Animation" );
pTab->InsertItem( 1, "RichEdit" );
pTab->InsertItem( 2, "DateTime" );
pTab->InsertItem( 3, "IP Address" );
```

Making Other Windows Children of the Tab

SDK

One common method for handling the hiding and showing of pages in a Tab control is to make the pages or controls that will be displayed child windows to the Tab control, rather than the dialog itself as is normally done. In order to do this, we can create the controls on the dialog and then programmatically change the parent with the SetParent() function. We might also want to size and reposition the controls to fit within their new parent.

Code 6–144 creates a RECT structure named Rect that will contain the display area of the tab control for positioning and sizing other controls.

Code 6–144

```
HWND hChild = GetDlgItem( hwndDlg, IDC_TABDEMO );
RECT Rect, TabRect;

// Determine the client display area for the Tab control
GetClientRect( hChild, &Rect );
TabCtrl_GetItemRect( hChild, 0, &TabRect) ;
Rect.top = 8;
Rect.left = 8;
Rect.bottom -= (8+TabRect.bottom);
Rect.right -=8;
```

We will be using this Rect structure to reposition and size our child controls. For example, if we placed an animation control on the same form with the Tab control and wanted to move that animation control into the display area of the Tab control, we would use Code 6–145.

The SetParent() function makes the animation control a child of the Tab control now. Note that now if we called GetDlgItem() to get its window handle, we would have to pass the HWND for the tab control in the first parameter and not the dialog window handle.

Code 6–145

```
hChild = GetDlgItem( hwndDlg, IDC_ANIMATE );
SetParent( hChild, GetDlgItem( hwndDlg, IDC_TABDEMO ) );
SetWindowPos( hChild, 0, 8, TabRect.bottom+8, Rect.right-8,
   Rect.bottom-8, SWP_NOZORDER );
```

For multiple controls on a page, you can create separate dialogs for each page, and then create the dialogs at runtime [with CreateDialog()] as child windows of the tab. Then hide and show the entire dialog window as needed.

MFC

One common method for handling the hiding and showing of pages in a Tab control is to make the pages or controls that will be displayed child windows to the Tab control, rather than the dialog itself as is normally done. In order to do this, we can create the controls on the dialog, and then programmatically change the parent with the SetParent() function. We might also want to size and reposition the controls to fit within their new parent.

Code 6–146 creates a RECT structure named Rect that will contain the display area of the tab control for positioning and sizing other controls.

Code 6–146

```
// Determine display area of the tab control
CRect Rect, TabRect;
pTab->GetClientRect( &Rect );
pTab->GetItemRect( 0, &TabRect);
Rect.top = 8;
Rect.left = 8;
Rect.bottom -= (8+TabRect.bottom);
Rect.right -=8;
```

We will be using this Rect object to reposition and size our child controls. For example, if we placed an animation control on the same form with the Tab control and wanted to move that animation control into the display area of the Tab control, we could now use Code 6–147.

Code 6–147

```
CAnimateCtrl * pAnimate =
      (CAnimateCtrl *)GetDlgItem( IDC_ANIMATE );
```

```
pAnimate->SetParent( pTab );
pAnimate->SetWindowPos( 0, 8, TabRect.bottom+8, Rect.right-8,
       Rect.bottom-8, SWP_NOZORDER );
```

The SetParent() function makes the animation control a child of the Tab control now. Note that now if we called GetDlgItem() to get its window handle, we would have to call it with pTab as the "this" pointer (for example: pTab->GetDlgItem (IDC_ANIMATE)) and not the dialog window "this" pointer.

Typically, a Tab control shows multiple controls on a single tab. This can be complicated to hide and show all the controls as each page is hidden and shown. For practical purposes, it is better to create a dialog for each page of the tab control and then hide and show that dialog.

With MFC, the ability to organize the message handlers of the tab control and its children dialogs becomes much easier than in an SDK program. This section describes how you would implement tab controls where each page was a specific dialog with child controls:

1. Create your dialog pages first in the resource editor.
2. For each new dialog, create a new class derived from CDialog (using ClassWizard)
3. In your main Dialog or View class, add a member variable for your Tab control using ClassWizards Member Variable tab.
4. In your main Dialog or View class, also add a data member for each of the types of classes for your dialog pages (classes created in step 2).
5. In the OnInitDialog() for your main dialog class (or OnInitialUpdate() of your view for view-based programs), use the CTabCtrl::InsertItem() to add the tab pages.
6. For each of your dialog page data members created in step 4, call its Create function, passing the ID of that dialog page and the address of the Tab control data member (this creates the dialog as a child control of the Tab).
7. Add a handler so that the tab changes are handled, and in that handler, hide and show the dialog pages as needed.

Assuming that m_MainTab is the member variable mapped to a Tab control (created in step 3 above), and CMainPage1 and CMainPage2 are the class names for your page dialogs (created in step 2 above).

In the main dialog class, declare the two dialog page members as illustrated in Code 6–148 (step 4 above).

In the main dialog's OnInitDialog() function, add the pages to the main control, and create the child dialog pages as shown in Code 6–149.

Code 6-148

```
CMainPage1 m_Page1;
CMainPage2 m_Page2;
```

Code 6-149

```
// Insert tabs for pages
m_MainTab.InsertItem( 0, "Page 1" );
m_MainTab.InsertItem( 1, "Page 2" );

// Create child pages, with taqb control as the parent:
RECT Rect;
m_MainTab.GetItemRect( 0, &Rect );
m_Page1.Create( IDD_DIALOG1, &m_MainTab );
m_Page1.SetWindowPos( 0, Rect.left+2, Rect.bottom+2, 0, 0,
      SWP_NOSIZE|SWP_NOZORDER );
m_Page2..Create( IDD_DIALOG2, &m_MainTab );
m_Page2.SetWindowPos( 0, Rect.left+2, Rect.bottom+2, 0, 0,
      SWP_NOSIZE|SWP_NOZORDER );
m_Page1.ShowWindow( SW_SHOWNA );
```

Add a message map for the Tab control in your main Dialog or View class for the TCN_SELCHANGE message. This is the function that will be called when the user changes the tab. In this tab, add Code 6–150.

Code 6-150

```
if( m_MainTab.GetCurSel()==0)
{
      m_Page2.ShowWindow( SW_HIDE );
      m_Page1.ShowWindow( SW_SHOWNA );
}
else if( m_MainTab.GetCurSel()==1)
{
      m_Page1.ShowWindow( SW_HIDE );
      m_Page2.ShowWindow( SW_SHOWNA );
}
```

Responding to Tab Change Events

SDK

When the user clicks on the tab pages of the Tab control, a TCN_SELCHANGE notification is sent with a WM_NOTIFY message. We will need to add a handler for this to the window procedure for the dialog. In this handler, we will want to hide and show the windows as appropriate for the tab selection. For example, we may hide the window controls from the first page and then show the windows for the second pages, if the user clicks on the second pages tab.

Code 6-151

Parse out data from a WM_NOTIFY message

Tab Control handler

```
LRESULT CALLBACK DialogProc( HWND hwndDlg, UINT uMsg, WPARAM wParam,
           LPARAM lParam   )
{
  int wID;
  int wNotification;
  HWND hChild;
  RECT Rect, TabRect;
  switch( uMsg )
    {
    case WM_NOTIFY:
      wID = (int) wParam;
      wNotification = ((NMHDR*)lParam)->code;
       hChild = ((NMHDR*)lParam)->hwndFrom;
      if( wID == IDC_TABDEMO && wNotification == TCN_SELCHANGE )
        {
        int Index = TabCtrl_GetCurSel( hChild );
        ShowWindow(GetDlgItem(hChild,IDC_ANIMATE),Index==0?SW_SHOW:SW_HIDE);
        ShowWindow(GetDlgItem(hChild,IDC_RICHEDIT),Index==1?SW_SHOW:SW_HIDE);
        ShowWindow(GetDlgItem(hChild,IDC_DATETIMEPICKER),Index==2?SW_SHOW:SW_HIDE);
        ShowWindow(GetDlgItem(hChild,IDC_MONTHCALENDAR),Index==2?SW_SHOW:SW_HIDE);
        ShowWindow(GetDlgItem(hChild,IDC_IPADDRESS),Index==3?SW_SHOW:SW_HIDE);
        }
      // Portions removed for readability
```

Hide or show certain
windows based on the
selected tab

Determine current tab selection

Code 6-151 demonstrates how this could be done using the GetDlgItem() function to get the desired child window handle to hide or show, then using ShowWindow() to hide or show the window. In Code 6-151, note how the selected tab (in the Index variable) is used to determine if a window should be made visible or invisible using the C/C++ ?: ternary operator.

MFC

The tab control unlike some other controls must be responded to immediately. When the user changes the tab selection, your program is responsible for swapping the controls that makes up the pages of the Tab control.

To respond to the Tab control notification of a tab change, use ClassWizard's Message Map tab. Make sure that the item in the Class Name is the parent window class for the Tab control (a Dialog or View derived class). Then, make sure the ID for the Tab control is selected in the Object IDs list and that the Messages list has the TCN_SELCHANGED item selected. Click the Add Function button and accept the default function name it suggests by clicking OK.

The function that was just added will be called when the user changes the tab selection, so we will most likely want to hide and display the various controls inside the tab display area. Assuming the controls (or dialogs) are already child windows of the tab, we can simply hide or show them using the CWnd::ShowWindow() function (regardless of their actual window types). An example is shown in Code 6–152.

Code 6–152

Page 1

```
void CMFC_CmnControlDlg::OnSelchangeTabdemo(NMHDR* pNMHDR, LRESULT* pResult)
{
    CTabCtrl* pTab = (CTabCtrl*)GetDlgItem( IDC_TABDEMO );
    int Index = pTab->GetCurSel();
    CWnd* pWin;
    pWin = pTab->GetDlgItem( IDC_ANIMATE );
    pWin->ShowWindow( Index==0? SW_SHOW : SW_HIDE );
    pWin = pTab->GetDlgItem( IDC_RICHEDIT );
    pWin->ShowWindow( Index==1? SW_SHOW : SW_HIDE );
    pWin = pTab->GetDlgItem( IDC_DATETIMEPICKER );
    pWin->ShowWindow( Index==2? SW_SHOW : SW_HIDE );
    pWin = pTab->GetDlgItem( IDC_MONTHCALENDAR );
    pWin->ShowWindow( Index==2? SW_SHOW : SW_HIDE );
    pWin = pTab->GetDlgItem( IDC_IPADDRESS );
    pWin->ShowWindow( Index==3 ? SW_SHOW : SW_HIDE );
    *pResult = 0;
}
```

Page 3

Page 4

Page 2

Animation Controls

An animation control is a control that has the ability to play simple AVI animation files, without sound. The animation starts on a separate thread (managed automatically by the animation control), so your program does not pause while the animation sequence takes place.

Under Windows, common examples of the Animated control in action is the animation when the file finder is doing a search, or when Explorer is coping with large files. In fact, with Visual C++, many of these same AVI files are now available with the compiler, permitting you to easily do the same animation sequence (look in the Video folder of your CD).

The Animation control has the ability to play an AVI file or an AVI file that is stored as a resource in your program (as long as they have no sound). Storing the AVI file in your resources means that you can then compile it into your EXE file, and you don't have to distribute as many separate files.

Importing an AVI file into your Resources—SDK and MFC

The steps for importing an AVI file into your project are the same for either SDK or MFC programs. Once you have done this step, the AVI file will become part of your EXE file when compiled, and you won't have to worry about having separate files or the client's accidentally removing the file.

To import an AVI file:

1. From the Insert menu, select Resource.
2. From the Insert Resource Dialog, click the Import button.
3. The Import Resource dialog will appear, where you can select a file. Search for and open the AVI file you want to include.
4. Once you have selected a file, you are prompted for the Custom Resource Type (as pictured in Figure 6–16).
5. Enter a custom resource type of AVI and click OK.
6. The AVI file will now be visible in your Resource View tab, on the left side of Visual Studio. If you look at the actual data in the resource, you will just see hexadecimal values.

That AVI file is now imported into your EXE file. You can change the ID of the AVI resource if you like, as it should default to IDR_AVI1 for the first AVI file imported. Next, we will show how to load this resource into an animated control at runtime.

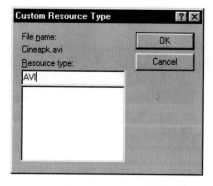

Figure 6–16   Load and play an AVI file.

Loading an AVI File or Resource for Playing

SDK

To load and play an AVI file, we use the Animate_Open() and Animate_Play() functions. The Animate_Open() function takes either the filename of an AVI file or the ID of an AVI resource, using the MAKEINTRESOURCE macro as shown in Code 6–153. Here, hWnd is the handle to the animation control, and lpszName is the file name of the AVI file or MAKEINTRESOURCE with the ID of an AVI file in the resources.

The Animate_Play() function takes four parameters as shown in Code 6–154: hWnd is the animation control to start playing; iFrom is the frame to start at, with zero being the beginning; iTo is the frame to stop at, with –1 meaning stop at the end of the clip; and iRep is the number of times to repeat the animation, with –1 meaning to repeat it continuously. An example of calling this function with the CAnimateCtrl class is shown in Code 6–155.

Code 6–155 assumes that IDC_ANIMATE is the ID of an animation control and IDR_AVI1 would be the ID of an AVI file that was imported into the resources. This code would be called from the dialog or window procedure for the window that was the parent of the animation control.

Code 6–153

```
BOOL Animate_Open( HWND hWnd, LPSTR lpszName );
```

Code 6–154

```
BOOL Animate_Play( HWND hWnd, int iFrom, int iTo, int iRepeat );
```

Code 6–155

```
HWND hChild = GetDlgItem( hwndDlg, IDC_ANIMATE );
if( Animate_Open( hChild, MAKEINTRESOURCE(IDR_AVI1) ) != FALSE )
    Animate_Play( hChild, 0, -1, -1 );
```

MFC

To load and place an AVI file, we use the CAnimateCtrl::Open() and CAnimate-Ctrl::Play() functions. The Open function is overloaded as follows to take either a file name or the ID of an AVI file that was loaded into the Resources, as illustrated in Code 6–156.

Code 6–156

```
BOOL Open( LPCTSTR lpszFileName );
BOOL Open( UINT nID );
```

The first version takes a filename parameter and the second takes the ID of the AVI resource that was previously imported. The Play() function takes three parameters as shown in Code 6–157; nFrom is the frame to start at, with zero being the beginning; nTo is the frame to stop at, with –1 meaning stop at the end of the clip; nRep is the number of times to repeat the animation, with –1 meaning to repeat it continuously. An example of calling the above functions with the CAnimateCtrl class is shown in Code 6–158.

Code 6–158 assumes that IDC_ANIMATE where the ID of an animation control, and IDR_AVI1 would be the ID of an AVI file that was imported into the resources. This code would be called from the main dialog or view class that was the parent window of the animation control.

Code 6–157

```
BOOL Play( UINT nFrom, UINT nTo, UINT nRep );
```

Code 6–158

```
CAnimateCtrl * pAnimate = (CAnimateCtrl *)GetDlgItem( IDC_ANIMATE );
if( pAnimate->Open( IDR_AVI1 ) != FALSE )
     pAnimate->Play( 0, -1, -1 );
```

Date Time Picker and Month Controls

The Date Time Picker control (see Figure 6–17) is a combo-box-type control where the user can enter a date. However, if the user clicks the down-arrow on its right, he or she is presented with the Month Calendar control (pictured on bottom of

Figure 6–17   Data time picker and Month controls.

Figure 6–17). The month control can also be used as a separate control on its own to display or get information for the date.

Before an SDK program can use a Date Time Picker control, it must call InitCommonControlsEx() to initialize that control. MFC programs will do so automatically for typical Dialog and View-based programs.

The Date Time Picker has the ability to alter its format for date display. As you interact with the control, however, you will be getting and setting a SYSTEMTIME structure to set or retrieve the date in the control. The SYSTEMTIME structure has as data members:

WORD wYear	WORD wHour
WORD wMonth	WORD wMinute
WORD wDayOfWeek	WORD wSecond
WORD wDay	WORD wMilliseconds

Initializing the Date Time Picker

SDK

Initializing the Date Time Picker control requires Code 6–159. The dwICC member of the INITCOMMONCONTROLSEX structure contains a bitmask for various controls to initialize. As you call InitCommonControlsEx(), it is an accumulative progression. That means that if you call it once to initialize the Date Time Picker control, then call it again to initialize the IP Address control, the Date Time Picker is still initialized.

Code 6–159

```
INITCOMMONCONTROLSEX icex;
icex.dwSize = sizeof(icex);
icex.dwICC = ICC_DATE_CLASSES;
InitCommonControlsEx(&icex);
```

Setting and Retrieving the Date Time Picker Value

SDK

In order to set the date and/or time in a Date Time Picker control, you need to initialize a SYSTEMTIME data structure and pass it off to the control with a DateTime_SetSystemTime() function call as shown in Code 6–160.

Code 6–160

```
BOOL DateTime_SetSystemtime( HWND hWnd, DWORD dwFlag, SYSTEMTIME* lpSysTime);
```

The hWnd parameter is the window handle to the Date Time Picker control to set. The dwFlag is GDT_VALID if you're passing a valid date or GDT_NONE to clear out the date. The lpSysTime parameter is a pointer to a SYSTEMTIME structure to initialize with the date and time from the control. An example of calling this function is shown in Code 6–161.

Retrieving the date and time from the Date Time Picker control requires a call to the DateTime_GetSystemtime() function as shown in Code 6–162. In this function, hWnd is the window handle for the Date Time Picker control, and lpSysTime is a pointer to a SYSTEMTIME structure that will contain the time from the Date Time Picker. An example of calling this function is illustrated in Code 6–163.

Code 6–161

```
HWND hChild = GetDlgItem( hwndDlg, IDC_DATETIME );
SYSTEMTIME SysTime;
GetSystemTime( &SysTime );
DateTime_SetSystemtime( hChild, GDT_VALID, &SysTime );
```

Code 6–162

```
DWORD DateTime_GetSystemtime( HWND hWnd, LPSYSTEMTIME lpSysTime);
```

Code 6–163

```
HWND hChild = GetDlgItem( hwndDlg, IDC_DATETIME );
SYSTEMTIME SysTime;
DateTime_GetSystemtime( hChild, &SysTime );
```

MFC

The MFC CDateTimeCtrl class provides functions for interacting with the Date Time Picker control. In order to get or set the time from or to the Date Time Picker control, we can call the CDateTimeCtrl::GetTime() and CDateTimeCtrl::SetTime() functions shown in Code 6–164.

Code 6–164

```
BOOL GetTime( COleDateTime& timeDest ) const;
DWORD GetTime( CTime& timeDest ) const;
DWORD GetTime( LPSYSTEMTIME pTimeDest ) const;

BOOL SetTime( const COleDateTime& timeNew );
BOOL SetTime( const CTime* pTimeNew );
BOOL SetTime( LPSYSTEMTIME pTimeNew = NULL );
```

The GetTime() and SetTime() functions both work with either COleDateTime or CTime objects or SYSTEMTIME structures. An example of calling the SetTime() function to set the current date into the Date Time Picker control is shown in Code 6–165.

Code 6-165

```
CTime Now = CTime::GetCurrentTime();
CDateTimeCtrl* pDateTime = (CDateTimeCtrl*)GetDlgItem( IDC_DATETIME );
pDateTime->SetTime( &Now );
```

Remember

○	Common controls must be initialized using InitCommonControls() or IntCommonControlsEx.
	Common controls send WM_NOTIFY messages to inform their parent of an event (not WM_COMMAND).
○	Common controls all use some form of the NMHDR structure for event notifications.
	Tree and list views can both make use of image lists.
○	Image lists contain a set of images, but are not visual controls like the others (they have no appearance on their own).

Chapter 7

Printing

- Mapping Modes
- Printers and Margin Settings
- Default Margins
- Invoking the Page Setup Dialog for Margins
- Obtaining Current Printer DC
- Margins, Mapping Modes, and Nonprintable Areas
- Determining Output Width of Text
- Pagination and Report Starting/Stopping
- Complete Printing Function
- Printing with MFC
- Determining Print versus PrintPreview in MFC
- Multiple Report Types

Printing in Windows requires an understanding of the Graphical Device Interface (GDI). GDI is a set of functions that perform graphic and text output (the text output as graphics). Functions such as TextOut(), Rectangle(), and Ellipse() are all examples of GDI functions.

Imagine GDI functions send output to a "canvas," called the device context. The device context is represented as an HDC data type in SDK programs and a CDC class in MFC programs. Device contexts are normally thought of as screen devices, but they are also used for printer and memory devices.

In this chapter we will examine the printing process, dialogs that are commonly invoked during printing, and the actual text output for a report. We will also discuss the print spooler, commonly referred to just as the spooler. The basic process for printing is to get a device context for the printer, initialize document information for the spooler, send output to the device context (text and/or bitmaps), and release the device context.

The print spooler in Windows is a program that gathers printer output from an application and slowly feeds the output to the printer. From the *Start* button, when you select *Settings*, and then *Printers*, you will see the print jobs that the spooler has waiting, or being processed. Each print job that the spooler keeps has a name, which we will demonstrate how to set up.

In communicating with the spooler, we will call StartDoc(), EndDoc(), and Abort-Doc(). These functions start, end, or cancel a print job in the spooler. We will also discuss BeginPage() and EndPage() functions, which will begin and end a printed page in the printout.

Mapping Modes

A mapping mode is a coordinate system for the GDI functions. Any of the GDI functions that use coordinates require a standard way of determining the location of the coordinate, which is accomplished using the mapping mode. The mapping mode plays a key role in printer output because it specifies common units of measurements like inches that are used to position the output on the page.

The default mapping mode for the screen or any device context handle is MM_TEXT. This uses coordinate 0, 0 as the upper-left corner of the output device (screen or printer), and each increment corresponds to a physical position on the output device. For screens, the output device measurement is in pixels, for a printer the measurement is the smallest dot the printer can make. You can think of this as the printer resolution, such as 600 DPI for 600 dots per inch.

So, if you knew that your printer was a 600 DPI printer and you wanted to draw a line 1 inch long and 1 inch from the top and left of the paper, you could do something like Code 7–1.

Code 7–1

```
MoveToEx( hPrinterDC, 600, 600 );
LineTo( hPrinterDC, 1200, 600 );
```

Code 7–1 assumes that the hPrinterDC variable is a device context for a printer. This works fine except that printer resolutions can change depending on the model of the printer being used. For example, the same code would not print the same line on a 1200 DPI printer as is printed on a 600 DPI printer because the resolution is different.

While it is possible to determine the current printer resolution with the GetDeviceCaps() function, there is a simpler way to implement consistent positioning and sizing for reports without worrying about the printer resolution—by using the mapping modes.

By changing the mapping mode, the coordinates and coordinate system change. Therefore, we use logical units instead of device units to specify the coordinates. A logical unit is a unit of measurement in the mapping mode. A device unit is a unit of measurement for an output device. These units may not be the same, and in fact they only are in the MM_TEXT mapping mode. We will use logical units, since these are independent of an output device.

You can change the mapping mode of any device context handle or CDC class by calling the SetMapMode() function, which we will see later. Mapping modes not only determine the size of our logical units, they also dictate how the coordinates work based on the X and Y values and the relative position of the coordinate. The possible values for the mapping modes are shown in Table 7.1. Note that only MM_TEXT (the default) has a mapping of one logical unit to one device unit.

Table 7.1 indicates how the value of Y increases or decreases to alter position. This means that for an X and Y coordinate where 1 is added to the X value, the original X position moves to the right. For the Y coordinate, some mapping modes will increment Y to move down and others will decrement Y to move down.

For example, in the MM_TEXT mapping mode coordinate X-1, Y-1 would be to the left, and above (X, Y). But in MM_HIENGLISH mapping mode, coordinate X-1, Y-1 would be to the left and below the original (X, Y) coordinate. So, to draw a line now using mapping modes, 1 inch from the top left and 1 inch long, use Code 7–2.

Table 7.1 Values for Mapping Modes

Mapping Mode	Meaning
MM_ANISOTROPIC	Logic units are mapped to device units based on the definitions of the SetWindowExtEx and SetViewportExtEx functions.
MM_HIENGLISH	Logical units are 1/1000", X increases to the right, and Y decreases going down.
MM_HIMETRIC	Logical units are 1/100 of a millimeter, X increases to the right, and Y decreases going down.
MM_ISOTROPIC	Similar to MM_ANSIOPTROPIC, except that logical units are mapped with equal scaling along axes.
MM_LOENGLISH	Logic units are 1/100", X increases to the right, and Y decreases going down.
MM_LOMETRIC	Logical units are 1/10 of a millimeter, X increases to the right, and Y decreases going down.
MM_TEXT	Logical units are mapped directly to physical units of the output device, X increases to the right, and Y decreases going down.
MM_TWIPS	Logical units are 1/1440", X increases to the right, and Y decreases going down.

Code 7–2

```
SetMapMode( hPrinterDC, MM_HIENGLISH );
MoveToEx( hPrinterDC, 1000, -1000 );
LineTo( hPrinterDC, 2000, -1000 );
```

Notice in Code 7–2 how the mapping mode of the printer device context is changed to MM_HIENGLISH, so that we didn't have to worry about the resolution of the output device. We simply placed the device context into MM_HIENGLISH mapping mode, which set the logical unit to 1/1000 inch in size. Also notice that the Y coordinate (−1000) is negative. Since the 0, 0 coordinate is still the upper left of the output device, we have to decrement Y to move down the page or screen (for HiEnglish mapping mode).

When printing a report, you should be concerned with the width of the printed text because the text might exceed the right or bottom margins of the document. An additional concern arises when the text uses a proportional font where the space alloted to each character of the text can be a different size. For example, in a Times Roman font, which is a proportional font, the text "iiii" takes up much less space than the text "WWWW," even though both are four characters wide.

Another concern is that characters within the text might be of different point sizes, which also changes the width of the character. For example, compare the width and height of W and W—both are the same characters, but each are in different point sizes.

Because of this sizing and spacing and the user's ability to select different fonts, it is impossible to hard-code a program to always print well-formatted text within margins. However, the Windows GDI functions include functions like GetTextExtentPoint32() and the MFC CDC:: GetTextExtent() function to help us write code to handle character-width issues. These functions permit you to determine the physical space need to print text before printing, so you can decide how much text to print to fit within our margins.

Notice that example programs in this chapter cut off any text that exceeds the user's margin settings. It would be a fairly straightforward task to modify the code so that it continued to print the text that was cut off on the next line. In this way, we could achieve word wrapping on our report.

Printers and Margin Settings

A primary concern with printers is that each model has its own printable and nonprintable areas. For example, a printer may have a 0.17-inch nonprintable area around the physical page. This means that if you fill the entire page with solid ink, there would still be a 0.17-inch area along the edge of the paper where the printer will not print. Part of this is due to the hardware design of the printer itself and the fact that printing on the very edge of the paper can become unreliable.

Figure 7–1 could be the upper-left corner of a page, with the gray area indicating the nonprintable area for the printer. The margins set by calling the PageSetupDlg() function do not take into account nonprintable areas. To properly handle margins, you need to subtract from the user's margin settings the dimensions of the nonprintable area.

In order to create a report, we need top, left, bottom, and right margins. The standard Page Setup dialog is used in order to permit the user to change margins (see the Page Setup Dialog in Chapter 3). The Page Setup Dialog can be used to retrieve the user selection for margin settings, as well as information about the nonprintable area to the specific printer.

Figure 7–1   The printable area of a page.

SDK versus MFC and Printing

In the example programs in this section, the SDK and MFC versions have slightly different base program types. The SDK program is a normal Windows program that creates an edit child window that will fill the entire main window. The MFC program is a dialog-based program that has an edit box on its main form. Similar processing is done for both when implementing printing.

It is worth noting that in MFC programs that involve Document/View architecture require minor changes because the ability to print is built into the program. These changes will be discussed in the *Printing with MFC* section later in this chapter. You can use the AppWizard to generate a program that starts out as a complete text editing and printing program without any code changes by simply choosing a CEditView as the view type in the last dialog of AppWizard. MFC topics in the first few sections are not based on the Document/View architecture.

Default Margins

SDK

Default margins are important in case the user creates a new document and tries to print it without setting the margins. In order to implement default margin settings in an SDK program, we will declare a global PAGESETUPDLG structure variable to contain the current margin settings. This declaration would simply look like PAGESETUPDLG PageSetup.

Next, in the WinMain() function we will call the PageSetupDlg() function to set up the dialog with default margin settings. We provide a helper function to simplify this task as shown in Code 7–3.

Code 7–3 sets up a PAGESETUPDLG structure with information for default margins. Because the Flags member of the PAGESETUPDLG has the PSD_RETURNDEFAULT flag on, it will not display the page setup dialog. Instead, it will merely initialize the data members of the PAGESETUPDLG with default values for the currently selected printer. Typical default margins are 1 inch for top, left, right, and bottom margins, which are stored in the rtMargin data member of the PAGESETUPDLG structure in 1/1000-inch units. This means the top is 1000 = 1 inch. Call this function (Code 7–4) from WinMain() and pass it the global variable that we setup earlier.

Code 7-3

Setup the lStructSize member with the size of the structure

Set all members to zero

```
void PNPageSetupInit( PAGESETUPDLG* PageSetup )
{
    memset( PageSetup, 0, sizeof(PAGESETUPDLG) );
    PageSetup->lStructSize = sizeof(PAGESETUPDLG);
    PageSetup->Flags=PSD_RETURNDEFAULT | PSD_INTHOUSANDTHSOFINCHES;
    PageSetupDlg( PageSetup );
}
```

Invoke the PageSetupDlg() function to initialize the structure

Set the flags to return default values, in thousands of an inch.

The above does not display the page setup dialog, because of how we initialized the Flags data member

Code 7-4

```
int APIENTRY WinMain(HINSTANCE hInstance, HINSTANCE hPrevInstance,
      LPSTR lpCmdLine, int nCmdShow)
{
      // Initialize the Margin settings for the page setup
      PNPageSetupInit( &PageSetup );
```

MFC

Default margins are important in case the user creates a new document and tries to print it without setting the margins. In order to implement default margin settings in an MFC program, declare a member variable of CPageSetupDlg type for our main View or Dialog class. The initialization of the default margins is done in the constructor of the View or Dialog class in an initializer list. Add the Code 7-5 to your View or Dialog class. Our example uses a MFC_NopePadDlg class, defined in MFC_NopePadDlg.h.

Modify the constructor of the View or Dialog class that now contains the m_PageSetupDlg data member so that it includes an initializer for m_PageSetupDlg as shown in Code 7-6.

Code 7-5

```
CPageSetupDialog m_PageSetupDlg;
```

Code 7-6

The LoadIcon does not require a subsequent DestroyIcon in Win32

The ClassWizard will add member initialization here

```
CMFC_NopePadDlg::CMFC_NopePadDlg(CWnd* pParent /*=NULL*/)
        : CDialog(CMFC_NopePadDlg::IDD, pParent),
          m_PageSetupDlg( PSD_RETURNDEFAULT|PSD_INTHOUSANDTHSOFINCHES )
{
    //{{AFX_DATA_INIT(CMFC_NopePadDlg)

    //}}AFX_DATA_INIT
    m_hIcon = AfxGetApp()->LoadIcon(IDR_MAINFRAME);
    m_PageSetupDlg.DoModal();
    m_PageSetupDlg.m_psd.Flags &= (~PSD_RETURNDEFAULT);
}
```

Turn off the GetDefaults flag

Invoke dialog function (without diplaying) to get margin defaults

The initializer passes the PSD_RETURNDEFAULT and PSD_INTHOUSANDS-OFINCHES flags to the m_PageSetupDlg constructor function. These flags indicate that the object should be initialized with data but that the dialog should not be displayed yet.

The m_psd data member of the CPageSetupDlg class is a PAGESETUPDLG structure that contains a data member rtMargin that holds the left, top, right, and bottom margins. Typical default margins are 1 inch for top, left, right, and bottom margins, which are stored in the rtMargin data member of the m_psd data member in 1/1000-inch units. This means the top is 1000 = 1 inches.

Invoking the Page Setup Dialog for Margins

SDK

Since the SDK program has a global PAGESETUPDLG structue named PageSetup, we can call the SetupPageDlg() function to permit the user to change the margin settings. Be sure to include a menu item that calls this function, such as IDM_PAGESETUP, and place a menu handler to the window procedure as shown in

Code 7-7. The PNPageSetup function shown in Code 7-8 is a helper function that makes it easy to call the SetupPageDlg().

Code 7-7

```
LRESULT CALLBACK WndProc(HWND hWnd, UINT message, WPARAM wParam, LPARAM lParam)
{
        int wmId, wmEvent;

        switch (message)
        {
                case WM_COMMAND:
                        wmId = LOWORD(wParam);
                        wmEvent = HIWORD(wParam);
                        switch (wmId)
                        {
                                case IDM_PAGESETUP:
                                        PNPageSetup( hWnd, &PageSetup );
                                        break;
        //Portions of code removed for readability
```

Code 7-8

TRUE if user hit OK, FALSE if not

Window handle to the parent or main window

Initialize the fundamentals of the struct

Pointer to the PAGESETUPDLG struct to initialize

```
BOOL PNPageSetup(HWND hWnd, PAGESETUPDLG* PageSetup)
{
    PageSetup->lStructSize = sizeof(PAGESETUPDLG);
    PageSetup->hwndOwner = hWnd;
    if(- PageSetup->rtMargin.left > 0 )
       PageSetup->Flags |= PSD_MARGINS;
     return( PageSetupDlg( PageSetup ) );
}
```

Invoke the PageSetupDlg() function to display the dialog

If so, use it as initialization

Is there any left margin?

In Code 7–8, the lStructSize and the hwndOwner members of the PAGESETUPDLG structure are initialized and then the PageSetupDlg function is called.

When the IDM_PAGESETUP menu item is selected, the Page Setup dialog is displayed and the user selections are stored in the global PageSetup variable we created. That variable is also required when we actually do the printing.

MFC

With the CPageSetupDlg data member we added earlier, we need to add a menu item that will call the Page Setup dialog. We recommend creating a menu item with the ID of IDM_PAGESETUP in your resource editor, but the actual name or ID can be whatever you prefer.

Once the menu item is added, you add a Message Map using the Message Map tab of ClassWizard. The message map should be added to either the main View or Dialog class for your program (MFC_NopePadDlg in our example). Once you have added the message map, you will see an empty function that looks like Code 7–9.

Modify Code 7–10 function to call the DoModal() function of the m_PageSetup data member we created earlier.

When the user selects the Page Setup menu item, the OnPageSetup() function is called (message map) and the dialog is displayed. Any user changes are stored in the m_PageSetupDlg member variable. We will need this margin data later when we actually perform the printing.

Code 7–9

```
void CMFC_NopePadDlg::OnPagesetup()
{
        // Add your command handler code here

}
```

Code 7–10

```
void CMFC_NopePadDlg::OnPagesetup()
{
        // Invoke the Page Setup dialog
        m_PageSetupDlg.DoModal();
}
```

Obtaining the Current Printer DC

SDK

In order to print, we will need to get a device context handle (HDC) for the currently selected printer. This is used to send our document to the printer. However, the document is first held by the Windows spooler then slowly sent to the printer. Use the PrintDlg() function to obtain the current printer device context. Similar to the PageSetupDlg() function previously shown in this chapter, we will not actually display the printer dialog.

Code 7–11 is a helper function has been created to simplify the task of getting the printer DC.

The print routine should resemble Code 7–12. Notice how we call the PNGetPrinterDC() to get an HDC for the printer. Next, the if test verifies that we succesfully obtain the DC handle. At the end of the if test we release the DC handle once printing is completed. The comment "Do your printing" indicates where we would place the TextOut and other GDI functions to output data to the printer.

Code 7–11

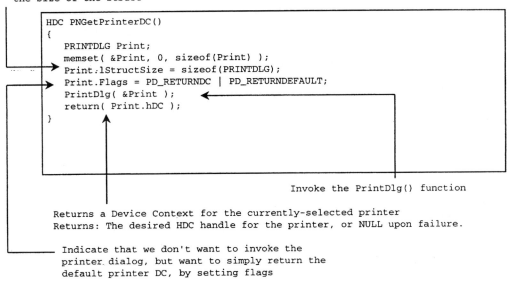

```
Initialize the Print structure with zeros, and
the size of the struct

HDC PNGetPrinterDC()
{
    PRINTDLG Print;
    memset( &Print, 0, sizeof(Print) );
    Print.lStructSize = sizeof(PRINTDLG);
    Print.Flags = PD_RETURNDC | PD_RETURNDEFAULT;
    PrintDlg( &Print );
    return( Print.hDC );
}
```

Invoke the PrintDlg() function

Returns a Device Context for the currently-selected printer
Returns: The desired HDC handle for the printer, or NULL upon failure.

Indicate that we don't want to invoke the printer dialog, but want to simply return the default printer DC, by setting flags

---

Code 7-12

```
void DoPrint( HWND hWnd )
{
        HDC PrintDC;

        PrintDC = PNGetPrinterDC();
        if( !PrintDC )
                MessageBox( hWnd, "Unable to open printer", "Information", MB_OK );
        else
{

                // Do your printing

                // Release the printer DC when we are done printing
                DeleteDC( PrintDC );
        }
}
```

MFC

In order to print, we will need to get a device context handle class (CDC) for the currently selected printer. This is the device context of the printer used for printing our document. The document is held by the Windows spooler then fed to the printer. To obtain the current printer CDC, we will use the CPrintDialog class, but as explained in the CPageSetupDialog shown previously in this chapter, we will not actually display the printer dialog.

Add a menu item for the Print functionality under the File menu in your program. We recommend that you use IDM_PRINT for its ID. Then, add a message map using ClassWizard for the menu item to your main View or Dialog class (MFC_NopePad-Dlg class in our example). When you have added the function, it will look like Code 7-13. Modify the code so that it looks like Code 7-14.

Code 7-13

```
void CMFC_NopePadDlg::OnPrint()
{
        // Add your command handler code here
}
```

Code 7-14

Invoke the GetDefaults() function, which will only
retrieve the printer DC

Create the
CPrinterDialog object
with the flags for
retrieving the current
printer DC.

```
void CMFC_NopePadDlg::OnPrint()
{

CPrintDialog Printer(FALSE);
Printer.GetDefaults();
if( !Printer.m_pd.hDC )
   MessageBox( "Unable to open printer" );
else
  {
  CDC PrinterDC;
  PrinterDC.Attach( Printer.m_pd.hDC );



  }

}
```

For convenience, create a CDC object, and attach the printer
HDC to it. The destructor for the CDC will automatically
destroy the HDC when we leave these french braces.

Do your printing here

Margins, Mapping Modes, and Nonprintable Areas

SDK

In order to print correctly when the user specifies a 1-inch margin, we have to remember to subtract the nonprintable area from the margin before printing. The
margin and the nonprintable area can be found inside the PAGESETUPDLG global
variable PageSetupDlg that we created earlier. The math for doing the adjustments
is easy but cumbersome, so we will put the code into a helper function shown in
Code 7-15.

Code 7-15

```
void PNEzMargins( PAGESETUPDLG* PageSetup, int* Left, int *Top, int* Right,
int* Bottom )
{
        *Left = PageSetup->rtMargin.left - PageSetup->rtMinMargin.left;
        *Top = -(PageSetup->rtMargin.top - PageSetup->rtMinMargin.top);
        *Right = PageSetup->ptPaperSize.x - PageSetup->rtMargin.right
                - PageSetup->rtMinMargin.left;
        *Bottom = -(PageSetup->ptPaperSize.y - PageSetup->rtMargin.bottom
                - PageSetup->rtMinMargin.top);
}
```

We call Code 7-15 to determine and set the left, right, top, and bottom print areas of the desired page, based on the PageSetup structure variable. We will also set the mapping mode for the printer device context to a mode (MM_HIENGLISH) that is easy to read and does not depend upon the resolution of the printer. If we didn't set the mapping mode, it would default to MM_TEXT. This means that for a 600 DPI printer the user would have to select a left margin of 600 for a 1-inch margin (something we will avoid). Because our earlier page setup examples all used the MM_HIENGLISH mapping mode, which relies on 1/1000 inch measurements, we will continue to use that mapping mode as shown in Code 7-16.

Code 7-16

```
void DoPrint( HWND hWnd )
{
        HDC PrintDC;
        int Top, Left, Bottom, Right;

        PrintDC = PNGetPrinterDC();

        if( !PrintDC )
                MessageBox( hWnd, "Unable to locate printer", NULL,
                        MB_ICONEXCLAMATION|MB_OK );
        else
        {
                SetMapMode( PrintDC, MM_HIENGLISH );

                // Determine our true printable margins
                PNEzMargins( &PageSetup, &Left, &Top, &Right, &Bottom );

                // Do printing here
        }
}
```

Code 7-16 initializes the PrintDC variable with a device context for the current printer by calling the PNGetPrinterDC() function. The new code we added (in bold) sets the mapping mode for the DC to MM_HIENGLISH. This means that measure-

---

ments are in 1/1000 of an inch, X increases to the right, and Y decreases as we move down the page. The PNEzMargins() function is then called with the PageSetup global variable, which is a PAGESETUPDLG data structure that contains the user's margins and the nonprintable printer area information for the printer.

If the user selected 1 inch for top and bottom margins, we assume that the Left and Top local variables contain the correct values to position the document 1 inch from the left and top of the paper. This takes into account the nonprintable area of the printer.

MFC

In order to print correctly when the user specifies a 1-inch margin, we have to subtract the nonprintable area from the margin before printing. The margin and the nonprintable area found inside the CPageSetupDlg class's m_psd data member. Use the member variable of this type that we added earlier. The math for doing the adjustments is easy but cumbersome, so we will put the code into a helper function as shown in Code 7–17.

Code 7–17

```
void CMFC_NopePadDlg::PNEzMargins(CPageSetupDialog &pPageSetup, int &Left,
int &Top, int &Right, int &Bottom)
{
        Left = pPageSetup.m_psd.rtMargin.left - pPageSetup.m_psd.
        rtMinMargin.left;
        Top = -(pPageSetup.m_psd.rtMargin.top - pPageSetup.m_psd.
        rtMinMargin.top);
        Right = pPageSetup.m_psd.ptPaperSize.x -
        pPageSetup.m_psd.rtMargin.right -
                pPageSetup.m_psd.rtMinMargin.left;
        Bottom = -(pPageSetup.m_psd.ptPaperSize.y - pPageSetup.m_psd.
        rtMargin.bottom -
                pPageSetup.m_psd.rtMinMargin.top);
}
```

We can now call the Code 7–17 to determine and set the left, right, top, and bottom print areas of the desired page, based on the PageSetup object passed. We will also need to set the mapping mode for the printer device context to a mode that is easy to read and does not depend upon the resolution of the printer. We will use the MM_HIENGLISH mapping mode, which uses 1/1000-inch measurements. We use this mapping mode to be consistent with earlier examples.

Be sure to add a Print menu item to the program. The menu item should have a message map handler created using the ClassWizard. In this example, we place the code needed to do the actual report in ClassWizard. Code 7–18 demonstrates how to determine the margins with our helper function and how to set the mapping mode.

Code 7-18

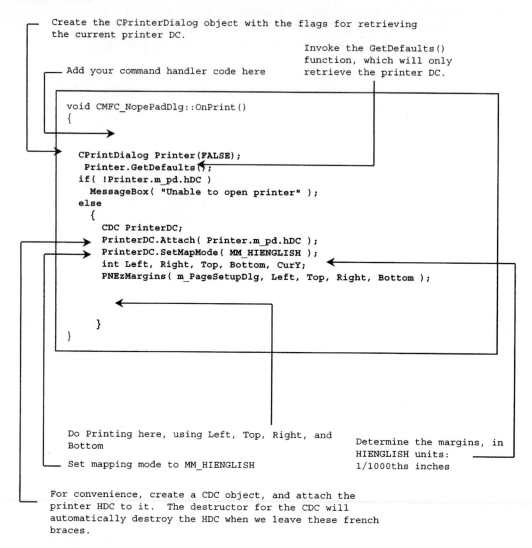

Create the CPrinterDialog object with the flags for retrieving the current printer DC.

Invoke the GetDefaults() function, which will only retrieve the printer DC.

Add your command handler code here

```
void CMFC_NopePadDlg::OnPrint()
{

    CPrintDialog Printer(FALSE);
    Printer.GetDefaults();
    if( !Printer.m_pd.hDC )
      MessageBox( "Unable to open printer" );
    else
      {
        CDC PrinterDC;
        PrinterDC.Attach( Printer.m_pd.hDC );
        PrinterDC.SetMapMode( MM_HIENGLISH );
        int Left, Right, Top, Bottom, CurY;
        PNEzMargins( m_PageSetupDlg, Left, Top, Right, Bottom );



      }
}
```

Do Printing here, using Left, Top, Right, and Bottom

Set mapping mode to MM_HIENGLISH

Determine the margins, in HIENGLISH units: 1/1000ths inches

For convenience, create a CDC object, and attach the printer HDC to it. The destructor for the CDC will automatically destroy the HDC when we leave these french braces.

In Code 7–19, the CPrintDialog class is used to acquire a printer device context by calling the CPrintDialog::GetDefaults() function. The if test verifies is we received the device context in the m_pd data member (a PAGESETUPDLG struct) of the Printer local variable. For convenience, we create a CDC object named PrinterDC and use the CDC::Attach() function to associate this object with the printer device context.

The mapping mode is changed to MM_HIENGLISH by calling CDC::SetMapMode(), and then the PNEzMargins() function is called to calculate the actual printing margins. Once the PrinterDC object goes out of scope, the desctructor is called to destroy the PrinterDC object.

Determining Output Width of Text

SDK

Although the left and right margins are set, we must be sure that the printing does not exceed the right margin. We will use the GetTextExtentPoint32() function to determine the output area or space needed to print the text and then to determine if the text will fit within the margins. If the text does not fit, then we keep testing smaller and smaller portions of the text until we determine that the text fits. Once the text fits, we will then print the text. Code 7–19 illustrates this technique. Code 7–19 assumes that PrintDC is a Device context handle to the printer, Right and Left

Code 7–19

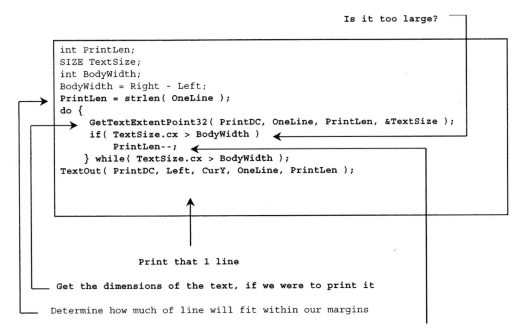

```
                                                            Is it too large?

    int PrintLen;
    SIZE TextSize;
    int BodyWidth;
    BodyWidth = Right - Left;
    PrintLen = strlen( OneLine );
    do {
        GetTextExtentPoint32( PrintDC, OneLine, PrintLen, &TextSize );
        if( TextSize.cx > BodyWidth )
            PrintLen--;
        } while( TextSize.cx > BodyWidth );
    TextOut( PrintDC, Left, CurY, OneLine, PrintLen );
```

Print that 1 line

Get the dimensions of the text, if we were to print it

Determine how much of line will fit within our margins

If so, decement the number of characters to test

are integers with current margin values, OneLine is the string to print, and CurY is the Y position to print at.

Notice in Code 7–19 how the do...while loop keeps looping until the TextSize.cx, which is the text width if printed, is less than the BodyWidth. The BodyWidth is determined as the right margin minus the left margin or size of the horizontal space we have to print. The GetTextExtendPoint32()prototype functions is Code 7–20.

Code 7-20

```
BOOL GetTextExtentPoint32( HDC hDC, LPCTSTR pszText, int nCount, LPSIZE pSize );
```

The hDC parameter is the device context handle for the text size. Whatever font is selected for the device context is the font used to determine the physical size. The pszText parameter is a pointer to a text to be tested. The nCount parameter indicates the number of characters in the string that is to be tested. The pSize parameter is a pointer to a SIZE structure that will contain the width and height of the text. The structure is populated after the function is called. Notice that the nCount parameter allows us to determine how many characters will fit within a specified area. Once we have determined the number of characters that will fit within the margins, we pass that number as the last parameter to TextOut() to control the number of characters it actually prints.

MFC

Once the left and right margins are set, make sure that our printing does not exceed the right margin. Use the CDC:: GetTextExtent() function to determine the size needed to print the text and determine if the text fits within the margins. If it does not, keep testing the text to determine if the text will fit, then print the text. Code 7–21 illustrates how this is done.

Code 7-21

```
CSize TextSize;
int BodyWidth, LineSize;
CString Text;
CDC PrinterDC;

// Initialize PrinterDC, Text, Left and Right here

BodyWidth = Right - Left;

LineSize = Text.GetLength();
do {
        // Determine size of text if printed upto 'LineSize' characters
        TextSize = PrinterDC.GetTextExtent( Text, LineSize );
        if( TextSize.cx > BodyWidth ) // If too big, decrement size and try
        again
```

```
            LineSize--;
} while( TextSize.cx > BodyWidth );

// Print the line (or only the portion that fits on the page)
PrinterDC.TextOut( Left, CurY, Text, LineSize );
```

Notice how the do...while loop keeps looping until the TextSize.cx, which is the text width if printed, is less than the BodyWidth. The BodyWidth is determined as the right margin minus the left margin. The CDC::GetTextExtent() prototype function (it is overloaded) is shown in Code 7–22.

Code 7–22

```
CSize CDC::GetTextExtent( LPCTSTR pszText, int nCount ) const;
CSize CDC::GetTextExtent( const CString& sStr ) const;
```

Both versions of the CDC::GetTextExtent() function returns a CSize object that contains the height and width of the text. Whatever font is selected for the device context is the font used to determine the size of the text. The pszText parameter is a pointer to text that is to be tested. The nCount parameter indicates how many characters in the text to test. The second version of the CDC::GetTextExtent() function uses a CString parameter named sStr, which will be tested in its entirely for printed dimensions. Notice that the nCount parameter allows us to determine the number of characters that will fit within a specified area. Once we have determined the number of characters that will fit within the margins, we pass that number as the last parameter to TextOut().

Pagination and Report Starting/Stopping

SDK

To start and stop a report, you must call the StartDoc() and EndDoc() functions. If you want to cancel a report in the middle of printing, then call AbortDoc() instead of EndDoc(). The StartDoc() function requires you to initialize a DOCINFO data structure with information about the print job, which will be displayed in the print manager program during printing (Figure 7–2). Code 7–23 initializes the DOCINFO structure then call StartDocs().

Code 7–23

```
// Setup the DOCINFO structure, for Print Manager
DOCINFO DocInfo;
memset( &DocInfo, 0, sizeof(DocInfo) );
DocInfo.lpszDocName = CurFile;

// Start the Document
StartDoc( PrintDC, &DocInfo );
```

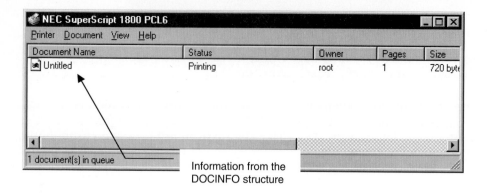

Figure 7–2   The printer queue.

In Code 7–23, the lpszDocName member of the DOCINFO structure is a pointer that must be initialized to point to the name of your document being printed (our example assumes that CurFile is a variable that contains the document name). Once the DOCINFO structure is initialized, pass its address to the StartDoc() function, along with the printer device context handle (PrinterDC in our example). At the end of the report or upon canceling the report, you should call either EndDoc() (Code 7–24) to finish it, or AbortDoc() to cancel it (see Code 7–25).

You must call the StartPage() function at the start of a page and the EndPage() function at the end of a page. If you want to generate a blank page in the report, you can simply call EndPage() immediately after StartPage().

Code 7–24

```
EndDoc( PrintDC );
```

Code 7–25

```
AbortDoc( PrintDC );
```

MFC

The CDC::StartDoc() and CDC::EndDoc() functions must be called to start and stop a report. Call the CDC::AbortDoc() instead of EndDoc() if you want to cancel a report that is being printed. The StartDoc() function requires you to initialize a DOCINFO data structure with information about the print job, which will be displayed in the print manager program during printing. This is shown in Figure 7–2.

Initializing the DOCINFO structure is exactly the same as described in the *Pagination and Report Starting/Stopping, SDK* section in this chapter. Once the DOCINFO structure is initialized, you can pass it to the CDC::StartDoc() function as shown in Code 7–26.

At the end of the report(or upon canceling the report), you should call *either* CDC::EndDoc() (Code 7–27) to finish it or CDC::AbortDoc() (Code 7–28) to cancel printing.

You must call the CDC::StartPage() function at the start of a page and the CDC::EndPage() function at the end of a page. If you want to generate a blank page in the report, call EndPage() immediately after StartPage().

Code 7–26

```
// Start printing the document
PrinterDC.StartDoc( &DocInfo );
```

Code 7–27

```
PrinterDC.EndDoc();
```

Code 7–28

```
PrinterDC.AbortDoc();
```

Complete Printing Function

SDK

Code 7–30 combines all of the previous SDK program topics discussed in this chapter and prints a document with pagination, margins, and headers. The text to be printed is taken from a single multiline edit box window and printed one line at a time. Code 7–30 uses the global variables shown in Code 7–29, which must be initialized before calling Code 7–30. Code 7–30 be called from the WndProc() function in response to a Print menu choice by the user.

Code 7–29

```
HFONT CurFont;
PAGESETUPDLG PageSetup;
char CurFile[MAX_PATH];
```

Code 7-30

```
// hWnd is the main window handle, that contains the edit window
void DoPrint( HWND hWnd )
{
    HDC PrintDC;
    static char OneLine[1024]; // We will print 1 line at a time
    HFONT ReportFont;
    SIZE TextSize;
    int End;
    bool PageStart=true;
    int Top, Left, Bottom, Right, BodyWidth, CurY;
    int LineHeight, PrintLen;

    PrintDC = PNGetPrinterDC();

    if( !PrintDC )
        MessageBox( hWnd, "Unable to locate printer", NULL, MB_ICONEXCLAMA-
        TION|MB_OK );
    else
    {
        HWND hEdit = GetDlgItem(hWnd, IDC_EDIT );
        int LineCount = SendMessage( hEdit, EM_GETLINECOUNT, 0, 0 );

        // CurFonts Height is based on screen DC. Make one for the printer DC
        ReportFont = PNCreatePrinterFont( hWnd, CurFont );
        SelectObject( PrintDC, ReportFont );
        SetMapMode( PrintDC, MM_HIENGLISH );

        // Determine our true printable margins
        PNEzMargins( &PageSetup, &Left, &Top, &Right, &Bottom );
        BodyWidth = Right - Left;

        if( LineCount )
        {
            // Determine Text height for the current font
            GetTextExtentPoint32( PrintDC, "Hy", 2, &TextSize );
            LineHeight = TextSize.cy;

            // Setup the DOCINFO structure, for Print Manager
            DOCINFO DocInfo;
            memset( &DocInfo, 0, sizeof(DocInfo) );
            DocInfo.lpszDocName = CurFile;

            // Start the Document
            StartDoc( PrintDC, &DocInfo );

            StartPage( PrintDC );
            EndPage( PrintDC );
```

```
// Print each line from the multi-line edit (the report)
for( int i = 0; i < LineCount; i++ )
{
      // Prints header for report
      if( PageStart )
      {
         if( i > 0 ) // Is this the start of a second or greater page?
               EndPage( PrintDC );

         // Start a new page
         StartPage( PrintDC );

         // Printer header
         TextOut( PrintDC, Left, Top + TextSize.cy+100, CurFile,
               strlen(CurFile) );
         MoveToEx( PrintDC, Left, Top + 100, NULL );
               // Remember: +100 means 'up the page'
         LineTo( PrintDC, Right, Top + 100 );

         // Set StartPage flag to false until needed again, and set
         // CurY back to top
         PageStart = false;
         CurY = Top;
      }

      // Get line from edit control
      *(int*)OneLine = sizeof( OneLine );
      End = SendMessage( hEdit, EM_GETLINE, (WPARAM)i,
      (LPARAM)OneLine );
      OneLine[End]='\0';

      // Determine how much of line will fit within our margins
      PrintLen = strlen( OneLine );
      do {
         GetTextExtentPoint32( PrintDC, OneLine, PrintLen,
         &TextSize );
         if( TextSize.cx > BodyWidth )
               PrintLen--;
      } while( TextSize.cx > BodyWidth );

      // Print that 1 line
      TextOut( PrintDC, Left, CurY, OneLine, PrintLen );
      CurY -= TextSize.cy; // Move CurY down the page

      // If we have atleast 1 more line, and it would be below
      bottom margin,
      // then we indicate a new page start is needed
      if( i+1 < LineCount && (CurY-TextSize.cy) <= Bottom )
         PageStart = true;
}
```

```
        // End the current page, and the report.
        EndPage( PrintDC );
        EndDoc( PrintDC );
    }
    // Release the Printer DC when done printing
    DeleteDC( PrintDC );
    }
}
```

MFC

Code 7–32 combines all of the above topics in an MFC function to print a document with pagination, margins, and headers. The text to be printed is taken from a single multi-line edit box window and printed one line at a time. This function uses data member variables shown in Code 7–31, which must be initialized before calling Code 7–32. Add Code 7–32 as the message map handler (callback function) for the Print menu item in your program.

Code 7–31

```
CPageSetupDialog m_PageSetupDlg;
CString m_CurFile;
```

Code 7–32

```
void CMFC_NopePadDlg::OnPrint()
{
    // TODO: Add your command handler code here

    // Create the CPrinterDialog object with the flags for retrieving
    //the current printer DC.
    CPrintDialog Printer(FALSE);
    // Invoke the GetDefaults function, which will only retrieve the
    printer DC, and
    Printer.GetDefaults();

    if( !Printer.m_pd.hDC )
        MessageBox( "Unable to open printer" );
    else
    {
        // Get CEdit* for the Edit control in the window
        CEdit* pEdit = (CEdit*)GetDlgItem( IDC_EDIT );
        // For convenience, create a CDC object, and attach the printer HDC
        // to it. The destructor for the CDC will automatically destroy the
        // HDC when we leave these french braces.
        CDC PrinterDC;
        PrinterDC.Attach( Printer.m_pd.hDC );

        // Start Printing
```

```
PrinterDC.SetMapMode( MM_HIENGLISH );
// CurFonts Height is based on screen DC. Make one for the printer DC
CFont ReportFont;
PNCreatePrinterFont( pEdit, ReportFont );
PrinterDC.SelectObject( ReportFont );

// Determine the margins, in HIENGLISH units: 1/1000ths inches
int Left, Right, Top, Bottom, CurY;
PNEzMargins( m_PageSetupDlg, Left, Top, Right, Bottom );

// Setup the DOCINFO structure so that Windows Spooler shows an
// intelligent name for our print job
DOCINFO DocInfo;
memset(&DocInfo, 0, sizeof(DocInfo));
DocInfo.cbSize = sizeof(DocInfo);
DocInfo.lpszDocName = (LPCSTR)m_CurFile;

// Start printing the document
PrinterDC.StartDoc( &DocInfo );

// String to hold our text
CString Text;

// Determine the line height for our font, and the
// width of the report body
int LineSize, FontHeight;
CSize TextSize = PrinterDC.GetTextExtent( "Hy" );
FontHeight = TextSize.cy;
int BodyWidth = Right - Left;
int PageNum=1;
CString Header;

// A flag to indicate that the header should be printed
bool PageStart=true;

// Iterate through the lines of the Edit control
for( int i = 0; i < pEdit->GetLineCount(); i++ )
{
    if( PageStart )
    {
        // If we already printed something, then we have to remember
        to end the
        // previous page
        if( i > 0 )
                PrinterDC.EndPage();

    // Tell Spooler to start a new page
    PrinterDC.StartPage();
```

```
// Print page header
PrinterDC.MoveTo( Left, Top + 100 );
PrinterDC.LineTo( Right, Top + 100 );
Header.Format( "%s - Page %d", (LPCSTR)m_CurFile, PageNum++);
PrinterDC.TextOut( Left, Top + 100 + FontHeight, Header );

// Set the PageStart flag to false until needed again, and
// set the CurY position back to the top margin
PageStart = false;
CurY = Top;
        }


// Get the line of text for the report from our multi-line edit box
LineSize = pEdit->GetLine(i, Text.GetBuffer(1024), 1024 );
Text.ReleaseBuffer(LineSize);

// Determine if the line fits in our printable areas
do {
        TextSize = PrinterDC.GetTextExtent( Text, LineSize );
        if( TextSize.cx > BodyWidth )
                LineSize--;
} while( TextSize.cx > BodyWidth );

// Print the line (or only the portion that fits on the page)
PrinterDC.TextOut( Left, CurY, Text, LineSize );

// Decrement the current Y position to move down by 1 line
CurY -= TextSize.cy;
        }
// End the last page
PrinterDC.EndPage();

// Stop printing the document
PrinterDC.EndDoc();


    }
}
```

Printing with MFC

MFC programs simplify printing because they contain the built-in print preview feature. This feature is included in a Document/View-style program, but more work is necessary to create a dialog-based program. As a guideline, create a Document/View-style program whenever you want to simplify printing and offer a print preview feature in your application.

There are five functions use to print a document using MFC. These are OnPreparePrinting(), OnBeginPrinting(), OnPrepareDC(), OnPrint(), and OnEndPrinting(). These functions are member functions of the View class and are called automatically as the framework to generate reports and print previews.

Your job is to create or modify the bodies of these functions for your report. Don't be concerned about the menu handling or print preview setup since the framework automatically addresses these.

When the user selects the Print or Print Preview menu item of an MFC Document/View program, the framework calls the OnPreparePrinting() function and then the OnBeginPrinting(). Framework then calls the OnPrepareDC() and OnPrint() functions repeatedly, once per page in your report. At the end of the report, framework calls the OnEndPrinting() function.

OnPreparePrinting()

OnPreparePrinting() (Code 7–33) is called primarily to set the minimum and maximum page numbers for your document and to otherwise control the appearance of the Printer dialog. You have the option to supply information using the pInfo parameter for information such as the number of pages to be printed. Add your code to alter the pInfo object before the call to DoPreparePrinting(), which you will find inside the OnPreparePrinting function (Code 7–34).

Code 7–33

```
virtual BOOL OnPreparePrinting( CPrintInfo* pInfo );
```

DoPreparePrinting() calls the Print dialog box, which alters the pInfo class. You can provide your own printer dialog, but it is not recommended since the DoPreparePrinting() function calls the standard Windows Print dialog box. If you comment out the call to DoPreparePrinting(), then no printer dialog is displayed.

Call the CPrintInfo::SetMaxPage() function within the OnPreparePrinting() to specify the maximum page. If you can't calculate the page in a reasonable amount of time, then don't call SetMaxPage(). If you do not specify the maximum number of pages, then you must write code in the OnPrepareDC() function to terminate the report. In addition, the standard Windows Print dialog usually provides an option to select a range of pages to print. By not setting the Max page, the from edit in that dialog will be blank.

Let's say it takes five minutes to determine the number of pages in a report because you are writing a report from a database. The delay is caused by the large number of records that comprise the report. You may decide not to perform the page count since this requires the program to spend five minutes to read all the records after the user selects the Print option.

DoPreparePrinting() (see Code 7–34) is automatically placed in your view class On-PreparePrinting function by AppWizard when the program is created, and is called once per report run. If OnPreparePrinting returns FALSE, then the report is canceled.

Code 7-34

```
BOOL CWhateverView::OnPreparePrinting(CPrintInfo* pInfo)
{
        // default preparation
        return DoPreparePrinting(pInfo);
}
```

OnBeginPrinting()

Code 7–35 is the prototype of the function that is called to create the GDI objects for your report, such as the fonts or bitmaps. OnBeginPrinting() is called once prior to the start of printing and is created by ClassWizard. The pInfo parameter contains information about the report. Code 7–36 illustrates the OnBeginPrinting() function created by the ClassWizard.

Code 7-35

```
BOOL OnBeginPrinting(CDC* pDC, CPrintInfo* pInfo)
```

Code 7-36

```
void CWhateverView::OnBeginPrinting(CDC* /*pDC*/, CPrintInfo* /*pInfo*/)
{
        // Add extra initialization before printing
}
```

Fonts and bitmaps must be member variables of the View class. If they are local variables, then as soon as this function ends, they will be destroyed and you won't be able to use them in your reports. Code 7–37 shows an example of how to create a font for later use in a report. Code 7–37 assumes that m_Header is a CFont data member of the View class.

Code 7-37

```
void CWhateverView::OnBeginPrinting(CDC* pDC, CPrintInfo* /*pInfo*/)
{
        // Add extra initialization before printing

        // Create a 14-point Times New Roman font. Note the point
        // size is in 1/10 points, so 140 = 14 points
        m_Header.CreatePointFont( 140, "Times New Roman", pDC );

}
```

OnPrepareDC()

Code 7–38 is the prototype of a function that is provided for you to set up the device context for the printer and to terminate the report output. The pDC parameter is the device context that represents either a printer or print preview window. The pInfo parameter is the same parameter pass to all the other MFC print functions and contains information about the report.

Code 7-38

```
void OnPrepareDC(CDC* pDC, CPrintInfo* pInfo)
```

Code 7–38 selects the GDI objects and sets the mapping mode of the device context to MM_TWIPS or MM_HIENGLISH. These mapping modes enable you to print proportional documents without knowing the printer's resolution. In Twips mapping mode, each coordinate is 1/1440th of an inch, and in High English each coordinate is 1/1000th of an inch. If you change GDI objects often, such as in a report with multiple fonts per page, then assign GDI objects into the pDC parameter in the OnPrint() function rather than using the OnPrepareDC() function.

The OnPrepareDC() function must have the m_bContinuePrinting member variable of the pInfo structure set to TRUE to continue the report or set to FALSE to end the report. This presents a way to terminate a report because the OnPrepareDC()function is called automatically by the framework. If you did not specify the maximum number of pages in the OnPreparePrinting() function, you must use m_bContinuePrinting to terminate the report.

The OnPrepareDC() function is also called prior to calling the OnDraw() function of the View class. For this reason, it is important to know when OnPrepareDC() is being called to prepare the device context for the screen or for print, which includes print preview output. If the pInfo parameter is 0 (or NULL), then it is being called for OnDraw(); if not, it is being called for OnPrint().

Normally, reports go from page 1 to page 2, and so on. But remember that this same function will be used for the print preview feature. If the user views page 1, then page 2, he or she can hit the Back button to go back to page 1. This is especially of concern if you are writing a report for a database, where you might assume (incorrectly) that you can iterate through the records of a dataset sequentially.

The OnPrepareDC()function is called repeatedly, once for each page of the report. AppWizard does not create this function. You must create it yourself.

Since the framework calls the OnPrepareDC()function automatically for print and print preview, you must terminate your report one of two ways:

1. By specifying in the OnPreparePrinting() function the maximum number of pages the report contains by using its pInfo parameter.
2. By setting the m_bContinuePrinting data member of the pInfo structure in the OnPreparePrinting() function to FALSE when the last page is printed, otherwise this data member is set to TRUE.

If you set m_bContinuePrinting to FALSE, the report terminates and the OnPrint() function will not be called again. Code 7–39 illustrates pseudo code and how the two methods above can cancel/end the report.

Code 7–39

```
CView View;
CPrintInfo PrintInfo;
//pseudo code!

if( View.OnPreparePrinting( &PrintInfo ) )
{
        CDC PrinterDC;
        PrinterDC.CreateDC( PrinterDriver, PrinterDevice, Output, &DevMode );
        View.OnBeginPrinting( &PrinterDC, &PrintInfo );
        for( int Pages=0; Pages < PrintInfo.GetMaxPage() ; Pages++ )
        {
                View.OnPrepareDC( &PrinterDC, &PrintInfo );
                if( PrintInfo.m_bContinuePrinting == FALSE )
                        break;
                View.OnPrint( &PrinterDC, &PrintInfo );// print 1 complete page
        }
        View.OnEndPrinting( &PrinterDC, &PrintInfo );
}
```

TIP

The OnPrepareDC() function is easy to add to your project using ClassWizard, instead of manually making the entries yourself in the .h and .cpp files of your project.

OnPrint()

Code 7–40 is the prototype of a function called when a page of a report is printed. OnPrint() is called to print one entire page, including any headers, footers, and the body of the text. The OnPrint() function is called once for each page in the report, and may be called multiple times for a single page if output is for a print preview. Page number information is available in the pInfo class, in the m_nCurPage data member.

Code 7-40

```
void OnPrint(CDC* pDC, CPrintInfo* pInfo)
```

Code 7-41 shows how to use the GDI functions in the CDC class to perform print the report.

Code 7-41

```
void CWhateverView::OnPrint(CDC* pDC, CPrintInfo* pInfo)
{

        CString Title;

        CFont* pOldFont = pDC->SelectObject( &m_Header );
        Title.Format( "Sample Report - Page %d", pInfo->m_nCurPage );
        pDC->TextOut( 1000, -500, Title );
        pDC->MoveTo( 1000, -1000 );
        pDC->LineTo( 7500, -1000 );

        // Select the original font
        pDC->SelectObject( pOldFont );

        // Do rest of page printing here.

        CView::OnPrint(pDC, pInfo);
}
```

Notice in Code 7-41 that hard-coded coordinates 1000 and -500 are used to print the header. It would be better to implement margins as discussed in the previous section. But, in the MM_HIENGLISH mapping mode, the report title and page number print roughly 1 inch from the left and ½ inch from the top of the page. Code 7-41 also prints a line separator about 1 inch from the left and 0.9 inch from the top, going to about 1 inch from the right margin.

You can use many CDC class functions, including TextOut(), DrawText(), Rectangle(), Ellipse(), and BitBlt() (for printing bitmaps).

The OnPrint() function is not provided by AppWizard and must be added with ClassWizard. The OnPrint() is called once per page for the report.

OnEndPrinting()

Code 7-42 is the prototype of the OnEndPrinting() function shown in Code 7-43. The OnEndPrinting() function is called at the end of a report to release any resources used by the report. This function is added to the View class when App-Wizard generates the program. However, you must provide the body of the function.

Code 7-42

```
void OnEndPrinting(CDC* pDC, CPrintInfo* pInfo)
```

Code 7-43

```
void CWhateverView::OnEndPrinting(CDC* /*pDC*/, CPrintInfo* /*pInfo*/)
{
        // Add cleanup after printing

        // Release the font object we initialized in OnBeginPrinting
        m_Header.DeleteObject();
}
```

Invoking a Report

A report is normally printed when the user selects the Print option from the menu or toolbar, with no additional coding on your part. You can generate the report from your own Print button by calling the OnFilePrint() for the OnFilePrintPreview() member function of the View class base class as shown in Code 7-44. The code above might be the message map added to handle the click of the button on the View form.

Code 7-44

```
void CWhateverView::OnPrintPreviewButton()
{
        OnFilePrintPreview();
}
```

Determining Print versus PrintPreview in MFC

There are two methods to determine if your program is printing to a printer or displaying the report in Print Preview. Normally, this won't be a concern for you, but sometimes in longer reports you may want to buffer data for print preview, but not for an actual print because the print preview may need to re-create page 2 after page 1.

You can either rely on the m_bPreview data member of the pInfo parameter that is passed to all the MFC print functions or you can call the CDC::IsPrinting() function from the passed CDC pointer as shown in Code 7-45.

Code 7-45

```
void CWhateverView::OnPrint(CDC* pDC, CPrintInfo* pInfo)
{

        if( pDC->IsPrinting() )
        {
        // it's printing
        }
        else
        {
                // Print Preview
        }
}
```

Important Members of CPrintInfo

TheCPrintInfo class describes a report and is used to track a document (DocObject) and a report. In a report, there is a distinction between a printer page and a document page. A printer page is a physical sheet or paper. A document page is includes the layout of the document—for example, a folded brochure document might have four pages that print on two printer pages (front and back). The information provided in Tables 7.2 and 7.3 address printer pages and not document-pages.

Table 7.2 Data Members

Member	Usage
m_bDirect	Set this option to TRUE in OnPreparePrinting to bypass the printer dialog box.
m_bPreview	Indicates if the report is a preview.
m_bContinuePrinting	Set this to FALSE in OnPrepareDC to terminate the report.
m_nCurPage	Contains the current page number (incremented automatically).
m_nNumPreviewPages	Indicates how many pages are visible in a preview. You can set this value to 1 or 2 in the OnBeginPrinting function to control the number of pages displayed side-by-side for print preview.
m_lpUserData	A pointer to data for your own use, not used by MFC. You can put anything you want in this value, including an indication of the type of report you want to print.
m_rectDraw	A rectangle, indicating the printable page area.
m_strPageDesc	Contains a format string for printing the page #, for example: "Page %u" or "Pages %u-%u."
	These are the default strings provided, but you needn't use them. Note that by default the two strings appear as one string in the data member, separated by a carriage return.

Table 7.3 Member Functions

Function	Usage
SetMinPage()	Sets number of the first page to print.
SetMaxPage()	Sets the number of the last page to print.
GetMinPage()	Returns the number of the first page to print.
GetMaxPage()	Returns the number of the last page to print.

Multiple Report Types

A common misconception of the MFC CView class printing framework is that the framework only supports one report because there is only one OnPrint() function. Several types of reports can be accommodated by writing a function for each report format then calling the appropriate function from the OnPrint() function as needed. Codes 7–46 and 7–47 illustrate this technique. You can write similar routine for the OnPrepareDC() function to select fonts or determine when a report is finished.

Code 7–46

```
void CWhateverView::OnPrintPeople( CDC* pDC, CPrintInfo* pInfo )
{
     // Do output of people report here
}
void CWhateverView::OnPrintPlaces( CDC* pDC, CPrintInfo* pInfo )
{
     // Do output of place report here
}
```

Code 7–47

```
void CTest11View::OnPrint(CDC* pDC, CPrintInfo* pInfo)
{
     // Determine and output correct type of report
     if( m_ReportType== 0 )
          OnPrintPeople( pDC, pInfo );
     else
          OnPrintPlaces( pDC, pInfo );
     CView::OnPrint(pDC, pInfo);
}
```

Remember

◯	Use the PageSetupDlg() function or CPageSetupDialog class to implement margins in your reports.
	Use the PrintDlg() function or the CPrintDialog class to get a Device Context to the current printer.
◯	Once you have the Device Context for the printer, you output text and shapes the same way you would to the screen with TextOut(), Rectangle(), BitBlt(), and other GDI functions.
	All printers have a nonprintable area that must be deducted from the user's margin settings for accurate placement.
	Mapping modes like MM_TWIPS or MM_HIENGLISH will make it much easier for you to deal with proportionate appearance, given different printer resolutions.
◯	The Document/View architecture of MFC provides Print and Print Preview with very little coding on your part.

Databases

Database Concepts

This chapter shows you how to create a database program using MFC classes (and not using SDK) because they greatly simplify database access and can also be used with non-MFC programs by simply including the database classes in the program.

A database is a collection of data and one or more programs with the ability to sort, search, and correlate that data. While Visual C++ is not a database program, it will permit you to create a front-end program that can present data from a database to users and permit them to sort, search, add, and edit the data.

A database is made up of two primary pieces: The data that is stored in the database and the programs that interact with the data. Some examples of database programs include Microsoft Access, Microsoft SQL Server, and Oracle Server. Sometimes the database program is said to be a back end.

A database application asks the database back end to search, sort, insert, or change records in the database. Figure 8–1 illustrates the relationship between your program and the database.

In Figure 8–1 the application (left) makes calls to functions to access the database program (middle). The database program accesses the database (right). When the database program is finished, it returns the results to your application. The term "front end" is often used to refer to the application program. The database program can be an application or a dynamic linking library (DLL) with database access capabilities. The term "Database Driver" is commonly used when a DLL is used as our interface to a database.

A database is comprised of one or more phyiscal files on a disk. Database software manufacturers determine the number of physical files used. For example, Microsoft Access stores all of its data in a large single file with an .MDB extension, and Microsoft FoxPro stores data in separate files with .DB extensions.

Database software such as Microsoft Access and Microsoft FoxPro are referred to as local databases because the application program directly accesses data files. Direct access is possible even if the files are stored on another computer and are linked using a network.

Figure 8–1   A database program interfaces with an application program.

SQL Server and Oracle are examples of a client/server database. A client/server database requires an application program (client) to send a request to the database program (server). The applications program does not directly interface with the database. Instead, the applications program communicates to the database program, which directly accesses the database. Client/server databases are normally more robust and secure than local databases and provide features such as stored procedures and transaction processing.

Data in a database is organized into tables similar in structure to a spreadsheet, where rows are called records and columns are called fields. Data that is similar to other data is stored in a field. For example, all first names are similar data and therefore stored in the same field.

Data that is related to other data is stored in the same record. For example, John is data in the first name field and Smith is data in the last name field. Both John and Smith are in the same record because the first name is related the last name (see Table 8.1).

Relationships

Data is organized into tables based on normalization rules, which assures that the same data does not appear in more than one table. This makes it efficent to locate a record. Normalization is discussed later in this section.

Data in two tables are logical joined together by using a common value. Databases that use this technique are called *relational databases*, because the database can relate one record to another record.

In the Stock example shown in Figure 8–2, records are identified by a unique ID that is used to relate tables. Using the Portfolio table, you can see that it contains the StockID field. When looking at a specific Portfolio record, you can link the stock table and the trade table by using the StockID field. By searching the Stock table, you can retrieve the company name for the portfolio record from the Stock table and the current price of the stock from the Trade table. Figure 8–2 is further explained in *The Stock Database Example* section that follows. We will now examine several types of relationships between records.

Table 8.1   Columns Represent Pieces of Data

FirstName	LastName	Age	Sex
John	Smith	24	M
Maria	Valdez	32	F

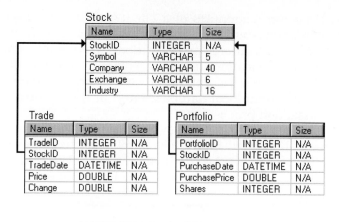

Figure 8–2 Tables in the Stock database are related to each other by common data.

One-to-One

A one-to-one relationship is where one record in a table matches to only one record in another table.

One-to-Many

A one-to-many relationship is where one record in a table matches two or more records from another table. In our example, one Stock record may have many Trade records or many Portfolio records.

Many-to-Many

A many-to-many relationship is where two or more records in a table match two or more records from another table. Creating a many-to-many relationship is typically considered bad database design.

Normalization

Normalization is the process of applying normalization rules to remove redundant data in a database and place one copy of the data in a table. Redundant data takes up unnecessary space and can cause unexpected side effects such as variations in the spelling of data.

Imagine there are fifty trades in our Trade Table, all for Microsoft. If the name of the stock were part of the trade record, then Microsoft's name is repeated fifty times in the trade table. Let's assume that sometimes "Microsoft" was used for some records and for other records "Microsoft, Inc." is used. A search of the table for "Microsoft, Inc." would not return "Microsoft." This is one of the disadvantages of having redundant data in a database. While normalization can reduce disk space and increase searching performance, overnormalization can be detremental to performance.

Structured Query Language (SQL)

SQL is a language for querying and modifying most popular database systems. The databases themselves—such as Access or SQL Server—execute SQL statements. MFC programs execute SQL commands by using the CDatabase and CRecordset classes to interact with databases.

Record Selection

A SELECT statement is used to select records from one or more tables. The format for the SELECT statement is shown in Code 8–1. Code 8–2 illustrates various ways to use the SELECT statement. The first SELECT statement returns all records sorted in order by the Company field from the Stock table, where the exchange field is equal to "Technology."

The next SELECT statement returns the number of persons over the age of 50 contained in the person table.

The last SELECT statement returns all records from both the Company and Trade tables where the StockID is the same in both tables and the price in the Trade table is greater than 15. These records are sorted by price and trade date.

Code 8–1

```
SELECT fieldlist FROM tablelist [WHERE criterialist] [ORDER BY orderlist]
```

Fieldlist is a list of fields, or "*" to indicate all fields. Tablelist is a list of one or more tables. Criterialist is a criteria list, such as "AGE = 50 and STATE = 'NY'," and is optional. Orderlist is a list of fields to order the results by and is optional.

Code 8–2

```
SELECT * FROM Stock WHERE Exchange='Technology' ORDER BY Company
SELECT count(*)FROM person WHERE age > 50
SELECT * FROM company, Trade
       WHERE Trade.StockID = Company.StockID
       AND Trade.Price > 15.00
       ORDER BY Trade.Price, Trade.TradeDate
```

The Stock Database Example

Throughout this section, we will be referring to a Stock database, which is used for tracking stocks in the stock market. The database will be extremely simple since its only purpose is to serve as an example. However, the database will have several tables that are related to each other.

The definition of the tables in a database is called its data model. There are four tables in our Stock database (see Figure 8–2): Stock, Trade, Portfolio, and TableIDs.

Stock Table

The Stock table contains information about a company in the stock market. The columns for this table are shown in Table 8.2. The StockID field is an integer, or numeric data field, while the rest are character- or string-type fields.

Trade Table

The Trade table contains information requires to record a stock trade (see Table 8.3). The trade is linked to a stock table record using the StockID field to form a relationship in the database. A stock may have many trades, but a trade will have only one stock.

This relationship is also called a *master/transaction* relationship. This means that between the two tables, we can see the activity of the stock throughout the day, much like your credit card bill has transactions for the month.

Portfolio Table

The Portfolio table (see Table 8.4) is used to keep track of the stocks in a customer's portfolio. Information contained in the Portfolio table includes the data of the pur-

Table 8.2   Columns for the Stock Table

Column	Purpose
StockID	A unique numeric ID that will help in locating the company.
Symbol	The symbol for the company as listed in the stock market. For example, "MSFT" is the symbol for Microsoft.
Company	The full name of the company—for example, "Microsoft, Inc."
Exchange	This is the stock market exchange where the company's stock is traded—for example, NASDAQ (National Association of Securities Dealers Automated Quotation) or NYSE (New York Stock Exchange).
Industry	The industry that the company is involved in—for example, Technology or Finance.

Table 8.3   Columns for the Trade Table

Column	Purpose
TradeID	Unique numeric ID for the trade record.
StockID	A numeric ID that will help in locating the company for the trade in the stock table.
TradeDate	The symbol for the company as listed in the stock market. For example, "MSFT" is the symbol for "Microsoft."
Price	The price of the trade.
Change	The change in price since the previous trade.

Table 8.4   Columns for the Portfolio Table

Column	Purpose
PortfolioID	Unique numeric ID for the portfolio record.
StockID	A numeric ID that will help us in locating the company for the porfolio record.
PurchaseDate	The date and time that the stock was purchased (added to the portfolio).
PurchasePrice	The amount paid for each stock share.
Shares	The number of shares purchased.

Table 8.5   Associate the Table Name with the Last Unique ID Used for the Table ID Table

Column	Purpose
TableName	Name of the table we want an ID for.
LastID	Last unique ID used in that table.

Table 8.6   Data in the Table ID Table

TableName	LastID
Stock	25
Trade	134
Portfolio	5

chase, number of shares, and purchase price per share. The Portfolio table also has a relationship to the Stock table by using the StockID field.

TableIDs Table

The TableIDs table has nothing to do with stocks. It was created as a method for producing unique IDs for each of the other tables. Later we will discuss several methods for creating unique IDs, but in our example this table has the format shown in Table 8.5. Table 8.6 is an example of how this table might appear.

Let's assume that the TableIDs are used to track the last ID. Therefore, the last Stock table ID is 25. The next Stock ID is 26. We will be demonstrating how to write sample code to easily use the TableIDs table to keep track of IDs.

How to Connect to Database Management Software

Figure 8–3 demonstrates the various methods used by an application to access to data stored in a database. These include:

ODBC—Open Database Connectivity: A generic, relatively simple, and time-tested means to access a wide variety of database types without modifying application source code.

DAO—Data Access Objects: A newer technology than ODBC offering improved performance over ODBC when working with certain ISAM type databases such as

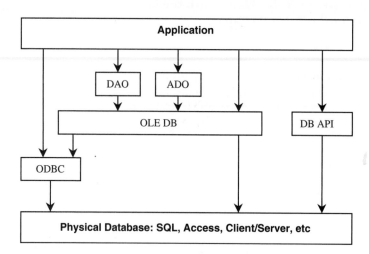

Figure 8–3 Various ways an application can access data.

Microsoft Access. Also has the ability to work with ODBC itself. DAO is also designed to appear similar to the database objects of Visual Basic.

ADO—ActiveX Database Objects: This is newer than DAO with similar capabilities. ADO tends to be a bit more generic than DAO and does not provide some DAO features such as table compaction for Access.

OLE DB—Object Linking and Embedding Database Base: This is a lower-level data access method than DAO and ADO but is used by both. Think of DAO and ADO as simpler interfaces to using the OLE DB directly.

DB API: This method is specific to a selected database. While DB API performance is sometimes better than the other options, it means that you must use nonstandard API calls unique to the database and your program will require major changes if you decide to use a different database.

DB API is also referred to as RDO—Remote Data Object. This method can still be used, but it has never caught on to the degree of the other methods mentioned above, so we will not cover it in detail here.

ODBC Connection

ODBC is a set of DLL files and database drivers that permit a standard way to access different databases. ODBC acts as a translator between your application and the database. You can write a program to access the data generically and your program will work with any database that provides an ODBC driver. For example, ODBC provides a way to write your program to use ODBC functions that ODBC then translates to either Access or SQL Server function calls.

Here's how your application works with ODBC and a database. Your application communicates with ODBC, which in turn communicates with the database ODBC driver. The ODBC driver then communicates with the database. ODBC has a setup applet in the Control Panel (see Figure 8–4) that enables you to setup information about the database. Figure 8–5 displays your application's connection to an ODBC driver.

Each database that is set up in the ODBC Data Source Administrator has a name called a Data Source Name or DSN, which is used by your program to connect to the database (see Figure 8–6).

In Figure 8–4, PNStocks data source name has already been created. You can see that it is a Microsoft Access database because it uses the Microsoft Access driver. By selecting the Configure button, you'll see the Microsoft Access database setup dialog (see Figure 8–6).

The PNStocks data source name is a Microsoft Access database that is physically located on the D:\work\Docs\Book\Chap8 folder. The name of the physical data-

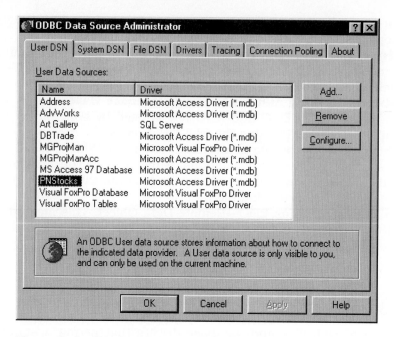

Figure 8–4 The ODBC Control Panel Applet.

base file is PNStocks.mdb. Once the database is configured, your application simply asks ODBC to open that data source name without regard to the type of database.

DAO Connection

DAO is also a generic way for your program to access a number of different types of databases and include features different than ODBC. These include:

- A more efficient to access the "Jet" database engine, which is the Microsoft Access database engine.
- Access to any ODBC data source.
- Direct access to ISAM-type databases such as DBase, Paradox, and Fox-Pro and also installable drivers.
- DAO is COM- or OLE Automation–based, where ODBC is API–function based.

Figure 8–5 The ODBC data source relationship.

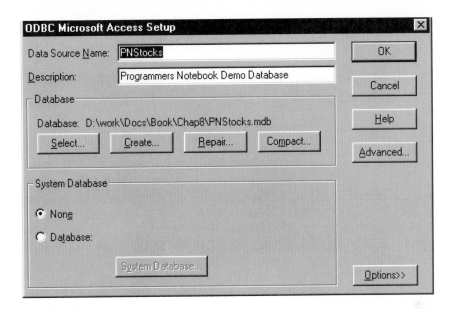

Figure 8–6 The ODBC Microsoft Access Setup dialog box.

Dealing with COM or OLE programming requires the use of objects and classes defined in other applications. The data types involved in COM are a bit more complicated to work with if you are familiar with the C++ data types such as CString, but conversion classes and macros are available. API programming means that you simply have a set of data types and functions that work against those types to achieve your goal.

For MFC programs, access to databases via ODBC or DAO are nearly identical. When your application uses ODBC, you'll use the CDatabase and CRecordset classes. When you use DAO, you'll use the CDaoDatabase and CDaoRecordset classes. The CDatabase and CDaoDatabase classes and the CRecordset and CDaoRecordset classes are nearly identical.

The DAO method of database access also provides another set of classes for accessing databases refered to as the dbDAO classes. The primary difference between the dbDAO classes and the CDaoRecordset classes are that dbDAO:

- Is not tied into ClassWizard as the other classes are and is therefore slightly more tedious to work with.
- Is modeled after the Visual Basic methods for accessing a database, while the CDaoDatabase is modeled after the CDatabase.
- Has classes to assist in the access of data, such as VARIANT data type access, where the MFC versions do not.

- Is not tied to the other MFC classes such as CTime and CString the way that CDatabase and CDaoDatabase are.

We will not discuss the dbDAO classes in this chapter; however, we will offer demonstrations of DAO access using the CDaoDatabase and CDaoRecordset classes.

Installing DAO

If you installed Visual C++ using typical install parameters, then DAO may not yet be installed on your machine. In order to install DAO so that you can use the dbDAO classes in your application, refer to the online documentation that came with your compiler. Normally, on one of the Visual Studio CDs there will be a \DAOSDK\Retail folder. In that folder will be a set of folders named Disk1, Disk2, and so on. Run the Setup program in the Disk1 folder to install the DAO libraries.

The \DAOSDK folder also contains a Redist folder. This folder contains several folders named Disk1, Disk2, and so on. These folders contain the disk images for the DAO installation that you should provide to anyone to whom you distribute your program, so that those people can install the needed DAO components.

ODBC is now a part of the Windows operating system. You can assume this is already installed, although your custom data source names may need to be set up.

ADO Connection

ADO is the standard way for Microsoft products to access a database. ADO requires a stronger knowledge of COM than the other methods of database access.

ADO is implemented in MFC programs as a series of unique classes that are not directly tied to MFC classes. This means that non-MFC programs can use the ADO classes, but also means that MFC programs that use them can not take advantage of the features like ClassWizards Member Variable tab to map an edit box directly to a field in a table (it can be done manually).

The ADO classes are COM-based classes and will present an extra learning curve to anyone not already familiar with COM programming, specifically in data handling, and COM interface method calling.

Should You Use ODBC, DAO, or ADO?

It depends on your needs. ODBC is standardized and is a time-tested, while DAO provides more functionality for database management and improved performance when dealing with Microsoft Access databases. The following list is a summary of the key advantages of the three types of database access.

ODBC

- Best when a project already supports ODBC.
- Best when you want good access to a wide variety of databases.
- Best when you want access to relational SQL server-style databases.
- MFC classes and ClassWizard can work with ODBC recordsets.

DAO

- Best if you are familiar with Visual Basic.
- Improved error handling and batch processing.
- An efficient means of working with Access databases.
- MFC classes and ClassWizard can work with DAO recordsets.

ADO

- Good if you are familiar with COM programming.
- More standard in non-MFC programs (though ODBC and DAO will work).
- Asynchronous in certain function calls.
- Supports component-based ActiveX data-aware controls.

Database and Recordset Connections

Before we can access a table in a database, we need to create an instance of a database connection object to connect to the database. A database connection object serves two purposes:

- To serve as a constant connection to the database in the event a login and password is required to access the database.
- Ability to execute database SQL commands against tables in the database.

CDatabase/CDaoDatabase

The CDatabase/CDaoDatabase classes provide a connection between your application and either an ODBC- or DAO-accessible database (respectively). While the CRecordset and CDaoRecordset provide connections between your application and one or more tables, they do so using the connection provided by these database classes. If you create a CRecordset or CDaoRecordset object, without supplying a CDatabase or CDaoDatabase, then the recordset object will simply create its own database connection object. This ability for each recordset object to create its own database object can cause undesirable side effects however, such as when a database connection requires a logon and password.

Let's assume that your application needs access to a database that requires a logon and password (such as SQL Server). Imagine you coded the program so that each recordset object you created was not given a database object, and had to create its own (database object). Each time a recordset object was instantiated and opened, it would create and open its own database connection object, which in turn would pop up a logon dialog.

In contrast, if you coded the program so that you created and opened one database object (CDatabase or CDaoDatabase), and then used that same open connection with all new recordset objects (CRecordset or CDaoRecordset), then the login process would only need to be done once. This approach is basically several record-set objects sharing, or pooled, with one database connection. Code 8–3 contains the prototypes for the constructors of the CRecordset and CDaoRecordset, which is where you can specify the database object to be shared.

Both constructors take a pointer to their respective types of databases with a default parameter of NULL. If you do not provide a CDatabase object or CDaoDatabase object to these functions, then each of the recordsets creates its database connection.

Code 8–3

```
CRecordset( CDatabase* pDatabase = NULL);
CDaoRecordset( CDaoDatabase* pDatabase = NULL );
```

Retrieving and Sorting Data from a Database

A C++ class called a recordset is used to manipulate data stored in a database such as retrieving and sorting data. A query is created using SQL to request records from the database. Code 8–4 illustrates a typical SQL query.

Code 8–4

```
SELECT * FROM stock
WHERE symbol='MSFT'
```

The SELECT SQL clause specifies the fields of the records that we want to retrieve. An asterisk as shown in Code 8–4 is a wild card character and requests to see all fields of records that match the criteria.

The FROM clause specifies the table that contains the requested fields. In this example we are requesting all the fields from the Stock table that match the criteria.

The WHERE clause specifies the criteria that must be matched for the database to return the requested fields. In this example, symbol is the name of a field in the Stock table and MSFT is the value within the symbol field that we want to match. MSFT is a literal value and therefore is enclosed with signal quotations.

The sort order for a recordset defines how to the order in which matching records will be retrieved. Code 8–5 illustrates a typical SQL query that specifies a sort order. In this example we are retrieving all the fields in every record of the Stock table because there isn't a WHERE clause that sets a criteria for matching particular records.

Code 8–5

```
SELECT * FROM stock
ORDER BY industry, company, exchange DESC
```

The ORDER BY clause lists fields names whose values dictate the sort order of the records. Three fields are used in this example. Records will be sorted by industry, then within industry by company, then within company by exchange.

The sort order is accending by default. In this example we want to use decending order therefore we use the DESC attribute to specify the direction of thesort order.

Using ODBC, DAO, or ADO in Your Projects

Adding ODBC, DAO, or ADO to your projects is accomplished by your selections made in the MFC AppWizard Step 2 of 6 dialog. Make sure that when running App-Wizard, in the Step 2 of 6 dialog you indicate some sort of database support other than "None" (which is the default) whenever you use the ODBC or DAO recordset classes in your MFC project. If you selected "None" in the dialog, then you must manually add a #include for the afxdb.h file to your stdafx.h file to use the database classes.

Database Connections with ODBC and CDatabase

The CDatabase class provides key functions as shown in Code 8–6 for connecting and disconnecting to a database.

Code 8–6

```
virtual BOOL Open( LPCTSTR lpszDSN, BOOL bExclusive = FALSE,
        BOOL bReadOnly = FALSE, LPCTSTR lpszConnect = "ODBC;",
        BOOL bUseCursorLib = TRUE );
virtual BOOL OpenEx( LPCTSTR lpszConnect, DWORD dwOptions = 0 );
virtual void Close( );
```

The Open() and OpenEx() functions open a database connection and Close() will close the connection. If the Open call fails because either an ODBC data source is not found or the database that the ODBC data source name refers to is not valid, then a CDBException is thrown by the Open() or OpenEx() function.

The parameters passed to Open() and OpenEx() indicate which ODBC data source name to open and may also contain extra parameters for the connection such as a logon name and password for the desired database. In its simplest form, the Open() function can be called with just the ODBC datasource name as shown in Code 8–7.

Code 8–7

```
CDatabase X;
X.Open( "PNStocks" );
```

The lpszDSN parameter in Code 8–6 is the name of the ODBC data source to open. The bExclusive and bReadOnly parameters are Boolean parameters that indicate if the database should be opened in an exclusive (no other users can access the database while open) or read-only (you cannot make any changes to the database or its tables) mode. The lpszConnect string indicates extra parameters you might want to pass to an ODBC data source, as well as (optionally) the data source name. If you place the datasource name in the lpszConnect parameter, then the lpszDSN parameter should be NULL.

Code 8–8 shows how to connect to an ODBC data source for SQL server that might have a logon and password required for access.

Code 8–8

```
CDatabase X;
CString Connect;

Connect.Format( "ODBC;DSN=Art Gallery;UID=%s;PWD=%s", UserName, Password );
X.Open( NULL, FALSE, FALSE, Connect );
```

Code 8–8 assumes that UserName is a character string with the user logon name and Password is a character string with their password. The lpszConnect parameter for both Open() and OpenEx() is broken down into sections shown in Table 8.7.

The fifth parameter for Open() is a flag to indicate if the cursor library should be used. This is a library that provides certain update abilities, forward and reverse record reading ability (some ODBC drivers support forward-only movement through a table), and support for dynaset style recordsets. If you are going to use a recordset directly for simple queries, then you can make the library parameter FALSE (by default, it is TRUE).

If a database requires a logon and password, and you do not provide one, then a logon box will be displayed automatically, such as shown in Figure 8–7.

Table 8.7 The Values the lpszConnect Parameter

Setting	Meaning
ODBC;	Indicates this is an ODBC connect string and is required.
DSN=	Indicates the desired ODBC data source name, as setup in the ODBC control panel applet.
UID=	Indicates the name to be used for the logon. This is optional.
PWD=	Indicates the password to be used for the logon. This is optional.

Code 8–9 demonstrates how to use a dynamic, read-only query to retrieve the count of records from the Stock table of the PNStocks data source (database).

Code 8–9

```
// Create and open the database
CDatabase db;
db.Open( NULL, FALSE, FALSE, "ODBC;DSN=PNStocks", FALSE );

// Create a recordset, and open it with a SQL Select statement
CRecordset R(&db);
R.Open( AFX_DB_USE_DEFAULT_TYPE, "select count(*) from Stock" );

// Retrieve a field from the open recordset
CString Count;
R.GetFieldValue( (short)0, Count );

// Count now has the count of records, in a CString variable
```

Normally, you won't use CRecordset directly except for SQL operations as shown in Code 8–9. For recordsets that can be edited or records inserted or deleted, you create table-specific recordsets, as described later in this chapter, which are derived from CRecordsets.

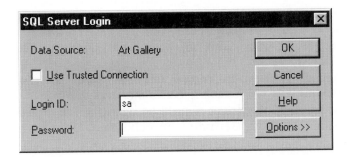

Figure 8–7 Log into the database if you previous did not provide login information.

If you create a CDatabase object that will be used by recordset objects throughout your program, they would normally be created as data members of your View or application class objects.

Database Connections with DAO and CDaoDatabase

First, insert Code 8–10 into the stdafx.h file. Make sure that the path to the msado15.dll file (in italics) is correct for your computer. The rename options for the #import will rename the EOF and BOF properties from the DLL to IsEOF and IsBOF to look a bit more like the standard MFC recordset classes.

The #import line should be all one line. #import will open the specified DLL file, and create interface files in the DEBUG or RELEASE folder named msado15.tlh and msado15.tli, which the compiler will use automatically. Other than the #import line, there are no extra steps to start using the COM classes in the msado15.dll file from your program.

Code 8–10

```
#import "C:\Program Files\Common Files\System\ado\msado15.dll" no_namespace
        rename("EOF", "IsEOF") rename("BOF", "IsBOF")
```

The CDaoDatabase class provides key functions as shown in Code 8–11 for connecting and disconnecting to a database.

Code 8–11

```
virtual void Open( LPCTSTR lpszName, BOOL bExclusive = FALSE,
     BOOL bReadOnly = FALSE, LPCTSTR lpszConnect = _T("") );
virtual void Create( LPCTSTR lpszName, LPCTSTR lpszLocale = dbLangGeneral,
     int dwOptions = 0 );
virtual void Close( );
```

The second, third, and fourth parameters to the Open() function are indentical to the parameters to the CDatabase::Open() function discussed previously and can specify exclusive and read-only access to a database as well as an ODBC datasource name, logon, and password options for the desired database. The *lpszName* parameter for Open is the path of an Access database (with a .mdb extension).

The Create() function can be used to create a new Access database file. The *lpszName* specifies the path to create the Acceess file, and the *lpszLocale* parameter indicates what type of language driver should be used for the new database (such as dbLangGeneral for English, German, French, and others, or dbLangArabic, dbLangGreek, etc.).

The *dwOptions* parameter to the Create() function indicates options like what type of Access database should be created, such as dbEncrypt, or dbVersion30.

An example of creating a CDaoDatabase object and opening the database in the current (working) directory of the executable program is shown in Code 8–12.

If you create a CDaoDatabase object that will be used by recordset objects throughout your program, they would normally be created as data members of your View or application class objects.

Code 8–12

```
CDaoDatabase db;
db.Open( ".\\pnstocks.mdb" );
```

The _bstr_t and _variant_t Types in ADO

ADO utilizes COM, which means you must use COM data types when passing parameters or retrieving return values from functions in the COM family such as BSTR and VARIANT. BSTR is really a double-byte wide character array data type. COM does not use single-byte wide characters such as used in C++ by default. Instead, for international language support, it utilizes a two-byte-per-character method. So, in normal C++, where you might expect to see Code 8–13 you use Code 8–14.

Code 8–13

```
char Name[32];
```

Code 8–14

```
short Name[33];
```

The char_w data type in C++ is similar to a double-byte character string array for support of international languages, as is Unicode on the Windows platform. Since this would cause all sorts of problems with normal string functions such as strlen or strcpy, there are helper classes and macros for dealing with the double-byte character strings such as _bstr_t. The _bstr_t object has functions to convert back and forth between normal strings and double-byte wide strings. It also supports the dynamic memory management for these strings using the Windows SysAllocString() and SysFreeString() functions. The _bstr_t object provides functions for conversion to and from normal char array strings and BSTRs.

The VARIANT is really a combination of a structure and a union. It is an interesting data structure in that it has the ability to represent any type of data including an "empty" or NULL value. The actual VARIANT type is defined as shown in Code 8–15.

Databases

Code 8-15

```
typedef struct tagVARIANT {
        VARTYPE vt;
        unsigned short wReserved1;
        unsigned short wReserved2;
        unsigned short wReserved3;
        union {
                unsigned char bVal;
                short iVal;
                long lVal;
                float fltVal;.
                // Portions removed for readability
                VARIANT FAR* pvarVal;
        void FAR* byref;
        };
};
```

The VARIANT data type stores in its vt member, which is the actual data type that it holds. Then, based on the value of vt, you would look in the specific data members of the union for the real data, such as iVal or lVal. An example of initializing a VARIANT is shown in Code 8-16.

Code 8-16

```
VARIANT V;
V.vt = VT_I4; // Set for a 4-byte integer
V.lVal = 123456789; // Initialize the lVal data member with the data
```

The _variant_t data type is a helper class for the VARIANT data type (MFC also provides a COleVariant class for a similar purpose). The _variant_t provides functions for conversion between variant and normal data types, as well as the ability to convert a variant from one type to another (i.e., from a BSTR to an integer).

Database Connections with ADO and _ConnectionPtr

Later in this chapter we will provide an ADO helper class that will simplify some of the more tedious tasks of using ADO in your programs. For now we'll show how to create a database connection without using the helper class.

Using ADO, we establish a database connection using the _ConnectionPtr class, which is created by the #import statement described in *Using ODBC, DAO and ADO in Your Projects*. Each recordset that you open is established from this _ConnectionPtr object. To use the _ConnectionPtr object, you must first instantiate it, then create the COM object for C++ object, and then provide database connection information.

There is an important aspect to be aware of for the ADO classes like _Connection-Ptr and _RecordsetPtr. This is that you will see the "." and "->" operators intermixed with the same object. This is a technique of using the ADO classes in that each provides a C++ operator-> function that returns another type of object.

So, where you would normally see the "->" operator used with pointers, you will now see it often with objects and not pointers as shown in Code 8–17. This is still normal C++, just slightly advanced in nature. If the SomeClass has an operator-> function, it would not be uncommon to see statements as shown in code 8–18. Even though Object was *not* declared as a pointer to an object. Code 8–19 demonstrates the code needed to create and initialize an ADO _ConnectionPtr data object:

Code 8–17

```
SomeClass Object;
Object.MemberFunc();
```

Code 8–18

```
SomeClass Object;
Object->MemberFunc();
```

Code 8–19

```
// Call CoInitialize to initialize COM (required for ADO
CoInitialize(0);

// Create a _ConnectionPtr object
_ConnectionPtr Connection;

// Initialize the object with an ADODB Connection COM object
Connection.CreateInstance( "ADODB.Connection" );

// Open the connection to an Access database in the current folder
Connection->Open( "Provider=Microsoft.Jet.OLEDB.4.0; Data Source=.\\PNStocks.mdb",
"", "", -1 );
```

In the Code 8–19, the CoInitialize() function should really be placed in the CWinApp::InitInstance function of your project. We place it here to emphasize that it must be called at least once (and preferably only once) in order for ADO to work. Next, a _ConnectionPtr object named Connection is instantiated. Then, the CreateInstance() function of the _ConnectionPtr function is called to initialize the COM aspect of the object. The Connection object is now linked to an ADODB Connection COM object. The CreateInstance() function is overloaded and can also take the CLSID of the ADODB Connection object, but the form above is much easier to read.

Finally, the connection to the database is opened. Note the use of the "->" operator and not the "." operator, as discussed earlier in this topic. The Open() function for a _ConnectionPtr takes four parameters as shown in Code 8–20.

Code 8–20

```
HRESULT Open( _bstr_t ConnectionString, _bstr_t UserID, _bstr_t Password,
long Options );
```

The first parameter, ConnectionString, indicates the connection string to the database and optionally provides information about the type of database, as well as the name or location of the database.

Next, the UserID and Password parameters indicate the logon and password name for the user to connect to the database, and may be blank ("") if none are needed. The Options parameter indicates options for opening the database such as shown in Code 8–21.

Code 8–21

```
adAsyncConnect          Indicates to open the connection asynchronously
adConnectUnspecified    Indicates the connection to be opened synchronously.
```

The ConnectionString Parameter and ADO Providers

The _ConnectionPtr object and ADO work on the concept of a data provider. A data provider is another name for a database engine. Examples of data providers are SQL Server, Access, and Oracle. The _ConnectionPtr object has a Provider property that you can set separately or you can specify the provider from within the ConnectionString parameter As shown in Code 8–22 and Code 8–23.

Code 8–22

```
Connection->Provider = "Microsoft.Jet.OLEDB.4.0";
Connection->Open( "Data Source=.\\PNStocks.mdb", "", "", -1 );
```

Code 8–23

```
Connection->Open( "Provider=Microsoft.Jet.OLEDB.4.0; Data Source=.\\PNStocks.mdb",
       "", "", -1 );
```

Both Codes 8–22 and 8–23 accomplish the same thing—that is, to open the PNStocks.MDB Access file in the current folder using the Microsoft Jet (Access) data provider. Notice how, in both cases, the provider is defined as a string. Possible data providers and their provider strings are shown in Table 8.8.

Table 8.8 Data Providers and Related Strings

Provider String	Provider/Database Type	Notes
Microsoft.Jet.OLEDB. 4.0	Access database	Data Source=? indicates location of MDB database file.
SQLOLEDB	Microsoft SQL Server	Data Source=? indicates name of SQL server. Has extra parameter of "DATABASE=?" to define the database name to work in.
MSDAORA	Oracle SQL Server	Data Source=? indicates name of SQL server.
MSDASQL	An ODBC data source	Supports use of DSN=? to define the ODBC data source.

Retrieving Data Using ODBC and CRecordset

> **NOTE**
>
> Before using the code and steps in this topic, you must make sure that your desired ODBC data source has been set up in the ODBC Administrator applet of Control Panel.

The CRecordset is the main class when interfacing with tables in a database using ODBC. You will not often work directly with the CRecordset, however. Instead, use ClassWizard to generate classes derived from the CRecordset class. This new custom class will inherit all the functionality of the CRecordset and will also have member variables that will be automatically bound to fields in the data table.

Later in this chapter, we will show how to map the member variables of these custom CRecordset classes directly to on-screen controls with very little coding.

We will demonstrate how to create a recordset for the Stock table from our PN-Stocks sample database. The Stock table in the database contains unique ID, stock symbol, company name, industry, and exchange fields. When we are done creating our custom class, it too will have those fields as data members. We will refer to the new class as the CStockSet class.

First, go to ClassWizard from the View menu choice. Click the Add Class button in ClassWizard and select New from the drop-down menu. The New Class dialog will appear, as shown in Figure 8–8.

In the New Class dialog, we have already entered CStockSet in the Name field, and we have changed the Base Class to be CRecordset. Click OK.

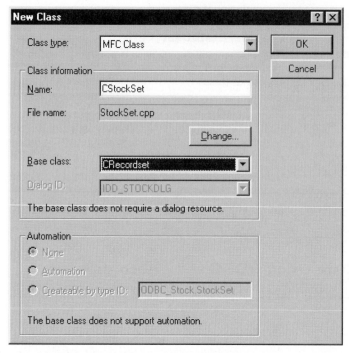

Figure 8–8   Adding a new CRecordset-derived class.

Once you have clicked OK, ClassWizard will display the Data base options dialog, where we can select ODBC, DAO, or OLE DB. Select ODBC in this dialog, and then select the ODBC datasource name for the database.

For this demonstration, the ODBC datasource name is PNStocks. A snapshot recordset type will buffer records in your queries so that if another user alters a record in your query, you will not be aware of the changes.

A dynaset on the other hand will show you the latest data even if another user has changed the data after you opened the query. Click OK on this dialog, and you will next see the Select Data Tables dialog, as shown in Figure 8–9.

In the Select Database Tables dialog, you can select one or more tables from the ODBC data source you previously selected. For now, just select the Stock table and click OK. To select multiple tables you would simply click on more than one table. If you were to select multiple tables for an SQL join statement, then you would be responsible for defining the join portion of the where clause in the m_strFilter data member of the new class (this will be discussed later).

Once you click OK on the above dialog, you will be returned to ClassWizard. You can now close ClassWizard.

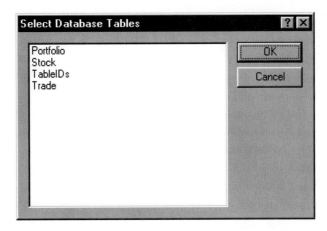

Figure 8–9 Select the required tables from the Select Data Tables dialog box.

The process above would have added a new class to your project named CStockSet. Code 8–24 shows some of the key portions of that new class, which can be found in the StockSet.cpp and StockSet.h files.

Code 8–25 contains the key points of the code from the CStockSet.cpp file (which will also be in any other CRecordset-derived class you make with ClassWizard). Now that we have the CStockSet class, we can use it in our program as shown in Code 8–26. Remember not to forget to #include the StockSet.h file.

Code 8–24

```
class CStockSet : public CRecordset // Derived from CRecordset
{
public:
        // Constructor takes pointer to CDatabase, but may be NULL or blank
        CStockSet(CDatabase* pDatabase = NULL);
        DECLARE_DYNAMIC(CStockSet)

        // Field mappings between the table, and member variables. Note how ClassWizard
        // uses comments //{{AFX and //}}AFX to denote portions of the class that
        // it will maintain. Basically, this means "don't touch".
// Field/Param Data
        //{{AFX_FIELD(CStockSet, CRecordset)
        CString m_Company;
        CString m_Exchange;
        CString m_Industry;
        long    m_StockID;
        CString m_Symbol;
        //}}AFX_FIELD
// Overrides
```

```
        // ClassWizard generated virtual function overrides
        //{{AFX_VIRTUAL(CStockSet)
        public:
        virtual CString GetDefaultConnect(); // Default connection string
        virtual CString GetDefaultSQL(); // Default SQL for Recordset
        virtual void DoFieldExchange(CFieldExchange* pFX); // RFX support
        //}}AFX_VIRTUAL
};
```

Code 8-25

```
CStockSet::CStockSet(CDatabase* pdb)
        :CRecordset(pdb)
{
        // Note the //{{AFX comments meaning "Don't touch". ClassWizard put
        // Initializations here for each data member it added.
        //{{AFX_FIELD_INIT(CStockSet)
        m_Company = _T("");
        m_Exchange = _T("");
        m_Industry = _T("");
        m_StockID = 0;
        m_Symbol = _T("");
        m_nFields = 5;
        //}}AFX_FIELD_INIT
        m_nDefaultType = snapshot;
}


CString CStockSet::GetDefaultConnect()
{
        // GetDefaultConnect returns the ODBC data source name for this recordset.
        // If you wanted to change the datasource name later, you don't have to
        // re-create the class, just change the string that appears here.
        return _T("ODBC;DSN=PNStocks");
}


CString CStockSet::GetDefaultSQL()
{
        // GetDefaultSQL returns the name of the table(s) in the query, with each
        // table surrounded by [ and ].
        return _T("[Stock]");
}


void CStockSet::DoFieldExchange(CFieldExchange* pFX)
{
        // DoFieldExchange is the function that will move data back and forth
        // between the table in the database and the data members in the
        // CStockSet class.
        //{{AFX_FIELD_MAP(CStockSet)
        pFX->SetFieldType(CFieldExchange::outputColumn);
        RFX_Text(pFX, _T("[Company]"), m_Company);
```

```
RFX_Text(pFX, _T("[Exchange]"), m_Exchange);
RFX_Text(pFX, _T("[Industry]"), m_Industry);
RFX_Long(pFX, _T("[StockID]"), m_StockID);
RFX_Text(pFX, _T("[Symbol]"), m_Symbol);
//}}AFX_FIELD_MAP
}
```

Code 8-26

```
CString Symbols;
CStockSet StockSet;

StockSet.Open();
while( !StockSet.IsEOF() )
{
        Symbols += StockSet.m_Symbol;
        Symbols += " ";
        StockSet.MoveNext();
}
```

Retrieving Data using DAO and CDAORecordset

When you want to use DAO to access a table in a database, you use the CDaoRecordset. In fact, you will be using ClassWizard to create a new custom class derived from CDaoRecordset.

The steps for create a CDaoRecordset-derived class are the same as those previously mentioned for ODBC and CRecordset except that in the Database Options dialog you will select DAO instead of ODBC and you will be prompted afterwards for the location of your Access database file. After this selection, the process is identical.

Opening and Closing a CRecordset/CDaoRecordset

Both the CRecordset-derived and CDaoRecordset-derived classes contain the functions for opening, refreshing, or closing a recordset object as shown in Code 8–27.

Code 8-27

```
virtual BOOL Open( UINT nOpenType = AFX_DB_USE_DEFAULT_TYPE,
        LPCTSTR lpszSQL = NULL, DWORD dwOptions = none );
virtual void Close( );
virtual BOOL Requery( );
```

Table 8.9   Possible Values of nOpenType

Option	Meaning
CRecordset::dynaset	The resulting list of records will reflect changes made by other users while the recordset stays open when you move onto the changed record.
CRecordset::snapshot	The resulting list of records will not reflect changes made by other users while the recordset stays open. To see the changes, you will need to close and reopen the query. The resulting list of records is buffered in this case.
CRecordset::dynamic	Similar to dynaset, except that changes made by other users may alter the membership or ordering of records in your query.
CRecordset::forwardOnly	A read-only recordset with only forward scrolling (you cannot move back a record, only forward).

The Open() function permits you to open a query and optionally provide filtering and sorting criteria. The nOpenType parameter may be one of the values listed in Table 8.9. Using AFX_DB_USE_DEFAULT_TYPE means to use the open method specified when the Recordset class was created

For CRecordset, the default value is CRecordset::snapshot. The default value mechanism allows the Visual C++ wizards to interact with both ODBC CRecordset and DAO CDaoRecordset, which have different defaults.

The lpszSQL parameter is an optional parameter that represents a SQL command to run against the table. Notice that this SQL query should include the list of field names that was defined in the DoFieldExchange() function. The dwOptions parameter is a bitmask parameter, which you can use to set options such as read-only recordsets or bulk-record operations.

The Close() function closes an open recordset.

Requery is similar to, but faster than, closing and reopening a query if it's already open. This function is normally called after m_strFilter or m_strSort has been changed.

Filtering and Sorting
with ODBC\CRecordset
and DAO\CDaoRecordset

Both the CRecordset and the CDaoRecordset provide a means to open the recordset with a SQL command. However, they also provide a means to perform searching and sorting of data in tables using two data members, m_strFilter and m_strSort. To understand how these two will work, we need to take a quick look at a typical SQL query string.

The SQL statement in Code 8–28 retrieves records that contain 'Technology' in the Industry field. These records are then sorted by the company field.

Code 8–28

```
SELECT * FROM Stock
WHERE Industry='Technology'
ORDER BY Company
```

CString m_strFilter; The m_strFilter data member of CRecordset and CDao-Recordset is used to specify filter criteria, which is Industry='Technology' in Code 8–28. If m_strFilter is blank, then all records are included. You can also specify one or more AND and OR Boolean operators. Remember that string fields need a single quote around them and numbers do not. The m_strFilter member variable should not contain the WHERE portion of the filter.

CString m_strSort; The m_strSort data member of the CRecordset and CDaoRecordset is used to specify one or more field names to be used for sorting re-sults. Sorting is ascending by default, but you can optionally do descending sort by adding DESC after the desired fieldname. The m_strSort member variable should not contain the ORDER BY portion of the SQL statement.

Code 8–29 illustrates how to open the CSocketSet class whether derived from CRecordset or CDaoRecordset.

Code 8–29

```
CStockSet StockSet;

StockSet.m_strFilter = "Industry='Technology' ";
StockSet.m_strSort = "Company";
StockSet.Open();
```

Code 8–30 demonstrates how our Stock example program retrieves a stock the user asked for by symbol. It is called when the user clicks a Fetch button.

Code 8–30

m_Symbol is the Stock symbol the user
wants to fetch from the database

Create a CStockset recordset, and
search for the entered stock symbol

Get values from on screen controls
into mapped member variables

```
void CStockPage::OnFetch()
{
    UpdateData();
    if( m_Symbol.IsEmpty() )
        MessageBox("Please enter stock symbol to retrieve" );
    else
    {
        CStockSet StockSet;
        StockSet.m_strFilter.Format( "symbol='%s'", (LPCSTR) m_Symbol );
        StockSet.Open();
        if( StockSet.IsEOF() )
            MessageBox( "No records found" );
        else
            PopulateControls( StockSet );
    }
}
```

If not found, tell the user, otherwise, populate the onscreen controls

Inserting Records with ODBC\CRecordset and DAO\CDaoRecordset

In order to insert a record to a table, we will first need to call the AddNew() function to place the record in an insert mode. Next, we place data into the member variables of the recordset object and call the Update() function of the recordset object. We can cancel the update by calling the CancelUpdate() instead of Update().

A new record often requires a new unique ID value. This will be addressed later in detail. In this example, we will assume that there is a GetNextID() function that returns to us the next unique ID for the table.

Code 8–31 illustrates how to insert with the StockSet class whether it is CRecordset-derived or CDaoRecordset-derived.

Code 8-31

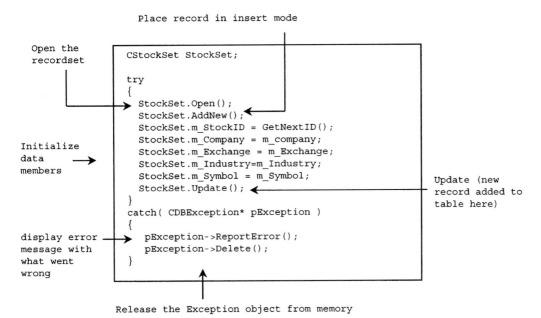

Place record in insert mode

Open the recordset

Initialize data members

Update (new record added to table here)

display error message with what went wrong

Release the Exception object from memory

```
CStockSet StockSet;

try
{
    StockSet.Open();
    StockSet.AddNew();
    StockSet.m_StockID = GetNextID();
    StockSet.m_Company = m_company;
    StockSet.m_Exchange = m_Exchange;
    StockSet.m_Industry=m_Industry;
    StockSet.m_Symbol = m_Symbol;
    StockSet.Update();
}
catch( CDBException* pException )
{
    pException->ReportError();
    pException->Delete();
}
```

In the field assignments as shown in Code 8–32, we assume that the m_Company is a variable that contains the desired data to be inserted into the table. Values are manually assigned to each field to avoid data binding.

Notice that Code 8–31 is in a try/catch block. If any of the Open(), AddNew(), or Update() functions encounters a problem, the function will throw an exception. The CRecordset classes will throw a CDBException, while the CDaoRecordset classes will throw a CDaoException. So, to change Code 8–31 to work with the DAO classes, simply change CDBException to CDaoException (see Code 8–32).

You can also add new records to a table by using a SQL INSERT command, which is discussed later in the *Executing SQL Commands* section of this chapter.

Code 8-32

```
catch (CDaoException* pEXception)
```

Editing Records with ODBC\CRecordset and DAO\CDaoRecordset

In order to edit a record, first you need to open a recordset and move to the desired record. Next, you need to call the Edit() function and modify the desired fields. Finally, you must either call the Update() function to save the changes or the CancelUpdate() function to cancel the changes and leave the record unchanged. Code 8–33 illustrates how this is done.

Notice that this code uses a try/catch block as discussed in the *Adding Records* section. You can also add edit records in your database table by using a SQL UPDATE command. We will discuss this later in the *Executing SQL Commands* section of this chapter.

Code 8–33

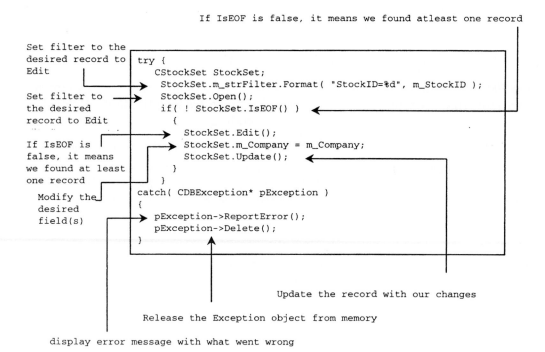

```
                                    If IsEOF is false, it means we found atleast one record

Set filter to the
desired record to     try {
Edit                      CStockSet StockSet;
                          StockSet.m_strFilter.Format( "StockID=%d", m_StockID );
Set filter to             StockSet.Open();
the desired               if( ! StockSet.IsEOF() )
record to Edit            {
                              StockSet.Edit();
If IsEOF is               StockSet.m_Company = m_Company;
false, it means           StockSet.Update();
we found at least         }
one record            }
                      catch( CDBException* pException )
    Modify the        {
    desired               pException->ReportError();
    field(s)              pException->Delete();
                      }
```

Update the record with our changes

Release the Exception object from memory

display error message with what went wrong

Deleting Records with ODBC\CRecordset and DAO\CDaoRecordset

In order to delete a record from a recordset, we will call the Delete() function. First, use the Open() function to open the recordset, then locate a record (using either the m_strFilter criteria before the open or by using the MoveNext/MovePrev functions), and then call the Delete() function to remove the record from the database. Unlike the AddNew() or Edit() functions, you do not need to call the Update() function to actually remove the record since the Delete() function will do it all. Code 8–34 illustrates this technique.

Notice that this code uses a try/catch block as discussed in the *Adding Records* section. You can also add edit records in your database table by using a SQL UPDATE command. We will discuss this later in the *Executing SQL Commands* section.

Code 8–34

```
try {
        CStockSet StockSet;

        // Set filter to the desired record to delete
        StockSet.m_strFilter.Format( "StockID=%d", m_StockID );

        // Open the table
        StockSet.Open();

        // If IsEOF is false, it means we found atleast one record
        if( ! StockSet.IsEOF() )
             StockSet.Delete();        // Delete it
}
catch( CDBException* pException )
{
        // display error message with what went wrong
        pException->ReportError();
        // Release the Exception object from memory
        pException->Delete();
}
```

Binding Fields to On-screen Controls with CRecordset and CDaoRecordset

Examples in this chapter use a program to manipulate data in a database. Another way to do this is to bind the data to controls on the user interface. This is called *data binding* and is where you associate an on-screen control with a member variable (or field) from the recordset class using ClassWizard.

Let's illustrate this technique by creating a dialog for editing an adding new stock records such as the one shown in Figure 8–10 by using the stock table and the CstockClass.

Step 1: Create the dialog—In your dialog editor, create the dialog with controls for each field you want to map to the stock table as shown in Figure 8–11. Each control in the dialog should have an ID. Edit boxes in this example should be created with the following IDs: IDC_SYMBOL, IDC_COMPANY, IDC_INDUSTRY, and IDC_EXCHANGE. Also change the ID of the dialog, so that the ID describes the purpose of the dialog such as IDD_STOCKDLG.

Step 2: Create a class for the new dialog—With the new dialog still open in the editor, open ClassWizard from the View menu choice. ClassWizard will display a dialog that will ask you if you want to create a new class for the dialog as shown in Figure 8–12.

Click Ok on this dialog. ClassWizard will ask you some information about the new class before creating it, as shown in Figure 8–13.

In the New Class dialog, entered the name of CStockDlg for the new dialog class. The Base Class will default to CDialog and the Dialog ID will default to the ID of the dialog resource we just created in step 1.

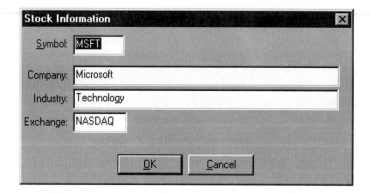

Figure 8–10   Data is entered into the stock table by using the Stock Information dialog.

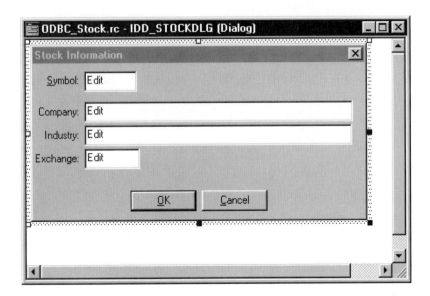

Figure 8–11   Create the Stock Information dialog as shown here.

Step 3: Set up the Foreign Class definition—The Foreign Class definition is the key to data binding. This enables a dialog to have a CRecordset or CDaoRecordset as a foreign class that will be used to map member variables to on-screen controls.

To define the foreign class, go to ClassWizard and select the Class Info tab. Make sure that the name of your new dialog class (CStockDlg in our example) is highlighted in the Class Name field.

In the Foreign Class field of ClassWizard, select the recordset class that you want to bind to fields on the dialog. In our example, it is CStockSet. In the Foreign Variable field, type the name of the data member for the class (m_pSet is recommended), which is shown in Figure 8–14.

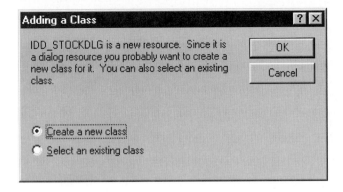

Figure 8–12   Select Create a new class.

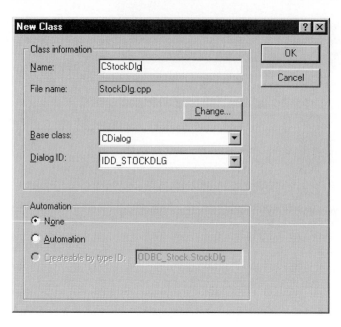

Figure 8–13 Enter information about the new class into the ClassWizard.

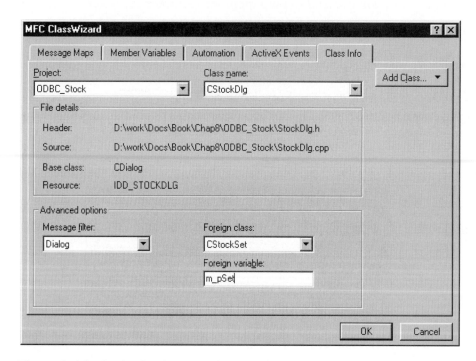

Figure 8–14 Setting Foreign class information in ClassWizard.

Step 4: Map field variables to on-screen controls—Now that the dialog has been setup with the controls and the foreign class, we can create the automatic binding between the on-screen controls and the fields in the database table.

To do this, go to the Member Variable tab of ClassWizard. This is the same tab where we have added member variables for on-screen controls before. Highlight the IDC_COMPANY control in the list of controls and click the Add Variable button.

Now, the Add Member Variable dialog should appear. If you look carefully, you will notice that the Member Variable Name field is now a drop-down list, instead of an edit box as we have seen in previous examples. This occurs because we set up the foreign class variable.

If you click the down arrow on the Member Variable Name field, you will see a list of the field names from the recordset we added as the foreign class in step 3. Simply select the desired field names (m_Company in our example) and click OK. That field is now bound to that on-screen edit control. Repeat this Add Variable step for each control, mapping it to its table field counterpart.

An example of what the Add Member Variable dialog might look like appears like Figure 8–15.

Step 5: Initializing the m_pSet member variable—The last step to actually using our stock dialog is to initialize the m_pSet foreign class variable that we added in step 3. The definition of this variable from the header file would look like Code 8–35.

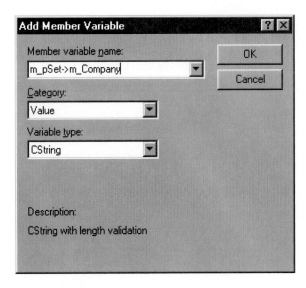

Figure 8–15   The Add Member Variable dialog.

Notice that it is a pointer to a CStockSet object, not an actual CStockSet object. In the constructor for the dialog, you can find Code 8–36 as the default initialization.

Code 8–35

```
CStockSet* m_pSet;
```

Code 8–36

```
m_pSet = NULL;
```

Since the constructor sets the object to NULL, if we attempt to use the dialog without initializing m_pSet, the program will crash (NULL pointer assignment).

One simple means to initialize the m_pSet member variable is to do so from the View class that will invoke the dialog shown in Code 8–37.

Code 8–37

```
CWhateverView::OnEdit()
{
        // Create a socket, and retrieve the desired record to edit
        CStockSet StockSet;

        StockSet.m_strFilter.Format( "StockID=%d", m_StockID );
        StockSet.Open();
        if( ! StockSet.IsEOF() )
        {
                // If found, then create an instance of our CStockDlg dialog
                CSockDlg SockDlg;
                // Initialize its m_pSet variable with our CStockSet object
                SockDlg.m_pSet = &StockSet;

                // Place the recordset in edit mode
                StockSet.Edit();

                // Invoke the dialog
                if( SockDlg.DoModal() == IDOK ) // User hit OK button?
                        StockSet.Update(); // If so, then update the record
                else
                        StockSet.CancelUpdate(); // Otherwise, cancel the update
        }
}
```

Extending Data Bound Dialogs

The technique discussed in the previous section can be improved. Keep in mind that anything you write in a View class will not be easily reusable in your next project. So the calls to Edit(), Update(), and CancelUpdate() will have to be re-created in the next project that requires the same dialog.

To make the dialog more reusable and more self-sufficient, we will make some changes to it. We will over-ride the DoModal() function of the dialog, and the OnOK() and OnCancel() handlers to call the Edit/AddNew() and Update/CancelUpdate() functions for us.

Step 1: Add an m_IsNew data member—In the CStockDlg header file, add the data member shown in Code 8–38.

Code 8–38

```
bool m_IsNew;
```

Step 2: Add a DoModal function—Using ClassWizard, go to the Message Map tab and make sure that the CStockDlg class is selected in the Class Name field. Then, make sure the name CstockDlg is selected in the Object IDs list, and that DoModal() is selected in the Message List, and click the Add Function button.

ClassWizard will add a DoModal function similar to Code 8–39.

Code 8–39

```
int CStockDlg::DoModal()
{
        // Call base class DoModal to display the dialog
        return CDialog::DoModal();
}
```

You will need to modify the DoModal() function in the header file of the CStockDlg class to accept the parameters shown in Code 8–40.

Next, modify the function definition for DoModal() inside the StockDlg.cpp file and make it look like Code 8–41.

Code 8–40

```
virtual int DoModal( CStockSet& pSet, bool IsAdd );
```

Code 8–41

```
int CStockDlg::DoModal( CStockSet& Set, bool IsAdd )
{
        // This is our overloaded DoModal function

        // Setup our m_pSet variable with the passed recordset.
        m_pSet = &Set;
        // If the record set isn't open, then open it
        if( !m_pSet->IsOpen() )
                m_pSet->Open();

        // If IsAdd is true, then we should add a new record, otherwise
        // we are being asked to edit the current record
        if( IsAdd )
                m_pSet->AddNew();
        else
                m_pSet->Edit();

        // Save the IsAdd parameter in member variable, for the OnOk function
        m_IsNew = IsAdd;

        // Call base class DoModal to display the dialog
        return CDialog::DoModal();
}
```

In Code 8–41, notice how the m_pSet parameter is initialized with the CStockSet object that was passed as the first parameter. The second parameter, IsAdd indicates if the dialog is being invoked to add (true) or edit (false) the CStockSet record.

The first if test in the code determines if the recordset is already open, and if not opens it. The second if test determines if this should be an add or edit of a record in the Stock table. For an add, it calls the AddNew() function, and for an edit it calls the Edit() function. It then saves the IsAdd parameter into the m_IsNew member variable, where we will use it in the OnOk handler (which we add next).

Finally, it invokes the dialog by calling the base class CDialog::DoModal() function.

Step 3: Add the OnOk and OnCancel handlers—Using ClassWizard again, add the Message Map tab, and add message maps for the BN_CLICKED message of the IDOK and IDCANCEL object IDs. Change these functions to look like Code 8–42:

Code 8–42

```
void CStockDlg::OnCancel()
{
```

```
// Cancel Edit or AddNew on m_pSet
m_pSet->CancelUpdate();
CDialog::OnCancel();
}


void CStockDlg::OnOK()
{
        // Move data from on-screen controls into member variables
        UpdateData();

        int NewID;

        // If this is a Stock addition, get the next Stock ID
        if( m_IsNew )
                NewID = m_pSet->GetNextID();

        // Update the record (doesn't matter if AddNew or Edit)
        m_pSet->Update();

        if( m_IsNew )
        {
                // If a newly-added record, go right back to it.
                m_pSet->m_strFilter.Format( "StockID=%d", NewID );
                m_pSet->Requery();
        }

        // Call default OnOk handler, to close the dialog
        CDialog::OnOK();
}
```

As you can see by examining the OnOk handler, it first calls UpdateData (to move data from the on-screen controls into the member variables of the m_pSet recordset). Then, if this was an insert (the m_IsNew member variable is true), we call the GetNextID function to determine the next unique ID value for that table. Next, the m_pSet->Update() function is called, which saves the user's changes or additions to the database table. Finally, if it was an insert, the newly added record is retrieved back into the CStockSet object that m_pSet points to. Now, using this dialog to add a record is shown in Code 8–43. To edit a record using this dialog, we would use Code 8–44. See *Determining Unique IDs for New Records* for more information on GetNextID().

Notice how all the AddNew/Edit and Update/CancelUpdate logic has been removed from the code that invokes the dialog and placed into the CStockDlg itself.

Code 8–43

```
        CStockSet StockSet;
        CStockDlg StockDlg;
        StockDlg.DoModal( StockSet, true );
```

```
CStockSet StockSet;
CStockDlg StockDlg;

// Set filter to retrieve the current stock
StockSet.m_strFilter.Format( " StockID = %d ", m_StockID );

// Invoke dialog to edit, and update, the selected stock
StockDlg.DoModal( StockSet, false );
```

Working with Non-bound Recordsets

While there is no question that data-bound controls can make life simpler, it is not a complex task to implement controls that you bind to fields manually. And of course, this will give you experience to working with field objects directly, which can come in handy in other programming requirements such as reports, data analysis, or conversion programs.

Once you have your data in a field, it is no different to move the data from the field to an on-screen control and vice versa than with any other type of data. You can use things like SetWindowText or map member variables using ClassWizard and then call UpdateData to transfer the data.

A good example of this approach is when the stock demo program displays the Portfolio table. In the portfolio tab of the program; all the records from the Portfolio table are listed, along with the stock symbol from the Stock table, and the most recent price from the Trade table. In other words, a combination of several tables displays usable data. The display of the portfolio information is shown in Figure 8–16. The code needed to implement this logic is fairly small as shown in Code 8–45.

Code 8-45

```
void CPortfolioPage::RefreshData()
{
    // Refresh the Portfolio page (which is really a dialog inside a tab control)
    CPortfolioSet PortfolioSet;
    CStockSet StockSet;
    int Index;
    CString Text;

    // Remove the contents of the Portfolio ListView control
    m_List.DeleteAllItems();

    // Set our portfolio recordset to be sorted by date
    PortfolioSet.m_strSort = "PurchaseDate";
```

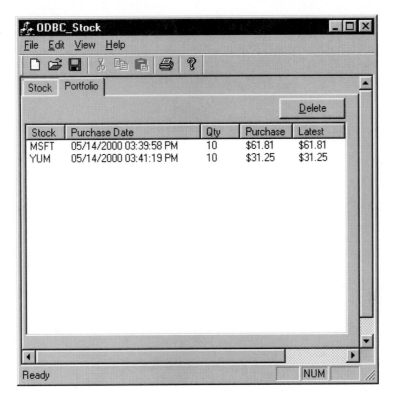

Figure 8–16 Portfolio information.

```
// Open the portfolio table, and iterate through records
PortfolioSet.Open();
while( !PortfolioSet.IsEOF() )
{
    // Lookup the stock from the portfolio, to get gurrent price
    if( StockSet.Lookup( PortfolioSet.m_StockID ) )
    {
        // Add entries to the List control, for the stock information
        Index = m_List.InsertItem( m_List.GetItemCount(), StockSet.m_Symbol );
        // Save the Unique ID of the Portolio record in the List control
        // also, as 'Item Data'.
        m_List.SetItemData( Index, PortfolioSet.m_PortfolioID );

        Text=PortfolioSet.m_PurchaseDate.Format("%m/%d/%Y %I:%M:%S %p");
        m_List.SetItemText( Index, 1, Text );

        Text.Format( "%d", PortfolioSet.m_Shares );
        m_List.SetItemText( Index, 2, Text );

        Text.Format( "$%.2f", PortfolioSet.m_PurchasePrice );
        m_List.SetItemText( Index, 3, Text );
```

```
        Text.Format( "$%.2f", StockSet.GetLatestPrice() );
        m_List.SetItemText( Index, 4, Text );

    }
    // Moce to the next portfolio record
    PortfolioSet.MoveNext();
    }
}
```

The flexibility of the code above offers us some slightly more flexible ways of displaying the data, such as the $ formatted prices, or the retrieval of the most current price. We don't have to worry about how to trick a database grid into displaying this format or altering the query to make use of a join statement.

In other words, sometimes what appears to be the simplest means initially may not work out in the long run. As a programmer, you have know when it's time to switch from one method to another, which is something learned with experience.

Determining Unique IDs
for New Records

As discussed in the earlier in this chapter, tables have unique IDs that represent a unique record in that table. In our Stock table, we assumed that there was a StockID field and each stock record in the table had a unique ID.

There are a number of common means for determined a unique ID for a new record:

- Some databases provide an auto-increment or counter-type field that will automatically be assigned to the new record when saved. The problem here is that you won't know the ID of the new record until after it is saved (this may or may not present problems).

- You can open the table in a recordset, move to the last record, get its unique ID, and add 1 to it. This provides some problems if two users perform the action at the exact same time (they might both get the exact same unique ID).

- You can create a table whose sole purpose is to keep track of the last-used ID for a given table. This requires a bit more setup and management than the other methods.

Let's examine the last method, because it tends to be the most flexible method across different database systems. In the Stock database, we have created a table named TableIDs. This table layout was described in detail in the Stock Database Sample section of this chapter.

A recordset object (derived from CRecordset or CDAoRecordset) that was created for the TableIDs table would have the data members as shown in Code 8–46.

Code 8–46

```
long m_LastID;
CString m_Tablename;
```

We would add a helper function to this class to provide the logic to retrieve the last unique ID for another table from the TableIDs table, add 1 to it, and store it back to the TableIDs table. This function was refered to as GetNextID when we discussed adding records in previous topics. The function, which is the only addition to the CTableIDs recordset class, would look like Code 8–47.

Code 8–47

```
int CTableIDs::GetNextID(const char *Tablename)
{
        // This helper function will look up Tablename in the TableIDs table
        // in the database, and return the LastID field for that table, and add
        // 1 to that ID in the table.
        int NewID;

        // If already open, then close it
        if( IsOpen() )
                Close();

        // Set the filter to search the TableIDs table for a specific tablename
        m_strFilter.Format( " Tablename='%s' ", Tablename );

        // Open the query
        Open();

        // Was the Tablename found?
        if( IsEOF() )
        {
                // If not, insert the tablename, with an ID of 1
                AddNew();
                m_Tablename = Tablename;
                m_LastID=1;
        }
        else
        {
                // Otherwise, Just add 1 to the current ID
                Edit();
                m_LastID++;
```

```
        }

        NewID = m_LastID;
        // Save the new ID and/or record back to the table
        Update();

        // Return the new ID
        return( NewID );

}
```

The code above does nothing fancy. Basically, it searches for the Tablename para-meter in the TableIDs table. If it is not found, then the table name is added to the table, with a Last ID of 1. If it is found, then the ID is retrieved, incremented, and then saved back to the TableIDs table.

Keep in mind that the TableIDs table and the CTableIDs recordset were created to help provide unique IDs for our data tables. They are not part of the data model that relates to stock quotes, but it does make it easier to make the data model work.

In order to use the CTableIDs class, we would add a GetNextID function to our "real" stock classes, like the CStockSet, which might look like Code 8–48.

Notice how the CStockSet version of GetNextID() creates a CTableIDs object locally, then calls its GetNextID() function with the return value of CStockSet::GetDefault-SQL(). Remember that GetDefaultSQL() returns the tablename of the recordset.

Code 8–48

```
int CStockSet::GetNextID()
{
        // Helper function that determines the next Unique ID for the Stock
        // table in the database. It uses the TableIDs table and recordset
        // to determine the next ID
        CTableIDs Tmp;
        m_StockID = Tmp.GetNextID( GetDefaultSQL() );
        return( m_StockID );
}
```

Extending Recordset Classes

One good practice in programming with CRecordset- and CDaoRecordset-derived classes is to add functionality to the class in the form of member functions, rather than requiring the repetition of code in a View or Dialog class. We saw an example of this in the *Extending Data Bound Dialogs* earlier.

This is more a generic approach than a specific code example. Any functionality that you think might be useful or executed often against a particular class of recordset can usually be implemented as a member function of that recordset.

For example, going back to our CStockSet class, which represents a company in the stock market, we might like to see a function that will retrieve the latest price for the stock. But, the Stock table doesn't store any pricing information. Instead, the Trade table has a list of trades for the company's stock, and we will assume that the last trade price is the latest known price of the stock. (This is not true in the real world, but OK here for point of discussion.)

So, in the CStockSet class, we might add the function as shown in Code 8–49. The logic in Code 8–49 is not complex and can easily be implemented in a View or Dialog class. However, by adding this functionality to the CStockSet (with the help of the CTradeSet class), we have extended the ability of the class and therefore the reusability of the class.

The next project that needs access to a stock record may simply reuse this class, rather than re-create it with ClassWizard. If we have a recordset class that we haven't made any changes to or extended in any way, then there is no harm in re-generating it from project to project.

Code 8–49

```
double CStockSet::GetLatestPrice(int StockID)
{
        // Helper function for the Stock table in the database, to determine
        // what the latest stock price is, based on the trades. Note that
        // it demonstrates how to search (m_strFilter) and sort (m_strSort)
        // a database table.
        if( StockID == -1 )
                StockID = m_StockID;

        CTradeSet Tmp;
        // Set the Trade table filter to the unique StockID
        Tmp.m_strFilter.Format( "StockID=%d", StockID );

        // Set the database table sort specifier to use the TradeDate field
        // in DESCending order
        Tmp.m_strSort = "TradeDate DESC";

        // Open the table
        Tmp.Open();

        // If IsEOF is true, then there are no records
        if( Tmp.IsEOF() )
                return( 0.0 );
        else
                return( Tmp.m_Price ); // Otherwise we can return the price found
}
```

Executing SQL Commands
with ODBC or DAO

You can perform bulk updates, deletions, and insertions using SQL commands with either the CDatabase/CDaoDatabase classes. You can also use them with the CRecordset/CDaoRecordset classes because these classes contain a pointer to a CDatabase/CDaoDatabase object. Code 8–50 contains examples of SQL commands.

Code 8–50

```
INSERT INTO Phones Values( 1, 'Home', '212-555-1212' )

UPDATE Inventory SET Price = Price * 1.10

DELETE FROM Invoice WHERE InvDate < 1/1/1980
```

SQL commands can return one or more records and is executed using the ExecuteSQL() command in a CDatabase or the Execute() command in the CDaoDatabase. Use these functions to query a database, which would return a list of records in a result set.

Code 8–51 demonstrates how to call the Execute command from a CRecordset object. In our stock example, we assume that a stock record may have many related records in a Trade table and a Portfolio table. If the user deletes the stock record, we should also delete the records from the Trade and the Portfolio tables as well.

Code 8–51

```
void CStockPage::OnDelete()
{
        // User hit the Delete stock button
        if( m_StockID==0 )
        {
                MessageBox( "Please fetch a stock to delete first" );
                return;
        }

        if( MessageBox(
        "Are you sure you want to delete this stock and its transactions?",
        "Confirmation", MB_ICONQUESTION|MB_YESNO ) == IDYES )
        {
                // Create a recordset object, and locate the desired stock
                CStockSet Tmp;
                Tmp.m_strFilter.Format( "StockID=%d", m_StockID );
                Tmp.Open();
```

```
// Delete Transactions (trades) for the stock
CString strSQL;
strSQL.Format( "delete from Trade where StockID=%d", m_StockID );
Tmp.m_pDatabase->ExecuteSQL( strSQL );

// Delete stock from portfolio (if it's there)
strSQL.Format( "delete from Portfolio where StockID=%d", m_StockID );
Tmp.m_pDatabase->ExecuteSQL( strSQL );
// Note: For CDaoRecordsets, use Execute, not ExecuteSQL

// Delete this Stock record itself
Tmp.Delete();

// Populate the controls (should now clear out all the data
// from the screen)
Tmp.Close();
Tmp.m_StockID=0;

}
```

Notice how Code 8–51 first retrieves the main stock record to be deleted. This action opens the CStockSet class. Once open, the m_pDatabase member of the recordset is used, which is a pointer to a CDatabase (or CDaoDatabase for CDaoRecordsets). The CDatabase and CDaoDatabase classes provide the functions shown in Code 8–52 for executing SQL commands.

For both of these functions, lpszSQL is the SQL command to execute. The CDaoDatabase::Execute() function has an optional nOptions parameter to indicate features like record locking during execution.

Code 8–52

```
void CDatabase::ExecuteSQL( LPCSTR lpszSQL );
void CDaoDatabase::Execute( LPCTSTR lpszSQL, int nOptions = 0 );
```

ADO Basics and a Helper Class

ADO requires a bit more work to implement than the ODBC and DAO method described earlier. The ADO classes do not get tied directly with MFC, meaning that you can't use ClassWizard to implement field binding as we did for the CRecordset and CDaoRecordset classes.

There are ADO bound dialog classes available in Visual C++ Enterprise, in the Component Gallery. The utilize a complex means of binding fields of fixed type directly to a separate class, which is in turn bound to the recordset.

For reasons of simplicity, we will not cover data binding here. Instead, we will treat the ADO classes as generic recordset classes, and this will require us to add manual updating to get field values moved between the table in the database and the recordset class.

The helper class we will present here is called CPNADORecordset. It wraps most of the common initialization and COM interfacing needed when working with ADO. The method of the class includes Code 8–53. Code 8–53 is used to execute an SQL command. Code 8–54 is used to connect to an ADO database. It is assumed that there will be only one database, with multiple tables. Code 8–55 opens a table, or query, with filtering and sorting ability.

Code 8–56 contains functions to get or set a field value for an open recordset. Code 8–57 contains a function that returns the next unique ID for a table, based on our TableIDs scheme described in *Determining Unique IDs for New Records*.

Code 8-53

```
static HRESULT PNExecute( const char* Command );
```

Code 8-54

```
static HRESULT PNConnect( const char* Datasource, const char* Provider=0 );
```

Code 8-55

```
HRESULT PNOpen( const char* Query );
```

Code 8-56

```
bool PNGetField( const char* Fieldname, CString& Dest );
bool PNSetField( const char* Fieldname, const CString& Dest );
```

Code 8-57

```
int PNGetNextID( const char* Tablename );
```

As we discuss the aspects of working with an ADO data source, we will give example code from this CPNADORecordset class and demonstrate how to use it. Make sure to read the section *Database Connections with ADO and _ConnectionPtr* before proceeding to the ADO topics below. The CPNADORecordset class is derived from the _RecordsetPtr class. The class definition looks like Code 8–58, but is listed in its lengthy entirety in Code 8–71.

Code 8-58

```
class CPNADORecordset : public _RecordsetPtr
{
};
```

This means that the same unusual use of the "." and "->" operators as described in Database *Connections with ADO and _ConnectionPtr* will occur with this class. However, functions we add to the class will all be prefixed with a PN in their name, and you will use an "." and not a "->" to access the members. Normal _RecordsetPtr members will still require the use of the "->" operator, so don't get confused when you see them intermixed.

Opening and Closing an ADO Recordset

Opening a records in ADO consists of calling the _RecordsetPtr::Open() function as illustrated in Code 8–59.

However, before you can Open a _RecordsetPtr object, you must initialize it, and initialize COM as well. Assuming that you read the *Database Connections with ADO and _ConnectionPtr* section, you should be able to initialize COM and create a _ConnectionPtr object. From that _ConnectionPtr object, we can open a recordset in ADO as shown in Code 8–60.

Code 8–59

```
HRESULT Open( const _variant_t & Source,
    const _variant_t & ActiveConnection, enum CursorTypeEnum CursorType,
    enum LockTypeEnum LockType, long Options );
```

Code 8–60

```
CoInitialize(0);
_ConnectionPtr Connection;

Connection.CreateInstance( "ADODB.Connection" );
Connection->Open( "Provider=Microsoft.Jet.OLEDB.4.0; Data Source=C:\\Test.mdb", "",
        "", -1 );

_RecordsetPtr Recordset;
Recordset.CreateInstance("ADODB.Recordset" );

HRESULT hr;
try
{
    hr = Recordset->Open( "Select * from Stock", Connection.GetInterface(),
        adOpenDynamic, adLockOptimistic, -1 );
}
catch( _com_error* E )
{
        MessageBox( E->Description() );
}
```

Code 8–60 (in bold) first creates an _RecordsetPtr object named Recordset. It then initializes it by calling the CreateInstance function. There are several versions of CreateInstance(), but this is probably the most understandable format.

CreateInstance will create a COM ADO recordset object, and it will now be associated with the Recordset variable. In order to access the functions of the COM object, we will need to use the -> operator, even though Recordset is *not* a pointer. As you can tell in the call to CreateInstance(), and the call to Open() below it, the "." and "->" operator calls are intermixed.

The Open() functions first parameter is either the table name, or a SQL SELECT statement for opening a query. The second parameter is a variant that can be either a COM interface to a _ConnectionPtr object, or a variant-type string that contains the same type of connection string as the Connection->Open function contains. The second parameter can easily be achieved as demonstrated, by calling the GetInterface() function for the Connection object. The third parameter to the Recordset->Open call is a flag that indicates the cursor mode (how you will iterate through records) and can be one of the values shown in Table 8.10. The fourth parameter to the Recordset->Open() parameter determines the record locking strategy as shown in Table 8.11. The final parameter to the Recordset->Open() function indicates the type of statement being used to open the query (the string passed as the first argument) as shown as Table 8.12.

To Close the _RecordsetPtr, simple call its Close() function as shown in Code 8–61.

Code 8–61

```
Recordset->Close();
```

Using the CPNADORecordset Class

In order to connect to an ADO data source and then open an ADO query using the CPNADORecordset class, you would simply use Code 8–62.

Table 8.10   Definition of the Third Parameter

Value	Meaning
adOpenDynamic	Modifications by other users are visible, and all types of movement through the Recordset are allowed, including bookmarks if the data provider supports them.
adOpenForwardOnly	Default. Identical to a static cursor, except that you can only scroll forward through records. If you are going to make a single pass through data records, then this offers improved performance.
adOpenKeyset	Like a dynamic cursor, except that records other users add are not visible, while records other users delete are removed from your Recordset. Updates by other users are visible.
adOpenStatic	A static copy of a set of records that you can use to find data or generate reports. Modifications other users are not visible until the recordset is closed and reopened.
adOpenUnspecified	Does not specify the type of cursor.

Table 8.11   Definition of the Fourth Parameter

Value	Meaning
adLockBatchOptimistic	Optimistic locking for batch processing.
adLockOptimistic	Optimistic locking on an individual record basis. The record is locked only when the Update actually occurs.
adLockPessimistic	Pessimistic locking on an individual record basis. The record is locked when an edit is begun.
adLockReadOnly	Indicates read-only records. You cannot alter the data.
adLockUnspecified	Does not specify a type of lock.

The CPNADORecordset class will be presented in its entirety at the end of this section.

Code 8–62

```
if( CPNADORecordset::PNConnect( "..\\PNStocks.mdb" ) != S_OK )
    return( FALSE );
CPNADORecordset TradeSet;

if( TradeSet.PNOpen( "Select * from Trade Order by TradeDate" ) != S_OK )
{
        MessageBox( "Unexpected error opening Trade table" );
        return(0);
}
```

Filtering and Sorting with ADO Recordsets

The _RecordsetPtr class provides two methods for specifiying the types of records you want to work with in a table and the order in which you want them sorted. The first method is refered to as "properties," where you set a filter and sort value, and

Table 8.12   Definition of the Fifth Parameter

Value	Meaning
adCmdUnspecified	Does not specify the command-type argument.
adCmdText	The first parameter is a SQL command or stored procedure call.
adCmdTable	The first parameter is a table name to be opened.
adCmdStoredProc	The first parameter is a stored procedure name.
adCmdUnknown	Default, –1. Means the type of command is unknown.
adCmdFile	The first parameter is a filename if a stored Recordset.
adCmdTableDirect	The first parameter is the name of a table, and all rows and columns are returned.

then call the Open() function. In ADO documentation, they are refered to as the Filter and Sort properties and they are function calls in a Visual C++ program (see Code 8–63).

Code 8–63

```
_variant_t GetFilter( );
void PutFilter( const _variant_t & Criteria );
_bstr_t GetSort( );
void PutSort( _bstr_t Criteria );
```

The second method is to place the entire SQL SELECT statement into the first parameter of the Open() function. Code 8–64 accomplishes the same thing using the two methods.

The Open() method will then return only records matching your filter and ordered by your sort order. If you choose to use the CPNADORecordset class, you can still use either method. The primary difference is that the PNOpen() function in the PNADORecordset class only takes one parameter.

Code 8–64

```
// Using Filter and Sort Properties
Recordset->PutFilter( "TradePrice>100" );
Recordset->PutSort  ( "TradeDate, TradePrice" );
Recordset->Open( "Trade", Connection.GetInterfacePtr(), adOpenDynamic,
        adLockOptimistic, -1 );

// Using Direct SQL Select:
Recordset->Open( "SELECT * FROM Trade WHERE TradePrice>100 ORDER BY
TradeDate, TradePrice",
Connection.GetInterfacePtr(), adOpenDynamic, adLockOptimistic, -1 );
```

Adding Records with ADO Recordsets

Using the _RecordsetPtr class already opened to a table in the database, you call the AddNew() function to place the recordset into insert mode, populate the fields, and call the Update() function when done as shown in Code 8–65.

Code 8–65

```
Recordset->Open( "Trade", Connection.GetInterfacePtr(), adOpenDynamic,
adLockOptimistic, -1);

Recordset->AddNew();
// Place values into fields
Recordset->PutCollect( "TradeID", GetNextID() );
Recordset->PutCollect( "TradeDate", (DATE) ColeDateTime::GetCurrentTime() );
Recordset->PutCollect( "TradePrice", m_Price );
```

```
Recordset->PutCollect( "StockID", m_StockID );
Recordset->PutCollect( "Change", m_Change );
if( ReallySave )
        Recordset->Update();
else
        Recordset->CancelUpdate();
```

The CPNADORecordset class does not provide any replacement functions for AddNew(), Update(), or CancelUpdate(), so you can use the _RecordsetPtr versions, as shown in Code 8–65. However, the CPNADORecordset class does provide a PNSetField function, which provides some extra interface between fields and MFC data types, such as CString and COleDateTime.

Notice that records can also be added by executing a SQL INSERT command.

Editing Records with ADO Recordsets

To edit a record in ADO, we first need to locate the record to modify, then change it's field values, and update the record. Unlike the CRecordset and CDaoRecordset of MFC, there is no Edit() function to call. Any record not in read-only mode is automatically considered in edit mode. Code 8–66 updates a record.

Code 8–66

```
Recordset->Open( "select * from Trade where TradeID=105",
Connection.GetInterfacePtr(),
adOpenDynamic, adLockOptimistic, -1);

// Place values into fields
Recordset->PutCollect( "TradeID", GetNextID() );
Recordset->PutCollect( "TradeDate", (DATE) ColeDateTime::GetCurrentTime()
);
Recordset->PutCollect( "TradePrice", m_Price );
Recordset->PutCollect( "StockID", m_StockID );
Recordset->PutCollect( "Change", m_Change );
if( ReallySave )
        Recordset->Update();
else
        Recordset->CancelUpdate();
```

The CPNADORecordset class does not provide any replace functions for Update() or CancelUpdate(), so you can use the _RecordsetPtr versions, as shown in Code 8–66. However, the CPNADORecordset class does provide a PNSetField function, which provides some extra interface between fields and MFC data types, such as CString and COleDateTime.

Notice that records can also be updated by executing a SQL UPDATE command.

Deleting Records with ADO Recordsets

To delete a record, we need to locate the desired record, and then call the Delete() function as shown in Code 8–67.

The Delete() function takes a single parameter, which indicates how many records are to be deleted. While the parameter is not a simple count of records, "1" does indicate to delete just one record (the current record); 2, however, would mean delete all records that match the current filter, no matter how many records there were.

The CPNADORecordset class does not provide any replace functions for Delete(), so you can use the _RecordsetPtr versions. Notice that records can also be deleted by executing a SQL DELETE command.

Code 8–67

```
Recordset->Open( "select * from Trade where TradeID=105",
Connection.GetInterfacePtr(),
      adOpenDynamic, adLockOptimistic, -1);
Recordset->Delete( 1 );
```

Binding Fields to On-screen Controls with ADO

The binding of fields from an ADO record to on screen controls is possible and can even be done with the ADO Data Bound dialog found in the Component Gallery of Visual C++. However, we will discuss the manual binding of on-screen controls to ADO field values in the demonstration program.

Executing SQL Commands with ODBC or DAO

To execute a SQL command, such as a DELETE, INSERT, or UPDATE statement, the _ConnectionPtr class provides an Execute() function shown in Code 8–68.

Here, the CommandText parameter is the SQL command to execute. The Records-Affected parameter will contain the number of records modified when the function returns. The Options parameter permits you to select options such as asynchronous execution (meaning the function will return before the command has finished executing). An example of deleting records is illustrated in Code 8–69.

Code 8–68

```
Execute(BSTR CommandText, VARIANT *RecordsAffected, long Options);
```

Code 8–69

```
CoInitialize(0);
_ConnectionPtr Connection;
Connection.CreateInstance( "ADODB.Connection" );
Connection.Open( ConnectString, "", "", -1 );
Connection->Execute( "DELETE ROM Trade WHERE TradeDate< 1/1/1970" );
```

Using the CPNADORecordset class, the PNExecute() function provides a simpler interface to accomplish the same task (see Code 8–70).

Code 8–70

```
CPNADORecordset::PNConnect( "C:\\test.mdb" );
CPNADORecordset::PNExecute( " delete from Trade where TradeDate< 1/1/1970" );
```

The CPNADORecordset Class

The CPNADORecordset class, as discussed in previous ADO programming examples, is a class derived from _RecordsetPtr and designed to make certain common operations simpler to perform. The source code listing is provided here in its entirety (see Code 8–71).

Code 8–71

```
// Programmers Notebook: Helper class for _RecordsetPtr objects and
// ADO database access.

class CPNADORecordset : public _RecordsetPtr
{
public:

        CPNADORecordset()
        {
                // Initialize the _RecordsetPtr base class
                CreateInstance( "ADODB.Recordset" );
        }

        static HRESULT PNExecute( const char* Command )
        {
                // Execute a SQL command
                _bstr_t bstrCommand = Command;
                _variant_t Records;

                // Note: Documentation incorrectly states Execute requires 4
                parameters,
                // when in reality it only requires 3.
                return( m_Connection->Execute(bstrCommand, &Records, -1 ) );
        }
```

```
static HRESULT PNConnect( const char* Datasource, const char* Provider=0 )
{
        // Connect to a database, initializing COM and the m_Connection
        member
        static bool Initialized=false;

        if( !Initialized )
        {
                // Initialize COM. Not a problem if done repeatedly.
                CoInitialize(0);
                m_Connection.CreateInstance( "ADODB.Connection" );
                Initialized = true;
        }

        if( m_Connection->GetState() & adStateOpen )
                m_Connection->Close();

        CString StrConnect;
        StrConnect.Format( "Provider=%s; Data Source=%s;",
                Provider?Provider : "Microsoft.Jet.OLEDB.4.0",
                Datasource );
        _bstr_t bstrConnect = (LPCSTR)StrConnect;

        return( m_Connection->Open( (LPCSTR)StrConnect, "", "", -1 ) );
}


HRESULT PNOpen( const _variant_t & Query )
{
        // Open a table or SQL Select statement
        HRESULT Result;
        if( (*(_RecordsetPtr*)this)->GetState() & adStateOpen )
                (*(_RecordsetPtr*)this)->Close();
        Result = (*(_RecordsetPtr*)this)->Open( Query, m_Connection.
GetInterfacePtr(), adOpenDynamic, adLockOptimistic, -1 );
        return( Result );
}


HRESULT PNOpen( const char* Query )
{ // Overloaded for CString ease of use
        HRESULT Result;
        if( (*(_RecordsetPtr*)this)->GetState() & adStateOpen )
                (*(_RecordsetPtr*)this)->Close();

        Result = (*(_RecordsetPtr*)this)->Open( Query, m_Connection.
GetInterfacePtr(), adOpenDynamic, adLockOptimistic, -1 );
        return( Result );
}


bool PNGetField( const char* Fieldname, CString& Dest )
```

```
{
        // Retrieves a field value, and converts it into a CString
        bool IsNull;
        _variant_t FieldVal = (*(_RecordsetPtr*)this)->GetCollect( Fieldname );
        IsNull = FieldVal.vt == VT_NULL;
        if( IsNull )
                Dest.Empty();
        else
                Dest = (char*) _bstr_t( FieldVal );
        return( !IsNull );
}
void PNSetField( const char* FieldName, const char* Src )
{
        // Sets a field value from a string
        (*(_RecordsetPtr*)this)->PutCollect( FieldName, Src );
}


bool PNGetField( const char* Fieldname, int& Dest )
{
        // Retrieves a field value, and converts it into an integer
        bool IsNull=false;
        _variant_t FieldVal;
        if( (*(_RecordsetPtr*)this)->GetState() & adStateOpen )
        {
                FieldVal = (*(_RecordsetPtr*)this)->GetCollect( Fieldname );
                IsNull = FieldVal.vt == VT_NULL;
        }

        if( IsNull )
                Dest = 0;
        else
        {
                FieldVal.ChangeType( VT_INT );
                Dest = FieldVal.intVal;
        }
        return( !IsNull );
}
void PNSetField( const char* FieldName, int Src )
{
        // Sets a field value from an integer
        (*(_RecordsetPtr*)this)->PutCollect( FieldName, (long)Src );
}


bool PNGetField( const char* Fieldname, double& Dest )
{

        // Gets a field vlaue from a recordset, into a double variable
        bool IsNull=false;
```

```
        _variant_t FieldVal;
        if( (*(_RecordsetPtr*)this)->GetState() & adStateOpen )
        {
                FieldVal = (*(_RecordsetPtr*)this)->GetCollect( Fieldname );
                IsNull = FieldVal.vt == VT_NULL;
        }


        if( IsNull )
                Dest = 0;
        else
        {
                FieldVal.ChangeType( VT_R8 );
                Dest = FieldVal.dblVal;
        }
        return( !IsNull );
}


void PNSetField( const char* FieldName, double Src )
{
        // Sets a field value from a double
        (*(_RecordsetPtr*)this)->PutCollect( FieldName, Src );
}


bool PNGetField( const char* Fieldname, COleDateTime& Dest )
{
        // Gets a field vlaue from a recordset, into a COleDateTime variable
        bool IsNull=false;
        _variant_t FieldVal;

        if( (*(_RecordsetPtr*)this)->GetState() & adStateOpen )
        {
                FieldVal = (*(_RecordsetPtr*)this)->GetCollect( Fieldname );
                IsNull = FieldVal.vt == VT_NULL;
        }


        if( IsNull )
                Dest = COleDateTime();
        else
        {
                FieldVal.ChangeType( VT_DATE );
                Dest = FieldVal.date;
        }
        return( !IsNull );
}
void PNSetField( const char* FieldName, COleDateTime& Src )
{
        // Sets a field value from a COleDateTime object
```

```
                (*(_RecordsetPtr*)this)->PutCollect( FieldName, (DATE)Src );
        }

        int PNGetNextID( const char* Tablename )
        {
                // Helper function to retrieve the next unique ID for a table,
                // from the TableIDs table. Demonstrate record insertion and
                // editing.
                int Ret=0;
                CString Str;
                Str.Format( "SELECT * from TableIDs where Tablename='[%s]'",
                (LPCSTR)Tablename );
                CPNADORecordset TableIDs;
                if( TableIDs.PNOpen( Str ) == S_OK )
                {
                        if( TableIDs->GetIsEOF() )
                        {
                                TableIDs->AddNew();
                                Ret=1;
                                TableIDs.PNSetField( "LastID", Ret );
                                Str.Format( "[%s]", Tablename );
                                TableIDs.PNSetField( "TableName", Str );
                        }
                        else
                        {
                                TableIDs.PNGetField( "LastID", Ret );
                                Ret++;
                                TableIDs.PNSetField( "LastID", Ret );
                        }
                        TableIDs->Update();
                }
                return( Ret );
        }

        static _ConnectionPtr m_Connection;

};
```

The Stock Sample Programs

There are three sample programs that demonstrate ODBC, DAO, and ADO database access. These programs are completely identical in operation except for their database access method, and all work against the same Microsoft Access database. The programs are called ODBC_Stock, DAO_Stock, and ADO_Stock. Sample screens from these programs are shown in Figure 8–17, Figure 8–18, and Figure 8–19.

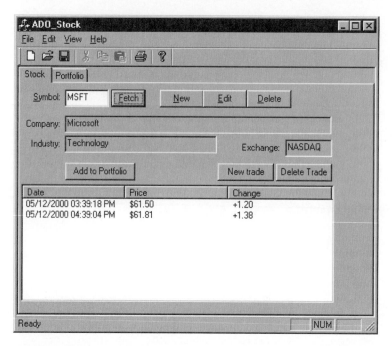

Figure 8–17 The Stock dialog.

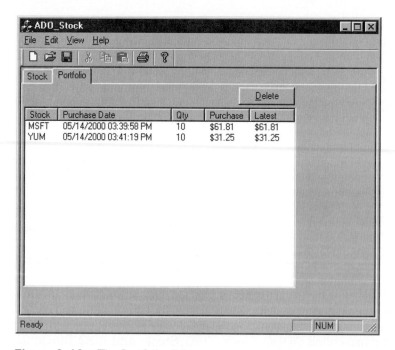

Figure 8–18 The Portfolio dialog.

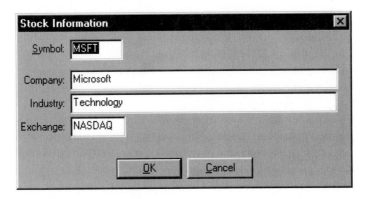

Figure 8–19 The Stock Information dialog.

ADO Controls

ADO also supplies a set of ActiveX controls that can be dropped on a form for quick Access to data. There are not a great number of controls, but certain ones are very handy, like the Grid control. To use the Grid control in one of your programs, it should be either a dialog-based application or a View application that is derived from a CFormView cview class:

- Go to the Project menu item, select Add to Project, then select Components and controls.
- In the Component Gallery dialog, enter the Registers ActiveX controls folder.
- In this folder, select the Microsoft ADO Data Control, Version 6.0 item, and click Insert.
- In the Confirm Classes dialog, click OK.
- Next, select the Microsoft DataGrid Control, Version 6.0 in the Registered ActiveX folder, and click Insert.
- In the Confirm Classes dialog, click OK.

You can now close the Components and Controls gallery. Back in your project, bring up the main dialog in the dialog editor. You should now notice two new controls in the tool palette. Drop one of each of these controls on your form.

One control is the Data control and the other is the Grid. Change the properties of the grid so that in the All tab, the DataSource property is IDC_ADODC1 (this should be the ID of the grid you dropped on the form.

Next, change the properties of the the Data Control, specifically:

- In the Control tab, make sure that the Use Connection String item is selected.
- Click the Build button, which will take you through a series of dialogs to help you build an ADO connection string.
- In the RecordSource tab, enter a sql statement like: SELECT * FROM Stock

If you compile and run the program, you should see something similar to Figure 8–20. Notice that this was created without writing a single line of code!

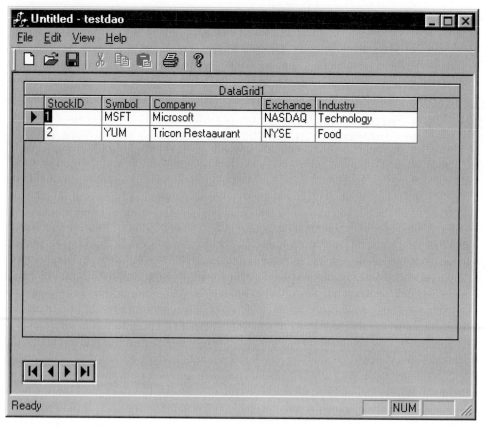

Figure 8–20 Return value from the query of the database.

Visual C++ Tips for Databases

The CRecordset/CDaoRecordset is your primary form of access to a table. You can use a single CRecordset to access multiple tables as with a join. You can specify search criteria and order criteria with them as well.

The CDatabase/CDaoDatabase class is a connection to a database, but you don't often need it in Access. Each CRecordset will make its own CDatabase if you don't provide it with one. Using a CDatabase is helpful when a database has a login and password needed for access.

In AppWizard, it's usually best to select "Header files only" when asked about database support. If you select a data source in appWizard, then your program is really designed to work with only one table, which is not a practical approach.

Your database will most likely be a SDI, CFormView project (not CRecordview).

You may find that your Document class goes mostly unused. This is not abnormal, given a database approach, which has no "document." But, don't use the dialog-based application or remove Document/View architecture, because with the View class you get easy print and print preview abilities. You may also find yourself removing the File/Open, /Save/, etc., options from the menu and toolbar.

You will be creating a variety of CRecordset-derived classes for different tables. Get into the practice of adding functions unique to that table to its class. In other words, if you have a class called CEmployee that works with an employee table, it might be a good idea to add a function called Find() that accepts the name of an employee to search for.

It is possible to associate field from a table/recordset with on-screen controls using ClassWizard (just like you could map member variables to on-screen controls).

In MFC, the CRecordset and CDaoRecordset classes have a member called m_strFilter that matches the criterialist and m_strSort that matches the orderlist in the SQL SELECT statement.

Chapter 9

Internet and Intranet Programming

- Client-Server Programming
- Common Gateway Interface (CGI)
- CGI with Database Access
- Socket Communications
- Service Protocols
- Initializing Windows Sockets
- Primary Socket Functions
- SMTP Classes
- Creating the CPNSMTP Class from CPNCommandSocket
- HTML Display
- ISAPI Filter

Internet and intranet programming normally takes the form of a client and a server program, which you can create using Visual C++. In this chapter we will be discussing various forms of programs that can be used in an Internet or intranet environment—both client- and server-style programming.

An intranet uses Internet technology to create a private internet within an organization. An intranet has many of the same features as the Internet, such as email, web pages, and file transfer, but access is restricted to within the organization. From a programmer's perspective, there is no difference between internet and intranet style of programming.

Client-Server Programming

A client/server application consists of two programs, a client and a server. A client program interfaces with the user and makes a request from the server program. The server program receives the request and responds to the client program.

Technically, there isn't a substantial difference between the client and server. Both programs send and receive data. Probably the most common demonstration of a client/server pair is a web browser client (such as Internet Explorer or Netscape Navigator) and a web server.

A web browser functions as a client. When you visit a web page, your browser-client attempts to connect to the web server at that site. The web server software runs 24 hours a day, 7 days a week, waiting for clients to make connections.

Most servers can perform more than one process at a time. For example, the main thread of the web server waits for incoming client requests. When a request arrives, the web server creates a child thread to process the requests, then the main thread waits for the next client's request.

Most client/server interaction for the Internet is performed using a *socket*, which is similar in concept to a file handle. A file handle provides an application with read/write access to data stored in a file. A socket gives an application read/write access to another program and enables applications to communicate with each other whether the applications both reside on the same computer or on a remote computer connected through the Internet or intranet.

Another form of a server application is called the Common Gateway Interface (CGI). A CGI application resides and is executed on a web server at the request of a client (browser). The results of a CGI program, which, in many cases, is a dynamically generated web page, are returned to the client.

Web Servers Are Free to Fly

Throughout this chapter, we will be referring to the use of a web server. The following is a list of the most commonly used web servers, which are available free of charge:

Microsoft Internet Information Server (IIS)

Microsoft's high-end web server, intended for professional web hosting, provides HTTP, FTP, and some SMTP support and is currently up to version 5. This software needs either NT Server to run, or will run with Windows 2000. You can download it free from Microsoft or get it from the NT Option Pack CD for Windows NT; it is included on the Windows 2000 CD.

Microsoft Personal Web Server (PWS)

Microsoft's personal-level web server, an excellent choice for most software-development needs, provides HTTP support and can run ASP and other extensions just as IIS can. It requires Win95/98, NT, or 2000 and is available for download or from the Windows NT Option Pack CD. It is included on the Win98 and Win2000 CDs.

Apache

Apache is a primarily Unix-based web server, but now has a Windows version as well. It runs CGI programs in its Windows version, but presently does not directly support ASP or ISAPI extensions as do IIS and PWS.

Each of the these servers is available free of charge and can be set up on a single machine without the need for a network connection for development purposes (to actually "publish" a web site for the world to see, you would need a full time Internet connection). We strongly recommend the use of PWS for development purposes because it is free, easy to install and manage, and mimics IIS very closely. Chances are good you already have it on a CD.

Developing Client/Server Programs on a Single Machine

In internet programming, we will often be referring to client and server machines. But, there is no reason that the two cannot be the same machine, the perfect example being a single machine running a web server and a client browser.

Throughout this chapter, we will be referring to the IP address or the URL for a server machine. When you are doing single-machine development, you don't always need a connection to the Internet, or a network at all, to use some of these programs.

The TCP/IP protocol (which the Internet runs on) defines the IP address of 127.0.0.1 as the name localhost. This special address refers to the local machine itself. If you have server software such as PWS or IIS installed, you can enter a URL of HTTP://localhost or HTTP://127.0.0.1 in order to have your browser connect to the web server on your own machine.

Common Gateway Interface (CGI)

CGI Programming

CGI (Common Gateway Interface) programs are programs that exist and are run on a web server. They are normally run on the server at the request of a client computer by clicking a button or link in the client's browser program. CGI programs usually perform some task, such as searching or storing information on the server and generating a dynamic HTML page in response to the user's request such as data from a database.

Figure 9–1 demonstrates the basic flow for CGI programs:

A. The user clicks on a link or a submit button on their browser. The browser sends the request to the web server.
B. The web server identifies the request as one to run a CGI program. It takes any related data from the client's request (such as fields from a form) and runs the CGI program, passing it that data.
C. The CGI program has run and performed whatever operation it was requested to do (such as searching a database). The CGI program outputs the results to the standard output device using HTML.
D. The web server takes the redirected results from the CGI program and sends them back to the client browser that made the original request. When the client receives the results, which is in HTML format, the client displays the results within the browser window.

Notice that it is the web server's responsibility to send the results of the CGI program back to the client. The CGI program needn't be concerned with coordinating results returned to users or having multiple users. The web server handles this.

CGI programs are developed as console or text applications and not GUI programs that contain Windows controls. CGI programs can be written in just about any language that can perform the following basic input and output requirements of CGI:

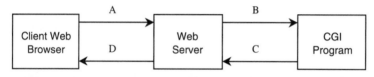

Figure 9–1   The basic flow for CGI programs.

- The program must be able to read from the standard input device (keyboard) or get values from the system environment.
- The program must be able to write to the standard output device (display).

The basic (yet most challenging) parts of starting a CGI program involve input and output. These items are described here and a basic understanding of HTML (Hyper Text Markup Language, the language used to create web pages) is assumed.

CGI Output

A CGI program outputs results by sending the data in a specific format to the standard output device, such as cout in C++.

The most common format is HTML text, but you can also output an image, sound, or any other file type that a web browser will recognize. We use the HTML text format in this chapter since it is by far the most common.

A CGI program must begin its output with the following string: Content-type: text/html followed by two carriage returns. This is illustrated in Code 9–1.

Code 9–1

```
cout << "Content-type: text/html\n\n";
```

Next, the CGI must output the entire web page using HTML tags. The minimum requirements are the start and end BODY and HTML codes. You can insert any web page code between the start and end codes as shown in Code 9–2.

Code 9–2

```
cout << "Content-type: text/html\n\n";
cout << "<HTML><BODY>\n; // \n isn't needed, but makes HTML source more readable
cout << "Hello world<P>\n"; // <P> is an HTML paragraph tag
cout << "</HTML></BODY>" << endl;
```

Some servers put a time-out period on programs so they don't become "runaway" processes. Normally, if your program doesn't complete its task and output its data in 10 seconds, the program will be terminated by the web server and an error message returned to the client by the server. Don't forget that even error messages from the program must appear in the HTML format.

Creating a Simple CGI Program

A CGI program must be run from a web server program. This means that you must have software such as IIS or PWS installed and running on at least one machine to work with these CGI examples.

Create a basic CGI program in Visual C++ as a Win32 Console application:

1. From the File menu choice in VC++, select New.
2. Make sure the Projects tab is selected in the New dialog that appears.
3. Select the Win32 Console Application item in the list of possible project types.
4. Enter a name for your project, such as SimpleCGI, in the Project Name field (see Figure 9–2).
5. Click OK.
6. In the Win32 Console Application Wizard—Step 1 of 1 dialog, click An Application that supports MFC option.
7. Click Finish, and then OK.

Notice in step 6 that we could have selected just about any type of application. We selected MFC because in future versions of CGI we will be using MFC classes such a CString and CRecordset for database access. The _main function created by the AppWizard will look like Code 9–3.

We need to change this code to output its text in HTML format including the CGI header requirements as shown in Code 9–4.

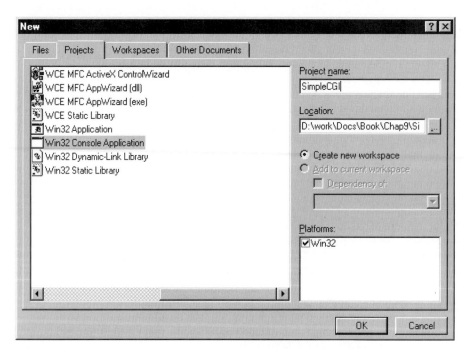

Figure 9–2 Creating a console application in AppWizard for CGI.

Code 9-3

```
int _tmain(int argc, TCHAR* argv[], TCHAR* envp[])
{
        int nRetCode = 0;

        // initialize MFC and print and error on failure
        if (!AfxWinInit(::GetModuleHandle(NULL), NULL, ::GetCommandLine(), 0))
        {
                // TODO: change error code to suit your needs
                cerr << _T("Fatal Error: MFC initialization failed") << endl;
                nRetCode = 1;
        }
        else
        {
                // TODO: code your application's behavior here.
                CString strHello;
                strHello.LoadString(IDS_HELLO);
                cout << (LPCTSTR)strHello << endl;
        }


        return nRetCode;
}
```

Code 9-4

```
int _tmain(int argc, TCHAR* argv[], TCHAR* envp[])
{
        int nRetCode = 0;

        // Output standard HTML CGI header
        cout << "Content-type: text/html\n\n";
        cout << "<HTML><BODY>" << endl;

        // initialize MFC and print and error on failure
        if (!AfxWinInit(::GetModuleHandle(NULL), NULL, ::GetCommandLine(), 0))
        {
                // TODO: change error code to suit your needs
                cout << "Fatal Error: MFC initialization failed<P>" << endl;
        }
        else
        {
                // TODO: code your application's behavior here.
                cout << "<H1>" << endl;
                cout << "Hey! This is my first CGI response!<P>" << endl;
                cout << "</H1>" << endl;
        }
}

        // Output standard HTML CGI footer
```

```
        cout << "</HTML></BODY>" << endl;

        return nRetCode;
}
```

Change the project so that it uses the statically linked version of MFC. You won't need the MFC42 DLL files to run the application this way.

1. Go to the Project menu item, and select Project Settings.
2. In the General tab of the Project Settings dialog, change the Settings For field to say *All* Configurations.
3. Change the Microsoft Foundation Classes combo box to say Use MFC in a Static Library.
4. Click OK to close the Project Settings dialog.
5. Compile and build the program.

If you attempt to run the program in debug mode, it will simply pop up and disappear before you have a chance to read its output. If you run it normally (by pressing Ctrl-F5, or selecting the Build/Execute menu items), then you should see its output as shown in Figure 9–3.

Notice that the `Context-type: text/html` text appears first, then a blank line followed by the HTML tags <HTML> and <BODY> appear.

You need to copy the SimpleCGI.exe file from our project (should be in the Debug folder) into the directory structure used by the web server software. We need to copy it into a web server folder whose security permits program or script execution.

For both PWS and IIS software, this is typically the C:\InetPub\Scripts folder, if you selected the defaults when you installed the web server. Copy the SimpleCGI.exe file from the Debug folder to the C:\InetPub\Scripts folder.

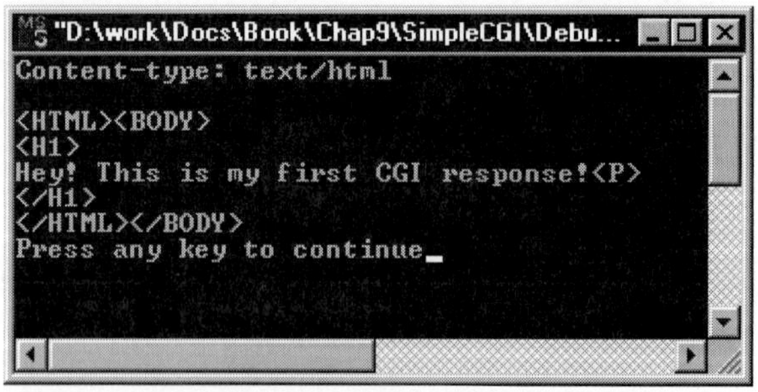

Figure 9–3   Output of running the CGI program.

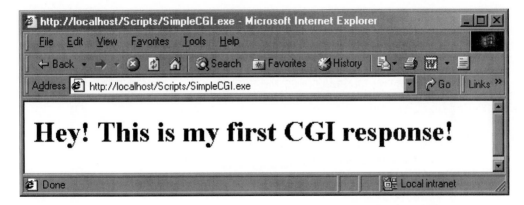

Figure 9–4   The output of the CGI program in a web browser.

Start your web browser and as a URL enter the web address of your web server followed by the server location of the CGI program such as http://localhost/Scripts/SimpleCGI.exe. You should see the output from the CGI program now appear in your web browser such as Figure 9–4.

If you were to select the View menu item in the browser and then the Source submenu item, you would be able to see the source code that made up the HTML page as show in Code 9–5.

Code 9–5

```
<HTML><BODY>
<H1>
Hey! This is my first CGI response!<P>
</H1>
</HTML></BODY>
```

Notice how the `Context-type: html/text` is missing from the HTML source code even though our CGI program sent it as its output. This is because that text is used to identify to the browser the type of data that we sent it and defines how the data should be displayed.

CGI Input

Input to the CGI originates as a user's response to a web page. The input to a CGI program includes the contents of fields from a web page and various information about both the server and the client.

To understand this, it's helpful to think of the web page as a form with edit controls or fields. Each field is assigned a name and a value. This is shown in Figure 9–5.

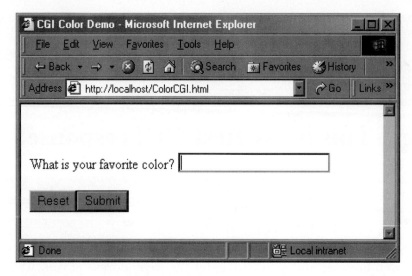

Figure 9–5　A browser based form.

The web page in Figure 9–5 has three controls on it: an Edit or Text field, a Reset button, and a Submit button. The HTML source code for this page is shown in Code 9–6.

Code 9–6

```
<HTML>
<HEAD>
<TITLE>CGI Color Demo</TITLE>
</HEAD>
<BODY>

<FORM ACTION="Scripts/ColorCGI.exe" METHOD="POST">
<P>What is your favorite color?
<INPUT NAME="Color" TYPE="text" SIZE="25"></P>

<INPUT NAME="name" TYPE="reset" VALUE="Reset">
<INPUT NAME="name" TYPE="submit" VALUE="Submit">

</FORM>
</BODY>
</HTML>
```

In Code 9–6, statements shown in Code 9–7 are key to our demonstration.

Code 9–7

```
<FORM ACTION="Scripts/ColorCGI.exe" METHOD="POST">
</FORM>
```

Code 9–7 defines the page as a form, by using the FORM tag. The FORM tag also defines the CGI program to be run when the user clicks the Submit button and whether it is a POST or a GET method. This example will run the Scripts/ColorCGI.exe CGI program using the POST method.

The INPUT tag (see Code 9–8) defines the Edit or Text box on the form and gives it the name of "Color."

Code 9–8

```
<INPUT NAME="Color" TYPE="text" SIZE="25"></P>
```

The TYPE specifier (Code 9–9) for the INPUT tag can define the Reset button on the form. If a Reset button is clicked on a form, it clears out all the users selections for the form.

Code 9–9

```
<INPUT NAME="name" TYPE="reset" VALUE="Reset">
```

The VALUE tag (Code 9–10) defines the Submit button on the form. When the user clicks this button, the web browser gathers all the user selections and sends them to the web server along with a request to run the CGI program that was specified in the FORM tag in Code 9–7.

Code 9–10

```
<INPUT NAME="name" TYPE="submit" VALUE="Submit">
```

Running a CGI Program via a Link

You can also run a CGI program via a link instead of a Submit button approach. To do this, the HTML tag for the link would include the path to the CGI executable on the server as well as any parameters to the CGI program hard-coded into the link as shown in Code 9–11.

Code 9–11

```
<A HREF="/Scripts/ColorCGI.exe?Color=Black">Favorite Color is black</A>
```

When the link above is displayed on the web page and the user clicks it, the client browser will tell the web server to run the ColorCGI.exe program, with a parameter of Color=Black.

GET vs. POST

The difference between the GET and POST is how the information from the form is sent to the CGI program from the server.

The GET method provides the user's input to the CGI program as an environment variable called QUERY_STRING. The CGI program reads this environment variable (using the getenv() function) and parses the string to get the user's input. The GET method also shows the input data to the user in the URL area of the browser, showing a string as in Code 9–12.

Code 9–12

```
http://www.somewhere.com/Script/ColorCGI.exe?Color=Black
```

A CGI program can read the data from the user's browser (submitted with the GET method) by including Code 9–13.

Code 9–13

```
char InputData[512];
strcpy( InputData, getenv( "QUERY_STRING" ) );
```

The GET method is acceptable for small amounts of data and is the default method when a CGI program is run via a link.

The POST method will provide the user's input to the CGI program as if it were type at the keyboard using the standard input device or cin in C++. If POST is used, then an environment variable called CONTENT_LENGTH indicates how much data is being sent. A CGI program can read this data into a buffer by including Code 9–14.

Code 9–14

```
char InputData[512];//612 byte limit-just for demonstration
int InputLength = atoi( getenv("CONTENT_LENGTH") );
cin.read( InputData, InputLength );
```

Your CGI program should inspect the REQUEST_METHOD environment variable to determine if the form was a GET or POST method and take the appropriate action to retrieve the form. In the *Parsing Input* section we demonstrate a helper function named PNGetAllParams() to determine the input method, which is used in the ColorCGI sample.

Parsing Input

Once the input is received via a POST or GET method, it must be parsed. All field values passed to the CGI program by either POST or GET appear as one long string. Each value is separated by an ampersand (&). For example, a two-value string might look like: `FavColor=Black&FavFood=Twinkies`

Here, `FavColor` and `FavFood` would be the names of two input fields from the form and `Black` and `Twinkies` are the values entered by the user.

The web browser and the web server convert data sent between them. Your CGI program needs to reverse these conversions in order to work with the received data. The conversions that the web server performs that your CGI program must reverse are:

- All spaces are converted to a + character
- Special characters (like \n) are converted to a % character followed by the ASCII code for the character
- Parameters are separated with the ampersand (&)

For example, the text This is a test\n is passed to your CGI program appears as:

```
This+is+a+test%0A.
```

Your CGI program needs to convert the string back to its original format (we will provide a helper function named PNGetParam() for this in the ColorCGI sample).

Once the string is parsed, store the input parameters in either an array of strings or in a long string of values. You would probably also want a function that searches the stored parameters to retrieve their values.

The ColorCGI Sample

This simple program demonstrates how to process a single field from a web client in a CGI program. As with the SimpleCGI demonstration, you will need to have a web server such as IIS or PWS installed and running on your computer (or your test server) in order to run through the demo.

Creating the ColorCGI Program

1. Follow the steps for creating the SimpleCGI program above.
2. Change the _main() function of the SimleCGI program to look like Code 9–15.

Code 9–15

```
int _tmain(int argc, TCHAR* argv[], TCHAR* envp[])
{
    int nRetCode = 0;

    // Output standard HTML CGI header
    cout << "Content-type: text/html\n\n";
    cout << "<HTML><BODY>" << endl;

    // initialize MFC and print and error on failure
    if (!AfxWinInit(::GetModuleHandle(NULL), NULL, ::GetCommandLine(), 0))
    {
```

```
        // TODO: change error code to suit your needs
        cerr << "Fatal Error: MFC initialization failed<P>" << endl;
    }
    else
    {
        // TODO: code your application's behavior here.
        PNGetAllParams();
        CString UsersColor;
        PNGetParam( "Color", UsersColor, "" );
        if( UsersColor.IsEmpty() )
            cout << "Hey, enter a color!" << endl;
        else
        {
            if( UsersColor.CompareNoCase( "blue" )==0 )
                cout << "Cool, I like blue also"<< endl;
            else
                cout << (LPCSTR) UsersColor << " is nice, but I prefer blue" <<
                endl;
        }
    }

    // Output standard HTML CGI footer
    cout << "</HTML></BODY>" << endl;

    return nRetCode;
}
```

3. Add the InputData global variable and the PNGetAllParams function (see Code 9–16) to your source code.

Code 9–16

```
char InputData[4096];

void PNGetAllParams()
{
    // Determing if was a POST or GET method
    if( getenv( "REQUEST_METHOD" ) == 0 )
    {
        cout << "No REQUEST_METHOD, must be running in DOS mode" << endl;
        return;
    }
    if( strcmp( getenv("REQUEST_METHOD"), "POST" ) == 0 )
    {
        // If POST, then get data from
        int InputLength = atoi( getenv("CONTENT_LENGTH") );
        cin.read( InputData, InputLength );
    }
    else
        // Otherwise it's a GET method, and retrieve from environment variable
```

```
        strcpy( InputData, getenv( "QUERY_STRING" ) );
}
```

The `InputData` is a global variable that will contain variables passed by the web browser to the web server and from the web server to the CGI program. The PNGet-AllParams() function determines if the parameters are available via the POST or GET method (as defined by the original FORM tag of the originating HTML page) and initializes InputData accordingly.

4. Add the PNGetParam() function to help extract parameters from the pass data as shown in Code 9–17.

Code 9–17

```c
int PNGetParam( const char * Name, CString& Dest, const char* Default )
{
    Dest.Empty();

    // Helper macro to convert two-character hex strings to character value
#define ToHex(Y) (Y>="0"&&Y<="9"?Y-"0":Y-"A"+10)
    // Search for the desired parameter name in InputData
    char* pArg = strstr( InputData, Name );
    if( pArg ) // If found
    {
        // Go to the start of the parameter
        pArg += strlen(Name);
        if( *pArg == "=" ) // Make sure there is an "=" where we expect it
        {
            pArg++;
            // Loop until we hit the end of this parameter value
            while( *pArg && *pArg != "&" )
            {
                // If the character is a "%", that means 2-character hex value follows
                if( *pArg == "%" )
                {
                    // Convert it to a single ASCII character and store at our
                    destination
                    Dest += (char)ToHex(pArg[1]) * 16 + ToHex(pArg[2]);
                    pArg += 3;
                }
                else
                    if( *pArg=="+" ) // If it's a "+", store a space at our destina-
                    tion
                    {
                        Dest += " ";
                        pArg++;
                    }
                    else
```

```
                Dest += *pArg++;
                // Otherwise, just store the character at our destination
        }
        return(1);
    }
}
Dest = Default; // If param not found, then use default parameter
return(0);
}
```

Code 9–17 can now be used to retrieve values from the InputData global variable, which PNGetAllParams initialized. The _main portion of code demonstrates how to call these two helper functions (see Code 9–18).

Code 9–18

```
CString UsersColor;
PNGetAllParams();
PNGetParam( "Color", UsersColor, "" );
// UsersColor now contains the text from the users web form.
```

5. Build the ColorCGI project and copy the exe file into the folder where your web server stores its CGI files (such as C:\InetPub\Scripts).
6. Create the HTML file for the form that will run the ColorCGI program (see Code 9–19).

Code 9–19

```
<HTML>
<HEAD>
<TITLE>CGI Color Demo</TITLE>
</HEAD>
<BODY>
<FORM ACTION="Scripts/ColorCGI.exe" METHOD="POST">
<P>What is your favorite color?
<INPUT NAME="Color" TYPE="text" SIZE="25"></P>
<INPUT NAME="name" TYPE="reset" VALUE="Reset">
<INPUT NAME="name" TYPE="submit" VALUE="Submit">
</FORM>
</BODY>
</HTML>
```

7. Store this file in the folder where your web server looks for html files (such as c:\Inetpub\wwwroot). Now, in your web browser, enter a URL to your web server machine and the ColorCGI.html file. This is shown in Figure 9–6.
8. Enter a color (or leave it blank) and select the Submit button. The Submit button tells the web server to run the ColorCGI.exe file with your form data. You should next see (if you entered a color of Green) a replica of Figure 9–7.

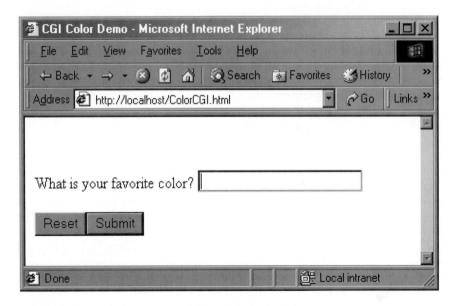

Figure 9–6 Display the ColorCGI.html file in the browser.

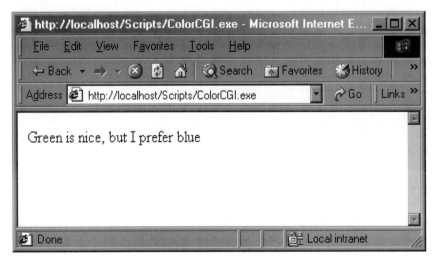

Figure 9–7 The Submit button causes the ColorCGI program to run.

CGI with Database Access

Using the MFC database classes in a CGI program is a fairly straightforward process. The demonstration here will utilize the PNStocks database from Chapter 8, *Databases*, with an ODBC connection.

ODBC Data Sources and CGI Programs

Normally, ODBC data sources are set up on a user basis. This means that each user name on a computer has its own set of ODBC data source settings. However, when a web server such as IIS is running, it is possible for it to run as a Service. This means that ODBC data sources may be running even before a user has logged in to the computer.

Since the web server runs the CGI program and it is possible for the web server to run without anyone logged in, the ODBC settings on a user-by-user basis won't apply to the CGI application.

To work around this, you need to make sure that any ODBC data sources that you want your CGI application to access are defined as a System DSN. This means that the DSN is available to all users of the computer and not just the user who actually set it up. You can do this in the ODBC administrator in the Control Panel (in Win2000, the ODBC administrator is inside the Administrator Tools, which is inside the Control Panel).

Creating the StockCGI Program

Create the StockCGI program by using the following steps.

1. Follow the steps as described in the creation of the ColorCGI program except make sure that _main() looks like Code 9–20.

Code 9–20

```
int _tmain(int argc, TCHAR* argv[], TCHAR* envp[])
{
    int nRetCode = 0;

    // Output standard HTML CGI header
    cout << "Content-type: text/html\n\n";
    cout << "<HTML><BODY>" << endl;

    // initialize MFC and print and error on failure
    if (!AfxWinInit(::GetModuleHandle(NULL), NULL, ::GetCommandLine(), 0))
    {
        // TODO: change error code to suit your needs
        cerr << "Fatal Error: MFC initialization failed<P>" << endl;
```

```
    }
    else
    {
        // TODO: code your application's behavior here.
        PNGetAllParams();
        CString Stock;
        PNGetParam( "Stock", Stock, "" );
        if( Stock.IsEmpty() )
            ListStocks();
        else
            ListTrades( Stock );
    }
    // Output standard HTML CGI footer
    cout << "</HTML></BODY>" << endl;

    return nRetCode;
}
```

2. In the stdafx.h file of your new project, add the following line:

```
#include <afxdb.h>
```

3. Add the two new functions (see Code 9–21) ListStocks and ListTrades to your .cpp file.

Code 9-21

```
void ListStocks()
{

    try
    {
        // Create the CDatabase object and connect it to the database
        CDatabase Db;
        Db.Open( NULL, FALSE, FALSE, "ODBC;DSN=PNStocks", FALSE );

        // Create CRecordset object, and pass the CDatabase to its constructor
        CRecordset Rs( &Db );

        // Open the SQL query with the CRecordset (Read only mode)
        Rs.Open(AFX_DB_USE_DEFAULT_TYPE,
            "select Symbol, Company from Stock order by Company" );

        CString Symbol, Company;
        cout << "Symbols and companies:<BR>" << endl;

        // Loop through list of all the Stock records found
        while( !Rs.IsEOF() )
        {
            // Get the Stock symbol and company name from the recordset
            Rs.GetFieldValue( (short)0, Symbol );
```

```
            Rs.GetFieldValue( (short)1, Company );
            // And output in HTML format
            cout << (LPCSTR)Symbol << "    ";
            cout << (LPCSTR)Company << "<BR>" << endl;
            Rs.MoveNext(); // Move to next record
        }

    }
    catch( CDBException* pE )
    {
        // Report any errors
        char Tmp[512];
        pE->GetErrorMessage( Tmp, sizeof(Tmp) );
        cout << "Error: " << Tmp << "<BR>" << endl;
    }

}
void ListTrades( const char* Symbol)
{

    try
    {
        // Create the CDatabase object and connect it to the database
        CDatabase Db;
        Db.Open( NULL, FALSE, FALSE, "ODBC;DSN=PNStocks", FALSE );

        // Create CRecordset object, and pass the CDatabase to its constructor
        CRecordset Rs( &Db );

        // Build Query string with the stock symbol, and open the
        // Trade and Stock tables with it
        CString Query;
        Query = "select Trade.TradeDate, Trade.Price from Trade, Stock ";
        Query += " where Stock.Symbol='";
        Query += Symbol;
        Query += "' and Stock.StockID=Trade.StockID ";
        Query += " order by Trade.TradeDate DESC";
        Rs.Open(AFX_DB_USE_DEFAULT_TYPE, Query);

        CString TradeDate, Price;
        if( Rs.IsEOF() )
            cout << "No trades found for " << Symbol << "<BR>" << endl;
        else
        {
            // Loop through all the Trade records for the specific stock symbol
            cout << "Trades for " << Symbol << ":<BR>" << endl;
            while( !Rs.IsEOF() )
            {
                // Retrieve the TradeDate and Price field values from the query
                Rs.GetFieldValue( (short)0, TradeDate );
```

```
        Rs.GetFieldValue( (short)1, Price );
        // Output in HTML format
        cout << (LPCSTR)TradeDate << "    ";
        cout << (LPCSTR)Price << "<BR>" << endl;
        Rs.MoveNext(); // Move to next record
      }
    }

  }
  catch( CDBException* pE )
  {
      // Report any errors in HTML format
      char Tmp[512];
      pE->GetErrorMessage( Tmp, sizeof(Tmp) );
      cout << "Error: " << Tmp << "<BR>" << endl;
  }

}
```

Notice the basic database access is similar in the two functions: A CDatabase object is constructed and opened (see Code 9–22).

Code 9–22

```
CDatabase Db;
Db.Open( NULL, FALSE, FALSE, "ODBC;DSN=PNStocks", FALSE );
```

A CRecordset object is constructed with the CDatabase and then a SQL query is performed to open the table as shown in Code 9–23.

Code 9–23

```
CRecordset Rs( &Db );
Rs.Open(AFX_DB_USE_DEFAULT_TYPE,
    "select Symbol, Company from Stock order by Company" );
```

The Rs recordset now contains the open table connection with access to the records that match the SQL SELECT statement. This is followed by a loop that goes through all the records found and extracts the field values from each record as shown in Code 9–24.

Code 9–24

```
while( !Rs.IsEOF() )
{
    // Get the Stock symbol and company name from the recordset
    Rs.GetFieldValue( (short)0, Symbol );
    Rs.GetFieldValue( (short)1, Company );
```

```
// And output in HTML format
cout << (LPCSTR)Symbol << "    ";
cout << (LPCSTR)Company << "<BR>" << endl;
Rs.MoveNext(); // Move to next record
}
```

4. Compile and build the new StockCGI program.
5. Copy the StockCGI.exe program from the Debug folder, into the folder where your web server software looks for CGI programs (for example, C:\InetPub\Scripts).
6. Create an HTML file named StockCGI.html that will let the user enter a stock symbol with the Submit button as shown in Code 9–25.

Code 9–25

```
<HTML>
<HEAD>
<TITLE>Stock CGI Demo</TITLE>
</HEAD>
<BODY>
<FORM ACTION="Scripts/StockCGI.exe" METHOD="POST">
<P>Enter Stock Symbol: <INPUT NAME="Stock" TYPE="text"
SIZE="25"></P>
<INPUT NAME="name" TYPE="reset" VALUE="Reset">
<INPUT NAME="name" TYPE="submit" VALUE="Submit">
</FORM>
</BODY>
</HTML>
```

7. Copy the stockCGI.html file to the folder where your web server keeps html files (for example, C:\InetPub\wwwroot).
8. On the web server, make sure that the ODBC administrator has a System DNS setup for the PNStocks data source name and that it is set up to point to the location of your PNStocks.mdb Access database file.
9. Test the CGI program with your browser by going to the web address http://localhost/StockCGI.html. Example screens and the StockCGI.HTML file in browser are shown in Figure 9–8.

Results of clicking Submit with no stock symbol entered (lists all stocks) as shown in Figure 9–9.

Results of clicking Submit with MSFT entered as a stock symbol is shown in Figure 9–10.

In this Database and CGI example, we opted to create a read-only recordset, which was easy to use for dynamic queries. We also could have created CRecordset-derived objects for our database tables (as described in Chapter 8).

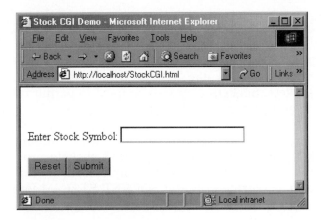

Figure 9–8 The display of the StockCGI.HTML program.

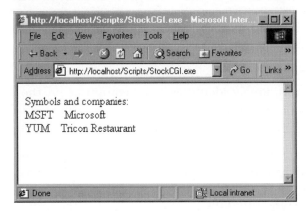

Figure 9–9 All stocks are shown if you don't enter a stock symbol.

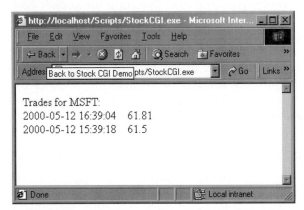

Figure 9–10 The results when the MSFT stock symbol is entered.

Socket Communications

A socket represents a connection between two processes that permits them to exchange data. Internet programs like FTP, web browsers, and chat programs all communicate via sockets. Sockets may also be used to permit two processes on the same machine to communicate as well.

We will address sockets in a cursory fashion, while attempting to present a reusable C++ socket class. It is worth noting that sockets provide more flexibility than described here. We will use the TCP/IP style sockets and not Unix or Xerox NS type. We'll also demonstrate only the SOCKET_STREAM family of sockets, but the class should be able to handle others such as datagrams, and raw sockets.

Unix has similar functions for all the Windows functions mentioned in this chapter except read() and write(). This means that with very few changes, the code presented here could be used in both Unix and Windows environments. We will, however, target the classes to the Windows environment.

When a computer is connected to the Internet, the computer is assigned an IP address. This address uniquely identifies your computer on the net. Both the client and the web server are represented as a single IP address each (though larger sites like www.ibm.com may split their IP address by geographical divisions).

In order to create a connection, the IP addresses of the server must be known by the client. In addition to the IP address, the process must know the port the other process is listening on. An IP address is like a building address; a port is the apartment number within the building.

Throughout this discussion, we will use the terms server and client. A server is the process that is constantly running and listening for socket connections. The client process contacts the server as needed.

MFC provides certain high-level classes for the support of HTTP and FTP protocols. It is best to use those classes rather than to rebuild them with normal socket classes. The purpose of this section is to describe sockets in general and implementing protocols not supported by MFC such as the SMTP and POP3 email protocols. We will discuss the HTTP and FTP protocols and classes in a later section.

Why Not Use the CSocket and CAsyncSocket Classes?

Socket classes are provided by MFC and are relatively easy to use. The CAsyncSocket class provides nonblocking sockets, while the CSocket class provides blocking sockets. A nonblocking function is a function that yields even if it is not finished processing. A blocking function is one that will wait until all the processing on the socket (such as a read) is completed. A blocking function that is performed on a server that has suddenly crashed might wait forever, making your program appear as if it has crashed. In other words, if you call a blocking function, it will wait until its processing is complete; if you call a nonblocking function, it will return right away, whether its processing is done or not.

These classes are used for well-defined and well-behaved socket-style communications. However, with the CAsyncSocket classes, you must deal with all the timing issues yourself. And with the CSocket classes, you have to deal with the possibility that the server you are connected to has timed out, making your socket processing appear to have locked up.

The socket classes presented here will be both blocking and non-blocking and permit you to easily define a time-out value for the sockets. It is best to avoid using the CSocket class because it has all kinds of unusual tricks to deal with—such as the creation of invisible windows and timer events sent to those windows. These things have nothing to do with socket communications but can still cause the socket connection to fail. We can only assume that this logic is a leftover from the days of 16-bit socket programming, where multithreaded processing was not available.

The CSocket and CAsyncSocket classes do provide functionality not provided by the CPNSocket classes, such as the ability to work with the CSocketFile class. If you have the need to work with a CSocketFile, then use CSocket. In most other cases, you will find the CPNSocket classes easier and more flexible.

Service Protocols

Client and server programs communicate over a standard port using a standard protocol as defined by an Internet Request For Comment (RFC) document. This document describes how the client and server are to send data back and forth to each other. If you are writing a client or server program for a specific protocol such as File Transfer Protocol (FTP) or the Hyper Text Transfer Protocol (HTTP), then you start by locating and reading the RFC document for that protocol.

You can find the RFC documents (there are many of them) by searching the following web sites:

- http://www.faqs.org/rfcs/
- http://www.cis.ohio-state.edu/hypertext/information/rfc.html
- http://www.pmg.lcs.mit.edu/rfc.html

Some of these protocol documents can be quite lengthy and wordy, thus making for very complex reading. However, the end result is the same: They describe what your program must send and receive through a socket in order to communicate

---

with a client or server using a specific protocol. They will also describe the port number used by a particular service. Table 9.1 lists some of the most common port numbers used by services.

A server has software running 24 hours a day, 7 days a week to handle specific services as specified by the RFC document for that protocol. Not all web servers provide all services; they normally only provide HTTP and sometimes FTP.

While a detailed description of any protocol can be quite lengthy, we will present a very brief description of the SMTP protocol. SMTP is used to send email. A typical exchange between an SMTP client (such as Outlook or Outlook Express) and an SMTP server (such as IIS or Microsoft Exchange) is shown in Table 9.2.

Notice that the SMTP protocol defines only the prefixes of the strings from the server and not the entire text. A client program checks the prefix of the response from the server. The text after the prefix is usually a descriptive piece of text to give more detail on either a success or failed request.

In the SMTP protocol, the RCPT TO line may be repeated for multiple recipients. The DATA section, which defines the body of the message, is plain text. Attachments in an email are really embedded in the body of the message using the UUEncode and MIME definitions, which are beyond the scope of this section.

The sending and receiving of the strings in Table 9.2 takes place through a socket connection between the client and server programs.

Table 9.1 Port Numbers and Internet Protocols

Service	Port(s)	Meaning
FTP	21, 20	File Transfer Protocol
Telnet	23	Telnet, for remote login ability
SMTP	25	Simple Mail Transfer Protocol, for sending email
HTTP	80	Hyper Text Transfer Protocol, for web page viewing
POP3	110	Post Office Protocol, for receiving email
NNTP	119	Network News Transfer, for newsgroups
NTP	123	Network Time Protocol, for getting the correct time
SNMP	161	Simple Network Management Protocol, for managing your network

Table 9.2   An Exchange Between an SMTP Client and an SMTP Server

Event	Action
Client connects.	The server sends a greeting message to the client, starting with "220," which indicates success. For example: **"220 Hello User, welcome to xyz.com SMTP Server.\n"**
Client checks server response.	Any value other than 220 at the start of the message indicates an error and the client should disconnect. Otherwise, it is safe to continue.
Client sends HELO command.	A HELO command identifies the domain that the email will be coming from. For example: **"HELO somecompany.com\n"**
Server responds to HELO command.	A string is sent from the SMTP server starting with "250" if email is accepted from the specified domain. If email is not accepted from that domain, you will get a response back other than "250." For example: **"250 smtp.somewhere.com Hello 192.0.1.2, pleased to meet you\n"**
The client checks the response.	If the server sent back anything but a string starting with "250," then the client disconnects; otherwise, it proceeds.
The client sends MAIL FROM command.	The client sends a MAIL FROM command to identify who the email is coming from. The format of the string would be: **"MAIL FROM: mario@somecompany.com\n"**
The server sends back an acknowledgment of the sender name.	The server sends back a string that starts with "250" if the sender's email name is acceptable. If not acceptable, it will return something other than "250." For example: **"250 2.1.0 mario@somecompany.com... Sender ok\n"**
The client checks the response.	If the response from the server is anything but a string starting with "250," then it should disconnect; otherwise, it may proceed.
The client sends a RCPT TO command to indicate the email destination.	The client sends a RCPT TO command followed by the name of the intended recipient for the email. For example: **"RCPT TO: mario@openroad.org\n"**
The server sends back acknowledgment of the recipient name.	If the recipient name is acceptable to the server, it sends back a string that starts with "250." If the name is unacceptable, it sends back something other than "250." For example: **"250 2.1.5 mario@openroad.org... Recipient ok\n"**
The client checks the response.	If the response from the server was anything but a string starting with "250," then the client disconnects; otherwise, it proceeds.

(continued)

Table 9.2 An Exchange Between an SMTP Client and an SMTP Server (*continued*)

Event	Action
The client sends the DATA command.	The client sends a DATA command by itself. For example: **"DATA\n"**
The server sends back an acknowledgment of the DATA command.	The server sends back a string starting with "354" to indicate that it is ready to receive the body of the message. A string starting with anything else is considered an error. For example: **"354 Enter mail, end with "." on a line by itself"**
The client checks the response.	If the response from the server starts with anything other than "354," then the client should disconnect; otherwise, it proceeds.
The client sends the text of the body of the message.	The client sends the entire text of the message, possibly in several chunks. There is no response for each chunk. To end the sending of the data, the client sends a "." on a line by itself. For example: **"Hello Mario\n\tHow are you?\n.\n"**
The server acknowledges receipt of the message body.	The server sends back a message indicating that it has received the data for the message, starting with "250." If it returns a string with anything but "250," then an error has occurred. For example: **"250 2.0.0 e4M08lA08772 Message accepted for delivery\n"**
The client checks the response.	If the return string starts with anything but "250," then the client disconnects and reports the error. Otherwise, the message was accepted for delivery.

Initializing Windows Sockets

In order to establish a socket connection, you must first initialize the Windows Socket system by calling the WSAStartup() function if you created the application using the SDK. In an MFC program, you can use the AfxSocketInit() function. The Windows Socket system must be initialized from each thread that will be using it.

For client style programs, a good place to call AfxSocketInit() is within the InitInstance() function that ClassWizard added to your CWinApp-derived application class as shown in Code 9–26.

Code 9–26

```
BOOL CMailerApp::InitInstance()
{
        if (!AfxSocketInit())
        {
             AfxMessageBox(IDP_SOCKETS_INIT_FAILED);
             return FALSE;
        }
        // Portions of code removed for readability
```

If you are writing a server program, it is important to realize that a server will typically start a child thread to handle each client. This means that each child thread must call the AfxSocketInit() function for itself as shown in Code 9–27.

Code 9–27

```
UINT PortResponder( LPVOID lParam )
{
        AfxSocketInit(); // Each thread intializes Windows Sockets
        CString Tmp;

        SOCKADDR_IN SockAddr;
        int Size=sizeof(SOCKADDR);
        HOSTENT* pHost;

        CSocket Sock;
        if( !Sock.Create( (int)lParam ) ) // Someone already has that port
                return(-1);

        Sock.Listen( 5 );
        CSocket Connected;

        if( Sock.Accept( Connected ) )
        {
                // The Connected socket is now connected to a client
                // of this server.
                // Process that request as desired.
                Connected.Close();
        }
        return( 0 );
}

int CSomeView::MonitorPort(int Port)
{
        AfxBeginThread( PortResponder, (LPVOID)Port, THREAD_PRIORITY_LOWEST );
        return( 1 );
}
```

In Code 9–27, the MonitorPort() function is a typical View class member function. It calls AfxBeginThread() to start a child thread. That child thread calls the PortResponder() function and terminates when the port responder is ended.

The PortResponder() function, which now starts in a child thread, calls the AfxSocketInit() function to initialize sockets for that thread. It also demonstrates how to have a thread call the CSocket functions such as Create(), Listen(), and Accept() to wait for an incoming socket connection from a client program.

Primary Socket Functions

The following functions outline the operations for a socket connection. We will describe each Windows SDK function and its counterpart in the CPNSocket class.

SOCKET socket(int AddressFamily, int Type, int Protocol);
The socket() function creates a socket handle. It is not yet connected to another process. The parameters are shown in Table 9.3. A typical example of calling this function is shown in Code 9–28. The CPNSocket class calls this function in the constructor function is shown in Code 9–29.

Code 9–28

```
SOCKET Socket;
Socket = socket( AF_INET, SOCK_STREAM, 0 );
if( Socket != INVALID_SOCKET )
        // Function worked
```

Code 9–29

```
CPNSocket::CPNSocket( int nFamily=AF_INET, int nType=SOCK_STREAM, int nProtocol=0 )
{
        // Initialize the default timeout for sockets
        m_nTimeOut=10000;
        // Try to initialize the CPNSocket, using the socket system call
        m_nSocket = ::socket( nFamily, nType, nProtocol );
        if( m_nSocket < 0 && m_bThrowException ) // If an error, and we should
        //throw it
```

Table 9.3   Parameters Used in the SOCKET() Function

Parameter	Meaning
AddressFamily	Indicates the address family, which defines the network type. While values such as AF_IPX can be used for netware networks, the most common parameter is AF_INET for Internet family (TCP/IP protocol).
Type	Indicates the type of socket, either SOCK_STREAM for a reliable, sequenced, two-way connection between processes using the TCP protocol. SOCK_DGRAM is an alternative, which is not connection based, and packets may arrive out of order, using the UDP protocol. More often than not, you will be using SOCK_STREAM.
Protocol	Defines the protocol to be used for the specific address family type. Note: This is not a service protocol like FTP or SMTP. The definition of this parameter depends on the AddressFamily protocol, but for most cases of AF_INET for AddressFamily, you can use zero.

```
                    ThrowErrMsg( "socket() call failed: %d", m_nSocket );
        if( m_nSocket >= 0 )
                    IncRef();
}
```

int bind(SOCKET Socket, const struct sockaddr FAR *Name, int NameLen);
The bind() function is called to associate an unconnected socket with a name. For an Internet socket, the name defines the address family, a host address, and a port number (see Table 9.4). This function is called before the listen() function, which is used by servers to wait for an incoming connection request.

The Name parameter to bind(), which is actually a pointer to a sockaddr_in structure that has been type-cast to a sockaddr pointer, must have the data structure shown in Table 9.5 initialized.

The following two functions are available from the CPNSocket class for easier binding as shown in Code 9–30. An example us using the CPNSocket class for binding is shown in Code 9–31. The Bind functions are usually called by server-type programs.

Code 9–30

```
// Bind Functions
int CPNSocket::Bind( struct sockaddr* sapMyAddr, int nAddrLen ) const
{
    if( m_nSocket < 0 )
    {
        if( m_bThrowException ) // If not setup correctly
            ThrowErrMsg( ErrNotInit );
        return(-1);
    }
    // Call the bind system function to actually do connect.
    int Ret = ::bind( m_nSocket, sapMyAddr, nAddrLen );
    if( Ret < 0 && m_bThrowException ) // If there was an error, and we should throw
it.
        ThrowErrMsg( "bind() failed: %d", Ret );
    return( Ret );
}
```

Table 9.4   Parameters for the bind() Function

Parameter	Meaning
Socket	The socket to be bound. This would be the return value from the socket() function call.
Name	This is a pointer to a sockaddr structure, which defines the address and port we are binding to the socket. See example for initialization of the structure.
NameLen	Defines the number of bytes in the Name structure.

Table 9.5   Data Structure Members for the Name Parameter of the bind() Function

Member	Description
sin_family	This is the Address Family value for the type of networking protocol. For Internet and intranet style connections via TCP/IP, it will be AF_INET.
sin_addr	This is the TCP/IP address of the desired connection. In the case of preparing a server-style socket, this should be initiliazed with INADDR_ANY meaning that any IP address may connect to the server. See htonl description below.
sin_port	This is the port that the TCP/IP socket connection should utilize. For server-style sockets, it defines the port that the connection will be listening on for client connection requests. See htons description in box.

```
// Overloaded Bind functin, is easier to call then previous
int CPNSocket::Bind( int nPort, int nFamily=AF_INET, int nAddr=INADDR_ANY ) const
{
    struct sockaddr_inSrvrAdrs;
    memset( &SrvrAdrs, 0, size of( SrvrAdrs ) );
    SrvrAdrs.sin_family = nFamily;
    SrvrAdrs.sin_addr.s_addr = htonl( nAddr );
    SrvrAdrs.sin_port = htons( nPort );
    // Here, we call our 'other' Bind member function
    return( Bind( (struct sockaddr*)&SrvrAdrs, (int)sizeof( SrvrAdrs ) ) );
}
```

Code 9–31

```
CPNSocket Socket;
Socket.Bind( 25 ); // Binds to port 25, for SMTP connections
```

int closesocket(SOCKET Socket);

The closesocket() function closes the socket specified by the Socket parameter. The CPNSocket class takes special care called reference counting, in handling the closing of sockets. The CPNSocket() destructor automatically closes the socket it wraps when the object goes out of scope. But this behavior offers a bit of a challenge when also providing functionality for things like copy constructors and assignment operators. For example, image 2 CPNSocket Objects as shown in Code 9–32.

Code 9–32

```
CPNSocket A, B;
A = B;
```

In Code 9–32, A has been set to the same socket that B contains. The problem is that when the destructor for A is later called and its socket is closed, the B object now has an invalid socket handle because the two shared the same socket handle.

In order to work around this problem, the CPNSocket class implements reference counting, using the STL "map" class.

With reference counting, when you have a resource like a socket handle, you also track the number of object instances that are used or referenced. Then, in your destructor, decrement the reference count for that handle. If the count is zero, then no other class instances are using that specific socket and it can be safely closed.

The map class was selected because it lets you store two pieces of data called the "key" and the "value" for that key. The socket handle is the key, and its reference count is the key's value. You can look at the simple IncRef(), DecRef(), and GetRef() functions in the protected section of the class definition for the details as shown in Code 9–33. The CPNSocket::~CPNSocket destructor function is written as shown in Code 9–33.

Code 9–33

```
CPNSocket::~CPNSocket()
{
        if( m_nSocket >= 0 )
                Close();
}

// Closes socket, but pays attention to reference counting
int CPNSocket::Close()
{
        int Ret = m_nSocket;
```

```
        if( Ret < 0 && m_bThrowException )
                ThrowErrMsg( "Close called on a closed socket" );
        if( Ret > 0 )
        {
                // Decrement the count of objects using this socket
                DecRef();
                if( !GetRef() ) // If this is the last object
                        closesocket( m_nSocket ); // then really close it
                m_nSocket = -1;
        }
        return( Ret );
}
```

int connect(SOCKET Socket, const struct sockaddr FAR *Name, int Name-Len); The connect() function attempts to establish a connection to a server. This is called by a client-style program. The Socket parameter (see Table 9.6) is connected to a server socket. When the client program calls the connect function, the accept function on the server program returns (for nonblocking mode).

The Name parameter to connect, which is actually a pointer to a sockaddr_in structure, has been type-cast to a sockaddr pointer and must have the data structures initialized shown in Table 9.7.

The CPNSocket class provides two overloaded Connect() functions for simplified interaction with the connect SDK function. The server address is specified in string format such as "www.company.com" or "127.0.0.1" is provided as shown in Code 9–34. Using the CPNSocket class, it is now possible to connect to a server by simply using Code 9–35.

Code 9–34

```
// Connect - Establishes a socket connection to a server
BOOL CPNSocket::Connect( struct sockaddr * sapSrvrAdrs, int nLenAddr ) const
{
    if( m_nSocket < 0 )
    {
```

Table 9.6   Socket Parameter List

Parameter	Meaning
Socket	The socket to be used for the connection. It must not already be connected.
Name	This is a pointer to a sockaddr structure that defines the server IP address we want to connect to. See example for initialization of the structure.
NameLen	Defines the number of bytes in the Name structure.

Table 9.7   The sockaddr_in Data Structure

Member	Description
sin_family	This is the AddressFamily value for the type of networking protocol. For Internet and intranet style connections via TCP/IP, it will be AF_INET.
sin_addr	This is the TCP/IP address of the desired connection (the server). See htonl description in the bind function for more details.
sin_port	This is the port that the TCP/IP socket connection should utilize. For server-style sockets, it defines the port where the connection will be listening for client connection requests. See htons description in the bind function for more details.

```
        if( m_bThrowException ) // If not setup correctly
            ThrowErrMsg( ErrNotInit );
        return(FALSE);
    }

    // Call the connect system function to actually do connect.
    int Ret = ::connect( m_nSocket, (struct sockaddr*)sapSrvrAdrs, nLenAddr );
    if( Ret==SOCKET_ERROR )
    {
        if( m_bThrowException )
            ThrowErrMsg( "connect() failed", WSAGetLastError() );
        return( FALSE );
    }

    if( TimedOut(toWrite) )
    {
        if( m_bThrowException )
            ThrowErrMsg( "connect timed out" );
        return(FALSE);
    }
    if( Ret < 0 && m_bThrowException ) // If there was an error, and we should throw
    it.
        ThrowErrMsg( "connect() failed: %d", Ret );
    return( Ret==0?TRUE:FALSE );
}

// Overloaded Connection function, easier to call then previous version
int CPNSocket::Connect( const char* cpHostAddr, short sPort ) const
{
    // Setup and init the sock_addr_in struct, needed by real connect function
    struct sockaddr_in SrvrAdrs;
    memset( &SrvrAdrs, 0, sizeof( SrvrAdrs ) );

    // If szHostAddr looks like "127.0.0.1" then it's easy, just
    // call inet_addr to convert the string into a netword address ID integer
```

```
    if( isdigit(cpHostAddr[0]) )
        SrvrAdrs.sin_addr.s_addr = inet_addr( cpHostAddr );
    else
    {
        // Otherwise, it may be a host name. Get its IP address and use that.
        // For example, szHostAddr may be www.acme.com
        struct hostent * pHostEnt = gethostbyname( cpHostAddr );
        if( pHostEnt == NULL )
        {
            if( m_bThrowException )
             ThrowErrMsg( "Unable to determine IP for "%s"", cpHostAddr );
            return( -1 );
        }
        SrvrAdrs.sin_addr.s_addr = *(long*)pHostEnt->h_addr_list[0];
    }
    SrvrAdrs.sin_family = AF_INET;
    // Call htons, to convert out local pc short to format compatible with the "net"
    SrvrAdrs.sin_port = htons( sPort );

    // finally, call the other version of Connect, with the struct we set up
    return( Connect( (struct sockaddr*) &SrvrAdrs , (int)sizeof( SrvrAdrs ) ) );
}
```

Code 9–35

```
CPNSocket Socket;
Socket.Connect( "smtp.somewhere.com", 25 ); // Establish connection with
SMTP server
```

int listen(SOCKET Socket, int BacklLog); The listen() function places the specified socket Socket in "listen" mode, where the operating system knows that incoming connections on the specific port of the socket will be connected to it. This function is called from a server-style program, after a bind() function is called and before a listen() function call. The BackLog parameter indicates the number of connections the operating system should buffer before rejecting connections. A typical value for BackLog is five.

The CPNSocket class provides a Listen() function to simplify calling the listen SDK function as shown in Code 9–36.

Code 9–36

```
int CPNSocket::Listen( int nBackLog ) const
{
    if( m_nSocket < 0 )
    {
        if( m_bThrowException )
            ThrowErrMsg( ErrNotInit ); // Error string
        return( -1 );
```

```
    }
    // Call the system "listen" function
    int Ret = ::listen( m_nSocket, nBackLog );
    if( Ret < 0 && m_bThrowException )
        ThrowErrMsg( "listen() failed: %d", Ret );
    return( Ret );
}
```

SOCKET accept(SOCKET Socket, struct sockaddr FAR *Name, int FAR *NameLen); The accept() function is called by server-style programs and waits for an incoming connection. Table 9.8 lists the accept() parameters. The return value is a new socket connection, which is connected to a client socket. Notice when the client program calls the connect function, the accept() function returns (for non-blocking mode) (see Code 9–37).

Code 9–37

```
The CPNSocket class provides an Accept helper function for calling the accept SDK
function:
// Accept - Used by servers, to accept a socket connection from a client
int CPNSocket::Accept( CPNSocket& msrRet, struct sockaddr* sapClientAddr, int* npLen )
const
{
    int MyLen;
    struct sockaddr_in Client;
    // To make things easier on our caller, we can create the struct
    if( sapClientAddr == 0 )
    {
        sapClientAddr = (sockaddr*)& Client;
        npLen = &MyLen;
    }
    if( m_nTimeOut && TimedOut(toRead) )
    {
        if( m_bThrowException )
            ThrowErrMsg( "Timed out on Accept" );
        return( -1 );
```

Table 9.8   accept() Parameters

Parameter	Meaning
Socket	The socket to be used for the connection. It must not already be connected.
Name	This is a pointer to a sockaddr structure, which is where this function will store information about the client that connected, such as its IP address. See example for initialization of the structure.
NameLen	Defines the number of bytes in the Name structure.

```
    }
    // Call the system "accept" function
    int nRet = ::accept( m_nSocket, sapClientAddr, (int*)npLen );
    if( nRet < 0 && m_bThrowException )
        ThrowErrMsg( "accept failed: %d", nRet );
    msrRet = nRet;
    return( nRet );
}
```

int recv(SOCKET Socket, char FAR *Buffer, int Len, int Flags); The recv()
function is used to read data from a socket, assuming the program at the other end
has sent some data. Returns SOCKET_ERROR if an error occurred, otherwise the
number of bytes read. Table 9.9 contains the recv() parameters.

Reading data from a socket is similar to reading it from a file with one major exception. When you read from a socket, reading fewer bytes than anticipated does not
indicate the end of the data. For example, if you attempted to read 100 bytes from a
file, but only read 50, that would normally mean that you hit the end of the file.
But in a socket, attempting to read 100 bytes but only getting 50 may simply mean
that the other 50 haven't arrived yet. For this reason, you should perform your
reads in a loop until you get the needed amount of data.The CPNSocket class provides several helper functions for this function (see Code 9–38).

Code 9-38

```
// Reads data from a socket, a line (CR delimited) or a block
int CPNSocket::Receive( char *cpDest, int nSize, char Term ) const
{
    int ReadIn=0, Stat=0;
    if( m_nSocket < 0 )
    {
        if( m_bThrowException )
```

Table 9.9   The recv() Parameters

Parameter	Meaning
Socket	The connected socket to be read from.
Buffer	Pointer to buffer where to store read data.
Len	Number of bytes to read.
Flags	Flags controlling the read operation:
	MSG_PEEK—Data is copied into the buffer but not removed from the socket queue.
	MSG_OOB—Processes out of bound data, such as for DECNet protocols and UDP style sockets.
	0 – (zero) Read and remove data from the socket queue.

```
            ThrowErrMsg( ErrNotInit );
        return( 0 );
    }

    while( ReadIn < nSize-2 )
    {
        if( m_nTimeOut && TimedOut(toRead) )
        {
            if( m_bThrowException )
                ThrowErrMsg( ErrTimedOut );
            return( 0 );

        }
        Stat = recv( m_nSocket, cpDest+ReadIn, 1, 0 );
        if( Stat < 0 )
        {
            if( m_bThrowException )
                ThrowErrMsg( Stat==0?ErrConTerm:"ReadLine error: %d", Stat
);
            return( 0 );
        }
        if( cpDest[Stat+ReadIn-1]==Term )
            break;
        ReadIn += Stat;
    }
    cpDest[ReadIn+Stat-1]="\0";
    return( ReadIn+Stat );
}

int CPNSocket::ReceiveLine( char *cpDest, int nSize ) const
{
    int Ret=Receive( cpDest, nSize, "\r" );
    if(Ret)
    {
        while( strlen(cpDest)>0 && cpDest[strlen(cpDest)-1]<' ')
            cpDest[strlen(cpDest)-1]="\0";
        while( strlen(cpDest)>0 && cpDest[0]<" " )
            memmove( cpDest, cpDest+1, strlen(cpDest));
    }
    return(Ret);
}
```

int send(SOCKET Socket, const char FAR *Buffer, int Len, int Flags); The send() function is used to transmit data through a socket. When one end of a socket calls send(), send() assumes that the other end of the socket called recv() to get the data. It returns SOCKET_ERROR if an error occurred, otherwise the number of bytes written. Table 9.10 contains the send() parameters.

Table 9.10   The send() Parameters

Parameter	Meaning
Socket	The connected socket to be written to.
Buffer	Pointer to buffer with data to be sent.
Len	Number of bytes to be sent.
Flags	Flags controlling the write operation:
	MSG_DONTROUTE—Sends data without any routine. This flag may be ignored by the operating system.
	MSG_OOB—Sends out of bound data such as for DECnet protocol and UDP sockets.
	0—(zero) Write data to the socket queue normally.

As with the recv() function, you may need to write your data several times in a loop to receive all the data. The CPNSocket class provides the following functions (see Code 9–39) to assist in calling the send() function.

Code 9–39

```
// Writes a block of data to a socket
int CPNSocket::Send( const char *cpSrc, int Len ) const
{
    int Written=0;
    if( m_nSocket < 0 )
    {
        if( m_bThrowException )
            ThrowErrMsg( ErrNotInit );
        return( 0 );
    }
    while( Len>0 )
    {
        Written=send( m_nSocket, cpSrc, Len, 0 );
        if( Written <=0 )
        {
            if( m_bThrowException )
              ThrowErrMsg( Written==0?ErrConTerm:"Writing socket: %d", Written );
            return( 0 );
        }
        cpSrc += Written;
        Len -= Written;
    }
    return( 1 );
}

// Writes a line of text to a socket, like a string
int CPNSocket::SendLine( const char *cpSrc, char Term ) const
```

```
{
    int Written=0, Len;
    Len = strlen(cpSrc);
    if( Term=="\0" ) // If terminator is "\0", include that in data out
        Len++;
    return( Send( cpSrc, Len ) );
}
```

int select(int Ignored, fd_set FAR *ReadSockets, fd_set FAR *WriteSockets, fd_set FAR *ExceptionSockets, const struct timeval FAR *TimeOut); The select() function is called to determine if a socket is ready to be read or written to or if a socket has an error code to report. The select() function is used to perform time-out processing. For example, before calling the recv() function to read from a socket (which might hang if the socket never gets any data), you can call this function to determine if there is any data to be read. Table 9.11 contains the select() parameters.

The CPNSocket class uses this function internally before all operations when a time-out value has been specified with the SetTimeOut() function. CPNSocket calls the select() function without you having to understand the details of how it works. The TimedOut() function from the CPNSocket is not called by you directly, but is called by the other functions like ReadLine() as needed (see Code 9–40).

Code 9–40

```
int CPNSocket::TimedOut( toMode Mode ) const
{
        fd_set fdSet;
        struct timeval TimeToWait;
```

Table 9.11   The select() Parameters

Parameter	Meaning
Ignored	This parameter is ignored and is provided for compatibility with Berkley socket functions.
ReadSockets	An array of fd_set elements, indicating flags for which sockets to check for readability (data in the input queue).
WriteSockets	An array of fd_set elements, indicating flags for which sockets to check for write ability (data can be sent).
ExceptionSockets	An array of fd_set elements, indicating flags for which sockets to check for an error.
TimeOut	A structure that indicates how long the function should wait for a change in socket status (such as data available) before returning with an error.

```
    // Initialize the timeval struct
    TimeToWait.tv_sec = m_nTimeOut / 1000;
    TimeToWait.tv_usec = m_nTimeOut % 1000;
    // Initialize the fd_set variable with zeros, and then our cocket
    FD_ZERO( &fdSet );
    FD_SET( m_nSocket+1, &fdSet );
    int Ret;
    // Call select
    Ret = select( m_nSocket+1, &fdSet, &fdSet, &fdSet, &TimeToWait );

    return( Ret>0?0:1 );
}
```

Examples Using the CPNSocket Class

The CPNSocket class simplifies working with the Windows socket SDK functions. In particular, it provides the following features:

- Automatic creation and destruction of socket handles
- Simplified time-out processing
- Selectable generation of return codes or exceptions for function failures
- Simplified calling functions, including host name resolution

The functions of the CPNSocket are summarized in Table 9.12.

Table 9.12   CPNSocket Functions

Function	Description
Close	Closes an internet socket.
Connect	Connects to an internet server.
Bind	Sets up Binding information.
Listen	Sets up Listen information.
Server	Sets up a server-style connection to listen on a port.
Accept	Accepts incomming client connections on a server-style port.
SetExceptions	Determines if errors should return error codes or throw exceptions.
SetTimeOut	Sets the time-out period (if any) for a function.
Receive	Reveives a block of data.
ReceiveLine	Receives a line of text (\n).
Send	Sends a block of data
SendLine	Sends a line of text (\n).

SMTP Classes

While the CPNSocket class provides a simpler interface to general socket communications, we want to demonstrate a real-world application for it. As such, we will create several derived classes to implement the SMTP protocol. Some of the following classes and code can be found in the Mailer demonstration program, which provides the CPNSocket class, as well as an SMTP and a POP3 class, to simplify sending and receiving emails.

While you may not typically be asked to write an email program, there are two strong points for implementing the SMTP and POP3 classes:

- You may have a batch processing program, which, when it encounters a serious error, doesn't just display an error message, but also emails off a notification to a system administrator.
- You may need to write a custom email-reading program, such as an auto-responder to clients for requests for certain types of information.

The first class we will write is derived from CPNSocket is called CPNCommandSocket. This class is a type of socket that deals with sending and receiving commands and acknowledgments. Since many protocols like SMTP and POP3 are implemented like this, CPNCommandSocket should be a very reusable class. CPNCommandSocket is declared as shown in Code 9–41.

Code 9–41

```
class CPNCommandSocket : public CPNSocket
{
public:

    CPNCommandSocket( int TimeOutms=10000);

    bool SendCommand(const char *Command, const char *Data, CString* Dest,
        const char *OK=0 );
};
```

As you can tell from the Code 9–41, very little is added except for the SendCommand() function as shown in Code 9–42.

Code 9–42

```
bool CPNCommandSocket::SendCommand(const char *Command, const char *Data,
    CString* Dest, const char *OK )
{
    int i, Len;
    CString sCommand, LocalDest;
```

```
// Get Feedback from socket command locally if end user not interested in it
if( Dest == 0 )
    Dest = &LocalDest;

// If there is a command string
if( Command && *Command )
{
    // Format and Send the command throw the socket
    sCommand.Format( Command, Data );

    TRACE( "Send Command-> %-128.128s\n", (LPCSTR)sCommand);
    Len = sCommand.GetLength();
    i=0;
    if( Send( (LPCSTR)sCommand+i, Len-i ) ==0 )
        return( false );
}
else
{
    TRACE( "Send Command-> NULL\n", (LPCSTR)sCommand);
}
// If there is no "Ok" string, then just return
if( !OK )
    return( true );

// Otherwise, lets get the sockets response to our command
char* Buffer = Dest->GetBuffer( 2048 );

i = ReceiveLine( Buffer, 2048);
if( i <-0 )
    return(FALSE);

TRACE( "Reply: %s\n", (LPCSTR)Buffer );
Dest->ReleaseBuffer();

// And see if the Ok string we were passed as a parameter was inside response
// we received from the socket
if( OK )
    return( Dest->Find( OK, 0 )>=0 );

return( TRUE );
}
```

The SendCommand() function parameters are shown in Table 9.13. The return value is TRUE if we got back the OK string we wanted based on the command we sent, FALSE if we didn't.

Table 9.13   The SendCommand() Parameters

Parameter	Meaning
Command	String to send through the socket (should be a command, like HELO in the SMTP protocol)
Data	Optional parameter to send with the Command, a string. May be NULL.
Dest	Where to store the response from the server, if we want it. May be NULL if we don't care.
Ok	A string that indicates the command went "ok". For example, in response to the SMTP HELO command, we want a "250" back indicating success.

Creating the CPNSMTP Class from CPNCommandSocket

The CPNSMTP class is a class that supports the SMTP protocol for sending emails via an SMTP server. It is derived from CPNCommandSocket, which in turn was derived from the CPNSocket class. Its class definition is shown in Code 9–43.

The only functions we wrote inside this class are Connect(), SendMail(), and GetErrMsg(). The functions are defined in Code 9–44.

Code 9–43

```
class CPNSMTP : public CPNCommandSocket
{
public:
    BOOL Connect( LPCSTR lpszHostAddress, UINT nHostPort=25 );
    BOOL SendMail(LPCSTR From, LPCSTR To, LPCSTR Subject, LPCSTR Msg);
    CString& GetErrMsg();
    CString m_Error;
}
```

Code 9–44

```
BOOL CPNSMTP::Connect(LPCSTR lpszHostAddress, UINT nHostPort)
{
BOOL Ret = CPNCommandSocket::Connect( lpszHostAddress, nHostPort );
    if( Ret )
    {
        if( !SendCommand( 0, 0, 0, "220" ) )
            return( FALSE );
        else
```

```
            return( TRUE );
    }
    return( FALSE );
}
```

The Connect() function is used to connect to an SMTP server in preparation for sending an email. Parameters for the Connect() function are shown in Table 9.14. It returns TRUE if the connection was made, or FALSE if not (see Code 9–45).

Code 9–45

```
BOOL CPNSMTP::SendMail(LPCSTR From, LPCSTR To, LPCSTR Subject, LPCSTR Msg)
{
    CString Tmp;

    char *Domain = strchr( From, "@" );
    if( Domain )
        Domain++;
    else
        Domain="nowhere.com";

    if( !SendCommand( "HELO %s\n", Domain, &m_Error, "250" ) )
        return(FALSE);
    if( !SendCommand( "MAIL FROM: %s\n", From, &m_Error, "250" ) )
        return(FALSE);
    if( !SendCommand( "RCPT TO: %s\n", To, &m_Error, "250") )
        return(FALSE);
    if( !SendCommand( "DATA\n", "", &m_Error, "354" ) )
        return(FALSE);
    SendCommand( "To: %s\n", To, 0, 0 );
    SendCommand( "Subject: %s\n", Subject, 0, 0);
    if( !SendCommand( "%s\n.\n", Msg, &m_Error, "250" ) )
        return( FALSE );
    return(TRUE);
}
```

The SendMail() function is used to send an email message to an SMTP server for delivery. Table 9.15 contains parameters for the SendMail() function. It returns TRUE if mail is sent, or FALSE if not (see Code 9–46).

Table 9.14 The Connect() Parameters

Parameter	Meaning
lpszHostAddress	The name of the SMTP server to connect to for sending. For example, "smtp.someplace.com."
nHostPort	The port to use for SMTP protocol; will default to 25 (the SMTP protocol default).

Table 9.15   Parameters for SendMail()

Parameter	Meaning
From	The email name under which the email should be sent.
To	The email address we are sending the email to.
Subject	The subject of the email.
Msg	The body of the email message.

Code 9–46

```
CString& CPNSMTP::GetErrMsg()
{
    return( m_Error );
}
```

The GetErrMsg() returns the string sent to us if any command failed during the SMTP protocol transfer. It returns the string with the SMTP server response (including the status code).

Example of Sending Email

Sending an email (using our new classes) is shown in Code 9–47.

Code 9–47

```
CPNSMTP MailSrvr;
MailSrver.SetTimeOut( 30000 ); // Time out after 30 seconds

MailSrver.Connect( "smtp.somecompnay.com" );
MailSrver.SendMail( "mario@openroad.org", "BGates@Microsoft.com", "Hey bill",
    "When is Windows 3000 coming out?" );
```

FTP Example

Unlike the SMTP and POP3 protocols where we need to create our own socket communication classes, the FTP (File Transfer Protocol) does have support built into MFC. The demonstration here will show how to connect to an FTP server, get and send files, and get a list of files from the FTP server.

The classes used will include the CInternetSession class, the CFtpConnection class, and the CFtpFileFind class.

CInternetSession

This class provides a variety of internet capabilities, but the one we want to look at the most involve creating an FTP connection. Specifically, the CInternetSession class provides a GetFtpConnection() member function as shown in Code 9–48).

Code 9–48

```
CFtpConnection* GetFtpConnection( LPCTSTR pstrServer, LPCTSTR pstrUserName = NULL,
        LPCTSTR pstrPassword = NULL, INTERNET_PORT nPort = INTERNET_INVALID_PORT_
        NUMBER,
        BOOL bPassive = FALSE );
```

The parameters to the GetFtpConnect() function are shown in Table 9.16.

The return value of the GetFtpConnection() function is a pointer to a CFtpConnection object. This pointer may then be used for sending or receiving files, get a list of files on the server side, and other FTP operations.

CFtpConnection

This class provides the basic FTP operations once connected to an FTP server. Table 9.17 contains a list of functions in the CFtpConnection class.

Of special note are the PutFile() and GetFile() functions as shown in Code 9–49.

Code 9–49

```
BOOL PutFile( LPCTSTR pstrLocalFile, LPCTSTR pstrRemoteFile,
        DWORD dwFlags = FTP_TRANSFER_TYPE_BINARY, DWORD dwContext = 1 );

BOOL GetFile( LPCTSTR pstrRemoteFile, LPCTSTR pstrLocalFile, BOOL bFailIfExists
= TRUE,
        DWORD dwAttributes = FILE_ATTRIBUTE_NORMAL,
        DWORD dwFlags = FTP_TRANSFER_TYPE_BINARY, DWORD dwContext = 1 );
```

As you can tell from the prototypes in Code 9–49, most of the parameters in the two functions have default arguments and only need to be specified under certain circumstances. The bare minimum that you would need to specify in either function would be the local filename and the remote filename. These are the functions we will be using in our demonstration.

Table 9.16 Parameters for the GetFtpConnect()

Parameter	Meaning
pstrServer	The name or URL of the FTP server.
pstrUserName	The user name, or NULL (in which case "anonymous" is used).
pstrPassword	The users password, or NULL (in which case a blank password is sent).
nPort	The port for the FTP connection. The default will be turned into port 21, the FTP port.
bPassive	Indicates if connection is passive or not. Passive FTP connections uses a slightly different protocol than active connections.

Table 9.17   Functions in the CFtpConnection Class

Function	Task
SetCurrentDirectory()	Sets the current FTP directory on the server.
GetCurrentDirectory()	Gets the current directory for the server.
GetCurrentDirectoryAsURL()	Gets the current directory for the server as a URL.
RemoveDirectory()	Removes the specified directory from the server.
CreateDirectory	Creates a directory on the server.
Rename()	Renames a file on the server.
Remove()	Removes a file from the server.
PutFile()	Sends a file to the server.
GetFile()	Gets a file from the server
OpenFile()	Opens a file on the server.
Close()	Closes the connection to the server.

CFtpFileFind

The CFtpFileFind class is a class derived from CFileFind, which works in a similar way to retrieve a list of filenames. The main difference, of course, is that CFtp-FileFind will retrieve a list of files from a remote FTP server.

The constructor of the CFtpFileFind class requires a pointer to a valid CFtpConnection object on which to build a file list. The constructor syntax is as shown in Code 9–50.

Code 9–50

```
CFtpFileFind( CFtpConnection* pConnection, DWORD dwContext = 1 );
```

Like CFileFind, the CFtpFileFind class provides functions like GetNext() to retrieve the next filename and GetFileName to get the name of the file found. Since CFtp-FileFind is derived from CFileFind, we are able to build a single BuildFileList() function in our program that populates a list of filenames into a List Control, whether the files are on our machine or the remote FTP server (this is an aspect of C++ inheritance, not MFC internet classes).

NOTE

Though not documented in MFC, a single CFtpConnection can only be used once to retrieve a file listing. If you want to retrieve another file listing (for example, to update the list of files after a send to the server), then you must establish a new CFtpConnection object.

FTPDemo Program

Our example program is a very simple FTP program to demonstrate the basic steps of an FTP client. It does not take advantage of full FTP features, such as the ability to traverse folders or delete or rename files on the server, but it will demonstrate how to connect to an FTP server and transfer files.

Keep in mind that the FTP protocol, like others, can be used for other purposes outside its expected realm. For example, you may not need to write an FTP client, as there are already many high-quality ones available free. However, you might need to write a program that allows the user to perform updates to code or data files across the Internet, which can be simplified with FTP.

FTP Demo Screen Setup

Our FTP program is an MFC Document/View program whose view class is derived from a CFormView so that we can easily drop controls on it. On the main dialog of your program, add the following controls using the dialog editor:

- A STATIC control, whose Caption is &URL:
- An EDIT control, whose ID is IDC_URL
- A STATIC control whose Caption is &Login:
- An EDIT control whose ID is IDC_LOGIN
- A STATIC control whose Caption is &Password:
- An EDIT control whose ID is IDC_PASSWORD
- A BUTTON control whose ID is IDC_CONNECT and Caption is &Connect
- A LIST VIEW control whose ID is IDC_CLIENTLIST
- A BUTTON control whose ID is IDC_SEND and Caption is &>
- A BUTTON control whose ID is IDC_GET and Caption is &<
- A LIST VIEW control whose ID is IDC_SRVRLIST

Make sure that the two List View controls are in the Report Style by changing their properties and that the IDC_PASSWORD edit box has the Password property checked.

Once you have added the controls, go into ClassWizard from the View menu choice and select the Member Variables tab. Add member variables shown in Table 9.18. Make sure you have the View class name selected in the Class Name field.

The dialog should look something like Figure 9–11.

Table 9.18   Member Variables to Be Added the Class

Control	Variable Type	Variable Name
IDC_CLIENTLIST	CListCtrl	m_ClientList
IDC_LOGIN	CString	m_Login
IDC_PASSWORD	CString	m_Password
IDC_SRVRLIST	CListCtrl	m_SrvrList
IDC_URL	CString	m_URL

FTP Demo Member Variables

Add the following data members to your View class, in the header file as shown in Code 9–51.

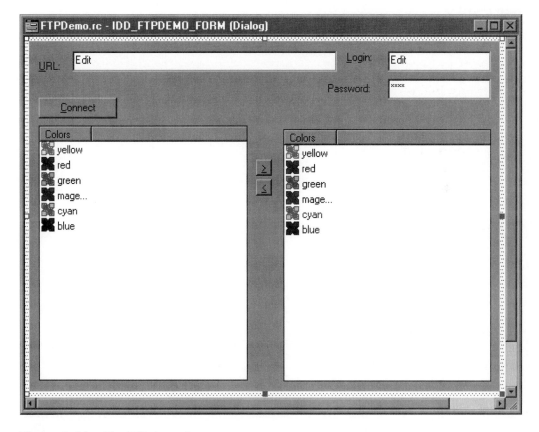

Figure 9–11   The FTP demo form.

Code 9–51

```
CString m_LocalDir; // Name of local directory
// Internet Access objects:
CFtpConnection* m_FTPConnection;
CInternetSession m_InternetSession;
```

The m_FTPConnection and m_InternetSession data members will provide the Internet access to the FTP server.

FTP Demo Helper Functions

You will need to add helper functions shown in Code 9–52 to your View class. You can add them manually by making entries in the .h and .cpp file, or by right-clicking on the View class name in ClassView. Do not attempt to add help functions with ClassWizards Message Map tab, since they are not in response to a message. Items in bold indicate FTP-specific.

Code 9–52

```
// BuildFileList
// This function gets a list of files names in a folder from either
// the local machine or the remote FTP server, and places the list into
// a List Control.
void CFTPDemoView::BuildFileList(CFileFind &Files, CListCtrl& List )
{
        int i, Count=0;
        BOOL bFound, NeedParent = TRUE;
        CString Str;

        // Remove any items already in the CListCtrl
        List.DeleteAllItems();

        // See if there are any files to place into the List Control
        bFound=Files.FindFile( );

        while( bFound ) // Loop through the files, if any
        {
                // Get information on the file
                bFound = Files.FindNextFile();

                Str = Files.GetFileName();
                if( Str!= "." ) // Ignore the "current folder" entry
                {
                        // Add the filename to our List control
                        i = List.InsertItem(Count++, Str, 0 );
                        // Add either the text <DIR> or the file size, to our List
                        Control
                        if( Files.IsDirectory() )
```

```
                    {
                            if( Str==".." )
                                    NeedParent = FALSE;
                            Str = "Dir";
                    }
                    else
                            Str.Format( "%d", Files.GetLength() );
                    List.SetItemText( i, 1, Str );
            }
    }
    if( NeedParent )
    {
            i = List.InsertItem(0, "..", 0 );
            List.SetItem( i, 1, LVIF_TEXT, "Dir", 0, 0, 0, 0 );
    }
}


// Populates list of files from FTP server into List Control
void CFTPDemoView::BuildSrvrFileList()
{
    if( MakeConnection() )
    {
            CFtpFileFind Files( m_FTPConnection );
            BuildFileList( Files, m_SrvrList );
    }
    else
            MessageBox( "Unable to establish connection" );
}


// Populates list of files from local machine into List Control
void CFTPDemoView::BuildClientFileList()
{
    CFileFind Files;
    BuildFileList( Files, m_ClientList );
}
// Establishes a connection to the FTP server
bool CFTPDemoView::MakeConnection()
{
    // Get current URL, Login and Password information into m_URL,
    // m_Login, and m_Password

    UpdateData();
    // Close the connection if already open
    CloseConnection();

    try
    {
            // Establish the FTP connection
```

```
                m_FTPConnection = m_InternetSession.GetFtpConnection( m_URL,
                        m_Login, m_Password );
        }
        catch(...)
        {       // Report Error
                if( !m_FTPConnection )
                        MessageBox( "Error establishing FTP connection" );
                return( false );
        }
        return( true );
}
// Closes the connection to the FTP server
void CFTPDemoView::CloseConnection()
{
        if( m_FTPConnection ) // Make sure we have a connection to close
        {
                // Close and then delete the CFtpConnection object
                m_FTPConnection->Close();
                delete m_FTPConnection;
                m_FTPConnection = 0;
        }
}
// This function enables or disables controls as needed, depending
// upon whether or not we are connected to the FTP server.
void CFTPDemoView::SetControls()
{
        CWnd* pWnd = GetDlgItem( IDC_SRVRLIST );
        pWnd->EnableWindow( m_FTPConnection!=0 );

        pWnd = GetDlgItem( IDC_CLIENTLIST );
        pWnd->EnableWindow( m_FTPConnection!=0 );
        pWnd = GetDlgItem( IDC_SEND );
        pWnd->EnableWindow( m_FTPConnection!=0 );
        pWnd = GetDlgItem( IDC_GET );
        pWnd->EnableWindow( m_FTPConnection!=0 );
        pWnd = GetDlgItem( IDC_URL );
        pWnd->EnableWindow( m_FTPConnection==0 );
}
```

FTP Demo Handler Functions

You will need to add handler functions shown in Code 9–53 to your View class. You should add them using the Message Map tab of ClassWizard. Items in bold indicate FTP-specific programming.

Code 9–53

```
// Handler for the Connect button, to connect to FTP server
void CFTPDemoView::OnConnect()
{
```

```
        UpdateData();

        // If not connected, then establish connection
        if( !m_FTPConnection )
        {
                if( MakeConnection() )
                {
                        // Connection established, change Connect button to
                        "Disconnect"
                        GetDlgItem( IDC_CONNECT )->SetWindowText( "Disconnect" );
                        if( m_LocalDir.IsEmpty() )
                        {
                                char Buffer[_MAX_PATH];
                                GetCurrentDirectory( sizeof(Buffer), Buffer );
                                m_LocalDir = Buffer;
                        }
                        // Populate list of files on local and remote machines
                        BuildClientFileList();
                        BuildSrvrFileList();
                }
        }
        else // Otherwise if already connected, then disconnect
        {
                GetDlgItem( IDC_CONNECT )->SetWindowText( "Connect" );
                CloseConnection();
        }
        SetControls();
}
// Handler for the Send File (">") button
void CFTPDemoView::OnSend()
{
        // Determine which name in the local list is selected
        int i = m_ClientList.GetNextItem( -1, LVNI_SELECTED );
        if( i >= 0 )
        {
                CString LocalName;
                // Get name of selected file from local list
                LocalName = m_ClientList.GetItemText( i, 0 );

                // Invoke CFtpConnection::PutFile function to send the file
                if( m_FTPConnection->PutFile( LocalName, LocalName ) )
                        BuildSrvrFileList(); // Refresh server file list
                else
                        MessageBox( "Unable to send file (upload security?)" );
        }

}
// Handler for the Get File ("<") button
void CFTPDemoView::OnGet()
{
```

```
      // Determine name of file selected in the Server list.
      int i = m_SrvrList.GetNextItem( -1, LVNI_SELECTED );
      if( i >= 0 )
      {
            CString Name;
            // Get name of selected file from server list
            Name = m_SrvrList.GetItemText( i, 0 );
            // Invoke the CFtpConnection::GetFile function to get the file
            m_FTPConnection->GetFile( Name, Name );
            // Refresh the local file list
            BuildClientFileList();
      }
}
```

Once you have made all the additions shown in Code 9–53, you can compile and run the program. Make note that by far the majority of the code above deals with user interface and not FTP processing. A bare-minimum example of FTP file transfer could simply be described as shown in Code 9–54.

Code 9–54

```
CInternetSession IS;
CFtpConnection * pFTP;
pFTP = IS.GetFTPConnection( "ftp.someplace.com" );
pFTP->GetFile( "somefile.txt", "somefile.txt" );
pFTP->Close();
delete pFTP;
```

HTML Display

MFC comes with a number of methods for displaying HTML pages within your application. The first form is the CHTMLView class, which is a view (as in, Document/View architecture) window class whose entire client area is filled with an HTML page. Another means of playing an HTML viewer in your program is by using the HTML ActiveX control WebBrowser.

Notice that all of the discussions on HTML displaying using MFC will assume that the target machine has Microsoft Internet Explorer installed. The examples will not work without it.

Using the CHTMLView Class

The CHTMLView class is a type of View that displays an HTML page in its client area. It will be a fully functional HTML window, capable of displaying links, graphics, and any Internet Explorer plug-in that is installed. This demonstration utilizes the CHTMLView class in a splitter window and it will display an HTML page on the

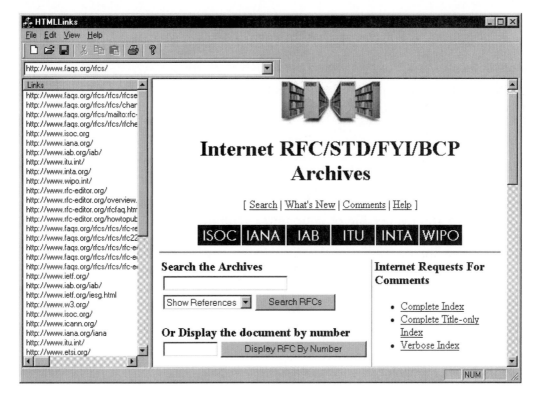

Figure 9–12   The display of the HTMLLinks program.

right and a list of links from the page on the left. The HTMLLinks program is illustrated in Figure 9–12. Perform the following steps to create the HTMLLink program.

Use AppWizard to Create the Template Program

1. From the File menu choice, select the New menu item.
2. Make sure Projects is the highlighted tab of the New dialog.
3. Select the MFC AppWizard (EXE) item and enter the Project Name (HTMLLinks). Click OK.
4. In the MFC AppWizard Step 1 dialog, select Single Document and click OK.
5. Click the Next button until you get to the MFC AppWizard Step 4 of 6 dialog.
6. Click the Advanced button.
7. In the Advanced Options dialog, click the Window Styles tab.
8. Check the Use Splitter item and click Close.
9. Click the Next button twice to get to the MFC AppWizard Step 6 of 6 dialog.
10. Change the Base Class item for the view class to CHTMLView.
11. Click Finish and then OK.

---

12. Compile the program by pressing F7. The program automatically displays the Visual C++ home page.

Creating the Link View for the Left Splitter Pane

The left pane of the splitter window contains a CListView object, which has a ListView control that fill the entire client area. In or to create this view:

1. Go to ClassWizard from the View menu choice.
2. Click the Add Class button, and then Add New...
3. For the name, enter ClinkView.
4. For the Base Class, select CListView.
5. Click OK.
6. In the header file of your new CLinkView object (CLinkView.h), add a #include for afxcview.h.

Modifying the Splitter Window for Left and Right Panes

The default splitter window (if selected in MFC AppWizard Step 4 of 6) is a dynamic splitter. In a dynamic splitter, each pane of the window must be of the same View class. We want a static splitter so that we can display our CLinkView window on the left and the CHTMLView on the right. To do this, we must modify the CMain-Frame::OnCreateClient() function, which should look like Code 9–55, and change Code 9–55 to Code 9–56.

Code 9–55

```
BOOL CMainFrame::OnCreateClient(LPCREATESTRUCT /*lpcs*/,
    CCreateContext* pContext)
{
    return m_wndSplitter.Create(this,
        2, 2,                // TODO: adjust the number of rows, columns
        CSize(10, 10),       // TODO: adjust the minimum pane size
        pContext);
}
```

Code 9–56

```
BOOL CMainFrame::OnCreateClient(LPCREATESTRUCT /*lpcs*/,
    CCreateContext* pContext)
{
    // PN: Change Splitter to a static splitter, and make the panes
    // a ListView and a HTMLView window.
    m_wndSplitter.CreateStatic( this, 1, 2 );
    m_wndSplitter.CreateView( 0, 0, RUNTIME_CLASS(CLinksView),
        CSize( 100, 100 ), pContext );

    // Setup the List View control appearance
    CListView* pListView = (CListView*)m_wndSplitter.GetPane(0,0);
```

```
pListView->GetListCtrl().ModifyStyle( 0, LVS_REPORT );
pListView->GetListCtrl().InsertColumn( 0, "Links" );
pListView->GetListCtrl().SetColumnWidth( 0, 1000 );

m_wndSplitter.CreateView( 0, 1, RUNTIME_CLASS(CHTMLLinksView),
    CSize( 100, 100 ), pContext );
return TRUE;
}
```

Code 9–56 creates a static splitter window with two panes. The CreateStatic() function in the CSplitterWnd class creates the splitter window. Code 9–56 begins by calling the mainframe class ("this" – the first parameter) as the parent of the splitter, and it has one row of two columns (the second and third parameters).

The CreateView() function of the CSplitterWnd class is called to create a new view in the left pane. Using the RUNTIME_CLASS macro in the third parameter, we define the CLinkView class as the view that should appear on the left.

Next, the List control in the CLinkView class is initialized to our desired style by getting the view from the pane (GetPane()) and calling the GetListCtrl() function for the CLinkView. This returns a reference to the ListView control of the CListView class. We then set up its style flags and width.

CSplitterWnd::CreateView() is called again, this time to create the CHTMLView window for the right pane of the splitter.

Notice that the m_wndSplitter data member was added to the CMainFrame class by ClassWizard.

Make sure that in the CMainFrame.cpp file that you add a #include for the LinkView.h file (the header for the CLinkView class).

Add the Dialog Bar with URL ComboBox

A Dialog Bar is like a toolbar except that it holds other types of controls in addition to buttons, such as the combo box for selecting a URL. MFC provides the CDialogBar class to help you create and work with Dialog Bars.

When the Dialog Bar gets user events, it sends notifications to its parent window. It does not handle them in the typical ClassWizard Message Handler fashion. In our Dialog Bar, we use a combo box for selecting a URL, and it will be subclassed by our own CPNComboBox class.

The CPNComboBox class has the ability to perform auto-completion of what the user types from entries in the drop-down list and can also automatically save and load its string list to and from the registry. Because of its complexity, the CPNComboBox class will be listed in the appendix section.

Figure 9–13 Create a dialog bar item using the Dialog Bar dialog.

To add the Dialog Bar to your project:

1. From Project menu choice, select Add To Project and then Components and Controls
2. Then, select Visual C++ Components
3. Select the Dialog Bar item from the list, and click Insert and then OK as shown in Figure 9–13.
4. Click OK.
   You will see the dialog shown in Figure 9–14.
5. Click OK.
6. Close the Component Gallery dialog.
   Steps 1–6 add a dialog that will be used by the program for the Dialog Bar. Its ID will be CG_IDD_MYDIALOGBAR by default. We need to edit this dialog and add a combo box with the ID of IDC_URL.

Figure 9–14 This message is displayed when the new Dialog Bar is added to the project.

7. Open up the CG_IDD_MYDIALOGBAR dialog (which was added by the steps above) in the dialog editor. Remove the static control and add a combo box. Change the combo box ID so that it is IDC_URL.

Modifying the CMainFrame Class

We will need to add several message/event handlers to pull the program together. Some will be MFC events and others Windows events. Most can be added with ClassWizard, but some must be added manually. We will note the ones that must be added manually.

First, in your CMainFrame class, create a CPNComboBox object and name it m_Dialog-BarCB. Place it in the CMainFrame class definition in MainFrm.h (see Code 9–57).

Code 9–57

```
CPNComboBox m_DialogBarCB;
```

CPNComboBox source is listed in the Appendix and not described here. You can also download it from the PTR ftp site at: ftp://ftp.prenhall.com/pub/ptr/professional_computer_science.w-022/winprog.

Next, add the following functions to the same CMainFrame class definition as shown in Code 9–58. Add the definitions of these functions (see Code 9–59) to the MainFrm.cpp file.

Code 9–58

```
void CBNavigate();
CListCtrl* GetListCtrl();
CString GetURL();
void SetURL(const char* URL);
```

Code 9–59

```
void CMainFrame::CBNavigate()
{

        // Add current string to combo box, in case not already there
        m_DialogBarCB.AddString();
```

```
        // Get current text from the combo box:
        CString Text;
        int Index = m_DialogBarCB.GetCurSel();
        if( Index >= 0 )
                m_DialogBarCB.GetLBText( Index, Text );
        else
                m_DialogBarCB.GetWindowText( Text );

        // Get pointer to the CHTMLView object in the right pane of the splitter,
        // and call Navigate to go to the new web page
        CHTMLLinksView* pView = (CHTMLLinksView*)m_wndSplitter.GetPane(0,1);
        pView->Navigate( Text );

}
CString CMainFrame::GetURL()
{
        // Retrieve current string from the URL combo box
        CString URL;
        m_DialogBarCB.GetWindowText( URL );

        return( URL );
}
CListCtrl* CMainFrame::GetListCtrl()
{
        // Return pointer to the List Control of the right pane CLinkView
        CListView* pList = (CListView*)m_wndSplitter.GetPane(0,0);
        return( &pList->GetListCtrl() );
}
```

The CBNavigate() function demonstrates the use of the Navigate function. This is the function in the CHTMLView class that permits you to change the page displayed in the HTML View class. Simply place the URL of the desired parameter in the first parameter of the Navigate function.

Also in the CMainFrame class definition file (MainFrm.cpp), add the following two lines of code (see Code 9–60) to the CMainFrame::OnCreate() function, at the end just above the return statement.

Code 9–60

```
        m_DialogBarCB.SetThisRegistrySave( true );
        m_DialogBarCB.SubclassDlgItem( IDC_URL, &m_wndMyDialogBar );

        return 0;
}
```

These functions help the CHTMLView interact with the Dialog Bar to get the URL and the CLinkView to populate it with links.

The call to SubClassDlgItem() is performed because the Dialog Bar is not its own class and we need to subclass the normal combo box in the Dialog Bar with our own CPNComboBox class. Normally, if this were a typical dialog we could simply add a member variable to the Dialog Bar for the combo box, specify a Category value of "Control," and specify CPNComboBox as the Type.

Modifying the Two View Classes

Both the CLinkView and CHTMLLinksView classes need to have a message handler added to respond to the user's making a selection in the URL combo box. Controls in the CDialogBar will not be listed in the Class Wizard Message Map tab, so we will need to add the handler manually.

1. In theCLinkView class definition file (CLinkView.h), add the following (see Code 9–61) entry to your MESSAGE MAP section.

Code 9–61

```
//{{AFX_MSG(CLinksView)
        // NOTE - the ClassWizard will add and remove member functions
        here.
//}}AFX_MSG
// PN: Note position of our manually-added Message Map entry
afx_msg void OnSelChangedURL();
DECLARE_MESSAGE_MAP()
};
```

2. Add the following (see Code 9–62) Message Map entry to your CLink-View.cpp file.

Code 9–62

```
BEGIN_MESSAGE_MAP(CLinksView, CListView)
        //{{AFX_MSG_MAP(CLinksView)
                // NOTE - the ClassWizard will add and remove mapping
                macros here.
        //}}AFX_MSG_MAP
        ON_CBN_SELCHANGE( IDC_URL, OnSelChangedURL )
END_MESSAGE_MAP()
```

3. Add the OnSelChangedURL function (see Code 9–63) to the end of your CLinkView.cpp file.

Code 9–63

```
void CLinksView::OnSelChangedURL( )
{
        CMainFrame* pMain = (CMainFrame*)AfxGetMainWnd();
        pMain->CBNavigate();
}
```

4. Make the same changes from steps 1–3 for the CHTMLLinksView .h and .cpp files.
5. In the CHTMLLinksView.cpp file, add a #include for the mshtml.h file. This allows us to interact with the web page control.
6. Using ClassWizard and the Message Map tab, add a message map for the OnDocumentComplete Message. It should create Code 9–64 for you.

Code 9–64

```
void CHTMLLinksView::OnDocumentComplete(LPCTSTR lpszURL)
{
        // TODO: Add your specialized code here and/or call the base
        // class

        CHtmlView::OnDocumentComplete(lpszURL);
}
```

Modify this function to look like Code 9–65.

Code 9–65

```
void CHTMLLinksView::OnDocumentComplete(LPCTSTR lpszURL)
{
    // OnDocumentComplete is called when the HTML web page is
    // finished loading.

    CHtmlView::OnDownloadComplete();

    // PN: IHTMLDocument2 is a COM object provided by Microsoft Internet Explorer
    // that gives us access to the HTML document contained in an HTML Window (like
    // our CHTMLLinksView class)
    // Get the COM IDispatch (or, LPDISPATCH) for the current document
    IHTMLDocument2* pDoc = (IHTMLDocument2*)GetHtmlDocument();

    // Get the Body of the HTML document
    IHTMLElement* pBody;
    pDoc->get_body( &pBody );

    // Get the HTML text for the document body, into a BSTR
    BSTR Body;
    pBody->get_outerHTML( &Body );

    // Move the BSTR COM data type into a CString
    CString Page( Body );
    ::SysFreeString( Body );

    // Temporary string variable for extracting links
    CString Link;

    // Get pointer to the Mainframe class, and the Lst control opn the left
```

```
CMainFrame* pMain = (CMainFrame*)AfxGetMainWnd();
CListCtrl* pList = pMain->GetListCtrl();

// Delete the items currently on the left ListView
pList->DeleteAllItems();

// Start parsing the HTML text looking for links (Start with "<A")
int Index;
while( (Index = Page.Find( "<" )) >=0 )
{
    Link.Empty();
    Page.Delete(0, Index+1 );
    if( Page.GetLength() > 8 && toupper(Page[0])=="A" && Page[1]==" " )
    {
        Index = Page.Find( """ );
        if( Index >=0 )
        {
            Page.Delete(0, Index+1);
            while( !Page.IsEmpty() && Page[0] != '"' )
            {
                Link += Page[0];
                Page.Delete(0);
            }
            if( Link.Find(".") < 0 ||
            ( Link.Find( "." ) > Link.Find("/") && Link.Find( "http:") != 0) )
            {
                // GetLocationURL returns the URL the Web page is at
                CString Home = GetLocationURL();
                if( Home[ Home.GetLength()-1 ] == "/" && Link[0]=="/" )
                        Link.Delete(0);
                Link = Home + Link;
            }
            pList->InsertItem( pList->GetItemCount(), Link );
        }
    }
}
// Update the URL in the combo box
pMain->SetURL( GetLocationURL() );
CHtmlView::OnDocumentComplete(lpszURL);
}
```

Code 9–65 demonstrates how to get the source code or the HTML content for the web page currently displayed in the CHTMLView window. The specific code for this is shown in Code 9–66.

Code 9–66

```
IHTMLDocument2* pDoc = (IHTMLDocument2*)GetHtmlDocument();
IHTMLElement* pBody;
```

```
pDoc->get_body( &pBody );
BSTR Body;
pBody->get_outerHTML( &Body );
CString Page( Body );
::SysFreeString( Body );
```

Once the HTML code for the page is stored in the Page CString variable, we move into the loop, which searches for all the HTML link tags and adds them to the List View (right pane).

Compile and build the program. Remember, the CPNComboBox class must be added to your program, as it was not covered here. You can find the source in the Appendix or you can download it (and this program) from the PTR ftp site.

The majority of the code in this example deals with user interface. Working with the CHTMLView class to display a web page in your program is fairly simple. We have demonstrated only three aspects of working with the HTML View class here:

1. To change the web page displayed in the CHTMLView object call the CHTMLView::Navigate() function.
2. To perform processing after the page is loaded add an OnDocument-Complete() message handler for the CHTMLView object, using Class-Wizard.
3. In order to get the HTML source of a page in the CHTMLView object, use the CHTMLView::GetHtmlDocument() function and then the IHTML Document2 and IHTMLElement COM classes.

The Navigate2() function in the CHTMLView class extends the Navigate() function by permitting the browser of special folders such as the desktop or network neighborhood.

Using the Web Browser ActiveX Control

If you have Internet Explorer installed, you also have the Microsoft Web Browser ActiveX control (SHDOCVW.DLL). The ActiveX control is a slight variance of the CHTMLView class example and has the same abilities of the CHTMLView class only the functions are located in a separate class. The CHTMLView class was actually a container for the Active X control.

To see the ActiveX control in action, create a dialog-based application with AppWizard. The ActiveX control can be used on any type of window or program, but we will use the dialog-based type because of its simplicity.

Once you have the base project created, add the Web Browser ActiveX control:

1. Go to the Project menu choice and select Add to Project.
2. Next, select the Components and Controls menu item.

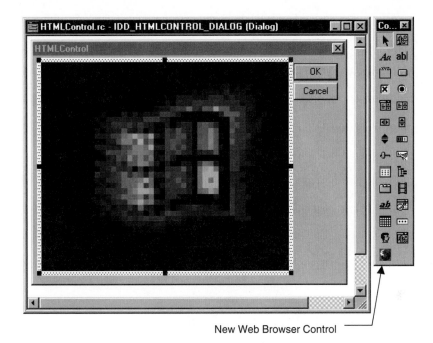

New Web Browser Control

Figure 9–15 The Web Browser control is added to the project.

3. In the Components and Controls Gallery, double-click the Registered ActiveX controls item.
4. Locate the Microsoft Web Browser item in the list and double-click it.
5. Click OK to insert the component.
6. Click OK at the Confirm Classes dialog (accepting all the defaults).
7. Close the Component Gallery dialog.

These steps added a CWebBrowser2 class to your project and also the Web Browser control to your tool palette. Go to the dialog editor for your main dialog and place a Web Browser control on your dialog (Figure 9–15).

In ClassWizard, go to the Member Variable tab and add a member variable for the Web Browser control you just dropped on the dialog. Call it m_Browser. Change the web page for the browser by calling the CWebBrowser2::Navigate2() function.

For example, add the following (see Code 9–67) to the OnInitDialog() function of your program, near the end just above the return statement.

```
// Change the web page in the Browser control
COleVariant Nothing;
COleVariant URL("http://www.openroad.org");
m_Browser.Navigate2( &URL, &Nothing, &Nothing, &Nothing, &Nothing );

return TRUE; // return TRUE unless you set the focus to a control
}
```

As with the CHTMLView demonstration of the previous section, you can also add Message Maps to your dialog to handle various events the Web Browser control will send, such as DocumentComplete() to get notified when a page is completely loaded.

ISAPI Filter

An ISAPI (Internet Server Application Program Interface) filter is a DLL that runs under the IIS or PWS web server program. Filters have the ability to monitor web access and data flow to and from the server as well as change that data flow. ISAPI programs can be thought of as similar to CGI-style programs with the following exceptions:

- CGI programs are executable files that start up and shut down at the request of the server. A filter is a DLL that is loaded once by the web server and remains in memory. Filters have a speed advantage.

- CGI programs are run with parameters to request information and must process data as a whole. Filters can respond to certain events, such as a connection request or a URL mapping, and handle only the events as desired.

- CGI programs are stand-alone programs, where the filters are extensions to the web server. This means that a filter becomes part of the web server. If the DLL crashes, the server will crash also. CGI programs have a robustness advantage (safer to run from a reliability standpoint).

- CGI programs can be visible to the web browser; with a filter the user may not know that he or she is running a server program.

The two key benefits are speed and safety. While the filter DLL is faster than the CGI program because it remains in memory, the CGI program is safer because it cannot crash the web server if it contains a bug.

We will create a simple ISAPI filter that restricts the access to the server based on IP addresses. We do so by creating an ISAPI filter that handles the URL request of the server, to redirect restricted IP addresses to an "Access Denied" web page.

This program requires you to have either IIS or PWS installed and running. Since this program is a DLL program, it will have no user interface. The only way to prove it is working is to deny access for a machine and then try to access the web server from that machine.

Creating the ISAPI Filter

1. Click the New menu item.
2. In the New dialog, make sure the Projects tab is highlighted.
3. Select the ISAPI Extension Wizard item, and enter in a Project Name of IPRestriction as shown in Figure 9–16.
4. In the ISAPI Extension Wizard Step 1 of 2 dialog, check the Generate Filter Object, and uncheck the Generate a Server Extension Object item (see Figure 9–17).
5. In the ISAPI Extension Wizard—Step 2 of 2 dialog (see Figure 9–18), select the priority of your filter (Low), the connection types (leave both checked), and the notifications you want to process (URL Mapping requests for this demo).
6. Click the Finish button, and then OK.
   AppWizard has created a filter project for you. Locate the OnUrlMap() function, which will be in the IPRestriction.cpp file. It will look like Code 9–68.

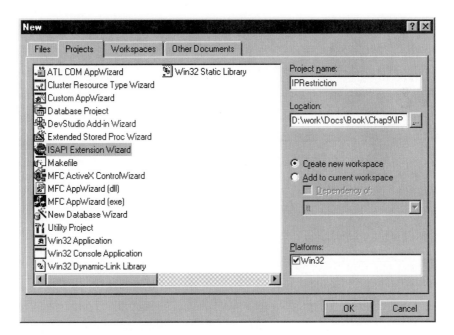

Figure 9–16   Select the ISAPI Extension Wizard.

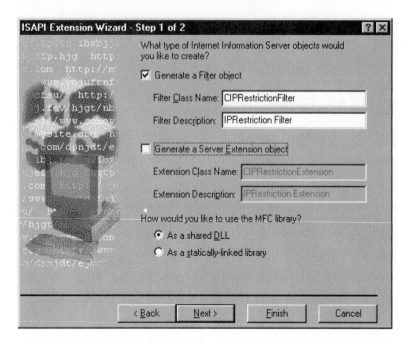

Figure 9–17   Check the Generate Filter Object and uncheck the Generate a Server Extension Object.

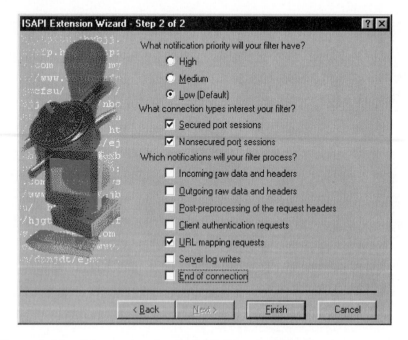

Figure 9–18   Select options for the ISAPI Extension Wizard.

Code 9-68

```
DWORD CIPRestriction::OnUrlMap(CHttpFilterContext* pCtxt,
    PHTTP_FILTER_URL_MAP pMapInfo)
{
    // TODO: React to this notification accordingly and
    // return the appropriate status code
    return SF_STATUS_REQ_NEXT_NOTIFICATION;
}
```

The OnUrlMap() function is the function that the web server calls before any web page is requested. This function has the ability to redirect the client's browser to another web page instead of the one being requested. Modify the function to look like Code 9-69.

Code 9-69

```
DWORD CIPRestrictionFilter::OnUrlMap(CHttpFilterContext* pCtxt,
    PHTTP_FILTER_URL_MAP pMapInfo)
{
    // TODO: React to this notification accordingly and
    // return the appropriate status code

    // Get IP of remote user
    char RemoteHost[128];
    DWORD Size=sizeof(RemoteHost);
    pCtxt->GetServerVariable( "REMOTE_ADDR", RemoteHost, &Size );

    // Load Text file with restricted IP addresses
    CFile IPs;

    bool Restricted=false;
    int Pos;
    // Note hard-coded file name and path, for our demo:
    if( IPs.Open( "c:\\inetpub\\wwwroot\\IPRestriction.lst", CFile::modeRead ) )
    {
        // Create CArchive to read strings easily:
        CArchive Ar( &IPs, CArchive::load );
        CString Line;

        // Load the text file, one line at a time:
        while( Ar.ReadString( Line ) && !Restricted )
        {
            // Truncate input line if it has an "*" wildcard
            Pos = Line.Find( "*" );
            if( Pos > 0 )
                Line.Delete( Pos, Line.GetLength() - Pos );

            // See if the remote host was in the line we just read:
            if( !Line.IsEmpty() && strncmp( RemoteHost, Line, Line.GetLength() ) ==
```

```
            0 )
                    Restricted = true; // If so, then they are restricted
        }

        // If restricted, then redirect them to our information html file, telling
        // telling them they are redirected.
        if( Restricted )
            strcpy( pMapInfo->pszPhysicalPath, "c:\\Inetpub\\wwwroot\\
            notallowed.html" );
    }


    return SF_STATUS_REQ_NEXT_NOTIFICATION;
}
```

Code 9–69 is mostly performing a file I/O. There are really only two lines in the Code 9–69 that reflect working as an ISAPI filter: Codes 9–70 and 9–71.

Code 9–70

```
pCtxt->GetServerVariable( "REMOTE_ADDR", RemoteHost, &Size );
```

The GetServerVariable() function allows you to get the server variables for the client connection. One such variable is the IP address of the client. Server variables are accessed by name, so we pass the string "REMOTE_ADDR" to the function to retrieve the IP address of the remote client. A list of other common variables can be found in the Appendix.

Code 9–71

```
strcpy( pMapInfo->pszPhysicalPath, "c:\\Inetpub\\wwwroot\\
notallowed.html" );
```

Specific to this type of filter event map is the pMapInfo parameter. This is a pointer to a structure that contains information we can modify if we want to redirect the web client to another page. By copying the full local path and filename of an HTML file into the pszPhysicalPath data member, we reroute the browser to that web page. In our example, we redirect the user to the notallowed.html file. Compile and build your program.

Installing the ISAPI Filter

To install the ISAPI filter, you must use the Registry editor (REGEDIT.EXE) for PWS, or you can use the configuration properties for IIS. Before setting this information, be sure to copy the IPRestriction.DLL file from our project to your web server. It is typically copied to the C:Windows\system32\inetsrv folder.

For PWS

1. Run RegEdit.EXE.
2. Open the following folder:

HKEY_LOCAL_MACHINE\SYSTEM\CurrentControlSet\Services\W3SVC\Parameters.

3. If not already there, add a new string value named "Filter DLLs."
4. In the value for "Filter DLLs," add the full path and filename to the location where you will copy your new Filter DLL. This is typically the %SYSTEM%\System32\INetSrv folder. MSDN Document # Q150312 also describes this process.

For IIS

1. Select your web server properties from either the IIS Management Console or your Control Panel Administrative services and select the ISAPI Filters tab (see Figure 9–19).

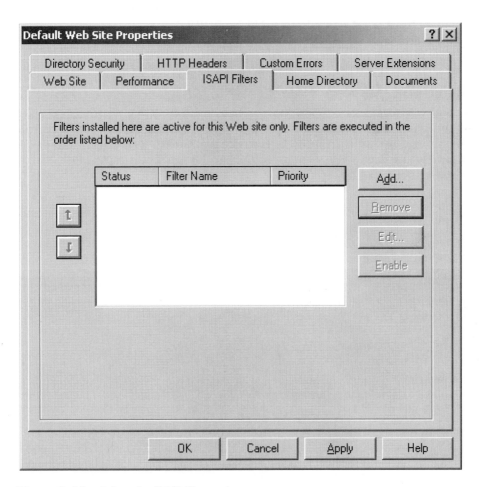

Figure 9–19   Select the ISAPI Filters tab.

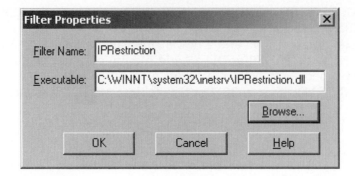

Figure 9–20   Enter the name and path of the new DLL.

2. Click the Add button to add your New Filter DLL. Enter the name and path of the new DLL. (see Figure 9–20).
3. Click OK and you see the filter displayed as shown in Figure 9–21.

Setting up the No Access Web Page

As mentioned earlier, any IP addresses that we want to restrict access from are placed into the IPRestrictions.lst text file. When one of those restricted machines attempts access, we want to redirect it to the No Access web page. Code 9–72 is the sample source for a No Access page, but it can be any valid HTML file.

Code 9–72

```
<html>
<title>You have been directed to this page because your IP address has been
denied access</title>
<body>

<p>You have been directed to this page because your IP address
has been denied access.</p>

<p>This is a test page of the IPRestriction ISAPI Filter,
written in Visual C++.</p>
</body>
</html>
```

This HTML file should be placed in the C:\InetPub\wwwroot folder, as it is referenced in the .cpp source code.

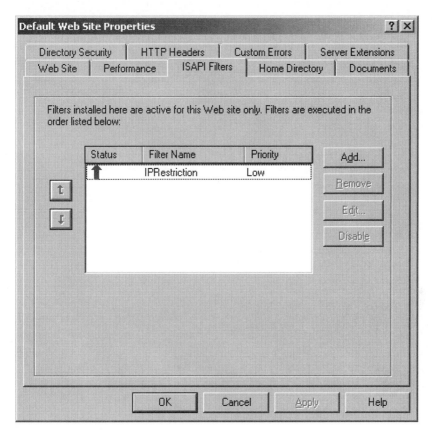

Figure 9–21   The ISAPI filter is listed in the Web Site Properties dialog.

Setting up the IPRestriction Text File

The IPRestriction.lst file contains a list of IP addresses or ranges that are to be denied access to our server. You should create a file named IPRestriction.lst in the c:\InetPub\wwwroot folder, as this is referenced by the .cpp file for the filter.

This file should contain lines of text where each line is an IP address. You can also use the (*) at the end of the IP address to indicate a wild card. For example:

```
192.4.5.32
192.5.*
```

The 192.5.* example will deny access to all machines on the 192.5 subnet, while the 192.4.5.32 will deny access only for that machine.

Testing the ISAPI Extension

To test the ISAPI extension, simply use your web browser to access the web server. You should see the normal web page displayed. Then, edit the contents of the IPRestriction.lst file to contain the IP address of your machine and attempt again to connect to the web server with your browser. On the second attempt request, you should see the No Access page, not the default web page.

Remember

◯	CGI programs are normal console-style programs.
	CGI programs usually offer better security than ISAPI extensions, but ISAPI extensions offer better speed.
	CGI or ISAPI programs are used to process forms from web browsers.
◯	Web servers like PWS and IIS are free to install and simplify single-machine development for Internet programming.
	Socket-style programming is another style of Internet, or client-server programming, which usually uses well-defined protocol standards.
◯	MFC provides support for Gopher, HTTP, and FTP protocols.

Chapter 10

Windows CE and Windows 2000 Programming

Windows CE Programming

The Windows CE environment is a trimmed-down version of Windows designed to run on a wide variety of general- and specific-purposes devices. Windows CE takes advantage of the well-known Windows API and MFC classes and visual components and brings them to these devices. These devices include palmtop, handheld, or automotive computers, as well as special purpose devices such as cable boxes and cameras.

Windows CE was built from the ground up with new kernel source code to take advantage of a wide range of CPU types. With all the current functionality of Windows CE, the memory requires a footprint of as little as 1.5 megabytes to run.

This section will concentrate on the three forms of Windows CE:

PocketPCs: A PocketPC represents the smallest type of computer. It typically has a touch-screen, several control buttons, FLASH expansion slot, and PC connection.

Handheld PC: A handheld PC typically has a keyboard, pointer device, infrared port, USB, serial, and VGA output, much like a typical laptop. Handheld PCs are typically half the size and weight of the smallest laptop PC and have no hard drive. They mimic normal PCs with the use of a keyboard.

AutoPC: The AutoPC edition of Windows CE is customized to work with AutoPC hardware installed in automobiles. Its primary difference is user interface and use of microphone and speakers for user interface to permit hands-free computer operation. AutoPCs also are tied into the audio system of an automobile, including the CD player that can be used for computer data.

Developing Programs for Windows CE

At this writing, Microsoft is releasing a new development tool for creating Windows CE programs named *eMbedded Visual Tools 3.0*. This new tool will serve as the future replacement for the Windows CE Toolkits described here. eMbedded Visual Tools 3.0 is a stand alone program for developing CE programs and does not require Visual Studio. However, you can continue to develop CE programs with the Toolkit and Visual C++, and the embedded Visual Tools 3.0 interface is almost identical.

Before you can develop a Windows CE program, you must purchase and install the *Windows CE Toolkit*. In addition, you should also download (or order for free) the latest update to the toolkit, which supports color, at `http://www.microsoft.com/msdownload/cetools/ppcsdk_color.asp`.

With these tools installed, you can create Windows CE programs using AppWizard just as we have throughout previous chapters. Before you install the toolkit, your selection of AppWizard projects might look something like Figure 10–1.

After installing the toolkit, the Figure 10–2 options will be available via AppWizard:

WCE Application: Creates an SDK-style Windows CE program.
WCE ATL COM AppWizard: Creates a DLL or Executable file that can serve as a COM server. Initially, it has no COM object classes, which you can add later.
WCE Dynamic-Link Library: Creates an SDK-style Windows CE Dynamic Link Library, that can be used by other Windows CE programs or DLLs.
WCE MFC ActiveX Control: Creates an ActiveX control that supports use of the MFC classes. The ActiveX control can then be used by other Windows CE programs.
WCE MFC AppWizard (dll): Creates a DLL file that can be used by MFC and Visual C++ programs.
WCE MFC AppWizard (exe): Creates an MFC-type program, optionally with the MFC Document/View architecture.

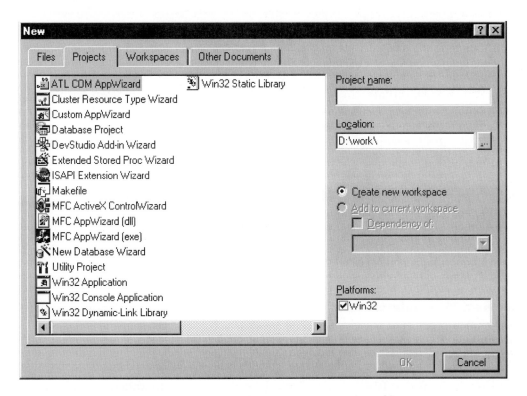

Figure 10–1   Available project formats before the installation of the CE toolkit.

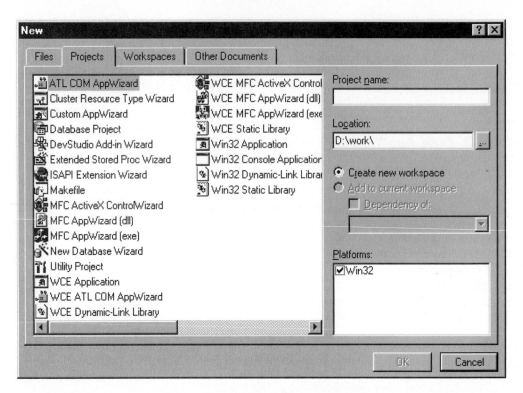

Figure 10–2 Available projects after the CE toolkit is installed.

These AppWizards create the skeleton of the Windows CE program with the bare minimum source and header files and project settings; these enable you to add functionality as needed. For all demonstrations here, we will be using the *WCE MFC AppWizard (exe)* option when creating new programs.

The Windows CE Emulator

Windows CE emulators are installed with the Windows CE Toolkit for C++. These are programs that enable you to run and test your Windows CE programs on a Windows NT and 2000 machine (Windows 95/98 supports the toolkit, but not the emulator program). There are two emulators installed by the Toolkit and one by the update:

Handheld PC Emulator: This program can be used to test and debug handheld PC programs.
Palm-sized PC Emulator: This program can be used to test and debug earlier Windows CE programs that do not support color.
Palm-sized PC Emulator 1.2: This program can be used to test and debug the newer color-enabled Windows CE programs. This is installed by the update. (PocketPC Emulator in the new E.V.T.)

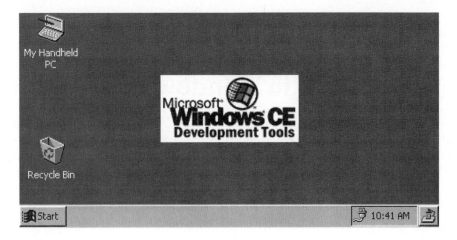

Figure 10–3   The Handheld Emulator as shown running in Windows NT.

The Handheld Emulator running under Windows NT is shown in Figure 10–3; the Palm-size Emulator 1.2 running under Windows NT is shown in Figure 10–4. There is no AutoPC emulator installed with the toolkit.

These emulators provide a complete Windows CE operating system and enable interactive debugging with your test programs. This means that you can still use the

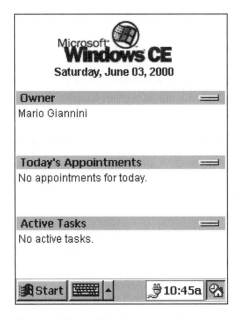

Figure 10–4   The Palm-sized Emulator
as shown running in Windows NT.

same debugging abilities of Visual C++ such as breakpoints, variable watches, and the call stack, as you would in a typical Visual C++ program.

Key Differences in Windows CE Programs

Windows CE uses Unicode strings. This means that each character of a string is 16 bits and not 8 bits as in a typical C++ program. Unicode is also an option on Windows NT programs, but Windows 95/98 offers only minimal support for Unicode strings. In order to have your constant strings converted to Unicode, enclose them in the _T() macro. This will also work with normal Windows programs and Unicode as shown in Code 10–1.

Code 10–1

```
// 8-bit string:
MessageBox( "Hello world" );

// 8-bit or Unicode, as determined by compiler settings:
MessageBox( _T("Hello World" );
```

When loading strings from the string table resource or using CStrings, the difference can mostly be ignored. For other string functions, avoid the use of the standard string functions like strcpy(), strcat(), and strcmp() and instead use the Windows functions such as wcscpy(), wcscat(), and wcscmp().

Windows CE Displays

You should design your user interface for a 240 × 320-pixel display area for a palm-sized PC and between 480 × 240 to 800 × 600 for handheld PCs. Resolution on Windows CE is not adjustable as on desktop PCs (based on your video card).

In addition, palm-sized PCs have an input panel that may pop up over your application. Try to lay out your screens so that this input panel does not cover important information. Also, a palm-sized PC favors vertical layout of controls (the display is taller than it is wider), where the handheld PC favors vertical layout (it is wider than it is taller).

Finally, some palm-sized PCs still operate in monochrome or a limited color set. Where possible, design your programs so that color or rich color selection is not important. For instance, if you must put a bitmap on a button, try to use only the primary Windows colors.

Program Termination

A Windows CE device does not have a power-off capability. Instead, it offers a standby mode where the major device operations are displayed, such as sound and display. However, it is possible that when your application is started, it may remain running for weeks or months even though you think you have turned off the device.

This brings several things into play, primarily in the area of resource management. If your program has a memory leak or a handle leak of some sort, those leaks are released in a typical Windows program when it terminates or when the user turns off the computer. You will have no such safety net in Windows CE. Thus, you will need to be careful in your resource management.

Standby mode should not be confused with the hibernate mode. When Windows CE starts to run low on memory, it will send a WM_HIBERNATE message to applications asking them to go into hibernation mode. In response, the application should release any unneeded memory or resources. While in hibernation mode, the program may then receive either a WM_CLOSE or WM_ACTIVATE message, indicating that the program is being closed or activated. The CE program should respond to the WM_CLOSE by terminating, or to a WM_ACTIVATE by possibly reallocating the resources it previously released.

Using Hardware Buttons

Windows CE for PocketPCs takes advantage of special hardware buttons on the device that can be associated with a particular application. Specifically, the hardware button is used to run an application, and, if held down for half a second, the application is requested to create a new document.

For your application to determine if there is an associated hardware button, you should call the SHGetAppKeyAssoc() function with your executable filename. For example, Code 10–2 could be placed near the end of the InitInstance() function of your CWinApp-derived application class. Then, add a FileNew() function to your CWinApp-derived application class as shown in Code 10–3. Finally, in your CMainrame class add a WM_TIMER handler using ClassWizard as shown in Code 10–4.

Code 10–2

```
// m_bKey is defined as a BYTE member variable
m_bKey = SHGetAppKeyAssoc( _T("MyApp.exe") );
if( m_bKey )
{
        BOOL Registered = RegisterHotKey ( m_pMainWnd->GetSafeHwnd(), 1000,
                MOD_WIN, m_bKey);
// If we registered the hotkey, set timer for 1 second, for a new document:
        if (Registered && GetAsyncKeyState(m_bKey) < 0)
                m_pMainWnd->SetTimer( 9000, 1000, 0);
}
```

Code 10–3

```
void CCETest2App::FileNew()
{
```

```
        OnFileNew(); // Call the normal MFC OnFileOpen
}
```

Code 10-4

```
void CMainFrame::OnTimer(UINT nIDEvent)
{
        KillTimer( nIDEvent );
        CCETest2App* pApp = (CCETest2App*)AfxGetApp();

        // If the hotkey is still down, then create a new document
        if( GetAsyncKeyState(pApp->m_bKey) < 0 )
        {
                // Create new Document
                pApp->FileNew();
        }

        CFrameWnd::OnTimer(nIDEvent);
}
```

Limited Memory Management

Memory space on a Windows CE device is always at a premium. When dealing with dynamic memory management, design your code to favor less memory rather than to favor speed. For example, instead of implementing link list type structures, consider implementing dynamic arrays that requires less memory.

Also, refer to the Program Termination for information about the hibernation mode, where your program may be asked to conserve memory by releasing any noncrucial dynamic storage.

File Storage

Windows CE does not support drive letters, though it does support folder storage. Data files are stored in the My Documents folder and program files are stored in the Programs folder. Programs may also create their own subfolders in either of these two folders. From a user interface standpoint, you should use the GetOpenFile-Name() and GetSaveFileName() functions for implementing dialogs that keep the user within the My Documents folder. (These functions and their MFC counterparts are discussed in Chapter 3, *Dialog Boxes*.)

Program Installation

A Windows CE program is prepared for installation by using the Windows CE Toolkit to create a .CAB file that contains all the required files for your application. This process is discussed later in this chapter. You can also purchase third-party software such as Install Shield for Windows CE to create installation programs for CE applications. Installations are done using the Windows CE Program Manager, which resides on the desktop to which the CE device is connected as synched.

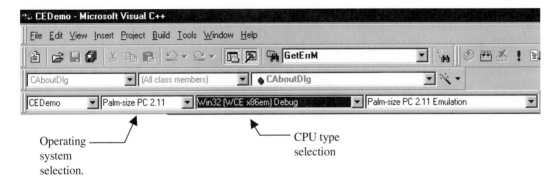

Operating system selection.

CPU type selection

Figure 10–5   The WinCE 2.11 is the target for the emulator.

Target CPU Type

The Windows CE Toolkit can target a number of different types of CE device CPUs, specifically: ARM, MIPS, PPC, SH3, SH4, and x86emu. The x86emu is for testing and debugging in the emulator. The others are device CPUs that will depend on the type of Windows CE device. You can create multiple target types.

Common devices with MIPS type CPUs include CASIO E-100/E105, Compaq Aero, MaxTech, Philips Nino and Velo, Trogon Palm, and Uniden.

Common devices with SH3 type CPUs include: Casio A20, PA-2400, HP Jornada, Palmax, Hitachi HPW 200.

It is possible to create a program with multiple CPU types, in which case you will have multiple executable files. As with a typical Windows program built in Visual C++, each type of executable is placed in its own subfolder from the project. If you build a MIPS and a x86emu project in debug mode, then you would find a WMIPSDbg and a x86emDbg folder containing the executable files generated.

Our demonstration image (Figure 10–5) shows the WinCE 2.11 (color) operating system program, targeted for the emulator. We could change the CPU selection for actually building the executable for a specific device.

MFC Class Difference for Windows CE

Table 10.1 contains a list of the primary classes that behave differently in the Wince version of MFCm than in the normal Windows version. There are additional class and method differences, that can be found in the online documentation.

Table 10.1   Classes in Wince

Class	Major Changes
CAsyncSocket	Only partial event notifications and the GetLastError() function is not supported.
CBitmap	The following is not supported: CreateDiscardableBitmap(), GetBitmapBits(), LoadMappedBitmap(), SetBitmapBits().
CBrush	The LOGBRUSH structure, used by this class has been modified for Windows CE. Windows CE does not currently support hatched brushes.
CComboBox	Does not support the Dir() function.
CComandLineInfo	Does not provide the following members: m_bRunAutomated, m_bRunEmbedded, m_strDriverName, m_strPortName, and m_strPrinterName.
CCommonDialog	Only the following common dialogs are available: CColorDialog(), CFileDialog(), CFindReplaceDialog(), CPrintDialog().
CDC	The following functions do nothing and are only available for portability reasons: DptoLP(), GetWindowExt(), GetViewportExt(), GetWindowOrg(), GetViewportOrg(), and LptoDP().
CDocument	Does not support OnFileSendMail() and OnUpdateFileSendMail().
CEdit	Does not support GetHandle() and SetHandle().
CFile	Does not support the Duplicate, LockRange(), and UnlockRange() functions.
CImageList	Image lists cannot contain cursors.
CListBox	Does not support the DIR() function.
CListCtrl	Does not support the CreateDragImage() function.
CMenu	Does not support GetMenuContextHelpId(), LoadMenuIndirect(), SetMenuContextHelpId(), or SetMenuItemBitmaps().
COleDateTime	Does not support constructor that uses a DOS file timestamp.
CPropertyPage	Does not support the OnWizardBack(), OnWizardNext() or OnWizardFinish() functions.
CSocket	Use the CceSocket() class instead of Csocket() for sockets.
CStatic	Does not support GetCursor(), GetEnhMetaFile(), GetIcon(), SetCursor(), SetEnhMetaFile(), or SetIcon().
CStdioFile	Does not support ReadString(), WriteString() functions of the m_pStream data member.
CString	Does not support AnsiToOem(), Collate(), FormatMessage(), or OemToAnsi().
CTabCtrl	Does not support GetToolTips(), SetToolTips(), or SetItemExtra() functions.
CTime	Does not support GetGmtTm(), Format(), or FormatGmt().
CWnd	Does not support a wide variety of functions, relating to drag and drop, tool tips, clipboard management, regions, and scrolling.

MFC Global Functions Not Supported

The following functions are not supported by the WinCE version of MFC:

AfxDaoInit()   AfxDaoTerm()   AfxDbInit()

AfxDaoInit()	AfxDaoTerm()	AfxDbInit()
AfxDbInitModule()	AfxGetInternetHandleType()	AfxInitRichEdit()
AfxNetInitModule()	AfxOleCanExitApp()	AfxOleGetMessageFilter()
AfxOleGetUserCtrl()	AfxOleLockApp()	AfxOleLockControl()
AfxOleParseURL()	AfxOleSetEditMenu()	AfxOleSetUserCtrl()
AfxOleTypeMatchGuid()	AfxOleUnlockApp()	AfxOleUnlockControl()
AfxThrowDaoException()	AfxThrowDBException()	

Creating a Windows CE Program with MFC

After installing the Windows CE Toolkit and the updates, you can create a Hello World program by executing the following steps:

1. From the File menu choice, select New...
2. In the New dialog (see Figure 10–6), make sure the Projects tab is selected:
3. In the New dialog, select the WCE MFC AppWizard (exe) option.

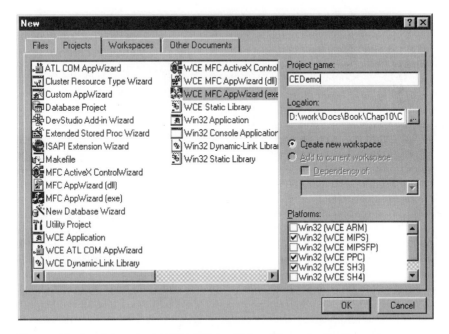

Figure 10–6   Select the WCE MFC AppWizard from the Projects tab.

4. Fill in the Project Name (CEDemo in our example).
5. If desired, select the desired platforms (Device CPU types) from the Platforms list. Make sure you have Win32 (WCE x86em) selected so you can debug on your desktop computer (if you are running Windows NT or 2000). Click OK.
6. In WCE MFC AppWizard (exe) step 1 of 4, select (see Figure 10–7) your desired project type. Our example uses Dialog based.
7. Click Next.
8. In the WCE MFC AppWizard (exe) Step 2 of 4 dialog, select (Figure 10–8) any options you want to add to your program and click Next. (Note: The selections you make here are based upon the type of program you will be creating. If you want to support sockets, online help, or ActiveX controls, then mark those selections now.)
9. In the WCE MFC AppWizard (exe) Step 3 of 4 dialog make your selections (see Figure 10–9) for comments, and whether or not you want to use MFC classes in a DLL or static library, and click Next.
10. In the WCE MFC AppWizard (exe) Step 4 of 4 dialog (see Figure 10–10), there is nothing to change in terms of options. Simply click Finish.
11. Click the OK button on the New Project Information dialog to create your project. If we had done the typical Single Document interface selection in our first dialog instead of a dialog-based program, we would have options for controlling the menu and toolbar appearance as well.

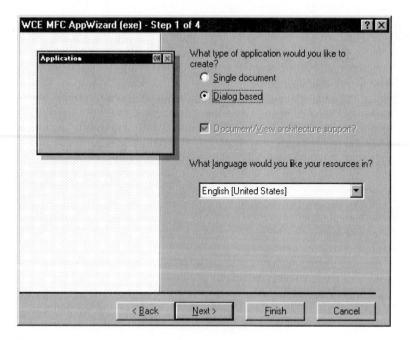

Figure 10–7 Select the Dialog-based project type.

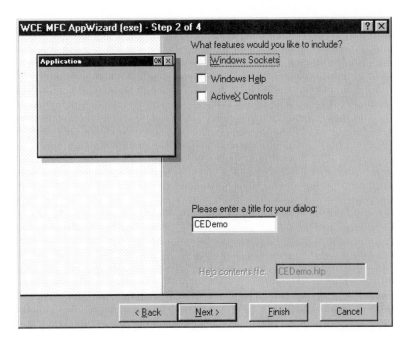

Figure 10–8 Select the options that you want to include in the project.

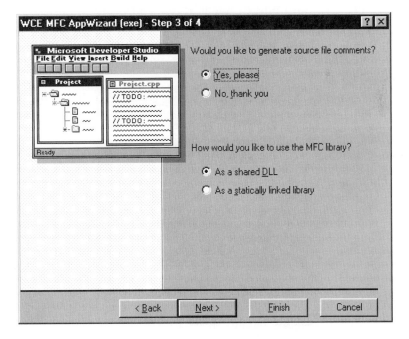

Figure 10–9 Select source code comments and shared DLL.

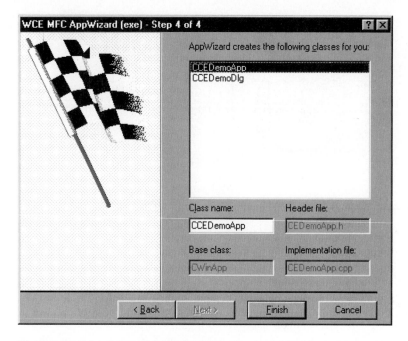

Figure 10–10   Select Finish to execute the AppWizard.

12. Change the Operating System and CPU types for your project, as Palm-size PC 2.11, and Win32 (WCE x86emu) Debug.

13. Edit the IDC_CEDEMO_DIALOG dialog in the dialog resource editor and add a button (see Figure 10–11). Change the button so that its ID is IDC_HELLO, and its caption is &Hello.

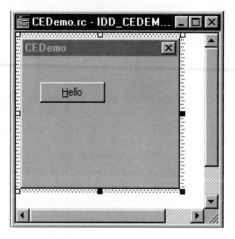

Figure 10–11   Insert a button on the CEDemo dialog.

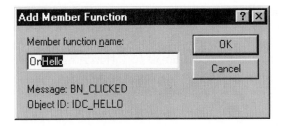

Figure 10–12 Add a click handle by double-clicking the Hello button.

Figure 10–13 The initial program in the emulator.

Figure 10–14 Click the Hello button and a message appears.

---

14. Resize the dialog so that it is about 120 × 90.
15. Double-click on the Hello button while in the dialog editor to add a click handler (see Figure 10–12) (you could also do it via ClassWizard).
16. Click OK to accept the default function name of OnHello. You should now be placed into the dialog.cpp source file by Visual Studio, at the new handler, which looks something like Code 10–5. Modify this code to look like Code 10–6.

Code 10–5

```
void CCEDemoDlg::OnHello()
{
        // TODO: Add your control notification handler code here

}
```

Code 10–6

```
void CCEDemoDlg::OnHello()
{
        MessageBox( _T( "Hello World!" ) );
}
```

17. Compile your program by pressing F7.
18. Run your program by pressing Ctrl-F5.

Your initial program, in the emulator, should look like Figure 10–13. If you click the Hello button, you should now see the message box appear as shown in Figure 10–14. Notice how the OK and Cancel buttons on message boxes in Windows CE are displayed on the top right of the window, not as separate window buttons.

Creating a Windows CE Installation

The steps in the previous section demonstrate how to create a typical Hello World program for Windows CE with MFC. Here we will discuss installation options.

Windows CE supports two means of program installation: You can use the tools included with the CE toolkit to create a CAB file that will work with the CE Application Manager, or you can purchase or download a third-party installation utility. A third alternative exists in which you can create your own installation program, but this topic would be beyond the scope of this section.

Third-Party Tools

Third-party tools can be used to create custom, professional installation programs that install your software directly onto the Windows CE. The CE machine would need to be connected to a desktop, and the desktop would run the setup utility. The following companies offer installation utilities for Windows CE.

Install Shield: The InstallShield for Windows CE product is a commercial product that can be ordered at `www.installshield.com`.

NStall Wizard: This utility, if you can still find it, was a $65 shareware program. It has since been taken over by InstallShield. The companies website, `www.nstall.com`, now redirects you to the InstallShield website.

CuteInstall: This freeware utility is made by AcerTech software (Acer) in Shaghai. Very little support is provided, and there is no official website. It can be downloaded at `www.cegadgets.com/download.htm`.

Using Toolkit Utilities

Creating an installation based on the utilities included with the CE toolkit is a straightforward process, though not as easy to implement as with the third-party tools. Basically, you will need to create an INF file to create a CAB file, as well as an INI file. Once this is done, you will need to distribute your programs in the form of the INI and CAB file.

The toolkit utilities rely on the CE Application Manager (ceappmgr.exe) to install and remove programs. The end user can run this program from the Tools menu option of the ActiveSync program, which is included with Windows CE and is a desktop program to configure the Windows CE device.

Creating the INF and CAB Files

The CAB file needed for installation is created from an INF file using the CAB Wizard (cabwiz.exe) program from the Windows CE Toolkit. We will first review the sections needed for creating an INF file and then examine the steps to create the CAB file from it.

The INF file is a text file that you can create with Notepad. It should have a name similar to that of your project, so we will call ours CEDemo.inf. Code 10–7 contains the sections needed for the INF file, which you should add to your INF file.

Code 10–7

```
[Version]
Signature=""$Windows NT$""
Provider="ProgrammersNotebook"
CESignature="$Windows CE$"
```

The Version section lists the Provider and Signature values. The Provider is the company distributing the program. The Signature must be "$Windows NT$" or "$Windows 95$" and CESignature must be "$Windows CE$."

The INF file is similar to the old-style make files and makes extensive use of macro names and strings. The CEStrings section defines string names to be used for a CE setup. In Code 10–8 we have defined the AppName to be CEDemo and the Install directory to be %CE1\%AppName. These string macros (AppName and InstallDir) will now be used later on in the INF file. Table 10.2 contains %CE?% string macros are predefined.

Code 10–8

```
[CEStrings]
AppName="CEDemo"
InstallDir=%CE1%\%AppName%
```

The CEDevice section defines the target operating system versions and the processor type. In Code 10–9, the target is Windows CE 2.11, and the ProcessorType is an SH3 processor.

Code 10–9

```
[CEDevice]
VersionMin=2.11
VersionMax=2.11
```

Table 10.2   CE String Macros

Macro	Definition
%CE1%	\Program Files
%CE2%	\Windows
%CE3%	\Windows\Desktop
%CE4%	\Windows\Startup
%CE5%	\My Documents
%CE6%	\Program Files\Accessories
%CE7%	\Program Files\Communication
%CE8%	\Program Files\Games
%CE9%	\Program Files\Pocket Outlook
%CE10%	\Program Files\Office
%CE11%	\Windows\Programs
%CE12%	\Windows\Programs\Accessories
%CE13%	\Windows\Programs\Communications
%CE14%	\Windows\Programs\Games
%CE15%	\Windows\Fonts
%CE16%	\Windows\Recent
%CE17%	\Windows\Favorites

```
;Processor type is 10003 for SH3 and the MIPS is 40000
ProcessorType=10003
```

The DefaultInstall section (see Code 10–10) lists the names of other sections to follow, which define the files to be installed: Files.Program definition for Copyfiles and Shortcuts.All for CEShortCuts. The definition for CEShortCuts can be found further down in this section. Both CopyFiles and CEShortCuts are predefined values that specify files to copy and shortcuts or links to create, respectively. Possible other values under this section include AddReg for registry settings, CESetupDLL for DLL copying, and CESelfRegister for registering DLL (ActiveX/COM) files.

Code 10–10

```
[DefaultInstall]
CopyFiles=Files.Program
CEShortCuts=Shortcuts.All
```

The ShortCuts.All is a section (see Code 10–11) we created to list the links or shortcuts that should be created. The strings are formatted as three items: the link name (without the lnk extension), 0 if the link is to a file or nonzero if to a folder, and finally the item the link is set to. By default, the InstallDir defines where the third item is located on the Windows CE device, but you can optionally provide a fourth item on the line to define an alternative.

Code 10–11

```
[Shortcuts.All]
CEDemo,0,CEDemo.exe
```

The SourceDiskNames define a logical disk where the various files can be found for placing into the CAB file. In Code 10–12, we define disk 1 to be called CEDemo Files and give its full physical path (on the local desktop machine).

Code 10–12

```
[SourceDisksNames]
1 = ,"CEDemo Files",,D:\work\Docs\Book\Chap10\CEDemo\WCESH3Rel
```

SourceDiskFiles defines where the files we will be copying are located based on the logical disk number, defined in the SourceDiskNames folder. In Code 10–13, we specify only one file, our CEDemo.EXE file, from SourceDiskName 1.

Code 10–13

```
[SourceDisksFiles]
CEDemo.exe=1
```

The DestinationDirs section defines where on the Windows CE we should place our files. Each file section we define (like Files.Program) can have its own installation directory. Our example will place the installed files into the Install Directory (see Code 10–14).

Code 10–14

```
[DestinationDirs]
Files.Program=0,%InstallDir%
```

The Files.Program section (see Code 10–15) (which is our own definition from Code 10–14) defines a list of files that should be copied. In our demo, we only copy one file, our CEDemo.exe file.

Code 10–15

```
[Files.Program]
CEDemo.exe,,,0
```

Once the INF file has been set up and its paths are correct, we can run the AB Wizard program (CabWiz.exe). The CabWiz.exe file is run from the command line with command line switches, so you may need to indicate the entire path to the executable. From the command line, type Code 10–16.

Code 10–16

```
"C:\Windows CE Tools\WCE211\ms palm size pc\support\appinst\bin\cabwiz.exe"
"CEDemo.inf" /err CEDemo.err /cpu sh3
```

Code 10–16 assumes that the cabwiz.exe file is located in the C:\Windows CE Tools\WCE211\ms palm size pc\support\appinst\bin folder. The program is run with "CEDemo.inf," the name of the inf file we want to use to create the CAB file. Errors are logged in the CEDemo.err file, with the /err option. The /cpu option is also used to indicate we are creating a CAB file for an SH3 CPU type.

Once you have run the above command (it should be a single line on the command line), the cabwiz.exe program will generate a CEDemo.sh3.cab file that can then be used for the installation. We next have to make the ini file, and we are ready to install.

Making the ini File

In order to install your CAB file, you must also create an ini file for the CE Application Manager (ceAppMgr.exe). A typical ini file is shown in Code 10–17.

Code 10–17

```
; Note:
; Do not edit CEAppManager Version!
; Refer to Help for more information.
```

```
[CEAppManager]
Version = 1.0
Component = CEDemo

[CEDemo]
Description = CEDemo
CabFiles = CEDemo.sh3.cab
```

The CEAppManager section defines the component being installed and its version. The component being installed is referred to as CEDemo. The CEDemo section lists a description of the component or program being installed and then the CAB files used for the install.

Bringing It All Together

Copy the CEDemo.ini and CEDemo.sh3.cab files into a folder named CEDemo inside the child folder of the ActiveSync folder. The ActiveSync folder is typically in the C:\Program Files\Microsoft ActiveSync folder. From that folder, run the CEAppMgr program and specify the .ini file name as shown in Code 10–18, which should be one line of code.

Code 10–18

```
C:\Program Files\Microsoft ActiveSync\ceappmgr "C:\Program Files\Micro
soft ActiveSync\CEDemo\CEDemo.ini"
```

Notice that you can create a program to automate the above steps, to copy the CAB and INF files into the correct location and run the CEAppMgr.exe file. To determine where a machine has the ActiveSync program installed, examine the registry key in Code 10–19.

Code 10–19

```
HKEY_LOCAL_MACHINE\SOFTWARE\Microsoft\Windows\CurrentVersion\App
Paths\CEAPPMGR.EXE
```

Windows 2000 Programming

While Windows 2000 brings a slew of technological advances over Windows NT, its effect on the typical application programmer is somewhat limited. In this section, we will discuss the overall new services provided by Windows 2000, some of the changes to the user interface, and any special programming considerations.

Compatibility

Windows 2000 is basically Windows NT 5. As such, your Win32 programs should work on it without any problems. If anything, Windows 2000 extends the abilities of Windows NT and Windows 98, so existing code can reliably work.

Windows 2000 does modify the "thunking" procedure when dealing with 16-bit programs, though. Thunking is the term used to describe the ability for a 16-bit program to call 32-bit functions (such as in a DLL) or 32-bit code to call 16-bit functions. Where Windows 9x provides this feature in something called *flat thunking*, Windows 32 provides a new method called *generic thunking.*

In generic thunking, one 16-bit application can call 32-bit functions and can provide a callback function to 32-bit code so that it (the 32-bit code) can call it back (the 16-bit code). However, it no longer supports the ability for 32-bit code to call directly into 16-bit code. For the most part, given the age of 16-bit code, we assume that it will be easier to port it to the newer 32-bit platform than to dive deeply into thunking requirements.

A thunk itself is a small piece of code that translates data types between 16- and 32-bit applications. For the most part, it is hidden from the programmer.

Determining Windows Version

If your program uses features specific to a type of Windows 32 OS (such as Windows 98 or Windows 2000), you should verify the version of the operating system at program startup. If the version is not what you need, then the program should indicate such and terminate. To determine the version of Windows, call the GetVersionEx() function (see Code 10–20).

Code 10–20

```
BOOL GetVersionEx( LPOSVERSIONINFO lpVersion );
```

The GetVersionEx() function needs a pointer to an OSVERSIONINFO structure, which will be used for both input and output. The structure contains data members shown in Table 10.3.

An example to building a string with the current OS version is shown in Code 10–21.

Code 10–21

```
OSVERSIONINFO vi;
vi.dwOSVersionInfoSize = sizeof(vi);
```

Table 10.3   Data Members of the OSVERSIONINFO Structure

Member	Meaning
DWORD dwOSVersionInfoSize	Indicates size of the structure used for input.
DWORD dwMajorVersion	Indicate the returned major version of the OS; 3 and 4 indicates Windows NT 3 or 4, and 5 indicates Windows 2000.
DWORD dwMinorVersion	Indicates the minor version of the OS.
DWORD dwBuildNumber	Indicates the build number for Windows NT and 2000, or the build number and the major and minor version numbers for Windows 9x.
DWORD dwPlatformId	Indicates the platform ID and is one of the following: VER_PLATFORM_WIN32s for Win32s on Windows 3.1, VER_PLATFORM_WIN32_WINDOWS for Windows 9x, or VER_PLATFORM_WIN32_NT for Windows NT and 2000.
TCHAR szCSDVersion[128]	Indicates the last installed Service Pack, or empty if no service packs installed.

```
GetVersionEx( &vi );
CString Full, Version;
TCHAR *Platform = "Unknown";

if( vi.dwPlatformId == VER_PLATFORM_WIN32s )
    Platform = "Win32s on Windows 3.11";
else
if( vi.dwPlatformId == VER_PLATFORM_WIN32_WINDOWS )
{
    if( vi.dwMinorVersion )
        Platform = _T("Windows 95");
    else
        Platform = _T("Windows 98");
}
else
{
    if( vi.dwPlatformId == VER_PLATFORM_WIN32_NT )
```

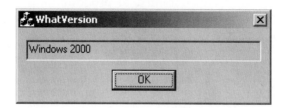

Figure 10–15   A simple dialog-based application running on Windows 2000.

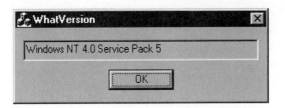

Figure 10–16 A simple dialog-based application running on Windows NT.

```
{
    if( vi.dwMajorVersion == 3 || vi.dwMajorVersion == 4 )
    {
        Platform = _T("Windows NT");
        Version.Format( _T("%d.%d"), vi.dwMajorVersion, vi.dwMinorVersion );
    }
    else
    if( vi.dwMajorVersion == 5 )
        Platform = _T("Windows 2000");
    }
}

Full.Format( _T("%s %s %s"), Platform, (LPCSTR)Version, vi.szCSDVersion );
SetDlgItemText( IDC_VERSION, Full );
```

Code 10–21 finally uses SetDlgItemText() to set the text of a STATIC control to contain the entire string. An example of a simple dialog-based application that executes Code 10–21 on a Windows 2000 machine is shown in Figure 10–15. Notice that no Service Pack was installed, and the Build number was not displayed. The same program running on Windows NT is shown in Figure 10–16.

Visual Studio Plus Pack/Windows 2000 Readiness Kit

At the time of this writing, Microsoft offers a free Windows 2000 Developer's Readiness Kit to help you become accustomed to programming for the Windows 2000 platform. This package is part of the Visual Studio 6.0 Plus Pack. If you do not have the Plus Pack CDs, the majority of its components can be downloaded from http://msdn.microsoft.com/vstudio/downloads/updates.asp. The Plus Pack contains the following items:

Windows 2000 Readiness Kit: The Windows 2000 Readiness Kit contains an online training and documentation that takes advantage of the latest Windows 2000 technologies. Topics covered include generic Windows 2000 development topics (i.e., API and COM additions and changes), common compatibility issues with existing software, requirements for the Windows Logo program, COM+ resources, and the Visual Studio Installer.

The Visual Studio Installer is a new common installation mechanism for program installations now standard on Windows 2000, and it can be added to Win9x and Windows NT. The installer makes it possible for you to create professional install and uninistall programs for your application, without requiring the purchase of a third-party utility like InstallShield. A demonstration of the Windows installer is provided later.

Microsoft Data Engine (MSDE): The Microsoft Data Engine is Microsoft's latest definition for database management. Also included is a personal version of SQL Server 7.0. These two tools together will permit you to create programs that will work on a retail version of SQL Server without having to change any code in your application.

Developer Training for MSDE: This CD consists of online documentation to help you learn and implement MSDE in your programs.

Windows NT 4.0 Service Pack 4.0: Though Microsoft is currently on Service Pack 6.0a at the time of this writing, the components for Windows 2000 development require at least Service Pack 4.0. If you have already installed a later service pack, then you will have no problems with the other tools.

Using Win2000 Options

Before you can take advantage of some of the latest Windows 2000 abilities, you will probably need to update your Platform SDK in Visual C++. The Platform SDK is the portion of Visual C++ that has the header files and libraries for target platforms. Even with Service Pack 3 installed with Visual C++, you will still need to get the latest SDK.

The latest version of the Windows SDK can be downloaded from `http://www.mi-crosoft.com/msdownload/platformsdk/setuplauncher.htm`. Depending on the options, the download from Microsoft may be between 18 and roughly 200 megabytes. We recommend the "typical" option for installation.

Depending on your compiler version, you may or may not need to install the latest SDK. You should check your compiler by testing out some of the user interface programs below. If you get compiler errors then you probably need the latest SDK.

User Interface Changes

User interface changes are included in the following DLL files: Comctl32.dll, Shell32.dll, and Shlwapi.dll. While Windows 2000 comes with version 5.81 of comctl32.dll to give you its new features, they can also be installed (with minute differences) by installing Internet Explorer 5.0. Many of the changes described here can also be implemented on a Windows NT or 98 computer that has Internet Explorer 5.0 installed.

Notice that if any of the sample code here causes compiler errors, you may need to download the latest Windows Platform SDK, as described in the previous section.

The core list of controls in Windows 2000 remains the same as that in Windows 95, except that the styles that can be applied to them have changed to make the controls appear or function differently than previous versions.

The list of style changes is too broad to cover in this topic. Basically, you can review the styles for a particular type of controls using the online help, which should tell you what version of the control supports a given style.

The following example demonstrates how to utilize the new latest tooltip styles (see Table 10.4).

In our example, we will use the TTS_BALLOON style, as shown in Figure 10-17.

Using MFC, we can change the style of a window by calling the CWnd::ModifyStyle() or CWnd::ModifyStyleEx() functions. For normal styles (not extended styles), we want to call ModifyStyle().

In order to add the tooltip ability to our program, we need to declare a CToolTipCtrl data member in our main Dialog class (CWhatVersionDlg.h in Figure 10-17). This is illustrated in Code 10-22.

Code 10-22

```
class CWhatVersionDlg : public CDialog
{
// Construction
public:
        CWhatVersionDlg(CWnd* pParent = NULL);// standard constructor

// Dialog Data
        //{{AFX_DATA(CWhatVersionDlg)
```

Table 10.4   Tooltip Styles

Style	Meaning
TTS_BALLOON	The tooltip appearance will represent a rounded balloon, not a rectangular tooltip.
TTS_NOANIMATE	Disables sliding tooltip animation on Win98 and Win2000.
TTS_NOFADE	Disables fading tooltip animation on Windows 2000 systems.

Figure 10–17 The TTS_BALLOON style.

```
enum { IDD = IDD_WHATVERSION_DIALOG };
CEdit m_Version;
CButton m_Ok;
//}}AFX_DATA

// ClassWizard generated virtual function overrides
//{{AFX_VIRTUAL(CWhatVersionDlg)
public:
virtual BOOL PreTranslateMessage(MSG* pMsg);
protected:
virtual void DoDataExchange(CDataExchange* pDX);   // DDX/DDV support
//}}AFX_VIRTUAL

// Implementation
protected:
        HICON m_hIcon;
        CToolTipCtrl m_ToolTips;

        // Generated message map functions
        //{{AFX_MSG(CWhatVersionDlg)
        virtual BOOL OnInitDialog();
        afx_msg void OnSysCommand(UINT nID, LPARAM lParam);
        afx_msg void OnPaint();
        afx_msg HCURSOR OnQueryDragIcon();
        //}}AFX_MSG
        DECLARE_MESSAGE_MAP()
};
```

Next, we need to create the tooltip control, which we do inside the OnInitDialog()
handler for the dialog, and then turn on our desired balloon style using Modify-
Style() as shown in Code 10–23.

Code 10–23

```
BOOL CWhatVersionDlg::OnInitDialog()
{
        // Portions of code removed for readability

        // Create the tool tip control
        m_ToolTips.Create( this );
```

```
        // Modify its style to take advantage of Win2000 baloon style:
        m_ToolTips.ModifyStyle( 0, TTS_BALLOON );
        // Enable tooltips for each child window
        GetDlgItem(IDC_VERSION)->EnableToolTips( TRUE );
        GetDlgItem(IDOK)->EnableToolTips( TRUE );

        // Add the desired text caption for the tool tip, for each control
        m_ToolTips.AddTool( &m_Version, "Version information" );
        m_ToolTips.AddTool( &m_Ok, "Click to Close" );

        return TRUE; // return TRUE unless you set the focus to a control
}
```

We are using ModifyStyle() to alter the Windows style to include the new "balloon" style. The remaining few lines of code has nothing to do with the new Windows style. Calls to EnableToolTips() enable the tooltips for those windows and the calls to AddTool() associate the tooltip text with a specific window.

The m_Version and the m_Ok are member variables in the Dialog class that were created using the ClassWizard Member Variable tab (they are both "control category" type variables).

Our final step in activating the tooltip control is to add a PtretranslateMessage() function for the Dialog class, using ClassWizard's Message Map tab. The function added by ClassWizard will look like Code 10–24. Modify it to call the RelayEvent() function of the m_ToolTips object as shown in Code 10–25.

Code 10–24

```
BOOL CWhatVersionDlg::PreTranslateMessage(MSG* pMsg)
{
        return CDialog::PreTranslateMessage(pMsg);
}
```

Code 10–25

```
BOOL CWhatVersionDlg::PreTranslateMessage(MSG* pMsg)
{
        // Add tooltip processing
        m_ToolTips.RelayEvent( pMsg );

        return CDialog::PreTranslateMessage(pMsg);
}
```

Now, when the program runs, if you let the mouse hover over a control in the dialog, its tooltip is displayed with the new balloon style, as pictured at the start of this topic.

The Windows Installer

The Windows Installer is a new Visual Studio tool that will permit you to create small installation programs without the need for a third-party tool such as Install Shield. The end user will have the ability to uninstall the program by using the Control Panel Add/Remove Programs applet.

There are two main methods for creating an installable program using the new Windows Installer: to include the installer itself or not to include the installer. If you do not include the installer itself, then the size of your program will be very small, but will only work on computers that already have the Windows Installer program set up on the machine. If you do include the installer, then your distribution will be larger and consist of multiple files, but can be run on any Win32 machine.

If you choose to include the installer itself in your distribution, it will then set up the Windows Installer on the target machine, meaning that in subsequent installs or patches, you only need to distribute the smaller setup file (without the Windows Installer itself included).

For example, we will demonstrate how to create an installation program for the WhatVersion program which had portions explained in the "Determining Windows Version" and "User interface changes." The installation that does not include the Windows Installer will be a single file, 178K in size. The version that does include the installer will be an additional 2.5 megabytes in size, with four additional files.

The Windows Installer gives you the means to set up what files should be copied to the user's computer, what registry settings should be defined, and what icons should be placed on the target machine's desktop.

Creating a Windows Installer Project

We will create an installation for the WhatVersion program discussed earlier in this chapter. We will assume that you have created that file, WhatVersion.exe, in preparation for the installation. You can in reality use any executable file you want, such as Notepad.exe, in order to go through the steps here as long as you keep the file names straight. This way you don't need to create the WhatVersion in advance.

The Installer program is the DEVENV.EXE file, which can normally be found within your Start menu, under Programs, and then the Microsoft Visual Studio 6.0 submenu. Look for the Visual Studio Installer item in that menu, or perhaps in a submenu. Run the Installer application from that menu item.

When the Installer starts, you may see the logo message for Java or Visual Basic. Don't get confused, this will allow us to make new Installation projects also.

Starting the Installation Project

Once you have started the Visual Studio Installer, you will be in the Microsoft Development Environment main window.

1. From the main menu, select the File menu item, then the New Project... menu item. You should see a dialog similar to Figure 10–18.
2. Open the Visual Studio folder, and in that you will see a Visual Studio Installer Projects node. Select that node.
3. Enter a Name for your new project (WhatVersion, in the image below), make sure that the Location is where you want to store the file, and then click Open (see Figure 10–19).

The Project view window (see Figure 10–20) displays the structure of your Installation project. For our sample, we are going to indicate the EXE file to copy to the target machine, where we will install it on the target machine and also add a menu item to the Start Button to run our program.

Adding the Executable File to the Installation Project

1. Double-click on the File System node in the Project explorer window; this should open the Project – File System window as shown in Figure 10–21.
2. Right-click on the Application Folder item, and select Add Files... from the popup menu that appears.

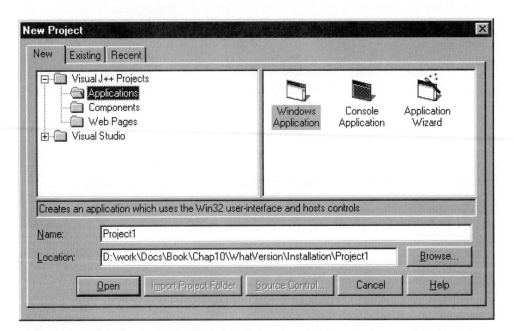

Figure 10–18 Select a new applications project.

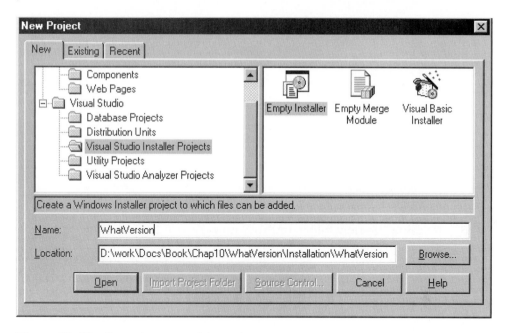

Figure 10–19 Enter the name of the project.

3. In the file open dialog that appears, locate the WhatVersion.exe file (the name of the program you want to create an install disk for), and double-click that filename. Once the file is added, the File System will appear like Figure 10–22.

4. Select the User's Start Menu folder, again on the File System window, and right-click on it.

5. From the pop-up menu that appears, select the Add Folder menu item. A new folder will be added.

Figure 10–20 Here is the structure of the installed project.

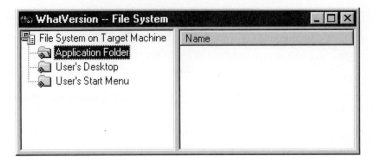

Figure 10–21   The File System lists the file system on the target computer.

6.   Rename the new folder to Programs. Your File System window will look like Figure 10–23.
7.   With the Programs folder selected (as pictured in Figure 10–23), right-click in the Name window on the right, and this time select the Create Shortcut item in the menu that pops up.
8.   You should see a list of the files in your project appear as shown in Figure 10–24.
9.   Highlight the name that you want the shortcut to refer to (this shortcut will be displayed in the Program menu on the target machine) and click OK (see Figure 10–25).
10.   Click once on the ShortCut to WhatVersion.exe item, and the properties for the item should be displayed in the Properties window (see Figure 10–26).
11.   Change the Name property to just say WhatVersion.
12.   From the main menu, select the Build menu item, then the Build submenu item.

Once you have done all the steps above the program should have created a folder in your original project location named Output\Disk_1. If you look inside this folder

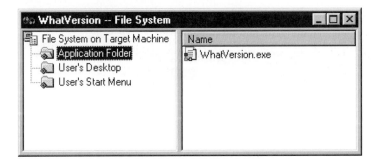

Figure 10–22   Select the Application Folder to display the program.

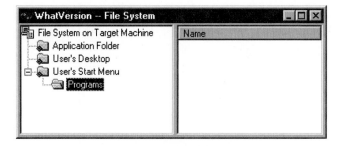

Figure 10–23   Rename the new folder to Programs.

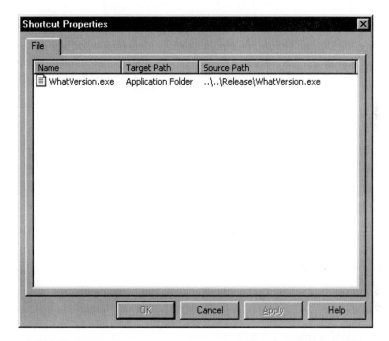

Figure 10–24   The program appears in the File tab in the Shortcut Properties dialog.

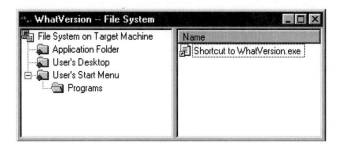

Figure 10–25   Highlight the program to create a shortcut.

Figure 10–26 Set the properties for the shortcut.

you should find the single WhatVersion.msi file. You can test your new installation file by double-clicking it, and you should see Figure 10–27.

Clicking the Next button will start a series of dialogs that will complete the installation process.

Other Installer Components

Though the above example did not utilize them, you can also change the banner used at the top of the installation dialogs by double-clicking the User Interface node in the Project Explorer window. Once you have done this, the User Interface window appears (see Figure 10–28).

In the properties for each of the nodes, you can specify the bitmap to be displayed at the top of that dialog. You can also turn on or off the display of some of the installation dialogs (each child node indicates a dialog during program installation).

You can also modify the registry settings in preparation for the actual installed programs first run. If you double-click the Registry item in the Project Explorer window, you will see the registry editor appear (see Figure 10–29).

To add a new key to the registry, simply right-click on the desired parent and add the key. Note that you may have to create several keys because registry settings are never at the root level, as is shown in the Figure 10–29.

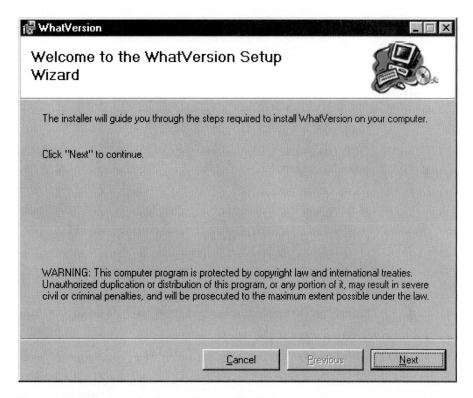

Figure 10–27 Double clicking the new file displays this dialog.

You can also create file associations with your installer, so that if your program uses a data file, the user can open a data file just by double-clicking it in Windows Explorer. To create this type of association (which MFC programs will also do automatically, the first time they are run), double-click on the Associations node in the Project Explorer window (see Figure 10–30).

You can define new document type associates, MIME associations, or COM objects or type libraries for your installation.

Including the Installer Loader

If you want to be safe, you might want to make your distributed programs available in two formats: one with the Windows Installer itself as part of the distribution and one without it. Ideally, if everyone had the Windows Installer on his or her machine, it would be a simple choice.

By default, the setup files created by the Windows Installer will generate only the setup file and will not include the required executables if the target machine does not already have it installed. If you want to make the distribution so that any computer can use it (with or without Windows Installer), then do the following:

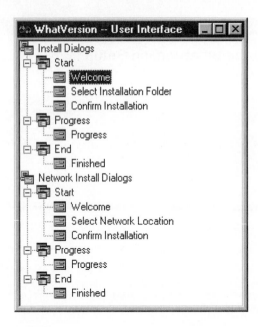

Figure 10–28 Double-clicking the User Interface displays the User Interface dialog.

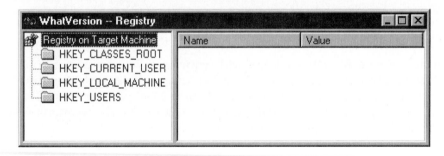

Figure 10–29 Double-click the Registry to display the registry editor.

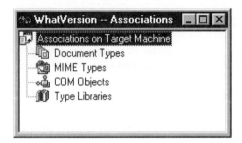

Figure 10–30 Double-click Associations to display the Associations dialog.

1. Open the desired project.
2. Go to the Project menu item.
3. At the bottom of the menu, select the Properties menu item.
4. In the new project Properties dialog, change the build type (see Figure 10–31).

Running Your Install

To run your new install, simply double-click either the SETUP.EXE file (if you opted to include the Windows Installer) or the WhatVersion.msi file (if you didn't include the Windows Installer). The first screen of the installation process will be displayed (see Figure 10–32).

To Remove the Installed Program

Removing an installed program simply requires going to the Control Panel Add/Remove Program applet. Once that is loaded, you should be able to locate your program (see Figure 10–33).

Click the Add / Remove button to remove the application.

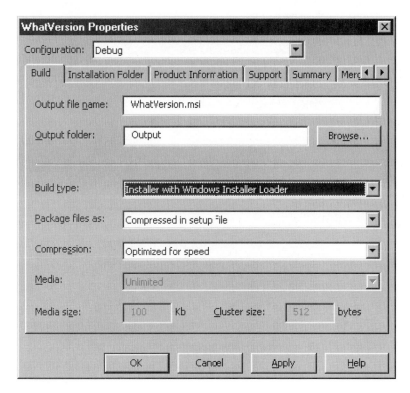

Figure 10–31 Change the build type in the application's properties dialog.

Figure 10–32 Double-click SETUP.EXE to run the application's install wizard.

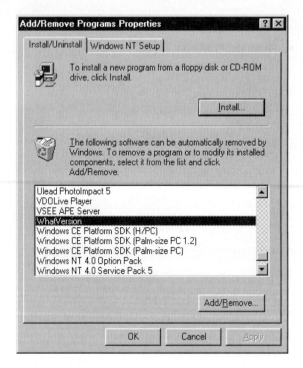

Figure 10–33 The Add/Remove Programs Properties dialog is used to remove an installed program.

Active Directory Services

Active Directory Services is an extremely large topic, far too large for several pages of text. Rather than providing a programming example, we will simply describe what it is and how you might use it.

Active Directory Services, a new feature to Windows 2000, is actually made up of several core components. The basic principle of ADS is that a computer manages a directory of objects. Those objects may be drives, folders, files, printers, users, etc. ADS is a means to provide a standard method for working with these objects.

In terminology, a directory is similar to a database, only it is not designed to contain extremely large amounts of data, nor is that data intended to change often. This makes it ideal to store things like system configurations and network segments. Directories are designed to present their data hierarchically in a standard and rapid fashion.

In addition to the database-style analogy, a directory can also be compared to the type of object stores found in email systems. Departments, groups, users, and emails are all objects found in the object store, or directory. Users do not frequently alter their emails or sort and search them, so they are good candidates for a directory-type implementation. The standard directory methods would permit us to iterate through a list of objects, determine the properties of those objects (such as name, type, size, etc.), determine if that object had any children, and then repeat the process.

In a very basic sense, Active Directory Services provide a standard means of working with hierarchical object stores. The type of object is almost unimportant (except, of course, we hope they are the objects we want to ultimately work with). ADS provides an API called the Active Directory Services Interface (ADSI) to enable you to work with ADS objects. The ADSI is divided into two types of programs: clients and providers. A client is a program that makes use of ADS, and a provider is a program (or DLL) that provides ADS access to a type of resource or data.

This is similar to the ActiveX protocol. ActiveX controls define standard "Stock" properties that the control implements. The Control itself would be called the provider. The user of the control can utilize standard functions for getting and setting the properties, as well as to determine how many properties there are and what they are called. The program using the control would be called the client.

Much in the same way you can add new ActiveX controls to your computer to use new controls, you can also add new ADS providers. For example, if you were to write an ADS provider that would expose your company hierarchy chart (of workers) to ADS, then an ADS client could use that provider to iterate the chart. The provider may store the actual hierarchical data as a database or a text file.

Active Directory Services Programming

ADSI is a set of COM interfaces that provide access to ADS. The actual interface class names are IADs and IDirectoryObject. IDirectoryObject objects provides a performance benefit for ADS, but also requires a deeper knowledge of the Directory object itself, which in part nullifies the advantage of a generic interface. For automation clients, IADs should be used,

Using the IADs core interface requires the creation of an Active Directory Service object. From this object, you can instantiate the other COM interfaces of ADS. Using the MFC OLE classes like COleDispatchDriver, you can implement IADs interfaces. After that, normal COM programming plays a role in using the ADS objects.

Active Directory Services require the Windows 2000 server to run, and they must be installed using the DCPROMO.EXE program. Once installed, Microsoft sets up a standard set of object types, such as users and domains.

Remember

○	The majority of new Windows 2000 abilities concern user interface, as far as an application programmer is typically concerned.
	You may need to download an updated SDK package to take advantage of new user interface styles.
○	The Windows Installer is the new standard means to create installations for your application.
	Developing programs for Windows CE requires either the Windows CE toolkit, or the embedded Visual Tools.
○	Windows CE programs are installed on the CE device with the help of the ActiveSync program.

Chapter 11

Messages, Timers, and Threads

- Message Pumps
- Timers
- Threads

Message Pumps

Every Windows graphical program contains at least one message pump or loop. Events from the user or from an application are stored in a message queue for your application. It is Windows' responsibility to place messages such as mouse movements, key presses for user interface, and timer events into this queue. It is the job of the message pump to remove them from the queue and process them.

Figure 11–1 illustrates the path of a message in the Windows programming model. First, the mouse moving over a window generates a message. Windows takes that message and places it into the appropriate application message queue. The application itself contains one or more message pumps that takes that message out of the queue and dispatches it to the appropriate message handler or Window Procedure [WndProc()]. The message handler may also put additional messages back into the message queue.

Code 11–1 uses the GetMessage() to retrieve a message from the application message queue. When a WM_QUIT message is taken from the queue, GetMessage() returns FALSE, which will cause the loop to terminate, and then the program will terminate. Anything other than WM_QUIT, however, is handled inside the loop. Inside the loop, DispatchMessage() is called to send the message to the appropriate window procedure for the window that the message was intended for.

Code 11–1

```
MSG Msg;
while( GetMessage( &Msg, NULL, 0, 0 ) )
{
        DispatchMessage( &Msg );
}
```

Windows takes care of all of the processing here: You simply need to call the two functions shown in Code 11–1. The message handler or window procedure receives the message (MSG structure) in its four parameters. Code 11–2 is an example of a window procedure.

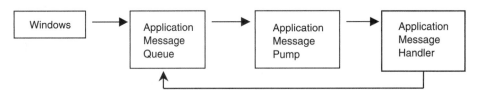

Figure 11–1   The message pump.

Code 11-2

```
LRESULT CALLBACK WndProc( HWND hWnd, UINT uMessage, WPARAM wParam, LPARAM
lParam )
{
    HDC DC;
    PAINTSTRUCT PaintStruct;
    switch( uMessage )
    {
        case WM_PAINT:      // Draw Hello world in client area
            DC = BeginPaint( hWnd, &PaintStruct );
            TextOut( DC, 0, 0, "Hello World", 11 );
            EndPaint( hWnd, &PaintStruct );
            break;
        case WM_CLOSE:
            // Place a WM_QUIT message into the application queue
            PostQuitMessage(0);
            break;
        default:
            return( DefWindowProc( hWnd, uMessage, wParam, lParam ) );
    }
    return( 0 );
}
```

If the message in Code 11-2 was WM_PAINT, then the text "Hello World" is displayed. This happens any time the window must be displayed, such as when it is first run or when another window that was covering it is removed. If the WM_PAINT message were not handled, then the appearance of the window would not be accurate.

The WM_CLOSE message is also handled in Code 11-2. This is a demonstration of a handler placing another message back into the application message queue. When the main window receives a WM_CLOSE, it calls PostQuitMessage(). PostQuitMessage() places a WM_QUIT message in the application message queue, which would later be taken out of the queue by our message pump, causing the loop to end and our program to terminate.

Though not immediately apparent, when we call DispatchMessage() in the message pump, it will call the WndProc() function. When the WndProc() function returns, DispatchMessage() will also return.

When Your Program Gets Busy

Now, consider that your program is busy doing some long, repetitive task. Maybe it has to sort 100,000 records. Normally, while it is doing that task, the message pump is not executing. If the message pump is not getting called, then messages are not being processed. As a result, the window will not have its appearance updated until the task is completed.

Since button clicks are also based on message processing, the same would happen if you were to place a Cancel button on a form. If the user clicked the Cancel button while the lengthy task was executing, the message would go into the queue, but it would not be handled until after the task was completed. Of course, this makes for poor user interface.

One final example might be a progress indicator of some type. Though your program is updating the progress indicator, that indicator isn't getting any WM_PAINT messages because the message pump isn't executing. So, you wouldn't see the progress indicator change until the task had finished running. This is not a very good use of a progress indicator.

Using Additional Message Pumps

In order to solve the problem of the application message pump not executing during our lengthy progress, we will simply write another one and call it from within our application. We will use the PeekMessage() function to determine if there are any messages waiting and then call the MFC CWinThread::PumpMessage() function. The CWinThread::PumpMessage() is an undocumented MFC function, so you won't find it in the online help. Since CWinApp is derived from CWinThread, we can call it using our CWinApp object or by using AfxGetApp.

The MFC source code for PumpMessage() with the comments and debugging information removed looks like Code 11–3. Notice that this code is already in MFC, you don't need to write it.

Code 11–3

```
BOOL CWinThread::PumpMessage()
{
    if (!::GetMessage(&m_msgCur, NULL, NULL, NULL))
        return FALSE;
    if (m_msgCur.message != WM_KICKIDLE && !PreTranslateMessage(&m_msgCur))
    {
        ::TranslateMessage(&m_msgCur);
        ::DispatchMessage(&m_msgCur);
    }
    return TRUE;
}
```

In Code 11–3 the GetMessage() and DispatchMessage() function are needed for our message pump. The PeekMessage() function is defined as the following:

```
BOOL PeekMessage( LPMSG lpMsg, HWND hWnd, UINT wMsgFilterMin, UINT wMsgFil-
terMax, UINT wRemoveMsg );
```

The parameters are shown in Table 11.1.

Table 11.1 PeekMessage() Parameters

Parameter	Usage
lpMsg	Pointer to an MSG structure to receive the message information.
hWnd	The window handle to receive message for (or its children).
wMsgFilterMin	The lowest Window Message ID to retrieve.
wMsgFilterMax	The highest Window Message ID to retrieve.
wRemoveMsg	Indicates how to retrieve the message from the queue:
	PM_NOREMOVE: Message is not removed from queue.
	PM_REMOVE: Message is removed from queue.
	PM_NOYIELD: Can be combined with the above to prevent system yielding for WaitForInputIdle processing.
	For Windows 2000 and Windows 98, you can also specify:
	PM_QS_INPUT: Process mouse and keyboard messages.
	PM_QS_PAINT: Process WM_PAINT messages.
	PM_QS_POSTMESSAGE: Process all posted messages, including timers and hotkeys.
	PM_QS_SENDMESSAGE: Process all sent messages.

To demonstrate our message pump, create a dialog-based application with four buttons, and one static control.

1. Go to the dialog editor for your new project.
2. Edit the main dialog, which should already have OK and Cancel buttons on it.
3. Delete the Cancel button.
4. Add three buttons with the IDs of IDC_GONOPUMP, IDC_GOPUMP, and IDC_CANCEL.
5. Change the captions of the three buttons to be "No Pump," "Pump," and "Cancel," respectively.
6. Add a static control and make its ID IDC_STATUS.
7. Add the following data member to your Dialog class:

    ```
    bool m_Cancel
    ```

8. Using ClassWizard, add a BN_CLICKED handler to the Cancel button to look like Code 11–4.

Code 11–4

```
void CMessagePumpDlg::OnCancel()
{
        m_Cancel = true;
}
```

9. Using ClassWizard, add a click handler for the No Pump button as shown in Code 11–5.

Code 11–5

```
void CMessagePumpDlg::OnGonopump()
{
        CString Status;
        m_Cancel = false;

        // Simulate a lengthy process
        // m_Cancel does not work here, because there is no
        // message pump!
        for( int i=0; i < 40000 && m_Cancel == false; i++ )
        {
                // Update Status
                Status.Format( "On %d of %d", i+1, 40000 );
                SetDlgItemText( IDC_STATUS, Status );
        }
}
```

Notice how this piece of code does not implement a message pump. This means that when we click the No Pump button, if we click the Cancel button, then the click message won't get processed and the loop will not stop. In other words, this code contains a bug.

10. Using ClassWizard, add a click handler for the "Pump" button as shown in Code 11–6.

Code 11–6

```
void CMessagePumpDlg::OnGopump()
{
        CString Status;
        m_Cancel = false;

        MSG Msg;

        for( int i=0; i < 40000 && m_Cancel == false; i++ )
        {
                Status.Format( "On %d of %d", i+1, 40000 );
                SetDlgItemText( IDC_STATUS, Status );
                // Implement message pump
                if( PeekMessage( &Msg, GetSafeHwnd(), 0, 0, PM_NOREMOVE ) )
```

```
                    AfxGetApp()->PumpMessage();
        }
}
```

Notice that Code 11–6 is identical to the No Pump button, except that it contains a message pump using PeekMessage() and PumpMessage(). Now, it is possible for the message pump to call DispatchMessage(), which in turn could call the OnCancel() if the Cancel button were clicked. If that were to happen, then the loop would terminate, as we want.

Message Pump Performance

Message pumps usually favor the task they are executing, rather than the user interface. It is possible to have the loop call GetMessage() directly and take out only one message at a time, thus giving further time benefits to the task. We can go still further and call the PeekMessage() after, say, every ten iterations of the loop.

What the message pump permits us to do is let our user interface continue to work while performing a long repetitious process. It does not work well when we need to execute a single function call that might take five minutes, because we need to be able to periodically call the message pump code. We would also need to handle situations such as what happens if the user hit the Run button again while the first run was already going (we could simply disable it).

OnIdle() Processing

MFC programs that contain a CWinApp provide a means of utilizing application idle time. Idle time is defined as when the application is waiting for user input. This approach differs from the message pump in that instead of your lengthy process giving the message loop some time to run, the message loop gives your task some time to run.

The OnIdle() function is a virtual function in the CWinThread class from which the CWinApp class is derived. It is called by the CWinThread::Run() function when the application enters its main application loop. The Run function will call the OnIdle() function in between messages from the queue, or as the OnIdle() function requires additional time for processing. The Run() function is called by the MFC framework when your application starts and remains running while the program runs.

Code 11–7 was copied directly from the MFC source code ThrdCore.cpp files, and therefore retains all of the copyright information of that file.

Code 11-7

```cpp
int CWinThread::Run()
{
    ASSERT_VALID(this);

    // for tracking the idle time state
    BOOL bIdle = TRUE;
    LONG lIdleCount = 0;

    // acquire and dispatch messages until a WM_QUIT message is received.
    for (;;)
    {
        // phase1: check to see if we can do idle work
        while (bIdle &&
            !::PeekMessage(&m_msgCur, NULL, NULL, NULL, PM_NOREMOVE))
        {
            // call OnIdle while in bIdle state
            if (!OnIdle(lIdleCount++))
                bIdle = FALSE; // assume "no idle" state
        }

        // phase2: pump messages while available
        do
        {
            // pump message, but quit on WM_QUIT
            if (!PumpMessage())
                return ExitInstance();

            // reset "no idle" state after pumping "normal" message
            if (IsIdleMessage(&m_msgCur))
            {
                bIdle = TRUE;
                lIdleCount = 0;
            }
        } while (::PeekMessage(&m_msgCur, NULL, NULL, NULL, PM_NOREMOVE));
    }

    ASSERT(FALSE);   // not reachable
}
```

The Run() function's main tasks are to call the CWinThread::PumpMessage() function to get and dispatch messages and to call OnIdle() as needed.

In order to take advantage of idle time processing in a Document/View program, you simply have to write the OnIdle() function for your CWinApp-derived class. We will discuss later how to do it in a dialog-based application.

To demonstrate idle time processing, create an SDI, Document/View MFC application with a CFormView View base class (our demo is called OnIdleDocView). Then place a static control on the main view dialog using the dialog editor and change its ID to IDC_STATUS.

Next, add the OnIdle() handler, which should be called COnIdleDocViewApp, to your CWinApp-derived application class using ClassWizard. Figure 11–2 illustrates how to add the OnIdle() handler: The handler will create a function that looks like Code 11–8; we want to change the function to look like Code 11–9.

Code 11–8

```
BOOL COnIdleDocViewApp::OnIdle(LONG lCount)
{
        return CWinApp::OnIdle(lCount);
}
```

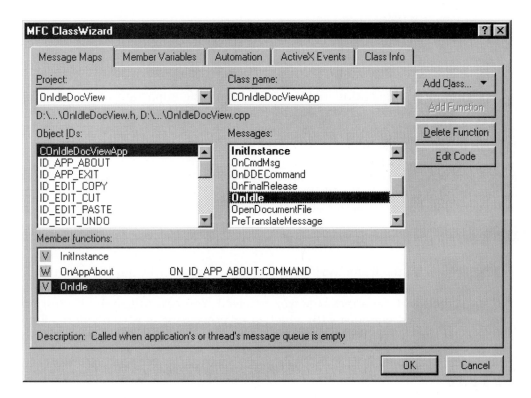

Figure 11–2   Enter the COnIdleDocViewApp in the ClassWizard.

Code 11-9

```
BOOL COnIdleDocViewApp::OnIdle(LONG lCount)
{
        static int Count;

        CString Tmp;
        Tmp.Format( "Processing #%d", Count++ );

        // Get pointer to out CMainFrame window
        CMainFrame* pFrame = (CMainFrame*)AfxGetMainWnd();

        // Using that CMainFrame, call GetActiveView to get active View
        class
        COnIdleDocViewView* pView = (COnIdleDocViewView*)pFrame->GetActive-
        View();

        // Set the status control for that Active view.
        pView->SetDlgItemText( IDC_STATUS, Tmp );

        CWinApp::OnIdle(lCount);
        return( 0 );
}
```

The code that we are executing inside the loop isn't the important part of this topic. What is important is the fact that during idle time (when the program is waiting for user input), our new OnIdle() function is called, and in there we can perform some brief task or portion of a task.

The code example calls the AfxGetMainWnd() function, which returns a pointer to our CMainFrame object, and with that we call the CMainFrm::GetActiveView() function to get a pointer to the active view. We then use the SetDlgItemText() function to update the text of our IDC_STATUS static control to reflect how many times our OnIdle() function was called.

OnIdle() is called by the framework with a single parameter (lCount) and returns an integer. The lCount parameter indicates the number of times OnIdle() has been called since the last time a message was received. You can utilize the lCount parameter to control the frequency with which your processing is actually done. For example, to perform your idle processing every ten calls, do something like Code 11–10.

Code 11-10

```
if( (lCount%10) == 0 )
        DoProcessing();
```

The return value from OnIdle() indicates if your program needs additional idle time or if it is done with its task. Return zero to indicate idle time isn't needed and returns non-zero to indicate a need for more time. An example is shown in Code 11–11.

Notice that the idle time processing does not occur when the program is executing a dialog or when menu commands are dropped down.

Code 11–11

```
BOOL COnIdleDocViewApp::OnIdle(LONG lCount)
{
        static int Count;

        if( Count < 100000 )
               Count++;

        // Do some small task here

        if( Count < 100000 )
               return( 1 ); // Still need more time
        else
               return( 0 ); // Don't need any more time
}
```

Idle Time Processing in a Dialog

The normal CWinApp::OnIdle() function will not work properly for dialogs or dialog-based applications—you must take a slightly different approach with them. When a dialog is invoked using the CDialog::DoModal() function, it will start executing the CDialog::RunModalLoop() function. The RunModalLoop() function such as the CWinThread::Run() function will intermittently perform idle processing.

Where the CWinThread::Run() and CDialog::RunModalLoop() functions differ is that the RunModalLoop() will send an MFC-specific windows message to the parent window called WM_KICKIDLE. This message indicates that the program is in idle time and to use that idle time you would add a handler for the WM_KICKIDLE message.

In order to add idle time processing to a dialog or dialog-based application, do the following:

1. Add a #include <afxpriv.h> to the top of your dialog class .cpp file as shown in Code 11–12.

Code 11-12

```
// PN: For the WM_KICKIDLE message
#include <afxpriv.h>
```

2. Add the OnKickIdle() (or similarly named function) to your Dialog class. You can't use ClassWizard since the WM_KICKIDLE is a normal Windows message. Add Code 11-13 to your .h file for your class.

Code 11-13

```
// PN: Add OnKickIdle handler function prototype
afx_msg LRESULT OnKickIdle(WPARAM, LPARAM);
```

3. Add the OnKickIdle() function body to the .cpp file for your dialog class as shown in Code 11-14.

Code 11-14

```
LRESULT COnIdleDlgDlg::OnKickIdle(WPARAM, LPARAM lCount)
{
        static int Count;

        CString Str;
        Str.Format( "Processing %d", Count++ );
        SetDlgItemText( IDC_STATUS, Str );

        return( 1 );
}
```

Notice that what we execute inside the function is not important for this demo and we will simply set a static control on the dialog to contain the number of times we were called. The lCount parameter is similar to that of the OnIdle() described above and indicates the number of times the function was called since the last message was received in the message queue.

The return value is also like that of OnIdle() described above. Returning non-zero indicates that you want additional idle time and returning zero means you don't want additional idle time.

WM_KICKIDLE is not a Windows message, but a custom MFC message that MFC will send to the parent window.

Idle Time Performance

Idle time processing usually favors the user interface from a performance standpoint. Instead of your repetitive task calling a message pump as desired, now the message pump calls your task function as desired. Another basic difference is the fact that in a message pump approach you can process your task in a simple loop, whereas with idle time processing you must write a function that would execute what would normally be done in one iteration of the for loop.

Timers

Windows supports a timer mechanism where you can instruct the operating system to periodically send a WM_TIMER message to a specific window or function. In the discussion of background processing, timers can be handy and easy to use for small background tasks, or reminders.

In order tell the operating system to send WM_TIMER messages to a window or function use the SetTimer() function. Our example will use the CWnd::SetTimer() function, which accomplishes the same thing with fewer parameters. The CWnd:: SetTimer() function is prototyped as:

```
UINT SetTimer( UINT nIDEvent, UINT nElapse, void (CALLBACK EXPORT* lpfn-
Timer)(HWND, UINT, UINT, DWORD) );
```

The parameters are shown in Table 11.2.

The lpfnTimer() function is declared as:

```
void CALLBACK EXPORT TimerProc( HWND hWnd, UINT nMsg, WPARAM wParam, LPARAM
lParam );
```

Table 11.2   SetTimer() Parameters

Parameter	Meaning
nIDEvent	The requested ID for the timer. A single window may have multiple timers (though it should be avoided as this may waste resources).
nElapse	The period on which to send WM_TIMER messages, in milliseconds (i.e., 1000 = 1 second, see Note below).
lpfnTimer	Pointer to a function to receive the timer message. If NULL, then the message is sent to the window.

TimerProc() can be any function name you want. This is not a normal member function for a CWnd class; it should be a nonmember function, or a static member function.

The return value for SetTimer() is the ID of the timer that was set. If the function returns zero, that means that the timer could not be set (timers are a limited resource).

NOTE

While the nElapse parameter indicates milliseconds, the timer can only reliably be counted on to be accurate to no more than 0.052 seconds. This means that if you were to set the timer to be called every millisecond (an nElapse value of 1), that the WM_TIMER message would only be sent roughly 18 times a second.

Our programming example is for a dialog that will automatically close itself after five seconds. We will assume that you have created a dialog in the dialog resource editor, that you placed a STATIC control on the dialog with the ID of IDC_REMAINING to display a countdown, and also that you have created a class for the new dialog named CTimeOutDlg using ClassWizard.

1. Use ClassWizard to add a WM_INITDIALOG message handler named OnInitDialog, which will look like Code 11–15. Modify it to call the SetTimer() function as shown in Code 11–16.

Code 11–15

```
BOOL CTimeOutDlg::OnInitDialog()
{
        CDialog::OnInitDialog();

        return TRUE;   // return TRUE unless you set the focus to
                       a control
                       // EXCEPTION: OCX Property Pages should
                       return FALSE
}
```

Code 11–16

```
BOOL CTimeOutDlg::OnInitDialog()
{
        CDialog::OnInitDialog();
```

```
m_SecondsLeft = 5;
SetTimer( 9000, 1000, 0 );
ShowSeconds();

return TRUE;   // return TRUE unless you set the focus to
               a control
               // EXCEPTION: OCX Property Pages should re-
               turn FALSE
}
```

2. Add the m_SecondsLeft data member to your Dialog class, in its .h file. Declare it as shown in Code 11–17.

Code 11–17

```
int m_SecondsLeft;
```

3. Add the ShowSeconds() function to your dialog class as a normal member function as show in Code 11–18.

Code 11-18

```
void CTimeOutDlg::ShowSeconds()
{
        // Display the remaining seconds in the IDC_REMAINING
        static control:
        CString Tmp;
        Tmp.Format( "Seconds remaining: %d", m_SecondsLeft );
        SetDlgItemText( IDC_REMAINING, Tmp );
}
```

4. Using ClassWizard, add a message map to the WM_TIMER message for your new dialog class as shown in Code 11–19. Modify it to look like Code 11–20.

Code 11–19

```
void CTimeOutDlg::OnTimer(UINT nIDEvent)
{

        CDialog::OnTimer(nIDEvent);
}
```

Code 11–20

```
void CTimeOutDlg::OnTimer(UINT nIDEvent)
{
    // Decrement seconds left and update the display
    --m_SecondsLeft;
    ShowSeconds();
```

```
                // If no more seconds left, then close the dialog
                if( !m_SecondsLeft )
                        EndDialog( IDOK );

                // Comment out the following line:
                // CDialog::OnTimer(nIDEvent);
                }
```

5. Add code that tests the new dialog as shown in Code 11–21. An example of such a dialog running would look like Figure 11–3.

Code 11–21

```
void CTimerDlg::OnDemo()
{
        // Declare an instance of our Time Out dialog
        CTimeOutDlg Demo;

        // Invoke it - Will return when user closes it, or when
        it times out:
        Demo.DoModal();
}
```

Timer Performance

Timer performance can be very erratic for the "background" task being executed. The timer message is considered a low-priority message, which means that only when there are no other messages in the message queue will the WM_TIMER be processed. If your application is busy and misses a WM_TIMER message, there is no "catch-up" or backlog of timer messages. Timer messages do not accumulate in the queue—there will be only one timer message in a queue at a time. For this reason, timers should only be used for trivial timing issues.

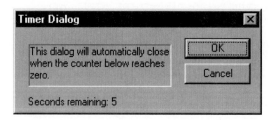

Figure 11–3   The timer dialog.

Threads

Multithreaded programs are a means of having your program do more than one task at a time. It is not done to increase performance, but to make the program more user-friendly or to handle certain types of programming requirements such as server programming.

Many people mistakenly think that if their program does two jobs at once, it will take half the time to do them simultaneously rather than sequentially. In fact, it will usually take longer to complete the same degree of processing in a multi-threaded manner. In order to understand this, we have to state the fact that by far the majority of computers have only one CPU to perform the work.

Even in multi-CPU computers, there are many other tasks running on the computer in addition to your program (my computer currently has 32 processes running and only 1 CPU). Imagine (see Figure 11–4) that you have two tasks you must perform, TaskA and TaskB. Each task takes 1 second when run sequentially.

Now imagine that your CPU runs at a fixed speed. The CPU executes each task in 1 second, if that was the only task it was doing. However, when you multithread your program, the operating system actually performs *time slicing*. This means that if both TaskA and TaskB were to run simultaneously, a second of CPU time would be divided into smaller fractions, and each task would be given one of those time fractions to execute.

For time slicing, the computer will execute a fraction of a second of one task and then suspend that task. It then resumes the other task, executes it for a fraction of a second, then suspends it. It keeps doing this, splitting its time between the two tasks. The outcome is that TaskA, which should only take 1 second to run, may

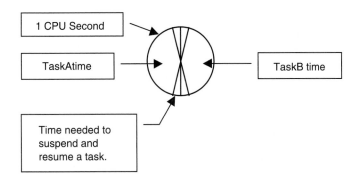

Figure 11–4 Time slicing enables computers to appear to do more than one thing at a time.

now take 2 seconds because it only gets fractions of a second in which to run (before being suspended by the operating system).

Time slicing happens so fast that it can be compared to a cartoon. A cartoon is really just a series of slightly different pictures, displayed at a rate of 30 pictures a second. Displayed in the right order at this speed, they take on the appearance of a single moving image.

Figure 11–5 represents a very simplistic view of a single CPU second of processing time divided in half. TaskA and TaskB both get to run in that time period but as far as each task is concerned, it has only run for half a second. In reality, a small amount of additional time is needed to suspend and resume each thread or task. This means that each of the tasks will receive slightly less than half a second of CPU time. You may have guessed from this logic that it will now take slightly more than two seconds to execute the two tasks. In other words, multi-threading your programs will actually degrade their performance, rather than enhance it.

Threads came to the Windows operating system with Win32 programming. Using threads, it is possible to run two or more tasks simultaneously, with little concern about how to coordinate the performance of one task against another.

Keep in mind that threads still utilize the time-slicing technique that was discussed above. Because of this, we will use threading to perform tasks that do not tie up the user interface or to implement server-style programs. They will not in themselves introduce a performance increase by executing two tasks simultaneously (instead, we can imagine that each task will now take twice as long to execute).

A thread should be considered as a thread of execution. We have already seen a single thread of execution where we have mentally followed the flow of a program from statement to statement, in and out of functions. A multithreaded program will call a function that will start a separate function that will also start executing simultaneously when we return from the called function.

When a thread starts another thread, the original thread is termed the main or parent thread, and the new thread is termed the child thread. The child thread will

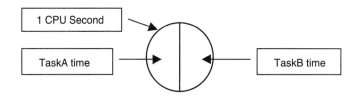

Figure 11–5   The CPU second of processing time.

typically inherit all the data from its parent thread and can place a value into a variable so that the parent thread will retrieve it.

Starting a Thread

SDK

A thread is started by calling a thread-starting function and passing to it at least the name of a function for the thread to execute. The new thread will start executing that function; when that function terminates, so will the thread. In all cases, you cannot use a normal C++ member function as the threading function, you must use either a nonmember function or a static member function. Code 11–22 SDK functions to start a thread.

Code 11–22

```
unsigned long _beginthread( void( __cdecl *start_address )( void * ), un-
signed stack_size, void *arglist );
```

_beginthread begins a thread with default security. Start_address is a pointer to the function to start the thread on, and arglist becomes the parameter to that function. stack_size indicates the stack size to be provided to the new thread. It returns the thread ID, or 0 upon failure as shown in Code 11–23.

Code 11–23

```
unsigned long _beginthreadex( void *security, unsigned stack_size,
        unsigned ( __stdcall *start_address )( void * ), void *arglist,
unsigned initflag, unsigned *thrdaddr );
```

Like _beginthread, except that security permits you to specify WinNT security values, and can start a thread in a suspended state. It returns the thread ID, or –1 upon failure as shown in Code 11–24.

Code 11–24

```
HANDLE CreateThread( LPSECURITY_ATTRIBUTES lpThreadAttributes, DWORD
dwStackSize,
        LPTHREAD_START_ROUTINE lpStartAddress, LPVOID lpParameter,
        DWORD dwCreationFlags, LPDWORD lpThreadId );
```

This function creates a thread with various attributes and security settings. If you are building an application that uses the threaded, statically linked, C runtime library (LIBCMT.LIB), you must not use the CreateThread function. It returns a handle to a thread, or 0 upon failure. The SDK example is shown in Code 11–25.

In Code 11–25, the three arrays will be sorted simultaneously, but each sort will take roughly three times longer. In other words, there is only so much raw CPU power available, and a thread divides that power.

Code 11–25

```
void SortArray( void* Array )
{
        SortStrings( (char**) Array );
        Done++;
}


char *Array1[]={ "Bill", "Betty", John", "Franke", Abe", NULL };
char *Array2[]={ "One", "Two", Three", "Four", Five", NULL };
char *Array3[]={ "Smith", "Jones", Wilson", "Lee", "Kim", NULL };

volatile int Done;
SortEm()
{
        Done=0;
        _beginthread( SortArray, Array1 );
        _beginthread( SortArray, Array2 );
        _beginthread( SortArray, Array3 );
        while( Done != 3 )   // Wait for threads to terminate
                ;
}
```

MFC

MFC makes a distinction between user-interface threads and worker threads. A user-interface thread has a user interface that can respond to user events (it looks like a normal window) and messages while a worker thread does not. The Sort demo in Code 11–25 would be an example of a worker thread, the most common type of thread.

The AfxBeginThread() function is the function used to start a child thread. MFC provides two versions of the AfxBeginThread() using standard C++ overloading. One is used to create a worker thread and the other to create a user-interface thread. The Sort example in Code 11–25 describes a worker thread and is very similar to using AfxBeginThread() to create one. The version of AfxBeginThread() that creates a user-interface thread looks like Code 11–26.

Code 11–26

```
CWinThread* AfxBeginThread( CRuntimeClass* pThreadClass,
        int nPriority = THREAD_PRIORITY_NORMAL, UINT nStackSize = 0, DWORD
        dwCreateFlags = 0, LPSECURITY_ATTRIBUTES lpSecurityAttrs = NULL );
```

In order to create a user-interface thread, you must perform the following basic steps:

1. Create a new class, derived from CWinThread.
2. Implement and use the DECLARE_DYNCREATE and IMPLEMENT_DYNCREATE macros in the new class.
3. Override the InitInstance() in the new class.
4. Call AfxBeginThread() with the RUNTIME_CLASS of your new class.

The InitInstance() of the new class is where the thread continues to execute. Once the function returns, the user interface thread will terminate.

For worker threads, the most common type of thread (as seen in the Sort demonstration in Code 11–25), the AfxBeginThread(), has a second overloaded version as shown in Code 11–27.

Code 11–27

```
CWinThread* AfxBeginThread( AFX_THREADPROC pfnThreadProc, LPVOID pParam,
        int nPriority = THREAD_PRIORITY_NORMAL, UINT nStackSize = 0,
        DWORD dwCreateFlags = 0, LPSECURITY_ATTRIBUTES lpSecurityAttrs =
        NULL );
```

As with the user interface example, most of the parameters are the same except the first. These parameters can typically be used at their default values.

In Code 11–27, the pfnThreadProc parameter is a pointer to a function that should be called by the child thread. The function should have the following prototype (see Code 11–28):

Code 11–28

```
UINT ThreadProc( LPVOID pParam );
```

The return value of the ThreadProc() function serves as a return value if the parent thread calls the SDK function ::GetThreadExitCode(). The pParam parameter to the function is whatever value you passed as the pParam parameter in the call to AfxBeginThread(). The pParam is our method of passing data to the child thread.

Stopping a Thread

When the function that was started with the thread terminates normally, the thread will also terminate. Whatever value the function returned (or was specified in an AfxEndThread() function call) will become the exit code of the thread.

The SDK provides a TerminateThread() function that can be used to terminate a thread immediately. This can be a dangerous function to call, as it will not give the child thread any ability to intercept or gracefully handle the termination. The thread is terminated, and any resources held by the thread (including synchronization object locks like critical sections or mutexes) will not be properly freed.

The best way to terminate a thread is to do so from the thread itself. The parent thread can terminate a child thread by communicating its request to the child thread, as through a global variable of some sort. The functions _endthread(), Exit-Thread(), and AfxExitThread() are functions that terminate a thread. However, they are called from the child thread and not the parent (they permit you to specify return codes from the thread to its parent). Calling ExitProcess() will immediately terminate the process and all its threads.

To retrieve the exit code for a thread, you can use the GetExitCodeThread() function from the parent thread. There will be no exit code if the thread was ended with TerminateThread(). You will need the thread handle of the child thread to call these functions. That data can be retrieved from the return value of AfxBeginThread() as shown in Code 11–29. Now, the pThread pointer can be used to return the exit code as shown in Code 11–30.

Code 11–29

```
CWinThread* pThread = AfxBeginThread( BarThreadProc, pBar ); // Start the
thread
```

Code 11–30

```
DWORD ExitCode;
::GetExitCodeThread( pThread->m_hThread, &ExitCode );
```

Synchronization

Programmers writing multithreaded programs for the first time face a new problem, referred to as thread synchronization. The basic intent in a multithreaded program is that the main thread continues its normal processing while the child thread performs some task. At some point, however, the two threads usually must communicate so that the child thread can give its results to the parent window.

One of our examples is a child thread that performs the task of searching your hard drive for a file. As it finds matching files, it places those files into a CString Array collection object. The main window will periodically (with the help of a timer message) go and check the CStringArray object for any newfound items to put into a list control to show the user. If the child thread was in the middle of adding an entry to the CStringArray while the parent thread was simultaneously trying to take items out, the program could crash.

This happens because the CStringArray, like almost all the MFC classes, is not Thread Safe. That means that two threads cannot work with the object at the same time—if, for example, one were to change the object while the other was reading from it. Imagine Code 11–31 in the OnTimer handler is running in the main thread.

Code 11–31

```
void CMFileFindDlg::OnTimer(UINT nIDEvent)
{

        int Index;
        while(m_Found.GetSize() )
        {
                Index = m_FoundList.InsertItem( 0, m_Found.GetAt(0) );
                m_FoundList.SetItemText( Index, 1, m_Found.GetAt(1) );
                m_FoundList.SetItemText( Index, 2, m_Found.GetAt(2) );
                m_FoundList.SetItemText( Index, 3, m_Found.GetAt(3) );
                m_Found.RemoveAt(0, 4 );
        }

        CDialog::OnTimer(nIDEvent);

}
```

Code 11–31 looks into the m_Found object, which is a CStringArray collection. If there is any data inside the object, it takes out four strings from the collection class and places them into a List Control (m_FoundList).

Now, imagine that the child thread, while running, finds a file (with the help of the CFileFind class) and wants to put its newfound data into the same m_FoundList object as shown in Code 11–32.

Code 11–32

```
UINT DoFind( LPVOID pParam )
{
        CStringArray* pFound = (CStringArray*)pParam;

        CFileFind Find;

        // Did we find any files?
        if( Find.FindFile( "*.*" ) )
        {
                // If so, add them to the CStringArray
                pFound->Add( Find.GetFileName() );
                pFound->Add( GetPath() );
                if( Find.IsDirectory() )
                        Str = "<DIR>";
                else
                        Str.Format( "%d", Find.GetLength() );
                pFound->Add( Str );
```

```
Find.GetLastWriteTime( Time );
pFound->Add( Time.Format( "%I:%M %p") );
    }
}
```

Code 11-32 is a function that might be our threading procedure. It receives a pointer to a CStringArray, where it will place its found data. You will note in the DoFind() function that if it finds a file, it places four strings in it—the same four strings that the timer will take out. We can imagine this thread procedure getting started by a call to AfxBeginThread(), which would be performed from the main thread as shown in Code 11-33.

Code 11-33

```
AfxBeginThread( DoFind, (LPVOID)&m_Found );
```

The problem here is this that the timer in the main thread expects four strings for each file. But what if the timer in the main thread executes at the same time the child thread is just starting to put the four values into the CstringArray? Maybe it has only had time to put in two of the four strings. The OnTimer() trying to retrieve four would cause the program to crash.

To insure against this type of problem, we have to synchronize the two threads. Synchronization is a technique where two threads that share the same resource (such as the CStringArray above) can coordinate their access to that resource. It basically is a way for one thread to let another thread know that it is using the re-source, so that the other thread waits until it is done.

There are actually a wide variety of synchronization techniques available, but we will only cover those that are termed as synchronization objects by Windows. These are objects specifically created for the purpose of thread synchronization. There are other techniques—such as the two threads creating a socket connection to each other to indicate their process—that we will not discuss. The following is a list of the basic synchronization objects.

Events: Provide a means of thread notification, signaling another thread when it is safe to access a resource.

Mutexes and Critical Sections: Provide mutually exclusive access to a resource, either in the same process of different process respectively.

Semaphores: Provide access to a resource based on a certain limit number (i.e., only five threads can access a resource).

Waitable Timers: Notify a thread that a certain time has arrived.

Most likely, your programming will involve the use of the critical section or mutex synchronization object. In staying with MFC classes, we will discuss all of the above except for the waitable timers, which do not have a direct MFC class for support.

The CSynchObject Class

The CSynchObject is the base class for the MFC classes that provide thread synchronization. This is an abstract class, which you would never instantiate on its own. Instead, it provides the framework for the other classes that follow. The CSynchObject only contains four functions: the constructor, Lock(), Unlock(), and a HANDLE() operator.

CSyncObject(LPCTSTR pstrName);
virtual ~CSyncObject( ); The constructor takes a string that refers to a named synchronization object, but can be NULL. This is specifically for classes that need a string, like a CMutex.

virtual BOOL Lock(DWORD dwTimeout = INFINITE); The Lock() function attempts to lock the synchronization object within the specified time. dwTimeout refers to the number of milliseconds to wait. If the object is locked by another thread, this function will wait until the time period before timing out and returning FALSE. If the object is not locked by another thread, it will return TRUE indicating that you now have it locked.

virtual BOOL Unlock( ) = 0;
virtual BOOL Unlock(LONG lCount, LPLONG lpPrevCount = NULL); The Unlock function will release a lock on an object. The first version is a pure-virtual function, which is provided in the derived classes. The second version takes parameters that indicate the number of accesses to release and a pointer to store the count of previous locks (used in Synchronization Access classes).

operator HANDLE( ) const; This function returns the handle to the actual synchronization object used by the class object.

CEvent() Synchronization

Event synchronization is designed to mimic signal-style processing, but it does not utilize a typical event or signal process. By this, we mean that an event or signal usually triggers a handler in some way, whereas these events will be periodically polled for the event. The MFC CEvent class is a wrapper class for this type of synchronization.

Where other synchronization objects will use the term "locked" to determine allowable access to a resource, the CEvent() will utilize the lock as the identification of a particular event. We will use the CEvent() object more for notification type action, rather than protecting a resource. This class requires a #include of afxmtmt.h.

CEvent(BOOL bInitiallyOwn = FALSE, BOOL bManualReset = FALSE, LPCTSTR lpszName = NULL, LPSECURITY_ATTRIBUTES lpsaAttribute = NULL); The constructor for CEvent(). The parameters are shown in Table 11.3.

Table 11.3   bManualReset() Parameters

Parameter	Meaning
bInitiallyOwn	Indicates whether the process initially has the "signaled" state.
bManualReset	Indicates whether the object is a manual reset. Automatic reset objects have their "signaled" state returned to not-signaled when another thread is released, and manual reset objects must have the Reset function called manually.
lpszName	This is the name for the Event object. Events have names so that other CEvents created can refer to the same event resource.
lpsaAttribute	A pointer to a structure that defines the security attributes for the event.

BOOL SetEvent( ); Sets the signal state to signaled. In automatic mode, the event is automatically set back to signal as soon as another thread is released from its wait state (its polling). Returns non-zero if function succeeded, zero otherwise.

BOOL PulseEvent( ); Sets the signal state to signaled releases all waiting threads, then sets it back to non-signaled again. For automatic mode events, only a single thread is released. Returns non-zero if function succeeded, zero otherwise.

BOOL ResetEvent( ); Sets the state of the event back to non-signaled. Returns non-zero if function succeeded, zero otherwise.

virtual BOOL Unlock( ); Releases the event object. Returns non-zero if the thread owned the event object and the event is an automatic event, zero otherwise,

Code 11–34 shows how to coordinate two threads using a CEvent object.

Code 11–34

```
UINT EventDemo( LPVOID vpParam)
{
      // Create CEvent object in child thread, with same name
      CEvent Event(FALSE,FALSE, "CEventDemo");

      // Set the event to 'signaled' (matches WaitForSingleObject in main
      thread)
      Event.SetEvent();

      // Do nothing for 4 seconds
      Sleep(4000);

      // Notify main thread that we are done.
```

```
        Event.SetEvent();

        return( 0 );
}

void CSynchDemoDlg::OnGoevent()
{
        // Create CEvent object in main thread
        CEvent Event(FALSE,FALSE, "CEventDemo");

        // Start the child thread
        AfxBeginThread( EventDemo, 0 );

        // Wait for the Event signal
        while( WaitForSingleObject( Event, 0 ) == WAIT_TIMEOUT )
                ;

        // Reset the signal state
        Event.ResetEvent();

        int Counter=0;
        CString TmpStr;

        // While the event signal is not received a second time,
        // display some text on screen.
        while( WaitForSingleObject( Event, 0 ) == WAIT_TIMEOUT  )
        {
                Counter++;
                TmpStr.Format( "Waiting (%d)...", Counter );
                SetDlgItemText( IDC_EVENTSTATUS, TmpStr );
        }
        SetDlgItemText( IDC_EVENTSTATUS, "We got our event notification" );
}
```

Code 11–34 demonstrates how to coordinate two threads activities using the CEvent(). In the main thread, the WaitForSingleObject() is used to wait for the signal event of the child thread, which is set by the child thread calling Event.SetEvent().

CMutex and CCriticalSection Synchronization

Both CMutex and CCriticalSection classes are MFC classes that are designed to assist in mutually exclusive access to resources between two threads. The primary difference between the two is that CMutex can be used between two processes, whereas CCriticalSection can only be used in the same process. For this reason, if you were to implement thread synchronization in a DLL, which might be used from two processes, you would select the CMutex.

Table 11.4 CMutex() Parameters

Parameter	Meaning
bInitiallyOwn	If TRUE, then the Mutex is locked by the creator, otherwise it is not.
lpszName	The name of the Mutex.If the name does not already exist in the system-managed list of Mutexes, then a new Mutex is created; otherwise, the same Mutex is used by all other instances.Each process or thread wanting to work with the Mutex must use the same name when declaring its Mutex.This is a system-wide name.
lpsaAttribute	A pointer to a structure that defines the security attributes of the Mutex.

The mutually exclusive access provided by these classes actually refers to the class objects themselves but is used to control access to another resource. Our example for both these items will be where the child thread places text into a string and the main thread retrieves the text. But, we don't want to have the two threads working with the string at the same time. So, the two threads will implement synchronized access to the string by using the Mutex/Critical Section.

When you want a single resource, such as the string in our demo, to be shared by two or more threads but you don't want there to be a collision of the two working with it at the same time, you should use the Mutex or Critical Section.

CMutex The CMutex class defines only a constructor function. The rest of the functions are inherited from the CSynchObject base class, like Lock and Unlock.

CMutex(BOOL bInitiallyOwn = FALSE, LPCTSTR lpszName = NULL, LP-SECURITY_ATTRIBUTES lpsaAttribute = NULL); This constructor is used to create a CMutex object (Table 11.4).

Code 11–35 demonstration shows how to use the CMutex to have two threads coordinate access to a single string variable, which is actually a local variable in the main thread.

Code 11–35

```
UINT MutexDemo( LPVOID vpParam)
{
   // Get the passes parameter into a char* for working
   char* pStr = (char*)vpParam;

   // Create a Mutex object, named CMutexDemo, for the main thread
```

```
    CMutex Mutex( FALSE, "CMutexDemo" );

    // Lock the Mutex, so no one else can use it
    Mutex.Lock();
    strcpy( pStr, "Mutex" );

    // Lets add a delay, for demonstration purposes.In reality, a
    // thread should attempt to unlock as quickly as possible.
    Sleep(4000);

    // When we are done working with the data, we unlock the Mutex
    Mutex.Unlock();
    return( 0 );
}

void CSynchDemoDlg::OnGomutex()
{
    // Create a Mutex object, named CMutexDemo, for the main thread
    CMutex Mutex( FALSE, "CMutexDemo" );
    char String[128];

    // Start the child thread
    AfxBeginThread( MutexDemo, String );

    // Give child thread time to start up
    Sleep(1000);
    CString TmpStr;

    SetDlgItemText( IDC_MUTEXSTATUS, "Waiting to access data..." );

    // Lock the Mutex, so we can have access to the String variable.
    // This line of code will wait until the Child thread unlocks its Mutex
    // object, at which point the Lock will return.You could optionally
    // specify a time-out period in milliseconds as a parameter to Lock.
    Mutex.Lock();

    TmpStr.Format( "We could access our data: %s", String );
    SetDlgItemText( IDC_MUTEXSTATUS, TmpStr );

    // Unlock the Mutex for the String variable.
    Mutex.Unlock();

}
```

The CCriticalSection object works in the same fashion as the CMutex, except that since it only works within the same process, it does not require a name in its constructor as shown in Code 11–36.

Code 11-36

```cpp
// A helper class:
class CriticalParam
{
public:
    CCriticalSection m_Critical;
    char m_String[128];
};


// Our Threading procedure:
UINT CriticalDemo( LPVOID vpParam)
{
    // Get the passed parameter (critical section and string data)
    CriticalParam* pCritical = (CriticalParam*)vpParam;

    // Lock the Critical Section, so no one else can use it
    pCritical->m_Critical.Lock();

    // Now it's safe to work with the data
    strcpy( pCritical->m_String, "CriticalSection" );

    // Lets add a delay, for demonstration purposes. In reality, a
    // thread should attempt to unlock as quickly as possible.
    Sleep(4000);

    // When we are done working with the data, we unlock the Critical Sec-
    tion
    pCritical->m_Critical.Unlock();
    return( 0 );
}


void CSynchDemoDlg::OnGocritical()
{
    // Create a CriticalParam object, with CriticalSection and String in it
    CriticalParam Critical;

    // Start the child thread
    AfxBeginThread( CriticalDemo, &Critical );

    // Give child thread time to start up
    Sleep(1000);
    CString TmpStr;
    SetDlgItemText( IDC_CRITICALSTATUS, "Waiting to access data..." );

    // Lock the Critical Section, so we can have access to the String vari
    // able. This line of code will wait until the Child thread unlocks the
    // shared Critical Section object, at which point the Lock will return.
    Critical.m_Critical.Lock();
```

```
    // It is now safe to access the data (resource).
    TmpStr.Format( "We could access our data: %s", Critical.m_String );
    SetDlgItemText( IDC_CRITICALSTATUS, TmpStr );

    // Unlock the Critical Section for the String variable.
    Critical.m_Critical.Unlock();
}
```

CSemaphore Synchronization

The CSemaphore class is designed not for mutually exclusive access to a resource but for a limited number of thread accesses to a resource. When creating the CSemaphore object, you specify how many threads may use the resource. When other threads or processes attempt to lock the semaphore, only the limited number will return immediately; any additional locks will have to wait until one of the original threads releases its lock.

If you wanted to write an interface to resources, such as a DLL that controlled access to software licensed for a certain number of users, then the DLL could be written to create a semaphore with the licensed number of users. You could then limit the number of users on a network that could simultaneously run the software.

The CSemaphore only defines a constructor. The Lock() and Unlock() methods are inherited from the CSynchObject class.

CSemaphore(LONG lInitialCount = 1, LONG lMaxCount = 1, LPCTSTR pstr-Name = NULL, LPSECURITY_ATTRIBUTES lpsaAttributes = NULL); The constructors of the class are shown in Table 11.5.

Code 11–37 shows how you might use a CSemaphore object. It creates a CSemaphore that has two allowable accesses. Notice the constructor in OnGosemaphore().

Table 11.5   Constructuctor Data Members

Parameter	Meaning
lInitialCount	The initial count of threads that may simultaneously access a resource.
lMaxCount	The maximum count of threads that may simultaneously access a resource.
pstrName	The name to be used for the semaphore. If the name does not already exist in the system-managed list of semaphores, then a new semaphore is created, otherwise the same semaphore is used by all other instances. Each process or thread wanting to work with the semaphore must use the same name when declaring their semaphore. This is a system-wide name.

It then creates two child threads that also create a semaphore with the same name, in which case they will reuse the same semaphore previously created. The two child threads lock the semaphore, replacing the maximum access count of two, and then they do nothing for four seconds.

Meanwhile, the parent thread also attempts to lock the semaphore. However, since this would be the third access to the semaphore and it was defined for only two, the main thread must wait for one of the child threads to unlock the semaphore. It doesn't matter which child thread unlocks, as shown in Code 11–37.

Code 11–37

```
UINT SemaphoreDemo( LPVOID vpParam)
{
    // Create semaphore object. Since the main thread created the
    // real semaphore, we will just get a handle to the existing one.
    // Because of this, the first two parameters to the constructor
    // are ignored.
    CSemaphore Semaphore( 1, 1, "CSemaphoreDemo" );

    // Lock the Semaphore. This decrements the allowable accesses by 1
    Semaphore.Lock();

    // Some bogus 4 second process
    Sleep( 4000 );

    // Unlock the semaphore. This increments the allowable accesses by 1
    Semaphore.Unlock();

    return( 0 );
}

void CSynchDemoDlg::OnGosemaphore()
{
    // Create a CSemaphore, with 2 allowable accessors
    CSemaphore Semaphore( 2, 2, "CSemaphoreDemo" );

    SetDlgItemText( IDC_SEMAPHORESTATUS, "Starting threads..." );
    CTime Start = CTime::GetCurrentTime();

    // Create 2 threads.This is the limit of allowable threads
    // finish.
    AfxBeginThread( SemaphoreDemo, 0 );
    AfxBeginThread( SemaphoreDemo, 0 );

    // Give those threads a moment to start up
    Sleep( 500 );
```

```
    // Then we try to access the semaphore. Since we would be
    // resource #3, we have to wait until one of the other two
    // threads releases the semaphore (about 4 seconds)
    Semaphore.Lock();

    CTime Stop = CTime::GetCurrentTime();

    CString TmpString;

    TmpString.Format( "Started: %s  Stopped: %s",
        (LPCSTR)Start.Format( "%H:%M:%S"),
        (LPCSTR)Stop.Format( "%H:%M:%S") );

    SetDlgItemText( IDC_SEMAPHORESTATUS, TmpString );
}
```

Message Notification

Message notification is not specific to threaded programming but can be a simple means for a child thread to tell the parent thread that something has occurred. The logic here is that the child thread posts a unique message in the application message queue indicating the event. An application can create its own custom window messages by using either the WM_USER or WM_APP message and adding an extra integer value to it. Our example will use WM_USER+1, which must be a unique message identifier within our program.

An example of a child thread that notifies its parent via the message notification technique might be as shown in Code 11–38.

Code 11–38

```
UINT NotificationDemo( LPVOID vpParam)
{
    // A threading function that demonstrate how to send windows messages
    // to the main thread to indicate an event.
    for( int i=0; i < 4; i++ )
    {
      Sleep( i*1000 );
      AfxGetMainWnd()->PostMessage( WM_USER+1, i+1 );
    }
    AfxGetMainWnd()->PostMessage( WM_USER+1, -1 );
    return( 0 );
}

void CSynchDemoDlg::OnGonotification()
{
    // Start the Notification demo thread
    AfxBeginThread( NotificationDemo, 0 );
```

```
}

void CSynchDemoDlg::OnNotification( WPARAM wParam, LPARAM lParam )
{
    // The handler function for the notification messages sent
    // by NotificationDemo.
    CString TmpString;
    if( wParam == -1 )
        TmpString = "Child thread finished";
    else
        TmpString.Format( "Child thread sent me %d", wParam );
    SetDlgItemText( IDC_NOTIFICATIONSTATUS, TmpString );
}
```

The OnNotification() function must be added manually to your main window, without the help of ClassWizard. You would make the following changes:

1. Add a handler to the message map section of your main window .h file as shown in Code 11–39.

   ### Code 11–39

   ```
   //{{AFX_MSG(CSynchDemoDlg)
   //}}AFX_MSG
   afx_msg void OnNotification( WPARAM wParam,  LPARAM lParam);
   DECLARE_MESSAGE_MAP()
   ```

2. Add the handler to the message map of your .cpp file for your main window class as shown in Code 11–40.

   ### Code 11–40

   ```
   BEGIN_MESSAGE_MAP(CSynchDemoDlg, CDialog)
     //{{AFX_MSG_MAP(CSynchDemoDlg)
     //}}AFX_MSG_MAP
     ON_MESSAGE( WM_USER+1, OnNotification)
   END_MESSAGE_MAP()
   ```

Notice that in both examples above, the code was added outside the //{{and //}} comments.

CSingleLock and CMultiLock

The CSingleLock() and CMultiLock() are helper classes—also known as accessor classes—to help you work with the CSyncObject classes above. The CSingleLock() permits synchronization on a single object, while the CMultiLock() provides synchronization for multiple objects.

To use these classes, declare your synchronization object and then construct a lock object that passes the synchronization object to its constructor. This is shown in example Code 11–41. Code 11–42 shows how to lock or unlock the object.

Code 11–41

```
CCriticalSection CS;
CSingleLock SL(&CS);
```

Code 11–42

```
SL.Lock();
// Do something
SL.Unlock();
```

A Multithreaded Example

The following program is a multithreaded demonstration. The program is a file-find utility, where the main thread starts a child thread to perform the file search. As the child thread finds files, it notifies the parent by sending a WM_USER+1 message to the parent thread message queue. It will also populate a CStringArray object with four pieces of data found on the file: Filename, path, size, and modify time. When the main thread gets the message from the queue, it looks into the CStringArray to get the found data and places it into a CListCtrl.

The program demonstrates critical section locking between the two threads to coordinate access to the CStringArray.

As a general rule, it is unsafe to pass MFC objects between threads. This is because an MFC thread maintains information about the objects created in each thread, and when an object from one thread appears in another, it may cause problems. The child thread will control some of the user interface in this demonstration. Because of the MFC general rule, we will not pass off CWnd objects for the controls to the thread but will use HWND objects instead.

The program is a dialog-based application.

Creating the Dialog

The main dialog for the program should have seven controls, as shown on Figure 11–6.

- A static control with the text &Named for its caption.
- An edit control, with the ID of IDC_NAMED.
- A static control with the text &Look in: for its caption.
- An edit control with the ID of IDC_LOOKIN.

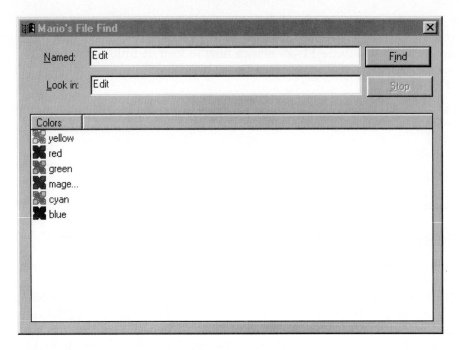

Figure 11–6   There are seven controls on the main dialog.

- A button, with the ID IDC_FIND and a caption of &Find.
- A button, with the ID IDC_STOP and a caption of &Stop (disabled by default).
- A list control, with the Report style set, and an ID of IDC_FOUNDLIST.
- Using ClassWizard, add member variables for the two edit controls and the list control, named m_Named, m_LookIn, and m_FoundList, respectively.
- Also using ClassWizard, add handlers for the Find and Stop button.

The CLookFor Class

This class is going to assist you in keeping track of what you are looking for, where you are searching, and the current status of the search (i.e., Running, Stopped, or Cancelled). Your Dialog class will need a member variable instance of this class, and the search function will need one as a local variable. The class has data members shown in Table 11.6.

Table 11.6 Data Members for the CLookFor Class

Variable	Purpose
CString m_In;	Pathname, or where to look.
static CString m_Named;	What to search for.
static HWND m_hFindButton;	Handle to the Find button, so it may be enabled and disabled.
static CStringArray m_Found;	Static string array for the names.
static HWND m_hStopButton;	Handle to the Stop or Cancel button, so it may be enabled and disabled.
static volatile bool m_bCancel;	Flag, indicating if cancel was requested.
static volatile bool m_bRunning;	Flag, indicating if child thread is still running.
static CCriticalSection m_CriticalSection;	This is the critical section used to synchronize the child thread with the parent.

Functions

void AddFound(CFileFind& Found); This function adds the file in the Found parameter to the m_Found array. Before doing so, it should lock the m_CriticalSection, then do add and then unlock it before returning.

It will lock the m_CriticalSection object, then add the information to the m_Found array, release the lock, and notify the parent thread using a window message notification as shown in Code 11–43.

Code 11–43

```
// Add information for a found item to collection class
void CLookFor::AddFound(CFileFind &Found)
{
        // Lock critical section, for exclusive access to the m_Found list
        m_CriticalSection.Lock();

        CString Str;
        CTime Time;

        m_Found.Add( Found.GetFileName() );
        m_Found.Add( GetPath() );
        if( Found.IsDirectory() )
                Str = "<DIR>";
        else
                Str.Format( "%d", Found.GetLength() );
        m_Found.Add( Str );
        Found.GetLastWriteTime( Time );
        m_Found.Add( Time.Format( "%I:%M %p") );
```

```
        // Unlock it when we are done
        m_CriticalSection.Unlock();

        // Tell the parent thread that data is available
        AfxGetMainWnd()->PostMessage( WM_MYFOUND );
}
```

void SetData(const CString& Named, const CString& Path, HWND hFind-Button, HWND hStartButton); Initializes all data members, except the m_bCancel and m_bRunning variables. This function must be called before any other function is called (with a few minor technical exceptions) as shown in Code 11–44.

Code 11–44

```
void CLookFor::SetData( const CString& Named, const CString& Path, HWND
hFindButton, HWND hStopButton )
{
        m_Named = Named;
        m_In = Path;
        m_hFindButton = hFindButton;
        m_hStopButton = hStopButton;
}
```

void SetPath(const CString& *Path*); Sets the pathname (m_In) variable from *Path*. This is for setting the nonstatic path string, because the search is a recursive one as shown in Code 11–45.

Code 11–45

```
void CLookFor::SetPath( const CString& Path )
{
        m_In = Path;
}
```

static void Start(); Disables the Find button and enables the Stop/Cancel button, then sets the Running flag to true and the cancelled flag to false as shown in Code 11–46.

Code 11–46

```
void CLookFor::Start()
{
        m_bRunning = true;
        m_bCancel = false;
        if( m_hFindButton )
                ::EnableWindow( m_hFindButton, FALSE );
        if( m_hStopButton )
                ::EnableWindow( m_hStopButton, TRUE );
}
```

static void Stop(); Enables the Find button and disables the Stop/Cancel button, then sets the Running and Cancel flags to false as shown in Code 11–47.

Code 11–47

```
void CLookFor::Stop()
{
        m_bRunning = false;
        m_bCancel = false;
        if( m_hFindButton )
                ::EnableWindow( m_hFindButton, TRUE );
        if( m_hStopButton )
                ::EnableWindow( m_hStopButton, FALSE );
}
```

static void Cancel(); Sets the Cancel flag to true. This is used by the file-searching routine in the child thread to determine when to stop searching as shown in Code 11–48.

Code 11–48

```
void CLookFor::Cancel()
{
        m_bCancel = true;

        while(  m_bRunning == true )
                ;
        if( m_hFindButton )
                ::EnableWindow( m_hFindButton, TRUE );
        if( m_hStopButton )
                ::EnableWindow( m_hStopButton, FALSE );
}
```

static bool IsCanceled() Returns status of the canceled flag as shown in Code 11–49.

Code 11–49

```
static bool IsCanceled() { return( m_bCancel ); }  // In the LookFor.h file
```

static bool IsRunning(); Returns the status of the running flag as shown in Code 11–50.

Code 11–50

```
static bool IsRunning() { return( m_bRunning ); }  // In the LookFor.h file
```

const CString& GetPath(); Returns the current path to search (m_In).

const CString& GetNamed(); Returns the current name to search for (m_Named) as shown in Code 11–51.

Code 11-51

```
const CString& GetNamed() { return( m_Named ); } // In the LookFor.h file
```

CLookFor(); Does nothing.

virtual ~CLookFor(); Does nothing.

void Lock(); Locks the m_CriticalSection static member variable as shown in Code 11–52.

Code 11-52

```
void Lock() { m_CriticalSection.Lock(); }// In the LookFor.h file
```

void Unlock(); Unlocks the m_CriticalSection static member variable as shown in Code 11–53.

Code 11-53

```
void Unlock() { m_CriticalSection.Unlock(); } // In the LookFor.h file
```

The Threaded DoFind() Function

In order to accomplish file searching, we will use the CFileFind class. This class enables you to get a list of names from a folder and also identify if a found name was a subfolder or not. The file searching function will need to be recursive, meaning that when a subfolder is found in a folder, the function calls itself to search that subfolder.

The file-searching routine is the function that should be passed to the AfxBeginThread() function to start the child thread. As its parameter, it should receive a CLookFor* that was typecast to an LPVOID. The file-searching function needs to be a standalone function and not a member of a class.

The search function has two main loops: First, it searches for files matching your request in a given folder. Then, it searches for subfolders in the same folder. For each subfolder found, the function will create a new local CLookFor object, initialize it, and call itself with that local CLookFor (this is the recursive part).

Note how the CLookFor::AddFound() function is used to add data to the m_Found CStringArray object. Remember from the previous class that the AddFound() function will lock and unlock the critical section as needed. It also calls the CLookFor::IsCancelled() function to determine if the search was cancelled, and the child thread should terminate as shown in Code 11–54.

Code 11-54

```
// This is the function that will execute in the child thread, to do
// the actual file finding.
```

```
UINT DoFind( LPVOID pParam )
{
    static int Depth;
    CTime Time;
    CString GenStr;
    BOOL MoreFiles;

    Depth++;
    CLookFor* pLookFor = (CLookFor*)pParam;
    CFileFind Find;

    // Step 1: Find matching files in Folder
    CString Path;
    Path = pLookFor->GetPath();
    if( Path.IsEmpty() )
    {
        char * pPath = Path.GetBuffer( _MAX_PATH );
        GetCurrentDirectory( _MAX_PATH, pPath );
        Path.ReleaseBuffer();
    }

    if( Path[ Path.GetLength()-1 ] != ':' && Path[ Path.GetLength()-1 ] !=
'\\' )
        Path += "\\";
    Path += pLookFor->GetNamed();

    if( Find.FindFile( Path ) )
    {
        do
        {
            MoreFiles = Find.FindNextFile();
            GenStr = Find.GetFileName();
            if( GenStr.CompareNoCase(".")==0 || GenStr.CompareNoCase("..")
              ==0 )
                    continue;

            pLookFor->AddFound( Find );

        } while( MoreFiles && !pLookFor->IsCanceled() );
    }
    // Step 2: Look for Sub-directories
    Path = pLookFor->GetPath();
    if( Path.IsEmpty() )
    {
        char * pPath = Path.GetBuffer( _MAX_PATH );
        GetCurrentDirectory( _MAX_PATH, pPath );
        Path.ReleaseBuffer();
    }
    if( Path[ Path.GetLength()-1 ] != ':' && Path[ Path.GetLength()-1 ] !=
```

```
'\\' )
    Path += "\\";
Path += "*.*";

if( Find.FindFile( Path ) )
{
    do
    {
        MoreFiles = Find.FindNextFile();
        GenStr = Find.GetFileName();
        if( GenStr.CompareNoCase(".")==0 || GenStr.CompareNoCase("..")
          ==0 )
            continue;
        if( Find.IsDirectory() )
        {
            CLookFor Next;
            CString Tmp;
            Tmp.Format( "%s\\%s", (LPCSTR)pLookFor->GetPath(),
            (LPCSTR)GenStr );
            Next.SetPath(Tmp);
            DoFind( &Next );
        }
    } while( MoreFiles && !pLookFor->IsCanceled() );
}
Depth--;
if( Depth == 0 ) // Last call
    pLookFor->Stop();
return( 1 );
}
```

The Dialog Class

The Dialog class for this demonstration needs to coordinate the running of the thread with the access to the found file information. Your Dialog class will be your main window and will handle the user interface. You will need to add the data members as shown in Table 11.7.

Table 11.7   Data Members for the Dialog Class

Variable	Description
CListCtrl m_FoundList;	The List Control, mapped to the list control.
CString m_LookIn;	The path to look in, mapped to the edit box.
CString m_Named;	The file to look for, mapped to the edit box.
CLookFor m_Start;	The starting CLookFor, where to begin the search.

Functions

virtual BOOL OnInitDialog(); Added by ClassWizard, this is where we will initialize the column names and widths for the list control, as well as the default path for the "Look In" edit box as shown in Code 11–55.

Code 11–55

```
BOOL CMFileFindDlg::OnInitDialog()
{
    CDialog::OnInitDialog();

    // Add "About..." menu item to system menu.

    // IDM_ABOUTBOX must be in the system command range.
    ASSERT((IDM_ABOUTBOX & 0xFFF0) == IDM_ABOUTBOX);
    ASSERT(IDM_ABOUTBOX < 0xF000);

    CMenu* pSysMenu = GetSystemMenu(FALSE);
    if (pSysMenu != NULL)
    {
        CString strAboutMenu;
        strAboutMenu.LoadString(IDS_ABOUTBOX);
        if (!strAboutMenu.IsEmpty())
        {
            pSysMenu->AppendMenu(MF_SEPARATOR);
            pSysMenu->AppendMenu(MF_STRING, IDM_ABOUTBOX, strAboutMenu);
        }
    }

    // Set the icon for this dialog. The framework does this automatically
    //  when the application's main window is not a dialog
    SetIcon(m_hIcon, TRUE);                    // Set big icon
    SetIcon(m_hIcon, FALSE);            // Set small icon

    // TODO: Add extra initialization here
    m_FoundList.InsertColumn(0, "Name" );
    m_FoundList.InsertColumn(1, "In Folder" );
    m_FoundList.InsertColumn(2, "Size" );
    m_FoundList.InsertColumn(3, "Modified" );
    CRect Rect;
    m_FoundList.GetClientRect( &Rect );
    m_FoundList.SetColumnWidth( 0, Rect.right / 3 );
    m_FoundList.SetColumnWidth( 1, Rect.right / 3 );
    m_FoundList.SetColumnWidth( 2, Rect.right / 8 );
    m_FoundList.SetColumnWidth( 3, Rect.right / 6 );

    char * pPath = m_LookIn.GetBuffer( _MAX_PATH );
    GetCurrentDirectory( _MAX_PATH, pPath );
```

```
m_LookIn.ReleaseBuffer();
UpdateData( FALSE );

    return TRUE;   // return TRUE  unless you set the focus to a control
}
```

afx_msg void OnFind(); Added via ClassWizard, this is the handler for the user clicking the Find button. This function clears out the data in the list control (m_FoundList) and initializes the m_Start variable with data from the m_LookIn and m_Named variables, as well as the HWND handles for the controls (i.e., the Find button, using GetDlgItem()) as shown in Code 11–56.

Code 11–56

```
void CMFileFindDlg::OnFind()
{
    // Clear out the list control
    m_FoundList.DeleteAllItems();
    UpdateData();

    // Initialize the m_Start CLookfor object
    m_Start.SetData( m_Named, m_LookIn, GetDlgItem( IDC_FIND )->m_hWnd,
        GetDlgItem( IDC_STOP )->m_hWnd );

    // Set the Start status flag
    m_Start.Start();

    // Start the searching thread
    AfxBeginThread( DoFind, (LPVOID)&m_Start );
}
```

afx_msg void OnStop(); Added via ClassWizard, this handler will simply call the Stop function of the m_Start member variables, which will cause the thread to terminate as shown in Code 11–57.

Code 11–57

```
void CMFileFindDlg::OnStop()
{
    m_Start.Cancel();
}
```

afx_msg void OnClose(); Added via ClassWizard to handle the WM_CLOSE message. This function is invoked when the user closes the program. It checks if the m_Start.IsRunning() function is true, meaning a search is taking place. If so, it calls m_Start.Cancel() and then waits for the child thread to terminate (by checking m_Start.IsRunning(), in a loop) as shown in Code 11–58.

Code 11-58

```
void CMFileFindDlg::OnClose()
{
        // Tell thread to terminate, then wait for it to terminate
        m_Start.Cancel();
        while( m_Start.IsRunning() )
                ;
        CDialog::OnClose();
}
```

afx_msg void OnFound(WPARAM wp, LPARAM lp); The window message notification handler for the WM_USER+1 message. It must lock the m_Start object, retrieve new data from the m_Found CStringArray, and then unlock the object as shown in Code 11-59.

Code 11-59

```
void CMFileFindDlg::OnFound(WPARAM wp, LPARAM lp)
{
    // Use Critical section to safeguard the m_FoundList collection
    m_Start.Lock();

    int Index;
    while( m_Start.m_Found.GetSize() )
    {
        Index = m_FoundList.InsertItem( m_FoundList.GetItemCount(),
            m_Start.m_Found.GetAt(0) );
        m_FoundList.SetItemText( Index, 1, m_Start.m_Found.GetAt(1) );
        m_FoundList.SetItemText( Index, 2, m_Start.m_Found.GetAt(2) );
        m_FoundList.SetItemText( Index, 3, m_Start.m_Found.GetAt(3) );
        m_Start.m_Found.RemoveAt(0, 4 );
    }
    m_Start.Unlock();
}
```

The OnFound() function must be added manually to the .h and .cpp files for your dialog as shown in Code 11-60 and 11-61. Code 11-60 shows changes for the .h file.

Code 11-60

```
// Generated message map functions
//{{AFX_MSG(CMFileFindDlg)
virtual BOOL OnInitDialog();
afx_msg void OnSysCommand(UINT nID, LPARAM lParam);
afx_msg void OnPaint();
afx_msg HCURSOR OnQueryDragIcon();
afx_msg void OnFind();
afx_msg void OnStop();
```

```
afx_msg void OnClose();
virtual void OnOK();
//}}AFX_MSG
afx_msg void OnFound(WPARAM wp, LPARAM lp);
DECLARE_MESSAGE_MAP()
```

Code 11–61 shows changes in the .cpp file.

Code 11–61

```
BEGIN_MESSAGE_MAP(CMFileFindDlg, CDialog)
    //{{AFX_MSG_MAP(CMFileFindDlg)
    ON_WM_SYSCOMMAND()
    ON_WM_PAINT()
    ON_WM_QUERYDRAGICON()
    ON_BN_CLICKED(IDC_FIND, OnFind)
    ON_BN_CLICKED(IDC_STOP, OnStop)
    ON_WM_SIZE()
    ON_WM_CLOSE()
    //}}AFX_MSG_MAP
    ON_MESSAGE(WM_MYFOUND, OnFound)
END_MESSAGE_MAP()
```

Remember

○	PeekMessage, DispatchMessage, and possibly Translate are used to implement a Message Pump.
	Timers, along with Message Pumps, can sometimes be a simpler alternative to threads.
○	SetTimer and KillTimer are used to start and stop the WM_TIMER messages.
	MFC Applications also provide an OnIdle handler for utilizing idle time.
○	Synchronization objects are used to synchronize access to a resource between multiple threads.

Chapter 12

COM, ActiveX Controls, and OLE Automation

- COM
- ActiveX Controls
- OLE Automation

COM

In this chapter, we cover the basics of COM programming and provide sample programs that implement those basics. By the end of the chapter, you should be able to create and use simple COM objects, ActiveX controls, and OLE Automation. Advanced topics such as aggregation (the COM version of inheritance), marshalling, DCOM (Distributed COM, across a network) and ATL (Active Template Library), manual Type Libraries, and ODL files will not be discussed in detail.

COM stands for Component Object Module. It is a combination of predefined API functions and an "architecture" that defines how one component can expose its abilities to another component or application, letting the latter use features of the former. OCX components and OLE automation are all based on COM. The term *component* is used to describe a program (EXE), Dynamic Link Library (DLL), or ActiveX control (OCX) that implements the coding requirements to become a COM server.

DCOM is Distributed COM. It is the ability for an application on one machine to work with a component on another machine.

COM objects provide their methods, properties, and events to their clients. A method is a function that you can invoke on a COM object. A property is like a data member in a C++ class, and an event serves as a means for the COM object to send event notifications to whatever piece of code is using it.

COM Properties and C++

Properties require a bit of additional definition here as they appear to work differently in C++ than other languages such as Visual Basic or Delphi. Imagine a clock COM object that has an AMPM property, which would be a boolean-type property indicating if time formatting is in AMPM or 24-hour military time. Let's call the imaginary Time COM object PNClock. We can easily picture a C++ class defined as show in Code 12–1.

Code 12–1

```
class PNClock
{
public:
        bool AMPM;
        ...
};
```

Now, to access the AMPM property, we simply access it directly as shown in Code 12–2. If a Visual Basic program were to use a PNClock COM object, it would merely do something like Code 12–3. In Delphi it would be similar. However, a property in a COM object is in reality a set of interface functions that really looks something like Code 12–4.

Code 12-2

```
PNClock AClock;

AClock.AMPM=true; // Use AMPM time.
```

Code 12-3

```
Dim AClock As Object
Set AClock = CreateObject("PN.AClock")
AClock.AMPM = True
```

Code 12-4

```
class PNClock
{
public:
        bool GetAMPM() { return( AMPM ); }
        void SetAMPM( bool Mode ) { AMPM=Mode; }
protected:
        bool AMPM;
        ...
};
```

Properties are implemented in the form of Get() and Set()/Put() interface functions. A C++ programmer calls these functions themselves. In VB and Delphi programs, the compiler itself turns the first statement in Code 12–5 into the second statement in Code 12–5.

Code 12-5

```
AClock.AMPM = True
```

into:

```
AClock.SetAMPM( True );
```

Keep this in mind as you examine the online help documentation where it refers to properties. The online help files are written for Visual Basic, not Visual C++. So, if you were to see a property in a COM object or ActiveX control such as Day, then the online help might give an example as shown in Code 12–6. It means that in C++ you would need to do something like Code 12–7. COM objects do not really give direct access to member variables, as it appears they do in VB or Delphi programs.

Code 12-6

```
Object.Day = 1
```

Code 12-7

```
Object.SetDay( 1 );
```

Servers, Clients, and Interfaces

COM objects are utilized in a client/server manner. If you write a program that makes use of a COM object, then that application is termed the client. The code (EXE, DLL, or OCX) that provides the COM functionality is termed a COM server.

When your program creates an instance of a COM object, it will be given an interface in the form of a pointer to a C++ class. The code behind that C++ class actually resides in the server application and the data will reside in the client application.

A typical example might be the use of a Microsoft Word document COM object. Microsoft Word is a COM server (to be more specific, it is an OLE Automation server, a special form of COM server). Word will expose its objects, such as the Document object, the Table object, the Spell Checker object, and so on, to any application that wants them.

When your application requests a Word Document COM object, the operating system will launch the MS Word application and ask the running Word application for the information needed to provide an interface to your application. Once you have that interface, you can invoke methods via that interface to perform operations such as loading and printing a document.

One important aspect of the COM specification states that once an interface (the methods, properties, and events) for an object is implemented by a COM server, that COM server must continue to provide that interface. In other words, it's a guarantee that older COM clients will continue to work with newer COM servers, as the newer COM servers must ensure backward compatibility.

In the event that a new interface is required or extremely beneficial, the common practice is to provide a second newer interface with a suffix of a version number. For example, in the Direct Draw COM objects, there is an interface named IDirectDraw. Later, newer interfaces named IDirectDraw2 and IDirectDraw3 were added. While IDirectDraw will continue to work, newly added features will be found in the later versions.

COM servers may also provide multiple interfaces to work with a single COM object. For example, a multimedia COM server may have an IPersistFile interface to support loading multimedia files and an IMediaPlayer interface to support the playing of the loaded file.

Creating COM Objects

A GUID is a Globally Unique Identifier, a structure that contains several numeric values. Its purpose is to provide a unique ID for a resource. A GUID is defined in Code 12–8.

Code 12–8

```
typedef struct _GUID {
    unsigned long Data1;
    unsigned short Data2;
    unsigned short Data3;
    unsigned char Data4[8];
} GUID;
```

A CLSID is a type of GUID that is associated with a COM object. When a COM server is registered with your operating system (installed or with the use of the REGSVR32.EXE program), it registers the unique CLSID for that server program in the operating system registry. Using the VC++ OLE-COM Viewer program, you can examine the CLSID for various controls and OLE types. You can also examine these values using the REGEDIT program.

When your program needs to make COM objects programmatically, you would use the CLSID of the desired COM object and call a function such as CoCreateInstance() to create an instance of a COM object.

When you create an instance of a COM object, you are asking Windows to load and execute the COM server file (it is an EXE, DLL, or OCX file). That file runs as a separate program or as an extension to your application (in the case of DLL and OCX files). What is returned for the COM object is really a piece of data that references the code inside the COM server.

While CLSIDs are difficult to work with, there is another means of identifying a particular COM object when you want to create an interface for a COM object. This is the Program ID. A Program ID is easier for humans to work with since it is a text-based identifier using common English, rather than the complex numeric values of the CLSID. For example, the Program ID for a Microsoft Word Document COM object would be "Word.Document."

If you know the Program ID for your desired COM object, then you can call the CLSIDFromProgID() SDK function to determine its CLSID and then use the CLSID to actually create the COM object instance, which is shown in Code 12–9.

Code 12–9

```
CLSID WrdCLSID;
if( CLSIDFromProgID( _T("Word.Document"), &WrdCLSID ) == NOERROR )
    // We can create the COM Object now using WrdCLSID
```

Another means of getting a needed CLSID for a COM object may be that it is already predefined by the operating system. For example, Win32 has an Active Desktop COM object. Since this is part of the Windows operating system, you will find that the CLSID for this COM object is already defined in the comdef.h header file as CLSID_ActiveDesktop and IID_IActiveDesktop. It can be used as shown in Code 12–10. The CoCreateInstance() function is defined as shown in Code 12–11 and parameters are defined in Table 12.1. A return value of S_OK means the function succeeded and anything else indicates a failure.

Code 12–10

```
IActiveDesktop * pIActiveDesktop;

CoCreateInstance ( CLSID_ActiveDesktop, NULL, CLSCTX_INPROC_SERVER,
            IID_IActiveDesktop, (void**) &pIActiveDesktop );
```

Code 12–11

```
STDAPI CoCreateInstance( REFCLSID rclsid, LPUNKNOWN pUnkOuter,
        DWORD dwClsContext,  REFIID riid, LPVOID * ppv );
```

Table 12.1   Parameters to the CoCreateInstance() Function

Parameter	Meaning
rclsid	Class identifier (CLSID) of the object.
pUnkOuter	Pointer to controlling IUnknown for agregate objects. Can be NULL for new objects (more common).
dwClsContext	Context for running executable code. This parameter defines how the object server is to be instantiated.
riid	Reference to the identifier of the desired interface.
ppv	Address of output variable that receives the interface pointer requested in riid. This pointer must be typecast to a void** (pointer to a void pointer) type.

Initializing and Shutting Down COM

Before you can use COM in your applications, you must initialize the COM system. An MFC program should call AfxOleIni()t once to initialize COM routines and Ole-Uninitialize() to shut it down. An MFC program should call CoInitialize() or CoInitializeEx() to initialize COM and OleUninitialize() to shut it down. For MFC, the CWinApp::OnInitInstance() is a good place to initialize COM; CWinApp::~CWinApp is a good place to shut it down.

COM initialization is on a thread basis. This means that if your program is multi-threaded and you want the child threads to utilize COM, then each thread must initialize and shutdown COM for that thread.

If, in ClassWizard, when you generated your application, you selected one of the *Compound Document* support options (dialog # 3 of AppWizard), then the initialization and shutdown will have been done for you.

The prototypes for CoInitialize and CoInitializeEx are shown in Code 12–12.

Code 12–12

```
HRESULT CoInitialize( void* pvReserved );
HRESULT CoInitializeEx( void* pvReserved, DWORD dwCoInit );
```

CoInitialize() works with all Win32 platforms and CoInitializeEx() works with all Win32 platforms except Win95 without DCOM installed. In both cases, the pvReserved parameter is reserved for future use and should be zero. For CoInitializeEx(), the dwCoInit parameter allows you to define the threading model for COM support and may be one or more of the values shown in Table 12.2.

Table 12.2 Values for the dwCoInit Parameter

Option	Meaning
COINIT_APARTMENTTHREADED*	Apartment Threading. This means that COM objects created in this thread will only be used from within this thread.
COINIT_MULTITHREADED*	Multi or Free Threading. This means that COM objects created by this thread may be freely acted upon by other threads.
COINIT_DISABLE_OLE1DDE	Disables DDE for OLE version 1 in the thread.
COINIT_SPEED_OVER_MEMORY	Favors execution speed over memory use for the COM system.

*COINIT_APARTMENTTHREADED and COINIT_MULTITHREADED are mutually exclusive, you cannot combine the two in a single call to CoInitializeEx().

When the apartment-threading model is used, the COM system controls access to the COM object for a single thread. Operations against these COM objects are performed during normal Windows Message processing. In the multi or free threading model, COM does not manage interaction with a COM object between threads and no message processing is needed. However, in the multithreaded mode, it is up to the COM server code to synchronize access to the object between various threads. This synchronization is performed using synchronization objects such as a Mutex or Critical Section.

Interfaces and IUnknown

The COM system describes an Interface as an interface to a COM object's abilities (abilities being what would more normally be called "properties" and "methods"). In both C and C++, an Interface is implemented as a pointer to a structure that contains pointers to functions. Notice that IUnknown is implemented as a struct in C and a class in C++, so it is usable by either.

COM objects usually have several interfaces to provide various abilities. For example, the ActiveMovie OCX object contains an IPersistFile interface for loading a new file, as well as an IMediaControl interface that provides the ability to play or pause the currently loaded movie.

Some Interface types are standard, such as IPersistFile, while some are specific to the COM object, such as IMediaControl. IPersistFile is commonly implemented in COM objects as an interface that provides the ability to save and load a file.

IUnknown

Each type of COM object has its own Interface definition, but they all support a single, top-level interface known as IUnknown. Using IUnknown, you can query the COM object about its other interfaces. In C++ terms, we would call IUnknown the base class of all other interfaces.

The IUnknown interface supports several basic functions (the functions are actually pointers to functions). These functions are:

QueryInterface()   Returns pointers to supported interfaces.
AddRef()   Increments reference count.
Release()   Decrements reference count.

Getting an IUnknown Interface

Before accessing QueryInterface to get access to the COM object's other interfaces, you must get an IUknown interface to the object itself. There are several ways to accomplish this:

- Call a COM Library API function that creates an object of a predetermined type, such as DirectDrawCreate().

- Call a COM Library API function that can create an object based on a class identifier (CLSID) and that returns any type of interface pointer requested, for example, CoCreateInstance().

- Call a method of some interface that creates another object (or connects to an existing one) and returns an interface pointer on that separate object, for example, QueryInterface().

- Implement an object with an interface through which other objects pass their interface pointers directly to the client.

IUnknown::QueryInterface

Even though the IUnknown interface is really a pointer to a struct with a series of pointers to functions in it, it is often referred to, described, and functions invoked, in a fashion similar to C++ classes. There is no IUnknown class or QueryInterface() member function of it. However, there is an IUnknown structure and a pointer to a function inside it called QueryInterface. Because of this, the syntax for invoking QueryInterface() is similar between C and C++, but it is not a class.

QueryInterface() is a key part of the COM approach. It provides the method by which you gain access to other interfaces for a COM object. QueryInterface() is used to ask for a specific type of interface from an object; it will fail if the object does not support that interface.

There is no way to use IUnknown or QueryInterface() to iterate through a list of the component's available interfaces. This was a conscious decision because even if you could get a list of interfaces, your program would need to be created at design time to call specific functions of specific interfaces.

Reference Counting

Reference counting is the ability to identify how many times a COM object is being used. This way, the operating system knows when the object is no longer needed and can remove it from memory when resources are low and it is no longer needed.

The AddRef() and Release() functions of IUnknown implement reference counting. When you use a COM object, you call AddRef() to increment its reference count and call Release() to decrement it.

Marshalling

Marshalling in COM is the ability to transfer data between an application and a COM object. When the two are on the same machine or in the same process, this is a simple task. However, COM automatically supports cross-process and even cross-machine applications and component communication.

Luckily, marshalling is handled and implemented by COM itself and the component. It is invisible to the application and component writer. It is possible for a COM server developer to implement his or her own IMarshal interface, if that developer feels it will add substantial benefit to his or her COM object.

IDispatch and OLE Automation

IDispatch is an interface designed to simplify OLE Automation. OLE Automation is the ability of one program to control a COM server in a dynamic manner. For example, the macro language of Microsoft Word (Visual Basic) is exposed via COM and OLE Automation. This permits another program to execute commands against Word. For example, you could tell Word to open a file, print ten copies, and close it.

IDispatch's main functions are GetIDsOfNames(), where you can give it the name of an exposed function (i.e., "File.Open"), and Invoke(), where it executes the function by the ID returned from GetIDsOfNames(). You can get an IDispatch pointer in the same way you get an IUnknown pointer. Though IDispatch is used for all forms of COM objects, we will cover it in more detail in the *OLE Automation* section.

Common Data Types

Because a COM object can be used by other languages such as VB or Delphi, it must provide only the standard OLE data types as part of its interface to those languages (methods, properties, and events). Of these data types, the following are not self-explanatory and require further explanation:

BSTR: The BSTR is double-byte, or "wide" string where each character is 16 bits wide, not 8. This type is also referred to as an OLECHAR*. You can specify a constant BSTR by using the "L" prefix, for example: L"Hello world."

To get a BSTR from a CString object, you can use the AllocSysString() and SetSysString() functions. To set a CString from a BSTR, you can simply use the overloaded CString::operator=() function (see VARIANT below).

DATE: The DATE data type is implemented in C++ as a double, but the ColeDateTime provides a wrapper for this type. Because of implicit constructors and DATE operators, the ColeDateTime can be used just about anywhere a DATE is needed (see VARIANT below).

CURRENCY: The CURRENCY data type is implemented as a 64-bit (non-standard) integer by VC++. The COleCurrency class is a wrapper for this type (see VARIANT below).

VARIANT: The VARIANT data type is a structure that contains a union that has the ability to represent any form of OLE data type in a single container. The actual definition of the structure looks something like Code 12–13.

Code 12-13

```
typedef struct tagVARIANT  {
    VARTYPE vt;
    unsigned short wReserved1;
    unsigned short wReserved2;
    unsigned short wReserved3;
    union {
        Byte                    bVal;           // VT_UI1.
        Short                   iVal;           // VT_I2.
        long                    lVal;           // VT_I4.
        float                   fltVal;         // VT_R4.
        double                  dblVal;         // VT_R8.
        VARIANT_BOOL            boolVal;        // VT_BOOL.
        // etc.
```

To correctly initialize a VARIANT object, you specify its data type and value, such as shown in Code 12–14.

Code 12-14

```
VARIANT lv;
l.vt=VT_I4; // Set to 'long' data type
l.lval = 0; // Set the value
```

The COleVariant is the wrapper for this type, and, like the COleDateTime, this class can be used just about anywhere a VARIANT is needed.

The COleVariant classes provide various functions for access, but the main means for initialization is via the constructors. The COleVariant class provides a lengthy list of overloaded constructors that can be used to create a COleVariant for a specific data type. An example of using the COleVariant to accomplish the same demo as above is shown in Code 12–15.

Since ActiveX controls and OLE Automation servers are based on COM, you may find the same data types are needed to interact with these items as well.

Code 12-15

```
COleVariant lv ( 0L ) ; // Create a long (VT_I4) variant object
```

A Simple COM Client Demonstration

This section will implement a simple COM demo using the Active Desktop COM object. This COM object is available on all 32-bit versions of Windows and is provided by the operating system itself. The interface that we will be using is called IActiveDesktop, and we will instantiate it using the CoCreateInstance() API function.

Figure 12–1 The main dialog.

The program will use the IActiveDesktop COM object to display information about the desktop, such as the selected wallpaper and pattern images.

To create the demo, go through AppWizard and create a dialog-based application. Add four STATIC controls to the main dialog using your dialog editor and set the properties for them as shown in Table 12.3. The main dialog should look something like Figure 12–1.

In the stdafx.h file for your project, you need to add a #include for wininet.h just above the #include of afxdisp.h as shown in Code 12–16.

Code 12-16

```
#include <wininet.h>
#include <afxdisp.h>          // MFC Automation classes
```

Though the demo program does not make use of any Internet COM abilities, the header files for afxdisp.h use conditional compilation to load other files such as COMDEF.h, where the CLSID_ActiveDesktop declaration is contained. In order to force COMDEF.h to be #included, we need to #include wininet.h as well.

Next, go to the OnInitDialog() function of your program and just before the last line where you should see a "return TRUE;" statement, add Code 12–17. When you run the program, it should look similar to Figure 12–2.

Table 12.3 Properties for Static Controls to the Main Dialog

ID	Caption
IDC_STATIC	WallPaper:
IDC_WALLPAPER	N/A
IDC_STATIC	Pattern:
IDC_PATTERN	N/A

Code 12-17

```cpp
// Needed variables
WCHAR Str[MAX_PATH];
HRESULT hr;
// Our Interface pointer
IActiveDesktop * pIActiveDesktop;

// Initiale the COM system
CoInitialize ( NULL );

// Retrieve a COM interface using CoCreateInstance
hr = CoCreateInstance ( CLSID_ActiveDesktop, NULL, CLSCTX_INPROC_SERVER,
    IID_IActiveDesktop, (void**) &pIActiveDesktop );

if( SUCCEEDED(hr) )
{
    // Invoke the GetWallPaper method
    hr = pIActiveDesktop->GetWallpaper ( Str, MAX_PATH, 0 );

    // Set the STATIC control Text, if worked or failed:
    if( SUCCEEDED(hr) )
        SetDlgItemText( IDC_WALLPAPER, CString( Str ) );
    else
        SetDlgItemText( IDC_WALLPAPER, "WallPaper retrieval failed" );

    // Invoke the GetPattern method
    hr = pIActiveDesktop->GetPattern ( Str, MAX_PATH, 0 );

    // Set the STATIC control Text, if worked or failed:
    if( SUCCEEDED(hr) )
        SetDlgItemText( IDC_PATTERN, CString( Str ) );
    else
        SetDlgItemText( IDC_PATTERN, "Pattern retrieval failed" );

    // Release our Interface:
    pIActiveDesktop->Release();
}
else
    MessageBox( "CoCreateInstance failed" );

// Shutdown the COM system:
CoUninitialize();

return TRUE;  // return TRUE  unless you set the focus to a control
}
```

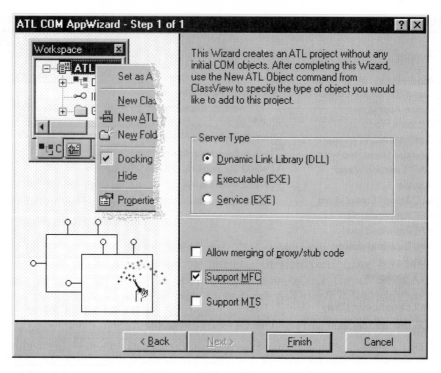

Figure 12–4 Step 1 of the COM Wizard.

The ClassView display of your new project should look like the following, with the items expanded as shown in Figure 12–5.

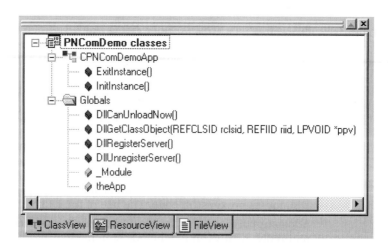

Figure 12–5 The ClassView display of the new project.

Since we haven't added any interfaces yet, all we have is the application class object and the global functions that will be managing the loading and registration of the COM server. We won't need to modify any of these for our demonstration. Next, we will add a COM object to the project, which will provide our interface, and we will add some properties to it.

Adding the COM Object

Our PNCOMDemo server will implement a "Clock" object. So, we need to add the Clock object to our project:

- From the Insert menu choice, select New ATL Object.
- From the ATL Object Wizard dialog, select Object in the Category list, and then the Simple Object from the Objects list, and click Next as shown in Figure 12–6.
- Fill out the ATL Object Wizard Properties dialog, by simply typing in the name of the object we want to create (Clock) in the ShortName field, and the rest of the fields will be modified as shown in Figure 12–7.
- Select the Attributes tab in the ATL Object Wizard Properties dialog and note the settings (see Figure 12–8). Other properties are contained in Table 12.5. We won't change anything here and will accept all the defaults.
- Click the OK button on this dialog.

  If you look in the ClassView display now, you should note two new nodes: CClock the C++ class, and IClock the COM interface to CClock as shown in Figure 12–9.

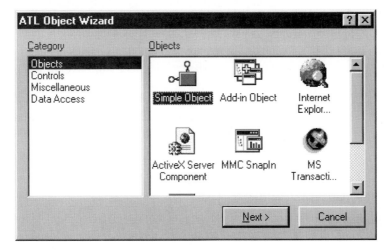

Figure 12–6   Select Objects from the ATL Object Wizard.

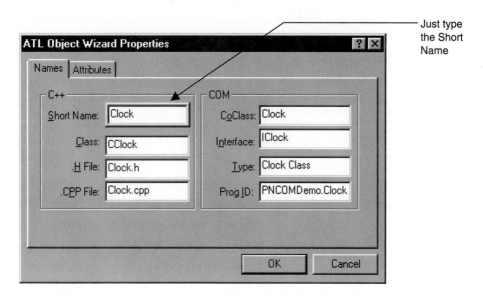

Just type the Short Name

Figure 12–7   Type Clock as the value for the shortname field.

Table 12.5   Options for the ATL Object Wizard Properties Dialog (Attributes Tab)

Option	Meaning
Threading Model	Defines how this COM object can be access from threads.
Interface	Defines the type of interface to be created and lets you choose whether IDispatch should be part of the interface.
Aggregation	Specifies if the object can be, cannot be, or must be used as an aggregate (for Yes, No, or Only, respectively).
Support ISupportErrorInfo	Means that the COM object will have an interface for handling errors.
Support for Connection Points	Means that the COM object will support connection points (a connection point is a form of communication between two COM objects; so far, we have only talked about an interface to a COM object, where a connection point allows that object to get an interface back to our code as well).
Free Threaded Marshaller	Supports efficient marshalling of data between multiple threads of the same process.

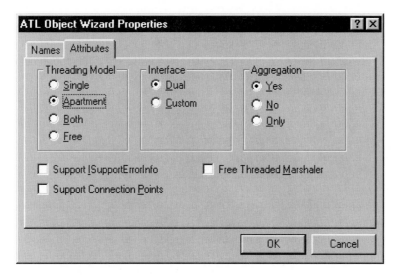

Figure 12–8   Select the Attributes tab.

Adding a Property to the PNCOMDemo.Clock COM Object

We are going to add two properties to our COM demo: the current time and an AMPM/24-hour format flag. Properties, methods, and events are all added by right-clicking on the interface name (IClock in our example) in the ClassView window and selecting Add Method, Add Property, or Add Event from the pop-up menu.

- Right-click the IClock item in ClassView and select Add Property from the pop-up menu.
- The Add Property to Interface dialog will appear.
- In this dialog, make the selections shown on Figure 12–10.

Notice that the Time property will be a read-only property. For this reason, we unchecked the Put Function checkbox option. The Property Type of BSTR means that the property will be a string type.

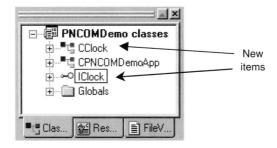

Figure 12–9   Two new items in the ClassView display.

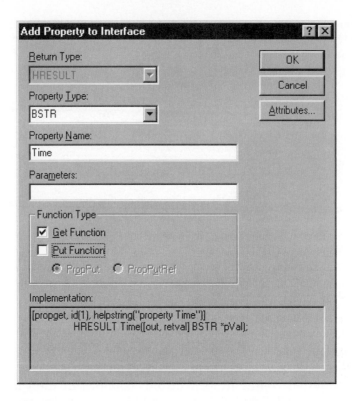

Figure 12–10   Add a property to the interface.

- Once you have made the changes, click OK, and Code 12–18 will automatically be added to the IClock interface item, inside the CClock class.

Code 12–18

```
STDMETHODIMP CClock::get_Time(BSTR *pVal)
{
      AFX_MANAGE_STATE(AfxGetStaticModuleState())

      // TODO: Add your implementation code here

      return S_OK;
}
```

- Modify the get_Time() function as shown in Code 12–19, so that it gets the current time, formats it as a string, and then returns it using the pVal parameter:

Code 12–19

```
STDMETHODIMP CClock::get_Time(BSTR *pVal)
{
```

```
AFX_MANAGE_STATE(AfxGetStaticModuleState())

// TODO: Add your implementation code here
CTime Now = CTime::GetCurrentTime();
CString Ret;

if( m_AMPM )
    Ret = Now.Format( "%I:%M:%S %p" );
else
    Ret = Now.Format( "%H:%M:%S" );

*pVal = Ret.AllocSysString();

return S_OK;
}
```

We need to add the AMPM property to the COM object, which, unlike the Time property, is a read/write property.

- Right-click the IClock item in ClassView and select Add Property from the pop-up menu.
- The Add Property to Interface dialog will appear.
- In this dialog, make the following selections:
  a. Property Type is BOOL.
  b. Property Name is AMPM.
  c. The rest of the items can be left at their defaults.
- Once you have made the changes, click OK, and the following functions have been added to the IClock interface item, inside the CClock class as shown in Code 12–20.

Code 12–20

```
STDMETHODIMP CClock::get_AMPM(BOOL *pVal)
{
    AFX_MANAGE_STATE(AfxGetStaticModuleState())

    // TODO: Add your implementation code here
    return S_OK;
}

STDMETHODIMP CClock::put_AMPM(BOOL newVal)
{
    AFX_MANAGE_STATE(AfxGetStaticModuleState())

    // TODO: Add your implementation code here

    return S_OK;
}
```

We need to change Code 12–20 so they work with our m_AMPM data member of our CClock class as shown in Code 12–21.

Code 12–21

```
STDMETHODIMP CClock::get_AMPM(BOOL *pVal)
{
        AFX_MANAGE_STATE(AfxGetStaticModuleState())

        // TODO: Add your implementation code here
        *pVal = m_AMPM;

        return S_OK;
}

STDMETHODIMP CClock::put_AMPM(BOOL newVal)
{
        AFX_MANAGE_STATE(AfxGetStaticModuleState())

        // TODO: Add your implementation code here
        m_AMPM = newVal;

        return S_OK;
}
```

Notice how the property interface functions normally provide an interface to some data member of our C++ class.

Finally, we need to add the m_AMPM data member to the CClock class. Locate the class definition for the CClock class (tip: double-click the constructor name in ClassView), and add the code in bold displayed in Code 12–22.

Code 12–22

```
///////////////////////////////////////////////////////////////////////////
// CClock

class ATL_NO_VTABLE CClock :
        public CComObjectRootEx<CComSingleThreadModel>,
        public CComCoClass<CClock, &CLSID_Clock>,
        public IDispatchImpl<IClock, &IID_IClock, &LIBID_PNCOMDEMOLib>
{
public:
        CClock()
        {
                m_AMPM = TRUE;
        }

        BOOL m_AMPM; // PN: Our AMPM property
        // Portions of code removed for readability
```

You should now be able to compile your COM object. Part of the COM compilation process will also register the new COM server (PNCOMDemo) with your system. On other machines that will use the COM server, make sure to use REGSVR32.EXE to register it.

> **NOTE**
>
> When you compile the COM object, it will not only create the DLL file for the server, but it will also create *Type Library* file, named PNCOMDemo.tlb. This file will be helpful later in another Visual C++ program when we want to use the COM object.

Testing the COM Server Demo

For debugging a COM object, see the section *Debugging COM, ActiveX, and DLLs.*

We will now provide a simple demo program that uses our PNCOMDemo COM server:

- Create a dialog-based application named PNCOMDemoTest.
- Modify the main dialog of your new program so that it looks like Figure 12–11. The controls should be set up as shown in Table 12.6.

Importing a Type Library

In order to simplify working with the COM object, we are going to use ClassWizard to create a wrapper class for the COM object. Importing the Type Library file, which was created by compiling the PNCOMDemo project, will do this. This wrapper class will be derived from the MFC COleDispatchDriver class. To create the wrapper class:

- Go into ClassWizard.
- Click the Add Class button, and then select From a Type Library from the drop-down menu.

Table 12.6 Setting for the Main Dialog Controls

Control	ID	Caption
Button	IDC_GETTIME	Get Time
CheckBox	IDC_AMPM	AM/PM
STATIC	IDC_TIME	N/A

Figure 12–11   The new look for the main dialog.

- In the Import from Type Library dialog, browse back into the PN-COMDemo project, and locate the .tlb file for that project as shown in Figure 12–12.
- Click the Open button.

This will create a new class named IClock in our project. This IClock class is the wrapper for the COM object. This wrapper class will simplify the creation of, and interaction with, the COM object. The class definition for IClock should look like Code 12–23.

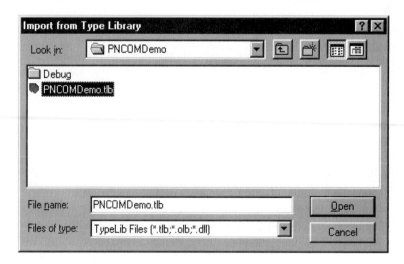

Figure 12–12   Select the PNCOMDemo.tlb library.

Code 12-23

```
class IClock : public COleDispatchDriver
{
public:
        IClock() {}                     // Calls COleDispatchDriver default constructor
        IClock(LPDISPATCH pDispatch) : COleDispatchDriver(pDispatch) {}
        IClock(const IClock& dispatchSrc) : COleDispatchDriver(dispatchSrc) {}
// Attributes
public:

// Operations
public:
        CString GetTime();
        long GetAmpm();
        void SetAmpm(long nNewValue);
};
```

Notice the functions in bold reflect the properties that we created in the previous project for the COM object (PNCOMDemo.Clock).

All that remains now is to add demonstration code to create an instance of the PNCCOMDemo.Clock COM object and use its properties. Add Code 12-24, using ClassWizard, as a message map handler to the Get Time button on your dialog.

Code 12-24

```
void CPNCOMDemoTestDlg::OnGettime()
{
        IClock Clock;

        // Initialize Clock with an interface to the COM object
        Clock.CreateDispatch( "PNCOMDemo.Clock" );
        // Determine if the AMPM box is checked
        CButton* pButton = (CButton*)GetDlgItem( IDC_AMPM );
        // Set the AMPM property of the COM object, based on checkbox status
        Clock.SetAmpm( pButton->GetCheck() ? TRUE : FALSE );
        // Set the STATIC control text to the Time property from the COM object
        SetDlgItemText( IDC_TIME, Clock.GetTime() );
}
```

At the top of your dialog's .cpp file, make sure you add the bold line in Code 12-25 to include the IClock class in your compilation.

Code 12-25

```
// PNCOMDemoTestDlg.cpp : implementation file
//
```

```
#include "stdafx.h"
#include "PNCOMDemoTest.h"
#include "PNCOMDemoTestDlg.h"

#include "PNComDemo.h" // PNComDemo.h was generated from Type Library

#ifdef _DEBUG
```

You should now be able to compile and run the test program. When you run the program, if you click the Get Time button, you should see the time displayed in the static control. This time string is coming from the COM object.

ActiveX Controls

Using ActiveX Controls

ActiveX controls are in reality small COM servers. A single COM server may contain one or more ActiveX controls. The process of using an ActiveX control in your applications is as easy as adding it to your project.

Notice, however, that when you add an ActiveX control to your project, you are really just creating a C++ interface class to interact with the ActiveX control. If you distribute your program, you must also distribute the ActiveX control. ActiveX controls are typically stored in DLL or OCX files.

For our demonstration, create a dialog-based application named ImageViewer. Follow all the default AppWizard options for this new program. The program will demonstrate how to use the Wang Image Edit ActiveX control and will create a simple image file display program. Please note: The Image Edit control may be Wang or Kodak, depending on the version.

Adding the ActiveX Control to Your Project

To add the Wang/Kodak Image Edit ActiveX control, go to the Project menu choice, and select Add To Project, and then Components and Controls.... In the Component Gallery dialog that appears, double-click on the Registered ActiveX controls folder. Scan through the ActiveX control list and locate the Wang Image Edit Control or Kodak Image Edit as shown in Figure 12–13.

Note that the Path To Control field tells you the location of the OCX file. This is the file you will need to distribute along with your application. Also note that the More Info button is enabled. The More Info button will provide you with online help on the methods, properties, and events that the OCX file uses (if a help file for the control is available, otherwise the More Info button is disabled).

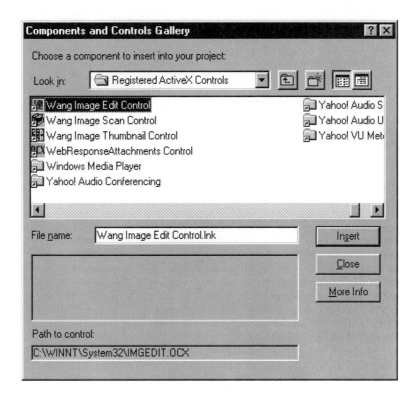

Figure 12–13   Locate the Wang Image Edit Control.

To add the control, click the Insert button. At this point, Visual Studio will inspect the ActiveX control and create a series of interface classes to work with the control. In the next dialog (see Figure 12–14) Visual Studio will confirm that you want to add the classes that it generated to your project. With all the classes selected (as is the default), click the OK button.

Now, if you go into the dialog editor for your main dialog window, you should see that the new control (Wang or Kodak Image Edit) has been inserted into your tool palette. Drop the new control on your form, along with several buttons, so that your dialog now looks like Figure 12–15.

Interacting with the ActiveX Control

You will now interact with the ActiveX control in the same manner you have with the other built-in Windows control types such as Edit boxes and List Boxes. You could use GetDlgItem() to get a pointer to the object, but we instead will add a member variable to the main dialog class. Go to ClassWizard and select the Member Variable tab. Make sure that your main dialog class name is selected in the

---

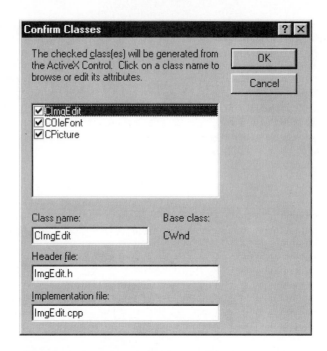

Figure 12–14 Click OK after selecting all the classes.

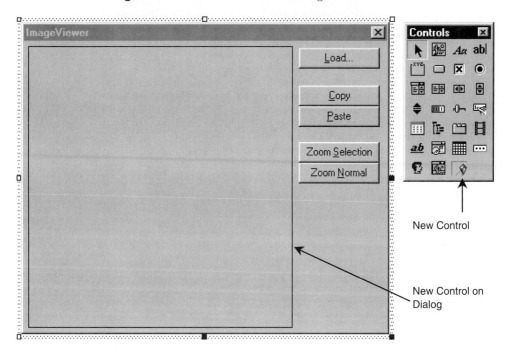

Figure 12–15 Add a member variable.

Class Name field; you should see a list of controls appear in the Control IDs listing (of the Member Variables tab).

Highlight the control ID for the new ActiveX control and click the Add Variable button. You should see a dialog similar to Figure 12–16.

Notice how the Variable type selection is CImgEdit. This is the same class name that was added when we added the ActiveX control to our project. This is the interface class to the ActiveX control.

We will now describe the message handler functions for the program. They will demonstrate how to interact with the ActiveX control (now a member variable named m_Image). Each function should be added via ClassWizards Message Map tab for the specific button. Items in bold are specific to working with the ActiveX control. Please note that certain operations such as SetImage are specific to the Wang/Kodak Image Edit ActiveX control. The handler for the Load button is shown in Code 12–26; the handler for the Copy button is shown in Code 12–27. Code 12–28 contains code for the Paste button. Code 12–29 contains code for the Zoom Selection button. Code 12–30 contains code for the Zoom Normal button.

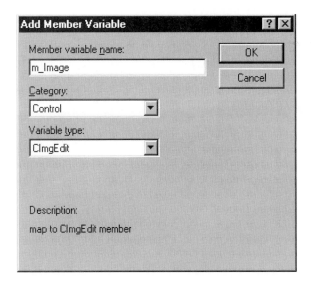

Figure 12–16 Add and place controls as shown here.

Code 12-26

```
void CImageViewerDlg::OnLoad()
      {
      CFileDialog X(TRUE);

      // Invoke file open dialog, to select image
      if( X.DoModal() == IDOK )
      {
            // Set the Selected filename as the Image in the OCX
            m_Image.SetImage( X.GetPathName() );

            // Create a BOOL type variant
            COleVariant vFalse( (SHORT)FALSE, VT_BOOL );

            // Tell the Image control to fit the image inside the control
            m_Image.FitTo( 0, vFalse );

            //  Tell the Image control to display the image
            m_Image.Display();
      }
}
```

Code 12-27

```
void CImageViewerDlg::OnCopy()
{
      // Create VARIANT-compatible parameters for ClipboardCopy function
      COleVariant Left( m_Left );
      COleVariant Top( m_Top );
      COleVariant Width( m_Width );
      COleVariant Height( m_Height );

      // Draw the selection rectangle
      m_Image.DrawSelectionRect( m_Left, m_Top, m_Width, m_Height );
      // Copy what is within the selection rectangle to the clipboard
      m_Image.ClipboardCopy( Left, Top, Width, Height );

}
```

Code 12-28

```
void CImageViewerDlg::OnPaste()
{
      if( m_Image.IsClipboardDataAvailable() )
      {
            COleVariant Zero((short)0);
            m_Image.ClipboardPaste( Zero, Zero );
      }
}
```

Code 12–29

```
void CImageViewerDlg::OnZoomsel()
{
        if( m_Width )
                m_Image.ZoomToSelection();
}
```

Code 12–30

```
void CImageViewerDlg::OnZoomnorm()
{
        COleVariant vTrue( (SHORT)TRUE, VT_BOOL );
        m_Image.FitTo( 0, vTrue );
}
```

To make the program work, we will also need to add an event handler or message map function for when the user has finished making a selection rectangle (for the Copy button). Using ClassWizard, we will add the message map in the same manner as any other Windows control:

- Go to ClassWizard and select the Message Map tab.
- In the Class Name field, make sure the name of your main dialog appears (CImageViewDlg in our example).
- In the Object IDs list, select the ID of the Image control (IDC_IMAGE in our example).
- In the Messages list, select the SelectionRectDrawn message (this is unique to the Wang/Kodak Image Edit Control).
- Click the Add Function button and click OK to accept the suggested function name of OnSelectionRectDrawnImage().Modify the OnSelectionRectDrawnImage() function to look like Code 12–31.
- Add the data members shown in Code 12–32 to the class definition for your main dialog class.

Code 12–31

```
void CImageViewerDlg::OnSelectionRectDrawnImage(long Left, long Top, long
Width, long Height)
{
        // TODO: Add your control notification handler code here
        m_Left = Left;
        m_Top = Top;
        m_Width = Width;
        m_Height = Height;
}
```

Code 12-32

```
long m_Left, m_Top, m_Width, m_Height;
```

Once done, you can compile and run your program. You should be able to load images files such as JPG or TIF images and display them now, with the help of the Wang/Kodak Image Edit ActiveX control as shown in Figure 12-17.

Creating ActiveX Controls

Visual C++ supports two methods for creating an ActiveX control: MFC and ATL. ATL is the Active Template Library, which can be used for creating small, compact OCX files. The MFC method creates larger OCX files, but provides full MFC benefits and is a bit easier to use. This section will discuss the MFC method.

We will create a simple AlarmClock ActiveX control. This control will display the current time when on a form, will allow you to set an Alarm time property, and when the alarm time is reached, it will send an event to the parent window.

We will also demonstrate a stock property. Stock properties are properties common to all ActiveX controls and are easy to implement. The stock properties are shown in Table 12.7.

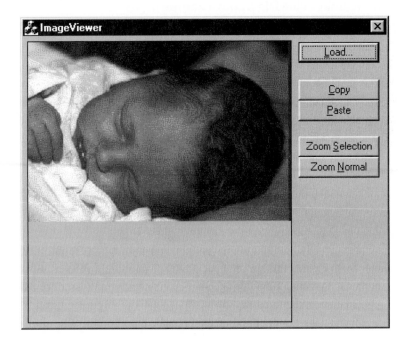

Figure 12-17 Display an image using the Wang/Kodak Image Edit ActiveX control.

Table 12.7   The Stock Properties

Property Name	How to Access
Appearance	Use the m_sAppearance variable.
BackColor	Call the GetBackColor function.
BorderStyle	Use the m_sBorderStyle member variable.
Caption	Call the InternalGetText function.
Enabled	Use the m_bEnabled member variable.
Font	Call the SelectStockFont function.
ForeColor	Call the GetForeColor function.
hWnd	Use the m_hWnd member variable
Text	See Caption property above.

Creating the Project

- From the File menu item, click New.
- Make sure the Projects tab is highlighted.
- Click the MFC ActiveX Control Wizard.
- Enter a Project Name and click OK (our demo is PNAlarmClock as shown in Figure 12–18).
- In the MFC ActiveX Control Wizard Step 1 of 2 dialog, you can normally accept all of the defaults. The options on this dialog are shown in Table 12.8.

Table 12.8   Options for the Dialog

Option	Meaning
How many controls would you like your project to have?	Change this option if you would like to put multiple controls in a single OCX file.
Would you like the controls in this project to have a runtime license?	A runtime license is a file that permits the OCX to be used on a specific machine. If you want to license or sell the OCX with a license file, select Yes for this option.
Would you like source file comments to be generated?	This very polite option allows you to specify whether the generated source code contains comments for common "to do" operations. You should leave this at "Yes, Please."
Would you like help files to be generated?	If you select this option, then a default set of help files will be generated that you can modify using MS Word. Your project will also be configured to compile the help files as well as the OCX itself.

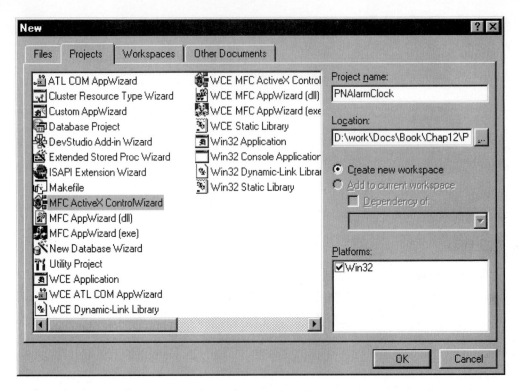

Figure 12–18   Creating an ActiveX control with AppWizard.

- In the MFC ActiveX Control Wizard Step 2 of 2 dialog, note the following:
  a. The Edit Names button permits you to change the name of your control(s) and associate property pages with the control.
  b. The Invisible At Runtime can be checked when the control should have no appearance during runtime (this means that it will not get a window handle and certain functions, like GetDlgItem(), will not work with it).
  c. You can Subclass the control, having it start out its basic appearance like a normal Windows control (button, edit, list, etc.).
- Normally, you can accept just about all the defaults, but this, of course, depends on the application as shown in Figure 12–19.
- Click OK and AppWizard creates the skeleton program for your control.

When AppWizard is done, you will have a ????Ctrl and ????PropPage class for each control created (where ???? is the name of the control). The ????Ctrl class is the code that will handle the control itself, and the ????PropPage is the class for displaying custom property pages. Our demonstration program will have classes like CPNAlarmClockCtrl and CPNAlarmClockPropPage, as shown in Figure 12–20.

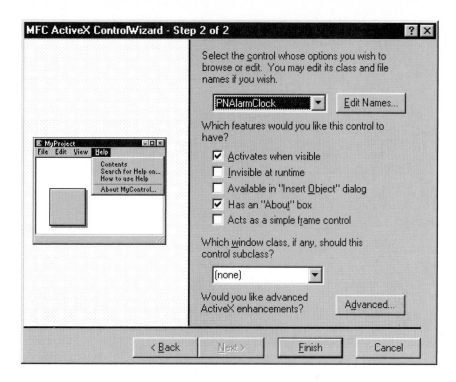

Figure 12–19   Accept the default settings.

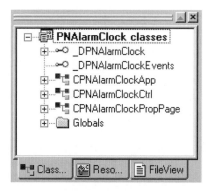

Figure 12–20   Classes for the demonstration program.

In the CPNAlarmClockCtrl class, take a look at the OnDraw() function. You will see something similar to Code 12–33.

Code 12–33

```
-void CPNAlarmClockCtrl::OnDraw( CDC* pdc, const CRect& rcBounds, const
CRect& rcInvalid)
{
    // TODO: Replace the following code with your own drawing code.
    pdc->FillRect(rcBounds,
    CBrush::FromHandle((HBRUSH)GetStockObject(WHITE_BRUSH)));
    pdc->Ellipse(rcBounds);
}
```

Like in the CView class, the OnDraw() function is where you want to add code for changing the appearance of your OCX. This is the function where later we will display the time.

Adding a Property.   Our demo control will have a one property: The alarm time that the control will send an event to its parent. We will also add the Font stock property, discussed later. To add a property to your ActiveX control, go into Class-Wizard and select the Automation tab (see Figure 12–21).

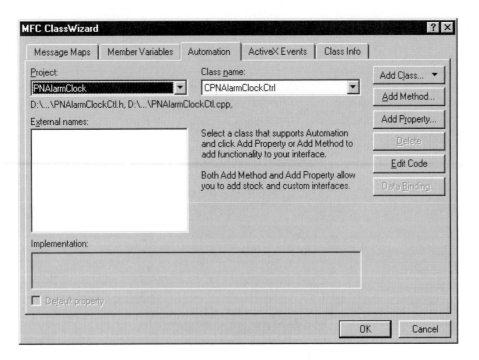

Figure 12–21   Select the Automation tab.

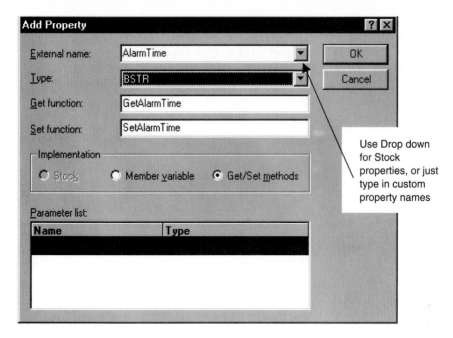

Figure 12–22   Enter the name of the new property.

Make sure that the Class name field shows the name of the CPNAlarmClockCtrl class that you want to add the property for.

Adding the AlarmTime Property
- Click the Add Property button on ClassWizards Automation tab.
- Fill in the Add Property dialog as shown in Figure 12–22.
- Click OK on the Add Property.

There are two forms of implementation for properties that work very similar. These are shown in Table 12.9.

Table 12.9   The Time Properties

Implementation	Description
Member Variable	In this implementation, a member variable is added (m_AlarmTime in our example) and a single function is created that will be called when the property is changed. Users of the ActiveX object will have access directly into the object for the variable.
Get/Set methods	In this implementation, two functions are created. A Getproperty() and Setproperty(), which will be called to get and set the property respectively.

While the two implementations work out to be very similar in the long run, it is recommended that if your control will change appearance based on getting or setting a value, you should use the Get and Set methods, otherwise use the Member Variable method. For consistency, we will only implement the Get/Set methods.

The third type of implementation, Stock, will be selected if a Stock property is added.

This will add two functions to your Ctrl class as shown in Code 12–34.

Code 12–34

```
BSTR CPNAlarmClockCtrl::GetAlarmTime()
{
       CString strResult;

       return strResult.AllocSysString();
}
void CPNAlarmClockCtrl::SetAlarmTime(LPCTSTR lpszNewValue)
{
       // TODO: Add your property handler here
       SetModifiedFlag();
}
```

Modify these two property functions so that they look like Code 12–35.

Code 12–35

```
BSTR CPNAlarmClockCtrl::GetAlarmTime()
{
       CString strResult;

       // Format Alarm time into a string, if it is valid
       strResult = m_AlarmTime;

       return strResult.AllocSysString();
}
void CPNAlarmClockCtrl::SetAlarmTime(LPCTSTR lpszNewValue)
{
       // TODO: Add your property handler here
       int H=-1, M=-1, S=-1;

       m_AlarmTime=lpszNewValue;
       if( lpszNewValue[0] == '\0' )
       {
              m_AlarmH=m_AlarmM=m_AlarmS=-1;
              m_AlarmTime = lpszNewValue;
       }
       else
```

```
        {
                H = atoi( lpszNewValue );
                while( *lpszNewValue && *lpszNewValue != ':' )
                        lpszNewValue++;
                if( *lpszNewValue )
                        M = atoi( ++lpszNewValue );
                while( *lpszNewValue && *lpszNewValue != ':' )
                        lpszNewValue++;
                if( *lpszNewValue )
                        S = atoi( ++lpszNewValue );
                if( H>=0 && H <=23 && M >=0 && M <= 59 && S >=0 && S<=59 )
                {
                        m_AlarmH = H;
                        m_AlarmM = M;
                        m_AlarmS = S;
                        m_AlarmTime = lpszNewValue;
                }
        }

        SetModifiedFlag();
}
```

The functions in Code 12–35 are the interface functions to our object's AlarmTime property. In order to make the property work, we still need to create member variables in the CPNAlarmClockCtrl class so that the property can be retained by the object. Add the following data members to your CPNAlarmClockCtrl class as shown in Code 12–36.

Code 12–36

```
int m_AlarmH, m_AlarmM, m_AlarmS;
CString m_AlarmTime;
```

The SetModifiedFlag() function is invoked to indicate that a property has been modified. We could also invoke the InvalidateControl() function, which would cause the control to be redrawn, if changing the property were to affect the control's appearance. We will use InvalidateControl() later in a timer message to have the time constantly displayed.

Placing Properties on the Property Page Dialog.   Along with the CPNAlarm-ClockCtrl class, AppWizard also generated a CPNAlarmClockPropPage class, which is the class responsible for presenting the property pages for our control to the user. Property pages are the pages that allow you to change a property of a control, such as when you right-click a control in the dialog editor and select the Properties menu item.

We will want to add the AlarmTime property to the property pages, but we will not add the Time property, since the Time property is a read-only, dynamically changing property.

Go to the property page dialog and modify it as shown in Figure 12–23.

- Go into ClassWizard and select the Member Variable tab.
- Make sure that the CPNAlarmClockPropPage class (the property page class for the dialog) is selected in the Class Name field of ClassWizard, and click the Add Variable button.
- Fill out the Add Member Variable dialog like Figure 12–24. Notice how the Option property name field contains the external name of our property.
- Click OK.

Now, when the user of the OCX invokes the properties of the control, he or she will see Figure 12–25.

When this dialog is invoked, the GetAlarmTime() function in the control class is called to initialize the contents of the edit box. When the user changes the value in the edit box and clicks OK or Apply, the SetAlarmTime() will be called, with the contents of the edit box. This calling of GetAlarmTime() and SetAlarmTime() happens automatically, and you don't need to write any code for it.

Adding a Stock Property.   Our ActiveX control will also use the Font stock property for displaying the time. In this section, we will add the property and also add a Font selection page to the Properties dialog.

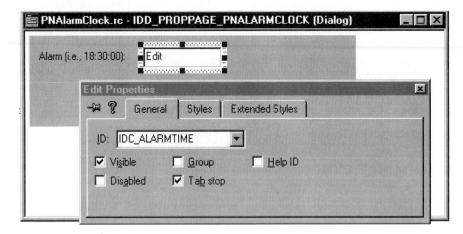

Figure 12–23   Modify the property page of the dialog as shown here.

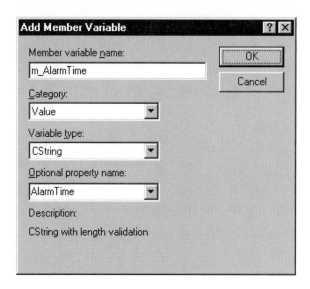

Figure 12–24 Enter information to create a new member variable.

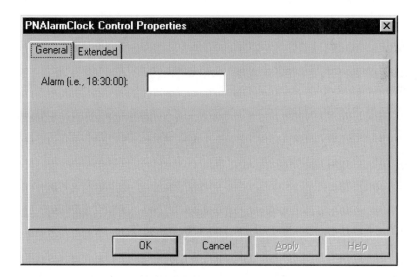

Figure 12–25 Here's what the user sees when selecting the OCX properties of the control.

- Go to ClassWizard, and select the Automation tab.
- Click the Add Property button.
- For the External name field, click the down button and select the Font item.
- Click OK.

We will also want to add a Font selection page to the Properties dialog, so the user can select the font. The MFC framework for ActiveX controls uses an array of property pages that simplify this task for us. In your CPNAlarmClockCtl.cpp file, locate the array of property pages, which should look like Code 12–37.

Code 12–37

```
BEGIN_PROPPAGEIDS(CPNAlarmClockCtrl, 1)
    PROPPAGEID(CPNAlarmClockPropPage::guid)
END_PROPPAGEIDS(CPNAlarmClockCtrl)
```

Make the following changes:

```
BEGIN_PROPPAGEIDS(CPNAlarmClockCtrl, 2) // 2 property pages now
    PROPPAGEID(CPNAlarmClockPropPage::guid)
    PROPPAGEID( CLSID_CFontPropPage ) // The predefined Font property page
END_PROPPAGEIDS(CPNAlarmClockCtrl)
```

You can also add predefined property pages for a color property page and a picture property page by adding Code 12–38. We won't be using these properties in our demo, however.

Code 12–38

```
PROPPAGEID( CLSID_CColorPropPage )
PROPPAGEID( CLSID_CPicturePropPage )
```

When we display the time, we will do so using the Font stock property, with the help of the SelectStockFont() function. That section is coming up soon.

Saving Property Values. In Visual C++, when you add an ActiveX control to a form or dialog and set various properties, if you save the project and then reload it later, those same properties are still there. These are referred to as persistent properties. These same property settings, though not the default for the ActiveX control, will need to be set when the actual program is run.

To complete our work on our properties, we need to add the ability for the ActiveX control to save and load its properties when requested. We will do this work in the CPNAlarmClockCtl class, in the DoPropExchange() function.

DoPropExhchange() is called whenever an ActiveX object should save or load a set of persistent properties. If the properties don't need to be persistent, then no additional work is needed. DoPropExchange() is similar to the CRecordset::DoField Exchange() and CWnd::DoDateExchange() in that it will transfer data to and from the object using a single function call for each piece of data (or property, in our case).

DoPropExchange() calls one of the PX_???? functions, where ???? is the data type of the property. For example, since our AlarmTime property is a string, we would call the PX_String function, such as `PX_String( pPX, "AlarmTime," m_AlarmTime )`, and then set the m_AlarmH, m_AlarmM, and m_AlarmS by calling SetAlarmTime.

Adding an Event.   An ActiveX control can send a notification to its parent in the form of an Event. When you create an event, a function is added to the control class, and any time you want to send that event notification to the parent, you "fire" it, by calling the "fire" function that was added.

- Go to ClassWizard in the ActiveX Events tab.
- Click the Add Event button.
- Fill out the Add Event dialog as shown in Figure 12–26.

Figure 12–26 creates an event named Alarm. It will create a function in your control class named FireAlarm. Anytime you want the control to send this Alarm event to its parent, simply call the FireAlarm() function from within your control code.

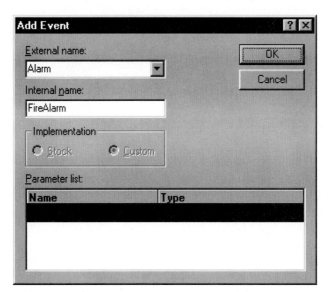

Figure 12–26   Create a new event using the Add Event dialog.

There are also stock events such as Click. We will not be using any of these events in this demonstration.

When a Visual C++ project uses this ActiveX control in a program, it will be able to use ClassWizard's Message Map tab to add handler functions for ActiveX events.

Adding the Time Display and Alarm Ability.   Now that we have the Alarm event added, we want our control to display the current time every second and also to fire the Alarm event when it reaches the designated alarm time. In displaying the time, we must also make sure to use the Stock Font property to display the time in the current font. Modify the CPNAlarmClockCtl::OnDraw() function as shown in Code 12–39.

Code 12-39

```
void CPNAlarmClockCtrl::OnDraw(
                    CDC* pdc, const CRect& rcBounds, const CRect& rcInvalid)
{
        // Set Timer, if not already done
        if( !m_TimerSet )
        {
                m_TimerSet = true;
                SetTimer( 1, 1000, 0 );
        }

        // Clear out control area and draw border
        pdc->FillRect(rcBounds, CBrush::FromHandle((HBRUSH)GetStockObject
        (WHITE_BRUSH)));
        pdc->DrawEdge( (RECT*)&rcBounds, EDGE_SUNKEN, BF_RECT );

        // Select the Stock Font property into the DC
        CFont* pOldFont = SelectStockFont(pdc);

        // Get the current time
        m_Now = CTime::GetCurrentTime();

        // Output the current time
        pdc->TextOut( 4, 4, m_Now.Format( "%I:%M:%S %p" ) );

        // Restore the original font
        pdc->SelectObject( pOldFont );
}
```

The OnDraw() function, note how the m_TimerSet variable is checked. If it is false, then a SetTimer() call is invoked. SetTimer() is invoked so that Windows will send our control window a WM_TIMER message every second.

The FillRect() and DrawEdge() functions are called to erase the window control and redraw its area and border. Since we are going to display the time, we use the SelectStockFont() function to select the stock font on our CDC pointer for display purposes.

The CTime::GetCurrentTime() function is called to get the current time into the m_Now data member, and then TextOut is used to output the m_Now time object as a string (with the help of the CTime::Format() function).

Finally, we put back the original font as it was before we called SelectStockFont(), using SelectObject.

You need to add the following (Code 12–40) data members to the CPNAlarm-ClockCtl class.

Code 12–40

```
bool m_TimerSet;
CTime m_Now;
```

We also need to add a handler for the WM_TIMER message. The time was set to go off every second, by the OnDraw() function. Using ClassWizard's Message Map tab, add a handler to the CPNAlarmClockCtl class for the WM_TIMER windows message. Once you have done this, the Code 12–41 is added to your project. Modify this function to look like Code 12–42.

Code 12–41

```
void CPNAlarmClockCtrl::OnTimer(UINT nIDEvent)
{
        COleControl::OnTimer(nIDEvent);
}
```

Code 12–42

```
void CPNAlarmClockCtrl::OnTimer(UINT nIDEvent)
{
        // Force control to be redrawn, to display new time
        InvalidateControl();

        // Check to see if new time is the Alarm Time
        m_Now = CTime::GetCurrentTime();
        if( m_Now.GetHour() == m_AlarmH && m_Now.GetMinute()==m_AlarmM
        && m_Now.GetSecond()==m_AlarmS )
                FireAlarm(); // If so, fire the Alarm Event
        COleControl::OnTimer(nIDEvent);
}
```

Now, we can see that every second (in response to the WM_TIMER message), this code will invalidate the control forcing OnDraw() to be called again. It will also get the current time and see if it matches the hour, minute, and second alarm time. If it does match the alarm time, then the Alarm event is fired by calling FireAlarm().

Our ActiveX Control in the Test Container

If we run the ActiveX Test Control Container program and use the Edit menu choice to add our PNAlarmClock control, we can change the properties to set the AlarmTime and the font. In Figure 12–27, we changed the font to a Times New Roman font and set the alarm time to 14:44:15 (2:44:15 PM). Note the bottom window (see Figure 12–27) where it displays events such as the font being changed and the Alarm event being fired.

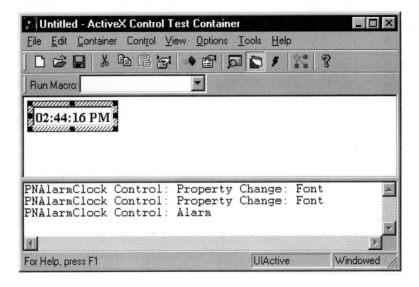

Figure 12–27   Events appear in the bottom window.

OLE Automation

OLE Automation, which is built on COM, is where the COM server is typically a complete application and not a small control as in an ActiveX object. An OLE Automation server program will expose its abilities through the COM system for other applications to use.

MS Word is an example of an Automation server that does this. We can write a Visual C++ program to load a Word document and print it, using OLE Automation. We will write a quick simple program to do just this and will also demonstrate how to use a Type Library to generate wrapper classes in C++ for the COM interfaces that Word supports.

Creating the Project

Using AppWizard, create a dialog-based application. In the MFC AppWizard Step 2 of 4 dialog, make sure you check the Automation checkbox. Modify the main dialog, so that it looks like Figure 12–28. The new controls are defined in Table 12.10.

Using ClassWizard and the Message Map tab, add a handler for the Browse button as shown in Code 12–43.

Table 12.10   Definition of New Controls

Control Type	Control ID	Caption
STATIC	IDC_STATIC	File
Edit	IDC_FILENAME	
Button	IDC_BROWSE	&Browse...
Button	IDC_PRINT	Print

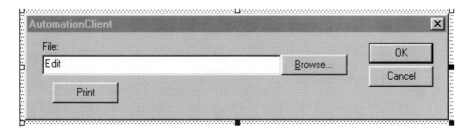

Figure 12–28   The main dialog should look like this.

Code 12-43

```
void CAutomationClientDlg::OnBrowse()
{
        CFileDialog FileDlg( TRUE );

        if( FileDlg.DoModal() == IDOK )
                SetDlgItemText( IDC_FILENAME, FileDlg.GetPathName() );
}
```

Using the Word Type Library

Here, we will create the wrapper classes for the COM objects from Microsoft Word, using its type library. A type library is a file that is distributed with COM servers that expose their COM interfaces. Visual Studio has the ability to create wrapper classes for the COM interfaces from these type libraries.

To import the Type Library for Word, do the following:

- From ClassWizard, click the Add Class button.
- Select the From a Type Library item from the pop-up menu.
- The Import From Type Library dialog will appear.
- In this dialog, go into your Microsoft Office folder and locate the MS-Word8.olb file (this is the type library for Word 97).

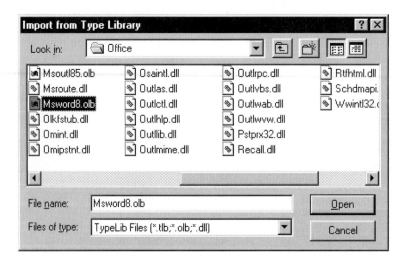

Figure 12-29   Click Open after highlighting the OLB file.

- Highlight the OLB file and click Open as shown in Figure 12–29.

  Visual Studio will now build a list of interfaces found in that type library. There will be many, but we only need the _Application, Documents, and _Document COM interfaces.

- In the Confirm Classes dialog that now appears, select the _Application, _Documents, and Document classes only, and click OK (see Figure 12–30).

Visual C++ will now create the msword8.h and msword8.cpp files with the three wrapper classes we selected. Back in the .cpp file for the dialog (AutomationClient-Dlg.cpp in our demo), add a #include for the msword8.h file as shown in Code 12–44.

Code 12–44

```
#include "msword8.h"
```

Adding the COM Interface Code

Now we will write the code for using our new classes to interface to the COM interfaces in MS Word. Using ClassWizard's Message Map tab, add the following handler for the Print button on our dialog as shown in Code 12–45.

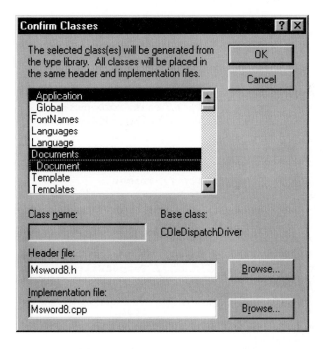

Figure 12–30 Confirm the classes that will be generated.

Code 12–45

```
void CAutomationClientDlg::OnPrint()
{
        _Application MSWord;

        COleVariant vTrue((short)TRUE);
        COleVariant vFalse((short)FALSE);
        COleVariant vOptional((long)DISP_E_PARAMNOTFOUND, VT_ERROR);
        COleVariant vOne(1L);
        CString Filename;
        GetDlgItemText( IDC_FILENAME, Filename );
        COleVariant vFilename( Filename );
        LPDISPATCH Dispatch;

        // Create an instance of the Word Application COM Object
        if (!MSWord.CreateDispatch("Word.Application"))
        {
                MessageBox("Couldn't get Word object.");
                return;
        }
        MSWord.SetVisible(TRUE);   //This shows the application.

        // Create an instance of the Word Documents collection object
        Documents Docs( MSWord.GetDocuments() );

        // Create an instance of the Word Document object
        _Document Doc;

        Dispatch = Docs.Open( vFilename, vFalse,    // Confirm Conversion.
                        vFalse,     // ReadOnly.
                        vFalse,     // AddToRecentFiles.
                        vOptional, // PasswordDocument.
                        vOptional, // PasswordTemplate.
                        vFalse,     // Revert.
                        vOptional, // WritePasswordDocument.
                        vOptional, // WritePasswordTemplate.
                        vOptional); // Format.
        Doc.AttachDispatch( Dispatch );

        Doc.PrintOut(vFalse,                // Background.
                vOptional,          // Append.
                vOptional,          // Range.
                vOptional,          // OutputFileName.
                vOptional,          // From.
                vOptional,          // To.
                vOptional,          // Item.
                vOne,               // Copies.
                vOptional,          // Pages.
                vOptional,          // PageType.
```

```
                    vOptional,          // PrintToFile.
                    vOptional,          // Collate.
                    vOptional,          // ActivePrinterMacGX.
                    vOptional );        // ManualDuplexPrint.

        MSWord.Quit(vFalse,   // SaveChanges.
                    vTrue,    // OriginalFormat.
                    vFalse);  // RouteDocument.

}
```

Code 12–45 performs the following basic steps:

Declares an _Application object named MSWord: This is a wrapper for the Word Application COM interface. It is initialized with the line as shown in Code 12–46. Notice the use of the Program ID, which is passed to the CreateDispatch function.

Code 12–46

```
if (!MSWord.CreateDispatch("Word.Application"))
```

Declares several COleVariant variables: This step is done for convenience. When we call functions via the COM interface wrapper classes, most of them will be passed via a VARIANT data type, and the COleVariant is a helper class for working with VARIANTs.

A Documents object is created: The Documents object is an MS Word Documents collection class. Our Documents class is a wrapper for the COM interface to the Documents collection. The Docs variable is initialized as shown in Code 12–47. This means that the return value of MSWord.GetDocuments, which is an LPDIS-PATCH (long pointer to an IDispatch), is used in the constructor of the Docs object.

Code 12–47

```
Documents Docs( MSWord.GetDocuments() );
```

Document file is opened: Using the Documents::Open() function, we open a word document. When a Documents object opens a Word document, it also returns an LPDISPATCH. This LPDISPATCH is really a COM interface to an MS Word Document object. This LPDISPATCH is saved in the Dispatch variable with the Code 12–48.

Code 12–48

```
Dispatch = Docs.Open( vFilename, vFalse,   // Confirm Conversion.
                      vFalse,    // ReadOnly.
                      vFalse,    // AddToRecentFiles.
```

```
        vOptional, // PasswordDocument.
        vOptional, // PasswordTemplate.
        vFalse,    // Revert.
        vOptional, // WritePasswordDocument.
        vOptional, // WritePasswordTemplate.
        vOptional); // Format.
```

Notice the lengthy parameter list for the Open() function and how we pass our COle-Variant variables to it as needed. Some of the parameters are described as optional; and for those, we pass the vOption variable. We then intialize the Doc variable using the AttachDispatch() function as shown in Code 12–49.

Code 12–49

```
Doc.AttachDispatch( Dispatch );
```

Doing the Printout: Now that we have an MS Word Document COM object that we can work with via our Doc variable, we can invoke the PrintOut() method of that COM object as shown in Code 12–50. Notice the lengthy parameter list and the use of our COleVariant variables.

Code 12–50

```
Doc.PrintOut(vFalse,          // Background.
        vOptional,            // Append.
        vOptional,            // Range.
        vOptional,            // OutputFileName.
        vOptional,            // From.
        vOptional,            // To.
        vOptional,            // Item.
        vOne,                 // Copies.
        vOptional,            // Pages.
        vOptional,            // PageType.
        vOptional,            // PrintToFile.
        vOptional,            // Collate.
        vOptional,            // ActivePrinterMacGX.
        vOptional );          // ManualDuplexPrint.
```

Closing the COM server: Once the printout has been done, we don't need the MS Word server anymore. We quit the COM server for MS Word by calling the Quit function of the _Application object as shown in Code 12–51.

Code 12–51

```
MSWord.Quit(vFalse,   // SaveChanges.
        vTrue,    // OriginalFormat.
        vFalse);  // RouteDocument.
```

Knowing What Is Available

One of the most perplexing issues in dealing with a COM server like MS Word is trying to identify what features or functions are available for you to use. For example, how did we know to call the PrintOut() function?

The answer is that it will depend on each Automation server. In the case of MS Word, the use of the VB programmer's online help will detail the objects and methods that are provided. While they won't specifically describe them as COM objects, we assume that they are because MS Word is an Automation server.

In other server programs, you may be lucky enough to find documentation specific to using the program via COM. And you can always look at the code generated by importing the type library and "hack" it out yourself.

Debugging COM, ActiveX, and DLLs

Debugging a COM server, ActiveX control, or DLL is different than debugging a typical application because they don't really do anything on their own. You must have a second client or container program that use them in order to have their code executed.

Visual Studio has a method for debugging these types of projects by specifying some other executable file as the executable for the debug session. That executable will be run, and it should be a program that uses functionality of your COM/ActiveX/DLL project.

In your COM/ActiveX/DLL project:

- Go to the Project menu choice and select Settings.
- Make sure that the Debug tab is selected.
- Make sure that General is selected in the Category combo box.
- You can specify the executable name to be used to test your project in the Executable for Debug session field. The button to the right of this field lets you select three options as shown in Table 12.11.

Table 12.11   Definition of Options Available from the Button

Option	Meaning
Browse	Lets you select any executable file.
ActiveX Test Control Container	Uses the ActiveXTest Control Container program, a tool in Visual Studio that lets you interactively work with ActiveX controls, changing their properties, invoking methods, and seeing events.
Default Web Browser	Uses your web browser as the test program.

Once you have specified the debugging executable, when you run the program in debug mode, that executable is started. It is assumed that the executable makes the call into your COM/ActiveX/DLL project. If you set breakpoints within your source code, you will now be able to reach them and watch your code execute (see Figure 12–31).

Set the breakpoints with the source code so you can watch your code execute.

The ActiveX Test Control Container is also accessible from the Tools menu choice. It lets you drop an ActiveX control on a form and then examine or change its properties, invoke its methods, or indicate when the control fires an event.

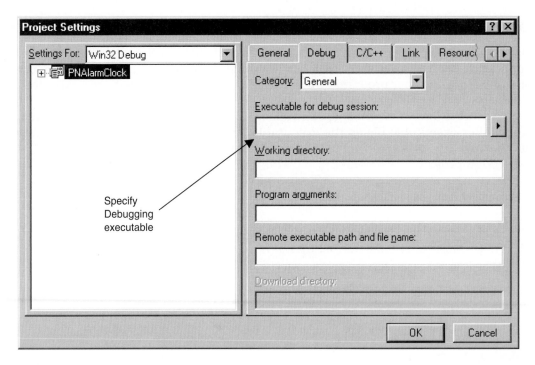

Figure 12–31   Set the breakpoint in your source code.

Remember

○	ActiveX controls can be created with either MFC or ATL.
	Using an ActiveX control is done by adding it to your project with the project menu item.
	ActiveX controls and COM object properties are really a set of get and set/put functions in Visual C++.
○	Using ClassWizard to import type libraries will greatly simplify your job of working with automation servers.
	To add MFC support to exe-type COM servers you should first create a normal MFC application and then add an ATL COM object to it.
○	To debug COM objects, set the Executable name to a test exe file in project settings, and/or use the ActiveX test container program.

Appendix

The CPNImageButton Class

The CPNImageButton class is an MFC class that extends the abilities of the normal CButton by allowing you to specify both an image and text to appear on the button. Once you have these class files, you can simply add them to any project, then create a member variable of CPNImageButton type for a button using ClassWizard's Member Variable tab. You can specify what image a button is to use by calling the SetData function:

```
BOOL SetData( BOOL ImageOnLeft, UINT IDUp, UINT IDDown=0, UINT IDFocus=0,
              UINT IDDisabled=0);
```

Parameter	Meaning
ImageOnLeft	If true, image appears on left of text; otherwise, it appears on the right.
IDUp	The ID of a bitmap resource to display in the button.
IDDown	The ID of a bitmap resource to display the button in a "down" state. If zero, then the same image as IDUp is used.
IDFocus	The ID of a bitmap resource to display the button in a "focused" state. If zero, then the same image as IDUp is used.
IDDisabled	The ID of a bitmap resource to display in the button in a "disabled" state. If zero, then a greyed version of the IDUp image is used.

PNImageButton.h

```
#if
!defined(AFX_PNIMAGEBUTTON_H__D6751986_DDBD_11D3_9F4A_080009EE62AA__
INCLUDED_)
#define AFX_PNIMAGEBUTTON_H__D6751986_DDBD_11D3_9F4A_080009EE62AA__
INCLUDED_

#if _MSC_VER > 1000
#pragma once
#endif // _MSC_VER > 1000
// PNImageButton.h : header file
//
```

```
////////////////////////////////////////////////////////////////////////
// CPNImageButton window

class CPNImageButton : public CButton
{
// Construction
public:
        CPNImageButton();

// Attributes
public:

// Operations
public:

// Overrides
        // ClassWizard generated virtual function overrides
        //{{AFX_VIRTUAL(CPNImageButton)
        //}}AFX_VIRTUAL

// Implementation
public:
        BOOL SetData( BOOL ImageOnLeft, UINT IDUp, UINT IDDown=0, UINT
        IDFocus=0,
                UINT IDDisabled=0);
        void DrawTransparent(CDC* pDC, int x, int y, CBitmap* hbmImage,
                BOOL LowerLeft=TRUE, COLORREF crColor=0);
        void Emboss( CBitmap& Dest, CBitmap& bmSource );
        void DrawItem(LPDRAWITEMSTRUCT lpDrawItemStruct);

        // Bitmaps for image display
        CBitmap m_Up, m_Down, m_Focus, m_Disabled;
        // Bitmap height and width information
        int m_ImageWidth, m_ImageHeight;
        // Flag for image on left or right
        BOOL m_ImageOnLeft;

        virtual ~CPNImageButton();

        // Generated message map functions
protected:
        //{{AFX_MSG(CPNImageButton)
        //}}AFX_MSG
        DECLARE_MESSAGE_MAP()
};
```

PNImageButton.cpp

//

```cpp
//{{AFX_INSERT_LOCATION}}
// Microsoft Visual C++ will insert additional declarations immediately
before the previous line.

#endif //
!defined(AFX_PNIMAGEBUTTON_H__D6751986_DDBD_11D3_9F4A_080009EE62AA__
INCLUDED_)

// PNImageButton.cpp : implementation file
//

#include "stdafx.h"
#include "MFC_Controls.h"
#include "CPNImageButton.h"

#ifdef _DEBUG
#define new DEBUG_NEW
#undef THIS_FILE
static char THIS_FILE[] = __FILE__;
#endif

////////////////////////////////////////////////////////////////////////
// CPNImageButton

CPNImageButton::CPNImageButton()
{
    m_ImageOnLeft = TRUE;
    m_ImageWidth = m_ImageHeight = 0;
}

CPNImageButton::~CPNImageButton()
{
    if( m_Up.GetSafeHandle() )
        m_Up.DeleteObject();
    if( m_Down.GetSafeHandle() )
        m_Down.DeleteObject();
    if( m_Focus.GetSafeHandle() )
        m_Focus.DeleteObject();
    if( m_Disabled.GetSafeHandle() )
        m_Disabled.DeleteObject();

}

BEGIN_MESSAGE_MAP(CPNImageButton, CButton)
    //{{AFX_MSG_MAP(CPNImageButton)
    //}}AFX_MSG_MAP
```

```
END_MESSAGE_MAP()

//////////////////////////////////////////////////////////////////////
// CPNImageButton message handlers

void CPNImageButton::DrawItem(LPDRAWITEMSTRUCT lpDrawItemStruct)
{
    CRect Rect = lpDrawItemStruct->rcItem;
    SIZE DrawArea;
    int XOffset, YOffset, YTextOffset=0, YImageOffset=0;
    UINT nOffset = 0;
    UINT nFrameStyle=0;
    int nStateFlag;
    CBitmap* pImage;

    CString Text;

    CDC DestDC;
    DestDC.Attach( lpDrawItemStruct->hDC );

    // Based on the size of the button text, and the images, determine drawing
    // positions of each.
    GetWindowText( Text );
    DrawArea  = DestDC.GetTextExtent(Text);
    DrawArea.cx += (m_ImageWidth+4);
    if( DrawArea.cy > m_ImageHeight )
        YTextOffset = ( m_ImageHeight - DrawArea.cy ) /2;
    else
    {
        YImageOffset = (DrawArea.cy - m_ImageHeight) /2;
        DrawArea.cy = m_ImageHeight;
    }
    if( Text.Find( "&" ) >= 0 )
    {
        CSize Tmp;
        Tmp = DestDC.GetTextExtent( "&" );
        DrawArea.cx -= Tmp.cx;
    }
    XOffset = (Rect.right - DrawArea.cx)/2;
    YOffset = (Rect.bottom - DrawArea.cy)/2;

    // Determine if button is in the selected state
    if ( lpDrawItemStruct->itemState & ODS_SELECTED)
    {
        nFrameStyle = DFCS_PUSHED;
        pImage = m_Down.GetSafeHandle() ? &m_Down : &m_Up;
        nOffset += 1;
    }
```

```
// Determine if button is disabled
if( lpDrawItemStruct->itemState & ODS_DISABLED )
{
    nStateFlag = DSS_DISABLED;
    pImage = m_Disabled.GetSafeHandle() ? &m_Disabled : &m_Up;
}
else
{
    nStateFlag = DSS_NORMAL;
    pImage = &m_Up;
}


// Determine if button has the focus state
if ( lpDrawItemStruct->itemState & ODS_FOCUS )
    pImage = m_Focus.GetSafeHandle() ? &m_Focus : &m_Up;

// If button is selected, the use DrawFrameControl to display its frame
if( ! (lpDrawItemStruct->itemState & ODS_SELECTED) )
{
    // If the button is focused, then we need to draw the black
    rectangle,
    // and shrink the button a tiny bit (visual appearance of all
    buttons)
    if( lpDrawItemStruct->itemState & ODS_FOCUS  )
    {
            DestDC.Rectangle(Rect.left, Rect.top, Rect.right, Rect.bottom );
            Rect.DeflateRect(1,1);
    }
    DestDC.DrawFrameControl( &Rect, DFC_BUTTON, DFCS_BUTTONPUSH |
    nFrameStyle);
}
else
{
    // If its not selected, then drawing is more complex
    // Create out pens and brushes for drawing, and draw a rectangle.
    CBrush NewBrush;
    NewBrush.CreateSolidBrush( ::GetSysColor( COLOR_3DFACE ) );
    CBrush* pOldBrush = (CBrush*)DestDC.SelectObject( &NewBrush );
    DestDC.Rectangle(Rect.left, Rect.top, Rect.right, Rect.bottom );
    CPen NewPen;
    NewPen.CreatePen( PS_SOLID, 1, GetSysColor(COLOR_3DSHADOW) );
    CPen* pOldPen = (CPen*)DestDC.SelectObject( &NewPen );

    // Then, shrink the rectangle a tiny bit, and draw the inner
    rectangle
    Rect.left++;
    Rect.top++;
    Rect.bottom--;
    Rect.right--;
```

```
        DestDC.Rectangle( Rect.left, Rect.top, Rect.right, Rect.bottom  );
        DestDC.SelectObject( pOldPen );
        DestDC.SelectObject( pOldBrush );

    }

    if( m_ImageOnLeft )
    {
        // Draw the bitmap image, transparently, and then the text
        DrawTransparent( &DestDC, XOffset+nOffset, YOffset+nOffset+
        YImageOffset, pImage );
        DestDC.DrawState( CPoint(XOffset+m_ImageWidth+4+nOffset,
        YOffset+nOffset+YTextOffset),
                DrawArea, Text, DST_PREFIXTEXT|nStateFlag, TRUE, 0, (HBRUSH)0  );
    }
    else
    {
        // Draw the text, and then the bitmap image transparently
        DestDC.DrawState( CPoint(XOffset+nOffset, YOffset+nOffset+
        YTextOffset), DrawArea,
                Text, DST_PREFIXTEXT|nStateFlag, TRUE, 0, (HBRUSH)0  );
        DrawTransparent( &DestDC, XOffset+nOffset+DrawArea.cx+m_ImageWidth,
        YOffset+nOffset+YImageOffset, pImage );
    }

    // Draw the focus rectangle for the button
    if( ( lpDrawItemStruct->itemState & ODS_FOCUS ) )
    {
        RECT Rect2;
        Rect2 = Rect;
        Rect2.left += 3;
        Rect2.right -= 3;
        Rect2.top += 3;
        Rect2.bottom -= 3;
        DestDC.DrawFocusRect( &Rect2 );
    }
    DestDC.Detach();

// CButton::OnDrawItem(nIDCtl, lpDrawItemStruct);
}

// CPNImageButton::SetData - Sets image information for the CPNImageButton
class
//      ImageOnLeft - If TRUE then image appears to left of text, otherwise
        image appears to the right
//      IDUp - Must specified the ID for the bitmap to display when in the
        normal, 'Up' state.
//      IDDown - Specifies the image to use for the down state of the
        button.  May be zero.
```

```
//        IDFocus - Specifies the image to use for the focus state of the
          button.  May be zero.
//        IDDisabled - Specifies the image to use for the disabled state of
          the button.  May be zero.
// Returns: TRUE if successful, FALSE if not
// Comments: If IDDown or IDFocus are zero, then the Up image is used for
   those states.  If the
//        IDDisabled value is zero, then an embossed version of the up image
          is created and used.
BOOL CPNImageButton::SetData(BOOL ImageOnLeft, UINT IDUp, UINT IDDown, UINT
IDFocus, UINT IDDisabled)
{
    // If button already has data loaded, then delete the bitmaps
    if( m_Up.GetSafeHandle() )
        m_Up.DeleteObject();
    if( m_Down.GetSafeHandle() )
        m_Down.DeleteObject();
    if( m_Focus.GetSafeHandle() )
        m_Focus.DeleteObject();
    if( m_Disabled.GetSafeHandle() )
        m_Disabled.DeleteObject();

    // Load the 'Up' state bitmap (required).  Use it to specify height and
    width of all images
    m_Up.LoadBitmap( IDUp );
    BITMAP BM;
    m_Up.GetObject( sizeof(BM), &BM );
    m_ImageHeight = BM.bmHeight;
    m_ImageWidth = BM.bmWidth;

    // Store the ImageOnLeft value
    m_ImageOnLeft = ImageOnLeft;

    // Load other bitmaps as needed
    if( IDDown )
        m_Down.LoadBitmap( IDDown );
    if( IDFocus )
        m_Focus.LoadBitmap( IDFocus );

    // If a disabled image was specified, then load it, otherwise create an
    embossed version
    // of the 'Up ' image.
    if( IDDisabled )
        m_Disabled.LoadBitmap( IDDisabled );
    else
        Emboss( m_Disabled, m_Up );

    return(TRUE);
}
```

```
// DrawTransparent - Draws a bitmap with transparency
// Parameters:
//     DC - HDC to draw bitmap on
//     x - X coordinate on DC to draw bitmap at
//     y - Y coordinate on DC to draw bitmap at
//     hbmImage - Handle to bitmap to display
//     LowerLeft - If True, then transparency color is taken from lower
//        left of bitmap
//     crColor - If LowerLeft is false, then this must specify transparent
//        color for bitmap
void CPNImageButton::DrawTransparent(CDC* pDC, int x, int y, CBitmap*
hbmImage, BOOL LowerLeft, COLORREF crColor)
{
    CDC hdcImage;
    CDC hdcTrans;
    CBitmap hbmTrans;
    BITMAP bmBitmap;

    hbmImage->GetObject( sizeof(bmBitmap), &bmBitmap );
    // Change Background and text color, saving values for end
    COLORREF crOldBack = pDC->SetBkColor(RGB(255,255,255));
    COLORREF crOldText = pDC->SetTextColor(RGB(0,0,0) );

    // Create Memory DCs to do our work in
    hdcImage.CreateCompatibleDC(pDC);
    hdcTrans.CreateCompatibleDC(pDC);

    // Select passed Image bitmap into Image memory DC
    hdcImage.SelectObject(hbmImage);

    // Create transparent bitmap, and select into transparent DC
    hbmTrans.CreateBitmap( bmBitmap.bmWidth, bmBitmap.bmHeight, 1, 1, NULL);
    hdcTrans.SelectObject( hbmTrans);

    // If LowerLeft is true, then determine transparent color from bitmap
    passed
    if( LowerLeft )
        crColor = hdcImage.GetPixel( 0, bmBitmap.bmHeight-1 );

    // Select background color (transparent color) for our image memory DC
    hdcImage.SetBkColor(crColor);
    hdcTrans.BitBlt( 0, 0, bmBitmap.bmWidth, bmBitmap.bmHeight, &hdcImage,
    0, 0, SRCCOPY);

    // Perform BitBlt operations (this is where the Masking occurs)
    pDC->BitBlt( x, y, bmBitmap.bmWidth, bmBitmap.bmHeight, &hdcImage, 0, 0,
    SRCINVERT);
    pDC->BitBlt( x, y, bmBitmap.bmWidth, bmBitmap.bmHeight, &hdcTrans, 0, 0,
    SRCAND);
```

```
    pDC->BitBlt( x, y, bmBitmap.bmWidth, bmBitmap.bmHeight, &hdcImage, 0, 0,
    SRCINVERT);

    // Retore original background and text colors for the passed DC
    pDC->SetBkColor(crOldBack);
    pDC->SetTextColor(crOldText);
}


// Emboss - Basic embossing ability
// Parameters:
//      bmDest - Destination bitmap
//      bmSource - Source bitmap to be embossed
// Comments: Uses brute force so we can maintain 3 colors on a disabled
bitmap:
//    the highlight, dark, and transparent colors
void CPNImageButton::Emboss( CBitmap& Dest, CBitmap& bmSource )
{
    CDC memDC, memDCEmbossed;
    CBitmap hbmOldBM, hbmOldBMEmbossed;
    BITMAP bmInfo;
    COLORREF crTransparent, crLo =
::GetSysColor(COLOR_3DHILIGHT),crHi=::GetSysColor(COLOR_3DSHADOW);
    COLORREF crCur, crNewTransparent = ::GetSysColor( COLOR_3DFACE );
    int Row, Col, ColorAvg=0, Total=0;

    // Determine information for the bitmap passed
    bmSource.GetObject( sizeof(bmInfo), &bmInfo );

    // Create memory DCs, and the return bitmap, for drawing and creation
    memDC.CreateCompatibleDC(NULL);
    memDCEmbossed.CreateCompatibleDC(NULL);
    memDC.SelectObject(&bmSource );
    Dest.CreateCompatibleBitmap( &memDC, bmInfo.bmWidth, bmInfo.bmHeight );

    // Select the new bitmap into the memory DC.  Now, when we draw on the
    memory DC, it
    // will manipulate the bitmap that is selected into it.
    memDCEmbossed.SelectObject( Dest );

    // Perform some basic color analisys, to determine what colors to use
    crTransparent = memDC.GetPixel( 0, bmInfo.bmHeight-1 );
    for( Row=0; Row < bmInfo.bmHeight; Row++ )
        for( Col=0; Col < bmInfo.bmWidth; Col++ )
        {
          crCur = memDC.GetPixel( Row, Col );
          if( crCur != crTransparent )
          {
            ColorAvg+=(GetGValue(crCur)+GetBValue(crCur)+GetRValue(crCur));
            Total++;
```

```
            }
        }
    ColorAvg /= Total;

    // Draw the original bitmap into the memory DC, which will set the color
    depth and
    // dimensions of the new bitmap.
    memDCEmbossed.BitBlt( 0, 0, bmInfo.bmWidth, bmInfo.bmHeight, &memDC, 0,
    0, SRCCOPY);

    // Now, go through each pixel, and make it one of 3 colors: Dark, light,
    and transparent
    for( Row=0; Row < bmInfo.bmHeight; Row++ )
        for( Col=0; Col < bmInfo.bmWidth; Col++ )
        {
            crCur = memDC.GetPixel( Col, Row );
            if( crCur != crTransparent )
            {
                if( (GetGValue(crCur)+GetBValue(crCur)+GetRValue(crCur)) >
                ColorAvg )
                    memDCEmbossed.SetPixel( Col, Row, crHi);
                else
                    memDCEmbossed.SetPixel( Col, Row, crLo);
            }
            else
                memDCEmbossed.SetPixel( Col, Row, crNewTransparent );
        }
    // Destructors clean up for us.
}
```

The CPNSocket Class

The CPNSocket class is designed as a replacement for CSocket, which permits easy
socket communications with a selectable time-out period. It is used by the Mailer
demonstration program to implement an SMTP and POP3 class for sending and receiving emails. The class serves as the base class for the CPNCommandSocket,
CPNSMTP, and CPNPOP3 socket classes.

PNSocket.h

```
// PNSocket.h: interface for the CPNSocket class.
//
/////////////////////////////////////////////////////////////////////

#if !defined(AFX_PNSOCKET_H__1A3533C8_EA58_11D3_9F5C_080009EE62AA__
INCLUDED_)
```

```cpp
#define AFX_PNSOCKET_H__1A3533C8_EA58_11D3_9F5C_080009EE62AA__INCLUDED_

#if _MSC_VER > 1000
#pragma once
#endif // _MSC_VER > 1000
#pragma warning(disable: 4786)
#include <map>
// disable warning C4786: symbol greater than 255 character,
// okay to ignore

using namespace std;

// The CPNSocket class
class CPNSocket
{
public:
    CPNSocket( int nFamily=AF_INET, int nType=SOCK_STREAM, int nProtocol=0 );
    CPNSocket( const CPNSocket& msSrc ); // Copy Constructor
    ~CPNSocket();

    int Close();
    // Socket operations (Client)
    int Connect( struct sockaddr * sapSrvrAdrs, int nLenAddr ) const;
    int Connect( const char* szHostAddr, short sPort  ) const;

    // Socket operation (Server)
    int Bind( struct sockaddr * sapSrvrAdrs, int nLenAddr ) const;
    int Bind( int nPort, int nFamily=AF_INET, int nAddr=INADDR_ANY) const;
    int Listen( int nBackLog=5 ) const;
    int Server( int nPort ) const; // Helper Function
    int Accept( CPNSocket& msrRet, struct sockaddr* sapClientAddr=0, int*
    npLen=0 ) const;

    // Atributes for normal- or exception-mode error reporting
    static bool m_bThrowException;
    static bool SetExceptions( bool bMode );

    // Operators
    CPNSocket& operator=( CPNSocket& msrSrc );
    CPNSocket& operator=( int Socket );

    // I/O functions
    int SetTimeOut( int MilliSeconds );
    int Receive( char *cpDest, int nSize, char Term='\r' ) const;
    int CPNSocket::ReceiveLine( char *cpDest, int nSize ) const;
    int Send( const char *cpSrc, int Len ) const;
    int SendLine( const char* cpSrc, char Term='\n' ) const;

    // Helper functions
    void ThrowErrMsg( const char* cpMsg, int nCode=0 ) const;
```

```cpp
    void ThrowErrMsg( const char* cpMsg, const char* cpInfo ) const {
    ThrowErrMsg( cpMsg, (int) cpInfo); }
    static bool WasConTermErr( const char* ErrMsg );
    const char* CPNSocket::GetErrMsg() const;

    // Typecast operator, so you can use this class anywhere you need a
    normal socket handle.
    operator int() { return( m_nSocket ); }
protected:
    SOCKET m_nSocket;
    long m_nTimeOut;
    char HostName[128];
    enum toMode { toRead, toWrite, toError };
    int TimedOut( toMode Mode ) const;

    // Support for reference counting, using STL map class
    static map<int,int> RefCount;
    void IncRef()
    { if( RefCount.find( m_nSocket )!=RefCount.end() ) RefCount[m_nSocket]++;
    else RefCount[m_nSocket]=1; }
    void DecRef()
    { if( RefCount.find( m_nSocket )!=RefCount.end() ) RefCount[m_nSocket]--; }
    bool GetRef()
    { return( RefCount.find(m_nSocket)!=RefCount.end()?
(RefCount[m_nSocket]?true:false): false ); }

};

#endif // !defined(AFX_MSOCKET_H__1A3533C8_EA58_11D3_9F5C_080009EE62AA__
INCLUDED_)

PNSocket.cpp
// PNSocket.cpp: implementation of the CCPNSocket class.
//
//////////////////////////////////////////////////////////////////////
// disable warning C4786: symbol greater than 255 character,
// okay to ignore
#pragma warning(disable: 4786)

#include "stdafx.h"
#include "PNSocket.h"
// disable warning C4786: symbol greater than 255 character,
// okay to ignore
#pragma warning(disable: 4786)

#ifdef _DEBUG
#undef THIS_FILE
static char THIS_FILE[]=__FILE__;
```

```
#define new DEBUG_NEW
#endif

//////////////////////////////////////////////////////////////////
// Construction/Destruction
//////////////////////////////////////////////////////////////////

// Common error strings, to save some space
static char ErrNotInit[] = "Socket not initialized";
static char ErrConTerm[] = "Connection terminated";
static char ErrTimedOut[]= "Connection timed out";

// m_szErrMsg is not part of the class, because of the const functions
throwing exceptions
// might modify it.  Size is probably overkill.  Unfortunately, my g++
compiler doesn't
// support the sstream class.
static char m_szErrMsg[256];

// Statics for the class
bool CPNSocket::m_bThrowException = true;
map<int,int> CPNSocket::RefCount;

/////////////////////////////////////// Start of the CPNSocket class
functions

// Constructors
CPNSocket::CPNSocket( int nFamily, int nType, int nProtocol )
{
    m_nTimeOut=10000;
    // Try to intialize the CPNSocket, using the socket system call
    m_nSocket = ::socket( nFamily, nType, nProtocol );
    if( m_nSocket < 0 && m_bThrowException ) // If an error, and we should
    throw it
        ThrowErrMsg( "socket() call failed: %d", m_nSocket );
    if( m_nSocket >= 0 )
        IncRef();
}

// Copy constructor
CPNSocket::CPNSocket( const CPNSocket& msrSrc )
{
    m_nTimeOut=10000;
    m_nSocket = msrSrc.m_nSocket;
    IncRef();
}
// Destructor
CPNSocket::~CPNSocket()
{
```

```
        if( m_nSocket >= 0 )
            Close();
}


// Closes socket, but pays attention to reference counting
int CPNSocket::Close()
{
    int Ret = m_nSocket;
    if( Ret < 0 && m_bThrowException )
        ThrowErrMsg( "Close called on a closed socket" );
    if( Ret > 0 )
    {
        DecRef();
        if( !GetRef() )
            closesocket( m_nSocket );
        m_nSocket = -1;
    }
    return( Ret );
}


// Connect - Establishes a socket connection to a server
BOOL CPNSocket::Connect( struct sockaddr * sapSrvrAdrs, int nLenAddr )
const
{
    if( m_nSocket < 0 )
    {
        if( m_bThrowException ) // If not setup correctly
            ThrowErrMsg( ErrNotInit );
        return(FALSE);
    }

    // Call the connect system function to actually do connect.
    int Ret = ::connect( m_nSocket, (struct sockaddr*)sapSrvrAdrs, nLenAddr );
    if( Ret==SOCKET_ERROR )
    {
        if( m_bThrowException )
            ThrowErrMsg( "connect() failed", WSAGetLastError() );
        return( FALSE );
    }

    if( TimedOut(toWrite) )
    {
        if( m_bThrowException )
            ThrowErrMsg( "connect timed out" );
        return(FALSE);
    }

    if( Ret < 0 && m_bThrowException ) // If there was an error, and we
    should throw it.
```

```
        ThrowErrMsg( "connect() failed: %d", Ret );
    return( Ret==0?TRUE:FALSE );

}
// Overloaded Connection function, easier to call then previous version
int CPNSocket::Connect( const char* cpHostAddr, short sPort ) const
{
    // Setup and init the sock_addr_in struct, needed by real connect function
    struct sockaddr_in SrvrAdrs;
    memset( &SrvrAdrs, 0, sizeof( SrvrAdrs ) );

    // If szHostAddr looks like '127.0.0.1' then it's easy, just
    // call inet_addr to convert the string into a netword address ID integer
    if( isdigit(cpHostAddr[0]) )
        SrvrAdrs.sin_addr.s_addr = inet_addr( cpHostAddr );
    else
    {
        // Otherwise, it may be a host name.  Get its IP address and use that.
        // For example, szHostAddr may be www.acme.com
        struct hostent * pHostEnt = gethostbyname( cpHostAddr );
         if( pHostEnt == NULL )
        {
            if( m_bThrowException )
                ThrowErrMsg( "Unable to determine IP for '%s'", cpHostAddr );
            return( -1 );
        }
        SrvrAdrs.sin_addr.s_addr = *(long*)pHostEnt->h_addr_list[0];
    }
    SrvrAdrs.sin_family = AF_INET;
    // Call htons, to convert out local pc short to format compatible with
    the 'net'
    SrvrAdrs.sin_port = htons( sPort );
    // finally, call the other version of Connect, with the struct we set up
    return( Connect( (struct sockaddr*) &SrvrAdrs , (int)sizeof( SrvrAdrs ) ) );
}

// Bind Function
int CPNSocket::Bind( struct sockaddr* sapMyAddr, int nAddrLen ) const
{
    if( m_nSocket < 0 )
    {
        if( m_bThrowException ) // If not setup correctly
            ThrowErrMsg( ErrNotInit );
        return(-1);
    }
    // Call the bind system function to actually do connect.
    int Ret = ::bind( m_nSocket, sapMyAddr, nAddrLen );
    if( Ret < 0 && m_bThrowException ) // If there was an error, and we
    should throw it.
```

```
        ThrowErrMsg( "bind() failed: %d", Ret );
    return( Ret );
}


// Overloaded Bind function, is easier to call then previous
int CPNSocket::Bind( int nPort, int nFamily, int nAddr ) const
{
    struct sockaddr_in SrvrAdrs;
    memset( &SrvrAdrs, 0, sizeof( SrvrAdrs ) );
    SrvrAdrs.sin_family = nFamily;
    SrvrAdrs.sin_addr.s_addr = htonl( nAddr );
    SrvrAdrs.sin_port = htons( nPort );
    // Here, we call our 'other' Bind member function
    return( Bind( (struct sockaddr*)&SrvrAdrs, (int)sizeof( SrvrAdrs ) ) );
}


// Listen - Tells Operating System we are ready to accept connections on a
// socket
int CPNSocket::Listen( int nBackLog ) const
{
    if( m_nSocket < 0 )
    {
        if( m_bThrowException )
            ThrowErrMsg( ErrNotInit );
        return( -1 );
    }
    // Call the system 'listen' function
    int Ret = ::listen( m_nSocket, nBackLog );
    if( Ret < 0 && m_bThrowException )
        ThrowErrMsg( "listen() failed: %d", Ret );
    return( Ret );
}


//Server - Helper function, for writing a Server application
int CPNSocket::Server( int nPort ) const
{
    int Ret;
    Ret = Bind( nPort );
    if( Ret >= 0 )
        Ret = Listen();
    return( Ret );
}


// Accept - Used by servers, to accept a socket connection from a client
int CPNSocket::Accept( CPNSocket& msrRet, struct sockaddr* sapClientAddr,
int* npLen ) const
{
    int MyLen;
    struct sockaddr_in Client;
```

```
    if( sapClientAddr == 0 ) // To make things easier on our caller, we can
    create the struct
    {
        sapClientAddr = (sockaddr*)& Client;
        npLen = &MyLen;
    }
    if( m_nTimeOut && TimedOut(toRead) )
    {
        if( m_bThrowException )
            ThrowErrMsg( "Timed out on Accept" );
        return( -1 );
    }
    // Call the system 'accept' function
    int nRet = ::accept( m_nSocket, sapClientAddr, (int*)npLen );
    if( nRet < 0 && m_bThrowException )
        ThrowErrMsg( "accept failed: %d", nRet );
    msrRet = nRet;
    return( nRet );
}


// Assignment operator, if from another CPNSocket.  Invokes the other
// operator=
CPNSocket& CPNSocket::operator=( CPNSocket& msrSrc )
{
    if( &msrSrc != this ) // Make sure caller didn't to X = X;
        *this = msrSrc.m_nSocket;
    return( *this );
}
// Asignment operator.  Pays attention to reference counting
CPNSocket& CPNSocket::operator=( int nSocket )
{
    if(  nSocket < 0 && m_bThrowException )
        throw "operator= called with bad socket";

    if( m_nSocket >= 0 )
        Close();
    m_nSocket = nSocket;
    IncRef();
    return( *this );
}


// TimedOut - Uses select() to determine if data is ready to be read, or
// written, with timeout period
int CPNSocket::TimedOut( toMode Mode ) const
{
    fd_set fdSet;
    struct timeval TimeToWait;
    TimeToWait.tv_sec = m_nTimeOut / 1000;
    TimeToWait.tv_usec = m_nTimeOut % 1000;
```

```
    FD_ZERO( &fdSet );
    FD_SET( m_nSocket+1, &fdSet );
    int Ret;

    Ret = select( m_nSocket+1, &fdSet, &fdSet, &fdSet, &TimeToWait );

    return( Ret>0?0:1 );
}

// Sets the exception operating mode for the class.  Throw exceptions, or
// return error codes.
bool CPNSocket::SetExceptions( bool bMode )
{
    bool Ret;
    Ret = m_bThrowException;
    m_bThrowException = bMode;
    return( Ret );
}

// Sets the time out for an individual socket.
int CPNSocket::SetTimeOut( int nMilliSeconds )
{
    int Ret = m_nTimeOut;
    m_nTimeOut = nMilliSeconds;
    return( Ret );
}

// Reads data from a socket, a line (CR delimited) or a block
int CPNSocket::Receive( char *cpDest, int nSize, char Term ) const
{
    int ReadIn=0, Stat=0;
    if( m_nSocket < 0 )
    {
        if( m_bThrowException )
            ThrowErrMsg( ErrNotInit );
        return( 0 );
    }

    while( ReadIn < nSize-2 )
    {
        if( m_nTimeOut && TimedOut(toRead) )
        {
            if( m_bThrowException )
                ThrowErrMsg( ErrTimedOut );
            return( 0 );

        }
        Stat = recv( m_nSocket, cpDest+ReadIn, 1, 0 );
        if( Stat < 0 )
```

```
        {
            if( m_bThrowException )
                ThrowErrMsg( Stat==0?ErrConTerm:"ReadLine error: %d", Stat );
            return( 0 );
        }
        if( cpDest[Stat+ReadIn-1]==Term )
                break;
        ReadIn += Stat;
    }
    cpDest[ReadIn+Stat-1]='\0';
    return( ReadIn+Stat );
}

int CPNSocket::ReceiveLine( char *cpDest, int nSize ) const
{
    int Ret=Receive( cpDest, nSize, '\r' );
    if(Ret)
    {
        while( strlen(cpDest)>0 && cpDest[strlen(cpDest)-1]<' ' )
            cpDest[strlen(cpDest)-1]='\0';
        while( strlen(cpDest)>0 && cpDest[0]<' ' )
            memmove( cpDest, cpDest+1, strlen(cpDest));
    }
    return(Ret);
}

// Writes a block of data to a socket
int CPNSocket::Send( const char *cpSrc, int Len ) const
{
    int Written=0;
    if( m_nSocket < 0 )
    {
        if( m_bThrowException )
            ThrowErrMsg( ErrNotInit );
        return( 0 );
    }
    while( Len>0 )
    {
        Written=send( m_nSocket, cpSrc, Len, 0 );
        if( Written <=0 )
        {
                if( m_bThrowException )
                    ThrowErrMsg( Written==0?ErrConTerm:"Writing socket: %d",
                    Written );
                return( 0 );
        }
        cpSrc += Written;
        Len -= Written;
    }
```

```
        return( 1 );
}

// Writes a line of text to a socket, like a string
int CPNSocket::SendLine( const char *cpSrc, char Term ) const
{
    int Written=0, Len;
    Len = strlen(cpSrc);
    if( Term=='\0' ) // If terminator is '\0', include that in data out
        Len++;
    return( Send( cpSrc, Len ) );
}

// ThrowErrMsg - Helper function to create a string, and throw it as an
// exception
void CPNSocket::ThrowErrMsg( const char* cpMsg, int nCode ) const
{
    sprintf( m_szErrMsg, cpMsg, nCode );
    throw m_szErrMsg ;
}

// WasConTermErr - Helper function, to determine if the connection was
// terminated
bool CPNSocket::WasConTermErr( const char* ErrMsg )
{
    return( strcmp(ErrMsg,ErrConTerm)==0);
}

const char* CPNSocket::GetErrMsg() const
{
    static char Msg[128];
    char* pMsg="";
    int ErrCode;

    if( 0 != (ErrCode=WSAGetLastError()) )
    {
      switch( ErrCode )
      {
        case WSAEADDRINUSE:
           pMsg = "The specified address is already in use.";
           break;
        case WSAEADDRNOTAVAIL:
           pMsg = "The specified address is not available from the local
           machine.";
           break;
        case WSAEAFNOSUPPORT:
           pMsg = "Addresses in the specified family cannot be used with
           this socket.";
           break;
        case WSAECONNREFUSED:
```

```
            pMsg = "The attempt to connect was forcefully rejected.";
            break;
        case WSAEDESTADDRREQ:
            pMsg = "A destination address is required.";
            break;
        case WSAEFAULT:
            pMsg = "The lpSockAddrLen argument is incorrect.";
            break;
        case WSAEINVAL:
            pMsg = "The socket is already bound to an address.";
            break;
        case WSAEISCONN:
            pMsg = "The socket is already connected.";
            break;
        case WSAEMFILE:
            pMsg = "No more file descriptors are available.";
            break;
        case WSAENETUNREACH:
            pMsg = "The network cannot be reached from this host at this time.";
            break;
        case WSAENOBUFS:
            pMsg = "No buffer space is available. The socket cannot be
            connected.";
            break;
        case WSAENOTCONN:
            pMsg = "The socket is not connected.";
            break;
        case WSAENOTSOCK:
            pMsg = "The descriptor is a file, not a socket.";
            break;
        case WSAETIMEDOUT:
            pMsg = "The attempt to connect timed out without establishing a
            connection. ";
            break;
        default:
            wsprintf(Msg, "Unknown error: %d", ErrCode);
            pMsg = Msg;
            break;
        }
    }
    return( pMsg );
}
```

The CPNComboBox Class

The CPNComboBox class is an MFC extension class derived from the CcomboBox. It implements behavior similar to that of Explorer: It will provide auto-completion for words in the drop-down list, and it will save and load its string to and from the registry. The HTMLLinks demo program uses it for accessing a URL.

To use the class, simply place a combo box on a form, and then use the ClassWizard Member Variable tab to add a member variable for that control, specifying CPN-ComboBox as the control type. These files must be added to your project.

PNComboBox.h

```
#if !defined(AFX_PNCOMBOBOX_H__C2CFA945_8CBB_11D3_9ECA_080009EE62AA__INCLUDED_)
#define AFX_PNCOMBOBOX_H__C2CFA945_8CBB_11D3_9ECA_080009EE62AA__INCLUDED_

#if _MSC_VER > 1000
#pragma once
#endif // _MSC_VER > 1000
// PNComboBox.h : header file
//


/////////////////////////////////////////////////////////////////////////////
// CPNComboBox window

class CPNComboBox : public CComboBox
{
// Construction
public:
        CPNComboBox();
        bool m_DoLookup; // MG: Do lookup flag

        int AddString( LPCSTR pNewString=0 ); // MG: AddString, to add current string
        to combobox list
// Attributes
public:

// Operations
public:

// Overrides
        // ClassWizard generated virtual function overrides
        //{{AFX_VIRTUAL(CPNComboBox)
        public:
        virtual BOOL PreTranslateMessage(MSG* pMsg);
        protected:
        virtual void PreSubclassWindow();
        //}}AFX_VIRTUAL
```

```
// Implementation
public:
        bool ShouldSave();
        static void SetAllRegistrySave( bool Mode );
        static bool m_RegistrySave;
        void SetThisRegistrySave( bool Mode ) { m_MyRegistrySave=Mode; }
        bool m_MyRegistrySave;
        virtual ~CPNComboBox();

        // Generated message map functions
protected:
        //{{AFX_MSG(CPNComboBox)
        afx_msg void OnDestroy();
        afx_msg void OnEditupdate();
        //}}AFX_MSG

        DECLARE_MESSAGE_MAP()

        bool m_DoPerLookup; // MG: Per-character lookup flag
};

///////////////////////////////////////////////////////////////////////

//{{AFX_INSERT_LOCATION}}
// Microsoft Visual C++ will insert additional declarations immediately before the
previous line.

#endif //
!defined(AFX_MEMORYCOMBOBOX_H__C2CFA945_8CBB_11D3_9ECA_080009EE62AA__INCLUDED_)
```

PNComboBox.cpp

```
// PNComboBox.cpp : implementation file
//

#include "stdafx.h"

#include "PNComboBox.h"

#ifdef _DEBUG
#define new DEBUG_NEW
#undef THIS_FILE
static char THIS_FILE[] = __FILE__;
#endif

///////////////////////////////////////////////////////////////////////
// CPNComboBox
bool CPNComboBox::m_RegistrySave=false;
CPNComboBox::CPNComboBox()
```

```
{
        m_DoLookup = m_DoPerLookup = true;
        m_MyRegistrySave = false;
}


CPNComboBox::~CPNComboBox()
{
}


BEGIN_MESSAGE_MAP(CPNComboBox, CComboBox)
        //{{AFX_MSG_MAP(CPNComboBox)
        ON_WM_DESTROY()
        ON_CONTROL_REFLECT(CBN_EDITUPDATE, OnEditupdate)
        //}}AFX_MSG_MAP
END_MESSAGE_MAP()

/////////////////////////////////////////////////////////////////////
// CPNComboBox message handlers

void CPNComboBox::PreSubclassWindow()
{
        if( ShouldSave()  ) // Should we load strings from registry?
        {
                CString Value;
                CString Family, Setting;
                int j, DialogID, ID;
                CWinApp* pApp = AfxGetApp();

                // determine ID for parent dialog and this combobox control
                DialogID = GetParent()->GetDlgCtrlID();
                ID = GetDlgCtrlID();
                // Set registry key for this specific dialog
                Family.Format( "PNComboBox%d", DialogID );
                j=0;
                do {
                        // Load each string from the dialogs settings (for this
                        // control)
                        Setting.Format("ComboBoxStr%d-%d", ID, j++ );
                        Value=pApp->GetProfileString( Family, Setting );
                        if( Value!="" )
                                AddString( Value );
                } while (Value!="");
        }
        CComboBox::PreSubclassWindow();
}

void CPNComboBox::OnDestroy()
{
        if( ShouldSave() )
        {
```

```
            int i, ID;
            CString Text, Family, Setting;
            CWinApp* pApp = AfxGetApp();

            // Set Family with the unique ID for the parent dialog
            Family.Format("PNComboBox%d", GetParent()->GetDlgCtrlID() );
            int OldItems = pApp->GetProfileInt( Family, "Count", 0 );

            ID = GetDlgCtrlID();
            pApp->WriteProfileInt( Family, "Count", GetCount() );

            for( i=0; i < GetCount(); i++ )
            {
                    GetLBText( i, Text );
                    Setting.Format( "ComboBoxStr%d-%d", ID, i );
                    if( !Text.IsEmpty() )
                            pApp->WriteProfileString( Family, Setting, Text );
            }

            while( i < OldItems ) // There's a better way: keep the count of items
            in registry, and delete only whats needed
            {
                    Setting.Format( "ComboBoxStr%d-%d", ID, i++ );
                    pApp->WriteProfileString( Family, Setting, NULL );
            }
        }
        CComboBox::OnDestroy();

}


BOOL CPNComboBox::PreTranslateMessage(MSG* pMsg)
{
        if( ::GetParent( pMsg->hwnd ) == m_hWnd && pMsg->message == WM_KEYDOWN )
        {
                if( pMsg->wParam==VK_RETURN)
                {
                        TRACE("Post message\n");
                        AfxGetMainWnd()->PostMessage( WM_COMMAND, MAKELPARAM
                        (GetDlgCtrlID(),CBN_SELCHANGE), (LPARAM)m_hWnd );
                }
                else
                {
                        if( pMsg->wParam == VK_BACK || pMsg->wParam == VK_DELETE )
                                m_DoPerLookup = false;
                }
        }
        return CComboBox::PreTranslateMessage(pMsg);
}


void CPNComboBox::SetAllRegistrySave(bool Mode)
```

```
{
      m_RegistrySave = Mode;
}


int CPNComboBox::AddString( LPCSTR pNewString )
{
      // Don't add duplicates
      CString Tmp;
      if( pNewString == 0 )
            GetWindowText( Tmp );
      else
            Tmp = pNewString;
      int Index = FindStringExact( 0, Tmp );
      if( Index < 0 )
            Index = CComboBox::AddString( Tmp );
      return( Index );
}


void CPNComboBox::OnEditupdate()
{
      if( !m_DoLookup || !m_DoPerLookup )
      {
            m_DoPerLookup = true;
            return;
      }

      CEdit* Tmp = (CEdit*)GetDlgItem( 1001 );
      int StartSel, EndSel;
      Tmp->GetSel( StartSel, EndSel );
      CString strTmp;
      Tmp->GetWindowText(strTmp );

      if( StartSel && StartSel == EndSel && StartSel==strTmp.GetLength() )
      {
            int Index;
            if( (Index=SelectString( -1, strTmp )) >= 0 )
            {
                  GetLBText( Index, strTmp );
                  SetWindowText( strTmp );
                  Tmp->SetSel( StartSel, strTmp.GetLength() );
                  return;
            }
            SetWindowText( strTmp );
            Tmp->SetSel( StartSel, StartSel );
      }
}


bool CPNComboBox::ShouldSave()
```

```
{
        // Determine if all are set to save,
        if( m_RegistrySave == true )
                return( true );
        return( m_MyRegistrySave );
}
```

The CPNDirTree Class

The CPNDirTree class is an MFC extension derived from CTreeCtrl. It automatically provides the ability for a tree control to display drive and folder information for a computer, as well as file names, and to optionally provide checkboxes for each item.

To use the CPNDirTree class, add the files to your project and then drop a Tree control on a form. Using ClassWizard, map a member variable of type CPNDirTree to the new tree control. Compile and run the program.

PNDirTree.h

```
#if !defined(AFX_TREEFOLDER_H__F52456D4_9D3F_11D3_9EDB_080009EE62AA__INCLUDED_)
#define AFX_TREEFOLDER_H__F52456D4_9D3F_11D3_9EDB_080009EE62AA__INCLUDED_

#if _MSC_VER > 1000
#pragma once
#endif // _MSC_VER > 1000
// TreeFolder.h : header file
//

/////////////////////////////////////////////////////////////////////////
// CPNDirTree window
#include <afxtempl.h>

class CPNDirTree : public CTreeCtrl
{
// Construction
public:
        CPNDirTree();
        virtual ~CPNDirTree();

// Attributes
public:
        bool m_ShowFiles;
        bool m_AutoRefresh;
        bool m_HasCheck;

// Operations
```

```
public:

// Overrides
        // ClassWizard generated virtual function overrides
        //{{AFX_VIRTUAL(CPNDirTree)
        protected:
        virtual void PreSubclassWindow();
        //}}AFX_VIRTUAL

// Implementation
public:
        void SetCheckStyle( bool Mode );
        void Reset();
        bool SetShowFiles( bool NewMode );
        BOOL IsFileFolder( const char* Path );
        BOOL IsFileFolder( HTREEITEM hItem=0 );
        void RefreshItem( HTREEITEM hNode );
        void CheckAll( BOOL Checked, HTREEITEM hNode=0 );
        int GetAllChecked( CStringArray& Dest );
        int GetAllChecked( CListBox& List );
        int BuildFileList( CStringArray& Dest, const char* Path, bool FullPath=true );

        void ExpandAll(HTREEITEM hNode );

        LPCSTR GetFullPath( HTREEITEM hNode );
        LPCSTR GetSubPath( const char* Str );

        // Generated message map functions
        void StartPath( const char* Start );
protected:
        void LoadDriveLetters(const char* OneDrive = 0 );
        int BuildFileListEx( CStringArray& Dest, const char* Path, bool FullPath=true );
        BOOL HasSubItem(const char *Folder );
        HTREEITEM AddPath(const char *Path, HTREEITEM hNode=TVI_ROOT, HTREEITEM
        hInsertAfter = TVI_LAST );
        void ExpandItem( HTREEITEM hNode, bool ExpandIt, bool Recursive = false );
        void LoadPath( HTREEITEM hNode, const char* Str );
        void CheckSearch( CStringArray& Dest, HTREEITEM hNode );
        void SlashPath( CString& Dest, bool MustHave );
        //{{AFX_MSG(CPNDirTree)
        afx_msg void OnItemexpanding(NMHDR* pNMHDR, LRESULT* pResult);
        //}}AFX_MSG

        DECLARE_MESSAGE_MAP()

        CString m_StartPath;
        static CImageList m_ImageList;
        static int m_ObjCount;
```

```
        CList<HTREEITEM,HTREEITEM> m_Expanded;

};

//////////////////////////////////////////////////////////////////////

//{{AFX_INSERT_LOCATION}}
// Microsoft Visual C++ will insert additional declarations immediately before the
// previous line.
#endif // !defined(AFX_TREEFOLDER_H__F52456D4_9D3F_11D3_9EDB_080009EE62AA__
INCLUDED_)
```

PNDirTree.cpp

```
// PNDirTree.cpp : implementation file
//

#include "stdafx.h"
#include "PNDirTree.h"

#include <stdlib.h>

#ifdef _DEBUG
#define new DEBUG_NEW
#undef THIS_FILE
static char THIS_FILE[] = __FILE__;
#endif

//////////////////////////////////////////////////////////////////////
// CPNDirTree
CImageList CPNDirTree::m_ImageList;

int CPNDirTree::m_ObjCount;

CPNDirTree::CPNDirTree()
{
      m_ShowFiles = false;
      m_AutoRefresh = true;
      m_ObjCount++;
}

CPNDirTree::~CPNDirTree()
{
}

BEGIN_MESSAGE_MAP(CPNDirTree, CTreeCtrl)
      //{{AFX_MSG_MAP(CPNDirTree)
      ON_NOTIFY_REFLECT(TVN_ITEMEXPANDING, OnItemexpanding)
```

```
        //}}AFX_MSG_MAP
END_MESSAGE_MAP()
///////////////////////////////////////////////////////////////////////
// CPNDirTree message handlers

void CPNDirTree::StartPath( const char* Start )
{
        if( !Start )
                LoadDriveLetters();
        else
        {
                DeleteAllItems();
                m_StartPath = Start;
                AddPath( Start );
        }
}

void CPNDirTree::LoadDriveLetters( const char* OneDrive )
{
        // Initialize control with list of valid drive letters
        if( IsWindowVisible() )
                SetRedraw( FALSE );
        DeleteAllItems();
        char  Drives[128], *CurDrive;
        CWaitCursor Wait;

        if( OneDrive )
        {
                AddPath( OneDrive );
                return;
        }

        ::GetLogicalDriveStrings( sizeof(Drives), Drives );

        CurDrive = Drives;
        while( *CurDrive )
        {
                AddPath( CurDrive );
                CurDrive += strlen( CurDrive ) + 1;
        }
        if( IsWindowVisible() )
                SetRedraw( TRUE );
}
BOOL CPNDirTree::HasSubItem(const char *Folder )
{
        // Determine if a folder has sub-items (files or folders)
        CFileFind Find;
        CString    Tmp = Folder;
        BOOL       Found;
```

```
        SlashPath( Tmp, true );
        Tmp += "*.*";

        Found = Find.FindFile( Tmp );

        while ( Found )
        {
                Found = Find.FindNextFile();

                if( Find.IsHidden() )
                        continue;

                if ( Find.IsDirectory() )
                {
                        if( !Find.IsDots() )
                                return TRUE;
                }
                if ( !Find.IsDirectory() && m_ShowFiles )
                        return TRUE;

        }
        return FALSE;
}


void CPNDirTree::PreSubclassWindow()
{
        // Initialize the control
        SHFILEINFO ShFileInfo;
        HIMAGELIST hImageList = NULL;

        if( !m_ImageList.GetSafeHandle() )
        {
                hImageList = (HIMAGELIST)SHGetFileInfo( "C:\\", 0, &ShFileInfo, sizeof(
                ShFileInfo ),
                        SHGFI_SYSICONINDEX | SHGFI_SMALLICON );
                CImageList Tmp;
                m_ImageList.Attach( ImageList_Duplicate( hImageList ) );
        }
        SetImageList( &m_ImageList, TVSIL_NORMAL );

        m_HasCheck = (::GetWindowLong( m_hWnd, GWL_STYLE ) &TVS_CHECKBOXES ) ? true :
        false;

        LoadDriveLetters();
        CTreeCtrl::PreSubclassWindow();
}


HTREEITEM CPNDirTree::AddPath(const char *Path, HTREEITEM hNode, HTREEITEM hIn-
sertAfter )
{
```

```
        // Adds path to tree, and gets the icon for the file specified.
        SHFILEINFO shFileInfo;
        int iIcon, iIconSel;
    CString Tmp = Path;
        HTREEITEM Ret;
        HIMAGELIST hImageList;

        SlashPath( Tmp, true );

        // Get Icons
        hImageList = (HIMAGELIST)SHGetFileInfo( Tmp, 0, &shFileInfo, sizeof
        ( shFileInfo ),
                SHGFI_SYSICONINDEX | SHGFI_ICON | SHGFI_SMALLICON );
        iIcon = shFileInfo.iIcon;
        SHGetFileInfo( Tmp, 0, &shFileInfo, sizeof( shFileInfo ),
                SHGFI_SYSICONINDEX | SHGFI_OPENICON | SHGFI_SMALLICON );
        iIconSel = shFileInfo.iIcon;

        m_ImageList.DeleteImageList();
        m_ImageList.Attach( ImageList_Duplicate(hImageList) );

        // Perform insertion
        if ( hNode == TVI_ROOT )
                Ret =  InsertItem( Path, iIcon, iIconSel, hNode, hInsertAfter );
        else
                Ret = InsertItem( GetSubPath( Path ), iIcon, iIconSel, hNode,
                hInsertAfter );

        if( HasSubItem( Path ) )
                InsertItem( "", 0, 0, Ret);

        return( Ret );
}


LPCSTR CPNDirTree::GetSubPath(const char *Str)
{
        static CString Path;
        int i;

        Path = Str;
        SlashPath( Path, false );
        i = Path.ReverseFind( '\\' );
        if ( i != -1 )
            Path = Path.Mid( i + 1);

        return (LPCTSTR)Path;
}
void CPNDirTree::OnItemexpanding(NMHDR* pNMHDR, LRESULT* pResult)
{

        NM_TREEVIEW* pNMTreeView = (NM_TREEVIEW*)pNMHDR;
```

```
        // When an item is expanding, make sure its sub-items are loaded:
        ExpandItem( pNMTreeView->itemNew.hItem, pNMTreeView->itemNew.state & TVIS_
        EXPANDED?false:true );

        *pResult = 0;
}

void CPNDirTree::RefreshItem(HTREEITEM hNode)
{
        // Known Bug: If you:
        // 1. Expand a folder
        // 2. Collapse the folder
        // 3. Delete a File or folder in that folder
        // 4. Recreate a Folder of file for the deleted File or Folder (respectively)
        // 5. Expand the folder
        // Then, the icon for the file is no longer correct (But, it will still have a
        // '+' for subitems)

        CStringList CurFiles;
        CStringArray NewFiles;
        CString S, S2;
        BOOL Found, IsFolder, IsCurFolder;
        HTREEITEM hInsert, hOld, hChild = GetChildItem( hNode );

        BuildFileListEx( NewFiles, GetFullPath( hNode ), false );

        // Test current items in tree, and see if file is still there
        while ( hChild )
        {
                S = GetItemText( hChild );
                Found = FALSE;
                for( int i=0; !Found && i < NewFiles.GetSize(); i++ )
                {
                        S2 = NewFiles[i];
                        IsFolder = (S2[0] == 'A' );
                        S2.Delete( 0, 1 );

                        if( S.CompareNoCase( S2 ) == 0 )
                                Found = TRUE;
                }

                hOld = hChild;
                hChild = GetNextSiblingItem( hChild );
                if( !Found )
                        DeleteItem( hOld );
                else
                        CurFiles.AddTail( GetItemText( hOld ) );
        }
```

```
//Now, test to see for newly added items
for( int i=0; i < NewFiles.GetSize(); i++ )
{
      S = NewFiles[i];
      IsFolder = (S[0] == 'A' );
      S.Delete( 0, 1 );
      hChild = GetChildItem( hNode );
      Found = FALSE;
      hInsert = hChild;
      while ( hChild && !Found )
      {
            S2 = GetItemText( hChild );
            IsCurFolder = IsFileFolder( GetFullPath( hChild ) );
            // What if its the first file, after the folders?
            if( S2.CompareNoCase( S ) < 0 || !IsFolder && IsCurFolder )
            {
                  if( IsFolder ==  IsCurFolder || !IsFolder && IsCurFolder
                  )
                        hInsert = hChild;
            }

            if( S.CompareNoCase( S2 ) == 0 )
            {
                  Found = TRUE;
                  S = GetFullPath( hChild );
                  if( HasSubItem( S ) )
                  {
                        // Make sure children are there
                        if( !GetChildItem( hChild ) )
                              InsertItem( "", hChild ); // New sub
                              // items
                  }
                  else
                  {
                        // Make sure children no longer there
                        HTREEITEM hTmp = GetChildItem( hChild );
                        POSITION Pos;
                        while( hTmp )
                        {
                              DeleteItem( hTmp );
                              Pos = m_Expanded.Find( hTmp );
                              if( Pos )
                                    m_Expanded.RemoveAt( Pos );
                              hTmp = GetChildItem( hChild );
                        }
                  }
            }
            else
                  hChild = GetNextSiblingItem( hChild );
```

```
                }
        if( !Found )  // It's New
        {
                S2 = GetFullPath( hNode );
                SlashPath( S2, true );
                S = S2+S;
                hInsert = AddPath( S, hNode, hInsert );
        }
    }

}


void CPNDirTree::ExpandAll(HTREEITEM hNode )
{
     // Expands (and populates if needed) all child nodes of a node
     static int Running;
     if( !hNode )
            return;

     if( !Running++ )
     {
            ExpandItem( hNode, true, true );
            Expand( hNode, TVE_EXPAND );
     }

     HTREEITEM hChild = GetChildItem( hNode );
     while( hChild )
     {
            Expand( hChild, TVE_EXPAND );
            ExpandAll( hChild );
            hChild = GetNextSiblingItem( hChild );
     }

     Running--;
}
void CPNDirTree::ExpandItem(HTREEITEM hNode, bool ExpandIt, bool Recursive )
{
     CString Path;

     // Expands an item.  Can be called to do so recursively
     if ( ExpandIt )
     {
            if( m_HasCheck )
            {
                    if( m_Expanded.Find( hNode ) ) // Already populated
                    {
                            if( m_AutoRefresh ) // Refresh anyway?
                                    RefreshItem( hNode );
                            return;
```

```
                }
                m_Expanded.AddTail( hNode );
        }

        HTREEITEM hChild = GetChildItem( hNode );
        while ( hChild )
        {

                DeleteItem( hChild );
                hChild = GetChildItem( hChild );
        }

        Path = GetFullPath( hNode );
        LoadPath( hNode, Path );
        if( Recursive )
        {
                HTREEITEM hChild = GetChildItem( hNode );
                while( hChild )
                {
                        ExpandItem( hChild, ExpandIt, Recursive );
                        hChild = GetNextSiblingItem( hChild );
                }

        }
    }
}


LPCSTR CPNDirTree::GetFullPath(HTREEITEM hNode)
{
        // Gets the full path for a Node
        static CString Path;
        CString Tmp;

        Path.Empty();
        while ( hNode )
        {
                Tmp  = GetItemText( hNode );
                SlashPath( Tmp, true );
                Path = Tmp + Path;
                hNode = GetParentItem( hNode );
        }
        SlashPath( Path, false );
    return( Path );

}


int CStringCmp( const void* A, const void* B )
{
        // Comparison for two CStrings, for qsort call below
```

```
        return( ((CString*)A)->CompareNoCase( *(CString*)B ) );
}

int CPNDirTree::BuildFileList( CStringArray &Dest, const char *Path, bool
FullPath )
{
        // Builds a list of file names for a path.
        int Ret = BuildFileListEx( Dest, Path, FullPath );
        for( int i=0; i < Ret; i++ )
                Dest[i].Delete( 0, 1 );
        return( Ret );
}
int CPNDirTree::BuildFileListEx( CStringArray &Dest, const char *Path, bool FullPath)
{
        // Builds a list of file names for a path.  This also sorts the list
        // and precedes folder names with 'A' and file names with a 'B'.
        CFileFind Find;
        CString MyPath = Path;
        BOOL Found;
        CWaitCursor Wait;

        SlashPath( MyPath, true );
        MyPath += "*.*";

        Found = Find.FindFile( MyPath );
        while ( Found )
        {
                Found = Find.FindNextFile();
                if ( Find.IsDirectory() && !Find.IsDots() )
                        Dest.Add( "A" + (FullPath?Find.GetFilePath():Find.
                        GetFileName()));
                if ( m_ShowFiles && !Find.IsDirectory() )
                        Dest.Add( "B" + (FullPath?Find.GetFilePath():Find.
                        GetFileName()));
        }

        qsort( (void*)Dest.GetData(), Dest.GetSize(), sizeof(CString), CStringCmp );
        return( Dest.GetSize() );
}

void CPNDirTree::LoadPath(HTREEITEM hNode, const char *Path)
{
        int i;
        CString Tmp;
        BOOL IsFolder;
        CStringArray Files;
        CWaitCursor Wait;

        // Populates a single node with its file-list information
```

```
        SetRedraw( FALSE );
        BuildFileListEx( Files, Path );

        for( i = 0; i < Files.GetSize(); i++ )
        {
                Tmp = Files[i];
                IsFolder = (Tmp[0] == 'A' );
                Tmp.Delete( 0, 1 );
                AddPath( Tmp, hNode );
        }
        SetRedraw( TRUE );

}
void CPNDirTree::SlashPath(CString &Dest, bool MustHave)
{
        // Insures that a path either has, or does not have, a slash at the end
        char Now='\0';

        if( !Dest.IsEmpty() )
                Now = Dest[Dest.GetLength()-1];
        if( MustHave && Now != '\\' )
                Dest += '\\';
        else if( !MustHave && Now == '\\' )
                Dest.TrimRight( '\\' );
}


void CPNDirTree::CheckSearch(CStringArray &Dest, HTREEITEM hNode)
{
        HTREEITEM hCurNode;

        // Builds a list of Checked items and stores then in a CStringArray
        // Search can start from a specific node
        if( hNode )
                do
                {
                        if( GetCheck( hNode ) )
                                Dest.Add( GetFullPath( hNode ) );
                        if( (hCurNode = GetChildItem( hNode )) )
                                CheckSearch( Dest, hCurNode );
                        hNode = GetNextSiblingItem( hNode );
                } while ( hNode );

}


int CPNDirTree::GetAllChecked( CStringArray& Dest )
{
        // Builds a list of Checked items and stores then in a CStringArray
        Dest.RemoveAll();
        CheckSearch( Dest, GetChildItem(TVI_ROOT) );
```

```
        return( Dest.GetSize() );
}

int CPNDirTree::GetAllChecked( CListBox& List )
{
        // Builds a list of Checked items and stores then in a listbox

        CStringArray Dest;
        CheckSearch( Dest, GetChildItem(TVI_ROOT) );
        List.ResetContent();
        for( int i=0; i < Dest.GetSize(); i++ )
                List.AddString( Dest[i] );
        return( Dest.GetSize() );
}

BOOL CPNDirTree::IsFileFolder(const char *Path)
{
        // Determines if 'Path' is a file or folder.
        CFileFind Find;
        if( Find.FindFile( Path ) )
        {
                Find.FindNextFile();
                return( Find.IsDirectory()? TRUE : FALSE );
        }
        return( FALSE );
}

BOOL CPNDirTree::IsFileFolder( HTREEITEM hItem)
{
        // Determines if path for a node is a file or a folder
        return( IsFileFolder( GetFullPath( hItem ) ) );
}

bool CPNDirTree::SetShowFiles(bool NewMode)
{
        // Sets the ShowFiles property to true or false.
        bool Ret = m_ShowFiles;
        m_ShowFiles = NewMode;
        LoadDriveLetters();
        return( Ret );
}
void CPNDirTree::CheckAll(BOOL Checked, HTREEITEM hNode)
{
        HTREEITEM hCurNode;

        // Checks all child nodes from a node.  Populates node items
        // as needed
        if( !hNode )
        {
```

```
                hNode = GetSelectedItem();
                if( !hNode )
                        return;
                SetCheck( hNode, Checked );
                ExpandItem( hNode, true, true );
                hNode = GetChildItem( hNode );
        }
        if( hNode )
        {
                do
                {
                        SetCheck( hNode, Checked );
                        if( (hCurNode = GetChildItem( hNode )) )
                                CheckAll( Checked, hCurNode );
                        hNode = GetNextSiblingItem( hNode );
                } while ( hNode );
        }
}


void CPNDirTree::Reset()
{
        if( m_StartPath.IsEmpty() )
                LoadDriveLetters();
        else
                StartPath( m_StartPath );
}


void CPNDirTree::SetCheckStyle(bool Mode)
{
        // Bummer: You can't just change the Checkbox style
        // for a tree, you need to destroy and re-create it.
        CWnd* pParent = GetParent();
        int ID = GetDlgCtrlID();
        int ExStyle = ::GetWindowLong( m_hWnd, GWL_EXSTYLE );

        int Style = ::GetWindowLong( m_hWnd, GWL_STYLE );
        if( Mode )
                Style = Style | TVS_CHECKBOXES;
        else
                Style = Style & (~TVS_CHECKBOXES);

        m_HasCheck = Mode;
        CRect Rect;
        GetWindowRect( &Rect );
        GetParent()->ScreenToClient( &Rect );
        DestroyWindow();
        CreateEx( ExStyle, "systreeview32", "TreeView", Style, Rect, pParent, ID );
        SetImageList( &m_ImageList, TVSIL_NORMAL );
        ShowWindow( SW_NORMAL );
        Reset();
}
```

The CPNStatic Class

The CPNStatic class is an MFC extension class derived from the CStatic class. It provides added support for font changing and also provides the ability to have a static control act as a web link (when the cursor moves over it, it changes to a hand cursor, and if the user clicks it, his or her browser will be opened to the specified page).

To use the CPNStatic class, place a static control on your form and make sure that its Notify property is checked. Then, using ClassWizard, map a member variable to the static control, of type CPNStatic.

To set the object to act as a URL link, call the following function:

```
CPNStatic:: SetURL(const char *lpszCaption, const char *lpszURL);
```

where lpszCaption is the text to display in the static control, and lpszURL is the URL to launch of the user clicks the control. For example:

```
m_URL.SetURL( "www.openroad.org", "http://www.openroad.org" );
```

CPNStatic.h

```
#if !defined(AFX_PNSTATIC_H__BD23328A_C284_11D2_A3F2_0004ACC6A5DD__INCLUDED_)
#define AFX_PNSTATIC_H__BD23328A_C284_11D2_A3F2_0004ACC6A5DD__INCLUDED_

#if _MSC_VER > 1000
#pragma once
#endif // _MSC_VER > 1000
// PNStatic.h : header file
//

/////////////////////////////////////////////////////////////////////////////
// CPNStatic window

class CPNStatic : public CStatic
{
// Construction
public:
        CPNStatic();

// Attributes
public:

// Operations
public:
```

```
// Overrides
        // ClassWizard generated virtual function overrides
        //{{AFX_VIRTUAL(CPNStatic)
        //}}AFX_VIRTUAL

// Implementation
public:
        void SetForeColor( bool Mode, COLORREF Color=0 );
        bool SetItalic( bool Mode );
        void SetFontAttr(const char *Fontname, int Height=-1, int Width=-1, int
        Bold=-1, int Italic=-1, int Under=-1, int Fore=-1, COLORREF FontClr=0 );
        void UseHandCursor( bool Mode );
        void SetURL( const char* lpszCaption, const char* lpszURL );
        void SizeRectToFit();
        void SizeFontToFit( int Mode =0 );
        void SetText( const char* lpszCaption, const char * lpszCommand=0 );
        bool SetBold( bool Mode );
        bool SetUnderline( bool Mode );
        void DestroyCursor();
        bool LoadCursor( LPCSTR lpszResource );
        bool LoadCursor( UINT ID );
        bool bNoExecute;
        virtual ~CPNStatic();

        // Generated message map functions
protected:

        bool bSharedCursor, bBold, bItalic, bUnderlined, bForeColor;
        COLORREF crForeColor;
        HCURSOR hCursor;
        CFont    cFont;
        CString Command;

        //{{AFX_MSG(CPNStatic)
        afx_msg BOOL OnSetCursor(CWnd* pWnd, UINT nHitTest, UINT message);
        afx_msg void OnClicked();
        afx_msg void OnPaint();
        //}}AFX_MSG

        DECLARE_MESSAGE_MAP()
};

////////////////////////////////////////////////////////////////////////

//{{AFX_INSERT_LOCATION}}
// Microsoft Visual C++ will insert additional declarations immediately before the
previous line.

#endif //
!defined(AFX_PNSTATIC_H__BD23328A_C284_11D2_A3F2_0004ACC6A5DD__INCLUDED_)
```

CPNStatic.cpp

```
// PNStatic.cpp : implementation file
//

#include "stdafx.h"
#include "PNStatic.h"

#ifdef _DEBUG
#define new DEBUG_NEW
#undef THIS_FILE
static char THIS_FILE[] = __FILE__;
#endif

// MG: This class can be imported into another project.  It is an extended CStatic
// class, that has the ability to control appearance a little easier, as well
// as act like a 'link' where it will execute a program when clicked (like
// a URL link on a web page).
////////////////////////////////////////////////////////////////////
// CPNStatic

CPNStatic::CPNStatic()
{
      hCursor = 0;
      bForeColor = bSharedCursor = false;
      bNoExecute = true;
}

CPNStatic::~CPNStatic()
{
      DestroyCursor();
}

BEGIN_MESSAGE_MAP(CPNStatic, CStatic)
      //{{AFX_MSG_MAP(CPNStatic)
      ON_WM_SETCURSOR()
      ON_CONTROL_REFLECT(BN_CLICKED, OnClicked)
      ON_WM_PAINT()
      //}}AFX_MSG_MAP
END_MESSAGE_MAP()

////////////////////////////////////////////////////////////////////
// CPNStatic message handlers

// OnSetCursor - Called by framework when mouse moves over the control
BOOL CPNStatic::OnSetCursor(CWnd* pWnd, UINT nHitTest, UINT message)
{
      if( hCursor )
      {
            ::SetCursor( hCursor );
```

```
                return( TRUE );
        }
        return CStatic::OnSetCursor(pWnd, nHitTest, message);
}


// LoadCursor - Helper function - Loads cursor via its unique ID
// Parameters:      ID = ID of cursor to load, from the resource script
// Returns:         TRUE if successful, FALSE upon error
// Comments:  Calls LoadCursor(LPCSTR lpszResource) function, setting cursor
//                  for the static control
bool CPNStatic::LoadCursor(UINT ID)
{
        return( LoadCursor( MAKEINTRESOURCE(ID) ) );
}
// LoadCursor - Loads cursor via its resource name
// Parameters:      ID = ID of cursor to load, from the resource script
// Returns:         TRUE if successful, FALSE upon error
// Comments:  Sets cursor for the static control
bool CPNStatic::LoadCursor(LPCSTR lpszResource)
{
        DestroyCursor();

        if( !(hCursor = AfxGetApp()->LoadCursor( lpszResource )) )
        {
                if( !(hCursor = ::LoadCursor( NULL, lpszResource )) )
                {
                        bSharedCursor = true;
                        return( true );
                }
                bSharedCursor = false;
                return( false );
        }
        else
        {
                bSharedCursor = false;
                return( true );
        }
}


// DestroyCursor- Unloads Cursor, if one was loaded
void CPNStatic::DestroyCursor()
{
        if( hCursor && !bSharedCursor )
                ::DestroyCursor( hCursor );
        hCursor = 0;
        bSharedCursor = false;
}


// SetFontAttr - Sets various font attributes for the static control
```

```
// Parameters:       Fontname is the name of the new font, null to leave unchanged.
//                   Height is the new height for the font, or -1 to leave
//                   unchanged
//                   Width is the new width for the font, or -1 to leave
//                   unchanged
//                   Bold is 0 to turn off, 1 to turn on, or -1 to leave
//                   unchanged
//                   Italic is 0 to turn off, 1 to turn on, or -1 to leave
//                   unchanged
//                   Underline is 0 to turn off, 1 to turn on, or -1 to leave
//                   unchanged
//                   Fore is 0 to not use FontColor, 1 to use it, or -1 to leave
//                   unchanged
//                   FontColor is new font color (based on 'Fore' parameter).
// Comments:  Sets cursor for the static control
void CPNStatic::SetFontAttr(const char *Fontname, int Height, int Width, int Bold,
int Italic, int Under, int Fore, COLORREF FontClr )
{
    CFont *Font;
    LOGFONT lf;

    Font = GetFont();
    if( Font->GetObject( sizeof( lf ), &lf ) )
    {
        if( Fontname )
        {
            memset( lf.lfFaceName, 0, sizeof(lf.lfFaceName) );
            strncpy( lf.lfFaceName, Fontname, sizeof(lf.lfFaceName) );
        }
        if( Height!=-1 )
            lf.lfHeight = Height;
        if( Width!=-1 )
            lf.lfWidth = Width;
        if( Bold != -1 )
            lf.lfWeight = Bold ? FW_BOLD : FW_NORMAL;
        if( Italic != -1 )
            lf.lfItalic = Italic ? TRUE : FALSE;
        if( Under != -1 )
            lf.lfUnderline = Under ? TRUE : FALSE;
        if( cFont.GetSafeHandle() )
            cFont.DeleteObject();
        cFont.CreateFontIndirect( & lf );
        SetFont( &cFont );

        bBold = lf.lfWeight==FW_BOLD;
        bItalic = lf.lfItalic==TRUE;
        bUnderlined = lf.lfUnderline==TRUE;
    }
    if( Fore != -1 )
```

```
        {
            if( Fore )
            {
                bForeColor = true;
                crForeColor = FontClr;
            }
            else
                bForeColor = false;

        }
}


// SetBold - Helper function to turn Bold font on or off
// Parameters:      Mode: true to set to bold, false to set to normal
// Returns:         Previous setting
bool CPNStatic::SetBold(bool Mode)
{
    bool Ret = bBold;
    if( bBold != Mode )
        SetFontAttr( NULL, -1, -1, Mode?1:0);
    return( Ret );
}


// SetItalic - Helper function to turn Italics font on or off
// Parameters:      Mode: true to set to italic, false to set to normal
// Returns:         Previous setting
bool CPNStatic::SetItalic(bool Mode)
{
    bool Ret = bItalic;
    if( bItalic != Mode )
        SetFontAttr( NULL, -1, -1, -1, Mode?1:0);
    return( Ret );
}


// SetUnderline - Helper function to turn Underline font on or off
// Parameters:      Mode: true to set to underline, false to set to normal
// Returns:         Previous setting
bool CPNStatic::SetUnderline(bool Mode)
{
    bool Ret = bUnderlined;
    if( bUnderlined != Mode )
        SetFontAttr( NULL, -1, -1, -1, -1, Mode?1:0);
    return( Ret );
}


// SetForeColor - Helper function set text color
// Parameters:      Mode: true to set color on, false to use defualt
//                  Color: New color, if Mode is true
void CPNStatic::SetForeColor( bool Mode, COLORREF Color )
```

```
{
        SetFontAttr( NULL, -1, -1, -1, -1, -1, Mode?1:0, Color );
}


// OnClicked - Indicates user clicked the control
// Comments:   If the bNoExecute parameter is false, then the 'Command'
//                   is executed
void CPNStatic::OnClicked()
{
        if( ! bNoExecute )
        {
                if( !Command.IsEmpty() )
                        ShellExecute( *GetParent(), "OPEN", Command, "", "", SW_NORMAL
                        );
                else
                {
                        CString Tmp;
                        GetWindowText( Tmp );
                        ShellExecute( *GetParent(), "OPEN", Tmp, "", "", SW_NORMAL );
                }
        }
        else
        {
                // If this window had SS_NOTIFY, then send the BN_CLICKED off to the
                // Message Map of the main frame, as if a normal windows message.
                if( GetWindowLong( *this, GWL_STYLE ) & SS_NOTIFY )
                        AfxGetMainWnd()->OnCmdMsg( GetDlgCtrlID(), BN_CLICKED, 0, 0 );
        }
}


// SetText - Sets the window text, and the 'Command' option
// Comments:   If the bNoExecute parameter is false, then the 'Command'
//                   is executed when the user clicks the control
void CPNStatic::SetText(const char *lpszCaption, const char *lpszCommand)
{
        if( lpszCaption )
                SetWindowText( lpszCaption );
        Command = lpszCommand?lpszCommand:"";
}


// SizeFontToFit- Helper function to size the font to fill the window size
// Parameters:       Mode is 0 to perform sizing based on height only
//                          1 to perform sizing based on width only
//                          2 to perform sizing based on height and width
void CPNStatic::SizeFontToFit( int Mode )
{
        CRect Rect;
        GetClientRect( &Rect );
        if( Mode == 0 )
```

```
                SetFontAttr( 0, Rect.bottom, 0 );
        if( Mode == 1 )
                SetFontAttr( 0, 0, Rect.right  );
        if( Mode == 2 )
                SetFontAttr( 0, Rect.bottom, Rect.right  );
}


// SizeRectToFit- Sizes the child static window to fit the current font setting
void CPNStatic::SizeRectToFit()
{
        CDC* pDC = GetDC();

        CString Tmp;
        GetWindowText( Tmp );
        pDC->SelectObject( GetFont() );
        CSize Size = pDC->GetTextExtent( Tmp );
        SetWindowPos( 0, 0, 0, Size.cx, Size.cy , SWP_NOMOVE|SWP_NOZORDER );

        ReleaseDC( pDC );
}


// SetURL- Helper function to setup static control to reflect a URL link
// Parameters:     lpszCaption: Text to display in window
//                 lpszURL: URL to go to upon click
// Comments:  Sets text color, cursor, and underline to look like a link
void CPNStatic::SetURL(const char *lpszCaption, const char *lpszURL)
{
        SetText( lpszCaption, lpszURL );
        SetForeColor( true, RGB( 0, 0, 255 ) );
        SetUnderline( true );
        UseHandCursor( true );
        bNoExecute = false;
}


// OnPaint- Handles display of the static control, called by framework.
void CPNStatic::OnPaint()
{
        CPaintDC dc(this); // device context for painting

        CString Tmp;
        GetWindowText( Tmp );

        dc.SelectObject( GetFont() );
        dc.SetBkMode( TRANSPARENT );
        if( bForeColor )
                dc.SetTextColor( crForeColor );
        dc.TextOut( 0, 0, Tmp );

}
```

```
// The followig is the bit data for the hand cursor image.  Placed
// here to make the class easier to use without additional bitmap resources.
HCURSOR CreateMhandCursor(); /* Prototype */

unsigned char MhandCursorAndBits[]={
      0xFF, 0xFF, 0xFF, 0xFF, 0xFF, 0xFF, 0xFF, 0xFF, 0xFF, 0xFF, 0xFF, 0xFF,
      0xFF, 0xFF, 0xFF, 0xFF, 0xFF, 0x8F, 0xFF, 0xFF, 0xFF, 0x8F, 0xFF, 0xFF,
      0xFF, 0x07, 0xFF, 0xFF, 0xFF, 0x07, 0xFF, 0xFF, 0xFF, 0x07, 0xFF, 0xFF,
      0xFF, 0x07, 0xFF, 0xFF, 0xFF, 0x07, 0xFF, 0xFF, 0xFF, 0x00, 0xFF, 0xFF,
      0xFF, 0x00, 0x0F, 0xFF, 0xFF, 0x00, 0x00, 0xFF, 0xFF, 0x00, 0x00, 0xFF,
      0xFF, 0x00, 0x00, 0xFF, 0xFF, 0x00, 0x00, 0xFF, 0x83, 0x00, 0x00, 0xFF,
      0x81, 0x00, 0x00, 0xFF, 0x80, 0x00, 0x00, 0xFF, 0x80, 0x00, 0x00, 0xFF,
      0xE0, 0x00, 0x00, 0xFF, 0xF0, 0x00, 0x00, 0xFF, 0xF8, 0x00, 0x00, 0xFF,
      0xFC, 0x00, 0x00, 0xFF, 0xFE, 0x00, 0x01, 0xFF, 0xFE, 0x00, 0x01, 0xFF,
      0xFF, 0x00, 0x03, 0xFF, 0xFF, 0x00, 0x03, 0xFF, 0xFF, 0x80, 0x03, 0xFF,
      0xFF, 0x80, 0x03, 0xFF, 0xFF, 0x80, 0x03, 0xFF
};


unsigned char MhandCursorXorBits[]={
      0x00, 0x00, 0x00, 0x00, 0x00, 0x00, 0x00, 0x00, 0x00, 0x00, 0x00, 0x00,
      0x00, 0x00, 0x00, 0x00, 0x00, 0x00, 0x00, 0x00, 0x00, 0x20, 0x00, 0x00,
      0x00, 0x70, 0x00, 0x00, 0x00, 0x70, 0x00, 0x00, 0x00, 0x70, 0x00, 0x00,
      0x00, 0x70, 0x00, 0x00, 0x00, 0x70, 0x00, 0x00, 0x00, 0x70, 0x00, 0x00,
      0x00, 0x77, 0x00, 0x00, 0x00, 0x77, 0x70, 0x00, 0x00, 0x77, 0x76, 0x00,
      0x00, 0x77, 0xF6, 0x00, 0x00, 0x7F, 0xFE, 0x00, 0x00, 0x7F, 0xFE, 0x00,
      0x38, 0x7F, 0xFE, 0x00, 0x3C, 0x7F, 0xFE, 0x00, 0x1E, 0x7F, 0xFE, 0x00,
      0x0F, 0xFF, 0xFE, 0x00, 0x07, 0xFF, 0xFE, 0x00, 0x03, 0xFF, 0xFE, 0x00,
      0x01, 0xFF, 0xFC, 0x00, 0x00, 0xFF, 0xFC, 0x00, 0x00, 0x7F, 0xFC, 0x00,
      0x00, 0x7F, 0xF8, 0x00, 0x00, 0x3F, 0xF8, 0x00, 0x00, 0x1F, 0xF8, 0x00,
      0x00, 0x1F, 0xF8, 0x00, 0x00, 0x00, 0x00, 0x00
};


int MhandCursorHotSpotX=10, MhandCursorHotSpotY=5;

HCURSOR CreateMhandCursor()
{
      return( CreateCursor( GetModuleHandle(NULL), MhandCursorHotSpotX,
      MhandCursor-HotSpotY, 32, 32,
            MhandCursorAndBits, MhandCursorXorBits) );
}


// UseHandCursor- Helper function to set static control to use a hand cursor
// Parameters:      Mode: true to use a hand cursor when mouse moves over window,
false to use default cursor.
void CPNStatic::UseHandCursor(bool Mode)
{
      DestroyCursor();

      if( Mode )
```

```
    {
        // Note: Windows 2000 and many latest patches include a Hand
        cursor.  To be more more portable,
        // we will create our own hand cursor.
        bSharedCursor = true;
        hCursor = CreateMhandCursor();
    }
}
```

The CGI/ISAPI Server Variables

The following table lists the environment variables accessible by a CGI program. To access one of the pieces of data, you can use the getenv function, which will return a string pointer to the desired data (or NULL if the environment data was not found). These environment variables will only be available to programs run as CGI programs and not normally executed applications.

Variable	Meaning
AUTH_TYPE	The type of authorization in use, when present.
CONTENT_LENGTH	Number of bytes of data sent from client to the server.
CONTENT_TYPE	The content type of the information supplied in the body of a request by a POST variable.
GATEWAY_INTERFACE	The version of the CGI specification that the server implements.
HTTP_ACCEPT	Special-case HTTP header. Values of the Accept: fields are concatenated, separated by a comma.
PATH_INFO	Additional path information, as given by the client. It is the path of the CGI program.
PATH_TRANSLATED	This is the value of PATH_INFO, but with any virtual path name expanded into a directory specification.
QUERY_STRING	The data from the client URL request, which follows the '?' character portion of the URL.
REMOTE_ADDR	The IP address of the client.
REMOTE_HOST	The host name of the client.
REMOTE_USER	The user name supplied by the client and authenticated by the server, if present.
REQUEST_METHOD	The HTTP request method, either GET or POST.
SCRIPT_NAME	The name of the CGI program being run.
SERVER_NAME	The server's host name (or IP address) as it should appear in self-referencing URLs.

SERVER_PORT	The TCP/IP port on which the request was received.
SERVER_PROTOCOL	The name and version of the information-retrieval protocol relating to this request, usually HTTP 1.0.
SERVER_SOFTWARE	The name and version of the web server that ran the CGI program.

Index